PREACHING JUSTICE

Volume II

CONTRIBUTIONS OF DOMINICAN SISTERS
TO SOCIAL ETHICS IN THE TWENTIETH CENTURY

Preaching Justice

Volume II

Contributions of Dominican Sisters

− TO −

Social Ethics

− IN THE −

Twentieth Century

Edited by

Helen Alford OP

and

Francesco Compagnoni OP

DOMINICAN PUBLICATIONS

First published (2016) by
Dominican Publications
42 Parnell Square
Dublin 1

ISBN
978-1-905604-31-9

British Library Cataloguing in Publications Data.
A catalogue record for this book is available
from the British Library.

Cover design by David Cooke

Index by Julitta Clancy

Printed in Ireland by
Naas Printing
South Main Street
Naas, Co. Kildare

Contents

CONTENTS

[7]

Abbreviations

All the official documents of the Church for which abbreviations are given here can be found in English on the official Vatican website: www.vatican.va

ACAID – Association of Committees for Aiding Internee's Dependents (Northern Ireland)

ANC – African National Congress

ANISP - National Association of Private Educational Institutions (Italy)

ATHECAK - Association of Women Theologians and Canonists of Kinshasa

AWR – Association of Women Religious (South Africa)

AZAPO – Azanian People's Organisation (South Africa)

BCM – Black Consciousness Movement

BEC – Basic Ecclesial Community

BVM - Sisters of Charity of the Blessed Virgin Mary (USA)

CARA – Centre for Applied Research in the Apostolate

CBIS – Christian Brothers Investment Services

CEDHU – Ecumenical Commission for Human Rights (Ecuador)

CE.FO.RAS – Centre for Women's Formation and Remedial Training (DRC)

CELAM – *Consejo Episcopal Latinoamericano* (Latin American Bishops' Conference)

CFDT – *Confédération française démocratique du travail* (French Democratic Confederation of Work)

CFTC – *Confédération française de travailleurs chrétiens* (French Confederation of Christian Workers)

CGT – *Confédération générale du travail* (General Confederation of Work – in France)

CGT-FO – *Force ouvrière* (A breakaway union from the CGT, it added the words "Workers' force" to the CGT name)

CHW – Catholic Healthcare West (USA)

CIS – Corporate Information Center – later ICCR (USA)

CLAR – Latin American Conference of Religious

CM – Congregation of the Mission

CODALC – Confederation of Dominican Sisters of Latin American and the Caribbean

CODESA – Convention for a Democratic South Africa

CORI – Conference of Religious of Ireland

CP – Passionists

CPT – Pastoral Land Commission (Brazil)

CRSD – *Congrégation Romaine di Saint Dominique* (a congregation of Dominican sisters often referred to as the "Roman Congregation" in English)

CVR – Truth and Reconciliation Commission (Peru); the acronym 'TRC' is also sometimes used

DIP – *Dizionario degli Istituti di Perfezione* (Dictionary of the Institutes of Perfection)

DRC – apart from chapter 8, Democratic Republic of Congo; in chapter 8, Dutch Reformed Church (South Africa)

DSE – Dominican Sisters Europe (a region of DSI)

DSI – Dominican Sisters International

ECAR – Education Conference of Religious (South Africa)

EMPSA – Ecumenical Monitoring Program for South Africa

ENIM - *Ente Nazionale Insegnamento Medio*: National Association for Middle School Teaching (Italy)

EPA – Environmental Protection Agency (USA)

ESAT – Établissement et service d'aide par le travail (Establishment and Help Service for Work – in France)

ESG – Environment, Social, Governance (criteria used in SRI decisions)

ESPZ – English-speaking zone (of DSE)

FEDHU - *Frente Ecuatoriano de Derechos Humanos* (Ecuadorian Human Rights Front)

FMS – Marist Brothers

FUCI – *Federazione Universitaria Cattolica Italiana* (Italian Catholic University Federation)

FUNDEHI – Corporation for Integral Human Development (Colombian NGO)

GHG – Greenhouse gas

GS – *Gaudium et Spes*

HIV / AIDS – Human immunodeficiency virus and acquired immune deficiency syndrome

IBGE - *Istituto Brasileiro de Geografia e Estatistica* (Brazilian Institute for Geography and Statistics)

ICC – Irish Council of Churches

ICCR – Interfaith Center for Corporate Responsibility (USA)

IEC – Independent Electoral Commission (South Africa)

IFEE – Independent Forum for Electoral Education (South Africa)

IFP – Inkatha Freedom Party (South Africa)

IICM – Irish Inter-Church Meeting

INSEE – *Institut National de la Statistique et des Etudes Economiques*
(National Institute of Statistics and of Economic Studies – France)

IRA – Irish Republican Army

ISE – Irish School of Ecumenics

JOC – *Jeunesse Ouvrière Chrétienne* (YCW - Young Christian Workers)

JOLT – Justice Organizers Leadership Treasurers (USA)

J&P – Justice and Peace

LA CLE – Lille Association 'Compter, Lire, Ecrire' (Count, Read, Write)

LUMSA – *Libera Università Maria Santissima Assunta*, the Free University
of Our Lady Assumed into Heaven (in Rome)

MFJP – Women's Movement for Justice and Peace (DRC)

MK - *Umkhonto we Sizwe* (The Spear of the Nation – underground
military wing of the ANC)

MM – Maryknoll Missionaries

MNI – Mediation Northern Ireland

NATRI - National Association of Treasurers of Religious Institutes (USA)

NCCR – National Coordinating Committee for Repatriation (South
Africa)

NCCRI – National Catholic Coalition for Responsible Investment (USA)

NCLCI – National Christian Leadership Conference for Israel (USA)

NDEA – National Defense Education Act (USA)

NGO – Non-Governmental Organisation

NI – Northern Ireland

NP – National Party (South Africa)

NPT - Treaty on the Non-Proliferation of Nuclear Weapons (Non-
Proliferation Treaty)

OCD – Discalced Carmelites

OFEDICO - *Organisation des Femmes pour le développement intégral
et communautaire*, Women's Organisation for Integral and
Communitarian Development (DRC)

OP – Order of Preachers

PAB – Portfolio Advisory Board (Adrian Dominican sisters)

PAC – Pan African Congress

PCB - Polychlorinated biphenyl (contaminant)

PCF – French Communist Party

RC – Roman Catholic

RE – Religious Education

RODHECIC - Network Organization of Human Rights and Civic Education of Christian Inspiration in the Democratic Republic of Congo

RSM – Sisters of Mercy

SACBC – Southern African Catholic Bishops' Conference

SACC – South African Council of Churches

SALT – Strategic Arms Limitation Treaty

SECAM - Symposium of the Bishops Conferences of Africa and Madagascar

SND – Sisters of Notre Dame

SOA – School of the Americas

SPRED – Special Religious Education

SRI – Socially-Responsible Investment

SRTE / SRTF – Sister Rose Thering Endowment / Sister Rose Thering Fund

START – Strategic Arms Reduction Treaty

S.Th. – Summa Theologiae (the most famous work of St Thomas Aquinas)

TEC – Transitional Executive Council (South Africa)

TRC – Truth and Reconciliation Commission (see CVR)

TRI CRI – Tri-State Coalition for Responsible Investment (USA)

UDF – United Democratic Front (South Africa)

UN – United Nations

UNAMIR – United Nations Assistance Mission for Rwanda

UNHCR – (Office of the) United Nations High Commissioner for Refugees

USCCB – United States Conference of Catholic Bishops

WCC – World Council of Churches

WCRP – World Conference on Religion and Peace

WMD – Weapons of Mass Destruction

Contributors

Helen Alford OP, of the Congregation of St Catherine of Siena, Newcastle (Kwazulu Natal, South Africa), is Vice Dean of the Faculty of Social Sciences at the Pontifical University of St Thomas (Angelicum) and Consultor to the Pontifical Council of Justice and Peace. Her publications are mostly on the use of Catholic social thought in business ethics.

Kaye Ashe OP (1930-2014), of the Sinsinawa Dominicans, received a PhD in history from the University of Fribourg and was a teacher, university administrator, and author in the fields of Church history and feminism. She was Prioress General from 1986 to 1994.

Mary Patricia Beatty OP, of the Dominican Sisters~Grand Rapids, serves as the director of the Congregational Library located at the Marywood Motherhouse in Grand Rapids, Michigan.

Cesarina Broggi, a religious of the Union of St Catherine of Siena of the Missionaries of the Schools, has taught literature in Italian state schools for 40 years and wrote the *Positio* on the foundress of her institute, the Venerable Luigia Tincani. Currently she is Secretary General of the Missionaries of the Schools.

Beatriz Alicia and **Maria Leonor Charria Angulo** OP, twin sisters from Colombia who are also both Dominican Sisters of the Presentation, have combined missionary life with academic work in the accompaniment and support of highly marginalized and impoverished people. In the light of the Word of God, this has given new sense and meaning to their life and vocation as Preachers.

Francesco Compagnoni OP, of the Province of St Dominic (North Italy), has taught moral theology at the University of Fribourg, Switzerland, and at the Angelicum. His publications are in the areas of human rights and bioethics.

Patricia Daly OP, a Dominican of Caldwell, NJ, directs the work of the Tri-State Coalition for Responsible Investment, the largest of the coalitions of Catholic investors in the Interfaith Center on Corporate Responsibility, based in New York. Throughout her life as a Dominican she has engaged with corporations to advance justice in economic systems, with a significant focus on climate change.

Marie-Laure Dénès OP, of the Congrégation Romaine de Saint Dominique

(Roman Congregation), is the former Secretary General of Justice and Peace France (2004-2011) and Justice and Peace Europe (2008-2011), as well as former co-promoter of Justice and Peace for Europe within DSI (2005-2010).

Imelda Farkas OP, of the Congregation of Dominican Sisters of Saint Margaret of Hungary since 1984, personally experienced what it means to live religious life in secret while it was banned by the Communist regime. She is particularly interested in the history of her religious community during that period.

Madeleine Fredell OP, of the Congrégation Romaine de Saint Dominique (Roman Congregation), is Prioress of the Swedish Vicariate of her congregation. She is Secretary General of the Swedish Justice and Peace Commission and has a BA in Classics and an MA in Contemporary Theology.

Roger Gaise OP, of the General Vicariate of the Democratic Republic of Congo, has assumed the functions of Rector of the University of Uele at Isiro in the Province of Haut Uele since 2001, as its management has been confided to the Dominicans of the DRC. Besides his work since 2003 as holder of the Chair of Eucharistic Theology in the Faculty of Theology of the Catholic University of Congo in Kinshasa, he is convinced of the necessity of engaging the Church on the side of the poorest and the most disinherited in Congolese society.

Marie Therese Hanna OP is former Prioress General of the Dominican Sisters of Saint Catherine of Siena in Iraq, 1992-2004. She has recently been displaced from Mosul and the Nineveh Plain, with 73 other sisters, to Kurdistan.

Svenja Ibscher-Holz studied Catholic Theology and History at the University of Bonn, after which she trained to become a teacher. From 2009 to 2011, she worked as a junior lecturer in the Department of Church History at the Faculty of Catholic Theology in Bonn, and since then has been teaching religious education and history at a grammar school.

Margaret Kelly OP, of the Congregation of the Irish Cabra Dominican sisters, has spent her religious life in South Africa. She worked promoting 'open schools' and Justice and Peace at the local level for many years and eventually became Secretary of the Justice and Peace Commission of the SACBC from 1987 to 1995, under the leadership of Archbishop Denis Hurley OMI.

Bernice Kita OP, MM, of the Maryknoll Missionaries, has spent most of her life serving the Mayan peoples of Guatemala. She is author of *What Prize Awaits Us, Letters from Guatemala*, as well as many articles for various publications.

Hannah Rita Laue OP, of the Dominican Sisters of Bethany, has a degree in theology and is currently serving the people of Latvia through giving bible studies and retreats, working with youth, and in the work of prison chaplaincy. She is the prioress of the community in Riga where she is based, and is also the archivist of her congregation.

Elena Cornejo Luna OP, a member of the *Hermanas Misioneras Dominicas del Rosario* (Dominican Missionaries of the Rosary), has lived and worked for justice and peace among the poor of Peru.

Mary McAleese served as the eighth President of Ireland from 1997 to 2011.

Luigi Mezzadri CM is Emeritus Professor of Church History at the Pontifical Gregorian University and Lecturer in the History of Papal Diplomacy at the Pontifical Ecclesiastical Academy.

Anna Morrone, a religious of the Union of St Catherine of Siena of the Missionaries of the Schools, has a degree in literature from the Free University of Our Lady Assumed into Heaven (LUMSA) in Rome. She was a missionary in Pakistan from 1973 until 1995, working as a formator of students, a task which she still undertakes today in Italy.

Emmanuel Ntakarutimana OP, of the Vicariate of Rwanda and Burundi of the Canadian Province, chairs the Office for Evangelisation of the Burundi Catholic Bishops' Conference and runs the Ubuntu Centre for the promotion of peace and reconciliation in Burundi and the Great Lakes Region. He has also chaired the National Independent Commission for Human Rights of the Republic of Burundi from June 2011 to June 2015.

Michelle Olley OP, of the Racine Dominican community, has served in a variety of educational ministries including 35 years in Catholic Education and Formation in Catholic Schools and Parishes, and for the Milwaukee Archdiocese. In 1972 Michelle was elected to the Racine Unified Public School Board for 6 years and in the 1990s taught planning and organisational development in 8 cities to over 250 communities of Catholic women and men religious.

Margaret Ormond OP, of the Dominican Sisters of Peace, a recently reconfigured congregation, served as its first Prioress from 2009-2015. Currently she is President of a young women's college preparatory academy in New York City, which is committed to global solidarity. Sr Margaret was also the first International Coordinator of Dominican Sisters International (DSI).

Irmã Madalena de Santos, OP, of the Dominican Congregation of Our Lady of the Rosary of Monteils, graduated in Jurisprudence from PUC-GO (Pontifical Catholic University of Goiás), Brazil, with a specialization in Human Rights, Labour Law, and Labour Administrative Procedure.

Geraldine Smyth OP, of the Dominican Congregation, Cabra, with a background in education, ecumenics and peacebuilding, is the former Head of the Irish School of Ecumenics, Trinity College Dublin. She has a Ph.D. in Ecumenical Theology (ecumenical ecclesiology and ethics) from Trinity College, Dublin, and an honorary doctorate from Queen's University, Belfast, for her contribution to peace and reconciliation.

Adriana Valerio is a lecturer in the History of Christianity and of the Churches in the 'Federico II' University of Naples. From 2003 until 2007 she was President of AFERT (*Associazione Femminile Europea per la Ricerca Teologica* European Women's Association for Theological Research) and currently directs the international and interconfessional project *La Bibbia e le donne. Collana di esegesi, cultura e storia.*

Honora Werner OP, a Sister of St. Dominic of Caldwell, NJ, directs and teaches in the DMin in Preaching program at Aquinas Institute of Theology in St. Louis, MO. Her own research includes a thesis project on reading Scripture in the light of the evolving Universe Story.

Foreword

MARY McALEESE

As a former pupil at the St Dominic's High School in the Falls Road, Belfast, I owe a huge debt of gratitude to the Dominican Order. What is learned in childhood is engraved in stone and the Dominican Sisters understood that the academic development of their young charges, while of course very important, should not be the sole or central point of a young person's education. Dominican education is concerned with the education of the whole person, and an imperative part of that education is the awakening and development of a sense of morality and an understanding of the importance of living life according to a sound ethical code. Within the school community we were taught to search for the truth about God and the world and to understand our social and moral duties to that world. Of course, at that age we did not put formal words around it or even understand the concept of social ethics. We simply learned that in life it was important to follow rules of simple decency and fairness, rules that, in adult life, would allow us to make decisions based on the needs of society.

The Dominicans, however, know that words alone are not enough and that it is essentially through the witness of their lives that they support and uphold a society where righteousness and justice go hand in hand. It is a righteousness that is witnessed, not in a pious standing in judgement over their fellow man, but by the placing of God's teaching at the heart of what they do, in particular the living out of the great commandment to love one another, understanding that such love is both a discipline and a decision much different from the notion of a transient emotion or feeling. This love is a form of ethical living, which insists on solidarity with those who are helpless, powerless or overlooked. It calls too for a steady and 'blind' compassion for all of humanity, as well as a profound faith in the capacity of the human person to change for the better.

As a former President of Ireland, I am enormously proud of the Irish Dominican Sisters' transcendence of apartheid policies in South Africa which demonstrated, in a practical way, how integrated schools could work successfully. By being amongst the first schools to open their doors to children of all races in South Africa, the Dominican Sisters were at the forefront of promoting change and bringing about a fair and just system where it is now the constitutional right of all children in South Africa to enter any school, irrespective of race.

In Ireland's long and difficult struggle for peace, the contribution of the Dominican Sisters was calm, purposeful and effective. In practical and spiritual ways, they provided an all-important haven in the midst of the chaotic and violent environment that enclosed many of their students who were growing up in a troubled Belfast. By surrounding those students with a secure and constant ethos – one that embraced a spirit of openness, intellectual curiosity, optimism and cross-community tolerance – the Dominican Sisters quietly embedded the goal of peace and reconciliation into the minds and hearts of their students and many of the families within their community. In so doing, they created a spiritual infrastructure which helped many of us to deal effectively with growing up in complex, unjust and violent times.

The Dominican Sisters' commitment to social justice evolves and refreshes anew in each generation, adapting to a rapidly changing world which is impinging greatly on their own demographics, age profile, vocation recruitment and capacity. Yet, despite these contemporary realities and pressures, one gets the strong sense of a body of women who trust implicitly in the guidance of the Holy Spirit. Their work is done in the now but their timeline is of a very different scale and their destination is prepared for in this world but is not of this world. Theirs are important voices of contradiction and certainty in a world of doubt and cynicism.

As we move through the twenty-first century it is reassuring to know that the Dominican Sisters continue to push out into the deep in the tradition of the apostles and of St Dominic. They believe in that 'farther shore' and they have faith in humanity's ability to reach it.

Introduction

HELEN ALFORD, O.P., AND FRANCESCO COMPAGNONI, O.P.

It is a great pleasure for us, eight years on from the publication of *Preaching Justice I: Dominican Contributions to Social Ethics in the Twentieth Century* (hereafter PJI), to be introducing this second volume. If producing the first one was full of ups and downs, both of which made the job worthwhile, producing this one has been even more eventful and, thereby, all the more worthwhile.

In some ways, working on this book involved doing something similar to PJI – searching for authors through similar networks, talking about what members of the Dominican tradition have been doing, looking at the same time period – but, of course, in other ways it was very different. The history and structure of the congregations of Dominican sisters is not that of the friars, and women and men are not in the same place in society and in the Church. Events in the twentieth century affected women Dominicans very differently from their male counterparts, especially the rise of feminism and the impact of Vatican II.[1]

Hence, although this book shares many of the features of PJI, it is also different. First of all, we needed a more extensive introduction to the situation and history of the sisters, not only because this is a lot less well known than that of the friars, but also because of the major changes that women as a whole have been through in the twentieth century. The first part of the book makes a limited attempt to deal with this; thankfully, anyone more interested in these questions can go more deeply into it through the burgeoning literature on the history of women religious that is now available, even if it is not well known outside the academic world. Secondly, the way the contributions themselves are presented is different from PJI, where they were split by time period across the twentieth century. In that book, the introduction included short summaries of the particular situations of the various countries in those time periods from which the various figures presented had come. One of the ways in which this book is strikingly different from PJI is in how few of the

---

1. In this paragraph, we use the terms 'Dominican sisters' and 'women Dominicans'. Elsewhere, we also use 'Dominican women'. The use of such terms is sometimes indicative of a particular position on issues like the role of women in the Church or in the Dominican Order or family. Here we use these terms interchangeably, since we can see advantages and disadvantages in all of them. We use each of them where it makes sense to us to do so.

contributions are about individuals, and how many of them include quite extensive discussions about the situations in which the particular stories that are being told are situated, making it less important for us to add this kind of historical context here in the introduction. Another thing that is striking is how many of the contributions are from the end of the twentieth century and move into the present day; given this temporal frame, dividing them up chronologically did not make sense. Furthermore, most of the texts are about practical work for social justice rather than about thinking or writing about it (with a few important exceptions), which represents another significant difference between the two books. As a result of these and other, less important factors, we decided on a different way of presenting the contributions in this volume, grouping them around a theme or topic in the hope that this could be a more illuminating way of presenting the contribution of Dominican women to social ethics in the twentieth century. It will be these topics that are introduced here, rather than the historical contexts of the contributions, as we did in PJI.

RELIGIOUS AND DOMINICAN LIFE FOR WOMEN:
HISTORICAL BACKGROUND AND TWENTIETH-CENTURY DEVELOPMENTS
The history of religious life for women has now become a major area of research in Church history, women's studies and theology.[2] Nevertheless, for many readers of this book, if not for the sisters themselves, this history will be largely unknown. When thinking about what to present here, we thought first that it would be useful to do two things: Firstly, to examine the move from enclosed or monastic religious life to active forms. The transition from being a 'monk' in a monastery to being a 'friar' who belonged to a province and who could move among communities and, in that way, be more available for mission than the classical monk, is part of the foundational idea of the Dominican friars. By recognising the first set of constitutions in 1216, Pope Honorius III was allowing that transition to take place for male religious.

However, a similar transition for women was a much more difficult goal to attain, and had to wait for a few more centuries after the recognition of this possibility for men. In the meantime, many women active in apostolic works were associated with the Dominicans in different ways, among whom

2. See, for instance, the websites of the Conference on the History of Women Religious: http://www.chwr.org/ and the History of Women Religious in Britain and Ireland network, http://historyofwomenreligious.org/. Several important Dominican contributions have been made to this literature by Dominicans, including Sr Mary Ewens OP in *The Role of the Nun in Nineteenth Century America*, 1978, Arno Press, New York, described by the Conference on the History of Women Religious in 1998 as a 'seminal work' (see http://www.chwr.org/1998-awards/).

the fourteenth-century 'mantellata', St Catherine of Siena, would be the most famous. Since this transition took much longer, was more complicated and is more recent for women, and since the Dominican order today includes both enclosed nuns and active apostolic congregations, taking a closer look at how, when and why this possibility for women religious emerged seemed to be in order at the beginning of this book. Secondly, we needed to look at what has been happening to women in the twentieth century. In regard to the first issue, it was in Europe that this historical transition took place; our contribution, by the Church historian Luigi Mezzadri, while not ignoring the rest of Europe, focuses particularly on the situation in Italy and France, which were at the centre of this change.

The fact that the contribution on the transition to active religious life was set in Europe influenced our choice of how to deal with the second issue. It would have been hard to do justice to the changes that have been taking place for women across the world as a whole in one contribution. There is no 'average' woman or Dominican sister; all of them experience the major changes that took place for women in the twentieth century in the very concrete, local circumstances of their lives.

Therefore, we decided to continue with a focus on Europe in this contribution too, and particularly on Italy, so as to form a kind of particular case study of what has been happening in one part of the world in a way that complements Mezzadri's contribution. Adriana Valerio focuses on the impact of the women's movements on the Church and on religious women in the Church in Italy. We are conscious that many women in the world today have, sadly, not experienced the changes she discusses, or at least, have not experienced all of them. Her account cannot do justice to their situation. Similarly, readers from the US, for instance, might argue that this contribution does not go far enough and that it also does not represent their experience.

We expect some readers to feel dissatisfied with the choices we made, and all we can say in response is to explain why we made those choices. To us, it made sense that the chapter on the transition from enclosed to active life and on the changes for women in the twentieth century should relate to each other, allowing them to show one particular example of how these changes have progressed through time, rather than trying to produce something more general and, necessarily, more abstract. Staying on a more local, concrete level is also in keeping with what the contributors themselves have done in their texts. Since all the contributions are about very concrete, specific stories about groups of, or individual, sisters, the way these two contextual chapters work mirrors the way the authors (most of them sisters themselves) present the work for justice of Dominican women in the rest of the book.

Mezzadri's article opens in a rather alarming way, in a Europe caught up in the changes of the Counter-Reformation and, thus, with the strict re-imposition of enclosure for women in religious vows. Grilles are given strict design rules; nuns who leave the monastery without permission are to be excommunicated; abbesses encourage the nuns in their community to consider the monastery as a 'precious monument that should bury them' with the Lord. We might also be disturbed by the fact that it was a Dominican pope, Pius V, who was responsible for the re-imposition of the enclosure (or, in the case of some communities, its imposition for the first time) in 1566. Yet, if the reader can make it through the opening part of the text, it becomes clearer why the author uses this kind of 'shock tactic' at the beginning.

For what then emerges is both the 'agony and the ecstasy' of the enclosure, to re-use the title of Irving Stone's 1987 biographical novel on Michelangelo. On the one hand, entering the enclosure can be about entering into freedom: in her autobiography, Isabella Tomasi (1645–1699) speaks of being 'freed from the prison of the world', indicating that she experiences the contemplative life of the enclosure as a 'liberation' from 'prison'. On the other, Arcangela Tarabotti (1604–1652) wrote passionately about the 'nunnish hell' of the enclosure, and that the words of Dante's *Inferno* could be written on the doors of all monasteries: 'Abandon all hope, ye who enter here'. Both of these experiences, and many less dramatic in between, characterised the life of the enclosure in that period; the latter type was at least in part a result of the social conventions of the day that required noble families to keep their patrimony intact for their eldest son and for a dowry for one of their daughters, and as the need for that function gradually fell away, the enclosure could gradually realise its proper purpose as a means, freely chosen, for creating space for God and for others.

However, it is perhaps one of the ironies of history that, just at the moment that ecclesiastical attempts to re-impose enclosure were at their height, we begin to see the first really organised attempts to create the possibility for active religious life for women in figures like Angela Merici (1474–1540), Mary Ward (1585–1645) and Vincent de Paul (1581–1660). Only the last manages to make the breakthrough to a stable, recognised institutional form for active religious life for women, and Mezzadri discusses why (Cardinal

Suenens in his book *The Nun in the World: Religious and the Apostolate*, adds interesting complementary information to what the author gives us here).[3] To the editors, it also seems important to note that Mary Ward was unsuccessful not only because she made recourse to Rome, but also because, unlike Vincent de Paul, with his good ecclesiastical contacts in Rome and his status as a cleric, she was an unknown outsider. Overall, this history indicates how difficult it was to make this breakthrough. Nevertheless, it was providential that it came about when it did. After the French Revolution and the Napoleonic period, it would be the active female congregations that would largely keep religious life alive in Europe until the older orders (including the Dominican friars) could get back on their feet again following their suppression and dispersal and the loss of their property.

Following these historical chapters, another deals with the way in which the congregations of Dominican sisters are structured and estimates their numbers across the twentieth century. We include more detail for the end of the twentieth century, partly because we have more accurate statistics for that period, but also because the bulk of the contributions come from this time period. It is striking that, despite the decline that most congregations have experienced since Vatican II, it is still almost certainly the case ('almost certainly', because we do not have complete data for the beginning of the twentieth century) that there were more Dominican sisters at the end of the twentieth century than at the beginning.

Part 1 of the book closes with a contribution from Sr Margaret Ormond, who was the first co-ordinator of Dominican Sisters International (DSI) and a close observer of that phenomenon and of the development of the idea of the Dominican family.

DOMINICAN WOMEN PREACHING JUSTICE: FIVE THEMES

The five themes around which the 22 contributions are grouped were not set in advance but were selected after reading the contributions themselves several times and trying to uncover what connected them. In presenting the themes, we move from those that are more focused on resisting oppression and fighting exclusion, towards more positive themes with an ever-widening focus: first, promoting women and children, then building peace and, finally, 'building a new vision'. Although we tried to let the themes emerge from the contributions themselves, given the nature of some of them, their allocation

3. Leon-Joseph Cardinal Suenens, *The Nun in the World: Religious and the Apostolate*, revised edition, 1963, London, Burns and Oates, pp. 41–42.

to one or other of the five themes is nevertheless somewhat arbitrary. The contributions on particular Maryknoll and Sinsinawa sisters, for instance, ranging across the twentieth century, as well as the history of the foundation and development of the Iraqi Dominican sisters, could have been included under any of the headings. Similarly, the five themes could, perhaps, have been reduced, with the two more 'negative' themes merged into one, under a heading such as 'resisting evil', and the three more positive themes could have been included under a heading such as 'working for a more just world'. Nevertheless, we think that the advantages of using these particular themes outweighs the disadvantages. The contributions grouped under 'resisting oppression' deal with situations that are more extreme, in terms of lack of respect for the most basic human rights, including the right to life, than those in the section on fighting exclusion. Similarly, a section focusing on women and children is especially appropriate for a book dealing with the apostolic activities of women, while peacebuilding provides a foundation for moving towards a new vision, and became a major topic of activity and study in the twentieth century, thereby meriting a section dedicated to it alone.

RESISTANCE TO OPPRESSION

The stories recounted in this section all come from the second half of the twentieth century and range from resistance to totalitarian Communism in Hungary and Vietnam, through resistance to the apartheid system in South Africa, to resistance against the genocidal frenzy that gripped Rwanda in the first half of the 1990s, reaching its peak in 1994. In each case, the resistance takes a particular form: in the case of the Communist regime, resistance regards the existence of the Church herself and the survival of religious life as part of her tradition; in the apartheid regime, it was a struggle for the recognition of human dignity and of basic human rights, regardless of skin colour; in the Rwandan context, it involved both remaining with the people (in the case of the Belgian sisters, who could have left) and being true Christian witnesses to peace and solidarity with others, irrespective of tribal affiliation, in the midst of an orgy of killing by people, most of whom also professed to be Christian.

We can also see the very particular difficulties that the sisters experienced in each case. In Hungary, the isolation of the actors is almost complete. The possibility to be in contact with the Church or the order outside the country is nil, and, thanks to the regime's capacity to use the weaknesses and difficulties of people to blackmail them and constrain them to spy and inform on their friends and family, the sisters always had to be aware of its possible infiltration even into their most intimate relationships. Resisting in these circumstances required a really heroic, even super-human, strength based on one's faith in God, since support from others could not be relied on. In such a context, it is extraordinary what the sisters and others like them managed to achieve, and in particular, that even 'base communities' could emerge; the author, Sr Imelda, uses this title advisedly, since these communities were linked with the base community phenomenon elsewhere, even if, ironically enough, in other places they were often seen as vehicles for promoting Communism. This contribution is also important because of its extensive use of the archives of the Hungarian secret service, where copies of the letters the sisters sent or received are still to be found, as well as detailed records of their movements and contacts with others. In a phrase about Sr Tarzicia, the prioress-general of the congregation at the time of the dissolution, Sr Imelda underlines the full irony of this detailed record: 'Her [Sr Tarzicia's] life and sacrifice was known only to the Lord – though it was almost as well known to the State Security system.'

Many of the worst moments in the South African story are contemporary with those of the Hungarian one, and, although the sisters themselves did not suffer the persecution of their Hungarian counterparts, the political and socio-economic exclusion of the majority black African population in the country and the violent repression of any attempts to remedy this, even in non-violent ways, called upon the Dominican sisters to get actively involved. Indeed, solidarity with others is one of the key elements that allowed the resistance of the sisters, along with many others, to be effective in bringing about change; the contribution, for instance, also covers what other congregations of Dominican sisters involved in the struggle, along with the Cabra sisters, were doing, such as the sisters of King William's Town and Newcastle. Solidarity also came from outside the country, not only from individuals and groups, but also from the new theological ideas that were emerging from Vatican II.

At the same time, precisely the fact that the sisters as a community could resist the regime put the communities and their schools at risk, and they had to make choices that were not easy (whereas the Hungarian sisters had no 'choice' – they were forced to resist heroically or lose everything). What stands out in the case of the South African sisters, then, is that they made a choice to resist when they could have chosen otherwise. The useful inclusion in this contribution of the Irish prehistory of the Cabra sisters may also give part of the explanation as to why they had the courage to start resisting as they did. Another twisted link with the Hungarian story was the claim of the apartheid government to be anti-communist and the accusation levelled at the sisters that they were promoting communism in resisting against it – the morning after the first whites-only school admitted its first black students in January 1977, the school walls were daubed with the graffiti: 'This school is run by a Communist'. Curriculum changes took the resistance beyond the level of admitting black students, in valuing the cultures and religious traditions from which the children came – when a Hindu child talked about meditating for an hour before coming to school, it was a 'healthy shock' for the Catholics. Beyond the school walls, the protest marches also created the solidarity that was gradually able to overcome injustice but which also provided a 'moment of vision – what the new South Africa could be – all races, all creeds, and none, walking arm in arm into danger for justice'. Unlike the Hungarian case, however, where the regime's grip started to weaken in the 1980s as it limped towards its end, the last few years of apartheid were 'almost the worst'. Also worthy of note is the role of the Church in the peaceful transition to democracy – the sisters and many others criss-crossed the country in the run-up to the 1994 elections, explaining to local people the connections between the Gospel message and democratic participation.

In both of the previous cases, well-established congregations were called upon to witness to their faith in dangerous circumstances. In the case of Rwanda, we see a newly formed congregation having to face the onslaught of senseless killing within ten years of its foundation, as well as a prolonged period of instability in the build-up to the unbelievably violent months of 1994 when over 500,000 and perhaps a million people died. Coming straight after the South African contribution, where the elections of 1994 represented a key moment of transition for the country from oppression to freedom, the poignancy of the Rwandan situation is all the clearer. In the killing machine that gripped the country, we see a kind of parody of the solidarity that was operative in South Africa, which, instead of contributing to freedom, dehumanised and robbed human beings of dignity. The presence of the sisters, as a sign of life, forgiveness and generosity in the midst of a meaningless descent into an inferno of violence, was a real act of resistance based on faith in God and trust in his mercy. Despite the youth of their community, in the years leading up to the worst of the killing, the sisters went through a period of spiritual purification while, in its midst, they continued their life: 'the perpetual profession of Sister Pudentiana Mujawabega took place October

24, 1994 in the Cathedral in lifeless Byumba in the context of a war, with the encouragement of Father Hozer, the Apostolic Vicar, since the bishop of the diocese and almost all of its priests had been murdered. There was only one survivor.'

Having passed through this baptism of fire, the sisters went on to use the courage they had developed by accepting missions in some of the most violent and abandoned neighbourhoods, not only in Rwanda but also in the Democratic Republic of Congo and the Central African Republic. The contribution includes the unforgettable words of an elderly Christian in one of the areas to which the sisters went to live and minister: 'Instead of the cries of wild beasts and the fire of war, now, for the first time, the Lord can be heard here.' Similarly, in one of the other missions, a sister wrote: 'Our presence in the population is very significant. This is very encouraging for us. When we go shopping in town with the car, at least one sister must remain at the convent, otherwise the people think we have left and they too would want to flee.' Their solidarity with the people is always the same. Somewhat like the South African story, with its back history in the centuries of resistance to oppression in Ireland, the role of the Dominican Missionaries of Africa in the drama of Rwanda also has its preparation in the work of other sisters in the region, and especially in the life and vocation of Sr Marie-Pascale Crevecoeur, a Dominican sister of Namur. Her own life, touched by the double tragedy of the loss of both her parents before she was a month old, symbolised and prepared her for what was to come in Rwanda and how she would need to strengthen her sisters there. The contribution very beautifully and effectively brings out this connection.

The contribution on the sisters in Vietnam, written by a sister from Sweden on the basis of three extensive visits to the country, is rather different from the previous three texts, and yet it also complements them in an important way. The contribution focuses on how the Vietnamese Dominican sisters build peace, focusing on three ways of doing so: promoting reconciliation; promoting the good of the people through social work, in the context of a rather 'raw' capitalist economy, despite the Communist government, and by promoting interfaith hospitality. As such, therefore, the contribution could have been included in the section on 'peacebuilding', but it is here because the sisters in Vietnam do all that they do in the face of a regime that continues to repress them, and therefore their action for peace could also be seen, in a very real way, as positive resistance against oppression. One of the important elements of their activity is to rebuild trust with those who have painful memories of the pre-Communist Diem regime and the way in which it unfairly promoted Catholics. Like Sr Marie Pascale Crevecoeur in Rwanda and the Hungarian sisters, the Vietnamese sisters have a similar figure in Sr Maria Nguyen Thi Men, someone whose long resistance in the face of oppression and fidelity to her vocation is an inspiration to the sisters and to all those who meet her and hear about her. We will meet the question of interfaith dialogue in several other parts of the book; in this contribution, it is played out in the context of the Asian culture with its tendency towards searching for and building social good. The sisters show themselves to be in solidarity with their people, and this stretches even to organising for a part of the formation of their young sisters to take place in monasteries of Buddhist nuns.

TAKING UP THE FIGHT AGAINST SOCIAL EXCLUSION

Resisting against oppression that is open, or against the direct violation of basic human rights or frenzied violence, is heroic. At the same time, it is also relatively clear in such situations that one should strive to have the courage to make such resistance. On the other hand, there are many other less obvious or hidden forms of oppression that are apparently non-violent, but that can lead to equally damaging effects for human beings and the human community. Social exclusion, marginalisation and unjust social structures would be some of the forms of this less obvious, but no less real, attack on the human person and human dignity. In this section of the book, we have two contributions from France and one from Brazil, covering the life and witness of a worker-sister, support to landless farmers and the non-formal education of immigrants, aimed at promoting their integration into French society.

The twentieth-century phenomenon of the worker-priests is relatively well-known; what is less well-known is that there were also worker-sisters. Elisabeth Voisin, who had been inspired to join the Petites Sœurs Dominicaines because she experienced their closeness to the poor, followed the situation of the worker-priests very closely. When the movement in France was suppressed by Rome for fear of infiltration by the Communist Party (the Hungarian contribution shows why such fear was not to be treated lightly, even if historical studies tend to show that it was misplaced in this case), she was challenged by Fr Chenu to take up the baton they had had to drop, and she let that challenge inspire her. The call she experienced was not initially accepted by her congregation, and she was tempted to leave as others had done, but she remained convinced that it would be within the congregation that she would carry out this mission. Eventually her superiors agreed, and she began her life as a worker-sister in the world of industrial laundries, mostly with Muslim immigrant women. She did not hide her faith – as the author says, '[i]f there are only very few persons who know about her commitment to the religious life, she never hides her faith. But she never waves it as a flag, either.' She was also as 'cunning as a serpent and harmless as a dove' in her dealings with the only realistic option regarding worker solidarity for these women – the Communist union. She made use of the union structures in order to help the women gain protection and support, but she never allowed the Communists to use it as a means to constrain these vulnerable women to join the Communist Party. She exercised the virtue of prudence to a great degree, as well as providing an example of new ways for the Church to be present in society.

The story from Brazil shows the Dominican Sisters of Monteils, along with Fr Henri des Roziers OP, living outside the safe zone of traditional religious life, participating in the everyday sufferings of the landless people of the Parà region and organising for their new members in formation to experience this situation as part of their formation journey. The 'Pilgrimages of Land and Water' allow these downtrodden people to draw on the resources of the faith in standing up for their dignity in the face of an 'ethically-blind capitalism'. Their accompaniment of the people represents a very important model for religious life, confronting the current problems of our day, especially as they are to be found in emerging and developing economies where a mixture of corruption and lack of skills and appropriate social institutions can lead to the kind of violent repression of those deemed a nuisance by the powerful. These processes are also closely connected with developments in the post-industrial world and the migratory pressures we experience today, raising fundamental questions for our socio-economic order. We need to find new ways of expressing solidarity, of allowing the poor and excluded of the world to unite and rise up, for their good and for the good of humanity as a whole. The example of support to these processes that the religious in this Brazilian example give is emblematic of one of the ways religious are called to carry out the mission of the Sermon on the Mount in our world of today.

In the association 'LA CLE' the sisters of the Roman congregation and the many volunteers who work with them fight social exclusion in another way – by providing the kind of education that can promote inclusion. The contribution shows how important personal relationships can be in overcoming exclusive barriers, and that the personality of the educator and evangeliser is key, in the relation of a dialogue partner, accompanying the migrants along their way to greater inclusion. The example of what LA CLE is doing will be reflected in the lives of many other Dominican sisters around the world, especially those who have retired from teaching, like the sisters featured here, and who turn their skills to being applied more directly to combating exclusion.

PROMOTING WOMEN AND CHILDREN
AND PROVIDING SOCIAL SUPPORT

This is the part of the book that could have included contributions from every congregation and even every Dominican community. Promoting women and children and providing social support is an integral part of the 'holy preaching' of every community of Dominican women. Still, in these contributions, there are some elements that stand out: in Pakistan and Iraq, the ongoing harshness of their context and their endurance in the face of it; the very specific charism of the Bethany Dominicans for allowing women to be 'rehabilitated' in this life, not only 'redeemed' in the next; the combination of a missionary focus with these characteristics across the twentieth century, as in the case of the Maryknoll Missionaries, as well as the striking figure of Sr Pétronille Kayiba with her theology of the role of women in Africa and her verve as a 'serial founder' of organisations and groups, many of which are specifically focused on women.

The need to focus on supporting women, especially through education, quickly became clear to the Missionaries of the Schools on their arrival in Pakistan, and they have maintained that focus, even when it meant that they had to make hard choices and abandon other missionary possibilities that were also promising. This has also brought them into living within the context of a Muslim-dominated, progressively radicalising society, in which the urgency for interreligious dialogue, especially on the level of everyday life, is ever greater.

Empowering women and girls was the 'foundational vision' of the lay community that would later become the Dominican Sisters of St Catherine of Siena of Mosul in Iraq. The extraordinary story of their foundation at the end of the nineteenth and the beginning of the twentieth century, focused around the witness of the three Susans, the 'Sausanat', and creating within itself the meeting of many different Eastern Christian rites and languages, continues through the twentieth century and on into our day as one of real resistance in the face of one life-threatening blow after another and through a period of chaotic history for the Iraqi people as a whole. As such, this contribution could well have been included in the section on 'resisting oppression', and yet what seems equally important about it to us is the focus of the sisters on developing women within a culture, not unlike the Pakistani situation, where this is not easy to do. The sisters have consistently focused on educating and developing their own members, and then on allowing sisters to put that education to good use, especially in raising up the position of women in Iraqi society and in promoting peace and reconciliation in a country racked by war and instability. Margaret Ormond's contribution on the founding of DSI in the 1990s shows the importance of the Iraqi sisters and their isolated witness in stimulating Dominican sisters worldwide to develop more solidarity between themselves for the sake of their common good and their shared mission. The contribution on Iraq also mentions the library to promote interreligious dialogue that the sisters joined the friars in setting up in Turkey in the 1990s.

Sr Pétronille Kayiba, working in the Democratic Republic of Congo, has very clearly understood her vocation as a sister and theologian in the context of this war-torn country to be at the border between life and death and to make the liberation of life from the chains that bind it a central theme of her preaching. Her ideas about women in this regard are intriguing and challenging to many others who work in the area of women's rights. For Kayiba, women are mothers in both individual and social senses; in the latter sense, they are called to non-violence and to care for a good social order. She strikingly views the exclusion of women from public decision-making as an attempt by men to take over the life-giving role of women, entrusted to them by the Creator:

> ... since men have often wanted to dominate, and even take the place of women, relegating them to nothing more than an erotic function, these men have 'given birth' to a society that is a horribly violent monster. In the process, they forget that 'giving birth' is a singular privilege given to women by God. Therefore, combined efforts must be made to rehabilitate women so that they can regain their originality as intended by the Creator. Only under these conditions can African women be fully fertile and able to integrate fertility dynamically into the economic, political, cultural and religious dimensions.

This powerful African reflection on the role and dignity of women adds an intriguing and enriching voice to the others in the book that take up this issue.

The history and foundational charism of the Bethany sisters further enriches our vision about women and about how Dominican sisters can promote their good. Their founder, Fr Lataste, had been deeply moved by the (now much debated) image of Mary Magdalene, and the possibility that great sinners also had the makings of great saints. Not only did he meet women as part of his pastoral experience in women's prisons who reminded him of this, he also realised that many women in prison were not necessarily fully responsible for the crimes committed, that others who were also responsible had not paid for their mistakes and crimes as these women had, and that these women, like all the rest of us, needed the possibility to be accepted back into society, to be 'rehabilitated'. This idea of rehabilitation became central to the founding charism of the Bethany Dominicans, but it also became recognised in French law with a particular meaning – the chance for women who had received a custodial sentence to spend it, or part of it, with a religious community instead of in a prison.[4] It was to allow all the sisters who joined the congregation to be on an equal footing that discretion and confidentiality, especially about each sister's past, was so crucial to the Bethany sisters. At the same time, this left them in some difficulty by the time of the second half of the twentieth century, so that they had to introduce some modifications in order to remain faithful to their original inspiration, while also being open to development in the light of 'the signs of the times'. Discretion in an age of transparency is not easy to handle. The Bethany story also encompasses the other half of this theme, the promotion of children, through the story of the children's home and villages, bringing out how innovative these sisters were in their ways of treating the children, given the generally accepted models of child care at the time.

The Maryknoll story is one of intense energy and dynamism in the spreading of the Gospel through all kinds of ministry: many types of health care in many different situations, supporting the Japanese interned

4. The situation in French prisons in the second half of the nineteenth century is not easy for us to understand today. The Third Republic was secular and anticlerical but historians tell us that it still had a religious vision of the penal system. In this context, female religious congregations oversaw the inmates in women's prisons until the end of the nineteenth century (and continued to do so even later in the two women's prisons in Paris). The Bethany sisters introduced an innovative element to this situation: the possibility of rehabilitation, not only of doing penance. For more on this, see Sophie Leterrier, 'Prison et pénitence au XIXe siècle': https://www.cairn.info/ revue-romantisme-2008-4-page-41.htm and Olivier Landron, *La vie chrétienne dans les prisons de France au XXe siècle*, Paris, Éditions du Cerf, coll. 'L'histoire à vif', 2011. A review of the book by Landron can be found at https://assr.revues.org/24639.

in US camps during the Second World War, combating racism in Hawaii, supporting prostitutes in Lima, running the communications system for the bishops during the Rhodesian crisis, presiding over the Truth Commission in Ecuador, rebuilding higher education in Cambodia, working with the elderly in Panama, dealing with the AIDS crisis in El Salvador and promoting an ecological lifestyle in the Philippines. All of these impressive developments grew out of the initial inspiration of the congregation which found its first application in China. Here, as the author, Sr Bernice Kita says, 'the Maryknoll Sister pioneers in China carried the Good News to women and children, staying in villages for weeks at a time. They desired to save souls, yet saving lives soon became a large part of their work. From the beginning, spreading the Good News by word went hand in hand with spreading the Good News by deed.'

PEACEBUILDING

Building peace became a major question for society as a whole, as well as the Church, in the twentieth century, such that, by the end of the century, peacebuilding had largely replaced the earlier focus on deciding whether a war might not be unjust (a more precise and accurate way of describing what is usually referred to the other way around, with the term 'the just war theory'). The peace movements were already well-established in the early twentieth century, and the companion volume to this one deals with early Dominican involvement in them, whereas the contributions on this topic here all come from the second half of the twentieth century.

The search for truth and for reconciliation after the terrible years of the atrocities committed both by the communist terrorist group, Sendero Luminoso, and the government in trying to defeat them, is a very important way of building peace in a post-conflict situation. In being involved in such activity, the Dominican Sisters of the Rosary carried on the medieval tradition of the Dominican friars, who would bring together all the parties in a violent dispute in order to find a way to reconciliation. Being close to the poor and promoting justice, peace and human rights meant that these sisters are particularly able to mediate between excluded groups and the more powerful in society in order to bring about the resolution of conflict.

Another part of the world where peacebuilding was extremely important before any official peace accord could be reached was Northern Ireland. As in much of Latin America, the roots of the violence in Ireland go back centuries, with the different communities having developed different histories of the injustices they had suffered with few links between them. The main work of the Dominican sisters in this situation, discussed by the author as a form of following Christ as 'King/Sage, Priest and Prophet', involved building bridges and bringing people together, sometimes for major events, but most often in simple, everyday ways, allowing the building of relationships and some kind of shared identity, healing the wounds from the past. One of the things that is so striking about this contribution is the diversity of forms that activity for peacebuilding took, and the length of time and patience that they required, since misunderstandings and hatreds that had been built up over centuries could not be healed quickly.[5]

With the advent of weapons of mass destruction, many times more powerful than those dropped with devastating effect on Japan at the end of the Second World War, the possibility of a war where they might be used became impossible to justify in any circumstance, as well as too terrible to contemplate. The three sisters of the Grand Rapids congregation who carried out symbolic, ritual acts at the sites of the weapons themselves, as well as many other forms of resistance, putting themselves on a collision course with state power and enduring imprisonment as a result, have expressed in practice what modern Catholic social thought would teach. This is also what Pope St John Paul II captured so movingly in his sermon at Coventry Cathedral in 1982, and in his yearly messages for the World Day of Peace: 'War should be part of the tragic past.'[6] Their actions are especially significant because they take place in the US, which remains the leading military power, as well as being a country where Christian values still have social impact.

BUILDING A NEW VISION

The seven contributions grouped together under this heading represent the most diverse group among the five themes presented in the book. If we are talking about 'building a new vision', however, in all its diversity and richness, this should come as no surprise. It should also be no surprise that many of the issues touched here are referred to elsewhere in the book – this theme draws together what has gone before in terms of a positive proposition of a good society, where oppression and exclusion have no place, and where the promotion of human rights, especially those of women and children,

5. The author of this contribution wanted it to be dedicated it to the memory of Fr Austin Flannery OP, and the editors are delighted to be able to note this here in the Introduction.

6. Pope St John Paul II, Sermon at Coventry Cathedral, 30 May 1982, available at http://w2.vatican.va/content/john-paul-ii/en/homilies/1982/documents/hf_jp-ii_hom_19820530_coventry.html (last accessed 19.01.16).

takes place in a context of active peace-building. Through the rather clumsy mixed metaphor of 'building' a 'vision', we are able to bring to the fore a sample of the variety of initiatives that Dominican sisters have taken, and are still taking, to witness to more human and sustainable ways of life and to the role that the spreading of the Gospel can play in these developments. Resisting oppression and taking up the fight against exclusion are also parts of these stories, since building the new vision also requires constant vigilance against its opposite; the wheat and the tares grow up together until the Lord comes.

This section opens with the figure of Luigia Tincani, the foundress of the Missionaries of the Schools, looked at from the point of view of her concern for justice. Tincani is an important figure in the development of the role of women in the Catholic Church in Italy, and the Missionaries of the Schools, the congregation she founded, gets as near to the concept of a lay movement as could be imagined a few decades before such institutes received official recognition from the Church. In the context of the Fascist period, with all the difficulties it created for Church institutions, she quite naturally accepted a leadership role with regard to the issues that religious sisters were facing with their schools (almost all Catholic schools were run by religious at that time). Unlike her, many of the sisters in other congregations at that time had not had access to the education that she had received; the combination of her broader and deeper knowledge with her religious consecration, bringing her close to the sisters as a whole, allowed her to be able to share with them in an especially fruitful way the 'fruits of her contemplation'. As the contribution shows, Tincani saw that the promotion of women 'spiritually and culturally' was 'an act of social justice', and in doing so, she was especially concerned about women's education and of opening up to them the possibility of an 'intellectual vocation … understood as the fundamental work of their lives and practised as a liturgical cult and an apostolate'. Seen like this, studying 'for the love of God', was, for those with this vocation, 'a quest for the life divine hidden in what we know … seeking the truth, with purity of heart and humanity, in nature; hearing the universal presence of God'. Tincani's story brings out how the full flowering of women's capabilities will be a part of the new vision that Dominican sisters are building together.

Kaye Ashe's masterful contribution on how the Sinsinawa sisters worked for justice across the twentieth century and in various fields is an appropriate next step in developing the vision, expanding on the previous contribution into a wider group in a different social context. In both contributions, the role of teaching and education is strongly present; in the contribution on Tincani, the way in which that education can bring a deep spirituality into the state or public school system is emphasised, whereas, in a complementary way, in the contribution on the Sinsinawa sisters we see how education can confront structural injustices in economic, political and social systems and promote a vision of society based on the Gospels and on the Church's Tradition. Putting together curricula on the social teaching of the Church, challenging racial and sexual prejudice, developing a vision of the economy based on the Gospels and on the teaching of St Thomas and – the story that will perhaps relate to the greatest number of sisters – working in parish life and through campaigning for justice in all walks of life, these sisters capture many facets of the Church's mission in the field of justice. In them we see more dimensions of the 'new vision': an education that forms a good character as well as imparting knowledge; resistance to prejudices that damage and block human development; a vision of the economy that starts and ends with the common good and human development, putting market mechanisms and private property in their proper place as means of achieving them; and the need to keep parish and community life ever vigilant against the encroaching evils of the misuse of state and economic power and of exclusion and humiliation in our midst.

One of the differences between the two contributions is the question of women's ordination. Most of what the Sinsinawa sisters were doing predates the 1994 document by Pope St John Paul II on the question, where he states explicitly that the non-admission of women to the priesthood is to be definitively held by all believers. Aware of the potential of such a statement to undermine the recognition of equality between men and women, the same pope also made an extended attempt, primarily through the talks at his Wednesday audiences, to think through the relation between men and women from a theological point of view, aiming to illuminate their equality as well as the significance of the difference between them. At least one thing can be said that links the work of Sr Albertus Magnus McGrath and Sr Dolores Brooks, as presented in this contribution, to the efforts of Pope St John Paul II to deal with this issue: these sisters, along with many others, kept raising it, not allowing it to be swept under the carpet or ignored, and in so doing they made an important contribution to drawing the attention of the papacy, and of theologians in general, to the question, creating the possibility for progress to be made in thinking it through and dealing with it.

In Rose Thering, we find a sister who had the courage to face up to anti-

Semitic prejudice in school curriculum materials that had nevertheless already received the *nihil obstat* and *imprimatur* from the appropriate Church authorities. In so doing, she was able to play a role in strengthening those at the Vatican Council who were behind the key document on religious freedom, *Nostra Aetate*. Her contribution to the 'new vision', as presented in this chapter, is the recognition of the 'spiritual patrimony common to Christians and Jews', and the desire she shared with the Council Fathers that all should 'forget the past and work sincerely for mutual understanding and [to] preserve as well as [to] promote together for the benefit of all mankind social justice and moral welfare, as well as peace and freedom'.[7]

The example of Rose Thering leads smoothly into the next contribution, taking the work of one sister on interreligious respect and dialogue to the level of living an intercultural community life. The story of the Swedish sisters of the Roman Congregation shows how difficult it was to walk along this path, but also provides insights that can help others be more aware of the pitfalls involved and thus more able to achieve what they did. As the author says: '[i]n understanding what a process of integration really means, the Dominican sisters in Sweden slowly moved from living *in* a multi-cultural context to an intercultural life as such *within* their community'. In this, they went through a process similar to that which the Catholic Church as a whole in Sweden has had to work through. From being a Church of immigrants trying to enter into Swedish society, or of Swedish converts, they had to learn how to be an intercultural Church. They went from trying to be a *Swedish* Catholic Church to being a Catholic Church *in Sweden*. At the time the contribution was completed, the Latin rite was being celebrated in 12 languages, while a vicariate of Oriental Catholics existed with five different rites; the Ethiopian/Eritrean community was celebrating their liturgy in Gheez and then, finally, there were the Swedes themselves, also using the Latin Rite. The contribution shows very well how dealing with cultural difference within the same community needs to be handled in a very clear and upfront way. As the author says: 'we have learnt to live with certain tensions. Above all, we have accepted that we are not equal and that we can never pretend to live like equals either. This may sound shocking, but if an intercultural relationship should ever be fruitful and create something new, we have to be humble enough to accept some fundamental facts of a specific situation. Living fraternal justice then, with generosity and love in

---

7. *Nostra Aetate*, n. 3 and n. 4, available at http://www.vatican.va/archive/hist_councils/ii_vatican_council/documents/vat-ii_decl_19651028_nostra-aetate_en.html.

the biblical sense of these words, is to realise the Dominican motto of Truth and Mercy.' This account, then, contributes to the 'new vision' that we are 'building' by showing how community life may become a microcosm of the situation of intercultural life in many of today's societies, where solutions to problems can be tried and tested and then shared with others.

The contribution from Colombia focuses on another aspect of the 'new vision': what the poor can offer and how the Dominican sisters can benefit from an experience of being with the poor. The contribution has a particular colour because it is written by two Dominican sisters who are also twins. They emphasise the importance of hope in the face of extreme inequality (according to statistics, Latin America experiences some of the greatest levels of inequality recorded in the world today), and their language and approach, though written before the current papacy, resonates with that of Pope Francis. After an extensive review of the situation in the country, they can say: 'current Colombian structures and policies tend to be more exclusive than inclusive'. Yet, despite their analysis, they can still make the startling claim that 'Jesus lived a life of poverty in the way the poor do. This insight is the greatest Latin American contribution to theological reflection, the so-called *irruption of the poor into the Church.*' There is something valuable in living as a poor person, and this is something that Jesus wanted to emphasise. There is much here in this contribution for a theological reflection related to how social ethics and social justice relate to our faith.

So far under this theme we have looked at the promotion of women, the promotion of justice through education, campaigning and economics, the promotion of a true intercultural encounter, within the community of Dominican sisters as well as beyond, and the value of a life lived in and with the poor. All these are part of the new vision that is being built by the Dominican sisters, as well as many others, within the Church. Along with these issues, we received contributions that deal with two other issues: the promotion of sustainable lifestyles and the implications this has for theology, and the way the sisters in the US have been using their financial resources through responsible investing to promote ecological and social sustainability as well as solid financial returns on their investments.

The ecological contribution was completed before Pope Francis was elected to the See of Peter, but the advantage of this is to see how strong the official teaching of the Church about the environment was even before his papacy. Furthermore, the contribution shows how the initial mission of St Dominic and his companions put valuing the goodness of creation at its core and therefore creates a strong basis for Dominican involvement in treasuring God's creation and in protecting it from what threatens it in our day. The contribution shows how particular sisters and congregations as a whole have committed to environmental education, to developing more sustainable lifestyles, especially through creating farms that promote sustainable forms of agriculture, legal and health care systems that embody environmental awareness, and to deepening a theology and spirituality of creation, offering possibilities for retreats and opportunities for formation in creation spirituality as part of their preaching apostolate.

In the contribution on how the sisters in the US have developed socially responsible ways of investing their resources, while still making reasonable returns on those investments, especially for the sake of supporting aged sisters, the first key point is that it is the sisters themselves who need to be awakened to the need for Christians to connect their faith to the way in which they invest. Through the actions of screening out unacceptable companies and 'screening in' those that are particularly concerned about social and environmental issues, engaging with companies through shareholder resolutions, voting on other resolutions and participating in dialogues with companies, as well as searching for opportunities to invest in communities, or for 'impact investing', as it is increasingly known, the sisters have become more and more expert at combining the need for returns on their investments with promoting a business system that is sustainable and which respects and promotes human dignity. Also worthy of note is how the bigger congregations of sisters, especially the Adrian congregation, have helped smaller ones through training and sharing competence, and how in general the responsible investing community of which the Dominican sisters are a part work through regional and national coalitions (especially the Interfaith Center for Corporate Responsibility, ICCR), creating the possibility for greater impact through solidarity.

Before concluding this introduction, we would like to thank all those who contributed to the PJII project – those who contributed time and effort, in various ways, and those who supported it financially. Here in Rome, we would like to acknowledge the contribution of Sr Christine Gautier OP, Fr Alejandro Crosthwaite OP, and Fr Allen Moran OP, all of whom helped in bringing the project to its fruition. Among those beyond Rome who helped us, special mention should be made of Sr Joan Shanahan OP, who gave us great help in securing the contributions from Latin America. Several congregations and a private foundation contributed to funding the project. We also thank the authors and translators. Responsibility for any errors or problems in the text lies with the editors alone.

1

Enclosure and Active Apostolates: Developments in Female Religious Life in Europe between the Council of Trent and Saint Vincent de Paul

LUIGI MEZZADRI, C.M.

'Is enclosure a prison?'[1] This is the question that Jean Leclercq posed in an attempt to define this specific term of monastic legislation. Enclosure as a word is derived from *claustrum*, that is, prison.

The Council of Trent decided to reinforce and deepen the norms contained in the 1298 decretal *Pericoloso* of Boniface VIII. Among other things, it also threatened to involve civil authorities, as Venice had been doing since 1521 when it constituted a commission, the *Provveditori sopra monasteri*, to oversee the monasteries.[2]

In the constitution *Circa Pastoralis* (May 29 1566), Pius V decided to impose enclosure on all nuns, even if for reasons of abuse or custom they had not been observing it; meanwhile, communities without vows could no longer receive novices. Since resistance developed against this, through the constitution *Decori* (February 1 1570), this same Pope declared that nuns who left the monastery without permission and those who welcomed them were excommunicated *ipso facto*. Gregory XIII (*Ubi gratiae*, June 13 1575) later suppressed the privileges accorded to noblemen to enter monasteries and created some order in the access given to cardinals, bishops and male religious superiors to the monastic enclosure (*Dubiis*, December 23, 1581). Restrictive norms regarding the parlours were promulgated by the Congregation of the Council in 1669 (for instance, a male religious who spoke at the grille of the parlour without permission had committed a mortal sin and was excommunicated) and in 1678 (for instance, a male religious who preached in a monastery could not be engaged in conversation in the parlour without

---

1. J. Leclercq, 'Le cloître est-il une prison?', in *Revue d'Ascétique et mystique* 47(1971)407-11 ; id., s. v. *Clausura*, in *Dizionario degli istituti di perfezione* 2(1975) 1166-1174.
2. *Conciliorum oecumenicorum decreta*, a cura di G. Alberigo et alii, Edizioni Dehoniane Bologna, Bologna 1991, pp. 777f

permission).

In the implementation of this reform, other figures were important. St Charles Borromeo in his first provincial council (1565) promulgated very precise norms regarding various points: the grille, which had to be double, and the size of its bars; the doors; the keys; the windows; the entrance and the exit from the monastery.[3]

In the constitutions of Mother Mechtilde di Saint Sacrement (Catherine de Bar, 1614-1698), the nuns are invited to consider the monastery as a 'precious monument that should bury them' with the Lord.[4] For this, the walls had to be of such a height that they could not be scaled. No trees could be near the walls. The door should have a threshold of a single block of stone, fixed in the earth, and another further inside. The keys of the doors had to be in the care of the mother prioress. The iron grille had to be covered with a thick, black piece of cloth. The confessionals had to have iron grilles with holes of three inches square, covered by a frame holding a plate of copper or tin-plate with holes in it, and over that was nailed a black canvas. In the sacristy there had to be a turnstile, three feet high and two feet in diameter. Another turnstile was in another room, to be used for passing the things required for the daily needs of the community. In the parlour the sisters had to be accompanied by an 'auditor', unless the nuns needed to speak about a question of conscience. During the conversation, the nuns were to keep their veil lowered below their chins and a cloth over the grille unless they were in the presence of relatives.

THE ENCLOSURE AS IDEAL

To understand these provisions we need to remember that they were inspired by an ascetic ideal, a certain idea of woman and a particular social situation.[5]

---

3. *Acta Ecclesiae Mediolenensis* I, Mediolani, 1595, 41-53. For the legislation itself, see: M. Bonacina, 'Tractatus de clausura', in *Opera omnia*, I, Venetiis, 1728, 591-697; F. Pellizzario, *Tractatus de monialibus*, Romae, 1761; *Analecta Juris Pontificii*, V[e] s., Rome, 1861.

4. Madre Mectilde du Saint Sacrement, *Costituzioni sulla Regola del Santo Padre Benedetto per le Monache Benedettine dell'Adorazione Perpetua del SS. Sacramento*, s.l., 1982, 9-18.

5. Regarding female religious life, the following are fundamental texts: G. Zarri, *Le sante vive. Cultura e religiosità femminile nella prima età moderna*, Torino, 1990; ibid., *Donne e fede. Santità e vita religiosa in Italia*, edited by L. Scaraffia-G. Zarri, Roma-Bari, 1994; ibid., *Recinti. Donne, clausura e matrimonio nella prima età moderna*, Bologna, 2000; *I monasteri femminili come centri di cultura tra Rinascimento e Barocco*. Atti del convegno storico internazionale, Bologna 8-10 dicembre 2000, edited by G. Pomata e G. Zarri, Roma 2005, 1-406; ibid., *La religione di Lucrezia Borgia. Le lettere inedite del confessore*, Roma 2006 ; id., *Le donne nella chiesa in Italia: rassegna storiografica*, in *Le donne nella Chiesa e in Italia*, edited by L. Mezzadri e M. Tagliaferri, Cinisello Balsamo 2007, 13-34; ibid., *Introduzione*, in *Storia della direzione spirituale*, III. *L'età moderna*, edited by G. ZARRI, Brescia 2008, 5-53.

At their root there was the contraposition between the two figures of Martha and Mary, one seen as the example of the active life and the other of the life of contemplation (Lk 10: 38-42), in which the second was to be preferred, in so far as Mary had chosen the 'better part'.[6]

In his work *De ascensione mentis in Deum,* which is clearly inspired by St Bonaventure, Robert Bellarmine (1542-1621) started from the presupposition that God is close to the human being, but the human being is far from God.[7] For human beings, to see God is an intrinsically good end, so the traces of God's presence are reviewed in synthesis. In this way, step by step, we arrive at a reflection on the essence, potency, wisdom, mercy and justice of God. This is an engaging and serene journey that puts the person in the condition of feeling loved by God. It is God, and only God, who can take away the miseries of human life. While things are 'objectively' good, God is simply 'every good'. For this reason, he exhorted contemplation of the great good in heaven, our true home country, 'if you would love God in this life'. All the works of God are like thuribles from which rise up sweet perfume to God's glory; if the person possessed interior hearing, he or she would perceive the mysterious concerto of the various instruments that praise God.

Isabella Tomasi (1645-1699), sister of Giuseppe Tomasi, both of the Tomasi di Lampedusa family, from the time of her vision at age seven, had a revelation of the essence of God.[8] Entrance into the monastery, built by her father and in which her mother and sisters also entered, was the beginning for her of a personal exodus. Should we be so taken aback if little girls were educated to 'fear' sin, to abhor the devil and hell, to mortify themselves in order to 'win' Paradise, to put the catechism in the first place in their lives and not frivolous things? Certainly, it is surprising to see the decision of Rosalia, the mother of Isabella and a woman of 39 years, who at that point preferred the monastery to conjugal life. This, however, leads us to think of how different the quality of life was in the Tomasi household compared to that in other noble families of the time and region. Paradoxically, it is precisely the voca-

6. As is well known, from Gregory the Great onwards we find an overlapping of identities between Mary Magdalene (Lk 8,2. 24,10; Jn 19,25. 20, 1-18), the sinner who was forgiven (Lk 7, 36-50) and Mary of Bethany (Lk 10, 38-42; Mk 14, 3-9; Jn 11, 1-44. 12, 1-8).

7. *De ascensione mentis in Deum per scalas rerum creatarum,* in R. Bellarimino, *Scritti spirituali (1615-1620)* I, Brescia 1997, 54-495.

8. S. Locatelli, *La Ven. Suor Maria Crocifissa della Concezione (Isabella Tomasi) e il Seicento mistico italiano,* in *Regnum Dei* 10(1954)205-18, 11(1955)3-26, 13(1957)39-77, 234-52; C. Gallerano, *Isabella Tomasi,* Sorrento 1963; S. Cabibbo-M. Modica, *La Santa dei Tomasi. Storia di suor Maria Crocifissa (1645-1699),* Torino 1989; L. Mezzadri, *"Contemplare a viso scoperto". L'esperienza di Isabella Tomasi (1645-1699) a tre secoli dalla morte,* in *Arte e Spiritualità nella Terra dei Tomasi di Lampedusa,* edited by M. C. Di Natale e F. Messina Cicchetti, Palermo 1999, 19-27.

tion of the mother that illumines that of the daughters. She, like her children, was convinced that the gift that one makes of oneself to God was the most sublime goal of life, and her decision was consequent upon that. At the very least, we can say that they were blessed with strong personalities.

In her autobiography she speaks of being 'freed from the prison of the world', an affirmation that is both countercultural and provocative. The prison is the world, or the prison is the enclosure? Like St Clare, she had chosen the enclosure as a space of freedom. Seen from within, the enclosure is a frontier place, in the sense that it is protected from the pressures of what is useless, futile, opaque, and from the sadness of evil.

Certainly the monastery had its crosses, its hardships, its battles, and Isabella was not spared these. However, she could see past this, to the Beyond, just as a recluse can hear knocking from the other side of the wall. She was interested in God, not in compromises.

In Isabella's spiritual odyssey, the basic terms are 'I' and 'You'. The protagonist is God, and so as a consequence, the 'I' has to be described as the opposite, as the shadow with respect to the light, emptiness with respect to fullness, as the less with respect to the more, like the negative pole with regard to the positive. Isabella imagines herself as *Nothing* with respect to the *All*, but these images do not denote a distorted anthropology. At its base there is the idea of the '*contemptus mundi*', which is to be 'despised' not in itself but in so far as it is 'sinful'. The human being is called to 'be love' in so far as he who would 'find God must first lose himself'.

Isabella Tomasi, who had contemplated the Passion, was called to stand next to the Crucified, like Mary. Intoxicated by love, she was taken down into a 'large subterranean cave', and was placed on the 'stony floor of a cavern'; desirous to contemplate the Divine Face, she was repaid with an abyss of darkness. She anticipated the condition of the man and woman of the new Millennium. She tasted the beauty of pure Love and witnessed to those of her time that the Cross is the penultimate happening, for the conclusion of the story is a door that opens into a house of Light and after this, there is the 'holy Paradise', the 'joyful banquet of God'. This was the measure of an enclosed life lived not as a prison but as liberated by contemplation.

From Spain came the reform of St Teresa of Avila (1515-1582), who tended to centre life on contemplation and prayer as friendship with Christ, within the framework of strict penitence, but also with an eye on the various situations in the world, such as the advance of the Protestants, the profanations of the Eucharist and the missionary adventure to the New World.

When France knew peace again after the wars of religion, she began to renew traditional monastic life. One of the instruments used to reform certain monasteries that had become lax was the restoration of the enclosure. But it was also imposed on new entities. In 1610, the bishops obliged all religious women to make solemn vows and to shut themselves into the enclosure. Three years later, the Congregation of Notre Dame of Pierre Fourier was constrained to adopt enclosure and to abandon its schools. Something similar happened to St Francis de Sales. He had not intended to found a community of service, but only a contemplative community with a form of life that was less austere than that of the Poor Clares and the Carmelites. He wanted those from noble families also to be able to enter a monastery, without laying exorbitant burdens on them, and so enclosure was not a part of his vision. When he wanted to found a second house, he chose the diocese of Lyon. In such a situation, however, with more than one house, the idea arose of creating an order. Now, a new order required enclosure and solemn vows, which is what the archbishop of Lyon, Denis di Marquemont, required them to observe. Francis de Sales and Jane de Chantal did not make any opposition to this new configuration, indicating that it was not in marked contrast with their intentions. The prodigious success of the Visitation demonstrates that it corresponded to a need of the time.

In fact, all the major monastic communities prospered. At the end of the seventeenth century the Poor Clares were 70,000, in 700 monasteries, with 141 in Italy.[9] Ten years after the death of the foundress, the Spanish Carmelites were already 600 in number, in 31 monasteries,[10] while in France they had 62 monasteries by the end of the seventeenth century.[11] The monastery of the Benedictines of S. Salvatore of Brescia had 200 nuns at the end of the 1600s, while S. Benedetto at Catania had 120 and S. Michele di Mazara del Vallo had 83.[12] Often it was reforming abbesses who took it into their hands to re-introduce and respect the enclosure, without waiting for the intervention of their respective bishops, such as Madeleine de Sourdis at Saint-Paul de Beauvais (1596), Marie de Beauvilliers at Montmartre (1599), Angelica Arnauld at Port-Royal (1609), Jeanne de Courcelle at Tart, near Dijon (1617) and Marguerite d'Arbouze at Val-de-Grâce (1619). Saint Frances de Sales wrote that 'the good order of everything else depends on the enclosure'.[13]

9. *Dizionario degli Istituti di Perfezione*, diretto da G. Pelliccia e G. Rocca, 10 vol., Edizioni Paoline, Roma 1974-2003 (DIP), vol. 4 (1977), col. 186.

10. DIP, vol. 2 (1975), col. 428.

11. DIP, vol. 2 (1975), col. 441

12. DIP, vol. 1 (1974), col. 1232.

13. *Oeuvres* XIII, Annecy, 1904, 97.

The Grey Franciscan Sisters were required to adopt the enclosure in the 1620s, which meant that they had to give up their service to the sick, increase the size of their monastic buildings and establish new sources of income.[14]

There were cases in which girls entered the monastery because this form of life, 'separated', 'more perfect', penitential, held a certain fascination for them. Catherine de' Ricci (1522-1590), who belonged to the noble branch of the Florentine family of the Albizzi, decided to enter with the Dominicans in Prato when she was eleven years old. Maria Arcangela Biondini (161-1712) entered a monastery at fourteen years of age. Catherine Paluzzi (1573-1645) confessed to having felt since the age of four 'a continuous inspiration that I should be a nun'.

THE ENCLOSURE AS A SOCIAL SAFETY NET

At the same time, this flowering of monastic life should not lead us to think that it only grew thanks to its own strengths and through simple, spontaneous attraction. If in Torcello, a diocese with 16,000 inhabitants, there were nearly 900 nuns, we cannot attribute this to a miracle. It was the families who decided the fate of their daughters and who pushed them into a monastery so as to keep the family patrimony intact, both for the firstborn son and for a reasonable dowry for one of their daughters.

This explains three things. Firstly, it allows us to understand the rise in monastic foundations within cities. It was in the interests of the nobility to have more places in which to place their daughters. Secondly, we can understand why members of the aristocracy were often allowed to administer the goods of the monasteries where they had relatives. These nobles had endowed these communities in some way, and so, becoming the administrators of those same goods for the monastery, they continued to have control over what had been theirs. Thirdly, it is clear that these families would never have allowed any nun to abandon the monastic habit. If research done in the archives of the Penitentiary demonstrates that there were few requests for dispensation from vows by women in convents, we can understand why.[15] Even if such requests had been accepted, the dispensed nuns would not have been able to return to their families since the latter would have felt themselves dishonoured.

Therefore, if on the one hand the Tridentine norms were very rigid – with

14. P. Moracchini, 'La mise sous clôture des sœurs grises de la province franciscaine de France Parisienne, au XVIIᵉ siècle', in *Les religieuses*, 635-658.

15. F. Tamburini, *Santi e peccatori: Confessioni e suppliche dai Registri della Penitenzieria dell'Archivio Segreto Vaticano (1451-1586)*. Milano 1995.

the support of the dominant classes – their application left a lot to be desired, since particular monasteries were often able to find self-interested support from the noble classes against the requirements of the ecclesiastical reformers.[16]

This explains the custom of 'forced enclosure'[17] as in the case of the 'nun of Monza',[18] and of Sr Arcangela Tarabotti (1604-1652).[19]

Tarabotti had been enclosed in the Benedictine monastery of St Anna in Venice by her father. She had a physical defect (she limped) and was not in good health, but she knew how to turn a problem into an opportunity. She had complete freedom to read and write, something which she probably would have been denied outside the monastery, and thereby she became a great writer. In *L'inferno monacale* (*The Nunnish Hell*), she accused fathers of condemning their daughters 'to the prison of the monastery in which they are forcefully and innocently condemned to suffer an eternal martyrdom of punishment that, as such, can reasonably be called a Hell'. And she added: 'the avarice and tyranny of fathers, with the simplicity, ignorance and untimely obedience of the daughters, give birth to these deplorable consequences!'

An educated woman, she wrote *La semplicità ingannata o Tirannia paterna* (*Simplicity Deceived or Paternal Tyranny*), published posthumously in 1654; *L'Inferno monacale* (*The Nunnish Hell*) and *Il Paradiso monacale* (*The Nunnish Paradise*), both published in 1643; *L'Antisatira* (*The Antisatire*), 1644, in reply to a short work, *I donneschi difetti* (*Womanish Defects*), that denigrated women by Giuseppe Passi; a book of letters and, under a pseudonym, an opera entitled *Che le donne sieno delle spetie delli huomini* (*That Women should be of the same species as men*).

Sr Arcangela wrote passionately against parents who forcibly placed their daughters in monasteries, meriting to be called 'tyrants of Hell, abortions of nature, Christians in name and devils in action'. They claimed to operate according to the Divine Will, while actually offending it.

In a letter, the Patriarch of Venice, Tiepolo, confirmed that more than 2,000

16. G. Zarri, *Recinti* cit., 43-143.

17. L. Fiorani, 'Monache e monasteri romani nell'età del quietismo', in *Ricerche per la storia religiosa di Roma* 1 (1977) 63-111; R. Canosa, *Il velo e il cappuccio. Monacazioni forzate e sessualità nei conventi femminili in Italia fra Quattrocento e Seicento*, Roma, 1991.

18. M. Mazzucchelli, *La monaca di Monza (suor Virginia Maria de Leyva)*, Milano, 1961, (this text is not very reliable). Better would be: *Vita e processo di suor Virginia Maria de Leyva, monaca di Monza*, edited by U. Colombo, Milano, 1985.

19. E. Zanette, *Suor Arcangela Tarabotti, monaca del Seicento veneziano*, Venezia-Roma, 1966; F. Medioli, *L'"Inferno monacale" di Arcangela Tarabotti*, Torino, 1990; A. Tarabotti, *Lettere familiari e di complimento*, edited by L. L. Westwater e M. Kennedy Ray, Torino 2005.

unmarried women 'live enclosed in the monasteries', and for this reason decided to moderate their discipline. Tarabotti affirmed that on the doors of the monasteries one could have written the words of Dante's Hell: 'Abandon hope all you who enter here'. We may note that Tarabotti does not mention any sexual disorder or sensual atmosphere, as does other literature of a more pathological kind from that time.

Overall, we can say that there were good and bad situations; we cannot generalise. Some of the nuns lived in the monasteries with enthusiasm and conviction, others were resigned, while a third group was embittered.

Opposition to enclosure, therefore, came both from those who denounced these kinds of abuse and from those who wanted to carry out a more positive role in the world. Thus, ten Cistercian communities in the diocese of Liège refused on several occasions to include the words 'sub clausura perpetua' in their formula for profession, while within the Franciscan family, there was the significant phenomenon that among the Grey sisters, 22 communities accepted enclosure, while five were against. In practice, this led to the gradual weakening of the non-enclosed communities as compared to those who had accepted it.

This insistence on the enclosure corresponded to the perception of woman as weak and inclined to evil, who needed guidance and defence. Figures such as St Angela Merici, Ludovica Torelli, St Francis de Sales and then St Vincent de Paul struggled against the enclosure, but all were unsuccessful except the last among them.

THE 'THIRD STATE': WOMEN CONSECRATED FOR SERVICE[20]
Despite the obstacles, canonical or not, to the presence and direct apostolate of women in society, it is precisely in this period that the Copernican revolution in the life of the Church represented by active religious life for women was achieved.

Angela Merici (1474-1540) had already anticipated this moment.[21] Her project, however, could not survive the canonical framework adopted by Charles Borromeo and Pius V, with its imposition of enclosure.

---

20. The expression 'third state (terzo stato)' is from Gabriella Zarri, and designates the condition of those women who put themselves outside the usual scheme of 'marriage-or-enclosure', choosing precisely voluntary celibacy. 'Third way (terza via)' has another meaning: DIP 9 (1997) coll. 1030-1035.

21. Sant'Angela Merici, Gli scritti. Regole, ricordi, testamento, edited by L. Mariani - E. Tarolli, Brescia, 1996; 'Angela Merici e la Chiesa', in P. Prodi, G. Zarri, L. Mezzadri, D. Castenetto, Angela Merici. Vita della Chiesa e spiritualità nella prima metà del Cinquecento, edited by C. Naro, Caltanissetta-Roma, 1998, 77-105; G. Zarri, Recinti, 391-480.

Mary Ward (1585-1645) came from a noble English family.[22] She entered the Poor Clares, whom she quickly left after having conceived an ambitious ideal: to found an institute that would actively participate in the action of the Church, primarily through the education of girls. She wanted to adopt the constitutions of the Society of Jesus and to form the feminine active branch of the Jesuits, setting up an institute under a general superior, who would report directly to the Pope. It would be recognised as a religious institute without enclosure, so that the religious could leave the convent freely for the apostolate. Immediately, however, opposition blew up to her foundation. Among the first to attack her were members of influential sectors within English Catholicism.

Several strands of opposition came together against Mary Ward, including that coming from a certain idea of woman and of the claim of these women to carry out an active apostolate. Her group was therefore suppressed in 1631. In 1632, they obtained permission to live together with Mary Ward in a private form, but the project as originally conceived had failed.

However, what Mary Ward had not been able to achieve was then obtained by St Vincent de Paul (1581-1660).[23] In 1633, Vincent courageously decided to embark on a new initiative. The experience of the 'Companies of Charity', which had multiplied, had revealed some important results: the greater propensity of women to work with the poor (the Companies had by now become exclusively female); the possibility of involving the upper and middle aristocracy and the need for charitable work to be carried out with commitment, on a full-time basis.

This last point induced Vincent to create a female community alongside the ladies who were volunteers, the Daughters of Charity. In St Louise de Marillac (1591-1660) he found an intelligent and well-prepared collaborator, able to interpret the general indications she received from Vincent's intuition.[24] As a result, it was possible to break through the mindsets that excluded religious women from the direct apostolate and breakdown the social barriers that reserved charitable activity to persons of means.

At first, the Daughters of Charity were legally a part of 'les charités'.[25] They were a parish 'charité' (1633-45), and then approved as a diocesan 'con-

22. A. Lopez Amat, *Mary Ward il dramma di una pioniera*, Trento, 1994.
23. L. Mezzadri, *Vincenzo de' Paoli, il santo della carità*, Roma 2009.
24. L. Nuovo, *Luisa de Marillac fondatrice delle figlie della Carità*, Roma 2010.
25. A. Vernaschi, *Una istituzione originale: le Figlie della Carità di S. Vincenzo de' Paoli*, Roma, 1968; M. Cocheril, 'Les Filles de la charité', in *Les religieux, la vie, l'art. II: Les ordres actifs*, Paris, 1980, 684-709; L. Mezzadri - M. Perez Flores, *La regola delle Figlie della Carità di s. Vincenzo de' Paoli*, Milano, 1986.

fraternity' (1646-68). St Louise composed a first draft for their rules of life (1634); later, Vincent wrote a more developed text (1645) when the Company was given ecclesiastical approval by the Archbishop of Paris, John Francis de Gondi. However, there was a clause in the instruments of approbation that St Louise, above all, did not like, that is, the submission of the sisters to the authority of the archbishop. The text was submitted to the civil authorities. During the negotiations, the text was lost. Later, the negotiations were taken up again and concluded successfully: on January 18 1655, the Archbishop of Paris, Cardinal Retz, who was in the debt of Vincent for the hospitality he had received from him in Rome, recognised that the Daughters of Charity were under the authority of the General Superiors of the Congregation of the Mission (Vincentians).

The institute presented various anomalies: the direction of the sisters was placed in the hands of the Superior General of the Congregation of the Mission, on whose behalf there was appointed a 'director'; the institute spread to various dioceses (Paris, Nantes, Angers and beyond, such as to Krakow), with the sole approval of the Archbishop of Paris. There was no precedent for an institute without vows that had spread across several dioceses.

In 1668, Cardinal Vendôme, as legate *a latere* of Clement IX, gave his approbation to the institute. For this, the Daughters of Charity, designated as a confraternity, community, congregation, society, company – rather fluid terms, but all used by St Vincent himself – became of pontifical right, under its own legal framework. They therefore 'represented in ecclesiastical law the only female society 'sine votis' (instead, they made private vows annually) and the only female non-religious community to be really exempt [from the jurisdiction of the local ordinary]'.[26]

At the beginning they envisaged very small communities, spread across a particular territory. Thus, in every village, apart from the superior, there was usually a sister for the village school, who only taught the poor girls and not the boys, and another for the housebound sick and those in the hospital. In the particular rules for the sisters in the parishes it was emphasised that they should reflect on the meaning of their vocation, that is, offering spiritual and physical help.

They were exhorted to practise in their lives acts of faith, hope, charity, of penance and of resignation to the divine will. They were recommended to make a good general confession. In cases where these particular spiritual exercises might compromise their service, they had to make sure that every-

26. DIP 3 (1976) col. 1543.

one was treated equally. They had to make sure that the sick did not lack the minimum service necessary, but always for God alone, treating both praise and blame with indifference.

So that their service should appear completely free, the sisters were prohibited from receiving gifts; rather, they should be convinced that it was they who were in debt to the poor, and that they should prefer the service of the poor sick to every other activity, even of a spiritual nature. However, they could not stay to eat or drink in the houses they visited, nor keep vigil overnight in the house of a sick person.

These sisters would get up a 4 o'clock, and after meditation, they were to bring medicine to the sick and then go to Mass. Then they were to go to the woman who prepared their food so as to receive the pot and its contents from her. From 9 to 11, they distributed food. After lunch, they had to read the prescriptions of the doctor and prepare the medicine to take to the sick, as well as bring back the empty pot to the woman charged with doing their cooking. In winter, at 6 pm, and in summer at 8 pm, the sisters finally closed their door behind them for the day.

The Daughters of Charity wore a characteristic headdress (the 'cornette') that was particular to the young women of the area around Paris. They succeeded in being fully recognised members of the Church, without having to assume enclosure, or depending on the local bishops, and without solemn vows but only private vows that were repeated annually. They succeeded in spreading widely, first through France, then Poland, and thence throughout the world.

We may ask ourselves why St Vincent managed to achieve this when Mary Ward did not. He was prudent, taking small steps in stages, without making recourse to Rome where every concession became a question of principle. He obtained in France, through Cardinal Vendôme, what he desired, without damaging the interests of any Gallican cleric. He found a formula that allowed vows to be made without this leading to the enclosure. In this way, he opened a way for women to be involved in the apostolate.

CONCLUSION

The history of female consecrated life, contemplative and active, has been through profound changes, both as regards its meaning and its social and spiritual impact.

The old interpretations of the oppression experienced in the cloister (life as a prison) have given way to a deeper appreciation of what nuns have created, in music and literature, for instance, and of their lives. When the idea of the monastery as a sort of social safety net was abandoned, there was a general collapse among them. It is not by chance that some were transformed into prisons (Regina Coeli in Rome and the Mantellate in Florence, for instance). Still, monasteries are still with us and are now seen primarily as places of contemplation, with a deep quality of spiritual and intellectual life, offering the possibility of genuine, palpable human development.

The active congregations, flowering in the 1800s and 1900s, after the period we have focused on here, have also offered women very extensive possibilities for development. The monasteries went through a crisis in the period we discuss in this contribution; an equivalent crisis for active congregations started some time ago and is still with us. Nevertheless, just as the monasteries were able to rediscover their raison d'être after a long period of soul-searching, we can similarly be hopeful that the active congregations too will find a new synthesis after their equivalent period of crisis and rethinking.

2

Changes in the Position of Women in Society and in the Church in the Twentieth Century, with a Special Focus on Italy

ADRIANA VALERIO

WOMEN IN A SOCIETY IN TRANSFORMATION

The questions raised by feminism have profoundly modified ancient cultural and religious paradigms in the twentieth century. Idealism, growing out of the principles of the French Revolution, and the great social transformations wrought by industrialisation, technology and the consequent improvements in living conditions, have given rise to radical role changes between the sexes. On the one hand, there has been women's struggle for the widening of educational opportunities, better access to the world of work and the acquisition of civil and political rights. On the other, there has been the reduction in maternal and infant mortality, the possibility of limiting the number of births and the lightening of domestic burdens through the use of household electrical appliances. These have contributed decisively to changing not only the conception of the quality of private life, but also to favouring an ever-greater insertion of women into social, cultural and political life.

Feminism is a constitutive part of western history. It is as much a theoretical approach as a political movement, and as much a search for vindication as a spiritual inspiration for a more just society. Provocative demands for equality have jostled with impassioned calls for diversity; denunciations of one's own condition of subordination are intertwined with the search for new identities and new ways to live the faith and to relate to the historical churches and their traditions.

Virginia Woolf (1882–1941) in *Three Guineas*, for example, when faced with the imminent danger of war, knew how to express powerfully the urgency for women to find 'new words' and to invent 'new methods' for affirming their specific diversity as a value. This would be an indispensable presupposition for avoiding war that is born from the abuse of power and the violence specific to a 'masculine approach' as it was dramatically expressed in the systems of power (economic, political, religious) present both in society and in the Churches.

In the complex cultural and political dynamics that have characterised the women's movements of the twentieth century and that are expressions of many different groups (liberal, socialist, anarchic and Christian), we can distinguish several phases.

The first phase of feminism (the so-called 'first wave'), which runs through the century until the 1960s, draws its strength from the principles of equality and emancipation. Knowledge of the same dignity of woman in relation to man (equality) and the consequent need to escape from a centuries-old dependence (emancipation) animated the struggles of women, with the aim of the recognition of the fundamental rights of the human person and the redrafting of family law so as to go beyond any patriarchal or hierarchical form.

Many times, on an international level, positions have been taken in favour of the equalisation of male and female rights: we may think of the pronouncements of the UN, the Universal Declaration of Human Rights in 1948; the Convention on the Political Rights of Women in 1952; the Convention on the Elimination of All Forms of Discrimination Against Women in 1979; and again, the results of the Third World Conference on Women held at Beijing in 1995 and the Conference of Non-Governmental Organisations in 2000. Within the Council of Europe, in 1987 a European Committee for the Equality between Men and Women was constituted, and was followed up in 1988 by the Declaration on the Equality between Men and Women. Since 1982, the European Commission has promoted programmes of action with the aim of encouraging member countries in the implementation of measures aimed at removing obstacles to putting into practice equal opportunities between the sexes.

A second wave of feminism, which developed in the 1960s, takes its inspiration and driving force not so much from the ideas of emancipation and equal opportunities but rather from the idea of liberation, understood both as an interior process that renders the woman an autonomous person, above all in her sexual and procreative life, and as a modification of institutions and cultural models for the construction of a society that recognises feminine subjectivity and its difference from that of men.

WOMEN AND THE MAGISTERIUM IN THE TWENTIETH CENTURY

The magisterium in the first half of the twentieth century was not particularly open to the claims and demands of women, except in so far as to underline feminine roles linked to the domestic sphere. The condemnation of modernity, in fact, had been the worried and distressed response of a Church that saw in the processes of secularisation a mortal threat to a Christian society whose basis was crumbling. Female emancipation seemed to contribute to this breakdown. For this reason, the Church closed itself in around a strenuous defence of the traditional and patriarchal family, all to the advantage of political and social conservation.

It is without doubt that Vatican II represented a change of direction in the history of the Catholic Church, including all that regards the question of women. John XXIII had already indicated the entry of women into public life as one of the 'signs of the times' (*Pacem in Terris*, 1963), opening up a process of positive recognition of the transformations taking place in society. In *Gaudium et Spes*, the council spelled out the meaning of this opening up, affirming 'the equal personal dignity of wife and husband' (n. 49) and the duty of all to 'acknowledge and favour the proper and necessary participation of women in the [sic] cultural life' (n. 60).

Since Vatican II, the main lines of development of the magisterium have underlined the recognition of equal dignity, but at the same time have also confirmed the differentiation of roles, emphasising the basic task of humanisation specific to the woman, as well as her incapacity for priesthood (*impedimentum sexus*).

In John Paul II's Apostolic Letter *Mulieris Dignitatem* (15 August 1988), the first specific document of the magisterium on woman, we find ourselves in the presence of an anthropological turning point that overcomes sexual subordination at the same time as affirming the reciprocity between male and female, both called to be in relation and to constitute, one for the other, reciprocal help. In this text, the pope spends time on that which he himself called the specific 'genius' of woman, but also underlined, in line with tradition, the different vocation of woman with respect to man: the woman, with her total self-giving, limitless fidelity and untiring devotion to work (cf. *Redemptoris Mater*, 1987), must help humanity not to fall into decay. God entrusts man to her. In this sense the pope intended to reinforce the maternal and educative role of the woman, even if in a wide sense.

The *Letter on the Collaboration between Men and Women in the Church and the World* – which, despite the title, speaks only of women in the text itself and never of men and their vocation – was published in August 2004 by the Congregation for the Doctrine of the Faith on the initiative of the then Cardinal

Ratzinger. It takes up again many themes that are dear to feminism and to the philosophy of sexual difference (dignity of woman, equal responsibility with man in the plan of salvation, specificity and gender difference ...) to underline again, however, a specific vocation of woman: a self-giving rather than antagonistic calling, capable of existing for others, not closing oneself off in individualism; a vocation that, however, excludes priestly ordination.

RELIGIOUS WOMEN

The sense of unease among Catholic women with regard to their specific condition of 'religious junior partner' as it has emerged in the last century, as well as practical ideas that have been developed by various groups for a Church that is more responsive to the changed roles of women, have encouraged women to intertwine their own journey of faith with that of society as it evolves. In parallel with the world of lay people, that of the religious has also been riven with profound wounds. Following on from the radical transformations that religious communities had suffered through the effects of the secularisation of the modern states and the laws of suppression at the end of the nineteenth century, women have had to find different forms of community identity, less focused on a style of life that is exclusively contemplative and more focused on work in the social sphere (through education and various kinds of assistance), carrying out an important role in changing structures and in adapting to a society that is constantly changing.

The principle of an open apostolate for women has picked up momentum in the Catholic world, both as a response to the combative nature of the lay movements and as a need on the part of religious women themselves to be an active part of the change processes taking place. As a result, new models for the consecrated woman who was attentive to the social apostolate were born, above all in the Franciscan and Dominican Third Orders, to which belonged the greater number of the leading protagonists of Italian Catholic feminism. Important experiences in the missionary field were also part of these developments, where religious women created new congregations of active life that were full of creativity and offered greater psychological and economic independence to the sisters.

The Società serafica di apostolato femminile (Seraphic Society of the Feminine Apostolate), founded in Rome in 1916; the Apostole del Sacro Cuore ([Women] Apostles of the Sacred Heart), founded in Milan in 1919; the Compagnia di San Paolo (Company of St Paul), founded in Milan in 1920; the Piccole Apostole di Cristo Re (Little [Women] Apostles of Christ the King), founded in Lucca in 1935; the Figlie di San Paolo (Daughters of Saint Paul), founded in Rome in 1944, were some of the institutes in Italy, even as they encountered strong resistance, who affirmed a direct and active apostolate for women. The religious women understood not only that modernity did not need to be rejected and condemned as a whole, as from a sterile fortress, but also that, precisely through the instruments of modernity, one could re-launch a different presence of the Church in the world. They understood that women had to become an active part of this work of theological and pastoral renewal, conscious of carrying out, with the men of the Church, a *shared* work in the various pastoral and apostolic tasks that were needed, no longer in a merely subsidiary role.

Being missionary became another intrinsic and urgent element from the perspective of the apostolate. Working abroad had become part of the initiatives of some female religious institutes that made a considerable contribution to the history of the missions, both as regards the fields of their activity (schools, orphanages, hospitals) and for the role religious women played as cultural mediators in the delicate processes of adaptation that are set in motion by any action that brings cultures into contact with each other. The Salesian sisters in 1908, the Pie Venerini Teachers in 1909, the Filippini sisters in 1910, and then the Daughters of St Paul in 1936, to mention only a few, revolutionised the post-Tridentine model of enclosed religious life that would have separated them from the world. The freedom of movement of the religious broke with the social prohibitions regarding spatial mobility. Accepting these changes, they broke through the circles of protection around them, acquired autonomy, gave greater substance to their individuality and opened new horizons to the minds of so many women. With their apostolate abroad they posed the question of the presence and the position of women in the Church and society in a new way. The cultural mediation that they carried out between ethnic communities (American, African, Asian), the hierarchy of the Catholic Church and the cultures from which they came helped them assume responsibility, conquer new levels of autonomy and management skill and redefine their roles and behaviour so as to strengthen the processes of assimilation and adaptation that were in action.

The religious woman had the capacity to create the conditions for constructing a new feminine identity. She was ready to measure up to traditional roles and then to redefine herself through the completely new possibilities that she now had through education, work and apostolic commitments in a Church that was ever more sensitive to the mediation between the proclamation of the faith and the needs of a complex and often contradictory world. At the same time, alongside the many signs of progress, there was no lack of obstacles and steps backward. In the 1994 Synod of Bishops on The Consecrated Life and its Mission in the Church and the World, it emerged that the consecrated woman still lived in a condition of marginality. A group of sisters, through Clara Sietman, the general superior of the Missionaries of the Sacred Heart, asked for religious women to be admitted to decision-making roles and positions of responsibility in the Church, including the Roman Curia.

ANTHROPOLOGICAL AND ETHICAL QUESTIONS
The search for an ethical renewal brought women to understand that the faith should not remain closed within the walls of the home or the enclosure, but should play a role in the dynamics of history. In recent decades the issue of women has been profoundly re-thought within the Churches, including the Catholic Church: anthropology, language, historical memory, the experience of God and daily life in the Church have all been enriched by new meanings, thanks to the contribution brought by women to the field of theological reflection. Feminist theology, having arisen in the USA in the 1960s and having become embedded in Europe at the end of the following decade, has begun a systematic process of revision of the biblical and ecclesial tradition that has justified the different treatment, and the subordination, of women. At the same time, it offers useful new criteria for interpreting and re-orienting an androcentric theology, thus favouring a more active participation of women in the life of the Church. Within feminist theology itself different perspectives should be distinguished, all of which are involved in the vast range of historico-theological work that needs to be done, and that by now involve women theologians from all over the world. One of the fruits of this development is the European Society of Women for Theological Research, founded in Switzerland in 1986.

In a society in transformation, the topic of citizenship has raised questions for women in relation to modernity; in its diversity, the thought of women has developed new interpretative categories that question society and church. In 1949, Simone de Beauvoir underlined (*The Second Sex*) how the role of women derives not from 'nature' but rather from social obligations transmitted through education ('one is not born a woman, one becomes one ...'), opening up a discussion that went to the root of her theoretical presupposition. In the 1980s, thanks to women's studies programmes that had developed in universities in Europe and the USA, the category of gender was introduced, which considers the relationship between the sexes no longer on the basis of a nature that is determined physiologically, but rather as a constructed social relation that is therefore continually in transformation.

The concept of nature, considered either as something fixed or in its historical dimension, is connected to different anthropologies that support different types of relationship between the sexes. The anthropology of *subordination* (used in the past by the Catholic tradition) sustains that woman, though equivalent to man in the order of grace, is included in the human genus as a subordinated member, since she is inferior 'by nature'. The anthropology of *complementarity* involves the division of roles and competences, where the public and political sphere pertains to men, while, in a complementary way, the private and domestic belongs to the woman. The anthropology of *equality* defends the equal identity of man and woman, both belonging to the same, common human reality. The anthropology of *reciprocity* negates, instead, the hierarchy of values that define the relationships between human beings, accepting that each one has the same rights and duties. The anthropology of *difference* explores the otherness of the feminine and her specificity against the assimilation of women into the forms of male existence that are codified in the social order. The anthropology of *co-responsibility* respects the equality of the two sexes, in their common life and responsibilities, for which men and women can carry forward not different roles but 'the same roles in different ways'.

It is clear that each anthropological presupposition refers back to a specific vision, not only of the human being but also of the life of society and its various elements and practical organisation, over and above any ethical or theological understanding. It is not, therefore, irrelevant to ask ourselves about the interrelation between the cultural and religious fields. Within Christianity, for instance, the paradigm of co-responsibility, or partnership, is more present within the Protestant tradition, while that of complementarity is more to be found in the Catholic Church. How much this depends on theological presuppositions and how much on economic and political contexts remains to be seen. It does seem that the countries that have been more influenced by the Reformation have reached a higher level of equality, and more quickly, in the spheres of politics, of autonomy of conscience with regard to reproduction, and equal identity on the liturgical and ministerial levels, than in Catholic countries.

Today, society faces other challenges. Among these, there is the procreative revolution, which, on the wave of continual biotechnological development, dissociates sexuality from procreation. The separation between the figure of the biological mother and that of the surrogate, if it opens the way to a plurality of possibilities that raise questions for the woman in her new-found liberty and responsibility, is at the same time a source of conflicts of ethical, religious and juridical orders that are difficult to resolve.

Furthermore, the inclusive model of participation and the ethics of equality re-open the subject of the exercise of authority on the part of women. To think of the ministerial roles in the Church means both to organise a community with many tasks to carry out in a multiplicity of situations, and to rethink traditional ecclesiological models according to the principles of communion and apostolic co-responsibility. Ministerial roles also open up the question of the government of the Church and of the representation of women at all levels: globally, at diocesan and parish level, in councils and synods and in relation to all the various fields that regulate the moral and pastoral life of the Church.

Finally, the principles of equality and of the universality of the law ask profound questions of the religions, all of which were born and developed in patriarchal and androcentric contexts, because they are called to re-define themselves and to establish a new, critical and problematic relationship with the sacred texts. Are the Torah, the Bible and the Qur'an the foundation on which to affirm the full dignity of being man and being woman? Interreligious dialogue needs to measure up to the question of human rights and, in particular, to the position that the woman occupies. Is it as a function of the man, or is she autonomous? Is she free to choose, to think and to express herself? Can she get access to education and to work? Does she have the same dignity in the cultic aspects of religion as man? Are the roles she can undertake in line with asymmetric gender models, or are they are in harmony with universal human rights as established by international law?

BIBLIOGRAPHY

Børresen, Kari Elisabeth, and Cabibbo, Sara (eds.), *Gender, Religion, Human Rights in Europe*, Roma, Herder, 2006.

Duby, Georges, and Perrot Michelle (series eds.), *Storia delle donne in Occidente*, IV. *Il Novecento, Francoise* Thébaud (ed.), Roma–Bari, Laterza, 1992.

Fiume, Giovanna (ed.), *Donne, diritti, democrazia*, Roma, XL edizioni, 2007.

Gaiotti De Biase, Paola, *Le origini del movimento cattolico femminile*, Brescia, Morcelliana, 2000 (first edition 1963).

Militello, Cettina (ed.), *Il Vaticano II e la sua ricezione al femminile*, Bologna, Dehoniane, 2007.

Perroni, Marinella (ed.), *Non contristate lo Spirito. Prospettive di genere e teologia: qualcosa è cambiato?*, Verona, Segno di Gabrielli, 2007.

Rocca, Giancarlo, *Donne religiose. Contributo a una storia della condizione femminile in Italia nei secoli XIX-XX*, Roma, Paoline, 1992.

Valerio, Adriana, 'Donne e teologia nei primi trent'anni del '900. La tensione irrisolta' in *Donna e Teologia. Bilancio di un secolo*, Cettina Militello (ed.), Bologna, Dehoniane, 2004, pp. 61–73.

3

Basic Characteristics of the Dominican Sisters in the Twentieth Century

HELEN ALFORD, O.P.

The stories of the Dominican sisters presented in this book arise out of the life of the Dominican sisters as a whole, and it is thus useful to put them in the context of that whole. This is especially so since the Dominican sisters have a rather complicated history, which has left them with a complex structure today, one that has been a lot less studied than that of the Dominican friars and that can be hard even for the sisters themselves to understand. Here we aim to give an overview of the structures, location and numbers of sisters in the twentieth century.

At the time of writing this text, we have been able to identify 174 congregations of Dominican sisters in the world, with at least four, one each in Democratic Republic of Congo, Italy, Vietnam and the USA, awaiting approbation from the Order, and another, in Bolivia, whose constitutions are approved *ad experimentum*. Here the word 'congregation' indicates an independent legal entity in canon law. By the time you are reading this text, however, this number may have changed, as it has changed throughout the twentieth century, through the creation of new congregations and the mergers of others.[1] Of this 174, 151 are affiliated to the movement known as Dominican Sisters International (DSI), founded in 1995 at a meeting of the prioress generals of 80 congregations of Dominican sisters.[2] Another important distinction is that between the congregations of pontifical right (a juridical form that developed slowly but which was only formally promulgated in 1900), and those of diocesan right. At the time of writing,

1. The number of 174 comes from the office of Dominican Sisters International. However, DSI may not know about all the congregations that have not joined DSI but which may still officially call themselves Dominican. In order for a congregation of sisters to be known as Dominican, they need to have approbation from the Master of the Order. A request to the Secretary General of the Order for an updated list of recognised congregations did not produce any result, so the best approximation we have is the number we received from DSI. It is likely that the number of congregations unknown to DSI is small, covering a small number of sisters, and all the contributions to the book come from congregations that are part of the DSI group. Using data from DSI as the basic framework for presenting the numbers and structures of the sisters therefore makes sense.

2. For more on this, see Chapter 4, 'The Contribution of Dominican Sisters International to the Development of the Dominican Family', pp. 76-84.

based on the incomplete data we have, about two thirds of the congregations are of pontifical right and one third of diocesan right, but again, these numbers could change. Diocesan congregations that are growing, such as those in Vietnam, may at some stage decide that it is better for them to become congregations of pontifical right. Although not many new congregations are being founded currently, it is possible that there may be some new ones created in the future, although this is not likely to be a major phenomenon. What is more likely is that there will be mergers or fusions of congregations, especially in Europe or North America, where the numbers of sisters are decreasing.

In this short chapter we first deal with the variation in the numbers of Dominican sisters across the twentieth century. After this, we will deal with their location and structure, but only according to the most recent data; it would have required too much work, in relation to the importance of this topic to this book, to try to go back further in history with this analysis.

OVERALL NUMBERS OF SISTERS

It is not easy to find out how many sisters there have been across the various congregations and down through the twentieth century. This is largely because of the way statistics are collected in the Catholic Church. The Congregation for Religious, an organ of the Roman Curia, collects statistics on congregations of pontifical right, whereas the statistics on congregations of diocesan right are collected at diocesan level. Since the foundation of DSI in 1995, this new co-ordinating body for Dominican sisters has also been collecting statistics on the numbers of Dominican sisters in the various congregations, but before that there was no central place where these statistics could be found. In order to obtain an accurate set of statistics, therefore, it would have been necessary to contact the generalates of all the diocesan congregations, a job that is made more difficult by the occasional fusion between congregations, the creation of breakaway groups or the founding of new ones.

Since this statistical presentation is only meant to create a sense of the overall numbers of Dominican sisters across the twentieth century, to help us in understanding the work of the sisters in the field of social justice and social ethics, it was not worth investing the time and effort needed to gather the most accurate statistics that could be found. Instead we decided to adopt a simple method: to contact the generalates of the congregations that are currently the biggest (we contacted ten) asking them to tell us how many sisters they each had in four specific years across the twentieth century: 1900, 1925, 1950, 1975. We then used this data, in a rather unscientific but not unreasonable way, to estimate the numbers of sisters overall, as explained below.

Taking these four dates not only gives us an even spread across the twentieth century, but also makes sense because of the major world events that took place in each period and allows us to get a sense of the effect that they had on the overall numbers of sisters. The year 1900 is obviously the starting point for the twentieth century, but it is also an interesting moment in Church history, a time of the rise of anticlericalism in France which, given the importance of France in the Dominican Order, is important for the sisters more generally. The next date, 1925, allows us to see the effect of the First World War, which, in terms of religious orders, was largely positive (indeed, we see that the numbers of sisters in all our sample congregations increased), and the same applies to the 1950 date, taking into account the effects of the Second World War. 1975 clearly has significance because we are in the post-conciliar phase; interestingly, only two of our ten sample congregations shows any decline by that time and, overall, numbers are still rising compared to the previous data point of 1950. After 1975, we no longer need to use the statistics from the ten sample congregations in order to create an estimate for the numbers of Dominican sisters in the world, since we have the data collected by DSI. As this covers almost all Dominican congregations, this data is much more reliable than any estimate we could make.

The estimates for the total numbers of sisters between 1900 and 1975 are made on a very simple basis. We started from the DSI data, which was collected in two rounds, in 1998 and 2009.[3] We worked out what proportion of Dominican sisters as a whole was represented by the sisters in our ten sample congregations at these two points, and took the average of the two proportions, which was 31 per cent. We then used this average as the basis for working out how many sisters overall were present in the world at the earlier dates. It is clear that many objections could be raised to this method from a scientific point of view, but it is relatively quick and makes sense in terms of the limited needs of this project.

As can be seen from Table 1 and Figure 1, all the congregations follow a very similar path across the twentieth century. Some had not yet come into existence by 1900, and of those that had, none had more sisters in 1900 than

___

3. Some of the data used in the 2009 survey had not been updated since 2004. This was especially true of the data from Africa.

Table 1: Numbers of sisters in the ten sample congregations at five dates across the twentieth century and in 2009.

Congregation[1]	Year					
	1900	1925	1950	1975	1998	2009
Adrian	0	554	1,612	1,841	1,079	815
Anunciata	931	1,185	1,638	1,683	1,206	1,030
Cabra	418	497	744	765	485	355
G. Rapids	114	440	645	651	367	257
Maryknoll	0	252	818	1,057	645	537
Presentation	1,658	1,658	4,078	4,388	3,159	2,527
Romaine	550	750	1,169	1,071	694	457
Rosario	0	236	521	840	810	748
S. Caterina	297	406	724	727	583	511
Sinsinawa	387	971	1,611	1,522	903	583

SOURCE: data for the dates 1900, 1925, 1950 and 1975 were collected by the editors through contacting the generalates of the ten congregations. Data for 1998 and 2009 come from DSI statistics.

1: The ten congregations are referred to either by the location of their motherhouse (which is often the way they refer to themselves), including Adrian, Cabra, Grand Rapids, Maryknoll, Sinsinawa, or by a key word from their official name: 'Anunciata' stands for 'Dominicas de la Anunciata'; 'Presentation' stands for 'Soeurs de Charité Dominicaines de la Présentation'; 'Romaine' stands for 'Congrégation Romaine de Saint Dominique'; 'Rosario' stands for 'Hermanas Misioneras Dominicas del Rosario'; 'S. Caterina' stands for 'Suore Domenicane di S. Caterina da Siena'. Four of these congregations have their generalate in the USA (Adrian, founded 1923; Grand Rapids, founded 1894; Maryknoll, founded 1912; Sinsinawa, founded 1847); three have the generalate in Italy (Présentation, founded 1696; Romaine, founded in its current form (after a merger) in 1959; S. Caterina, founded in its present form after the re-unification of two parts of the congregation that had become independent in the meantime, in 2005); two in Spain (Anunciata, founded in 1856; Rosario, founded in 1918) and one in Ireland (Cabra, founded in 1644). The source for all this information about these congregations is the *DSI Directory 2013*.

they had in 1998 (similarly, the three that were founded after 1900 also had fewer sisters in 1925 than they had in 1998). As the graph shows more clearly than the table, what we have witnessed in the twentieth century in the case of all the congregations is a significant increase in numbers up until the mid-1970s, after which a fall across all these congregations begins. Interestingly, however, even by 2009, only two of the ten congregations had fewer sisters than they had in 1900.

Combining these figures and using them to estimate the total numbers of sisters across the twentieth century, we get a graph with a very similar shape to that of Figure 1.

Figure 1

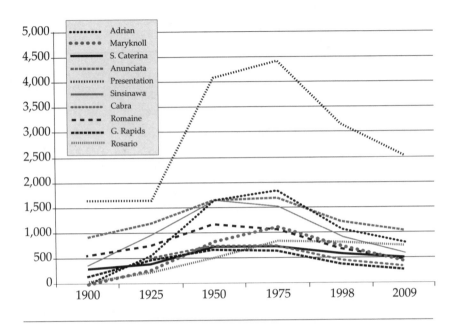

Table 2: Numbers of Dominican sisters overall at five dates across the twentieth century and in 2009.

For the dates 1900–75, the overall number of sisters is estimated on the basis of the average of the proportion of all sisters represented by the ten congregations in 1998 and 2009.

	Year					
	1900	1925	1950	1975	1998	2009
Total numbers of sisters in the 10 sample congregations	4,355	6,949	13,560	14,545	9,931	7,820
Estimated number of all sisters based on the sample	14,048	22,416	43,742	46,919	32,035	25,226

SOURCE: Data from Table 1 for the dates 1900–75; data from DSI statistics for the dates 1998 and 2009.

Figure 2: Estimated number of all sisters based on the sample

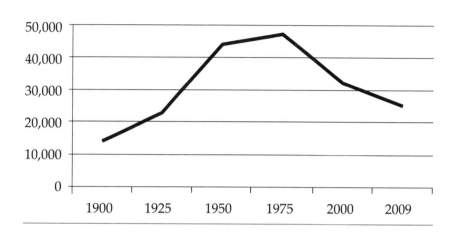

LOCATION AND STRUCTURE

So far, we have looked at the overall numbers of sisters at different points in time across the twentieth century. It is also interesting to look at where the sisters actually are, even if, due to the lack of data, we can only do this for the most recent years in which data has been collected, 1998 and 2009. Congregations of Dominican sisters are different from the provinces of Dominican friars in that they are much freer to send their sisters anywhere around the world, since they do not have a particular geographical area that is 'theirs'. Although congregations have a generalate house, which is often the first house founded by the congregation when it was set up, and many of the sisters of the congregation are often assigned to houses in the same regional area as the generalate, congregations may have other houses which are very distant from the generalate, in other continents of the world. This applies especially to congregations that have a 'missionary' charism, or to the largest congregations, such as the Présentation.

As a result of this, if we want to look at the data on where the sisters are, we need to look at it in two ways: firstly, we can look at how many sisters are in a congregation with a generalate in a particular region. Even if these sisters are assigned outside the region of the generalate, they will still have some kind of connection with that region and may well return to it. This is also the most reliable data that we can access, since congregations always know how many sisters they have in total.

Secondly, we can look at where the sisters have been assigned by their

Table 3: Locations of the sisters by generalate and by assignation, 2009.

	Region					
	Africa	Asia-Pacific	Europe	Latin America	North America	TOTALS
A: Number in the region by location of generalate	780	3,018	13,832	2,053	5,740	25,423
B: Number assigned outside region of generalate	206	184	5,366	128	442	6,326
C: row B as a % of row A	26%	6%	39%	6%	8%	25%
D: Total assigned to the region	1,393	3,934	7,685	5,646	5,784	24,442
E: Number assigned to region of their generalate	574	2,778	7,436	1,925	5,403	18,116
F: row E as a % of row D	41%	71%	97%	34%	93%	74%

SOURCE: DSI statistics; columns C and F include elaborations on these statistics by the editors.

congregations. In many ways, this information is more useful, but it is harder to get. Congregations are not always able to provide good and clear information on where all their sisters are, so it is useful to look at both sets of data.

Table 3 helps us get a feel for the differences between data presented by regional location of generalate and regional assignation of the sisters and the different insights we can gain from these two ways of presenting the data. Here we are looking only at 2009 data from DSI. The first row of data (row A) gives us the number of sisters in each region by location of the generalate. So the number given here for Africa, 780, includes all the sisters in the six congregations that have their generalates located in Africa. Similarly, 3,018 was the number of sisters in the 24 congregations with their generalates located in Asia-Pacific in 2009 and so on.

The fourth row of data (row D) tells us how many sisters are assigned to a region. These numbers include all the sisters assigned to the region, both from congregations that have their generalates in that region and from congregations whose generalates are elsewhere. It is possible to see here, for instance, that the number assigned to Europe is far smaller than the number according to location of generalate, meaning that many of the sisters who belong to congregations with their generalates in Europe are assigned outside Europe. In the case of North America, however, the two numbers are very similar (5,740 and 5,784). Latin America has a majority of sisters assigned to the region who come from congregations with their generalates outside Latin America.

The other rows help us to see two other things: for each region of the world, the proportion of sisters assigned outside the region of their generalate (row C) and the proportion of all sisters assigned to a region who come from congregations with generalates in that region (row F).

Looking at the totals column it can be seen that:
- the total number of sisters by assignation is about 1,000 fewer than the number by generalate (24,442 compared to 25,423). This is because data is missing and we do not know where all the sisters are assigned.
- the figure in row C of the totals column shows us that 25 per cent of sisters, on average, are assigned outside the region where their generalate is located. Similarly, the figure in row F of the totals column tells us that the average proportion of all the sisters assigned to each region that come from congregations with generalates in that region is 74 per cent (with rounding errors taken into account, this is 100 per cent of the sisters).

Looking at the rest of rows C and F, however, we can see that the percentages vary a great deal from one region to another, so the average does not tell us very much. A closer look at row C shows that the congregations with their generalates in the regions of Europe and Africa have significant proportions of their sisters assigned outside the region; the figure for Europe is the highest, 50 per cent higher than the average.

The other regions of the world have much lower percentages of sisters assigned outside the region of their generalate, ranging between 6 per cent and 8 per cent. It is interesting to consider why this might be so. We will probably find, for instance, that the European congregations that have many of their sisters outside Europe are among the biggest and the oldest; they are the ones that have developed the most missionary activity.

Equally interesting is row F. This shows us the proportion of all sisters assigned to each region who come from congregations with generalates in that region.

Europe again has the highest number in this column, meaning that almost all of the sisters assigned to the European region come from congregations with their generalates in Europe. Overall, then, we can say two opposite things about Europe: it is the most connected region with the other parts of the world in that so many of the sisters in congregations with generalates in this region are assigned outside Europe itself, but it is the least connected with the rest of the world in the sense of having sisters assigned to it who come from generalates in other parts of the world. It is likely that this may affect the experience of Dominican sisters in Europe.

The next highest number in row F is for North America. Again, like Europe, most of the sisters assigned to North America come from congregations with their generalates in North America. But unlike Europe, North America has only a small proportion of sisters assigned outside the North American region. Seen in this way, North America seems rather disconnected from the rest of the world. This again will more than likely affect the experience of being a Dominican sister in North America.

The number for Asia-Pacific in row F, although still relatively high, is significantly lower than it is for Europe or North America. This means that a significant proportion of sisters assigned to the Asia-Pacific region come from congregations with their generalates outside the region. At the same time, Asia-Pacific has one of the lowest proportions of sisters assigned outside the region.

In the two remaining regions, Africa and Latin America, more sisters are assigned to the region from congregations with their generalates outside the region than from those within. Africa is interesting in that it has relatively high proportions both of sisters from congregations with their generalates in Africa assigned outside the region and of sisters assigned to Africa from congregations with generalates outside Africa. In this sense, Africa is the most internationally connected of the DSI regions. Latin America is almost the opposite of Europe – two thirds of the sisters assigned to the Latin American region come from congregations with their generalates outside the region, but relatively few of the sisters from congregations with their generalates in Latin America (only 6 per cent) are assigned outside the region.

Overall, we can see that whether you are likely to be assigned outside the region of your generalate depends greatly on where your generalate is. The congregations based in each region show very different tendencies with regard to where they assign their sisters.

A few points on the question of structure are worth making, which here means the sizes of the congregations of sisters. Table 4 gives the numbers of congregations in different size brackets in 1998 and 2009. If we look at the overall totals for the two years, at the bottom left-hand corner of Table 4, it looks as if there was only one congregation fewer in 2009 than in 1998. However, compared to 2009 data, ten congregations were missing from the 1998 data set (three from Asia-Pacific, four from Europe, three from Latin America), so the number of congregations that are members of DSI fell over this period by 11 rather than just one.

Between 1998 and 2009, seven congregations merged in North America, and one other amalgamated with a bigger one, while three mergers of two congregations each took place in Europe and one took place between a

Table 4: Sizes of the congregations affiliated to DSI in 1998 and 2009.

		Location of Generalate					
Size of congregation	Year	Africa	Asia-Pacific	Europe	Latin America	North America	TOTALS
up to 50	1998	2	7	29	5	2	45
	2009	1	10	34	8	1	54
51–100	1998	0	5	9	4	7	25
	2009	1	3	17	2	5	28
101–200	1998	2	2	20	3	5	32
	2009	3	5	13	4	4	29
201–300	1998	1	6	8	3	4	22
	2009	1	5	7	3	6	22
301 or more	1998	2	0	17	1	11	31
	2009	0	1	13	1	6	21
Totals	1998	7	20	83	16	29	155
	2009	6	24	84	18	22	154

SOURCE: editors' elaboration based on DSI statistics.

European and a Latin American congregation. So the 15 congregations in 1998 that were involved in these mergers had become five congregations by 2009. One European congregation also withdrew from DSI, and one new congregation was founded in Asia and joined DSI before 2009.

If we look at the totals for each size category, we can see that the number of congregations in the smallest categories has increased between 1998 and 2009, while the number of larger congregations is decreasing.

North America demonstrates a different trend from elsewhere; the three

Table 5: Percentage of congregations in each size category in 1998 and 2009.

Size of congregation	% of all congregations	
Year	1998	2009
up to 50	27.8%	35.1%
51–100	17.7%	18.2%
101–200	19.6%	18.8%
201–300	15.2%	14.3%
301 or more	19.6%	13.6%
TOTAL	100.0%	100.0%

SOURCE: editors' elaboration on DSI statistics

smallest size categories for congregations have fewer congregations in 2009 than in 1998. A strategy of merger rather than a continuing reduction in the size of individual congregations has influenced this trend.

Over 60 per cent of congregations with generalates in Europe have 100 sisters or fewer. France has the highest number of small congregations (11). At the same time, Europe is the home (i.e. place of the generalate) of most of the big congregations. These are mostly based in Rome, with two based in Madrid.

RECENT CHANGES IN THE NUMBERS OF SISTERS
The more recent data that we have, from 1998 and 2009, is the most accurate, so it may be helpful to say something more on the basis of this data, which is also the most relevant to Dominican sisters at the time of the publication of this book.

Table 6: Changes in absolute and percentage terms in the numbers of sisters in the regions of DSI between 1998 and 2009, by location of generalate.

	Region					
	Africa	Asia-Pacific	Europe	Latin America	North America	TOTALS
Total 1998 (according to location of generalate)	957 (1340)	2,334	18,135 (17,752)	2,050	8,320	31,796
Total 2009 (according to location of generalate)	780	3,018	13,832	2,053	5,740	25,423
Change in absolute terms	-177	684	-4,303	3	-2,580	-6,373
Change in % terms	-18%	29%	-24%	0%	-31%	-20%

SOURCE: DSI data and editors' elaboration.

Looking at Table 6, we can see that by 2009 the number of sisters had fallen by 20 per cent compared to 1998 (some congregations that are included in the 2009 figures were missing from the 1998 data, so it is likely that the fall is somewhat bigger than it looks). However, the numbers of sisters in Asia, by generalate, were growing, even though this growth was not as much as it looks since three congregations were missing from the 1998 data (a new congregation was founded in Vietnam in 2004, but this does not affect the comparison between the two dates). The congregations missing from the 1998 data represent 12.5 per cent of the numbers of professed sisters in Asia in 2009. Most of the growth in Asia is in Vietnam, although Indonesia has also grown significantly (from a small base) and some congregations in the Philippines have grown slightly.

The data for Europe and Africa are shown with two numbers for 1998, one in parenthesis. This is because the Zimbabwe sisters moved their generalate to the European region between 1998 and 2009. To make an accurate comparison with the 2009 data (especially as regards Africa,) we also need to move the Zimbabwe sisters from the African region to the European region in 1998. The figures in brackets are the original ones for Africa and Europe in 1998. Those adjusted for the move by the Zimbabwe sisters are not in brackets, and these are the figures used to make comparisons with 2009.

In Africa, the entire drop between the two surveys is accounted for by congregations in South Africa; the congregations in Rwanda and Nigeria increased in size, and the congregation in Congo was stable.[4]

Europe lost 60 per cent more sisters than North America in absolute terms over this period (4,303 fewer sisters in Europe in 2009 compared to 1998; 2,580 fewer for the same period in North America). However, in percentage terms, the drop in North America was larger than that in Europe.

Latin America has seen no major change in terms of overall numbers in the region, if we only take into account congregations with their generalates in that region.

Table 7: Changes in absolute and percentage terms in the numbers of sisters in the regions of DSI between 1998 and 2009, by assignation.

	Region					
	Africa	Asia-Pacific	Europe	Latin America	North America	TOTALS
Total 1998 according to assignation	1,262	3,601	13,092	5,822	7,510	31,287
Total 2009 according to assignation	1,393	3,934	7,685	5,646	5,784	24,442
Absolute change	131	333	-5,407	-176	-1,726	-6,845
% change	10%	9%	-41%	-3%	-23%	-22%

SOURCE: DSI data and editors' elaboration.

According to Table 7, Africa has seen the biggest percentage increase in sisters present in the region by assignation. Asia has a similar increase of 9 per cent in the numbers assigned to the region, although in absolute terms the increase is significantly greater than in Africa (333 more sisters in the Asian region, compared to 131 more in Africa)

4. The data from Africa were not as up to date as those from other regions.

Europe (-41 per cent) and North America (-23 per cent) have seen significant reductions in the numbers of sisters assigned in their regions.

Interestingly, Latin America is practically stable in terms of the number of assignations to this region, which is reflected in the zero change in the numbers of sisters in congregations with their generalates in the Latin American region (as we saw in the two previous tables).

Table 8: Changes in the number of sisters in percentage terms in the Regions of DSI between 1998 and 2009, by location of generalate and by assignation.

Region

	Africa	Asia-Pacific	Europe	Latin America	North America	TOTALS
% change according to Location of generalate 1998-2009	-18%	29%	-24%	0%	-31%	-20%
% change according to location of assignation 1998-2009	10%	9%	-41%	-3%	-23%	-22%

SOURCE: editors' elaboration of DSI data.

In Table 8 we see the percentage change in the numbers of sisters in a region according to regional location of generalate and according to regional assignation of the sisters (these numbers are taken from Tables 6 and 7 and presented together in Table 8 to aid comparison).

This table shows us that regions may be declining in terms of numbers of sisters joining the congregations with generalates in the region, but growing in terms of assignation (the situation of Africa), or they may be increasing or declining by different amounts (Asia-Pacific, Europe, North America), or they may be more or less the same (Latin America). These different dynamics are explained by the movements in assignations of sisters, independently of the changing sizes of the congregations.

4

The Contribution of
Dominican Sisters International
to the Development of the Dominican Family

MARGARET ORMOND, O.P.[1]

What does it mean to be a member of a family? I offer one of my most poign-
ant experiences of kinship. It is a letter I received on 14 September 2001, from
Sr Marie Thérèse Hanna, Prioress General of the Dominican Sisters in Mosul,
Iraq. She writes:

> It is with sadness that we heard of the disaster that happened in America
> on Tuesday, the 11th of September. Having experienced such devastating
> attacks ourselves, we can imagine how difficult it has been for you. We
> are strongly against such barbaric acts of terrorism ... Please accept our
> solidarity and our sympathy on the loss of so many innocent people.

Dominican Sisters International (DSI) was formally launched in 1995,
only six years earlier, largely from the painful shock of our awareness that
these Iraqi Dominican sisters had been virtually alone during the war in
their country in the early 1990s. Now these same sisters were reaching out to
us in solidarity and prayer.

In a remarkable way it can be said of all members of the Dominican family, and most especially of apostolic Dominican sisters, that it was in the
twentieth century that we came to realise our full kinship in that family.
Moreover, it has been in and through our Dominican family that we have
made our most significant contributions to social justice in the twentieth century and beyond. Many factors contributed to that development, expressed
most powerfully among the apostolic sisters in the establishment of Dominican Sisters International in Rome in 1995. These values are clearly expressed
in the set of goals that were developed during the first multilingual gathering of DSI:

- To support one another in living out the Dominican charism and to

1. The author gratefully acknowledges the competent editorial assistance of Ruth Caspar OP,
of the Dominican Sisters of Peace, in the preparation of this chapter.

claim and promote our identity as women preachers.
- To facilitate communication and networking among Dominicans at both regional and international levels.
- To foster a more compassionate world order through the promotion of peace and justice, integrity of creation and human rights, especially those of women.
- To explore and foster collaborative initiatives among the Dominican family.

The goals that were articulated at that inaugural meeting remain in force today.

The same movements that inspired international co-operation and global consciousness among Dominican sisters were also being experienced by other branches of the family: the friars, the nuns, the laity, volunteers and youth. These graced stirrings of the hearts of Dominic's daughters and sons found expression in a document drafted in 2006 during the celebration of the 800th anniversary of the Order at Fanjeaux in southwestern France and endorsed as a 'Message to the Members of the Dominican Family'.[2] At that historic meeting, the members articulated a set of commitments designed to renew a vision of Dominic's family as the members work together in mission. They included a promise to be more welcoming to all branches of the Order and to come to know all these branches better, working together in harmony with mutual respect. Our preaching charism was affirmed as we committed ourselves to finding spaces to preach together as Dominic's family, and to finding new, innovative ways of preaching that would especially touch the poor, the young and the aged. The works of social justice were affirmed as we committed ourselves as members of Dominic's family to work together for justice, doing so in solidarity with those at the margins of society, while listening attentively to the needs of the world. And in all of this, we committed ourselves to link and nourish our prayer and mission.

Surely the same spirit, that of our Father Dominic, animated both the 1995 goals of Dominican Sisters International and the 2006 commitments articulated for the members of the Dominican family at the historic gathering in Fanjeaux.

THE DOMINICAN FAMILY: HISTORICAL AND GLOBAL VIEW
Founded in the thirteenth century by Dominic de Gúzman, the Order of

2. International Commission of the Dominican Order, May 2006. http://www.op.org/sites/www.op.org/files/public/documents/fichier/message_fanjeaux2006_en.pdf

Preachers has from the beginning included nuns, friars and laity. Over the ensuing centuries these foundational roots produced branches that took a variety of forms, from the Mantellata of fourteenth-century Siena, to the post-Reformation development of apostolic congregations of religious women, co-operator brothers, and a variety of lay associates and affiliates. A series of general chapters of the twentieth century endeavoured to define the constituents of the Order and the Dominican family.[3] By 1998 the Chapter of Bologna would state that the Dominican family is 'that communion of Friars, Nuns, apostolic Sisters, members of secular institutes, fraternities of priests and laity, associations attached to the Order, who, through a shared charism, are ordered to assume a similar mission of preaching and compassion'.[4] The shared mission of preaching and compassion unites us in a fabric of mutuality and support. Together we claim the heritage of Dominic in our profession to be preachers.

No one branch enjoys 'pride of place' in the Order: it is our mission that holds that place. In a letter announcing the fourth year of the novena approaching the 2016 anniversary, Fr Bruno Cadoré, Master of the Order, spoke of the role of Dominican women in evangelisation. Writing to the members of his far-flung family, he reminded them:

> At the beginning of this new adventure of evangelizing led by Dominic, it is in fact women who first come to join him, followed by the laity, providing for us a picture of the evangelization effort: a sort of 'small church', a community gathered by the power of the spoken Word, gathered to listen to this Word together and to take it to the world.[5]

As a family we have relatives in every continent of the world, and in nearly every country. By the end of the twentieth century there were approximately 32,000 sisters, 6,700 friars, 4,000 nuns and over 75,000 laity. Among the more recent developments of this remarkable family are the International Dominican Volunteers and the International Dominican Youth.

Two recent books provide dramatic witness to the variety of gifts brought to the service of the Word by these daughters and sons of Dominic, in each of the regions of the world. The *Dominican Way*, edited by Flemish writer and film producer Lucette Verboven, includes interviews with nine Domini-

---

3. See Tomasz Wytrwał, 'The legal relation of the Dominican Family to the Order of Preachers', *Angelicum* 86 (2009): 625–668.
4. Ibid., 631, quoting Chapter of Bologna 1998, 148.
5. Bruno Cadoré OP, '"Go tell my brothers!" (Jn 20:15): Dominican women and evangelisation', Curia Generalitia, 13 January 2012. http://curia.op.org/en/

can men and eight women.[6] Those interviewed for this anthology reflect the present reality of the Order's friars, monastic nuns, sisters and laity. Their ministries touch the lives of God's people in Europe (UK, Ireland, Italy, Norway, Belgium, France, Belarus); Africa (Benin, Nigeria), Middle East (Iraq, Egypt), Asia (Japan), North and South America (USA, Brazil). They include the heart-breaking accounts of two prioresses, one in Iraq and one in Nigeria, whose communities, caught in the cross-fire of ethnic and religious conflicts, have experienced persecution and dislocation. Dominican contributions to the arts are found in the powerful testimonials of a Korean painter and a Scottish composer, the latter a member of the Dominican laity. These Dominican women and men reflect with the interviewer on their lives as professors, scholars, peace builders, engineers fostering ecological agri-businesses and monastic nuns hoping to establish a foundation in Belarus.

Former Master of the Order Timothy Radcliffe notes in his introduction that the inclusion of nine men and eight women was a deliberate choice: 'First of all, the Church urgently needs the preaching of women if we are to be convincing. Secondly, the Dominicans have been a family of men and women from the beginning ... from the earliest days, a natural, relaxed friendship between men and women was part of our tradition.'[7]

A second book, *Building Bridges: Dominicans Doing Theology Together*, was developed jointly by Dominican Sisters International, the Pontifical University of St Thomas in Rome and the International Dominican Commission of Justice and Peace.[8] In these brief essays we invited 37 Dominican theologians to reflect on their experiences of 'doing theology', and what it meant to do so together as members of a family. Here we find friars and sisters sharing the amazing vitality of their diverse approaches to the study of God, each steeped in the foundational charism of the Order.

Keeping in mind the diversity of cultures and the different levels of education in the Dominican family among our theologians, there must be no dominance of west over east or north over south, and this desire is reflected in the contents. Each contributor to this project demonstrates the delight experienced by a sister or friar as study grounds ministry and ministry informs preaching. The region of Asia-Pacific is represented by theologians from Vietnam, the Philippines, New Zealand and India. Family members from Brazil, Peru, Venezuela, Argentina, Bolivia, Trinidad and Puerto Rico reflect

6. Lucette Verboven, *The Dominican Way*. London and New York: Continuum, 2011.
7. Ibid., p. 2.
8. *Building Bridges: Dominicans Doing Theology Together*. Margaret Ormond OP (DSI), Marco Salvati OP (PUST) and Joao Xerri OP (ICJP) Eds. Dublin, Ireland: Dominican Publications, 2005.

the Latin American and Caribbean experience. With the historical roots of the Order in Western Europe, that region is well represented with responses from Spain, France and Italy, but there are also contributions from Central/ Eastern Europe: Poland, Slovakia and the Czech Republic. Sr Petronille Kayiba of the Democratic Republic of Congo and Fr Albert Nolan of South Africa offer distinct views of doing contextual theology in Africa. Others speak for the USA, Ireland, Norway, Belgium and the Middle East.

Throughout the book we encounter men and women, friars and sisters from all over the world, each displaying the 'family resemblances' that mark them as sons and daughters of Dominic. Their ministries ground their study and their proclamation, whether these are the barrios of Peruvian missionary-theologian, Gustavo Gutierrez, or the rooms in the Vatican Palace of the Theologian of the Papal Household, Wojciech Giertych. In the reflections of Antoinetta Potente, we find the richly experiential theology of one who lives among the *campesinos* of Cochabamba, Bolivia, and teaches at the Catholic University of Bolivia. These brothers and sisters speak for us and to us. They inspire us to return to this critically important component of our charism – study – to give new life to our mission of preaching and compassion.

DOMINICAN SISTERS INTERNATIONAL TODAY

Today DSI is a global network of 151 congregations of sisters of the apostolic life, with nearly 25,000 members in 110 countries. As noted above, this organisation of apostolic congregations of Dominican women came about in 1995 when 80 prioresses general realised that we had challenges that we could best face together. At various levels there had been regional and even continental efforts towards co-operation, but at this point there was a new urgency. Our sisters were in need in troubled parts of the world, and we had to help them. How could we do it most effectively? At the invitation of Fr Timothy Radcliffe, at that time Master of the Order, we were offered facilities at Santa Sabina and the support of the Curia.

As a global organisation we have an international co-ordinator, and continental co-ordinators for the parts of the world in which our members are found. Numbers will vary, but in 2011 there were 720 sisters belonging to African congregations; 3,312 to congregations in Asia-Pacific; 13,158 to European congregations; 1,987 to congregations in Latin America and the Caribbean; and 5,461 in North American congregations.

From the beginning, we were drawn to the model given to us by the Visitation of Mary to Elizabeth. Among women there can be no better image of solidarity, presence, compassion and proclamation. It became for us more than a logo: it was the defining symbol of DSI, and wherever I travelled in those days, I collected pictures of this event. In each picture, although there are cultural differences, there are always two women in communion, usually standing together as one, embracing and connecting. We continue to be inspired by these two women, complete with their own humiliation and confusion, who dared to think beyond themselves and to embrace God's plan for the earth. 'God has put down the mighty from their thrones and lifted up those who are downtrodden, God has filled the hungry with good things and sent the rich away empty' (Lk 1: 52–3).

We were moved to respond to the concerns of our sisters in a world marked by widespread conflicts, ethnic clashes and harsh divisions between rich and poor. Increasingly aware of the needs of our members through global communications and technology, we wished to respond in a way that would emphasise our feminine impulse to develop relationships and to share our resources. We were determined to provide opportunities for women to talk in the Order, and a way for sisters to speak with each other across continental lines. We desired to find a way for us to be at home with each other.

The goals that were articulated in the formative years have continued to guide the initiatives of Dominican Sisters International through the successive terms of International Co-ordinators Sr M. Fabiola Velásquez Maya and Sr Marie Therese Clement. The DSI Newsletter and website report an impressive and inspiring list of programmes, projects and advocacy efforts spanning the various international regions. In many of these efforts, DSI has worked in close collaboration with Sr Toni Harris and Sr Celestina Veloso Freitas, International Promoters of Justice, Peace and the Integrity of Creation, as well as with Margaret Mayce, representative of the Dominican Leadership Conference at the United Nations.

It is now more than 20 years since the birth of Dominican Sisters International. As I reflect on these goals, and the variety of ways our members around the globe have endeavoured to fulfil them, I am truly filled with joy. I find the document developed at Fanjeaux, whose commitments were listed at the beginning of this paper, a great cause for hope. Even more reassuring is the above-mentioned letter from the Master, written to launch the year to celebrate Dominican women and preaching. At the same time, I know we could do so much more.

A DEVELOPING FAMILY: FROM GOOD TO BETTER TO BEST

From the foundation of the Order, the relationships among friars, nuns and laity have been good. Over the succeeding centuries, as new branches developed, new possibilities opened up and were affirmed by the Order, and new opportunities for collaboration were realised. The Order, now recognised as family, became more complete. Now we are challenged to look forward to what we can be for one another, at our best, since it is truly only when we tap into this deepest potential of our family heritage that we most effectively preach the Gospel. We are not there yet, but we have made remarkable progress, as the examples reviewed in this paper attest.

I have noted that the symbol we chose for Dominican Sisters International was that of the Visitation: Mary, Mother of Jesus, and her cousin Elizabeth in close communion, embracing and connecting. This is why I was so struck by the image chosen by Fr Bruno in his letter announcing the year of Dominican Women and Preaching. It is Mary of Magdala, at the dawn of the Resurrection, being sent forth: 'Go tell my brothers!' (Jn 20:15). When it first appeared on the Order's website, it was illustrated with the icon designed by Sr Thoma Swanson, depicting Mary torn between trying to embrace the Risen Christ, and turning as he sends her off on her preaching mission. Fr Bruno could not have chosen a more powerful image, and his words express, far better than anything I could craft, our deepest desire for the Dominican family. He writes:

> Since its foundation, when the first 'Dominican women' came to join Dominic, giving birth to the 'holy preaching of Prouilhe', our own 'communion for evangelisation', the Dominican family, has the need to be composed of men and women, religious and laity, so that it can be an image of the first community that walks along the paths with Jesus, learning from Him how to love and speak to the world, how to seek the Father, receiving everything from Him. All together, with our diversity and complementarity, as well as a mutual respect for differences and the common will to share in equality, we must all carry out this 'task of being brothers and sisters', in order to be *signs* in the world and the Church.

As a successor to our common father, Dominic, the Master knows that this goal is not yet realised, that there have been, and sadly there still remain, instances of prejudice, separation and exclusion suffered by some members as a result of the attitudes and practices of others. Yet the dream remains, as the letter continues:

Ours is a community of brothers and sisters that knows that the equal recognition of each member often suffers because of worldly limitations. In particular, there is still much to do so that everywhere the words of women and men may have equal value, rejecting all injustices and violence that still affect so many women throughout the world. Dominican women, in the adventure of the 'holy preaching', have the task of reminding all, even in the midst of many odds, that the world may not be «at peace » as long as these inequalities are not resolved. We must learn to become sisters and brothers, to identify the injustices, to fight them through this long and beautiful task of listening and of mutual esteem.[9]

His words bring us back to the most fundamental purpose of the Dominican family: fidelity to the mission. We will become the family we are meant to be through our common efforts to be faithful to the mission: preaching the Gospel for the salvation of souls and, especially, in doing justice. In so doing, we will be putting women's gifts at the service of something bigger than ourselves, so as to better humankind. Our common engagement in the works of justice will advance the common good.

As we reflect together in this book on the experiences of apostolic sisters working together in mission, we are moved to acknowledge the unique contributions that our international sisterhood has made to the Dominican family: belief in the power of the Holy Spirit to guide us and form us, a global consciousness with affective and apostolic bonds that has created solidarity among us, and a source of mutual inspiration and challenge that is bringing about a better world. This is the world that Jesus and Dominic are calling us to create.

This chapter in a book featuring contributions of Dominican women to preaching justice, opened with a question: 'What does it mean to be a member of a family?' In response to that question I noted how our realisation of the tragic isolation of our Dominican sisters in Iraq during the conflicts of the 1990s inspired the formation of Dominican Sisters International. I bring this chapter to a close by returning to more recent developments in Iraq, since nothing could more effectively demonstrate what it truly means to be a family living the spirit of our Father Dominic.

Delegations of US Dominicans, Voices of Veritas, visited Iraq and continued to offer family support during the build-up to the war that followed the attack on the World Trade Center in 2001, invoking the mantra, 'We have family in Iraq'. Dominican family resources were mobilised to provide assistance, support and advocacy. When the insurgency of the so-called Islamic State (2013–15) provoked a further crisis forcing the Mosul sisters into exile, they sent an urgent appeal and their Dominican family responded. In the USA, under the leadership of the North American Co-Promoter of Justice, we reconvened the Iraq Coordinating Committee. Two delegations, one of sisters and another of friars, visited Iraq in 2015, bringing our personal support as well as monetary aid. Funds were channelled through DSI, as well as through the financial offices of two US congregations of Dominican women. We have used all available media to make their plight known: articles in *Dominican Life/USA*, the Global Sisters Report of the *National Catholic Reporter*, media interviews and articles and the Facebook page 'I have family in Iraq'. On 14 August 2014, writing on behalf of 'our own brothers and sisters', Fr Bruno Cadoré, Master of the Order, directed a 'Plea for Urgent Action on Iraq' to the member states of the United Nations.

We continue to preach justice as we live ever more faithfully our vocations as members of the family of Dominic.

5

Dominican Sisters against Social Injustice in Hungary in the Communist Period

IMELDA ÉVA FARKAS, O.P.

The decree *Dignitatis Humanæ* of the Second Vatican Council, based on the social teaching of the Church, stresses that it is both the right and the duty of the Church to proclaim and teach the truths of the faith, as well as those regarding human nature and all the Gospel-based moral truths. The UN Declaration of Human Rights was promulgated to ensure the rights of each human person in every democratic society. Among these are the right to freedom of conscience and religion, and the right to peaceful assembly and association. Christian believers in Hungary, especially priests and religious but also lay people, were deprived of this most basic right for decades, as were the populations of the other Communist countries. The social teaching of the Church allows believers to protest and resist when these basic rights are not upheld and ensured in a given society.

As the life of religious orders was closely connected to the life of the Catholic Church, the changes in the relations between State and Church had a direct influence on the lives of the religious. In this essay the way in which some Hungarian Dominican Sisters resisted the unjust totalitarian Communist regime in their country is presented. I will put special emphasis on the witness of those remarkable sisters who, despite various prohibitions and threats, continued their apostolic work during the time of dispersion, and who supported the secret initial formation of new vocations. As a result of their sacrifice and work, when the Communist regime collapsed in 1989, the Congregation was able to reassemble with over twenty sisters who had been illegally accepted during that period.

Behind the Iron Curtain, which separated the Soviet zone of interest from the Western part of Europe and which was used by the Communist regime to protect its borders, many things were hidden from view. The unjust dictatorship and its crippling effect could only be seen to a limited extent from abroad. The party-state tried its best at political window dressing and put on a show to make it look as if all basic human rights were fulfilled. People slowly resigned themselves to the situation and for the most part took it for granted that neither freedom of conscience, nor the right to peaceful assembly and association, nor freedom of speech or press, nor many other human rights were ensured. I will outline the State institutions and instruments of oppression designed to employ political coercion, so that the reader could have a better understanding of the political and social situation of the period between 1945 and 1989.

The three sisters whose courage, commitment, deep faith, trust and fidelity is commemorated here, are: Sr Tarzícia Magdolna Takács OP († 5 June 1977), Sr Beáta Ibolya Maronyák OP († 17 November 2004), and Sr Ármella Mária Majoros OP, who is still with us, and still working tirelessly at the same place where she worked during the period described in this work. These three sisters of the Dominican Sisters of St Margaret of Hungary[1] stayed faithful to God's will and followed it in the hardest of times.

Almost no documents or correspondence survive in the relevant archives from the time that the permit for the religious orders to function was revoked. By Act no. 34 of 1950,[2] they ceased to exist as juridical personalities. Indeed, much of the older archive material was also destroyed and therefore it is difficult to research and reconstruct the events of this period. Information about the three sisters mentioned was obtained partly through conducting interviews with some elderly sisters and partly through researching the police forms and documents in the Historical Archives of Hungarian State Security.[3] Following Act no. III of 2003 and the permission of the board of trustees, the documents of the Secret Service Activities have been opened for public research. This corpus contains some valuable information in a number of documents, such as the photos of some of the sisters' letters, tracked by the police. The reports and accounts of the agents are somewhat less reliable, though of course these too provide some indications.[4]

SITUATION REPORT BETWEEN 1948 AND 1980

After World War II, following the occupation by the Soviet army, a number of

1. Founded in Kőszeg, Hungary, 15 October 1868.
2. *A Népköztársaság Elnöki Tanácsának 1950. évi 34. számú törvényerejű rendelete.* in Gergely Jenő *Az 1950-es egyezmény*, Vigilia, Budapest, 1990, p. 326.
3. The Archive was established by Act no. XXIII of 1994 to preserve and handle the documents of the state security bureau, which took the name Állambiztonsági Szolgálatok Történeti Levéltára (Historical Archives of the Hungarian State Security) in 2003.
4. I could only obtain a minimal amount of archival material pertaining to Tarzícia Magdolna Takács, whether this was material from the Order or police documents, while I knew Beáta Ibolya Maronyák personally. Ármella Mária Majoros has been an invaluable help in supplying many personal recollections but there is also a wealth of documents about her in the files of the secret service.

Hungarian Communist exiles started to return to the country, joined by their Soviet political advisers. The plans for turning Hungary into a Communist country had been previously made in detail in the Soviet Union. In this new social system the workers and the peasants would rule over their former exploiters. According to official propaganda this change would create 'the perfect, ideal, just society, free from all bourgeois ideology, religion and church influence, that will proclaim the fraternity and freedom of all peoples'.[5] Religion and the Church were considered to be some of the obstacles against reaching such a perfect society, so the Communist regime did everything in its power to diminish their influence over people, and, if possible, to put an end to them altogether. Since religious orders have always played an important role within the Church, the leaders of the new regime took meticulous care in hindering their work. The policies concerning church matters were formulated in new laws that shook the whole society at its roots. Communism saw its future in the young generations, so as a first decree, they forcibly removed the schools from under the Church's jurisdiction.

Some of the religious orders, such as the Dominican Sisters, served through teaching and education of children and young people. This possibility was denied them through Law no. 33 of 1948, by which the State took under its own jurisdiction the schools run and owned by religious orders or dioceses, and confiscated the buildings and all their properties. As a result the religious who worked in the field of education were forced to find work in other areas. Lots of the sisters ended up in factories or in smaller parishes as housekeepers. They were still allowed to live together in smaller groups, since they had been forced out of their own cloisters. Soon enough, another tragic decree followed that deprived the religious orders and their members of everything they ever owned. After the deportation of religious during the summer of 1950, Act no. 34 was issued on September 7, revoking any authorization that allowed the religious orders the right to function and work as religious in Hungary.

By then more than 600 religious houses (with all their valuables and furnishings) had already been confiscated by state authorities, and approximately 12,000 religious members were dislodged. Only four orders were allowed to function with as many members as the eight schools they were running (six for boys, two for girls) would need as educators.[6] The rest of

---

5. István Mészáros: *Kimaradt tananyag… Diktatúra és az egyház 1945-1956.* I. Márton Áron Kiadó, Budapest, 1994, p. 13.
6. This was only to keep up the appearance that the religious were free to function. Six grammar schools were run by the Benedictines, Franciscans and Piarists. The only female community

the religious from all orders were displaced, herded together and moved for a while to designated living quarters, and were told to expect being moved to Siberia and a life of forced labour. After the official dispersion of the orders, the members were not allowed to live together and were compelled to find positions as lay people. Officially they were no longer religious. Finding work proved to be especially difficult, since most places would not hire them for political reasons. For a while they still hoped that their situation would turn out for the best and they would be able to get back to their 'normal' religious life. Unfortunately, it did not happen. They had to find ways to live true to their vocation amidst their changed environment. Many of them did not wish to give up ministering to the young, and started illegal religious education groups for them.

During that period, the policy of the State regarding the Church was shaped according to the needs of the Communist party. The so-called 'agreements' between the State and the Church served only one purpose: to further the interest of the party and propagate in and outside the country their 'good relations'. All media were used to keep up appearances towards the whole of society in order to put a stop to all ecclesiastical activities and influence. This was reflected in party decisions calling upon members of the Communist Party to fight against the religious worldview. This attitude defined for decades the approach of Communists towards everything ecclesiastical, including practising Christians.

The first of these phony agreements was the one of 1950, born in the spirit of *fighting clerical reaction*.[7] It was preceded by a few other measures meant to intimidate and corner the Hungarian Bishops' Conference, putting them under pressure. One such event was the arrest of Cardinal József Mindszenty,[8]

---

allowed to run two grammar schools were the School Sisters. However, even they were not allowed to keep their convents besides the ones in school service. Their life was hindered by further restrictions, such as allowing only two classes in each year with two religious teachers per class, which limited the number of novices that a community could accept, also the constant state control in their schools and communities, etc. In many ways they were perhaps under greater pressure then those who had to leave their convents. Cf. Jenő Gergely: *A katolikus egyház Magyarországon 1944-1971*, Kossuth Kiadó, Budapest, 1985, p. 119

7. The expression 'clerical reaction' was widely used by the Communists in Hungary from 1945 till the mid 1970s. It was a political phrase, aimed at condemning all persons committed to the Church, priests, religious and lay people, as well as the Church's institutions and any movements associated with it, as directly endangering the regime. 'Clerical reaction' was usually used to signify any form of religious activity from administering or taking the sacraments through illegal catechism to the smuggling of religious books, and, less frequently, active resistance and rejection of the dictatorial regime, such as Cardinal Mindszenty's open protest.

8. 'An opponent of both Fascism and Communism, József Mindszenty was elevated to the College of Cardinals by Pope Pius XII on February 18, 1946. After he refused to permit the Catholic schools of Hungary to be secularized, the Communist government arrested him on charges of treason. Sentenced to life imprisonment in 1949 after a show trial tainted by a coerced

head of the Catholic Church in Hungary as the Archbishop of Esztergom, under false pretences, and his sentencing to life imprisonment in February 1949. He refused to let the Catholic schools be secularized and was an ardent defender of the rights of the Church; as such, he was considered a threat to the Communist regime. Another event meant to force the hands of the bishops was the deportation of religious, as well as a whole series of show trials against members of the Church. In the end the terrorized Bishops' Conference gave in and signed the agreement with the government, acknowledging the new state constitution shaped according to the Stalinist model. They hoped to save the religious orders by complying. However, notwithstanding the agreement, the orders were suppressed by Act no. 34 of 1950, a law that remained valid until 1990 following the fall of the Communist regime. The Church was reduced to total subjection to the ruling Communist Party.

With the uprising of 1956 the Hungarian people tried to get rid of their oppressors, but their victory was short lived. The Communist Party turned for help to Moscow, and after the entry of the Soviet army a bloody retaliation followed. The State requested another profession of allegiance from the Church, referring to events that had severed their 'good relations'. One such event was the activity of Archbishop Grősz, who, in a memorandum of the Bishops' Conference, demanded freedom of religion for the Church. Another event was the Holy See's excommunication of Hungary's collaborationist clergy, organized as the 'National Committee of Priests for Peace', also known as peace-priests,[9] as well as of those priests who remained members of Parliament in spite of a specific prohibition against this.[10] This was interpreted by the state as an open offensive on the Church's part; so the Communist Party retaliated by a decree requiring that a ministerial commissioner be at the side of every bishop at all times and that any appointments to ecclesiastical offices be subjected to state approval.[11] An official dispute

---

confession, his conviction generated world-wide condemnation. He remained in prison until the Hungarian uprising of 1956 and later sought asylum in the U.S. embassy in Budapest, where he remained for another 15 years.' Source: *New World Encyclopedia*.

9. The group of peace-priests included only about 300 of Hungary's 6,000 priests, but with government backing it was virtually in charge of the Hungarian Church in the years before 1989.

10. The prohibition was specific for Hungary. There was no blanket prohibition for priests going into politics, but in this case it was imposed because of the nature of the Communist regime and the fact that the government was not a democratically elected one. Furthermore, the civil rights of Catholics were severely curtailed by the government, which made any collaboration with it on the part of the clergy scandalous at best, betrayal of the Church at worst.

11. The State had formally intervened in Church government and personnel questions. The so-called Government Church Office (Állami Egyházügyi Hivatal) was established by Cabinet Order no. 110/1951. According to this, in order to implement the ecclesiastical policy of the Communist government, a ministerial commissioner was appointed to each diocese (they were popularly know as moustached bishops). Apart from regular inspections, these commissioners

arose between the Vatican and the Hungarian government because of these matters, which lasted until 1971.

Hungary's UN status was re-confirmed in December 1962[12] on condition that freedom of religion would be re-instated. This resulted in a general amnesty for a number of political prisoners, although the trials continued regardless. Indeed, there was a renewed wave of arrests in 1964-1965.

On 15 September 1964 a so-called partial agreement was signed between the Vatican and the Hungarian government, but, as its title suggests, only part of it was made public. As a result of this agreement the Pope was able to appoint five new bishops, several of the country's bishops were allowed to attend Vatican Council II and the *Pontificio Istituto Ecclesiastico Ungherese*, the Hungarian College in Rome, was re-opened to enable the studies of Hungarian seminarians at the pontifical universities in Rome. These events were announced as great results following the agreement, but the Party ensured that there were no real changes in the policy concerning the practice of religion. The Party's decision in 1958 to suppress all religion was in full force. The Kádár government's motivation to support the agreement and to make some concessions to the Church was to assure the Western world that there was indeed benevolence toward the Church in Hungary. Unfortunately, the Bishops' Conference too had started to emphasize to the faithful that full religious freedom was now secured, despite the obvious fact that there had been no substantial changes at all. Indeed, quite to the contrary: a large number of trials continued against the members of base-communities well into the 1970s and many priests and lay people were put in prison during this period.[13] Many of these arrests and trials were initiated after the 1964 agreement. Significantly, the State could maintain that it had not broken any law or legally binding regulation with its open oppression of the Church, since no law protecting the Church in this way existed. Instead, the State's

---

endeavoured to appoint peace priests into key Church positions: thus the head clerks of bishops' offices, bishops' secretaries and vicars of the dioceses were almost without exception from among the collaborating priests, appointed by state commissioners.

12. Hungary gained membership in the UN on 14 December 1955. Although the country had formally lost its membership after 1956, the UN's reaction to the Hungarian uprising was an informal suspension. After the military suppression of the uprising, an international committee was set up in January 1957 to examine the so-called Hungarian question. The investigation was closed in 1962, and Hungary's membership was once more confirmed, so that the country could finally start its full integration into the framework of the UN.

13. The term 'base-community' is mostly used with regard to Christian communities of lay people, created in South America; it is also associated with liberation theology. In Hungary it was used mostly to talk about informal Church structures, but the inspiration to establish such communities came initially from the South American example, where the Church was also fighting unjust regimes.

conduct was based on the Party's directives of 10 July 1958. According to these, the Church was allowed to organize youth activities only within the framework of catechesis taught at school, under extremely limited conditions and significant obstructions. All other religious activities were strictly forbidden. The practical observance of these regulations was strictly controlled at the parish level. The last Catholic youth trial came on 19 January 1974, in the course of which some Dominican friars were sentenced to prison.

Bishops, priests and lay people were equally intimidated and living under oppression until the mid 1970s. Gradually, the country's increasingly bad reputation abroad and its internal economic difficulties had made the enforcement of these religious policies impossible. Nevertheless, although the tight grip of the State started to loosen, the previously implemented process had already led to some deep changes in society. The long interference of the party-state had changed the worldview of the general public, especially of the younger generation. By the time of the collapse of the regime in 1989 a whole generation had grown up without even a cursory knowledge of any religion or religious culture. Both the school system and the media played a crucial role in this process.

A significant proportion of society suffered from the anti-religious attitude of the Communist regime, especially those who were educated, the country's intelligentsia. A Christian believer was considered only a second-class citizen. This attitude was made explicit to the students in their schools and to the employees at their workplace, especially when promotions, rewards or bonuses were considered. Practising believers were intentionally discriminated against in the sciences, in the academy, and in the arts, making life very difficult. Religious and teachers were at the centre of attention, as their vocation called them to foster and influence the younger generation. The political affiliation and ideological loyalty of teachers and educators was crucial for the future of Communism. The centrally issued national curriculum enforced an atheistic and materialistic form of education. Teachers were under strict control regarding any practice of religion. As a result, many religious and large numbers of teachers and professors were forced to leave the field of education and their teaching vocation.

Despite all efforts, however, in the wider society the acceptance of the Communist ideology was less than successful and it certainly did not fulfil the Party's expectations. Although a certain level of lethargy did gain a foothold, the need for the faith did not die, as the Party expected, and the Church did not become outdated and redundant. There remained a small core, which was faithful to the Church, for whom the official propaganda and ideology did not destroy their faith but reinvigorated it. Thus some new – and of course illegal – forms of practising faith began to spring up, in parallel, as it were, with the official activity of the Church: base-communities were born under the inspiration and leadership of priests, religious and some lay people. These were characterised by great commitment, deep faith and strong community spirit. Through its system of intelligence, the party-state tried very hard to disrupt and to make these small communities disintegrate, always justifying this with the aim of greater 'state security'.

The main motive behind the creation of these base-communities was the drastic decrease in catechesis. Decree no. 5 of 1949 by the State Council suppressed the hitherto compulsory teaching of catechesis in all state schools. Theoretically, catechesis was instead made optional but in practice it was greatly obstructed through the school system, while at the same time any religious activity outside the school environment was made practically impossible. The priests and religious leaders of the base-communities were therefore accused of high treason against the State, organizing the subversion of the political system. Even with such obviously concocted and extremely distorted accusations the State could rarely provide the necessary practical evidence to convict the accused. Nevertheless, significant efforts were made and resources mobilized to provide some condemning evidence.

To provide an effective tool against the activity of the Church, a political police force was set up within the Home Office, which operated a wide net of agents. The agents were recruited from both clerics and lay people. No method of recruitment was deemed too corrupt. The police employed persuasion, threats and blackmail in equal measure. The most numerous group of agents were those tracking and investigating religious. Their aim was to completely disable the work of religious by regular interrogations and intimidation, as well as by damaging their public reputation, often humiliating them, and sometimes even openly persecuting them. It was in these most impossible of situations and circumstances that the sisters of our Congregation tried to fulfil their vocation and to continue their pastoral mission.

THE SITUATION OF THE CONGREGATION IN 1948-1950
Before the dissolution of the orders the Congregation had eight houses around the country in the following towns and cities: Kőszeg, Vasvár, Szombathely, Hódmezővásárhely, Velem, Szeged, Szarvaskend, and Budapest. In 1948 the largest among these was the community of the motherhouse in

Kőszeg, with 34 choir sisters, 33 lay sisters, four novices and three postulants. The whole Congregation had 97 choir sisters, 94 lay sisters, nine novices and three postulants, with a total of 203 members. The sisters ran kindergartens, primary schools, secondary (high) schools, sixth form colleges[14], student hostels and teacher training colleges, teaching and educating children as well as young women.

As already mentioned, they too were caught up in the tragic events of 1948, when all their institutions were confiscated and nationalized. The chronicler of the Congregation describes this moment as follows:

Between 13-20 June all our schools and student hostels were taken over by the State, with all their equipment, collections and libraries, making an inventory of all our possessions. These were very sad days for all of us. All that the 80 year-old Congregation had created, the fruit of all our labour for the young, has been taken from us. The school – the site of our vocation – has been closed off from us. We have to retreat behind the walls of the enclosure in the spirit of sacrifice, asking that God, in his mercy, may leave us this at least.

Sadly, the party-state was not quite as merciful as God, and the sisters' worst fears were soon realised. In June 1950 the State started to remove the sisters from their convents. The first sisters were taken from Szeged, on the night of June 9. First they were taken to Pécel, to the convent of the Sacred Heart Sisters, but just 10 days later, their journey continued to Máriabesnyő, together with many other religious from different parts of the country. They were interned here until 15 September 1950. On the night of 19 June it was the turn of the sisters in Kőszeg, who were harshly treated and taken to the bishop's palace in Vác. Bishop József Pétery did everything is his power to make life easier for the large number of religious packed into the house. Many remembered his kindness with gratitude. The sisters' novitiate house was in Szarvaskend: on the warning of the Bishop of Szombathely, Sándor Kovács, all novices were sent home from there on 8 June, as a precautionary measure. Among these novices was Sr Ármella Mária Majoros. The remaining professed sisters were taken away in covered trucks just three days later, on the night of 11 June. They were interned in Mezőkövesd, as were the sisters from Szombathely. The community of Vasvár was taken only on 12 July. For three weeks they were kept at Klotildliget, in the convent of the Sisters of

14. 'Sixth form college' is a UK term for an educational institutional that offers pre-university training to the age group 16-18.

Charity, but on 2 August they were removed to the Cistercian Abbey of Zirc, where some 700 male and female religious were tightly packed together under strict house arrest.

The State apparatus applied great psychological pressure on these religious in the various internment camps to persuade them to renounce their religious habit and to return to secular life. With the exception of some infirm members they remained faithful to their vocation and their communities. By the beginning of September, however, the pressure changed to coercion: the religious were left no choice but to leave the camps within three days, without the habit or any means of livelihood. As much as they could, the sisters tried to stay together, two or three of them looking for a parish job wherever they could. The chronicler reports these events:

> The internment camp was empty by 1 October. The sisters were dispersed to the capital, Budapest, and to Vas and Zala counties. They had no money, no clothes, no home. Many had nowhere to go at all. Even if family members were able to take them in, they too were intimidated and afraid to jeopardise themselves. There was no possibility of correspondence or travel; they would not even have the money for these. [...] We were dispersed to the four corners of the world, some of us even rest abroad.[15]

> Spiritually we were well prepared for this big step. Our confessors and spiritual directors advised us wisely and we set off to the various parts of the country with faithful hearts. We carried the light of faith, the beam of hope and the warmth of love! It was not easy but we saw our mission; with this secret in our hearts we set off into the uncertain future.[16]

SR TARZÍCIA MAGDOLNA TAKÁCS

Magdolna Takács[17] was born in Szombathely on 15 August 1900. According to the register of the Congregation she entered the Order in Kőszeg on 31 January 1924. She was clothed on 12 June 1924 and received the name Tarzícia.[18] She was assigned to a teaching job in Hódmezővásárhely in 1930 and again to Budapest in 1938. In December 1949 we find her in the noviciate house in Szarvaskend, where she was the vicaress and the sub-novice mistress. In the autumn of the same year there was a general visitation in the convents of the Congregation, conducted by a Carmelite priest, Ignác Pálvölgyi OCD. At his

15. Krónika, p. 497.
16. Op. cit., p. 493.
17. Prioress General 1950-1977.
18. Belépő jelöltek könyve, no. 421.

suggestion the Bishop of Szombathely appointed Sr Tarzícia the Prioress General of the Congregation. It was an unusual mode of becoming a superior in the Order: by assignment rather than election. The Congregation's Necrology remembers her as a strict but loving superior, and so do the sisters who knew her. She was a strong-willed person, who demanded the observance of the Constitutions and who governed the Congregation with conviction.[19] No doubt she was chosen precisely because of these personal characteristics by the visitator to be the new superior of the community. It was during the time of her leadership that the dissolution of 1950 took place.

As early as April 1950, State Security had given orders that Sr Tarzicia should be investigated.[20] They also trailed her acquaintances and reported her every move any time she left her permanent address, even for the shortest of journeys. The documents contain all the details of this investigation. She was very closely followed. The report states, regarding her activity in Kőszeg, that 'she made hostile propaganda, as the leader of her subjects, and especially among the students.'[21]

At the time of the June deportations she lived in Kőszeg and was taken to the camp in Vác, together with the other sisters. She had to face a very difficult decision when the sisters were commanded to leave the camp and to take off their habits. They were looking for guidance from their superior, whether to obey the authorities or to stay together in that unpredictable situation. They had no notion of what was awaiting them as a result of either decision. They were threatened that they would be taken to Siberian labour camps and to work in the mines if they attempted to stay. Their memoirs testify to the fact that they were prepared even for this, only to be able to stay together as religious. Sr Tarzícia asked for her confessor's advice. The testimony of this is a letter of hers, dated 7 September 1950, which, with many others, was kept in her secret police file. Her letters were all checked, so the police also took a photo of the confessor's reply – the State Security thus knew of all her plans. In this letter the confessor advised the sisters to sign the so-called 'departure declaration' and to go back to their families, as far as possible. Mother Tarzícia should then move to her relatives at Szombathely, as her sisters would probably be living nearby and she could be of guidance to them.

She heeded the advice, and so, under obedience, the sisters were dis-

19. She is characterised this way even in the police reports. Cf. Report from 4 May 1950: Állambiztonsági Szolgálatok Történeti Levéltára, *Államvédelmi Hatóság*, ABTL 3.1.5. O-9177, p. 92.
20. Directive from 22 April 1950: op. cit., p. 89.
21. Report from 9 February 1951: op.cit., p. 128.

persed to wherever they could hope for a living and accommodation. Sr Tarzícia moved to the family of her widowed sister in Szombathely on 23 September 1950.

A police report from February 1951 informs us of her activities in Szombathely. Disregarding all observation by the police, and acting according to the plans envisaged earlier by her confessor, she began to make contact with the sisters and met regularly with the bishop and the superiors of the local seminary. She went to daily Mass at the former Franciscan church and then she did her administrative job at the presbytery. She also visited some 64 families who belonged to the parish and who lived in abject poverty and deprivation. Her correspondence with the sisters is well documented by the photographs of the letters in her police file. She supported the sisters both spiritually and financially, but there is also evidence that the favour was returned to her by some of the sisters. One of them, for example, sent Sr Tarzícia her embroideries, so that she could sell them and use the money for her living expenses.

A police report from 1951, based on the letters that Sr Tarzícia received from a number of her sisters, which were in turn seized by the secret police, summarises her work: 'she is trying to gather and support her former colleagues, both through correspondence and through personal meetings, [...] she is trying to govern them in whatever form she can.'[22] On 15 April 1951 she was put under even stricter surveillance, for the authorities wanted to know more of her illegal activity. They achieved this through recruiting an agent, a female teacher, intimidated into regular reporting because of her own 'clerical connection'. Agent 'Csöpi' rented a room as a lodger from Sr Tarzícia and quickly gained her trust and confidence. She had easy access to all of Sr Tarzícia's plans, including those regarding travel, and knowledge of her acquaintances.[23] Her reports were sent to State Security, which in turn reported them to the Home Office. We know that Sr Tarzícia was observed in this manner in order to build up condemning evidence against her, to be used in a future trial.

In all likelihood, Sr Tarzícia did not recognize this trap, because she continued to keep up her illegal connections with the sisters and the hierarchy and she spoke about these meetings openly to her lodger. There are many details of these conversations in the reports. A report from 19 May 1951, for example, states, that besides Sr Tarzícia's visits to the sisters, she had

22. Op. cit., p. 130.
23. Report from 12 February 1952: op. cit., p. 273.

also had regular contact with the bishop of Szombathely, Sándor Kovács, the bishop of Vác, József Pétery and the bishop of Veszprém, Bertalan Badalik OP. Because of these contacts the police opened a special file for Sr Tarzícia's case at the Budapest police force. From another report we learn that she was thought to have been a messenger between these bishops. Not long after the report was received by the Budapest police, József Pétery was arrested and Bertalan Badalik was interned by the Communist leaders. Thus her contact with the higher clergy was not without real dangers for all concerned. In fact Sr Tarzícia was discussing the future of Hungarian religious with these bishops. According to the agent, she was trying to arrange for a state pension (so-called mercy-pension) for the elderly and the infirm among her sisters. As they could not work or earn a living any more, and they usually had no family to look after them, without the support of the Congregation they could not hope for a living at all. She took great care to find a place for the elderly sisters in the newly established nursing home for the former clergy and religious, thus ensuring daily care and humane living conditions for them. A number of letters expressing the sisters' gratitude testify to this.

There is a denunciation among the documents, written by a member of the local Communist commission to his comrades. He accuses five sisters of 'local agitation and propaganda against popular democracy', for which they were expelled from the town. No further document follows.

From her conversations with agent 'Csöpi' we gain a clear picture of Sr Tarzícia's views on the political situation of the country. Her 'propaganda' consisted of disagreeing with the peace-priest movement, which served the Communist party; she considered the accusations against the arrested bishops false and saw them as propaganda directed against the religious. The reports also note that Sr Tarzícia showed interest in the so-called illegal religious movement, which in fact stood for the secret gatherings of the major superiors of different religious congregations. In this gathering she expressed the opinion that considering the adverse circumstances, the prioresses could not govern their sisters, but everyone had to consider their own situation and find a way towards an independent life. Still, she considered keeping in touch, visiting the sisters and helping them, to be essential, despite all prohibitions. 'Her activity shows that she is organising the dispersed members of her Order. They are expecting a political change and in the event of a war they would actively oppose our regime.'[24]

Still, in October 1952 the police had to acknowledge that the agent's

24. Op. cit., p. 340.

reports did not provide enough evidence for an arrest. So they decided to recruit a suitable agent from among the sisters, in order to expand and strengthen their trailing of Sr Tarzícia. With this aim they ordered a report on three sisters: Sr Róza Holler, Sr Márta Novotni and Sr Alexandra, but there is no evidence that any of them was deemed suitable for recruitment or that they would have agreed to spy on Sr Tarzícia.[25] Another decision was that in June 1953, Sr Tarzícia was let go from her administrative job at the Franciscan parish at the direct command of the State Office of Church Affairs. But even this was not enough for them; soon she had to leave her family, as she was ordered to move away not only from Szombathely but also from County Vas. She moved to Gönyü, a small village in County Győr-Sopron. Further reports of her surveillance cease here. She led a more secluded life from then on and they lost interest in her. She lived in Gönyü until November 1955, and then moved back to Szombathely.[26] The State Office initiated the closure of her file in September 1956,[27] but there is no evidence whether all that tracking ceased after this. Perhaps the case was dropped as a result of the Uprising just a month later.

The other source informing us about her whereabouts is the Congregation's Necrology. According to this, she did not stay long in Szombathely but soon moved to Tófej, a village in County Zala, where she lived for two decades with Sr Laurencia, working in the household and the kitchen garden of the local presbytery. In 1976, weakened by old age, she asked for a place in the Jászberény nursing home, which was already the residence of some of the sisters. They welcomed their prioress, who 'spent her days quietly, in prayer, until she gave back her soul to her Divine Spouse on 5 June 1977.'

We would know very little about the life and work of Sr Tarzícia if it were not for the trailing of the Communist authorities and their records of her every move and their copies of her correspondence. Despite all obstacles and prohibitions she visited and supported her sisters, both spiritually and financially, arranging for the infirm and elderly to be placed in nursing homes and caring for the families of the parish. She could not be imprisoned for lack of evidence against her but she was exiled and hidden away in small villages. Her life and sacrifice was known only to the Lord – though it was almost as well known to the State Security system.

25. Op. cit., p. 342.
26. Op. cit., p. 363.
27. Op. cit., p. 363.

SR BEÁTA IBOLYA MARONYÁK

Ibolya Maronyák was born in Szeged on 18 March 1922. She did her teacher training at the sisters' College in Kőszeg and it was during this time that she felt called to religious life. She entered the Congregation of Blessed Margaret of Hungary on 21 June 1941, where she was clothed on 25 January 1942 and received the name Beáta. She qualified as a teacher of biology and taught in the Congregation's school in Kőszeg until World War II, when she was assigned to the convent in Szeged. Here she studied physical education and art, then taught in the Congregation's school in a nearby town, Hódmezővásárhely.

After the nationalization of schools, like her other sisters, Sr Beáta taught catechesis in the surrounding settlements and isolated farms, and when this was also prohibited, the sisters earned their living by knitting and selling the knitwear. In the autumn of 1950 she too had to leave the convent but Providence allowed her a suitable job as a bell-ringer and sacristan at a nearby parish in Hódmezővásárhely, where she lived with four other sisters, two of whom were elderly, one blind and one paralysed. They all lived on Sr Beáta's miserably small salary.

Her memories of this period were very rich, full of apostolic tasks. Her job included the collection of Church taxes, which brought her into contact with virtually every Catholic family in the vicinity. She got to know their circumstances, talked to them and learned whether there was anybody infirm in the family or anybody wanting to receive the sacraments, especially Baptism and matrimony. She sought out those children and young people who were preparing for their First Communion and Confirmation, so the parish priest would know them and, whenever it was necessary, she also helped to instruct them. These visits went both ways: she visited the families but people also came to her. She learned to type so she could copy the material for catechesis for her charges. Typing was indeed playing with fire: the secret police was very careful to seek out every typewriter, every house search started with confiscating typewriters and any typed and copied material. Yet, for a few years she could continue this work untroubled, in secret.

In 1957, however, her illegal activity was discovered and she was taken to the Szeged police station. She was kept in custody for three weeks, during which time she was interrogated every night, deprivation of sleep being a very effective method of physical and psychological pressure. She was repeatedly asked about her connections but they could not obtain any evidence against her. She recalled these interrogations later, saying that she prayed very hard not to be weakened by the pressure and not to say any-one's name and bring trouble to them. No intimidation could break her or coerce her into talking and they obtained no information about her religious connections. Outraged, they finally tore up their notes and let her go. Not all religious were so fortunate: many spent years in prison for similar 'crimes'.

Soon after, the four sisters moved into nursing homes, and Sr Beáta moved to her parents' house in Orosháza. She could not hope for a teaching job in an ordinary school, as she was officially 'ideologically unreliable', but she was accepted into a special school. It was considered that – pushed to the margins – she could do no harm among disabled children with her 'religious attitude'.[28] She had to requalify by doing a degree in special education, and then she worked as a special needs teacher until her retirement. Although in this job she had less opportunity for direct apostolic work than earlier, she sought out every possibility by looking after the children and parents alike. She had many fond memories from this time because the disabled children were very open to God's love, and they listened to her most eagerly as she talked about God.

Towards the end of the 1970s the opportunity arose for lay people to study theology at the Theological Academy in Budapest. The decrease in priestly vocations necessitated the employment of more lay catechists, espe-cially in country towns and villages. After retiring, Sr Beáta started studying for a degree in theology and helped out an elderly priest as a catechist in two country parishes. Almost two decades since Vatican Council II, most priests in Hungary were still averse to employing lay catechists. Sr Beáta's parish priest, however, recognized the genuine need for their work, realizing also that the teaching of catechesis was not feasible without well qualified and faithful lay teachers. The local bishop did not dare to give open permission but it was with his tacit knowledge that a theological course, similar to the one in Budapest, was initiated in Szeged for lay catechists and pastoral as-sistants. He even asked for Sr Beáta's help, who thus taught pedagogy and psychology in the course.

Here the opportunity was finally opened to her to talk about her Domini-can vocation, though at first she only dared to mention it in great secrecy. The news about 'aunty Ibolya' having 'been a nun' was passed around in a whisper among the students. Some of them sought her out to talk about a religious vocation or Dominican spirituality. She talked about the conse-

---

28. Another sister found herself in a similar situation: she was employed as a teacher in a school at a sanatorium for children with pulmonary diseases.

crated life and how to recognize one's vocation with great joy and zeal. All the while she knew she was still risking another arrest, and perhaps prison, at any time. She helped many men and women to discern their vocation and to join the Dominican Order. The writer of this article was among them.

These events took place in the early 1980s, at the time of the so-called soft dictatorship, when the surveillance of the secret police was beginning to wane. As the constant stream of intimidation and assaults eased, the sisters began to meet up and to visit each other. Sr Beáta, together with Sr Ármella who lived in a nearby town, began vocations promotion work. Some priests in the vicinity invited them on Good Shepherd Sunday to talk to young people in their parishes and to give witness to their vocation. As a result, a few young women recognized their vocation to the Dominican life. The two sisters started giving initial formation in the Order through regular home visits. Despite being without the necessary means, such as a convent or spiritual literature, and still in the shadow of impending danger because of the illegal nature of this activity, they began to raise a new generation of vocations in close cooperation with God's grace, their only means being their own apostolic zeal and sense of mission.

Besides vocations promotion, Sr Beáta also received a new task from the then prioress general, Janka Gizella Tomka, who became the community's superior upon the death of Sr Tarzícia and who was already confined to a nursing home. Due to old age and infirmity she could not visit the sisters, so she entrusted the task to two others. Sr Beáta visited every sister in the Eastern part of the country twice a year, while a member of the former council, Sr Christofora Magdolna Csepreghy,[29] visited the sisters in the West. In the absence of community life these visits maintained the connection between the sisters and their affection for each other and helped them to share their joys and concerns. If a sister was in need of anything, the other members helped her out. Sr Beáta faithfully served in this dangerous task with great joy until her death.

After the fall of the Communist regime community life resumed with great hopes and Sr Beáta was appointed novice mistress to guide the first novitiate with its five novices. The small community gathered in a family home belonging to one of the sisters. The elderly sisters helped to support the novitiate from their pensions. The first convent was returned to the Congregation in 1990, albeit in a very bad state of repair. With the help of the local bishop it was renovated so that the community could resume a legal

---

29. Prioress General of the reassembling community in 1989.

existence once again in 1991 and accept new members officially. By this time, however, Sr Beáta's health had begun to decline rapidly: the difficulties and trials of the previous decades had taken their toll and undermined her physical and mental health. She could not cope with the demands and changes required by community life. Needing medical treatment she returned to her flat in Hódmezővásárhely, where she continued in the apostolic spirit and taught within the theology programme for a while. She died of heart failure on 17 November 2004, when the Lord called her home.

SR ÁRMELLA MÁRIA MAJOROS

Mária Majoros was born in Hódmezővásárhely, a town on the Great Plain in south-eastern Hungary, on 2 April 1929. She studied at the sisters' secondary school in her hometown and felt called to religious life. By the time she was due to take her A levels, the school had been nationalized. Her excellent marks would have ensured her a place in any university but she had decided to join the Congregation in Kőszeg. She felt an urgency to enter, as a change in the circumstances of religious was expected, even imminently, and she wanted to try out her vocation before the changes took place. Her father, though, expressed strong opposition and even threatened to disown her. But Mária entered the Order on 2 July 1949, at 20, and was clothed as Sr Ármella on 26 January 1950, just months before the dissolution. She recalls a very happy year in the novitiate house in Szarvaskend, which she had to leave on 8 June 1950 on the orders of the bishop of Szombathely.

Her family had a large farm, which prompted the Communist regime to declare them – with countless others – enemies of the State. Their lands and livestock were instantly confiscated. With the exception of a couple of rooms, even their house was taken away from them, so that they found themselves in great need. Sr Ármella became the sole breadwinner for the whole family immediately on her return, as she was the only member capable of work. She found a job in a canning and preserving factory, where she worked three shifts. Later on she found an administrative job in nearby Szeged. Here she was asked to do some further studies in accountancy, after which she received a promotion. While at college, she was taught the then compulsory Marxist-Leninist ideology, which she enjoyed, as it gave her the opportunity to get to know the views 'of the other side', though she could not be persuaded by them. Some Jesuit priests were allowed to stay on in her home town until 1952. They persuaded Sr Ármella to teach catechesis upon her return from Szarvaskend. She taught in four schools, without any official qualifications. While working to sustain her family she also tutored some students in mathematics. This was the beginning of her youth work.

By this time she was under police surveillance: the managing director of her workplace had connections with the State Office of Church Affairs. He informed them about the youth group organized by the Jesuits and entrusted to Sr Ármella when they were ordered by the police to leave the town. She was ordered in for a hearing and threatened, but she disregarded the intimidation and continued her work with the young.

She visited the families in the parish, seeking out those who were baptised but who had not received the other sacraments of initiation. She also taught catechesis in secret, in people's homes. Many adults visited her for the same purpose. A Jesuit priest, Fr János Németh, encouraged her to do Bible study with the students and to be careful to keep them all in the group. This activity did not go down well with the authorities and Sr Ármella was caught up in the show trial against the Jesuits. One night in 1955 armed policemen came to search her home. They were looking for a typewriter, for documents, names and other evidence of illegal connections. Despite the thorough search they could find nothing of interest – only lists of names: recently baptised, youth groups and their leaders. They did not know the meaning and significance of these lists and, leaving them behind, they left empty-handed. They promised to return, to keep her intimidated. Maintaining a constant state of terror was the most widely used method of intimidation by the regime.

Some time later a young woman came to her saying that she wanted to become a Dominican sister, because she was really captivated by the sacrificial life of her patron, Saint Margaret of Hungary (a Dominican nun), and by what she had heard from Sr Ármella about the beauty of religious life. Sr Ármella's first reaction was that of panic: 'it is impossible now...', 'how could she think of such a thing...', 'she is surely aware of the situation...'. But that same night she thought better of it: 'God knows the situation of religious life in Hungary. So why would the Holy Spirit awaken a new vocation now, when it's forbidden and dangerous? But I realized that no regime could cheat God and his grace and if he calls someone then that vocation must be fostered.'[30] This was the first time that the thought of vocations promotion occurred to her. 'We don't know or see what the future holds. But if God has granted this grace to somebody, that she wants to be a Dominican sister, we cannot dissuade her. Even if that means danger for the moment.'

30. Written testimony by Sr Ármella Majoros 1991 (no month and day).

It was soon apparent that some others were also thinking of a Dominican vocation, all together about 10 or 12 people, so she began to meet them regularly. A Divine Word priest served in a nearby village parish. The group began to visit this parish and the girls made a private vow of chastity into the priest's hands. Three girls made their vow together with Sr Ármella. Some made their promise for one or two years, but Sr Ármella made a perpetual vow. (Officially, as a Dominican sister, she could only make her final profession on 11 February 1978. This was still a secret profession into the hand of the above-mentioned prioress, Sr Janka M. Tomka.) The Divine Word priest was later assigned to a town where the State Office interrogated him about the groups in Hódmezővásárhely. They already knew the names of those attending these groups but as the groups no longer had any contact with this priest, nothing came of the interrogations.

Those who made a vow kept faithful to the group but did not have much opportunity to meet. They lived a committed life wherever they were. Later they obtained their degrees as catechists and taught catechesis alongside their day jobs. They never even dreamed of regular religious life in community. One of them met Fr Imre Bergou OP in Budapest, who supported them and took the risk of accepting these privately professed sisters into the Order. Their secret professions were later canonically recognized by the Sacred Congregation of Religious in Rome after the fall of the Communist regime.

According to Sr Ármella, there was always more opportunity to foster vocations when she was alone. As soon as an organized religious group was discovered, the regime immediately clamped down on it. Although she had had very little Dominican literature to rely on in her initial formation, she was able to pass on a few essential things: 'St Dominic talked always to God or about God – this is what I liked about him most. To serve God's purpose is the most wonderful thing of all. This service is helped by the Holy Mass, by prayer, by the true love of the dear Lord, love of the Bible and by walking in God's loving presence. This is what I had learned in the novitiate; this is what I talked about.' She formulated these principles as the Dominican charism, which she both lived and passed on in her apostolic work, wherever she lived. She also organized a community of lay Dominicans in the parish, uniting both single people and families who were interested in St Dominic and his Order's spirituality. They made their promises to observe the fraternity's constitutions and live the Order's mission in their own surroundings.

The secret police, however, did not approve of Sr Ármella's tireless work among the young. Their threat, following the house search, was not an empty one: their whole machinery was put into motion in 1955 to intimidate her for the next two decades. The documents dealing with the surveillance of Sr Ármella are now found in the Historical Archive. The file, aptly called 'Disciples', was opened by the political police force in 1966.[31] It contained evidence against Sr Ármella about her various illegal activities. In a document already dating from 1950 we find her name as a former religious, with ecclesiastical connections.

The methods used against her were the same as in Sr Tarzícia's case. After opening a personal register for Sr Ármella, they secretly made a survey of her family, her friends and acquaintances, and her Church connections. Then they organized the control and censoring of her correspondence and telephone calls – following her every step. She was soon aware of the situation, so she found it rather difficult to organize meetings or lessons of catechesis. Many times she tricked the secret police, who followed her even on the street, by circling round small streets on her bicycle, before finally going to her real destination.

As the local police could not catch her at this 'illegal and subversive activity against our State', they turned to their usual stratagem: the use of secret agents. First, they tried to recruit some of the young people Sr Ármella instructed, to give them reports of the meetings. They managed to convince one of them, claiming that reporting on Sr Ármella was carrying out a patriotic duty, because he was obstructing an activity harmful to society. He was registered under the name of agent 'László Fehér' in the documents of the secret police. Sr Ármella did not know of this until the young man, struggling with his conscience, told a friend in the group that he had been recruited by the police. From that time on, they kept all important events from him. Sr Ármella was also followed by another agent called 'Aranyosi'. A whole file was filled with his reports. The documents make it obvious that this agent was a priest who was well known to Sr Ármella. He was intimidated by the police: if he refused to collaborate, they said, his family would 'accidentally' come to some misfortune.[32] He did not dare to refuse. He agreed to observe the illegal youth work at Hódmezővásárhely.

The police were preparing various plans to eliminate the so-called 'clerical reaction', and 'activity preparing the subversion of the people's democracy', namely the illegal catechesis and the youth work and faith-centered gatherings outside the church building. They made every effort to damage

---

31. Történeti Levéltár, Csongrád Megyei Rendőrfőkapitányság, III./III. 205-19/57/66.
32. Sr Imelda Éva Farkas: Letter interview with agent 'Aranyosi', 14.02.2008.

the members' reputation, to disrupt and demoralize the groups and to isolate their leaders.[33]

In the police's action plans and realization report we read of several methods applied against Sr Ármella and her colleagues. These methods included anonymous letters containing false accusations, sent to the parents of the young people Sr Ármella catechised; chance encounters with agents or policemen on the street, which could further damage her reputation; regularly summoning and interrogating the young people at the police station. Several of them were threatened that if they did not sever all ties with the illegal group, they would lose their jobs or their places at university. Some were truly intimidated but Sr Ármella still encouraged them to persevere by her courage and faithfulness.

Despite all the agents, the tapping of her telephone, interrogations and threats, Sr Ármella continued her work with the youth group and vocations promotion. A number of times she was summoned at her workplace and warned because of her illegal activity, but nothing worse followed. Later she was assigned to a new but similar accounting job in a different town. This, however, did not hinder her in the work with the young people, since she could continue to keep track of them. She even considered this a fortunate move, as she was less directly under the watchful eye of the police.

The police, however, were determined to eliminate the groups. In their desperation, they did not shy away from the most sordid of methods, aiming to destroy Sr Ármella's reputation once and for all by treading on her honour. They sent several anonymous letters to the parents of the young girls in her groups, claiming that she was a lesbian who seduced their girls for her own gratification. Copies of these letters can be found in the police file, with various notes concerning the addressees and other instructions about their delivery. Most parents did not believe the slander, but, to stay on the safe side, they tried to keep their daughters from the meetings. In response, Sr Ármella tried to space the meetings out, and to organize them in different places.

Finally, by the late 1960s, as the secret service still could not produce any condemning evidence, they decided to close Sr Ármella's case. Her file was placed in the archive. The reason behind this move was similar to the two previous cases: the evidence was not enough to make a denunciation or for a

33. For instance: anonymous letters sent to parents about Sr Ármella Majoros, Állambiztonsági Szolgálatok Történeti Levéltára, *Államvédelmi Hatóság*, ÁBTL 3.1.5. O-13848/2 52., 1969; anonymous letters sent to priests and laymen about local priests, Állambiztonsági Szolgálatok Történeti Levéltára, *Államvédelmi Hatóság*, ÁBTL 3.1.5. O-13848/1/148., 1965.

feasible trial. In 1970 they concluded that the illegal youth groups had been successfully dissolved, their activity ceased and that Sr Ármella Majoros had retired from illegal activity.[34] They may have genuinely believed what they wrote, but the truth was quite different. Members of the group, who are Dominican sisters today, could easily disprove this. The call in their hearts could not allow them to conform to the approved state laws; indeed they committed themselves despite the lack of all external frameworks of religious life. The meetings, catechesis lessons, vocations discernment and spiritual exercises carried on in even greater secrecy.

In the 1980s, when the grip of the police loosened, vocations promotion witnessed a new upswing. As a result, several new members were accepted into the Order before the 1989 political transformation. The results of this tireless work are to be seen in the present situation of the Congregation: the sisters are active in four convents, and Sr Ármella continues her apostolic work, together with her sisters, in the same town where she suffered so much harassment.

CONCLUSION

Now that the documents of the secret service have become accessible for research, the true reality of the Communist State's persecution of the Church and of the activity of the religious finally unfolds. One can detect a great anxiety in the state apparatus' tense efforts. They really were afraid of committed Christians, of those who were faithful to the Church. They feared their influence on young people, because the Communist dictatorship wanted the youth for itself. Thanks to the Lord of history, there were still people, who, heeding the inspiration of grace and holding on to God's strength, dared to counter the injustice of political oppression and thus built the basis for a freer future, of which they themselves could have hardly dreamt.

---

34. Final report by Ferenc Nagy, Szeged, 23. 09.1970. Állambiztonsági Szolgálatok Történeti Levéltára, *Államvédelmi Hatóság*, ÁBTL 3.15. O-13848/242-248.

6

The Story of the Cabra Dominican Sisters in the Struggle against Apartheid in South Africa

MARGARET KELLY, O.P.

Stories are central to human life and to any reflection on it. Whether through fairy or family tales, through history or scripture lessons, we are all shaped by stories. Story is arguably one of the oldest forms of knowing and, fortunately, is part of the postmodern celebration of different ways of knowing. I shall therefore recall the story of the Cabra Dominican sisters in Ireland, tracing the impact this had on the Cabra Dominican sisters in South Africa as they responded to the unfolding events in their new homeland, and then reflect on the story.

THE STORY OF THE IRISH DOMINICAN SISTERS

Any records of the first 300 years of Dominican women in Ireland were lost or destroyed at the time of the Reformation. When the convents were disbanded their members were scattered. Some returned to their families and some fled to Dominican convents in Europe. The convent of Bom Sucesso was established for Irish Dominicans in Lisbon in 1639 and still continues under the Cabra Dominicans. Soon after that the political situation in Ireland appeared to improve and a group of women founded the first post-Reformation Dominican convent in Galway in 1644. In 1652 the sisters had to disperse again. In 1686 two of these, now elderly nuns, Sr Juliana Nolan and Sr Mary Lynch returned from Bilbao to Ireland to re-establish the Dominican monastery in Galway with the support of the Irish Provincial. Together with some new young sisters they began to live together without formal habit or enclosure. In 1717 one of the young sisters, Mary Bellew, led a little band of eight Galway sisters to Dublin, where they hoped to benefit from the religious anonymity of the capital city. Eventually the group settled in the Convent of Jesus, Mary and Joseph in Channel Row and continued there until 1808.

Over the years the convent became a centre of clandestine Catholic worship in Dublin and its numbers grew. Under Mary Bellew's leadership the nuns began to minister to others while maintaining their contemplative

[108]

traditions. As their numbers grew they took in lady boarders and educated the daughters of the upper tier of the Catholic gentry. 'These would be future leaders among the women in Irish society, even if by religion they were outlawed, and materially they had little else other than their titles.'[1] The convent flourished for several decades, after which the numbers in the community and in the school declined because the payment of punitive taxes over centuries meant the Catholic gentry could no longer afford education or dowries for their daughters. By 1808 there were only three sisters left: Eliza Byrne, Lydia Wall and Brigid Strong, but by 1819 the group had grown to five and moved with its new young leader, Anne Maher, to Cabra.

Life was changing in Ireland and religious tolerance increased; the British parliament passed the Catholic Emancipation Act in 1829. In this new climate the sisters gradually resumed the wearing of the Dominican habit and, with the support of their Dominican chaplains, began to restore and maintain full Dominican life. A few postulants joined them and they began again to take in boarders to educate young women from the emerging middle class. They also opened a free school for poor girls in 1820. By 1835 these schools were firmly established. In 1845 they founded a school for deaf children and thus were engaged in the three educational ministries that would characterise the Cabra sisters both at home and on the missions, namely the empowerment through Catholic education of young ladies, poor girls and deaf children. By the mid-nineteenth century the sisters were receiving requests to found convents in those places where Irish emigrants had settled, for example the USA and the expanding British Empire. They responded generously and among their new foundations were those in South Africa: Cape Town in 1863 and Port Elizabeth in 1867. These women brought with them the large travelling trunks of the time filled with the many practical, educational and religious items necessary for setting up new foundations. But, even more importantly, they brought the spirit of the Dominican Order with its traditions and values and the stories of how these had been lived faithfully throughout their own long history over many centuries.

The founding sisters, and those arriving in South Africa over the remaining decades of the nineteenth century, were expert at surviving in the ambiguous context of the British Empire. 'Part of their Irish inheritance was the capacity to evade penal laws and to treat the hostility of the Establishment if not always with contempt, at least with amused tolerance and indifference. Their Irish penal heritage also enabled them to adapt

1. G. Horgan (ed.), *Weavings: Celebrating Dominican Women*, Dublin, Glenprint, 1988, p. 10.

to their new environment in Cape Town and to set aside without scruple many of the minor conventual restrictions imposed in the more rarefied atmosphere of Cabra.'[2] It also set the tone for their relationship with the local bishops and clergy – one of partnership and mutual respect without which neither could have succeeded in building up the local Church. The main focus of their ministry was initially the spiritual and educational needs of the Irish Catholic diaspora so their focus was on the *ecclesia ad intra*. This was in accordance with the instructions given in 1837 to the Bishop of the Cape, Raymond Griffiths OP, from Propaganda Fide in Rome: 'Administer first to those of the faith and after to the native population.' As the number of convents grew during the last decades of the century their educational outreach gradually began to include new aspects.

The sisters set up schools for young ladies of all religions because they realised the important role educated women played in society. Within a few decades they prepared young women to enter the relatively new University of Cape Town. The sisters also trained primary school teachers in their state-aided schools for poorer girls. All their schools sought to inspire the young women with a love of truth, and to provide a pool of Catholic teachers who could expand the ministry of Catholic education. The outreach to the *ecclesia ad extra* also began. The sisters built and opened mission schools to educate the local 'non-white' population, which included any mix of African, coloured or Indian children in terms of the British policy of segregation. Sr Dympna Kinsella, the first prioress, came to the Cape with special training and experience in the field of educating deaf children, and in 1874 she opened the first special school for deaf girls and boys in Southern Africa at St Mary's, Cape Town.

The early history of the sisters in South Africa tells of grinding poverty, sickness and early deaths, but also of a lack of understanding of local problems and other ordinary human weaknesses. 'Nevertheless the record of the sisters' willingness to open and staff schools and convents, to accept a lifetime of punishing debt, and to endure the poverty of their daily lives, all bear witness to their commitment to the mission.'[3]

THE SOUTH AFRICAN STORY

The modern political history of South Africa can be divided roughly into four main phases: Dutch (1652–1806); British (1806–1948); Afrikaner (1948–

2. K. Boner, *Dominican Women: A Time To Speak*, Pietermaritzburg, Cluster Publications, 2000, pp. 42-43.
3. Ibid., p. 62.

93), and a post-1994 liberation phase. We take up the story of South Africa towards the beginning of the twentieth century. This period saw both the stabilisation of past trends and the introduction of changes that were to determine the future direction of the country. The discovery of diamonds in Kimberley in 1867 and of gold on the Witwatersrand in 1886 caused an increase in international interest in the remote British colony and a shift in South Africa itself from simple agriculture and trade to mining and industrialisation.

The Boer War (1899–1902), in which many Irish fought on both sides, resulted in a major alteration in the political landscape. In 1910 the state of the Union of South Africa was created. It seemed that the British were willing to yield political power so long as they could hold on to the economic wealth of the country, but the emerging African political leaders were excluded from representation. Within a few years the three major political parties, which would govern the country during the twentieth century, were founded. 1910 saw the establishment of the South African Party, later the United Party, which espoused co-operation between Boer and British within the British Empire. In 1914, the National Party (NP) was set up by more conservative Afrikaners who espoused self-rule and, ultimately, secession from the Empire. Both parties believed in white supremacy and rejected any suggestion of the mixing of the races. In 1912 the African National Congress (ANC) was founded to win inclusion and human rights for Africans in the social, political and economic spheres from which they were excluded, even though they formed the majority population group, worked both on the land and in the mines, and later fought in the First World War.

On the ecclesiastical front, too, there were changes. The new 1917 Code of Canon Law provided a way for all the convents in Ireland to unite as the Congregation of Cabra Dominicans, and then in 1938 the two groups in South Africa, in Cape Town and Port Elizabeth, were able to join the Congregation too. This formalised the supportive relationship that had continued for almost a century during which young white South Africans had joined the Irish sisters and Cabra had continued to send out young women who wanted to be missionaries to South Africa. In 1944 the sisters founded St Rose's Congregation in the Archdiocese of Cape Town, for young coloured past pupils who wished to join them and in response to Rome's promotion of local independent congregations. In 1974 the two groups formally amalgamated.

During all these decades the sisters in Cape Town were blessed to have the Dominican friars in Stellenbosch, some of whom, including Fr Albert Nolan, were past pupils. In Port Elizabeth, at the request of the local bishop, the Cabra sisters encouraged their African past pupils to join the Diocesan King William's Town Congregation for African Dominicans, set up in that diocese in parallel to the Pontifical Congregation of King William's Town in response to the difficulty created by the authorities for mixed communities of white and African sisters (this diocesan congregation and the pontifical King William's Town Congregation were amalgamated as soon as it was legally possible).

The sisters may not have been aware of the young Nelson Mandela and others who founded the ANC Youth League in 1944, but they were very much aware of the Second World War when rationing and blackouts were experienced. Against strong Nationalist opposition Prime Minister Jan Christiaan Smuts brought the nation into the war on the Allied side. South Africa became a Charter member of the United Nations in 1945, although Smuts refused to sign the Universal Declaration of Human Rights in 1948. While he gained prestige internationally, the more racist Afrikaner NP was gaining ground at home and Smuts was finally defeated in the 1948 elections. The NP government gradually brought in new apartheid laws to ensure that 'separate development' was forcibly implemented throughout the country. Great restrictions were imposed on blacks, coloureds and Asians and these groups were moved out of designated white areas. Over time, the Group Areas Act of 1950 forced about 1.5 million Africans to move to rural townships with few facilities, where they lived in abject poverty. Separate schools, hospitals, suburbs and stringent labour legislation also ensured ongoing poverty for those who managed to remain in urban areas.

A last attempt to change this direction was made by Harold Macmillan in his famous 'Winds of Change' speech to both houses of parliament of the Union of South Africa in February 1960. Macmillan tried to alert the government to the growth of African nationalism. He presented his analysis in story form, beginning his speech with 'Ever since the break-up of the Roman Empire one of the constant facts of political life in Europe has been the emergence of independent nations.' In listing the causes for the growth of nationalism throughout Africa he concluded that it was due to various reasons 'and, perhaps, more than anything else, to the spread of education'. Much of this education had been provided by Christian missionaries. In spite of Macmillan's efforts, when South Africa declared itself a Republic in 1961, it was dominated by a white minority and the black majority was rendered powerless. Thus, while many African and other Commonwealth countries were gradually gaining their independence, the white supremacist NP entrenched its draconian rule in South Africa.

EVOLVING POLITICAL STORIES

All groups, whether inside or outside parliament, responded differently to the new situation. The old South African Party/United Party became powerless before long. The members of the ruling NP were strict followers of the Dutch Reformed Church (DRC) and used scripture to legitimate their apartheid policies. The first NP prime minister, Dr Daniel Malan, a former DRC minister, made apartheid legal, and, over time, what had been more or less *de facto* became rigidly *de jure*.

The best known political group outside of parliament at the time was the ANC. The victory of the NP in 1948 came as a shock to them. The new racist legislation, including the new Suppression of Communism Act of 1950, threatened their future because their alliance included all racial groups as well as all religions and Communist Party members. It responded in 1952 with the nationwide Defiance Campaign against Unjust Laws, which, in its non-violent approach, honoured the tradition of the ANC since 1912. They viewed with even greater concern the pending legislation on education; as Mandela wrote: 'Since the turn of the century, Africans owed their educational opportunities primarily to the foreign churches and missions that created and sponsored schools ... we were limited by lesser facilities but not by what we could read or think or dream.'[4] In 1953, the Bantu Education Act was passed. It required all black mission schools to be transferred to government control by 1 April 1955 or to continue without state aid. 'The Act and Verwoerd's expression of it aroused widespread indignation from both black and white ... All the churches either closed their schools or handed them over to the Government with the exception of the Roman Catholics, the Seventh Day Adventists, and the United Jewish Reformed Congregation – who soldiered on without state aid.'[5]

The Defiance Campaign against the apartheid laws reached a climax at the Congress of the People in June 1955. The ANC and all groups who opposed apartheid sent 3,000 delegates to attend it. They set out the desired new future for South Africa in the Freedom Charter. Its main ideals were: 'The People Shall Govern, All National Groups Shall Have Equal Rights,

4. N. Mandela, *Long Walk to Freedom*, London, Abacus, 1995, pp. 194-5.
5. Ibid., p. 196.

The People Shall Share in the Country's Wealth, and The Land Shall Be Shared among Those Who Work It.' The Freedom Charter provided a vision of a happy ending to the freedom struggle. It would take almost 40 years to achieve it but it was important for, as the Bible says: 'Without a vision the people perish' (Pr 29:18). Many of the ANC leaders, who were past students of mission schools, would have recognised this quotation.

The response of the government was quick. In 1956 over a hundred ANC leaders were arrested on charges of high treason, though they were later found not guilty. Throughout its history, the ANC had been non-violent, although not pacifist; its leader, Chief Albert Luthuli, would be awarded the Nobel Peace Prize in 1961. However, by the time the prize was awarded, several major changes had taken place. In 1960, dozens of protesters had been killed in the Sharpeville Massacre and a national state of emergency had been declared. In 1961, the Pan African Congress (PAC) was formed by those who disagreed with the non-violent approach of the ANC. The ANC itself was banned and had to rethink its strategies. It became an underground movement and set up its military wing, Umkhonto we Sizwe (the Spear of the Nation), usually referred to as MK, as a distinct unit within the organisation, whose overall commitment was still to peaceful change.

Soon the government introduced laws allowing detention without trial, which could be extended indefinitely, and began rounding up Mandela, Sobukwe and other leaders. In late 1963, having captured the entire high command of MK, the famous Rivonia Trial began. The leaders were found guilty of 'recruiting people for training in sabotage and guerrilla warfare for the purpose of violent revolution'. In June 1964 sentence was passed. Thanks to world pressure and the moral standing of the accused, they were not executed but sentenced to life imprisonment and sent to Robben Island. This ended one of the most important chapters in the story of South Africa, but opened up a new era of far-reaching security legislation, indoctrination and repressive rule.

NEW THEOLOGIES AND NEW STORIES

The imprisonment of the ANC leaders startled the Dominican sisters. In fact the sisters found all the changes made since 1948 disturbing, especially those affecting education. They supported the decision of the newly formed Southern African Catholic Bishops' Conference (SACBC) to retain Catholic schools and heeded their call in 1957: 'To all white South Africans we direct an earnest plea to consider carefully what apartheid means: its evil and anti-Christian character, the injustice that flows from it, the resentment and bitterness it arouses, and the harvest of disaster that it must produce in the country that we all love so much.'[6] The sisters continued in their schools but found that apartheid slowly seeped into the whole education system. Soon Indian, African and coloured children could no longer be educated together. They also experienced the full impact of the law as they struggled to support their poorer black mission schools, which no longer received state aid. Fortunately, in the 1950s many young women were joining them, both from Ireland and South Africa. As they read of the end of a chapter in the story of South African politics, marked by the removal of the ANC leaders to Robben Island in 1964, they were nevertheless unaware that their own story was about to experience a new chapter, written by Vatican II, which at that time was concluding its meetings in Rome.

During the politically bleak and empty years following the imprisonment of all the black political leadership there was by contrast the slow blossoming of a theological springtime in the Church. The documents of Vatican II not only breathed new life into theological thinking about liturgy, ecumenism and other aspects of Church life but also into the relationship between the Church and the modern world. In writing about this, Archbishop Denis Hurley said 'Gaudium et Spes gave formal expression to the Church's acceptance of "the world" as an integrated part of God's plan for his kingdom.'[7] It was a call to address the current social and political reality as key dimensions of the Christian vocation. 'This means in the first place, overcoming the tendency to think in dualistic terms about history, that is to say, the tendency to separate the history of Salvation from the concrete history of economics and political events.'[8] Throughout the Third World Gaudium et Spes led to the development of contextual theology and liberation theology, with their emphasis on the preferential option for the poor. South African theologians, whether professional or amateur, were also influenced by these new theological trends.

By this time 80 per cent of the members of the Catholic Church in South Africa were black, though the leadership remained predominantly white. In the hostile atmosphere created since the coming to power of the NP in

6. Southern African Catholic Bishops' Conference, *The Bishops Speak*, vol. 1, 'Statement on Apartheid', Pretoria, SACBC, 1980, p. 17.

7. D. Hurley, 'Catholic Social Teaching and Ideology' in Andrew Prior (ed.), *Catholics in Apartheid Society*, Cape Town, David Philip, 1982, p. 33.

8. M. McKeever, 'A Medellin Spring? Thirty Years of the Theology of Liberation', in Joe Egan and Brendan McConvery (eds.) *Glimpses of the Kingdom, Milltown Institute of Theology and Philosophy*, Dublin, 2005, p. 14.

1948, however, the main aim of the minority Church was survival. The new government targeted three main enemies: the black threat, the Roman threat and the red or Communist threat. In 1948, the Catholic Church was already guilty on two counts, and over the years was to be accused of all three, so the stage was set for some interesting developments. In 1952, the first statement was issued by the recently formed SACBC. During the next ten years the bishops issued five pastoral letters in response to the increasing entrenchment of apartheid. The letters were cautious and conservative in tone. It was a small beginning, but enough to have the bishops labelled *kafferboeties* (nigger lovers). By 1957 the bishops had begun to call apartheid 'intrinsically evil'.

One way in which the Catholic bishops in Southern Africa responded quickly to the Council was by setting up Justice and Peace (J&P) commissions at both conference and diocesan levels. Some sisters joined their local commissions and were profoundly challenged by them. Some members were tortured, others slipped out of the country because they were on a hit list, and some missionary priest members were deported. This was at a time when groups were merely raising the consciousness of white Christians to the evils of the apartheid system, and the members themselves were only learning from Steve Biko and the emerging Black Consciousness Movement (BCM). One of the strengths of the Church was that the bishops interacted with such groups, listened as they told their local stories and responded positively. Both the bishops and their J&P commissions took to heart the document from the Synod of Bishops in Rome in 1971 which stated that 'Action on behalf of justice and participation in the transformation of the world fully appears to us as a constitutive dimension of preaching the Gospel.' In 1972, the SACBC issued one of their most important documents to date: *A Call to Conscience*. They highlighted Pope Paul's theme for the year: 'If you want peace, work for justice', and stressed that it 'is necessary to distinguish between party political action and the concern for justice in human relations which the Church must promote under any political system.'[9] They raised matters of concern, for example the impact on families of the migratory labour laws, unequal access to education, job opportunities and social welfare services and the lack of voting rights.

As these events were unfolding the sisters tried to respond in various ways, however small. They tried to bridge divides, bringing the children of black and white schools together for various activities and trying to make children

---

9. SACBC, *The Bishops Speak*, vol. II, 'A Call to Conscience', Pretoria, SACBC, 1980, p. 9.

of all races aware of the needs of the poor and to develop different ways of helping them. In several of their convents they developed night schools to provide education for young black adults in a wide range of subjects with high quality teaching. These schools were run in the same buildings as the day schools. The schools were seen as a way of empowering black people and consequently brought various threats from the authorities over the years. Many of the students were involved in the struggle. Literacy and sewing classes were also offered in some places. The night schools became very popular – in Vanderbijlpark, near Sebokeng, south of Johannesburg, the numbers grew from 60 to 530 within a few years.

In various places there were *ad hoc* responses to local needs; when approached by children for help, for instance, Sr Clare Harkin set up a 'bush school', and then negotiated with departmental officials until eventually additional classes were added to two local black schools so that all the children could be catered for. The sisters carried out these and many traditional charitable activities after a full day's work in school. In her unpublished master's thesis (1999) Sr Honor McCabe gives a summary evaluation of these works as follows: 'Today, speaking to the sisters about this period of quietly working with the oppressed, one does not find any sense of triumphalism. Some have a certain sense of satisfaction in having done all they could for the oppressed at the time. Others feel that *"working for change from within"* was not sufficient: *"We went along with the apartheid regime for too long"*.'[10] But this situation was soon to change.

THE STORY OF THE OPEN SCHOOLS
Even though the Catholic Church had bravely championed its schools, nevertheless between 1948 and 1975 more than half its African schools had been forced to close for lack of funding. Two surveys had been commissioned by the SACBC and the Education Conference of Religious (ECAR) between 1969 and 1974, but the reports were overtaken by changing circumstances. In a strange irony, having imposed rigid racial segregation at home, the government began to establish diplomatic relations with other African countries. The new African diplomats required good schools for their children, and in 1975 the government asked a few private white schools to admit them. The Catholic private schools were happy to oblige but this raised obvious ethical questions for them. At the beginning of the new school year in January 1976, a handful of local coloured children applied to Springfield

10. H. McCabe OP, *Living by the Truth*, 1999, p. 83, unpublished thesis.

Dominican Convent School in Cape Town. They were quietly admitted and soon afterwards one Indian pupil was admitted to Holy Rosary Convent School in Port Elizabeth. These were the first Cabra 'open schools', a term favoured as it conveyed the sense of freedom of choice.

The action was due mainly to the position taken by Sr Genevieve Hickey, the Region Vicar of the Cabra Dominicans, who was also an executive member of the Association of Women Religious (AWR). This body had resolved in September 1975 'to give practical Christian witness to social justice by accepting non-white Christians into their [white] schools'. The AWR, however, could only present the resolution to the SACBC at its meeting at the end of January 1976, after which the bishops passed a resolution that 'the Conference favours a policy of integration in Catholic schools'.[11] This statement was important, as law-abiding Catholic teachers and parents, who may have had scruples about breaking the law, were more likely to accept the policy on the authority of the bishops. However, by the time the resolution was formalised the school year had already begun quietly and few noticed the change, or indeed the bishops' statement.

Schools are rarely of interest to newspaper reporters but for a time they became the centre of many newsworthy storms. The first and greatest of these was the uprising of the African students in Soweto on 16 June 1976. At least 23 students were killed on the first day, and 566 in all during the following weeks. Hundreds more were imprisoned and thousands fled into exile. The protests began against inferior black education, as the government spent ten times more per capita on white education, but they soon targeted the whole system of apartheid and spread sporadically throughout the country during the following weeks, months and years. The brutal scenes shown on international television shocked world leaders, who began to put pressure on the South African government. Thus the growing intensity of the Black Consciousness Movement erupted onto the political scene and in many ways heralded the beginning of the final thrust against apartheid.

In January 1977, the Dominican sisters also became a focus for the media. One school will be taken as an example: Holy Rosary Convent School in Port Elizabeth. Throughout 1976 the staff and students had been prepared for the changes to come. 'By sharing concerts and choirs and sports days the young people learned to mix with a growing ease and poise with their peers of other races, languages and backgrounds.'[12] Yet all of this preparation had to be done

11. K. Boner, *Dominican Women: A Time To Speak*, Cluster Publications, Pietermaritzburg, 2000, p. 326.
12. *The Southern Cross*, Cape Town, January 1977, date not available.

in a subtle way as staff, students and visitors could have been put in danger if it was seen as preparation for direct confrontation with the government; one visiting Xhosa university lecturer, for instance, who had addressed the students on his culture, was afterwards taken in for questioning by the police. The sisters involved tried to analyse the situation and reflect on it in the light of scripture but they also sought to judge the morality of each action undertaken. The immorality of the apartheid structures was clear as was the morality of resistance, but the sisters knew that they could not use their students as mere pawns to make political statements, nor could they put any of the responsibility for their decisions or actions on the lay teachers, who were very vulnerable. The lay teachers remained loyal, even at the risk of having no jobs, and the local African King William's Town Dominican sisters were also very supportive as they quietly and discreetly arranged for some of their students to transfer to Holy Rosary High School as they finished primary school.

On 12 January 1977, the school welcomed 33 black students, who joined the approximately 550 white students. The students coped well and enjoyed getting to know one another. One student in the high school wrote in an essay how she had looked forward to giving 'Christian witness' and was delighted to find a black girl beside her, but added: 'I was in for a shock though. I soon realised that she was no different from me. She laughed, talked, sang and ate exactly the same as I did, except maybe she sang better than I did and I was more talkative than she.' In the junior school the little ones didn't even notice the difference. One father who had arranged for his daughter to sit beside a black student was frustrated when she said nothing at home and eventually asked, 'What colour is the girl beside you?' The unexpected response was, 'I don't know, Daddy, but I'll ask her tomorrow.' She then put her pale arm next to his tanned one and added, 'But she is more like you than me.' The official response was rather different. On the first day there was a phone call from the Director General of Education in the province insisting that the 33 students be sent away immediately.

The *Times* of London and *The New York Times* gave extensive coverage under the banner 'Threat of Closure to Catholic schools in Cape which mix Races'. A local paper quoted the new Region Vicar, Sr Marian O'Sullivan: 'The Dominican sisters' private schools have become "open" schools; they are accepting children without reference to so-called race classification.'[13] For days, photographers were at the school gates taking photographs as the

13. *The Argus*, Cape Town, January 1977, date not available.

children came and went and local people literally hung out of the windows of offices to behold this strange multiracial phenomenon. The international attention provided some protection for the sisters, as did the support of the Vatican and other Churches. In parliament, the opposition party also voiced their support. Even the most conservative Reformed Church said that, while it was illegal and they did not agree with the action, it was not immoral nor against Scripture. The most courageous support came from the lay teachers, Catholic and Protestant, English and Afrikaner, who worked away quietly. Most parents, too, were loyal, if somewhat bewildered and even frightened. Of course, the sisters were made aware of the opposition of the special security branch of the police. 'This school is run by a Communist' was painted on the wall one night, and often the principal would pick up the phone to hear heavy breathing at the other end. Even small mixed groups of parents who met in the evenings so that they too could get to know one another admitted that they suspected the school was bugged and their deepest sharing took place afterwards in the grounds.

In the Cape and the Transvaal, the two provinces where most of the open schools were situated, the administrators Lapa Munnik and Sybrand van Niekerk wanted the black children removed, or the schools closed. At national level, Dr Piet Koornhof was minister of education. Previously, as minister of sport, he had had practical experience of the international condemnation of apartheid. He called a meeting with the two administrators and the Catholic Church authorities. On 28 March he met with a delegation from the SACBC. It was led by the president, Archbishop J.P. Fitzgerald, and included Sr Marian O'Sullivan and Br Jude Pieterse FMS from ECAR. By then, the Cabra and Newcastle Dominicans and the Mercy Sisters had become the leaders in the open schools project. It was agreed that the matter of the open schools would be referred to the Cabinet. That year there were 227 children illegally in the schools, 90 of them in Cabra schools. Dr Koornhof understood the importance of world opinion; he also knew that the schools were in breach of the Constitution and understood the mentality of his conservative colleagues, so he played for time and delayed presenting the matter to the Cabinet until the following December.

It was decided that the Catholic Church could, in exceptional circumstances, accept a few children of African or coloured races into their schools, but that they would need to apply for permission for each child. In the Cape Provinces the permissions were given, but in the more conservative Transvaal no reply was received by the opening of school in

1978. In spite of hostility from officials, and threats from some local residents in that province, the Dominican and other Catholic schools went ahead and admitted more 'non-white' children. In 1978, there were 268 'non-white' students in that province alone, and by 1979 they had reached almost 500. But it was only after years of negotiations and mountains of correspondence between the bishops, together with ECAR and the government, that the matter was finally resolved.

At local level in Port Elizabeth, progress also continued; the curriculum was adapted, for instance, to include the teaching of Xhosa and African studies. Teachers also developed interesting ways for the students to teach one another about their religious and cultural differences. It was a healthy shock for Catholics to hear how a Hindu pupil would meditate for an hour before coming to school on a holy day. Muslims were equally impressive when sharing about their fasting. While treasuring their own faith, they were happy to attend church and usually did well in biblical studies. The African students were all Christian, but shared their traditional tribal stories, cultural traditions and magnificent singing.

This sharing was often a healing experience. One Indian mother wept when the principal thanked her for all she had done. She shared how her daughter had always been ashamed of being Indian. Suddenly, because she was leading a group at school, she wanted to learn all about her culture and how to wear a sari and dance in it to Indian music so that she could teach her group. Similar interaction and sharing took place in concerts and other areas of school life, but in the general social life of the school there were many challenges. Over time, as the school sports teams became racially mixed, some schools refused to compete with them. Eventually, the Education Department ruled that this was permitted but that the schools that refused would lose their league points. Likewise, barriers began to fall in various sports facilities; the local swimming pool in the city centre that was used by Holy Rosary Convent, for instance, eventually turned a blind eye to the changing school population.

Other moral challenges were whether to take students to cinemas that were for 'whites only', or to allow the open school to compete in inter-school activities such as quizzes and festivals, when these were open only to white schools. It took years to resolve all these moral and legal issues. But it was wonderful to experience the goodness of ordinary people who had grown up in a system that was geared to indoctrination and discrimination and to see the first small cracks appear in the monolithic structure of apartheid.

Following the lead of the private schools, over the next decade all the Dominican schools became open schools, including state-aided and special schools.

But, apart from the Education Department, the apartheid regime, and especially the security branch, grew daily more vicious, especially in the Eastern Cape. The most famous example of this was the cruel murder of Steve Biko, the Black Consciousness leader, on 12 September 1977. Together with the local people the sisters mourned his death. Some joined the crowd of over 10,000 people, including foreign diplomats, who attended his funeral. In this context the open school was a small but symbolic gesture of solidarity with the oppressed. In the words of Vatican II, the sisters were reading the signs of the times and trying to respond to them.

THE STRUGGLE STORY IN OTHER SCHOOLS

While the open schools were moving ahead the struggle was also growing in the much larger world of the schools in black and coloured townships. The Soweto protests of 1976 spread and by the early 1980s the schools' protest became part of the wider struggle against apartheid. Protest took various forms, including active public marches and passive boycotting of schools. In Cape Town in 1985, four sisters and several lay teachers took part in a schools protest march to Pollsmoor prison, to seek the release of Nelson Mandela. Two of the sisters were arrested. Sr Feargal Cassidy describes how this happened: 'As we reached a hill on the Kromboom Road, we found an army of police in front of us. A sergeant called us to halt and gave us one or two minutes to disperse. However this was deemed too little time to do so and it was decided we'd kneel down and pray the "Our Father". As we did so we were arrested and more or less dumped in an army lorry.'[14]

The march was shown on European television to the disadvantage of the apartheid government because, as Sr Aine Hardiman said, 'the government was meeting peace with aggression and put the churches in Europe more firmly behind us'.[15] It was little consolation that they were in the same jail as Mandela.

The 1980s saw increased repression of all new political organisations and of any religious groups who supported them. These new groups engaged in public protest marches and many sisters and students walked with them. All were committed to non-violence and most were led by ecumenical groups of

14. H. Mc Cabe OP, 'Living by the Truth', 1999, p.100, unpublished thesis.
15. Ibid., p. 100.

Church leaders. Sr Aine described one such march when they were met by a police blockade as follows: 'The silence deepened as we walked towards the massed array of force ... we clung to one another more tightly as we advanced and prayed softly. It was for me a moment of vision – what the new South Africa could be – all races, all creeds, and none, walking arm in arm into danger for justice.'[16] During the many marches to parliament in Cape Town the police would attempt to arrest hundreds of people. When all the police vehicles had been filled marchers would be escorted back to the nearest police station. Individual sisters would often slip away unnoticed with small groups of marchers and avoid arrest. They were mindful of the distinction between laws that are moral and those that are merely legal, and of the teaching of Aquinas that law is an act of reason, a means to the end of achieving human freedom and the common good, not a service to the will of dictators.

Sometimes direct confrontation was necessary; in July 1986, for instance, Sr Clare Harkin attended the funeral of a black student who had been killed by the police. She walked with another sister and some young people back to the family home for the traditional washing of hands. When she saw a policeman ill-treating a young boy she spontaneously ran between them and was arrested. She was taken to Pollsmoor prison and detained. She was not allowed to see a lawyer, interrogated almost every day and subjected to blaring music throughout the night. Sr Therese Emmanuel Dempsey, representing the Region Vicar, was allowed to visit her only after a fortnight had passed. The Supreme Court eventually found in Clare's favour in 1988.

In the Eastern Cape there were sporadic school boycotts and general unrest in major townships throughout 1984. In 1985, the intermittent boycotts came to a head in Langa near the small town of Uitenhage. After the shooting of some young men, the police forbade Saturday funerals, claiming that they were being used for political ends. On 21 March the people gathered to protest, and as they marched from Langa their numbers grew and grew. The police formed a barricade and seeing this, the leader of the protest raised his hand to stop the march. Nevertheless the police opened fire and many were killed. The official figure was 29, but most would claim that at least 40 were killed in the Langa Massacre. Later the police surrounded the hospital so that they could arrest anyone leaving it. They also refused to let the priests and sisters in. The local Catholic presbytery in the town became a makeshift

16. K. Boner, *Dominican Women A Time To Speak*, Pietermaritzburg, Cluster Publications, 2000, p. 332.

clinic, legal aid centre and a general place of refuge for the people. The Dominican sisters, the Black Sash women, and a few doctors who travelled from Port Elizabeth ministered to the wounded as all the local doctors were warned not to help anyone except in the hospital. The volunteers also helped people make affidavits, arrange bail and trace missing people by visiting morgues, hospitals, jails and police stations. It often took days for a child to find a parent in a mortuary or a parent to find a child badly beaten up in prison. As food ran out in the townships, Marymount convent became a distribution point for food; the old sisters especially helped in this work. The strongest memory of those days was of the absolute silence in the township. A while later, when school reopened, the greatest joy was hearing the voices of the children as they ran around the playground. Initially, the emphasis was on feeding and comforting them, but gradually life reverted to normal within the school. At the end of each day the principals, Sr Kathy Gaylor and Sr Bernadette Flinter, had to escort the children home as the army had cordoned off the township. They found it very moving to see how the children helped one another; the big boys would carry the little ones on their shoulders if they felt frightened and began to cry when they saw the soldiers.

In June of that same year there was another historic event involving a group that became known as the 'Cradock Four'. Matthew Goniwe was a great educationalist and leader of the United Democratic Front (UDF) who had been imprisoned and harassed for years by the police. On 27 June 1985 he left Port Elizabeth and sent a comrade to call into Holy Rosary Convent to collect a message from Sr Dorothy Balfe, then principal of the school. Sr Dorothy warned that the four should be careful on their return trip home to Cradock. She was assured that they would not stop except if they had to at an official police roadblock. They never reached Cradock and only later were the bodies of Matthew Goniwe, Fort Calata, Sparrow Mkonto and Sicelo Mhlauli found. From their injuries, it was clear that they had been assassinated. Their funeral was attended by all the liberation movements. On the same day President P.W. Botha declared a national state of emergency.

THE IRISH DOMINICAN STORY CONTINUED
If the struggle stories of the schools preoccupied many of the Dominican sisters in the decade following 1976 there were other internal concerns: there were very few new recruits, the sisters' numbers were dwindling and their age profile was rising. But in terms of ministry it was a very creative period. A more conscious option for the poor influenced new decisions taken

with regard to ministries. Many sisters availed of the freedom that came with retirement from schools to work in black or coloured parishes, visiting the poor, the old, the sick and the lonely or working as hospital chaplains. Individual younger sisters moved into specialised ministries using their professional qualifications at the service of the disadvantaged – lecturing in black universities, providing psychological services to black communities or engaging in full-time development, catechetical or pastoral ministries in black or coloured parishes.

While continuing to support the open schools that were vulnerable to government threats the sisters actively worked at handing over the running of their other schools to their lay colleagues, with a special emphasis on the Dominican ethos. Many who continued to teach also continued with a variety of weekend ministries. One special one that developed in Cape Town in the 1980s was assisting the families who came to visit their relatives who were political prisoners on Robben Island. The sisters would drive them from Cowley House down to the ferry and pick them up after their short visit. Listening to their heartbreaking stories brought tears, grace and conversion, such as the tale of a young woman of 20 whose father had been on the island since she was six months old.

Although the income from schools was decreasing the Region Council released some younger sisters to work for a mere stipend for Church bodies such as the Bishops' Conference or the Conference of Religious. One story may help give the feel of the times. Sr Margaret Kelly OP was freed to work with Sr Bernard Ncube CSA for the Conference of Women Religious, tasked with consciousness-raising among its members. They visited mainly rural communities who did not have easy access to information about current developments in the country. 'They dealt with such issues as the work of Justice and Peace Commissions and the scriptural basis for the church's teaching on justice. An analysis of the economic, social and political situation helped participants to come to a greater understanding of the main issues of justice and the role and responsibility of religious sisters in this work.'[17] 'The clarification of the scriptural base of justice and reconciliation was of great value to those who had seen the work for justice as simply a political response to the apartheid regime ... slogans or mere counter propaganda will not suffice.'[18] They also introduced the developing ideas of feminist theology into their talks and made sisters aware of the need for women's liberation

17. Ibid., p. 338.
18. Ibid., p. 339.

as part of national liberation. After 1994, Sr Bernard Ncube continued to strive for these ideals as an ANC member of parliament, following the first democratic elections.

These changes in ministry took place during increasing oppression throughout the country. It is difficult for people to realise that the last years of apartheid were almost the worst. There was no hint of even the possibility of change, and both apartheid and security laws were rigorously enforced; dozens of church workers, for instance, were detained throughout 1985–87. Even later, when the first group of top political prisoners was released from Robben Island at the end of 1989 and a public rally was held in a stadium in Johannesburg to celebrate, several political activists had to attend well out of view of the police as they were still under house arrest.

THE STORY OF THE CHURCHES

The story of Dominican schools in the struggle against apartheid can only be understood when seen in the context of the broader struggle of the Churches against apartheid in the 1970s and 1980s. During these years the critique of apartheid by the SACBC became more radical. This can be seen in their 1977 *Declaration of Commitment on Social Justice and Race Relations* in which they stated: 'We add our corporate voice … to the cry for a radical revision of the system … We affirm that in this we are on the side of the oppressed and … we commit ourselves to working for peace through justice in fraternal collaboration with all other churches, agencies and persons dedicated to this cause.'[19] True to their word, they issued many statements jointly with the South African Council of Churches (SACC) and joined with them in the Standing for the Truth Campaign during the 1980s. The bishops also bravely sponsored a radical secular newspaper called *The New Nation*. In 1987, when it was under attack and its editor, Zwelakhe Sisulu, was in prison, they restated their commitment to 'bringing to light information which otherwise would not have been made known and letting the voice of the oppressed be heard … to expose the truth is one of our pastoral concerns, for truth will set us free.'

In looking back over the increasingly brave and prophetic calls of the SACBC, one might well praise their stance. Even more, one could applaud the democratic process by which such statements were arrived at. Influenced not only by principle but also by the fact that they were a mainly white

19. SACBC, *The Bishops Speak*, vol. II, 'Declaration of Commitment on Social Justice and Race Relations Within the Church', Pretoria, SACBC, 1980, p. 42.

leadership in a mainly black Church, the bishops developed new ways of listening to the people. Consultations, study days and draft documents for comment became the normal process of dialogue, both within the Church and with trade unions and parties involved in the struggle, before the bishops issued public statements. One of the groups that was always consulted on social matters was the SACBC J&P Commission, to which Fr Bernard Connor OP was theological adviser. In this way, the bishops made dialogue part of their teaching ministry in the South African context. In their public statements and their internal training, the bishops helped Catholics adopt the ideal of seeking to be a 'Community Serving Humanity', the title they gave to their 1989 pastoral plan.

In hindsight, one can also trace a theological development in South Africa. Both the SACBC and the SACC moved only gradually from traditional theology to one influenced by such issues as black liberation, social analysis and economic structures. This journey lasted throughout the 1960s, 1970s and 1980s, and what emerged was a contextual theology suited to the South African situation. This empowered the Churches to play an important leadership role in the struggle against apartheid, especially in the 1980s.

Looking back, the roles played by the SACBC and the SACC can also be compared and contrasted. Both moved from merely condemning repressive legislation to actually giving leadership to the liberation movement in the late 1980s, as they filled the political vacuum left when all the political leaders were imprisoned. Each had their strengths and weaknesses. The SACC tended to be more bold and prophetic in its statements while the SACBC was more cautious and nuanced. The SACC represented the majority of Christians in the country, while the SACBC represented fewer than 10 per cent. The SACC, however, was only an umbrella body and had no power to insist that the member Churches accept its decisions and implement them, while the SACBC both consulted its members and brought its decisions back to them for implementation. Gradually this helped change Catholic thinking and action at many levels. In her book *Challenging the State*, Tristan Anne Borer also shows how these two bodies were influenced by their international context, in that the World Council of Churches (WCC) tended to have a progressive influence on the SACC, while the position of the Holy See was usually more conservative and restrictive. But what was more important than their differences was that the SACC and the SACBC complemented each other, and whenever possible they worked together to witness to the Gospel by both prophetic statements and symbolic actions.

THE CHURCH AND POLITICS

Anyone who watched President P.W. Botha declare a state of emergency on television in 1985 would have found it difficult to believe that his policy included some hints of reform. In 1983, his new constitution had been rejected by all the resistance movements who formed the UDF. Even the abolition of the pass laws in 1986 failed dismally to defuse internal resistance. Throughout the 1980s, the UDF continued a period of sustained protest, and there were sporadic township uprisings. Increased MK attacks on symbolic government targets, together with all the popular protests, caused Botha to extend the state of emergency until 1990.

During this time the state used extreme force to crush opposition; thousands of people were detained indefinitely, some held in solitary confinement and others tortured. In 1987, when Sr Margaret Kelly OP began to work as the co-ordinating secretary of the J&P Commission of the SACBC, her first task was to work for the release of J&P workers and others in prison. These included priests, such as Fr Peter Hortop OP, and leaders from political groups, trade and student unions. Soon Fr Smangaliso Mkhatswa, the secretary general of the SACBC, was also arrested. After some time, Sr Celia Smit OP (Oakford), his personal secretary, was allowed to visit him, and on her return could relate the tortures he had endured. To remind people to pray for those in detention, many churches and convents placed a candle ringed by barbed wire on their altars. Many other organisations were severely restricted or banned, as were public meetings and even funerals. 'Some churches and church leaders played an active role in the protests, and the SACC co-ordinated their opposition … With the effective banning of many organisations in 1987/1988, the churches became virtually the only legal voice of opposition for some time.'[20] The government was quick to respond, and in 1988 the security forces bombed the headquarters of both the SACC and the SACBC.

As the momentum for change grew, in 1989 the SACC committed member Churches to supporting non-violent action to end apartheid and joined the political activists to form the Mass Democratic Movement (MDM). Suddenly everyone was marching, as bishops and other Church leaders, priests and sisters, joined lay people and others in peaceful protest. The school marches and the arrests of Dominican sisters described earlier were part of this movement. Soon the most unusual behaviour of leading protest marches became normal for respectable Catholic bishops and other Church leaders.

20. J. Bottaro, P. Visser, N. Worden, *In Search of History*, Cape Town, OUP, 2009, p. 161.

They were imbued with the spirit of liberation theology, which had been captured in what became known as the Kairos Document (1989) to which Fr Albert Nolan had made a key contribution.

It was not only at home that pressure on the government grew; internationally also, pressure increased by means of boycotts, sports isolation and economic sanctions. Many ordinary people around the world helped put pressure on the apartheid government, to bring about reform and to win recognition for the ANC as the official representative of the people of South Africa. The defeat of the South African Defence Force in Angola, which resulted from the arms embargo, and their subsequent withdrawal from Namibia and the celebration of the independence of Namibia in 1989 was an admission by Pretoria that it was losing power. The collapse of communism internationally also stripped the government of any ideological claim to legitimacy or support from its capitalist allies. During the second half of the 1980s, delegations of prominent business leaders, opposition political leaders and even Church leaders travelled to different parts of Africa to meet the ANC leaders in exile. One Catholic bishop smiled as he recalled being addressed as 'comrade bishop'! Increasingly, the ANC was seen as the South African government in exile.

All of these factors: political pressure at home and abroad, the lack of military capacity, the threatened collapse of the economy and the currency, and the unrest throughout the country, challenged not only the legitimacy but also the power of the ruling National Party. By 1989, it was obvious that the strategy of mixing repression with limited reform had failed. The government now took little action against the marchers. It was preoccupied with disagreements within its own ranks, when suddenly P.W. Botha suffered a stroke. He was forced to step down by the members of his own cabinet and his place was taken by F.W. de Klerk. By the end of 1989, the stage was set for major change in South Africa.

ONE STORY TOWARDS ONE NATION

In the last years of the freedom struggle, most citizens came closer together as a new future slowly dawned and everyone tried to respond, including the Dominican sisters. Not everyone responded positively, however, and the last years felt more like a roller coaster ride than the last lap of a race. In January 1990, the SACBC held its meeting, as usual. The bishops issued a study document on negotiations, to help people look at the political issue of negotiations and reflect theologically on it. In their statement of 30

January, they expressed 'cautious hope', but warned that the cornerstones of apartheid were still in place and called on the government to remove these so as to open the way for negotiations.

In his opening address to parliament on 2 February 1990, F.W. de Klerk announced major new reforms, including the unbanning of the ANC, the release of political prisoners and the lifting of most restrictions, including censorship. Amazingly, these reforms echoed most of the demands made in the bishops' statement. It was a life-changing moment. The announcement that Nelson Mandela was soon to be released symbolised the end of apartheid. The people's dream of a just South Africa seemed fulfilled as they watched Mandela walk free from prison. Suddenly the demonised leaders of the ANC were appearing on television in people's own homes, and they were not only normal but also affable and likeable. Even the lives of ANC members in exile had been turned upside down as, after years abroad, they turned their thoughts towards home.

In spite of the good beginning, things were very unstable politically throughout 1990. Even when Mandela toured the world as an iconic hero, violence erupted constantly between the supporters of the ANC and those of other black parties, including the PAC and the Inkatha Freedom Party (IFP), while random criminal violence increased. Even within the ANC itself, different groups favoured different strategies; those returning from abroad, the exiles, had a different approach from those who struggled at home, the 'inziles', while the students had their own plans to continue in the mode of the 1970s, with radical protests and even violence. A special ANC Conference was held in December 1990 to try to resolve these differences.

But while the contest between violence and the shift to normal politics was being played out, the Churches continued to play an important role in the transition process as honest brokers. The National Co-ordinating Committee for Repatriation (NCCR), for instance, consisted of three religious bodies, the SACC, the SACBC and the World Conference on Religion and Peace (WCRP), as well as the three main liberation movements, the ANC, PAC and The Azanian People's Organisation (AZAPO). About 6,000 exiles were helped to return in 1990 and 1991 before the UNHCR brought in the first batch under its auspices. As the events of 1991 unfolded, the Churches found themselves playing the dual roles of prophets and servants. The Catholic bishops issued a document on religious rights and responsibilities; they denounced the violence which erupted constantly in various parts of the country and they provided shelter and services to the returning exiles through various Church bodies staffed by volunteers, both lay and religious.

On the political front the government and the ANC disagreed on many issues. Violence regularly broke out between various groups vying for power: radical blacks, right-wing whites and several of the 'independent Homelands' who sought either greater power at the negotiation table or complete autonomy as independent countries. On the economic front this resulted in tourism and investment falling dramatically and the almost total collapse of the rand. Happily the ANC elected a new united executive of exiles, 'inziles' and youth, which reiterated its commitment to negotiations when it joined 18 other parties in forming the Convention for a Democratic South Africa (CODESA) in December 1991. All except the radical black and white right-wing parties signed a declaration of intent, and working parties were set up to pave the way towards democracy. With the politicians involved in direct negotiations, the Church leaders could now retire from their brief careers in direct political leadership. But both politicians and Churches were learning from the mistakes of the past. At a meeting of Church leaders with the ANC, Mandela issued a warning: 'Never ask politicians what you can do to help because politicians will use you for their own ends. It is your mission to preach the Gospel and tell the truth because no politician ever wants to hear the truth.' In August 1991, the bishops again condemned violence in true prophetic style and called for a united political, social and economic effort in pursuit of the vision of a democratic future.

On a more humble level, those who had led the way in open schools felt vindicated when the government allowed each public school to decide to become open to all races, if the parent body desired it. These schools often approached their nearest Catholic schools for advice and guidance, because of their almost 20 years' experience in the field. Even Mandela encouraged the ANC leaders to visit the Marist Brothers' College in Johannesburg, which his grandchildren attended, so that they could see how their dreams had already been lived out there for nearly two decades.

1992 began in a general spirit of optimism, with South Africa's re-admission to international sport and the return home of many famous cultural and artistic exiles. This optimism increased when De Klerk called a referendum among whites to vote on whether they supported the reform process or not. Of these, 80 per cent registered and 68.7 per cent voted in favour. But violence continued in the background, as the Homelands police clashed with ANC supporters. In May, the CODESA talks again collapsed over arguments about majority rule, power sharing and regional powers. In the Boipatong Massacre, Zulu mine workers went on the rampage and killed 45 people. In response, the ANC and its allies began a campaign of 'Rolling Mass Action' throughout the country, with sporadic work stoppages, sit-ins and marches. In August, millions of black workers staged a stay-away and 200,000 marched on the Union Buildings in Pretoria, while some of the ANC staged a disastrous 'invasion' of the Ciskei homeland. The ANC leaders were worried by this turn of events, and the government was equally worried about the effect it was having on foreign investment. De Klerk held a summit with just the ANC, led by Mandela. Cyril Ramaphosa (ANC) and Roelf Meyer (NP) were appointed to work together to draft proposals to deal with the major contentious issues. At the bilateral talks, the two major players reached compromises that the multiparty CODESA could not, and both parties signed a Record of Agreement. While this was positive, the smaller parties felt left out, and the most conservative ones, black and white, began to form their own group.

In January 1992 the SACBC had issued a pastoral letter, which showed their concern about one all-controlling regime replacing another. In *A Call to Build a New South Africa*, they called on all people of good will in South Africa: 'If people of good will work together to solve local problems a healthy civil society will emerge. This will allow people to control many areas of their lives dealing with such things as religion, culture, welfare, sport and human rights without domination by either the market or the state.' In the course of the year, this position was given flesh, as the Churches worked with various NGO groups to monitor violence and to form the Independent Forum for Electoral Education (IFEE), from which political parties were excluded so as to ensure its credibility. A very real fear for all the Churches was that, within the ocean of democracy of the future South Africa, there would be large islands of oppression and despotism.

The 1993 January pastoral letter from the SACBC was called *Towards a Democratic Future*. It was a theological reflection on the links between democracy and Christian virtues such as justice, but included such practical issues as intimidation and bribery. It also quoted from letters of other African bishops' conferences, which made people aware that South Africa would no longer be isolated by apartheid. They said: 'We are not alone in this struggle for democracy; it is taking place throughout Africa. Many of the African Bishops' Conferences have spoken out about democracy. We have learned a lot from their pastoral letters and join our voices with theirs.'

On the national political front the bilateral talks were making real progress, even though violence still erupted regularly – the killing of Chris Hani in April and the storming of the World Trade Centre in Johannesburg in June led to suspensions in the negotiations. In July, it was agreed to hold elections early in 1994 and to set up a Transitional Executive Council (TEC) to oversee the transition to democracy. An interim constitution was agreed, and in September bills were passed by the TEC, allowing for an Independent Electoral Commission (IEC) and independent commissions for media and broadcasting. Great hope was ignited when, in October, Mandela and De Klerk were jointly awarded the Nobel Peace Prize. The other good news of that month was that the UN had lifted sanctions. The economy immediately began to recover, and the price of gold increased. At The National Economic Forum, the ANC and business groups reached an accommodation on each other's policies. The shares on the Johannesburg Stock Exchange rose within a few months from R501 billion to R737 billion. In November, Mandela and De Klerk had long meetings. They and their two chief negotiators managed to reach agreement on all the outstanding constitutional issues, and these agreements were accepted at the negotiating council. The chairman of the council congratulated the negotiators and predicted: 'This is the last mile to freedom.' Gradually, different opposition parties came on board; the PAC, for instance, abandoned the armed struggle and became part of the TEC in December 1993.

During the three years of negotiations, especially at times of violence, the Churches provided people with pastoral and material help as needed. But the people also looked to the church for guidance in political issues. As a founding member of the IFEE, the Catholic Church was actively involved in preparations for elections. Working with the IEC, the Churches helped train people as monitors and official observers. But the greatest effort was made in voter education, as many people were illiterate and most had never voted before. When the Electoral Act was passed, the J&P Commission trained leaders from around the country to teach people how to vote. These leaders then trained local leaders and teams so that they could teach local congregations and other groups on request. The basic training technique used was to explain the process of democratic elections, then to run mock elections and reflect on them afterwards, so as to learn from mistakes. Requests kept flooding in, since people experienced the Church as reliable and impartial. The work was done in every situation, even in buses and trains. In each workshop, the links between democracy and the Gospel were stressed so that people learned values as well as techniques. Again, Dominicans, other sisters and ordinary church workers did this work quietly on the ground, while the various political factions were engaged in the limelight. One story can serve as an example of many heart-warming experiences. At the Dominican School for Deaf Children in Hammanskraal, Sr Siobhan Murphy had arranged for some J&P workers to run a session on voter education. All the staff, teachers, carers and cleaners attended, as well as all the senior pupils, as none had ever voted before. During the presentation, a teacher interpreted the talk into sign language. At one point the speaker was taken aback when suddenly the teacher seemed to prance around like a devil with two fingers in front like horns and his other arm waving like a tail behind him. Failing to see any connection with what had just been said about not accepting bribes, an explanation was requested. The teacher explained that having given the warning, he had added as an example: 'Even if a politician offers you a goat as a bribe, you must reject it.' Much laughter confirmed that the serious point had been taken. The fact that less than 1 per cent of votes cast in 1994 were spoiled was testimony to the good work done. Throughout 1993, the Church also continued to be involved in attempts to bring about peace at local and regional levels, especially through its involvement in the Ecumenical Monitoring Program for South Africa (EMPSA). Catholics and others came from around the world to help monitor the violence in the country, and often formed human buffers between the police and hostile crowds.

By January 1994 the election campaign was in full swing. Some 'Homelands' and political parties had re-joined the TEC, as a result either of peaceful decisions or grassroots revolts. Clashes continued, however, led mainly by right-wing groups. It was estimated that 600 were killed and 1,400 injured between 1990 and March 1994. The Human Rights Commission reported that 111 were killed and over 400 injured in the last two weeks of March 1994. Fortunately, behind the scenes, Mandela and De Klerk managed to reach a peaceful settlement with Kwazulu–Natal, and on 25 April, the day before special votes were to be cast, Parliament met to amend the interim constitution to allow the Inkatha Freedom Party to participate. Alas, on the morning of 26 April, 20 minutes before polls opened for special votes, a right-wing white group exploded a car bomb at Johannesburg airport. The amazing thing was that, after all the violence, the voting days of 27–29 April were the most peaceful and crime-free days that South Africa had experienced for decades.

The SACBC invited the bishops' conferences from around the world to send delegates to be official observers at the South African elections. During the elections, there was an operations centre in their headquarters (which had been restored after the bombings) in Khanya House, and smaller ones in several dioceses. These were organised by the J&P Commission of the SACBC, under the leadership of Archbishop Denis Hurley OMI and Bishop Kevin Dowling CSsR, with Sr Margaret Kelly OP as co-ordinating secretary. These centres provided back-up services to the 50 international and over 500 domestic observers directly accredited by the IEC through the SACBC, as well as to hundreds of others. Needless to say, some Dominican sisters, working with diocesan commissions, were among the Church trainers and monitors, and each had her own moving story to tell of the elections. Through the media, millions around the world experienced the miracle of the elections in South Africa. One of the SACBC observers, Bishop Laridon of Bruges, Belgium, described it thus: 'Everywhere I passed, the people made me understand that, for them, it meant more than a political happening: they experienced it as a faith gift, as a miracle. What impressed me very much was the complete silence when people were standing in the queue at the voting office. Not just a normal silence, but a religious silence. It was a holy moment.'

The elections were declared free and fair when the results were announced a week later. Mandela and the ANC had won over 60 per cent of the votes. Speaking at an ANC celebration afterwards, he said: 'To the people of South Africa and the world who are watching ... this is a joyous night for the human spirit. This is your victory too ... You have shown such a calm, patient determination to reclaim this country as your own.' People remember his words, but they also treasure images of his inauguration as president, especially the sight of the South African Air Force aeroplanes flying overhead and trailing the colours of the new South African flag. The strongest symbol of apartheid was saluting the first black president and the new government of national unity, surrounded by heads of states from around the world, all united in peace, peace at last. These colours signalled the birth of the rainbow nation.

CONCLUSION

South Africa still struggles to be a home to many people with different stories, cultures and languages, even though this richness is now celebrated in its new flag and its multilingual national anthem. Some want to celebrate its liberation story, while others dismiss it and the liberation culture as overly optimistic and naive and want to learn from the experience others have had of liberators becoming dictators, while some even fear the dangers of genuine democracy when it is wedded to capitalism.

In conclusion I would like to invite you to reflect on how interiority, community and commitment to service played a part in the story of the Cabra Dominicans in their struggle against apartheid, as well as in your personal and community story as you struggle for truth and justice. We need to be inspired by our stories and to learn from their painful lessons of disenchantment. We can then reflect on the best ways we can all preach justice into the future because, like the story, the struggle for the Kingdom of God is ongoing, and we always need to be 'well on the way'. Farewell.

BIBLIOGRAPHY

Auret, Michael, *From Liberator to Dictator*, Cape Town, South Africa, David Philips Publishers, 2009.

Bausch, William J., *Storytelling, Imagination, and Faith*, Mystic, Connecticut, Twenty-Third Publications, 1984.

Bausch, William J., *In the Beginning, There Were Stories*, Mystic, Connecticut, Twenty-Third Publications, 2004.

Boner, Kathleen, OP, *Dominican Women: A Time To Speak*, Pietermaritzburg, Cluster Publications, 2000.

Borer, Tristan Anne, *Challenging The State, The Churches as Political Actors in South Africa*, Notre Dame, Indiana, University of Notre Dame Press, 1998.

Bottaro, J., Visser, P. and Worden, N., *In Search of History*, Cape Town, Oxford University Press, 2009.

Bradt, Kevin, MSJ, *Story as a Way of Knowing*, Kansas City, Sheed & Ward, 1997.

Calvin, John, *Commentaries on the First Book of Moses, called Genesis*, trans. John King, Grand Rapids, Eerdmans, 1948.

Egan, Joe and Mc Convery, Brendan (eds.), *Faithful Witness*, Dublin, Colour Books, 2005.

Elphick, R. and Davenport, R. (eds.), *Christianity in South Africa, A Political, Social and Cultural History*, Cape Town, David Philip, 1997.

Harford, Judith, *The Opening of University Education to Women in Ireland*, Dublin, Irish Academic Press, 2008.

Horgan, Dominique, OP (ed.), *Weavings: Celebrating Dominican Women*, Dublin, Glenprint, 1988.

Hurley, Denis, 'Catholic Social Teaching and Ideology' in Andrew Prior (ed.), *Catholics in Apartheid Society*, Cape Town, David Philip, 1982.

Loubser, J.A., *The Apartheid Bible, A Critical Review of Theology in South* Africa, Cape Town, Maskew Miller Longman, 1987.

Mandela, Nelson, *Long Walk to Freedom*, London, Abacus, 1995.

McCabe, Honor OP, *Living by the Truth*, 1999, unpublished thesis.

McKeever, Martin, 'A Medellin Spring? Thirty Years of the Theology of Liberation', in Egan, Joe and McConvery, Brendan (eds.), *Glimpses of the Kingdom, Milltown Institute of Theology and Philosophy*, Dublin, 2005.

Prior, Andrew (ed.), *Catholics in Apartheid Society*, Cape Town and London, David Philip, 1982.

Southern African Catholic Bishops' Conference, *The Bishops Speak* Volumes I and II (1980), Volumes III and IV (1989), Pretoria, SACBC, 1980 and 1989.

WCC and UNESCO, *The Role of Religion and Religious Institutions in the Dismantling of Apartheid*, Geneva, Final Report, 1991.

7

Resistance to the Madness of Evil and Injustice: Dominican Sisters Confront the Genocide and its Aftermath in Rwanda

EMMANUEL NTAKARUTIMANA, O.P.

INTRODUCTION

The candid faith of the Dominican Missionaries of Africa contrasts with the harshness and cruelty of the experience they had to face only ten years after the birth of their community. Psalm 137 serves as their companion:

> I give you thanks, O Lord, with my whole heart, ... I sing your praise; ...
> On the day I called, you answered me, you increased my strength of
>   soul....
> For though the Lord is high, he regards the lowly;
> but the haughty he perceives from far away.
> Though I walk in the midst of trouble, you preserve me....
> Your right hand delivers me.
> The Lord will fulfil his purpose for me!
> Your steadfast love, O Lord, endures for ever.
> Do not forsake the work of your hands.

This prayer is hard to say when you have to take the risk of hiding people who are fleeing from a systematically programmed killing machine of massive proportions. It is absurd to have to hide among corpses, or jump over them, in order to try to save what can still be saved, what remains of the living among the dead. It requires the prophetic gift of hope to continue to believe in the God of life and love when one has to negotiate one's passage between bands of killers or the military, all of whom are on the verge of lashing out from the stress of unceasing massacres. One is left with an experience of utter helplessness in the face of towering evil. When the sound of death around us becomes all-encompassing and the silence of God becomes deafening, how can we continue to believe that God is on our side and can dispel our fears?

The Dominican Missionaries of Africa were reluctant to share their experiences or to allow anyone to speak about them. Indeed, how could the unspeakable be expressed without hurting people? How could one be true to an indescribable experience, deeply embedded in one's flesh and heart? However, they finally agreed to risk a first witness to an outsider, after a long period of silence filled with the memories of violent and haunting death in their country.

From 1 October 1990, when clashes began in the north of the country, until 4 April 1994, the day on which the attack against the plane carrying the presidents of Rwanda and Burundi above Kigali airport signaled the first massacres that led to a paroxysm of genocide, the sisters had remained at their mission stations and continued to do so during the genocide itself. By mid-July 1994, they had begun to gather in Byumba, where their motherhouse is located. Overcoming unprecedented difficulties, they all arrived at their destination to find that they were all still alive. They remember: 'On arrival at Byumba, we had the joy of reunion. We created a framework for sharing our experiences of what had happened to us. No barriers hindered us from talking. Each sister was given the opportunity to say what she had experienced.'

These are the moments that we would like to relive with you, our reader. The long testimony exchanged within the community in Kigali on 11–12 May 2010, and other exchanges, continues to help the healing of memories. From the traumatising experiences the sisters lived through during those years, they have paradoxically drawn the strength to be able to participate in the renewal of the country, and that too is worth recounting. However, everything, before, during and after the genocide, comes from the long preparation that the founding of the congregation permitted.

SISTER MARIE-PASCALE CREVECOEUR:
BORN FOR JOY, FREEDOM AND INTELLECTUAL CLARITY
Georges Casalis, Protestant pastor and theologian committed to the poor, published a book in 1977 entitled *Correct Ideas Don't Fall From the Skies*. The coming together of circumstances, and the environment in which one lives, with personal choices always helps to form God's instruments for action.

This is what happened to Marie-Pascale Crevecoeur. From the comfort of her home town, Namur in Belgium, she never imagined the adventure that God had in store for her, but she had always wanted to be a missionary. The beginning of her life was marked by a considerable traumatic burden. The day after she was born in 1940, her mother died. The experience was too much for her father, who committed suicide a week later. Marie-Pascale grew up an orphan, with the words of Jesus she found in the Gospel: 'I am the resurrection and the life. Those who believe in me, even though they die, will live' (Jn 11:25). After visiting the graves of her parents several times, she came to the conviction that, if the words of Jesus, as recorded by the evangelist, were true, they must be proclaimed everywhere. Her missionary vocation thus came first, and only then her religious vocation, attached to another passage, found in the prophet Hosea: 'I will take you for my wife for ever; I will take you for my wife in righteousness and in justice, in steadfast love, and in mercy. I will take you for my wife in faithfulness; and you shall know the Lord' (2:19–20). Marie-Pascale thought, 'Let me be betrothed to Him who promises life beyond death!'

She would grow up without any further exceptional events taking place in her life. While still a child, she joined a children's group that assisted the missions. Later, she studied hard to earn her degree in philosophy and letters, developing a passion for knowledge and research in the quest for truth. As a teenager, she had felt very attracted to the climate of joy, freedom and intellectual clarity in her school, and in scouting, with the Dominican Missionaries of Namur. These sisters were dedicated to evangelisation in the east of the Congo, in the diocese of Niangara. After working for two years, Marie-Pascale decided to join them and in 1964, when she was 24 years old, she began her formation.

The congregation she joined was suffering through the political turmoil of the day. The Congo was still reeling from the turbulence that had rocked the country from 1961 to 1964, culminating in the outbreak of the Mulelist rebellion that had ravaged the eastern region from 1964 to 1966, in the context of a geopolitical confrontation between China and the western world.[1] The independence of the Congo, declared on 30 June 1960, had been followed by a long period of instability and violence. On 17 January 1961, Patrice Lumumba was assassinated in Katanga. The following month, Joseph Ileo's government used force against Katanga with the support of the United Nations. On 31 March 1961, Antoine Gizenga, starting in Stanleyville, formed a revolutionary government whose members were in exile. In August 1961, another government was formed by Cyrille Adoula. 1962 saw a series of

---

1. On this point, see Benoît Verhagen, 'Les rébellions populaires au Congo en 1964', in *Cahiers d'études africaines*, volume 7, n° 26, 1967, pp. 345–59.

For a better understanding of the history of the Congo, see the chronology by A. Sadi, J.B. Mbomio and Mutombo Kanyana, 'Chronique Congolaise', in *Regards Africains*, n° 40, 1997, p. 14, as well as Isidore Ndaywen è Nziem, *Histoire générale du Congo: De l'héritage ancien à la République Démocratique*, Collection 'Afrique Editions', Paris, Duculot, 1998.

negotiations between Moise Tshombe, Antoine Gizenga and Cyrille Adoula that lasted until the arrest of Gizenga in Kinshasa and the final offensive of the UN in Katanga. Tshombe fled to Spain in June 1963 when Pierre Mulele returned from China and started a rebellion in the Kwilu region. In October 1963, in Brazzaville, the National Liberation Committee was created by Gaston Soumialot and Laurent Kabila, with hostilities launched from the east of the Congo. Uvira was taken by the rebels in May 1964 and on 3 July Tshombe returned as a saviour to Leopoldville to form a new government there. Antoine Gizenga was set free, but the war in the east continued. By 7 August 1964, two thirds of Stanleyville was under the control of the rebels. The national army tried to liberate the city with the help of some mercenaries, but the city would ultimately be taken by Belgian paratroopers, supported by US aircraft, on 24 November 1964. Tshombe won the general election on 30 April 1965, but was ousted only six months later by President Kasavubu, who replaced him with Evariste Kimba as prime minister. On 24 November 1965, Joseph Desire Mobutu overthrew the government.

Among the many victims of this long crisis in the Congo were many nuns, monks and missionaries. Nine Dominican Missionary Sisters of Namur were killed on 26 November 1964, at the military camp in Watsa where they had been imprisoned.[2] The survivors had to resign themselves to returning to Belgium after having been beaten several times and having received death threats. Marie-Pascale, therefore, knew about the inherent risks of missionary life when she made her first profession on 16 April 1967, making her own the words of the Song of Songs, 'My Beloved is mine and I am His' (2:16).

A few months later, her dream of being a missionary was to become a reality. Forced to disperse as a result of the events taking place in the Congo, in 1966 the Dominican Missionaries of Namur had opened a house in Kivumu, Rwanda, to support a new health centre. The young Marie-Pascale, although formed to be a teacher, was sent to to be a nursing sister. Using the notes bequeathed to her by another sister, she studied alone at night for her classes at the African Catechetical Institute. The idea of a possible foundation can be traced back to this moment in time. At the end of an article devoted to Dominican life published in the diocesan journal of Nyundo, *Cum Paraclito*, she wrote: 'If it is true that in Rwanda "nothing is exchanged like the word" (according to the proverb "Ntabisanganwa nk'amagambo"), one can glimpse the apostolic wonders that God promises to achieve the day when

---

2. The account of these events is found in the booklet *Témoins de Dieu jusqu'à la mort*, Couvent des Dominicains, 5 rue Leys, Brussels, 1965.

Dominican life will find its Rwandan expression. In the warm atmosphere of the conversation "kuganira" we will break the bread of the Word, ponder on, and share that Word of fire which will continue to transform everything from hill to hill.'[3]

After this short but memorable stay in Rwanda, in October 1968 Marie-Pascale was sent to the Congo. The mission was started again because the sisters, who had nothing against the population, wanted to show their solidarity with this people whom they had come to love. Although the first attempt failed, because threats from other rebels forced the first three sisters to flee to Central Africa where they founded a new mission, others followed them into the field of the Congolese mission. This led Sr Marie-Pascale to spend a year teaching at the Ecole Normale in Niangara and four years at the Petit Séminaire in Rungu, where she lived with sisters who would play a role in the foundation of the congregation in Rwanda, including Sr Marie-Christine and Sr Miriam.

Politically, the situation remained difficult because of Mobutu's attempts to regain control of the country and organise an increasingly authoritarian government. The crisis between the Church and the state continued to grow, culminating in Mobutu's demand, on 13 January 1971, for the dismissal of Cardinal Joseph Albert Malula. That same year, the 'policy of authenticity' changed the name of the Congo to Zaire, and religious teaching was prohibited in the schools. Mobutism became the only acceptable religion, with Mobutu being its messiah. The sisters willingly relinquished the places of leadership in their schools, now nationalised, to lay people, and at the same time continued their work of education by extending it to include catechists and other pastoral workers.

This experience was highly instructive. People were traumatised by what they had gone through, but hope lived on in the formation of youth. It is in this context that Sr Marie-Pascale prepared for her solemn profession in Niangara, which she made in the hands of Sr Marie-Jeanne Landenne, along with Congolese sisters, in 1971. A slow maturation, and reference to the martyrdom of her sisters who had stayed despite the dangers, made her understand the full depth of another passage from scripture: 'Unless a grain of wheat falls to the ground and dies, it remains alone; if it dies, it bears much fruit' (Jn 12:24).

In 1974, Sister Marie-Pascale participated in her first general chapter of the

3. 'Dominicaines', p. 144, in *Cum Paraclito*, revue diocésaine du diocèse de Nyundo, special issue, 1968.

Dominican Missionary Sisters of Namur. She was entrusted with important responsibilities in the congregation that were renewed in the next chapter in 1978: general councillor, secretary, formator and missionary animator. She used this time to ponder deeply on the events she had experienced in Africa during the Congo crisis and her stay in Rwanda. Her memories of Rwanda were vivid with the great cultural wealth she encountered there. She devoted an exhibition to the country, entitled *Amazing Life*, based on its proverbs. Despite cultural differences, she remained fascinated by the fact that human beings are the same everywhere. She took the opportunity to make a collection of texts from different cultures on the theme of reconciliation without knowing how important this work would later become. She also nourished the hope of missionary vocations. While working on the renewed constitutions of her congregation, she became familiar with canon law. Everything is providential! She took part in the direction of religious life in Belgium as a member of the Permanent Council of the Union des Religieuses de Belgique (URB) and also that of the renewal of Dominican life for women in the Groupement Fraternel des Dominicaines de France et Belgique-Sud. Br Bernard Olivier, Vicar of the Master of the Order, urged her to give a lecture on 'Women devoted to the Word of God' in Madrid at the Missionary Congress of the Order of Preachers in 1982.[4]

'YOU HAVE A DOMINICAN GRACE FOR AFRICA'

By the 1970s, five different Dominican missionary congregations of sisters were attracting vocations in Rwanda. This created the problem that young Rwandan women wanting to join them were faced with five different congregations between which they had to choose.

By the late 1970s, members of the Dominican family began to wonder about whether each missionary congregation should do its own recruitment or whether it would be better to unite forces and create a typically African congregation, with its own style. Reflections and the discernment process took time, given the multiple views and the difficulty of finding people who wanted to engage in a possible joint project. In theory, there was a consensus that a new Dominican congregation should be formed, but it took some time for this consensus to become a reality. Several young Rwandan women wrote to the Dominican Missionaries of Namur asking for help. The General Chapter of 1982 gave a priority to answering this question from Rwandan

4. The text of this communication was published in the review *Vie Consacrée*, 15 January 1983, pp. 7–19.

women. After the chapter, Sr Marie-Christine Berhin, at that time Prioress General, called Sr Marie-Pascale and said to her, 'You can imagine that we thought of you when we said yes!' This call provoked feelings of joy as well as fear in the heart of Sr Marie-Pascale. Indeed, she knew neither the women in question nor the congregations in Rwanda. Nevertheless, willing to collaborate on the project, she agreed to go to Rwanda and Burundi with Sr Marie-Pierre Devoir at the beginning of 1983 to make contact with other Dominican entities, evaluate the chances of success for the initiative, and possibly also find a house.

The visit to Rwanda of the Master of the Order, Fr Vincent de Couesnongle, constituted the turning point for the birth of a new congregation. In fact, in his presence, it was decided that the Dominican family of Rwanda and Burundi would meet in Kigali on 7 March 1983. The foundation was entrusted to the Dominican Missionaries of Namur, who agreed to sponsor the new congregation until it reached maturity. All the other members of the Dominican family in Rwanda and Burundi – brothers, nuns and sisters – also gave their support. The founding trio was international: Marie-Pascale from Belgium; Sister Giulietta Primis from Italy (who was also a Dominican of Namur and who had spent several years in Kivumu in the Rwandan diocese of Nyundo) and a newly arrived Brazilian, Sr Regina Lucia Fuzisaka, who was a Dominican from the Congregation of the Most Holy Rosary of Monteils. A few months later, Fr de Couesnongle revealed to the pioneers of the project the value of their initiative by saying, 'You have a Dominican grace for Africa.' The inspiration had been given, and there was no reason to hesitate. The shared dream was to set up something very simple, close to the people, not a big institution. On 17 January 1983, Sr Marie-Pascale and Sr Marie-Pierre met Bishop Joseph Ruzindana, bishop of the new Diocese of Byumba, who was in favour of the project. On 9 March that year, he became the ecclesiastical superior of the congregation with the approbation of the Master of the Order. He provided the foundation with premises, though they were in need of restoration. The new congregation had its motherhouse in Byumba, in the northern part of the country.

On 1 October 1983, the novitiate was erected and the first three novices arrived: Maria Fides Gahongayire, Monique Kantamage and Mary Mediatrix Mukarusine. For the drafting and approval of the statutes of the Society, Sr Marie-Pascale proposed the name for the foundation: Dominican Missionaries of Africa (DMA). The decree of aggregation to the Order of Preachers was signed on 27 February 1984 by Fr Dominique Louis, Vicar of the Master of the Order.

Soon Sr Marie-Pascale began to work courageously and very energetically. It was necessary to ensure the promotion of vocations, to organise training programmess and, as young women entered, to involve African sisters in drawing up their own constitutions.

When the Master of the Order, Damian Byrne, visited the sisters on 29 March 1990, he encouraged them to follow their original intuition by referring to the three priorities of St Dominic: the hungry, those who do not know the Truth, and sinners. In the Rwandan milieu, as in the rest of Africa, there was clearly demand for this Dominican grace.

It is said that God writes straight with crooked lines. This expression reflects the growth of the Dominican Missionaries of Africa amidst great sociopolitical problems. Everyone remembered the experience of the Congo during the crises following its independence and how this experience had severely shaken the Dominican Missionaries of Namur. Even greater tragedy awaited the Dominican Missionaries of Africa.

AND WAR BREAKS OUT!

Indeed, only seven years after the foundation of the Dominican Missionaries of Africa, a war that had begun in Uganda started to spill over into northern Rwanda from 1 October 1990. The rebellion also entered the zone of Byumba. It is important to bear in mind that Rwanda had previously experienced a very serious socio-political crisis in 1959 when its balance of power was overturned. The Tutsi monarchy that had ruled the country for centuries was reversed, through a revolution that its initiators described as 'social'; power was placed in the hands of Hutus, with support from Belgium, to which the League of Nations – later the United Nations – had entrusted the guardianship and the administrative mandate of the country until independence on 1 July 1962. The reversal of the social equilibrium in Rwanda in 1959 was accompanied by violence and by massacres against the Tutsis. Many survivors had to seek refuge in neighbouring countries and elsewhere, making several unsuccessful attempts to return. Various military coups also failed, and this led the Kigali regime to harden its position on the issue of the return of refugees, arguing that there was not enough physical space to accommodate them.

The descendants of these refugees finally organised themselves into a large armed movement led from Uganda in 1990; it included mainly young people who had grown up in Burundi, Uganda and Zaire (now the Democratic

Republic of Congo). This happened at the moment when the geopolitics of the Great Lakes region of Africa was undergoing a deep transformation. The influence of Belgium gradually gave way to that of France. The Anglo-Saxon world was also progressively gaining influence there, with a clear desire to stem the spread of Islam towards the south of the continent. At the same time, the enormous wealth of natural resources attracted the attention of profiteers. The Democratic Republic of Congo became the weakest link in the region. The decline of Mobutu's power had resulted in an increased rate of plundering of these natural resources in the eastern region.

The armed movement of Rwandan refugees, the Rwandan Patriotic Front (RPF), launched an offensive from a geostrategic vantage point. The French support of the Kigali regime held back the first moments of the attack, but a low intensity war continued in an attempt to raise political bargaining positions. When political negotiations came to a standstill, the military confrontations once again became intense and, this time, extremely violent. On 4 April 1994, the plane carrying the presidents of Rwanda and Burundi to the umpteenth round of negotiations in Arusha was attacked as it approached Kigali airport. This event unleashed the killing madness whose images shocked the world. The violence even had symbolic significance since it coincided with the first Special Assembly of the Synod of Bishops for Africa. The major themes of the assembly were the Church as a family and the Church as communion. Rwanda, whose population was close to 80 per cent Christian, was ablaze with genocide. Some people asked questions about the role of the Church in building these notions of family and brotherhood in relation to the history of ethnic violence in the Great Lakes region.

By 1990, the young Dominican Missionaries of Africa had to deal with this new situation. From the beginning of the hostilities, they had to work actively. Here is a note that they made during the first days of the crisis:

In Byumba, all the sisters gathered in the motherhouse. Sister Miriam Gribomont arrived on October 3rd in the midst of troop deployments. On October 4th, Immaculate Nyirankuliza, from Rutongo, arrived to begin her postulancy, while the evacuations were already under way. The other candidate, Pierrette Lokosa, from Tadu DRC, was employed in the School of Social Work of Byumba as a teacher. She would help students to pass the first year of the war with sufficient confidence. On October 15th, Belgian soldiers conducted the evacuation of their nationals, but our Belgian sisters stayed in Rwanda. On November 3rd, we welcomed the first displaced persons. In addition, on November 14th, Sister Marie-

Christine arrived among us. The apostolate of the sisters was becoming more diverse in the service of the victims.

Indeed, the lives of the sisters were reorganised around emergency and crisis management. Up to that time, the sisters had been involved in the formation of basic ecclesial communities, vocational formation and other traditional apostolates. They were familiar with these ministries, but now they were working in a context of fragility and vulnerability. It was a period of extreme social tension, highly insecure, with some attacks. They had to face guerrilla activity. A renewed awareness of the poor as victims grew strongly in the sisters' souls. They wished to be present in the dangerous places where people did not go willingly.

As the war came a little closer to the house each day, the sisters felt challenged to respond to the catastrophic situation of more and more people displaced by the advance of the guerrillas. In addition to caring for the displaced in makeshift camps, it was also necessary to care for patients in the hospital, some of whom had been very seriously wounded by land-mines. The situation was difficult for the patients because their family members were scattered and could not visit them. It was a fantasy to think of family reunification in this chaotic context. The prison also called for the attention of the sisters. As the guerrillas advanced from Uganda, the number of arrests and detentions increased. It became impossible for their respective families to support the prisoners.

In 1992, two Oblate Sisters of the Assumption in Rushaki were killed in the Diocese of Byumba. The Dominican Missionaries of Africa welcomed the survivors of the community into their house.

These years brought the Dominican sisters through a phase of spiritual purification. The apostolate was accomplished in places where everything that usually constitutes human security had disappeared. When all that is humanly strong collapses, what else remains but the Word of God, the liturgy and the power of the Eucharist? The Liturgy of the Hours acquired new relevance, especially with the psalms of supplication that seemed to describe the situations they were really living through on a daily basis. The sisters bowed down in prayer not only in adoration but also to protect themselves from bullets. The Eucharist gave the sisters the strength to carry on. They recognised that Christ, crushed by the world, crushed by human evil, tortured and murdered, who left his testament in the celebration of the Last Supper, was at the heart of the Eucharistic action. This gift of self to the end became the heart of the lives of the sisters, with a renewed conscience of Christ's Last

Supper with his disciples. Christ in the Eucharist had to be brought to the people, and they were impressed by the comfort that his presence gave them in all the places to which they brought him. The Dominican Missionaries of Africa became a lynchpin for many in Byumba. They played a crucial role in the diocesan committee of assistance that brought together religious from different congregations present in areas where guerrilla warfare was raging, although sometimes they too had to leave and take refuge elsewhere.

> It was hot when we left Byumba. Sixteen Katyushas came down from the city. Bullets rained down. Even if there were as yet no injuries at home, it would take a miracle from above for us to survive. Death was present. We lived in total anguish. We did not know how to protect ourselves nor where to hide. We had no idea what was coming. We could neither eat nor sleep. The nights were a nightmare. The military communiqués brought drama after drama.[5]

While rescuing people, it was necessary to think strategically about the future. Despite the crisis, the formation of the novices and younger sisters continued. When the sisters were forced to leave Byumba, all too often under fire from the RPF, they were temporarily welcomed in the house of the Sisters of the Assumption in Kabuye. Sr Marie-Christine was looking for more stable lodging for the sisters in Kigali. A house under Canadian control was graciously made available and served some time for the temporary professed. Then she found a house for the novitiate in a neighbourhood of the capital, Kigali (Kicukiro), but the formation they received took a different turn. The novices helped in the camp for the displaced, in Nyacyonga, while the postulants visited the sick and wounded in the Kigali hospital. One sister had followed the evacuated prisoners from Byumba to the central prison in Kigali. With some of them, she was preparing for the outpouring of the Spirit! Many times, Sr Marie-Pascale and Sr Marie-Christine returned to Byumba in order to rescue some objects (including the entire library!) and continued going into the camps to support the displaced. Without realising it, the sisters developed a service of reception and listening, for many people bore wounds in their hearts. Many died of hunger and fatigue, and often families could not live normally because of their grief. Everything that the sisters were hearing had to be kept in their hearts. Discretion was a necessity. Several sisters followed the session of active nonviolence in Kigali organised by Hildegard Goss-Mayr and Alfred Bour. The leaders told them that they

5. Interview with the community of Rebero, Kigali, 11 May 2010.

had never seen a situation as dramatic as the one in Rwanda; one could feel the climax of the drama approaching.

On 17 January 1993, the sisters who had returned to Byumba were happy to receive the visit of the Master of the Order, Fr Timothy Radcliffe, with his socius for Africa, Fr Emmanuel Ntakarutimana, and Vicar Provincial for Rwanda and Burundi, Fr Yvon Pomerleau. Between Kigali and Byumba, these visitors had had to cross some checkpoints set up by the Interahamwe militia, masked and armed with studded clubs; thus, they had experienced what violence could represent during this time of crisis. They accompanied the sisters to the camp for internally displaced persons at Kisaro, and visited the hospital of maimed children and the prison. Timothy wept before returning home to celebrate the Eucharist ... The peace campaigner had just become aware of the realities of the war against which he had fought without knowing it. This visit so impressed the Master of the Order that he spoke of it several times in his books.[6]

The year 1993 marked the tenth anniversary of the founding of the congregation, and it was decided to devote this year to the writing of a rule, as a basis for the constitutions of the new congregation. The African sisters were beginning to be mature enough to take control of their future, but they still had to prove their capability to themselves. A general meeting was held for 11 professed sisters. Since it could not be held in Byumba, because of the insecurity there, nor in Kigali, because of the cramped quarters, they met in Ruhango, in the centre of the country. At this encounter the sisters were to review all issues, including their own ethnic problems in Rwanda, by sharing their backgrounds and all they had lived through in this area. Together they discussed their sufferings and developed a vision for the future. Here is what the pamphlet history of the congregation has to say about these days:

> From July 17th to August 15th, 1993, the first general meeting of professed DMA sisters was held in Ruhango. It was preceded by a retreat, preached by Father Bernardin Muzungu, O.P. The DMA sisters decided to take charge of their future. They asked the Dominican Missionaries of Namur to continue supporting them as long as necessary. The first part of the constitutions, devoted to the life of the sisters, slowly developed over the first ten years and already amended, was unanimously approved by the Assembly. (...). On August 21st, at the Christus Centre, the Acts

6. Especially Timothy Radcliffe, *Je vous appelle amis*, Paris, Cerf, 2000, pp. 44–45; *I Call You Friends*. London, Continuum, 2001.

of the Assembly were presented to Bishop Ruzindana. With great joy he celebrated the tenth anniversary with us and pointed out the specifically religious nature of our engagement during the war.[7]

Those years also presented challenges for continuing education. Sr Antoinette was studying by correspondence to be a pastoral associate. Sr Mediatrix had left to get her formation at the Institute of Integral Human Formation of Montreal. Sr Gertrude was at the Nursing School of Kagbayi, Sr Pierrette at the Pius XII High School in Bangui in Central African Republic, and Sr Josepha and Sr Maria Theresa at the African Catechetical Institute of Butare, in Rwanda.

AND GENOCIDE: GAMBLING AGAINST THE DEATH MACHINE

It is difficult to be a survivor. In an environment where rational arguments are no longer convincing and where everything is based on emotions, it becomes difficult to risk even a single word. One never knows how the words spoken will be interpreted. People must censor themselves. That is all one can do. One may even fall into self-blame with this nagging question: How is it that the others died and I'm still alive? We thought we could save a lot of people, but in fact we only saved a few.

The sisters recall the events of 1994 with mixed emotions. On 16 April, during Mass at the hospital in Byumba, the priest, who himself died a few days later, said, 'You have seen the child victims of mines, and others wounded by militias during the war. It is intolerable to see the innocent pay for the folly of grown-ups.' The next day, with the imposing entrance of the RPF in Byumba, the survivors of the genocide evacuated from Kigali had to be welcomed; it was necessary to listen to the accounts of the atrocities they had experienced, to sympathise with their grief, to visit the wounded, who were staying in a makeshift AMREF hospital close to the community. At the same time, the local population, who were also victims of repression, had to be listened to. The situation was extremely trying, but the Lord was there. The Emmanuel Community, who had survived and arrived from Kigali, were welcomed into the sisters' chapel, and the communion in prayer this provided was a great spiritual support.

The UN forces were conducting a new evacuation of foreigners. The expatriated sisters again had to choose between staying and leaving. Sr Marie-Pascale and Sr Marie-Christine decided to remain, and so did

7. Acts of the DMA General Assembly, 1993.

Françoise, a Congolese novice. Sr Marie-Pascale said she had to ask herself some questions in the midst of great inner turmoil, especially when the door of the last UNAMIR vehicle was closed: 'Am I not going beyond my strength? Will I be able to deal with this? But the duty of solidarity with my sisters and the people challenges me. I was revolted by apartheid in South Africa when I was young, so why should I leave the Rwandans to their fate when they are most in need of support and reassurance? Is my life worth more than theirs?'

After 24 April 1994, Christians in Byumba did not see their priests again. The witnesses say that they were taken away and murdered just as were people who had taken refuge in the pastoral centre. This was a great trial for the Dominican community. The sisters had few food rations, like other centres for the displaced and vulnerable. Groups were organised to support the different areas of life. There was one group for communication, one for social assistance and another for health. But how was it possible to deal with the misery that exceeded even the forces of big institutions? Despite this feeling of helplessness, they rushed to help people in the three-kilometre radius within which they were allowed to circulate. The visit of the Papal Nuncio in Kampala, Uganda, as well as that of Cardinal Roger Etchegaray as envoy of Pope John Paul II, brought a breath of fresh spiritual and apostolic air to the Church of Rwanda.

However, the situation in the other community, about 15 kilometres from Kigali, was much worse because it was situated in the area where the genocide was taking place. In September 1993, after the Assembly, the Dominican Missionaries of Africa had agreed to replace the Dominicans of the Immaculate Conception in the diocese of Kabgayi Gihara. They worked at the health centre run by a Spanish staff of Medicus Mundi, at the Foyer Social, and taught catechesis. The three young postulants had gone there with Sr Miriam. Hostilities were already approaching the capital. The testimony received from the sisters gives the following account of the situation in their area and the attack on their town:

The hordes of killers whistle around our centre. Despite the disturbance outside, we must constantly make decisions to intervene and save. The workers of Medicus Mundi are leaving for Spain, and so are the Spanish priests, after having done all they could. Sister Emerita, health auxiliary, must take full responsibility for the Health Centre. UNAMIR has suggested also that Sister Miriam leave. Without knowing what her sisters have decided in Byumba, she simply replies, 'No, thank you, I'm not leaving. I am with my sisters' and goes back to work. Fortunately, the good relations we have developed with our neighbours help us, because they often speak with the killers, saying: 'Please! Do not attack our sisters who have done so much for us. Respect the Health Centre; it's so useful.' Sister Miriam's rosary no longer leaves her hand. The community often surrounds the Blessed Sacrament. We managed to get a basket of consecrated hosts a few days ago, thanks to the military chaplain. Our biggest concern was how to protect the children and the young girls, to keep them from being molested. We cannot even change our clothes. The attacks are constant every day. Our poor health centre is overwhelmed; patients have to be taken to the hospital in Remera under the fire of the hostilities. In order to do this, we have to cross the militia's barriers risking our lives and those of the patients. Transporting the injured victims of the genocide is even more dangerous, because the militia's only desire is to finish them off. There was no exchange of news between our community and that of Byumba, because that zone was under the control of the Rwandan Patriotic Front, while we were in the area under government control. Militias were harassing us more than ever, as they sensed the imminent arrival of the RPF. We had to find a refuge. Apparently by chance, we found ourselves in the chapel with all the people we had hidden for some time, trying to gather in prayer and to share some provisions. People from the outside had already threatened us a few times, wanting to get rid of one of the people of a different ethnic background, as was done elsewhere. They wanted to finish the 'work' before the RPF invaded the place. Our driver was very sought after. They wanted to kill him. When the knife was already on his throat, we had the idea of paying to save his life. Young boys were also in great danger. Our Sister Perpetua, who was staying with her family, was in danger there, but she decided to join us, so as to die with us. Somehow she managed to escape the militias who killed all the Tutsis, in the places where she had to pass through. She spent one night in the home of Valerie, one of our former novices, then she was told to go to Kabgayi instead. She was received by the Sisters Hospitallers, where she found our Sister Gertrude, who had to finish her nursing studies. In fact, she also spent all of her time caring for wounded genocide victims, conscious that the killers could come at any moment and put an end to this activity. Sister Perpetua was assigned to accompanying those trying to flee to camps for displaced persons.

On June 24th, the Rwandan Patriotic Front arrived in Gihara. They found us thin as nails. We breathed a sigh of relief. For the first time after several weeks, we thought we could sleep peacefully. But at one o'clock in the morning, RPF soldiers came and told us that they were going to evacuate the areas already liberated. We asked them if they would allow us to take the books we use for the religious life, and they ordered us to take just a bag with useful things, so, we took a prayer book, the Bible, the basket of consecrated hosts and some clothing. The soldiers then put us into an escort. We did not go along the roads and paths. We passed through everything. The soldiers had given us the order to stay in a single line like they were. We had our first moment of rest only at 9 am, in Mugina. We had no idea where they were taking us. This break did not last long because we had to advance; the militia was pursuing us relentlessly.

It was already night when we arrived at Rugarika, and we slept there. Fortunately, there were people to welcome us and soldiers positioned in a van to guard us. The soldiers led us to Gitarama where we put ointment on our bodies after several weeks without even minimal hygiene. We put on slippers and we received some sweaters. At Kinazi, we lodged in the mayor's house and were told to relax even if the war continued. We learned about the terrible things that had happened in Kabgayi, and we realized at that moment how much the Church had also been hit by violence, especially with the assassination of three bishops. A few minutes before dying our Bishop had said to one of us, 'Above all always stay united.' We also realized the extent of the looting carried out. After two weeks in Kinazi, with Abizeramariya,[8] the first group was evacuated to Kibungo. They were lodged on the premises of the Benebikira Sisters in Rwamagana. Our lifestyle had come to be like that of the soldiers. We ate like them at 15:00. We went to greet the bishop, who had also been displaced. We found him with very friendly people, who managed to find papayas for Sister Miriam, who could barely eat anything. On July 4th, the liberation of the country was proclaimed with the announcement that the City of Kigali was controlled by the Rwandan Patriotic Front. We began to think about going back to Byumba. Sister Miriam, who could not stay in the place anymore, took the first opportunity, despite the danger,

---

8. This is a Rwandan word meaning 'Those who entrust themselves to Mary'. It is the name of a congregation of sisters founded in Rwanda, and since they have their roots in this country, these sisters do not like their name to be translated into other languages, since it is a typically Rwandan expression. Hence, we have kept their original name here.

to go to tell our sisters. Sister Marie-Christine immediately took the car to pick us up, and on July 12 we were reunited! Our big sister (Sr Marie-Pascale) also found the courage to go in search of the members of our families who were still alive and assure their safety. She did not hesitate, regardless of the ethnicity. The families of all the sisters were actually affected. We were able to share each other's misfortunes and the leaders supported us without discrimination. That was a very moving moment. For the sisters from ethnically mixed marriages, it would have been cruel to make distinctions. The fact that we knew the families of our sisters even before the deadly outbreak of 1994 helped us. Bonds were forged between our respective families. The sisters supported each other to see their families without distinction. We did whatever was possible to get news of the sisters and their families. Every time we learned some bad news, we organized an Office of the Dead in order to keep our communion with the dead and among us. We realized that we were all injured. Our option was to share all our wounds and unite with those of Christ. To overcome our collective trauma, we needed a retreat. The expected preacher could not come from Canada. We asked Sister Marie-Pascale to preach it to us, and she did so with Blaise Arminjon's book 'Sur la lyre à dix cordes',[9] which proposes a spiritual journey based on the meditation of the psalms. It was lived in an atmosphere difficult to describe, but what we can say is that the climate of silence allowed inner rebirth. How did we survive? How can we face life after these experiences? Each of us had to say to herself: It has become so difficult to confide in a person, how can I recover and say Yes to God?

Without delay, we thought of temporary profession for two of our young sisters, Frances and Mechtild. There was also a profession in perspective. How could these professions be interpreted in the face of death if not as a sign of invincible hope? Indeed, the perpetual profession of Sister Pudentiana Mujawabega took place October 24, 1994 in the Cathedral in lifeless Byumba in the context of a war, with the encouragement of Father Hozer, the Apostolic Vicar, since the bishop of the diocese and almost all of its priests had been murdered. There was only one survivor.

On the Feast of All Saints, the Master of the Order dedicated the only free day he had to be with his brothers and sisters to offer the condolences of the Order to those whose families had been affected by genocide and

---

9. Blaise Arminjon, *Sur la lyre à dix cordes: à l'écoute des psaumes au rythme des Exercices de saint Ignace*, Paris, Desclée de Brouwer, 1990.

massacres.

COMING OUT OF TRAUMA AND BROADENING HORIZONS

As early as August 1994, a wide dispersion of the sisters was projected for the future. Here is the their testimony concerning this plan:

> On the Feast of the Assumption, it was decided to disperse. 'If the grain is piled up, it rots; when dispersed, it bears much fruit.' This saying of St. Dominic will always inspire us. Sister Josepha left for Cameroon, accompanied by Sister Marie-Pascale as far as Nairobi, in a military aircraft of the UNAMIR. She would study nursing in Yaoundé. A few days later, Sister Marie-Pascale took Françoise and Immaculate to Bujumbura, via Rweza to greet the nuns. Sister Frances decided to study for a licence in social sciences at the Catholic University of Central Africa in Yaoundé. Sister Immaculate flew to Kinshasa where she would go to Kabinda and continue her normal primary studies with the Fichermont Dominican Missionaries. Sister Mary Theresa, who had left Byumba in June to visit her family in northern Zaire, joined her in Kabinda and would teach at the Lyceum for a year. Sister Nicole was already in Ivory Coast studying philosophy at the ICAO (Catholic Institute of West Africa), accompanied by Sister Victorine who was studying catechesis there. In September, our mission in Gihara would begin again with three sisters: Sister Pudentiana, who worked at the Nutrition Centre, Sister Emerita at the Health Centre, and Sister Mechtild at the Social Foyer. Sister Marie-Sophie, who had had to flee the Foyer of Charity of Remera-Ruhondo hurriedly in April, went to stay with her parents in Kinshasa. She then left for Belgium to complete her novitiate in safe conditions with Sister Miriam, who already had returned there on July 20. Sister Perpetua joined her there in a community for formation at the Ecole de la Foi and then at Mission Langues, where she would study French at a more advanced level. Thus, the mission and the intellectual formation of the sisters continued in the midst of everything.[10]

Sister Marie-Pascale was often on the road during this period. She devoted much of her time visiting the sisters, to be with them and encourage them. She continued to organise for sisters to study in rotation, allowing the sisters who had completed their studies to return so as to invest themselves in the rehabilitation of those traumatised by the genocide and all the violence

10. *Historique de la Fraternité des Dominicaines Missionnaires d'Afrique 1983–2005*, p.22–3.

experienced.

The missionary charism of the congregation continued to develop. Sr Mediatrix and Sr Marie-Grace already had experience with Dominican sisters from other congregations (in Bangui, Central African Republic, with the Sisters of Namur, and in Brazzaville, with the Petites Soeurs Dominicaines) The time had come to start their own community in Central Africa. The infamous neighbourhood of Les Combatants was chosen ... there are many drug addicts and criminals who hide in corners, and the zone did not yet have a parish. In 1997, between two mutinies in the national army, the house was inaugurated in Bangui and the sisters prepared the new parish of Titus and Timothy.

During the 1999 General Assembly, the new bishop of Byumba, Monsignor Nzakamwita, called for a foundation in the Mutara region in the very place where the war had begun. He offered several places, and the Dominican Missionaries of Africa, in keeping with their life so far, chose the most difficult one.

The foundations in Nyabwishongwezi in 2000 and Matimba in 2005 contributed to the new blossoming of Christian life in this abandoned region. Many sects had invaded the zone. It was not easy to unite the population, composed of former Tutsi exiles from Uganda, who were very hostile to the Catholic Church, which they considered responsible for their disgrace, Hutu peasants in search of land in this former hunting ground and Bahima nomads in search of pasture for their flocks. An elderly Christian exclaimed: 'Instead of the cries of wild beasts and the fire of war, now, for the first time, the Lord can be heard here.'

In the same vein, a request came from the renamed Democratic Republic of Congo to open a new diocesan socio-pastoral centre in Dondi (Watsa Parish, Diocese of Isiro). This is an inaccessible area, where the roads are often impassable, but the call was answered. It met the criteria of the congregation, forged during their hardships: a mission at the frontiers, where the less experienced dare not go. In subsequent years, the region would be attacked by LRA rebels from Uganda, aggressors who were even worse than the militia of the Rwandan genocide. A younger sister wrote,'Our presence in the population is very significant. This is very encouraging for us. When we go shopping in town with the car, at least one sister must remain at the convent, otherwise the people think we have left and they too would want to flee.' Their solidarity with the people is always the same.

LIFE MUST RISE FROM THE ASHES:
BELIEVING IN THE RESURRECTION

'God showed us His love and mercy!' This is the cry of a sister who was a postulant at the time of the 1994 crisis. When the criminals came looking for people who were hiding, the sisters did not leave, abandoning them to their fate. The sisters were there for everyone, without ethnic or regional preferences. They were always warned in time when someone was planning to harm them. They always did their work with confidence. They preserved some memories full of humanity in an ocean filled with cruelty. 'I saw people with a heart during the war. Even without speaking, some soldiers guided us; I saw soldiers caring for the wounded who were with us, treating their wounds and distributing food.'

The unity between the sisters remained flawless, and it was crucial to be able to maintain the challenge of evangelical witness in times of hardship. This internal sisterly unity of the Dominican Missionaries of Africa was strengthened by mutual encouragement between religious congregations. They were greeted and welcomed. It is true that the behaviour of the friars, the nuns and the people of the Church was not always rooted in evangelical witness, but it could not be said that the Church as a whole was unfaithful. At the end of the war, the wounds of the heart were large and widespread. Many survivors wanted to leave religious life and the Church. It was time to make great choices. Should one leave the congregation to go to care for orphans? How could help be found for the survivors of the members' or the sisters' families? Much attention had to be devoted to encouraging the religious. Twice, the congregation gave out rather substantial amounts of money so that each sister could help her own in what seemed most urgent.

Today the sisters give thanks to God for the experiences and lessons learned. They are sent to the sites of the mission with renewed faith. However, everything is not over yet. The legacy of past atrocities unconsciously rooted in both the victims and their communities produces a deep and abiding sense of fear and uncertainty. This can be seen first in those who have suffered physically or through segregation based on identity, and it spreads rapidly among their family members and then, by osmosis, to their community and to society in general. This sense of uncertainty leads to paranoia that in turn generates an inner demotivation and loss of capacity for initiatives.

In addition, people have gradually lost the ability to develop expectations and aspirations in relation to what they could reasonably expect. Having experienced frustration in their basic rights, these victims end up convincing themselves that they cannot expect anything good, and gradually the scope of their ambition shrivels. The poor, victims of violence and genocide, and people who have been labelled in some derogatory way develop a sense of self-censorship. These groups lose their aspiration to a fulfilling life and to social status on professional and economic levels. The courage to present claims to the authorities is diminished. The capacity to aspire to something better not only affects the individual's needs and desires, preferences or plans; it also affects social expectations.

In this milieu, the tendency to withdraw into one's family, clubs and communities is emphasised, thus reducing activity in the public sphere. This leads to withdrawal from social networks and reduces the dynamics of social solidarity in general, thus diminishing the elements of social capital.

These phenomena affect not only the victims. The dynamic of fear is contagious. The perpetrators of human rights violations eventually develop the same type of reflex of reclusion and closed solidarity as the victims, not only because of feelings of insecurity with respect to retaliation, but through the fear that history will be reversed. In this context, it becomes difficult for both victims and perpetrators to see each other as citizens of a country or a region, or to increase their opportunities to work together.

Another phenomenon that usually occurs in settings of violence is the loss of trust in institutions. We no longer believe in them. How can we respond positively to an authority or an institution if we are convinced that we do not share the same basic standards? Statements and decisions of the institutional authorities provoke resentment among victims that leave no room for the sense of voluntary co-operation in the execution of any programme. Institutions are thus obliged to resort to exerting force in order to implement their decisions, and this increases frustration, with the potential for violence that accompanies this. Social actors have the impression of being coerced into subscribing to social norms that contribute to the diminution of their dignity, exacerbating inequality and excluding themselves even more from access to goods and services.

These challenges are significant and common to all societies emerging from long periods of violence and dictatorship. They define the new framework in which the Dominican Missionaries of Africa accomplish their mission. Now joy, freedom and charity need to be revived. It is still important to take care of the hungry, those ignorant of the Truth, and sinners, and each must also care for herself, because the past, even if one has the will to overcome it, is indelible and induces unexpected behaviour when bad news comes again and awakens wounds. The sisters must regularly face moments that could upset their fragile equilibrium, such as a family member being imprisoned for some reason, a young survivor suffering a post-traumatic crisis, a person dying due to insufficient treatment, the convocation of a people's court, the burial of bones found and identified, and especially the emotions and memories that arise during the week of mourning each April.

Our sisters have realised that we should not stand idly by, ruminating over the past; but as the prophet says, if you take care of the unfortunate 'your healing shall spring up quickly' (Is 58: 8).

We must build the future on a sounder footing. In Mutara, the sisters give a deeper formation to catechists and leaders of grassroots communities; in groups of Enfance Missionnaire, children who have become friends of Jesus attract to him other children and even parents. The foundation of a Bible school allows Christians to draw from the wellspring of faith. To unite all these groups, the sisters have built a training centre with help from Germany.

In Byumba and elsewhere in the country, using the psycho-pedagogical approach of Dr Jeanine Guindon – the renewal of human life forces – some sisters form children to be 'small builders of peace'. They also touch their parents, who previously used violence to educate them.

Visits to prisoners continued in Byumba and Miyove, in the attempt to show God's mercy for the killers and to encourage the innocent who had been victims of arbitrary and summary trials.

In Gihara, the evangelisation of Rwanda's third ethnic group, the Batwa, considered inferior by the other two groups, has lead to the creation of basic ecclesial communities, and their members participate in events like the others.

Sr Marie-Pascale has found her way into courts, sessions, radio broadcasts and retreats, where she tries to promote interiority as well as more informed and engaged faith, in a setting of beauty and joy. She has even become known for her contribution to the biblical formation of politicians, who have assembled in a circle, under the patronage of Sir Thomas More, to deepen their Christian commitment.

The great challenge has been the construction of the house for the Generalate of the Dominican Missionaries of Africa in Kigali, on Rebero hill, which is also the centre of human and spiritual formation. Here groups of diverse sensitivities successively meet and enjoy the same reception.

WHAT CAN WE CONCLUDE?

The testimony of the Dominican Missionaries of Africa situates us at the heart of St Dominic's compassion in the context of a world that has collapsed, so that new life may emerge. Sr Marie-Pascale, at the heart of this experience, was herself born in a situation where life was faced with death. She began her mission in the Congo, when this country was on the border between life and death. The community of the Dominican Missionaries of Africa, which she was called to help found, was quickly confronted with an extreme situation, where they had to organise resistance against the madness of evil and injustice, while saving lives wherever possible and maintaining solidarity with the poor and vulnerable. The same mission is continuing today. Young Rwandan sisters and those from other African countries have fortunately learned from the experience in their own lives, by being immersed in the heart of the suffering of humanity. Today, they are assuming their responsibilities with determination and faith in the God of life.

In August 2005, Sr Emerita Nyiransabimana was elected Prioress General of the Society of the Dominican Missionaries of Africa. After four years of service in the novitiate and one year devoted to preaching retreats in Rwanda, Sr Marie-Pascale returned to Belgium to be Prioress General of the Dominican Missionaries of Namur. God's dream continues, and the two congregations will strengthen their collaboration in the same mission.

BIBLIOGRAPHY

De Greiff, P. and Duthie, R. (eds.), *Transitional Justice and Development: Making Connections*, Advancing Transitional Justice Series, New York, Social Science Research Council, 2009.

Guichaoua, A., *Rwanda: De la guerre au génocide – Les politiques criminelles au Rwanda (1990-1994)*, Paris, La Découverte, 2010.

Guichaoua, A. (ed.), *Les crises politiques au Burundi et au Rwanda (1993–1994). Analyses, faits et documents*, Paris, Karthala, 1995.

'Historique de la Fraternité des Dominicaines Missionnaires d'Afrique 1983–2005', unpublished text for internal use, 40 pp.

Ingelaere, B., 'The Gacaca courts in Rwanda', in Huyse, Luc and Salter, Mark (eds.), *Traditional Justice and Reconciliation after Violent Conflict: Learning from African Experiences*, Stockholm, IDEA, 2008, p. 25–59.

Ndaywel è Nziem, I., *Histoire générale du Congo: De l'héritage ancien à la République Démocratique*, Collection 'Afrique Editions', Paris, Duculot, 1998.

Reyntjens, F., *La guerre des Grands Lacs: Alliances mouvantes et conflits extraterritoriaux en Afrique Centrale*, Paris, L'Harmattan, 1999.

Ruzibiza, A.J. and Guichaoua, A., *Rwanda: L'histoire secrète*, Paris, Editions du Panama, 2005.

Sadi, A., Mbomio, J.B. and Mutombo Kanyana, 'Chronique Congolaise', in *Regards Africains*, n. 40, 1997, p. 14.

Sibomana, A. and Guichaoua, A., *Gardons espoir pour le Rwanda*, Paris, L'Harmattan, 2008.

Tutu, D., *Il n'y a pas d'avenir sans pardon: Comment se réconcilier après l'Apartheid*, Paris, 2000.

Verhaegen, B., 'Les rébellions populaires au Congo en 1964', in *Cahiers d'études africaines*, 1967, volume 7, n. 26, pp. 345–59.

8

An Appreciation of Peace-building: a Personal Encounter with the Dominican Sisters in Vietnam

MADELEINE FREDELL, O.P.

EXPLANATORY NOTE

In order to establish contact and exchange between the Swedish Vice-province of Saint Dominic's Roman Congregation, the Catholic Diocese of Stockholm and the Dominican Sisters in Vietnam, I have had the opportunity to travel three times to Vietnam and visit four Dominican congregations present in the country. These journeys took place in 2000,[1] 2002[2] and 2005[3] together with the then auxiliary bishop, William Kenney, of the Catholic Diocese of Stockholm.[4]

The three visits were quite different from one another in several aspects. The first one started with a rather thorough visit of North Vietnam, including religious congregations other than the Dominicans, as well as the local hierarchy. This gave an important historical and political background to the later visits to South Vietnam. The second and third journeys took place only in South Vietnam, including to the Mekong Delta and the region of Dalat. During the first two visits we were accommodated in hotels and could only be with the sisters during the daytime. It was not until 2005 that it was politically possible to stay as guests in one of the Dominican convents in Saigon.[5]

During these three visits we had the opportunity to experience how the Catholic religious community in general, and the Dominican sisters in particular, were creating confidence in a post-war society where religion, and especially the Catholic Church, had been, and still was, mistrusted by the political authorities. This confidence building was mainly done through a series of social and educational projects. The desire for reconciliation, despite all the hardships they had gone through since the peace accord in 1975, above all during the period from 1977 to the

---

1. 9–19 January 2000.
2. 18 February–1 March 2002.
3. 16–27 February 2005.
4. Bishop William Kenney CP is now Auxiliary Bishop of the Archdiocese of Birmingham, England.
5. Officially, Ho Chi Minh City, but many people still call it Saigon, so we use that name here.

beginning of the 1990s, runs as an underlying current throughout the life and work of the sisters.

The text of this contribution is an account of my personal experience during the three visits to Vietnam. None of the Vietnamese sisters should be held responsible for its contents. What I am sharing here is what I have heard and seen, interpreted through my own particular background. Even what may be called 'hard facts' are part of an historical interpretation, depending on how they are presented. When I was asked to write an essay on the recent history of the Dominican sisters in Vietnam from the perspective of 'preaching justice', I thought that I would do this in direct collaboration with a sister in Vietnam. However, various reasons prevented this. Therefore, I can only offer my own personal view of these three encounters with examples of Dominican life in Vietnam. They are deep learning experiences for myself, and I still often return to them with a continuous reinterpretation.

I would like to thank all the sisters whom I have met during my three visits to Vietnam. Their sharing of memories, their faithfulness through all hardships, their unconditional hospitality and their social commitment have strengthened my faith and especially my hope and my joy in being a member of the Dominican apostolic sisters.

A SHORT BACKGROUND TO THE PRESENCE
OF THE CATHOLIC CHURCH IN VIETNAM

My objective here is not to give an extensive historical background to the Christian mission in Vietnam, just to provide the religious context. The religious tradition in the country can be summarised by the concept of *Tam Giao*, 'Triple Religion', which refers to Confucianism, Taoism and Buddhism, and to which the large majority of the population belongs in one way or another. The whole Vietnamese culture is permeated by these eastern religious traditions. Their Buddhism is a form of the Chinese Mahayana version. A veneration of ancestors is seen everywhere, with a small altar of commemoration in every family. There is also a modern indigenous sect called *Cao Dai*, with Buddha, Jesus Christ and Cao Dai as the main spiritual influences. But whatever names we give to different religious traditions and however many people are affiliated to a special denomination, what is important to underline when it comes to the Vietnamese people is that they are imbued with a natural spirituality; they are, in a sense, naturally 'religious'. This is something you experience through their unconditional hospitality, especially among the Buddhists.

The roots of the Catholic mission go back to the first half of the sixteenth century, although this is known only through a decree banning Christianity from the country in 1533, the result of a Portuguese missionary endeavour in the region of Da Nang. A more continuous mission was carried out by Jesuits who had accompanied exiled Christians from Japan, settling in the same region at the beginning of the seventeenth century. These Jesuits were pioneers in studying the Vietnamese language, which then led to its transcription into Latin characters; this achievement is often ascribed to the Jesuit Alexander de Rhodes, the most famous Catholic missionary in Vietnam, although he was often exiled and had to move around the country with Macau as his base. Between 1640 and 1645 he worked in Hue, where he formed an indigenous group of catechists from which a local church was able to grow. The first Vietnamese priestly ordinations took place in 1668, after the appointment of two apostolic vicars in 1658.

During the eighteenth century Catholics were a minority that suffered discrimination, but a hundred years later the Catholic Church had created a rather stable structure, mainly in the northern part of the country. Much of the growth and strength of the Catholic Church in Vietnam during this time was due to French colonial activity and its hegemony in this area of Southeast Asia. From the eighteenth century, an important role was already being played by a group of Vietnamese religious sisters, the Lovers of the Holy Cross, who were engaged in the education of women. This is still a very flourishing congregation and its significance will become clearer later on.

The Vietnamese Catholics are proud of their martyrs during the Church's first centuries in the country. In 1988, Pope John Paul II canonised 117 Vietnamese martyrs, also known as the Martyrs of Tonkin, Andrew Dung-Lac and Companions or the Martyrs of Indochina. The total number of martyrs in Vietnam amounts to more than 130,000. Among these we find the Dominican and Jesuit missionaries of the seventeenth century, those killed in various persecutions during the subsequent 200 years, and finally, those who were martyred in the aftermath of the Communist takeover in the twentieth century. It is well known that the Vietnamese martyrs inspired St Thérèse of Lisieux to volunteer for the Carmelite convent in Saigon, which had been founded by her convent in Lisieux in 1861. Despite the persecutions of the Catholics in the South after 1977, the confiscation of buildings and other institutions, and the great difficulty of holding a monastic community together, the Carmelite sisters still managed to survive, and have been able to get back their original convent. Like all other religious orders, they are recruiting a large number of new members today.

With the Communist take-over of North Vietnam and the Geneva Conference in July 1954 which established the demarcation line on the 17th parallel, more than half of the Catholics from the North took refuge in South Vietnam.[6] Among the refugees were priests and religious, sisters and brothers. Almost all the sisters I met had their family roots in the North, and they could all tell of their parents or grandparents who were part of this exodus from the North to the South at that time. The Geneva peace accords gave all the Vietnamese the opportunity to choose if they wanted to remain in the Communist North or move to the South, or vice versa.

In South Vietnam, Ngo Dinh Diem became president after a fraudulent election in 1955. Diem was a devout Catholic and during his time in power until he was toppled in a coup in 1963, he promoted the Catholic Church in a rather unjust way. This was part of his political resistance against the Communists in the North, but also led to discrimination and eventually even persecution of the Buddhists and of ethnic tribal groups in the mountains. In early 1963, some Buddhist monks set fire to themselves and died as martyrs in protest against the dictatorship of Diem.

The Catholics who had remained in the North were cut off from contact with the rest of the Church and most of their religious practice had to be performed in secret. The institutions run by either the religious orders or the dioceses were closed and the buildings were confiscated. Despite this, the very few officials of the Catholic Church who stayed on in the North did whatever they could to keep the faith alive among ordinary people.

Cardinal Paul Joseph Pham Đình Tung, who died in 2009, was one of these examples. I had the opportunity of meeting him during my visit to Hanoi. He was appointed Bishop of Bac Ninh in 1963 and then Apostolic Administrator of Hanoi in 1990. In 1994, he became Archbishop of Hanoi. During most of his time as Bishop of Bac Ninh he lived under a kind of house arrest. There were only three priests left to minister to more than a hundred parishes in his diocese. In order to make Christian life survive locally, Bishop Tung formed councils of lay people to be responsible for parishes, and he also established a secular institute where young people were trained as catechists. He was appointed a cardinal in 1994 and resigned from his post in Hanoi in 2005.

Another Vietnamese with an international reputation was Cardinal Nguyên văn Thuân, who died in 2002. He was appointed Bishop of Nha

---

6. Some sources claim that more than 600,000 fled to the South, others up to a million people.

Trang in 1967 and Coadjutor Archbishop of Saigon in 1975, just a few days before the fall of the city. As he was a nephew of the former President Diem, he was immediately targeted by the Communists and put in a re-education camp for 13 years, nine of which he spent in solitary confinement. He is famous for his handwritten scraps of papers, which, smuggled out of the prison, circulated among his people and were eventually published as books. He was appointed President of the Pontifical Council for Justice and Peace in 1998.

After the fall of Saigon in 1975, and the unification of the country under the Communist regime of Hanoi, several hundred thousand people fled the country in small boats. This continued well into the 1980s, and among them were also priests and religious, sisters and brothers. A large number of Catholic priests were, like Cardinal Van Thuan, put in re-education camps without any formal trials. The religious sisters could usually stay on in their convents, or were forced to go back to their families, but almost all of them were assigned to forced labour in the rice-fields under inhuman conditions.

In 1977, a governmental decree on religion for the whole country imposed state control not only on the number of candidates to be accepted in seminaries and novitiates, but also on appointments, journeys and transfers within Vietnam as well as on travelling outside the country. This policy had already been in place for 20 years in the North, with the result that the Church had been drained of its resources. However, the Catholic faith lived on, and even thrived, through the devotion of the lay people and the few religious who remained in the North.

According to a report of the Plenary Assembly of the Vietnamese Catholic Bishops Conference in 2010, published by VietCatholic News, there were some six million Catholics in Vietnam in 2007.

THE HISTORY OF THE VIETNAMESE DOMINICAN SISTERS

The Dominicans arrived, together with other Catholic missionaries, during the seventeenth century. We know the names of two Dominican priests from that time, John of the Holy Cross and John de Arjona. Since then, the presence of Dominicans in Vietnam has been growing, despite persecutions.

In the eighteenth century, Dominican friars from the Philippines started a mission in North Vietnam. As part of their mission, they founded a kind of independent pious group of women in what was called *Nha Phuoc*, a 'Blessing House'. The first group goes back to 1715 in Trung Linh in the diocese of Bui Chu. These women made private vows and observed the

Rule of the Third Order of Penance of St Dominic. Seven such houses were made into a single religious congregation of Vietnamese Dominican sisters in 1951, when the Vietnamese Dominican Sisters of St Catherine of Siena was established in Bui Chu. Several new Dominican Congregations were founded in North Vietnam at this time, in the dioceses of Haiphong, Bac Ninh, Lang Son and Thai Binh.

With the partition of the country in 1954, most of the sisters were among the Catholics who fled to the South. The Congregation of St Catherine of Siena settled in Bien Hoa outside Saigon. A second Congregation of St Catherine of Siena was erected in 1958, also in Bien Hoa. The Dominican sisters from Lang Son formed a third congregation in Saigon. In 1973 a fourth Dominican congregation of sisters was established as St Rose of Lima at Thu Duc. Some Dominican sisters also remained in their original dioceses in the North, continuing their apostolic work among the Catholic population. Most of these sisters would live with their families, and as they were gradually cut off from contact with their counterparts in the South and were not allowed to accept any new candidates, they almost died out in the North. However, today there are two Dominican congregations registered in the North, one in Bui Chu, with its roots going back to 1951, and another one in the Thai Binh diocese, founded in 2004.

As was mentioned earlier, schools and other establishments of the religious orders were confiscated after the fall of Saigon in 1975 and further restrictions were introduced in 1977. A number of sisters witnessed the consequences of these confiscations, not only of buildings, but, more seriously, of the living of the religious, of their pastoral work and income. The sisters now had to work outside of their institutions and most often in forced labour teams on farms during long days. Under such circumstances, it was more or less impossible to keep up regular observance in the convent. Sometimes the sisters were also on the brink of starvation. Some sisters left religious life and returned to their families, some fled the country together with other refugees, and not a few lost their lives due to the hardships they suffered.

At the beginning of the 1990s, the Dominican sisters in Vietnam were allowed to rebuild their communities and receive new members. However, the number of new vocations was strictly limited by the government, and all convents suffered from hazardous police raids. As there were many who wanted to try their vocation, the congregations often adopted a system of officially legal candidates beside irregular candidates, who had to register as living with their families. The police raids mainly targeted these irregular candidates, who would have to stay in remote country areas or in the forests for several days, in order not to jeopardise the other sisters in the convent.

Dispossessed of their former institutions, the sisters often set up various forms of kindergarten which were in great demand at this time, and about which the local authorities could do very little. Some sisters would establish basic health care centres and a lot of general social and pastoral work was done through different local parishes.

There are some special characteristics of the Vietnamese Dominican sisters that are useful to keep in mind when looking at their way of living the Dominican charisma in the Vietnamese context today. They all have their roots in the North, with the dramatic events of 1954 and a French cultural past. On the other hand, the vast majority of the sisters have been recruited since the 1990s in the South, mainly in and around Saigon, even if, more often than not, they are descended from refugees from the North. Despite the Communist regime, this generation is very influenced by American culture, and most of them would have some knowledge of English. The sisters of this generation are also usually highly educated, many of them either entering with a university degree or getting one during their period of formation. The number of candidates is also high compared to other parts of the world. However, although there can be up to 50 or even 100 aspirants, only around ten sisters a year in each congregation make final profession.

Despite the fact that the Vietnamese Dominican sisters have more or less the same origin and share the same constitutions today, they are still divided into six different congregations. In addition to this, they are not of pontifical right but depend on their local bishops. It is difficult to tell if this is the result of the political situation and the rather different religious climate in various parts of the country. The sisters in formation are offered a common study period in order to get to know each other and to facilitate collaborative efforts.

The Dominican charism is extremely strong and visible among the Dominican family in Vietnam, including more than 150 friars and over 100,000 professed lay Dominicans. The four Dominican pillars of mission, study, prayer and community life are all lived out to the full.

SOME PERSONAL IMPRESSIONS FROM VISITING
THE VIETNAMESE DOMINICAN SISTERS

During my three journeys to Vietnam, I was mainly in contact with three congregations, the Dominican Sisters of St Catherine of Siena, Thanh Tam,

Bien Hoa, the Dominican Sisters of the Congregation of the Most Holy Rosary, Lang Son, and the Dominican Sisters of the Congregation of St Rose of Lima, Xuan Hiep. I also made two short visits to the Dominican Sisters of the Congregation of St Catherine of Siena, Tam Hiệp, Bien Hoa. To this should be added that the sisters of the Swedish Vice-province of St Dominic's Roman Congregation also had the great joy and opportunity to live and work together with two Vietnamese Dominican sisters in Stockholm and Gothenburg between 2000 and 2007. They belonged respectively to the Congregation of St Catherine of Siena, Thanh Tam, and the Congregation of St Rose of Lima, Xuan Hiep.

However, the very first convent I visited when arriving in Hanoi in 2000, was one of the Lovers of the Holy Cross. As mentioned earlier, they have a long history in Vietnam, and so it was of great significance to meet these sisters before going further into the Catholic community. The congregation was founded by the first vicar apostolic in 1670 and they have an unbroken history since then. Official statistics record more than 4,000 members in 2011, many of them living abroad. The community in Hanoi played a crucial part in the survival of the Catholic faith after the events of 1954. They not only continued their usual pastoral and social work among the population, but they also became the very presence of the Church, when most priests either fled to the South or were sent into camps or imprisoned. Thanks to these sisters, faith was carried on into the next generation.

In this community of the Lovers of the Holy Cross, I learnt about the police raids and how the sisters were handling these harassments, many of which were still taking place in 2000. The rather considerable number of the sisters in formation was irregular in relation to the number allowed by the authorities, but even after a look inside the enclosure of the convent it was impossible to determine any specific number of sisters living there! They had intelligently organised things such that one was completely confused by the organisation of the physical premises, as well as by their ordinary life. Despite the real threats to each sister's life, I was struck by their contaminating joy and their total dedication to serving the children in Hanoi, both those who had been orphaned and those who were attending their pre-school.

This first visit to a religious community in Vietnam pointed out three ways of building peace in a society that had suffered from a long period of war, and which was still suffering from the long-term effects of that war. There is widespread suspicion of the other, not only suspicion of the Catholics on the part of the Communist authorities, but also on the part of the Buddhists who had suffered during the Diem regime in the South. The Catholics who had enjoyed unjust privileges in the South during that time also have to recognise their part in the conflict. The sisters of the Lovers of the Holy Cross showed the will to remain in the country and work openly with all and everybody who needed their services, slowly but steadily creating confidence in those around them. This confidence-building is a way of promoting reconciliation between the different groups with regard to their past, and it is something I encountered during all three visits to Vietnam.

The second way of building peace is through the social work of different kinds to which the sisters commit themselves. There is an obvious necessity here, as the society as such does not have sufficient means to provide for even the most basic medical and social needs of the people. Vietnam may have a Communist regime, but it is permeated by a rather raw capitalism in the sense that there is no general social care, let alone social welfare, from which everybody can benefit.

Thirdly, in any East Asian context, there is a self-evident interfaith hospitality to be respected, if any confidence at all is to be built. At the core of their being, Asian people are naturally religious. Any doctrinal dialogue may be difficult, but a spiritual dialogue is part of hospitality. Your spiritual 'credentials' are appreciated through your personal behaviour, your ability to be attentive to the other, to nature, to all that is happening around you.

I would like to present here my personal impressions of the visits I made to Vietnam.

BUILDING CONFIDENCE AS RECONCILIATION WITH THE PAST
Confidence building and the work of reconciliation are closely linked to fidelity, to faithfulness. The Catholic population who remained in the North after the events of 1954 have truly followed that path, despite persecution and severe restrictions on living out their faith. To this must be added that they were also more or less forgotten by the rest of the world. Interest in Vietnamese Catholicism was focused on those who took refuge in the South, or who left the country altogether.

My strongest memory from all three visits to Vietnam is the encounter I had with the then oldest Dominican sister in the world, Sr Maria Nguyen Thi Men, 112 years old. She was living in the house of the newly appointed Bishop of Lang Son, where she still was able to fulfil some household chores and spend the rest of her time in prayer. Sr Maria Nguyen Thi Men had lived almost 50 of her 90 years as a Dominican sister alone, faithful to her vocation in preaching the Good News, despite everything that was against her. She must have been part of the very first Dominican sisters of Bui Chu and then of the Lang Son Dominicans. The perseverance of this Dominican sister, her faithfulness to her religious vocation, to the Church and to the population, all those who could not or did not want to leave the North in 1954, speak eloquently as to what confidence is about. She must have had faith, not only in her fellow Catholics but also in her 'enemies', otherwise she could not have endured. Obviously, she was not the only Dominican sister in the North, but many of the pioneers had died, and some left religious life as such, due to the circumstances. I also met three other Dominican sisters living in this area, one of whom was in a village further to the North. The second one was 90 years old and confined to bed, and the third was a relatively young sister, staying with her family in one of the villages.

After 1954, the diocese of Lang Son had more than 5,000 Catholics, but the bishop had only a single priest and one active Dominican sister to help with pastoral ministry. Religious sisters could live and minister in this region provided they were born there and lived with their families. At the time, it was difficult, if not impossible, to send candidates to the South for formation. Since 2000, the situation has changed for the better, but the whole region is still marked by poverty, and infrastructure is still far below the general Vietnamese standard.

It was an extremely deep and faith-challenging experience to travel in the Lang Son district with the sisters who originally came from this part of the country but who were now settled in the South. Officially, we were not allowed to travel around in the North, but we took the risk, as the most serious thing that could have happened to us would have been expulsion to the South. One of the most moving encounters in my life was with the inhabitants of a small village not far from the Chinese border, Thât Khê. It was in this village that the still active Dominican sister was living with her parents. As I was travelling with a bishop, and our arrival in the village was a big event for the Catholics there, we were received with traditional Vietnamese hospitality and openness. On a secret signal, all the faithful had gathered in the church, which was more or less in ruins, and we prayed the Angelus together. It would have been too dangerous to celebrate Mass, as some of the active lay people there were still under house arrest. But there was a dinner, shared in a small, dark room close to the church. We sat on small stools around a table with young and old villagers and were offered the best meal I have ever had in my life. When it was time to leave, once again, on a secretly given signal, up to a hundred people were kneeling on the road, in front of our car, to receive the episcopal blessing. I felt the shivers running down my spine, and wished we could have stayed on to celebrate the Eucharist. The people remained in front of the car for a couple of minutes, and then they all disappeared.

By staying on in this poor region, living under severe restrictions, these people, together with a sister like Maria Nguyen Thi Men, showed confidence and worked on reconciliation with a long perspective, beyond their own physical lifespan. They are the truly 'gentle who shall have the earth as their heritage'. To this must be added that sisters from the Congregation of the Most Holy Rosary, who had their origin in this region, tried to come from the South to minister to the people when possible. Today, there are also two established Dominican congregations in the North and there must have been a beginning of these groups already in 2000, even if we could not make contact with them at that time.

SOCIAL WORK

For obvious reasons, the sisters in the South have had to build confidence in a more active way through social work, rather than by living in an 'active silence'. As a face of the Catholic Church, the sisters also have had to restore trust among the different ethnic groups in the mountains, who were oppressed, and discriminated against, by the Diem regime. Even if most of the sisters were refugees from the North, they were still part of the leading social stratum in society, and through their institutions, mainly schools, were ministering to a middle class. This was completely broken down by the Communist take-over in 1975, and the subsequent further restrictions in 1977.

The very first steps they took after the events of 1975 and 1977 involved acting in a similar way to the Catholics in the North after 1954. Faithfulness was witnessed to by keeping the sisters together in a community, despite forced labour, which ruled out a normal religious schedule, and despite harassment and sometimes even starvation. It is easy to judge in hindsight, but how many of us would have stayed on as religious under these harsh conditions? It is a fact that very few sisters left religious life, even if they sometimes had to stay with their families for long periods, thus being separated from the rest of the community. Each personal story from this period of oppression and persecution is unique, but they all witness to faithfulness and to a strong hope that things would change.

Once things did start changing at the beginning of the 1990s, how did the sisters take their place in a society that had necessarily been profoundly transformed since the time that their congregations had been founded? To which needs did they respond?

What is striking is the number of pre-schools and nurseries the sisters operate. Taking care of children while their parents are at work was the first ministry the sisters were allowed to do by the official authorities. Some communities also have orphanages and others have built student hostels for the young people who come from the countryside to study at high schools or universities in Saigon. It is very obvious that the Vietnamese authorities themselves cannot satisfy these needs, and consequently see a cheap resource in the sisters' willingness to provide this kind of social care. We should not be blind to the state taking advantage of, or even using, the sisters for their own purposes. At the same time, by complying with this, the sisters not only have the possibility to minister to the children and to transmit faith, but they are also a part of the reconstruction of society on a broader level. And being part of this rebuilding of a war-torn society is creating confidence. It is a work of reconciliation, especially as they are caring for the whole population, far beyond the boundaries of the Catholic Church.

Some of the Dominican sisters are also partners in rebuilding the infrastructure of the poorest parts of the country. For these projects, they are relying on financial resources from abroad, and obviously this is to the benefit of the local authorities as well. In the province of Can Tho, in the Mekong Delta, a community of Dominican sisters, together with their parish priest, organised the building of nine bridges and put tarmac on several lanes for cycling. This was an urgent need in a region where flooding takes place every year and where children drown because of insufficient and badly maintained infrastructure. They also built a house where young schoolchildren would come to do their homework and receive a proper meal each day.

Several sisters were also working within the health sector, as doctors and nurses in ordinary hospitals, but also with traditional medicine in the remote countryside. I had the opportunity to visit health care centres both in Saigon and in small villages. People who could not afford to go to ordinary clinics came to the sisters for basic diagnoses and traditional medicine. Maybe what the sisters offered would not be considered up-to-date treatment according to western standards, but people were taken care of and treated with respect and dignity. Even in the west, we know that most people consulting a doctor do not need specialised medical care; what is more important is to be a good listener, someone who gives hope to those facing hardship and suffering.

Another problem in Saigon, as in so many other big cities around the world, is the number of street children. These children are left on their own, even though most of them have a family or relatives somewhere. The local authorities have been unwilling to acknowledge this problem, and hence the children easily become victims of violence or are drawn into criminal groups. One community of Dominican sisters was allowed to set up a primary school for these children, although they can use the premises for only half of the day, as the municipality requires the building for the ordinary school during the other half.

Many elderly people are also left on their own without any basic care. This is also a need to which the sisters have responded. As they rarely have sufficient resources to put up a nursing home with even the most basic equipment, I was struck by the inventiveness and love with which they carried out this ministry. Once again, these elderly were among the poorest people, those who had no family to care for them and who had lost everything during the war.

INTERFAITH HOSPITALITY

Even if you feel that you can literally 'touch' the religiousness of the Vietnamese people, there are still obstacles to interfaith hospitality that need to be overcome in post-war Vietnam. As mentioned earlier, the Buddhists were discriminated against by the Diem regime in the South (1955–63). Today, one would hardly see any obvious consequences of the interreligious turmoil that took place at the end of the dictatorship of President Diem. Nevertheless, confidence is still lacking and has to be rebuilt, and reconciliation has to be achieved.[7]

I was quite impressed by the efforts of the Dominican sisters to have regular contacts with Buddhist monasteries. There were social visits, but the junior sisters also had to spend a short time within the walls of such a

---

7. The Vietnamese Buddhist monk Thich Nhat Hanh is probably the most well known to westerners, but his impact in Vietnam itself is limited, since he has been living, studying and working in the west since the 1960s. During that decade he set up a lot of social projects in Vietnam to rescue people from the scourge of the war, but in 1973 he was formally denied the right to return to the country by the Communist regime. He was allowed to enter the country again in 2005, and has been returning regularly ever since then. He has become a symbol of peace and is an active dialogue partner with Christians all over the world. Nevertheless, the confidence-building on Vietnamese soil really has to be done at a grassroots level.

monastery as part of their formation. During my stays in Vietnam, I visited Buddhist monasteries, male and female, near Ho Chi Minh City, as well as in Dalat.

In one of the Buddhist monasteries for women outside Ho Chi Minh City, I was taken around the premises, offered tea and given quite a long time for sharing and questions. One thing that struck me on that visit was the way both the Buddhist nuns and the junior Dominican sisters lived. Their respective dormitories were completely similar, large rooms with big wooden boxes for beds, in which they also kept their personal belongings. There could be up to 50 bed-boxes like these in one room. This showed both the number of candidates they had within each religious tradition and the simple and serene living conditions they offered in each place. It very much testifies to the fact that religious life, whether monastic or apostolic, Christian or Buddhist, is very much a part of the Vietnamese culture and tradition. The interfaith experience in the exchange they had built up is a clear sign of confidence towards one another. It also gives strength to promote spiritual growth in a society that is still imbued with political hostility towards those who fully commit themselves to a religious life.

It was the visit to the Buddhist monastery of nuns in Dalat, however, that changed my own faith in a radical way. As I was welcomed by one of the nuns who spoke English, she uttered the rather disconcerting words, 'Welcome to our monastery, here we do not believe in God.' After hours of sharing our personal experiences of religious life, I could only conclude that 'the God you thought I believed in does not exist'.[8] But that was only the surface of our conversation. I have never been so challenged in my own faithfulness to religious life as when looking into the eyes of this nun. She owned no more than the clothes she stood up in, her head was shaved and she sat in Zen meditation for several hours each day and night, and for the rest of the time she worked on the premises of the monastery. She was travelling deep into the core of her own being, into the core of the human being as such, and there she was aware of the ultimate meaning of existence. Living like this is to be part of those gentle people who hold the world together in each moment of its being, of its continuous creation, by means of just breathing and being mindful. In one way we had both given our lives for the same

8. Note by the editors: this encounter emphasises the importance of recognising the different levels of interreligious dialogue. The most general level is that of the dialogue of life, as we see here; an encounter between two human beings sharing their understanding of their faith. On another level, there is theological dialogue; on this level, we would need to face the fundamental difference between Christianity and Buddhism regarding the possibility of thinking about God.

goal, albeit naming it quite differently. We were able to meet and recognise the way each one of us was walking. This is interfaith hospitality, when we take time to open our inmost and vulnerable selves to one another. Such an encounter leads to confidence and trust and must be valued as one of the most important ways of building peace in our world today.

We can never eliminate the wrongs and injustices that have been committed in the past, the injuries people have suffered, the fear people have felt, but we can find ways of building reconciliation. Maybe sitting in meditation and sharing of our life-giving sources are necessary means on the way to an intercultural and interreligious society where we can live in true solidarity with one another.

CONCLUSION

Are the Vietnamese Dominican sisters partners in the peace-building that is needed, and in the healing of the consequences of war in their country? One could only give a clear 'yes' in answer to that question. Still, there will always be new challenges to the lifestyle and ministries of the sisters. The candidates who are entering religious life today, whether on the Catholic or the Buddhist side, have not suffered the war directly, nor have they been the targets of direct discrimination or persecution because of their faith, although their families may have suffered from it. Do they experience and live by the same hope and perseverance as their older sisters?

The Vietnamese people are famous for keeping to their traditions, their language and their culture, wherever they have settled in the world. They are also known for their solidarity with one another, whether within the same family or in a refugee situation, within the whole group of compatriots. The religious sisters and brothers have a unique opportunity to build peace and confidence today through their faithfulness, their social commitment and their interfaith hospitality. Is the generation who suffered most during the war and from the restrictions and discrimination inflicted by the Communist regime that followed, whether in the North or in the South, capable of transmitting its experiences to the next generation, not only as a healed memory not to be forgotten, but as a life-giving force? Vietnam is heading towards a westernised and secularised society, not because of any regime but because of trade, new technology and globalisation. Will the seed of the martyrs still be the life-giving food for a growing Church, not with regard to numbers, but with regard to its faith?

9

A Battle for Dignity:
Elisabeth Voisin, Worker-Sister in France

MARIE-LAURE DÉNÈS, O.P.

Elisabeth Voisin was born in 1921. Having attended the school of the Dominican sisters of Pensier, she entered the Little Dominican Sisters (Petites sœurs dominicaines) in May 1940. It is a congregation that was founded at the end of the nineteenth century in Burgundy, France, which all through its history nourished a preferential love for the poor.

It was a time of formation, but also of the trials of war. Elisabeth became a nurse, working among people living in precarious situations. From 1958 to 1968 she took on the task of being novice mistress. At the end of her mandate she went back to her work as a nurse for a time, before being called to Brazzaville, Congo, where she stayed for three years.

The year 1972 marks a turning point. The chapter of *aggiornamento* of her congregation opened the doors to the working class for her, and she joined a small community established in a neighborhood of African migrants. This experience lasted for 14 years until 1986, when she was elected prioress general of her congregation. At the end of her two mandates she returned to a community established in a working-class suburb. Today she lives with another sister in a housing project, where she assures a fraternal presence among her neighbours while also visiting the sick in the hospital.

A LONG EVOLUTION: ANCIENT ROOTS

The battle that Elisabeth would fight for 14 years has its source in her life as an adolescent. It was at the age of 13 that a first realisation presented itself when she discovered the destitution of the children with whom she was in contact. Two years later, as leader of young girl scouts she found the same poverty in the working class to which these girl scouts belonged. For her, this poverty was an injustice, and she decided to become a lawyer to uphold the rights of the poor. She began her legal studies at the age of 17, all the while continuing to work with the young girl scouts. Gradually she discovered another type of poverty – ignorance of the existence of God. In these families, already so impoverished by the lack of possessions, this constituted another form of injustice.

She would later say that this was the moment when she became conscious of being called to respond to this double injustice. How? Something obvious became clear to her: she had known the Dominican order from having attended the school of the Dominican sisters of Pensier and she had loved it. Thus, she decided to become a Dominican.

Two fundamental acts in the life of St Dominic symbolise in themselves her choice of the Dominican life. While Dominic was studying at the university of Palencia in Spain, a severe famine was ravaging the country. Moved by the distress of the poor, Dominic decided to sell the parchments on which he studied, commented on with his own hand and indispensable for his studies, in order to distribute the income to the poor of the city who were dying from hunger. It is said that he explained this act in the following way: 'Would you have me study off these dead skins, when men are dying of hunger?' Later, coming back from Toulouse, Dominic stopped at an inn owned by a Cathar. Determined not to leave him in his error, it is said that Dominic stayed up the whole night, talking with the innkeeper, in order to bring him the Good News of the God of Jesus Christ.

From this moment on, Elisabeth would follow in the footsteps of Dominic.

In May 1940 she entered the congregation of the Little Dominican Sisters. She became a nurse working in people's homes, which led her to take care of the poorest. Through her ministry, she rediscovered her profound double intuition: to be with the poor as 'their little sister', and to comfort them in their distress, often also bringing them closer to God.

With time, however, this form of being close to the people started to raise questions in her. She became conscious of the discrepancy that existed between the harsh reality in which the people to whom she was sent were living and the lifestyle of the sisters of her congregation, and of religious in general.

THE FRENCH EXPERIENCE OF THE WORKER-PRIESTS

She was not alone in this sentiment. The 1950s was a decade which, in France, was marked by a general awareness of the distance that had developed between the working class and the Church. From the beginning of the industrial revolution, numerous initiatives had been made to remedy the inequalities to which that population was exposed. This movement, which came to be described as social Catholicism, found support in Pope Leo XIII's encyclical *Rerum Novarum*, the document that marks the birth of the modern social teaching of the Church.

But it was the Second World War that would bring about a decisive turning point. During this period almost a tenth of French priests became prisoners of war in Germany. Others would leave their houses in secret, together with the men requisitioned for mandatory work in German industry. There they would share in the everyday life of these workers at the very time when a great gap had opened up that separated them from the Church. In the work camps, the priests found that their ministry could be lived very differently from their experience of working in parishes. Sharing the life and working conditions of the men would take on a meaning that would be decisive for many of them in their later choices.

This realisation on the part of the priests, as they shared the fate of the prisoners of war and the men requisitioned for mandatory work, was far from being isolated. Things were also moving in the Catholic hierarchy. In 1941, Cardinal Suhard, the Archbishop of Paris, created the Mission de France with one clear objective: to educate priests destined to be sent out to the most dechristianised populations of the country. Two years later, in 1943, Fr Godin and Fr Daniel, two chaplains of the Jeunesse ouvrière chrétienne (JOC/Young Christian Workers) founded in 1927, published *La France, pays de mission?*[1] (France, a country of mission?), which would have a great impact all over the country. Cardinal Suhard, who was very affected by the publication of this book, went on to create the Mission de Paris. This was not about sending out priests to do 'missionary' work, but about creating a group of priests who would invest themselves in working-class areas outside the normal parochial structures. Very quickly, however, some of these priests wanted to go further, asking their bishops for permission to be employed as workers. Thus started the experience that will live in history as the adventure of the 'worker-priests'.

Elisabeth was well aware of this movement and related developments in the Church. Her sensibility regarding this question brought her in close contact with the French Dominicans who had invested themselves in this experience: Jacques Screpel, Joseph Robert, Albert Bouche. One of her own family members was one of the first priests of the Mission de France. Her younger brother and his wife, supported by Fr Michel Begouen-Demeaux OP, were also very involved with the worker-priests.[2]

1. H. Godin and Y. Daniel, Lyon, Les Éditions de l'Abeille, 1943.
2. Fr Begouen-Demeaux was a worker-priest in the fishing industry.

On 1 March 1954 Rome banned the movement, putting an end to the adventure of the worker-priests. This resounded like a clap of thunder in the Church in France. The international context of the Cold War and the fear of Marxism, the strong Communist influence in France and especially in the unions in which the worker-priests were involved as they sought to share all the battles of their colleagues, were all elements that contributed to the decision of the Holy See. The critique of the movement that the ban implied was not without foundation, and its promulgation would affect the kind of involvement that Elisabeth would later undertake. At the time, however, she felt very hurt by this decision. The question it raised for her was whether the work that had been started should be totally abandoned, and with it the working class. Her brother said, 'Now it is the time for you sisters to go out there. And why not you personally?' He had got to know some Dominican sisters from another congregation in Le Havre, who were the first ones to think of being employed in factories in order to replace the priests, and to invest their energies resolutely there. While the sisters directly involved found this experience worthwhile, their congregation did not allow it to be continued. This led to some painful choices. Supported by Fr Begouen-Demeaux, two of the sisters decided to leave. They wanted to remain Dominicans, but in a different way. They were later joined by two more sisters and then some other groups.

Elisabeth knew these sisters well. She understood them and admired them, but she did not consider leaving her congregation, convinced that it could evolve. 'Our founder wanted us to be here for the poor, for those that society rejects ...'

THE EXPLOSION OF VATICAN II

The question remained ... what does it mean to be Dominican? It belongs to the very essence of the Order, with its call to go out to the frontiers and preach, to go out to those who are furthest away from the Church, the 'Cumans' of St Dominic. His unrelenting cry was, 'My God, what will become of sinners?'

At around this time, Elisabeth was made novice mistress. She found herself confronted in a concrete way with what she perceived to be a discrepancy between the life of the worker and that of the religious. The novices that she received from a working-class environment did not feel at ease with religious practices which to them seemed 'bourgeois'. During this period, a Dominican brother paid her a visit, bringing a letter from Fr Marie-Dominique Chenu. In the letter, Chenu reproaches her congregation for being too distant from those for whom it was founded, and having in a way separated itself from the intention of its founder, Fr Chocarne. He wrote: '… the most miserable, all those marked by the scar of work that is too heavy, poverty that is too deep and whom the world oppresses with a level of contempt that is too great to bear, it is for them that "the work" exists in the first place. They must be jealously taken care of.' This again raised the idea that the sisters remained strangers to those for whom they were founded. What to do?

The spirit of Vatican II and the texts adopted by the council thus took on a particular dimension. *Ad Gentes* strengthened Elisabeth in the perception that the world is not saved from the outside. At the end of her mandate she asked for the permission to 'leave' in order to work. But for the time being, this request was denied her, while other sisters of the congregation did start to get involved in such work. Elisabeth was told, 'You are not cut out for this'.

So she returned to her work as a nurse, providing home help in a working-class suburb. She loved this work, where contacts and friendships are woven, but the reflections she heard from others strengthened her intuition. One day, somebody taunted her: 'You trail around your Church on your back, wearing that habit. It sends shivers down our backs.' Another day, she was told 'that which gives you happiness cannot give it to us. You are too different from us.'

She now remembers thinking at that time: 'Maybe by sharing everything in their life, by speaking even more their language, that which gives us happiness may also become theirs.'

When she joined the community in Brazzaville, which was established in a very poor neighbourhood, the idea of working in a factory faded away. Elisabeth thought she would stay in Congo for the rest of her life, but she returned to France after three years.

Things in the meantime had begun to move, encouraged by the spirit of openness to the world that swept through the Church after Vatican II. Pope Paul VI retracted the 1954 ban, paving the way for priests to work in the factories once again. The reverberations of the Medellin conference of the South American bishops in 1968, which affirmed the preferential option for the poor, arrived in May of that year in a France that was experiencing great turmoil. The document *Justice in the World*, published following the Synod of Bishops in 1971, confirmed very clearly that Justice and Peace is an integral part of evangelisation. Religious life was also touched by these developments and it was in this context, following Vatican II, that the important period of 'aggiornamento' of religious life began. The Little Dominican Sisters were no exception, as they celebrated their chapter in 1972. It allowed the sisters to engage in a return to their sources and to the spirit of their founder. 'To go out to them' took on the wider and more profound meaning 'to live with them', in the places where the people live: the towns, the neighbourhoods, the workplaces, the unions and the associations. Bit by bit, another model for an apostolic community life took shape, and the sisters found the means to ensure that it was an authentically Dominican religious life. The intuition was finally taking shape ...

A BATTLE FOR JUSTICE: THE DISCOVERY OF A REALITY
Elisabeth joined a small community of two sisters living in an African neighbourhood, and she 'left for work' as they had already done. One of them cleaned train carriages and the other washed dishes in a cafeteria, all in order to share the life of the poor and to offer them the joy of believing. Ever since her adolescence, Elisabeth had not stopped trying to pursue such a dual mission.

But she was about to discover an unexpected reality. She entered the world of an industrial laundry. At that time, these companies were very varied in size, with workforces comprising anything from 20 employees up to a thousand. The workforce was made up essentially of immigrants and French women from rural backgrounds, both groups unskilled. The working conditions were extremely hard; the workers were on their feet the whole day, except for a short 20-minute lunch break. The heat in the buildings was suffocating and could reach 50–55°C in the summer around the pressing machines. To that were added other hardships: the humidity, the acrid smells ... The work pace was fiendish: 'We never work fast enough!' At this time the industrial laundries functioned in a sector of French industry where exploitation was among the most blatant and where the presence of a union was still the exception.

To begin with, Elisabeth worked for a couple of years in a smaller company with some 20 other employees. Most of them were African or Yugoslavian. Beyond the physical fatigue that came from the conditions of work, she discovered a universe where humiliation is a permanent factor. The orders came without any explanation. There was never a time when the management appealed to the intelligence of the employees by explaining something. And worse, those who gave the orders were as ignorant as the workers themselves. Not being able to justify their promotion because of any specific skills, they resorted to other mechanisms for showing their superiority – mostly by using the humiliation to which they themselves had been subjected before. In a way, the system was self-sustaining. The situation seemed to be jammed and condemned to repeat itself forever. The most widely shared feeling was resignation. There was nothing you could do.

After the closure of the first company where she worked, her colleagues suggested that Elisabeth apply to be hired by a bigger company known for its tough methods. 'Try to get hired by them. It is a labour camp! There is work to be done there.'

This second company was much bigger than the first one. It employed 170 people. The conditions of work were no better, and the difficulties stemming from the work itself were aggravated by the management style.

The lack of respect for the employees was even more flagrant in this company than the last. Insults and humiliation were part of every working day. The boss even used physical violence on occasion, as against one woman whose hair he pulled, while another was dragged several metres by the shoulders, and yet another was severely beaten on the hands. Orders and counter-orders succeeded one another without any explanation, and cameras were installed everywhere in the factory to keep watch on every act and movement of the workers.

The room for freedom was extremely limited. Signs had been put up everywhere. 'Formal prohibition against ...' in big red letters – forbidden to talk, forbidden to go to the toilet within one hour of arrival or within one hour of the lunch break ... One employee was laid off for half a day for having transgressed just that prohibition.

The social legislation that applied to this company was deliberately ignored, and that was all the more easily done as most of the workers were unaware of their rights. Labour laws were constantly flouted and the collective labour agreement of the laundries was not displayed, which it should have been. Many of the workers were even ignorant of the fact that such an agreement existed. When someone ventured to mention the Labour Code, the boss would retort that in his company, he was the one who made the laws.

There is one very efficient way of putting pressure on, and of coercing, workers: money. Skills, margins and salaries were randomly valued and set, without any relationship to the work being carried out. The growing threat of unemployment in the aftermath of the first oil crisis in 1974, and the low degree of training of the majority of the workforce, made using blackmail easy. Arbitrariness reigned. A worker would lose 15 minutes' pay if he or she arrived one minute late for work, but the length of the working day could be extended if the boss wished. Minimum salaries were complemented by bonuses, but the latter were awarded without objective criteria and at the whim of the boss, applying Machiavelli's recommendation to 'divide and rule'. The bonus for diligence, which was the most important one, was taken away for the slightest lapse, whatever the reason, even an accident at work.

THE DECISION TO GET INVOLVED

This was Elisabeth's everyday life for 14 years. What she discovered would take her much further than she had ever imagined in the beginning. Her only ambition as she set out to work at the laundry had been to be present among the very poor and to manifest among them the presence of God in order to let them know that they are loved. But, as she would say later, she did not expect to encounter such injustices. The class struggle, very much in vogue in a France profoundly marked by a Communist Party that had not yet started to make the political adjustments that its European counterparts were doing, disturbed her. To her it did not seem evangelical, and she did not understand why some of her sisters had accepted positions in the unions. But these infringements of human dignity and freedom, these situations of humiliation, could not leave her cold and unmoved. God could not want this – that would be impossible! To do nothing, to say nothing, not to react to these abuses would have been to make herself an accomplice to these situations.

The first battle she had to take on was to convince the other employees that things could be changed. First, their awareness had to be awakened. Since they obeyed blindly, and because of the humiliations they suffered daily, some workers ended up believing that this situation was an inevitable part of the workplace. A Portuguese worker gave proof of this when he said one day: 'God wants us to obey the owner. He is the boss.' A feeling of resignation had become instilled. 'He is the owner. It's like that.'

Very often this was accompanied by the fear of losing one's job. 'In any case they are stronger than we are, because it is they who have the money.' In the latter part of the 1970s in France, the inexorable rise of unemployment and the implementation of austerity measures dampened the vague attempts by those, a minority, who wanted to act. In those tense times, the lack of skills of the majority of the laundry workers foreshadowed a difficult reordering of the labour market. Many of the employees were immigrants, and they feared for their personal situation. To lose one's job could mean having to go back to one's country, or make the chances of a bringing other family members to France even more remote than they were already. It could also lead to difficulties for the families at home, whose existence depended in part on the money that the workers were able to send back to them. These risks were real. The few who had tried to defend their dignity had had to pay a heavy price in more than one company. Inevitably those stories ended with the departure of that person, laid off for reasons that were more or less real, or induced to resign because of even tougher treatment by the management.

In these circumstances, and for years, Elisabeth thought that nothing could be done to confront such oppression. Still, it was important for her to be present with these workers, to share their working conditions, to pray with them and for them, and never to give up the efforts to make her colleagues conscious of the injustices of which they were victims. Elisabeth strove day after day to restore to each and every one of them their dignity in their own eyes. But this could only be a first step. To restore in each one of them their proper self-image should give them the courage to hold their heads high.

TAKING PART IN THE BATTLE

Only the establishment of a union presence in the company could radically change the situation. Some had to be encouraged to go for it, but Elisabeth herself could not stay aloof. To encourage the activity of a union necessarily implies personal involvement. Furthermore, the lack of education among her colleagues meant that she had to shoulder the leadership of the union. The priority given by the Order to Justice and Peace at the General Chapter of 1977, and the new International Commission of Justice and Peace, which was being formed at that time, encouraged her.

Elisabeth assumed this new responsibility and worked for the establishment of a union branch. Her intention in her first company was to set up a branch of the CFDT (Confédération française démocratique du travail/ French Democratic Confederation of Work), and she had some success.

In her second workplace it would be seven years from the beginning of her employment before a branch of the CGT (Confédération générale du travail/General Confederation of Work) could be set up, part of a union confederation that was close to the Communist Party.

First, she had to try to convince her colleagues that action can be successful if every one acts together. This was not self evident, since the general atmosphere in the company did not promote mutual confidence. Quarrels and tensions among the different nationalities working there were prevalent. Everyone was suspicious of anyone who 'wants to help you', thinking that the person in question must have some underhand motive – like the woman who could not understand why Elisabeth could defend her without asking for anything in return. Others feared the arrival of a union with a strong political identity. But some successes opened up the way, like that of the five or six workers, including Elisabeth, who for six months, never stopped demanding that a regenerator of trichloroacetic acid that was creating a toxic environment for them be placed elsewhere in the factory. After many long weeks they obtained what they ask for, and they realised 'that it is great what you can obtain if you stand up united'.

In 1981, five of the workers took the plunge and joined the CGT. The choice was strategic rather than ideological. The factory was situated in an administrative region that was very much marked by the presence of this union. A couple of years previously, it had tried to create a presence in the laundry but the management had put an end to it. In 1982, the union initiated a new presence in the company, and at the first elections by representatives of the staff the results were encouraging – it obtained 66 per cent of the votes.

The newly elected Elisabeth toured all the work stations, informing all the workers of their rights under the collective labour agreement, of which most were completely unaware. The owner followed her around indignantly: 'You make them think that they have rights.' The tone of voice was scathing.

Improvements were slowly achieved: greater respect for the employees, closer observance of the agreed working hours and break times, the display and implementation of the collective agreement, and the setting up of a mutual insurance system. The budget for professional training, which so far had had the management as its sole beneficiary, now allowed support to be given for literacy courses in particular. The work inspectorate, an administrative body that is tasked with surveying the implementation of employment law in the workplace, started to intervene frequently and vigorously in defence of the rights of the workers.

A court action was initiated against the management, which had paid out salaries below the minimum wage for the entire year of 1982. The employees were successful, and were reimbursed the arrears. This action was a turning point. As an employee from Mali put it, 'We have won. We have obtained the minimum wage. But most of all, now they respect us.'

But the battle was hard for the representatives of the employees. They were transferred from one work station to another, without any apparent reason. The quality of their work was constantly criticised. Sometimes these retaliations were also made against their colleagues. A number of Africans, with the agreement of the work inspectorate, had obtained the right to accumulate their paid holidays over two years in order to be able to make longer visits to their home countries every second year. Up until then, the company had always taken them back after their return. But after the creation of the union, some 30 workers from Mali found themselves unemployed on their return – the owner had refused to take them back after their two-month holiday. Furthermore, they did not qualify for unemployment benefits, since they were deemed to have left the company voluntarily. Elisabeth remarked that 'to fight for justice was getting to be very confrontational'. A number of union representatives resigned because of pressure, bullying and humiliation. It was hard to stand firm and go on, not least since, for many of them, this was their first union experience.

Furthermore, the management lost no time in setting up another union with a membership of people who were totally loyal to it. Elisabeth and her comrades were not spared political and personal attacks, including from those who called themselves Christians, and they therefore rejected the idea of being involved in the union. Anonymous letters arrived expressing the wish that she would die soon; a small coffin was left at her work station – she was spared nothing.

A UNIQUE BATTLE

Elisabeth was not the only one to experience this adventure of immersion in the world of the working class and of taking part in its battles. Her battle for a union was shared with others – priests and religious of both sexes. Even if she was the only religious in her laundry, she did not act alone. Her battle was nourished by the experiences, attempts, setbacks and successes of others who had launched this dynamic presence of the Church in the world of the workers.

This presence came to be known as the Mission ouvrière (Mission of the Workers), with the branch of the 'sisters in factories and companies' that includes some very dynamic and motivated Little Dominican sisters.

Elisabeth's experience was nourished by Vatican II and by putting down deeper Dominican roots. These factors combined to give her her own expression of her vocation, her personal touch. In this way, she has contributed to drawing up the contours of a possible position in society for religious that may very well still be fruitful today.

TAKING INCARNATION SERIOUSLY

At the heart of Elisabeth's involvement you find the dignity of the human person, the touchstone of the entire social teaching of the Church. And it is the Incarnation that is its foundation. She did not at first use the classical argument that the human person is created in the image and likeness of God, but the Christological argument unfolded by the Fathers of the Churches, especially Leo the Great. In the person of Christ, God has taken upon himself, once and for all, all that is human, thus conferring on each human being a unique dignity. This dimension is sometimes forgotten, but John Paul II was to develop it in his encyclical letter *Redemptor Hominis*, published in 1979, a couple of years after Elisabeth had begun her work in the factory. Signs of the times ... The pope wrote: 'With man – with each man and without any exception whatever – Christ is in a way united, even when man is unaware of it.'[3]

The love of Christ for humanity reveals to us our inherent dignity, and at the same time the humanity of each human being helps us to discover God. It is this conviction that gave Elisabeth support in her battle.

During a seminar organised in 1984 by the inter-provincial Commission of Justice and Peace of the Dominican Order in the convent of l'Arbresle, just outside Lyon, Elisabeth gave witness to this:

I have understood, thanks to Saint Thomas, how much the Incarnation is real, solid, and sure. Today I can say that the laundry and all our comrades, those of the companies where we work and those of our neighbourhoods, help me to discover the reality and the relevance of this Incarnation. (...) 'The humanity' of God, his 'weakness', his 'humility', so many everyday acts remind me of that. (...) How rich is the treasure of humanity among our comrades! They do not suspect that they reveal to us something of the God of Jesus Christ, of his tenderness, of his extraordinary closeness. He is there, present, acting, manifesting himself in these acts, much more than in any spoken words.

The face of God that I discover there is not one of Christ tolerating injustices or the oppression of the humble. Jesus put himself in danger

---

3. Pope John Paul II, *Redemptor Hominis*, 1979, n. 14, available at: http://www.vatican.va/edocs/ENG0218/_INDEX.HTM (last accessed 01.07.15).

for the truth. He made himself disliked by the powerful of this world, the people whose privileges he denounced, their hypocrisy … 'The servant is not greater than his Master.'

She goes on:

The Passover of Christ was the inevitable culmination of his battle for justice. We also are not spared the incomprehension, the severe criticism, and the rejection on the part of those for whom we fight. Only the God of Jesus is the source of Life for us in this, and it lets us be strong as the blows come down on us from all sides and nothing seems to amount to anything …

This dignity is something that she claims not only for her partners in the battle, but for everyone. Not these without the others, and not these against the others. This is what explains her reticence when it comes to the notion of the class struggle, which to her seemed, not without reason, so far away from the Gospel, because 'in his flesh he [Christ] … has broken down the dividing wall, that is, the hostility' (Eph 2: 14). Consequently she does not consider the class struggle as a means in itself, but only 'as something in which those who exploit us have taken the initiative. Therefore one has to defend oneself. It is the greatest service that one can render them, even if they do not appreciate it for the moment', because these situations of injustice are at the same time an abuse against the humanity of the management that resorts to these practices, as well as against the employees.

What we are talking about here is the collective dimension of salvation. In making us his sons and daughters, God makes of us brothers and sisters in Christ, who never stays indifferent to the fate of the other. 'Where is your brother?' (Gen 4: 9). The alliance with God makes us at the same time enter into an alliance with the human person, with all people, be they workers or bosses. We are participants in a game played by people and not simply by individuals, isolated particles. We are a people marching towards becoming a human community reconciled in Christ.

EVANGELISATION AND COMMITMENT

As we can see, faith and personal commitment are never separated in Elisabeth. In this she stays faithful to that which has carried her forward since her adolescence, and which led her to embrace the Dominican life and later brought her to the factory. Since the Kingdom of God is foreshadowed in what we accomplish here and now in our societies, we must contribute to the construction of a humane community, to a form of life where every person is respected unconditionally as a child of God – a living together that renders life itself more human. The Church as the community of the believers in the Resurrection of Christ has a special vocation to invite its members to be active socially, politically, and in the unions, in order to build a just order. One cannot separate action and spiritual life. The two are like the two faces of the same coin.

This fact is a strong support for Elisabeth. Through her commitment, it is the words of Paul VI in his apostolic exhortation *Evangelii Nuntiandi* (1975) on evangelisation in the modern world that she seeks to live and make understood by those who surround her, her congregation and beyond, in an ever wider circle. She has carried the words of the pope in herself for many years:

> Between evangelisation and human advancement – development and liberation – there are in fact profound links. These include links of an anthropological order, because the man who is to be evangelised is not an abstract being but is subject to social and economic questions. They also include links in the theological order, since one cannot dissociate the plan of creation from the plan of Redemption. The latter plan touches the very concrete situations of injustice to be combatted and of justice to be restored. They include links of the eminently evangelical order, which is that of charity: how in fact can one proclaim the new commandment without promoting in justice and in peace the true, authentic advancement of man?[4]

For Elisabeth the battle for justice is intrinsically tied to that of faith, and the opposite is true as well. This battle cannot be fought without nourishing oneself at the Source. In the context of her time, this is not self-evident. Elisabeth refuses to accept the phrase that she sometimes hears pronounced by priests or religious committed like her: 'Prayer is work.' Likewise she opposes the approach of a brother she knows, who wants to 'convert' people to Marxism before converting them to Jesus. She refuses this precondition; it is not at all how she understands things, which, instead, is rather along the lines of Madeleine Delbrêl:

> Once that we have gotten to know the Word of God, we do not have the

---

4. Pope Paul VI, *Evangelii Nuntiandi*, 1975, n. 31, available at http://www.vatican.va/holy_father/paul_vi/apost_exhortations/documents/hf_p-vi_exh_19751208_evangelii-nuntiandi_en.html (last accessed 01.07.15).

right to not receive it, once that we have received it, we do not have the right not to let itself be incarnated in us, once that it is incarnated in us, we do not have the right to keep it for ourselves; from then on we belong to those who wait for him.[5]

All the while she continues the indispensable part of her life, which is retreat, silence and prayer. Of course, as she often repeats, the factory and the daily companionship with her colleagues are privileged places to encounter God, 'but nothing comes automatically'. Together with the sisters of her community, committed like herself to this adventure, they use particular means to achieve their goals, but without making something absolute out of them – they let themselves stand back, they take long moments of personal prayer in the morning and come together for community prayer at night, they read again about the big and the small events of faith, and they grant themselves an entire day in 'the desert' of a monastery every month. Together with each other and with others, they study the Bible as often as possible with the support of Daniel Gobert, a Dominican brother of the convent of St Jacques in Paris, himself a worker-priest. In a wider context they continue their research in the Church, together with others who come together regularly, and with the group of 'sisters in factories and companies' to review what they are living. Sometimes, when you are engaged in an activity, it is important to have the help of others to find the right words to express what you live.

These are the moments that let you avoid being submerged by violence and fuelling an infernal spiral. These are the moments that let you, in the middle of your commitment, avoid yielding to the temptation of power and of domination that may be a threat when you are vested with responsibility. These are the moments that let you respect the time of the other, the long development of the other. These are the moments that help you avoid mistaking the means for the purpose …

Elisabeth willingly says that when she began to work in the factory, she did not leave anything of her Dominican life and its demands behind. If there are only very few persons who know about her commitment to the religious life, she never hides her faith, but she never waves it as a flag, either. Her purpose had never changed since she was 17 years old – to fight against injustice and to let others discover that someone Else is there. It was the fire of St Dominic that sparked in her, as she still says today. She thought that

5. M. Delbrêl, *Nous autres gens des rues*, Le Seuil, Paris, 1966, pp. 75–76 (*We, the Ordinary People of the Streets*, Grand Rapids, Michigan: William B. Eerdmans Publishing Company, 2000).

she could better share the Word of God with others by being one of them. But she quickly understood that this Word did not interest them if it was not accompanied by acts. 'The world of the workers mistrusts words. It is in the acts that it reveals itself. And it is in the acts that it puts its confidence' (the seminar in l'Arbresle, 1983). It was thus imperative for everyone to start together, by liberating themselves of injustices in order to gain mutual confidence, and then for Elisabeth to explain to the workers why and in whose name she had asserted that they had the right to be treated in a way other than as sub-humans. It was important not to advance too quickly in order not to force things. 'It is possible to come near to God, but very slowly,' she says.

FREEDOM

Keeping in mind the distance she had maintained from the practice of certain other priests and religious, one might be surprised by Elisabeth's decision to join a union.

As she began to work in the factory the question of engagement in a union soon posed itself, and a number of options presented themselves to her. At this stage it is necessary to describe in broad outline the situation of the unions in France in the beginning of the 1970s. Four organisations shared the most important position among the workers. The public authorities also recognised them as representatives of the workers, which in turn provided them with the opportunity to negotiate with the state. Historically, the first is the CGT, founded at the end of the nineteenth century. Its membership of 2.5 million made it the most important union in 1975. It is controlled by the French Communist Party, despite the Charter of Amiens (1906), which stipulates the independence of the unions in regard to political parties. The problem of the submission of the CGT to the Communist Party led to a split in 1947, which resulted in the formation of the CGT-FO (Force ouvrière / Workers' strength). The CGT-FO has always been very careful about its independence, not only with regard to political parties, in the tradition of the Charter of Amiens, but also in regard to state, Church and all other organisations.

The second organisation to be created was the CFTC (Confédération française de travailleurs chrétiens / French Confederation of Christian Workers). As its name indicates, it has a deliberately confessional character. In the 1970s it was the least important union because of a split that had taken place in 1964. When the majority then wanted to start a 'de-confessionalisation' of the movement 90 per cent of the membership split and created the CFDT.

The remaining 10 per cent kept the name CFTC.

When the moment arrived for Elisabeth to make her choice, involvement with the CFTC was quickly dismissed. Being openly Christian, this union could not respond to Elisabeth's ambition to involve the maximum number of workers, especially as some of them were Muslims or atheists. In the first laundry she chose the CFDT. This organisation has its roots in the Christian Union movement, and had distanced itself from the class struggle. But in 1970 it made a U-turn, once again identifying itself with the class struggle, and it approached the PSU (Parti socialiste unifié / Unified Socialist Party) of Michel Rocard for collaboration and support. The CFDT was then the second largest union by number of members.

Some years later, in the second laundry, Elisabeth chose to play the card of the CGT when she started a union branch.

Why did she make these choices, which might seem questionable and, at first glance, at odds with the spiritual dimension intrinsically linked to her action? They have been misunderstood by some Christians and by some sisters, particularly in a context where the French Communist Party seemed embroiled in the contradictions leading up to, and even supporting, the imposition of martial law in Poland in 1981.

Her first conviction, one might even say obsession, was the necessity of going forward with the others without hurrying or doing things for them in their place. She acted in the name of her faith, but at the same time she felt the need to join the others who did not share her conviction, on the shared ground of the battle for justice. If she chose the CFDT for her first experience and the CGT for her second, this was mostly on pragmatic grounds, since the union needed to be able to assemble the particular workers involved in the context of each laundry. The choice of the CGT was particularly clear in the second case – it was already familiar to the employees, as it had already tried to get a presence in the company. What counts is the possibility of changing the situation, rather than contenting oneself with denouncing injustice but going no further than just talking. To Elisabeth, starting the union was not about launching herself into a political battle, promising the moon, but about acting in order to assure that daily work takes place in an environment where the dignity of everyone is respected. The result of the elections of the representatives of the union seemed to prove her right – with two thirds of the votes, the legitimacy of the delegates was well underlined.

At the same time, concerns for efficiency could never justify accepting demands that one could not support. The policy from which Elisabeth never departs is – never cede to ideology, a position that can sometimes be difficult to maintain in practice. Because of her commitment to be supported by the union movement to which she belonged, by its activists and their experience, in her battle she could appear to expose herself to the occasion of sin. That was what worker-priests were reproached for just after the war. But she maintains her clarity and judgement at all costs. She said during the seminar in l'Arbresle: 'I meet remarkable activists, today of the CGT and yesterday of the CFDT. There are different ways to fight the battle. Anxious to be efficient, each union movement has a tendency to make its methods absolute, the ideologies tend to dominate, everyone defending his own. We refuse (I and my sisters committed in the same way in other companies) as Christians and religious to be forced to adopt such a stance. Our mutual and deep respect, the true friendship that links me to the activists of the CGT, does not change my critical opinion of the organisation. We are not devotees of the union. Our ambition is not first and foremost to help it succeed, but to make it mature through its conscience. The organisation helps us in our battle, and we can as freely express our agreements as our disagreements.'

She clearly shows her liberty in regard to the union organisation, out of respect also for those with whom and for whom she fights. She refuses to let them be used. This is why she fought against the demand of the Communist party that members of the CGT should also adhere to the Parti Communiste Français (PCF). Her action is a union one and is not political. Everyone should have the right to exercise freedom of choice when it comes to joining the PCF or not. But it was a difficult fight, and she had to carry it out in parallel to her other actions. It was difficult to keep the local union sections free from the domination of the party, but she always refused to have Communist Party pamphlets distributed at the entrance to the laundry. In spite of its support, she always refused to enter into this kind of deal with the Communist Party.

Being free in one's choices and adopting a rigorous stand even in the middle of particular choices taken, shows that to be a Christian in the social and political field is not to apply a ready-made programme. It is a call to be responsible, because there is never one single good solution that imposes itself. The Christian is called to keep a distance from ideologies and systems.[6]

---

6. Editor's note: it is important here to distinguish between individual and group responsibilities. The individual needs to make prudential decisions without being able, often, to influence the circumstances of the situation. At the level of groups of Christians, or of groups in the Church, it is necessary to develop a way of thinking (a 'system') and to work to influence social systems to make them more just.

Political or union work requires judgement, which takes form in relation to the particular demands of a situation, and within the scope that the social teaching of the Church proposes, all the while listening to what the Word of God has to say. The Gospel never stops evoking liberty and responsibility, an inventive and creative action anchored in reality, with all its circumstances and particularities. This is what Elisabeth has perfectly understood and put into practice. Her constant insistence on prayer and on the study of the scriptures says this perfectly. Opening genuine ways of liberation and of reconciliation in places of conflict and of oppression compels us to go past ideals that may sometimes be transformed into ideologies, and equally practices, while closely examining the Word of God.

The story of Elisabeth has a precious cornerstone, which is never to separate an activist's commitment from spirituality. This helps us to see the need to live an integrated life, making our commitment to spiritual action and prayer a political commitment ... Through her life, Elisabeth tells us that the God of Jesus is not a *deus ex machina*. He prefers to work through human beings, and he calls us to act in his name, to invent new answers to today's challenges, to be attentive to the signs of the time. Far from being an escape, prayer does not remove us from history; it writes us into it. It demands commitment, a commitment that needs constantly to return to its source.

BIBLIOGRAPHY

Delbrêl, M., *Nous autres gens des rues*, Paris, Le Seuil, 1966 [*We, the Ordinary People of the Streets*, Grand Rapids, Michigan, William B. Eerdmans Publishing Company, 2000].
Delbrêl, M., *Ville marxiste, terre de mission*, Paris, Cerf ,[1] 1957,[2] 1970.
Godin, H. and Daniel, Y., *La France, pays de mission?*, Lyon, Les Éditions de l'Abeille, 1943.
Leprieur, F., *Quand Rome condamne*, Paris, Plon / Le Cerf, 1989.
Poulat, E., *Les prêtres ouvriers. Naissance et fin*, Paris, Cerf, 1999 (revised ed.).

10

Working with the *Sem Terra* in Brazil

IRMÃ MADALENA DE SANTOS, O.P.

PROBLEM AND CONTEXT:
THE GEOPOLITICAL SITUATION OF THE REGION / DIOCESES

I am the earth, I am the life.
From my primordial clay came man.
The woman came to me and came to love.
Then the tree came, and the source.
The fruit is coming and the flowers.

Brazil is a country that covers 8.5 million km² with five major regions and 190 million inhabitants. Our discussion will focus on the southern part of the state of Pará, which is in the northern region. This area is about 175,000 km² and has 15 municipalities that form the diocese of Conceição do Araguaia.[1] According to the *Istituto Brasileiro de Geografia e Estatistica* (IBGE), the total population of this area is 406,000 inhabitants, with 154,838 – 38 per cent of the total – living in rural areas.

The state of Pará was marked historically by large migratory flows and violent territorial disputes. The struggle for land in the southern part of the state began to increase in the 1970s when the federal government granted tax incentives to colonise the Amazon. From this point on, many entrepreneurs received tax incentives to exploit the region's natural resources. However, there was no land reform programme to give the landless rural workers access to land. Instead, the small settlers and smallholders were systematically and violently expelled from their land by big businessmen who arrived with fake titles to these properties.[2] This led to open conflict, because much of the land in this region was seized violently and by means of *grilagem*.[3] Families,

1. Pau D`Arco, Redenção, São Félix do Xingu, Sapucaia, Tucumã, Água Azul do Norte, Bannach, Conceição do Araguaia, Cumaru do Norte, Floresta do Araguaia, Ourilândia do Norte, Rio Maria, Santa Maria das Barreiras, Santana do Araguaia and Xinguara,
2. Falsified documents are often used by loggers, ranchers and land speculators to seize public lands for their exploitation. The landowners act with the complicity of property registries to seize the public zones and use violence to evict squatters, indigenous peoples and traditional communities, who have legitimate rights to the land.
3. This term means 'grabbing', a practice of using forged documents to claim the possession of

especially those fleeing the poverty of the north-east, arrived in the region with the hope of finding better living conditions. They became cheap labour when they were not reduced to the condition of slaves on large farms. They encountered exploitation and an underdeveloped social infrastructure.

The Brazilian reality, especially in this region, created socially weakened migrant families, who then became victims of the various types of exploitation that mark this place: sexual exploitation, degrading labour conditions and nothing short of slave labour on farms. Large mining projects in the region have also attracted numerous families to the area in search of the promise of 'better living conditions'. Often the cities to which the families migrated were overwhelmed and unable to accommodate the newcomers. As a result, the population on the outskirts of cities swelled. Many families were at the mercy of violence, poverty, hunger and disease. The degrading conditions deprived them of their self-esteem and dignity.

The Dominican Sisters of Our Lady of the Rosary of Monteils arrived in the northern region of the country in 1902. Initially, they started their work in the town of Conceição do Araguaia. Later, they expanded to the region of Maraba. Both of these places are characterised by the regional exploitation mentioned above. In the 1970s, the northern region became the scene of attacks by the communist-inspired Araguaia guerrilla movement, giving rise to even greater violence from the government in response. The entire region where the sisters were established suffered greatly. The presence of these sisters in the basic ecclesial communities helped to ease the suffering and overcome the trauma caused by the torture inflicted by the military on workers, as well as on priests and sisters in the region who took a stance on the basis of their faith and commitment to the Gospel, engaging in the struggle for life alongside the suffering and marginalised people.

'HEAR THE CRY, COMING OUT OF THE GROUND,
THE PRAYER OF THE OPPRESSED'
Hearing the cry of the oppressed of the earth, of those whose dignity has been stolen and whose faces have been disfigured by a society characterised by possession and power, means committing oneself to the Gospel of Jesus Christ. It means being faithful to God's design and the Dominican charism. It means being merciful, and seeing all those who suffer with the eyes of Jesus.

---

a particular piece of land. To make them look old and authentic, the false papers are placed in a box with crickets and, over time, the insects make the documents look antique and used.

Since 1986, the Pilgrimages of Land and Water have been a major component of the mystical spirituality of the poorest in their struggle for land. They help to feed the hopes of rural workers during the arduous journey for the recognition and recovery of their dignity. In Brazil, more than 20 pilgrimages take place annually. These religious manifestations, affecting thousands of people, are organised and animated by the Pastoral Land Commission (CPT), together with the dioceses, churches and other local organisations, in order to draw the attention of society and of the government (municipal, state and federal) to the struggle for agrarian reform and access to water. The Pilgrimages of Land and Water allow faith and life to interact in making the people's cry heard in society and in the local Church.

The Pilgrimages of Land and Water also allow the Word of God to enter people's lives. These festivals are meant to prefigure the transformation of their social reality and to help construct a new world characterised by social justice, access to land for local people and recognition of their dignity. As such, these pilgrimages are meant to be a significant presence in the people's lives. To this end, material is prepared to strengthen popular participation in them and to help the people reflect on their experience. In this way, the spiritual life of the communities, churches and organisations is strengthened.

Sr Daniela, one of the sisters living in Pará, has aptly observed: 'The Pilgrimages of Land and Water are like the march of God's people and our ancestors in search of the Promised Land and the Kingdom of God.' They include moments of joy and celebration as well as space for the expression of faith and endurance; above all, they provide a place where hope and commitment to the struggle for life can be renewed.

The Dominican sisters realised that being in the 'missionary space' of Pará was and is formative for the sisters. With this in mind, they decided to situate their novitiate here. The young in formation have contact with the reality of urban and rural labourers and can maintain contact with the CPT, and they can participate in the Pilgrimages of Land and Water and other pilgrimages and Lenten walks, as well as in the various social movements. Formation includes integration into the life of a committed and active Church, helping to strengthen the basic ecclesial communities where faith and life are celebrated, introduction to the social organisations, unions, residents' associations and the study of contemporary Brazil. It is a time of empowerment for both the people and the young formators, who live in this special space of formation and mission. On this ground, where life is constantly threatened, the Dominican sisters evangelically witness to the preferential option for the poor. They have worked actively and effectively in these areas, giving priority to education, teacher training and the strengthening of local organisations. They have also worked to strengthen residents' associations, unions and the popular movements.

I remember an episode that marked my own formation: the eviction of an entire neighbourhood, the folha 28, in Marabá. We had been called upon to support the families. On arrival, we were faced with a battalion of military police with horses, dogs, heavy weapons and trucks. It seemed that we had come upon a battlefield. It was a shock. Women and children were crying. Men were being threatened by the police. There was a sense of horror in the air. Here, however, we also found pastoral workers, men and women religious, leaders.

We were invited by Sr Odette – a Dominican who lived on the folha 20 – to form a human chain, to act as a barricade and to isolate the police from the people. The police attacked, threatening to beat us with sticks. Sr Odette invited us to sing the national anthem, thinking that this symbol of national identity would be respected by the police. We sang vigorously, our vocal chords aching because we were singing with all our strength, so that the hymn could overcome the noise. We kept doing this for quite some time. It actually seemed that the police were pulling back, until orders came from a higher authority to proceed with the eviction. It was sad. Bulldozers knocked down shacks. Heads of families were arrested. The police were beating people. A woman with a child in her arms, who was close to us, took a blow from a truncheon and her daughter's arm was broken. People were crying, screaming and running in all directions. We felt helpless in the face of that devastation. The families' scarce belongings were thrown on top of trucks and taken to some unknown place. The scene we witnessed was unforgettable. Sr Odette, with the Bible in her hand, cried aloud: 'Woe to you who knock down the houses of the poor! Woe to you who beat and arrest the impoverished of this earth. Woe to you who accumulate assets and land and do not respect the sacred right of residence! Woe to you who gather wealth at the expense of the misery of homeless families, who have nowhere to lay their heads.'

I looked at Sr Odette with admiration, respect and pride. This was my sister. I thought: 'I want to be a sister with this strength and courage.' I wanted to live in Marabá and walk on the land of the north. I wanted to live with the sisters here who inspired me: Sr Eliene (Noka), who was doing a wonderful job with children and adolescents in the Movement for Adolescents and

Children (MAC); Sr Valeria, who frequently visited Cacimbas Street (where the most excluded from the community lived, especially those afflicted with leprosy) and conducted Bible studies in the community of Amapá; Sr Claudia, the novice mistress, who formed and integrated young women into the pastoral work of the Church, engaged and committed and involved in the social movements. Finally, I wanted to live among all the men and women religious who were part of this reality and receive a formation enriched by moments of participation in the struggle for justice. All this determined the kind of Dominican sister I would be.

PROTECTION OF HUMAN RIGHTS IN THE FIGHT FOR THE LAND

'... it is essential, if man is not to be compelled to have recourse, as a last resort, to rebellion against tyranny and oppression, that human rights should be protected by the rule of law.' (Universal Declaration of Human Rights, 1948)

The influence of an ethically blind capitalism is very strong in Pará, and its power is increasing as domestic markets become more and more integrated with others around the world. In the process, human dignity and human rights can be obscured. In today's world, to be modern is to be flexible and to relativise the suffering of the human person that must be sacrificed in favour of modernity. In this context, to speak out in favour of human rights is to be labelled an opponent of economic development, or, as in the case of northern Brazil, to be accused of standing in the way of advances in modern agriculture. The dynamics of modern society undermine many human values, and they reinforce ethical individualism and selfishness, creating a climate of indifference to the suffering of others. Private success is viewed as more important than the common good of the community.

Today human rights are violated in a systematic and continual manner by the few landowners who control such a large share of the terrain. Farm workers are forced to migrate to the city slums, swelling their pockets of misery. They often have to beg in the streets or submit to degrading work in the suburbs of large cities just to survive.

The CPT, which was established in 1975 during the military dictatorship, was born in response to the situations faced by landless rural workers and by those expelled from the land. The CPT emerged early as an unconditional defender of human rights in this regard, and worked methodically to seek outlets for justice for these people.

Among those who have been crucial in the development of the CPT we cannot fail to mention Dom Tomas Balduino, pioneer and founder of the CPT and its honorary president. He was a man of courage who was opposed to the dictatorship and the landowners and often risked his life and safety. Fray Henri des Roziers is also still influential. Fr Henri is a French Dominican priest and naturalised Brazilian, who lives in Xinguara-PA and has a strong presence in the region as a lawyer and human rights defender. He works tirelessly to combat slave labour and provide legal assistance to workers in the struggle for land. He has received numerous death threats because of his defence of rural workers, and has spent time living under police protection. He has received several awards from organisations that support the struggle for human rights, both in Brazil and abroad.

Fr Henri, along with the team of CPT Xinguara, have established a presence with the workers who are living in camps by the roadside. They engage in the legal fight for land and remain close to the settlers who are struggling to stay on the land. They work for better living conditions and alternative forms of production that would do less harm to the environment. CPT Xinguara and Fr Henri give legal advice to workers and act as their attorney in many court hearings. Despite his short and frail stature, his personal strength and the power of his words are very impressive. He has challenged anyone who has tried to exploit the workers politically. He would often challenge public institutions and authorities, making public both their responsibilities and their failure to act in various circumstances, resulting in irreparable harm to workers.

In his years of tireless legal service, Fr Henri found one case particularly important: the criminal trial of those who murdered João Canuto, a farmer and union leader.

João Canuto was a resident of Rio Maria. He engaged in the struggle for land reform and was pursued and threatened by farmers in the region. After several threats and much harassment he was found murdered with 18 gunshots in his body on 18 December 1985. The mayor of the city and a group of local farmers who were opposed to the struggle for agrarian reform in the region had plotted his murder; because of their political ties, justice did not come quickly. Fr Henri, then assistant to the prosecution, continued to monitor and keep the pressure of public attention on the case. Finally, in 2001, after international pressure from the Inter-American Commission on Human Rights of the Organization of American States (OAS) and various human rights organisations, two of the defendants were convicted of murdering João Canuto. In 2003 the two accused of ordering the killing of this union leader were sentenced to 19 years and ten months in prison. The former mayor of Rio Maria, however, had died of natural causes by this time, prior to being brought to justice.

The case of the murder of Expedito Ribeiro de Souza is another case worth mentioning in this regard. He had been the president of the Union of Rural Workers of Rio Maria until he was murdered by landowners on 2 February 1991. His assassination was ordered by Jeronimo Alves Amorim, a wealthy landowner in the region. The CPT had an important role in this case, which became the first criminal conviction of a wealthy landowner for the murder of a rural worker in the state of Pará. Fr Henri, as assistant to the prosecution, followed the entire process, from the police investigation until final judgment. Although the accused was sentenced to 19 years and six months' imprisonment, he served only one and a half years of the sentence. An appeals court pardoned him of the crime despite the fact that he was facing another criminal case for the murder of two people in the county of Xinguara in the same state of Pará.

The CPT has a historical commitment to the fight against the landowners of the region, who behave as if they were above the law. They kill workers and violate their rights, which are enshrined in and protected by the Constitution, while being regarded as citizens who contribute to the progress and development of the region. The workers, on the other hand, whose rights are violated, are often arrested and prosecuted for threatening the 'public peace'. When they are killed, criminal cases are treated with indifference by the judiciary and the authorities responsible for investigating and punishing these crimes. Those who commit crimes against the landless and the workers rely on the slowness of the Brazilian legal system to undermine justice.

The CPT, in contrast to this state of affairs, seeks to show the world the crimes of omission and cooperation in evil committed by those in authority. To that end, the Rio Maria Committee was created to be the focal point of these complaints, in partnership with the CPT. Fr Henri again assisted in the foundation of this committee and he worked closely with the CPT and the Rio Maria Committee for five years.

'Nothing of what we live makes sense, if it's not touching people's hearts.' (Cora Coralina)

DOMINICAN ADVOCACY AND THE PROTECTION OF HUMAN RIGHTS

Is she not also 'a daughter of Abraham'? (Lk 13:16)

'I cannot study at dead skins, while starving people extend their hands to beg.' (St Dominic de Gúzman)

'And are these not men? By what right?' (Bartolomé de las Casas)

In modern society, it is common to hear speeches in defence of human rights. Public agencies promote courses on human rights all the time, and one can find many groups working on behalf of the rights of others. This happens in part because of a growing awareness that human rights are foundational for the reconstruction of society.

I entered Dominican religious life in the 1980s, having been attracted by the life history and mission of the sisters that I knew. Reading the life of St Dominic inspired me, and I longed to be part of a religious congregation that was dedicated to protecting the rights of the less fortunate. At this point, I did not understand the full significance of human rights, but I was impressed with the compassion that I witnessed in the lives of St Dominic and Mother Anastasie.

Challenged by the Word of God, nourished by mysticism and the spirituality that is at the root of Dominican life, and with the firm conviction that peace is the fruit of justice, I began to study law at the Catholic University of Goiás. In my postgraduate specialisation I studied human rights issues. After completing my studies I was assigned to be a part of the congregation's CPT in which Fr Henri was also involved.

Commitment to the Gospel requires us to face the realities of the world, and the Church guides us in our judgements of these realities by the light of the Gospel and her social teaching. In an attempt to be faithful to the Gospel and to this teaching, believing that justice is the critical intervention of God in history, and that peace is based on our actions and is our ultimate goal, I served the people of the land on the staff of CPT Xinguara for five years. I tried to live in fidelity to a Church in the world today, with its many challenges, while maintaining a clear prophetic solidarity with, and a preferential option for, the poor. This commitment to build, little by little, a more human and fraternal world is directly linked to the promotion of justice and peace, which is a constituent element of our spirituality. In this regard it is worth remembering the words of the 1971 Synod of Bishops: 'Action for justice and participation in the transformation of the world fully appear to us as a constitutive dimension of the preaching of the Gospel, or in other words, of the Church's mission for the redemption of the human race and its liberation from every oppressive situation' (n. 6).

BIBLIOGRAPHY

Conflicts in the Field notebooks, National Archives CPT 2009: http://www.cptnacional.org.br/index.php/publicacoes/conflitos-no-campo-brasil (last accessed 01.07.15).

Girardi, Eduardo, author of a comprehensive and detailed atlas of the Brazilian agricultural sector, posted on the website of the Center for Studies, Research and Agrarian Reform Project (Nera) http://www.fct.unesp.br/nera/atlas (last accessed 01.07.15) .

Josaphat, Carlos, OP, *Las Casas: todos os direitos para todos*, Sao Paolo, Edições Loyola, 2000.

Sistema de Informações Territoriais: http://sit.mda.gov.br (last accessed 01.07.15).

11

'LA CLE' … A Key to Opportunity: Overcoming the Social Exclusion of Immigrants in France

MARIE-LAURE DÉNÈS, O.P.

The Roman Congregation of Saint Dominic (CRSD) is the result of a merger in the 1950s of five congregations, all with a long Dominican history. Their common denominator was that they were all congregations of teachers. After Vatican II and the *aggiornamento* of religious life, the fields of mission widened. Now it is no longer only in the institutions under the supervision of CRSD that the sisters live their vocation, but also outside, in other sectors of education or in wholly different fields of activity. One concern is constant, however: education in all its different forms.

The community in Lille, France, had its place in this movement at the beginning of the 1980s. Many of the sisters worked in a teacher training college, some involved in its direction. The community also received sisters from the province of northern France who were undergoing formation. It is in this environment that LA CLE was born.

THE FIRST STEPS

In 1984 in Lille (France): Sr Ancilla, who for many years had been the director of the training college for primary school teachers, retired from formal occupation, but not from the world of education. Ancilla was considering doing some type of volunteer work. She wanted to focus on school training or literacy with individualised follow-up for children and adults from disadvantaged backgrounds. Her objective was to help people integrate into society. She was looking for somewhere to offer her skills, but despite meeting several different project managers, nothing was a match for the thing she had in mind. She was, however, in contact with a special education school.

That is how two children arrived one day at the Dominican community in rue Jean Sans Peur, so that Ancilla could help them do their homework. The sisters did not suspect that this assistance would be the first in a long line of similar activities, nor that it would give birth to a beautiful adventure that would eventually celebrate its thirtieth anniversary.

Rapidly, by word of mouth, the requests for support grew. One day the mother of the first children knocked on the door and asked if the sisters would help her learn French. In the ensuing conversation, the mother expressed her bewilderment. She was unable to understand why all the public buildings of the French republic were inscribed with the motto 'Liberté, égalité, fraternité', when 'the poor are becoming poorer and poorer while the rich grow richer and richer'. Sr Ancilla offered the mother an introduction to the history of France and the history behind this motto. At the end the mother exclaimed, 'I have understood. From now on I am going to vote.'

The demands kept increasing until Ancilla asked for help from another of the sisters in the community, and then another one, and then yet another one. Ancilla and the sisters of the community welcomed the children into their house and offered them help with their homework after the school day was over. Sometimes this took place in the homes of the children, because the community house was becoming too small. Sometimes the sisters had to sit with the pupils in the stairwell in order to have enough space to teach.

Victims of their own success, the sisters had to start looking for some premises that would allow them to welcome larger numbers of children and in the best environment. One day a man came out of the house next door to the community. During their conversation with him the sisters learned that this building was about to be vacated and they asked to see it. They could see that the old building needed a really good paint job and some very important repairs. With the exception of the living room, which charmed the sisters, the house was very run down. But they could not dream of anything better – the size of the house and the proximity to the community made it an ideal place. And who was the owner? It was the hospital of Lille. One obstacle presented itself immediately. It would be impossible for private persons to rent the house, since it was let on a commercial lease. The sisters understood that the only way to get around this legal obstacle was to create an association according to the law.[1] The hospital went along with the idea.

The statutes of the association were submitted to the prefecture[2] on 17 June 1985. LA CLE (Lille Association: Compter, Lire, Ecrire / Lille Association: Calculate, Read, Write) was thus born, and could go ahead to rent the house. The hardest part, however, still remained. The necessary renovations of the

---

1. Loi 1901 (Law of 1901) regulates non-profit associations in France.
2. The prefecture is an administrative jurisdiction representing the French state, present in each one of the *départements* (counties) of the country.

house were going to require a lot of money and work. The community and the provincial council proved to be imaginative when it came to transforming the house into rooms capable of welcoming the pupils – and at the lowest cost possible. Once the heavy repairs were finished, the entire community rolled up their sleeves and got to work. Rub down, scrape off, repaint – it was as busy as a beehive. The adventure of LA CLE could now really begin. Individual attention was its founding principle. Being poor does not deprive one of the right to have the same quality of education as others. If it was impossible for the most fragile segments of the population to pay for special courses, it was then imperative to put solidarity to work and offer a different way: personalised school support, or the possibility of learning French at one's own pace. These were the sisters' founding convictions.

A DAZZLING DEVELOPMENT

The principle of 'one pupil, one companion' is a demanding one. The number of sisters in the community was soon insufficient for the demand, despite their best efforts. There were eight children being helped when the association was founded, but at the beginning of 1987 adults wanting to learn to read, write and calculate began to arrive at LA CLE, a total of 40 people. It was thus necessary to ask the parish for help, to look for volunteers outside of their circles of friends, to ask other parishes of the city for help, to look for help in the faculties and the elite schools … But the sisters quickly became aware of the fact that the volunteers, even those with diplomas, were not necessarily trained for this special task, and that they in turn needed to be supported and accompanied. It was also necessary to supply them with the educational texts that they needed. At the same time more space became necessary, and, thanks to the generosity of a sponsor, a new floor was constructed above the garage.

Little by little the volunteers came and helped add structure to the programme. By 1997 LA CLE had 200 volunteers for 250 pupils, divided into three different programmes. These programmes were put in place thanks to the know-how and educational discipline of Sr Ancilla and Sr Marie-Jo, who had joined Sr Ancilla in this adventure after her retirement from teaching in a different teacher training college. The first programme targeted children and adolescents who needed educational support anywhere from the earliest years to the last stages of school education. The second programme was designed to fight illiteracy, and was offered to an adult French public (often people with learning difficulties) or an adult French-speaking public (essentially people from Northern Africa). The third programme was intended for adults wanting to learn French as a foreign language, especially migrants.

The functioning of LA CLE was built exclusively on volunteer work and the total involvement of its founders, but in 1998 the decision was made to become professional. The association now had more than 300 persons being helped and 250 volunteer educators. Thus, the management of the association, fundraising, and the will to broaden the services offered, required a team of paid workers, even if the association still remained small. At first, this meant hiring a part-time secretary and a cleaner for a few hours a week. Two sisters now also devoted all of their time to LA CLE. The following year it was necessary to quicken the pace. Sr Anne-Marie was employed as a paid director and two qualified trainers/co-ordinators were recruited with an *emploi-jeune*[3] contract. The other sisters still remained very present in the organisation. Ancilla and Marie-Jo, especially, continued to give courses and to participate actively in directing the work. But the other sisters of the Lille community, whose number varied during these years, were also involved as volunteers. Two sisters of the neighbouring community of Roubaix[4] also received pupils in their house. Anne-Marie stayed for four years as the director of the association before she handed over these responsibilities to one of the two young women employed as teachers. This woman is still director today.

After having launched and developed the project and provided its direction, the sisters decided to transfer the direction of the programme to lay people, although they still maintain a supportive presence on the governing board and as voluntary teachers. They have kept their place in the association in order to become mentors and to pass on their experience, knowledge and humanity. Today the sisters continue their collaboration, but in a less intensive manner, on account of their advancing years. They are happy with the progress of the association since 1998. The number of volunteers had more than tripled to 556 during the academic year 2009/2010. During that same year 607 people regularly attended LA CLE, including 200 children.

3. The *emploi-jeune* contracts were created in 1997 in France and disappeared after 2002. This type of contract was introduced to favour the creation of jobs for young people in activities of social interest. The contracts were partly financed by the state.

4. The city of Roubaix is situated 11 kilometres from Lille, but it is a part of the same metropolitan area. CRSD has a community in this city.

THE SOUL OF LA CLE:

A CERTAIN VISION OF THE HUMAN BEING

The growth of LA CLE was unexpected. After all, there are other structures in Lille that also offer educational support or literacy courses. To what can its success be attributed? Several reasons become apparent as one reads the annual activity reports of the association: the way that the local media reports on its activities, and the way the people involved in the association talk about it. These reasons constitute, in a certain way, the soul of LA CLE, its spirit.

One characteristic of LA CLE is without doubt connected to the objective of the association, as described in article 2 of its statutes:

This association, which does not have any profit-making goal, has as its objective to ensure, with the appropriate means, the functioning of a centre of education, culture, help and support to young and adult persons having intellectual, psychological or social difficulties and coming from an underprivileged environment.

It achieves this objective notably in organising sessions of individual work or work in small groups free of charge dealing with literacy, educational support, assistance with the persons' integration into society, and, in general, all forms of teaching and education capable of supporting human training.

One of the areas that distinguishes LA CLE from other similar organisations is its commitment to individual and personalised attention. This constitutes 'the central principle that structures the entirety of the activities of the association'.[5] This was the first insight of the founding sisters, and it remains today the foundation on which LA CLE rests: in everything that is done, the attention given to the person, and the consideration that is taken of his or her particular situation and its context, are the top priorities.

Behind this principle there is a particular perception of the human being – of his or her uniqueness, frailty and dignity. The association was not founded in order to show how big it could grow. The objective of LA CLE was never to develop itself, to become a powerful association; from the outset the sisters did not even think about founding an association.

It is exactly this attention given to each person, and the care tailored to each one's needs, that attracted so many persons in difficulty. In LA CLE

5. The following lines are based on the ethical charter, 'Values, Principles and Rules of Conduct', given to everyone engaged in the association, and which amounts to a commitment on the part of each one of them. The board adopted this charter in November 2008.

each person is recognised for who he or she is. No one is seen as just another problem or statistic. 'One does not come to LA CLE before one has decided to tackle difficulties from a perspective of hope.'[6] And the association believes that, in facing the impossible, the unconquerable, each person has in himself or herself the resources needed to go on and to get back on their feet.

Each newly enrolled person undergoes an evaluation designed by LA CLE to gauge his or her skills, but the idea is not to expose that person's failures. On the contrary, the evaluations are aimed at establishing a personalised training programme adapted to the individual's current situation, and this gives each person's progress its own dynamic of success. LA CLE seeks to build on the skills that the individual already possesses. Constant adjustments are made to the programme, taking into account the individual's progress, so the programme adheres as closely as possible to his or her needs. At LA CLE, the fact that the courses are free does not mean that they are mediocre. They are free because they aim to be programmes of excellence that are available to all.

As already mentioned, it is precisely the attention given to each and every person that attracts the great number of volunteers ready to share the sisters' experiences – and because the customised care also extends to the support given to the volunteers. Still, too often, the word 'volunteer' is associated with incompetence and inconsistency. In some organisations the status of volunteer allows for vagueness and irregular attendance. Here there is nothing of that. A commitment to LA CLE is demanding, because the association aims for professionalism in its volunteer work. This is done firstly out of respect for the pupil, who has the same right to quality as everyone else even if he or she does not pay, as the sisters stated so clearly when the association was started. Secondly, it is also done out of respect for the volunteers who find recognition of and esteem for their labour. As one volunteer who is retired put it: 'For a retired person, it permits you to maintain a status as much in relation to the association as to the pupil and those around him or her.'[7]

Before starting to work with pupils, each volunteer benefits from an individual meeting with one of the trainers/co-ordinators. After four or five weeks' work the new volunteer meets again with the trainers/co-ordinators to make an assessment, to adjust the methods used, and to find help in

---

6. Luce Guillerm, President of LA CLE, in an editorial in the newsletter *Lettre de La Clé*, first quarter of 2009, no. 2.

7. Testimonial of a volunteer published in the presentation booklet of the association 2009/2010, p. 20.

resolving possible difficulties. The volunteers are also offered training courses every quarter, and a volunteer who would like closer supervision may appeal to the trainers/co-ordinators. Besides that, the continuing presence of the co-ordinators in the work of the association favours more informal encounters where specific problems can be resolved.

If the chemistry works, it is largely thanks to the fact that LA CLE builds above all on the quality of its relationships. The pupil/volunteer relationship is essential. To put one's heart into this relationship is not merely an educational method – it is first and foremost a human need. The bonds created between people thus become a foothold for the learning process. Everything takes place there, in the personal motivation that draws everyone, from one side or the other, to commit themselves to this approach. Everything takes place there, in the dialogue that is woven between people, which leads to a true encounter provided that each one accepts that his or her 'scenery' may be changed, sometimes in the obvious sense of that expression. Everything takes place there, in our desire to bond.

Attention is thus given to the intrapersonal relationship between pupil and volunteer, but equally care is given to the relations between the people active in the association. That may appear as a challenge in an association dedicated to one-on-one mentoring. Here it is impossible to count on the dynamics of and in the group, and the occasions when everyone meets are rare. As one volunteer stated: 'The sheer number of pupils and teachers makes every kind of associative life difficult during the work day,' but at the same time he stressed that 'the bond is remarkably and wholeheartedly assured by the permanent employees.'[8]

THE DREAM OF A HARMONIOUS SOCIETY

If one-on-one mentoring constitutes the basic principle of the activities of the association, LA CLE places all of its actions in the general framework of a mission towards the social integration of people with difficulties. To ensure respect for the human dignity of each person is to allow everyone a role in shaping their own future. It is to permit everyone to participate in the construction of our shared society. It gives everyone the opportunity to make their voices heard in the public debate. Article IV of the ethical charter of LA CLE underlines that the ultimate objective of the association is to 'facilitate access to autonomy, integration and social insertion'.[9]

8. Ibid.
9. Op.cit.

Far from restricting themselves solely to conveying knowledge, the volunteers have the duty to become points of reference for societal know-how. They are not only expected to teach the French language and help their pupils catch up to the levels of education commensurate with their age, but they are also expected to develop in their pupils familiarity with local institutions, and an understanding of and the ability to function in French society. They should promote respect for the values, rules and codes that constitute the foundation of the 'social contract'. Observing the codes of politeness, respecting common rules and commitments made, and accepting liberty of conscience and the convictions of others in the framework of a system based on a secular society[10] – these are all part of the educational effort of LA CLE.

This approach has two aspects. In order to live together in peace and harmony each member of society needs to acquire the values that underlie that society, but it also requires that everyone is able to express themselves, in one way or another, so as not to become prey to discrimination.

Thus, all those participating in the association's activities commit themselves 'to taking part in the positive recognition of the diversity of those received' and 'to encouraging, by favouring exchanges, a better reciprocal knowledge of the different cultures of origin present within the association'.[11]

The diversity among the people received by LA CLE – starting with French people and foreigners who know little or nothing of written French, to adults and adolescents with learnng difficulties, including school-aged children and adults in professional training or adult students who need to update their knowledge or bring it up to a certain level – is the concrete anticipation of, and a workshop for the construction of, the society of the future.

AN ASSOCIATION GROUNDED IN THE LOCAL REALITY

LA CLE is a spirit, but it is also firmly grounded. One of the foremost characteristics of the association is the ability to listen to the appeals from the world, being conscious of the needs of the population of the metropolitan area of Lille, and being able to plan and operate the best service possible, so that the people who come – whether young or of working age – may find their place in society.

10. *Laïcité*, which is an important and accepted pillar of French society.
11. Ibid., article I.

A territory with a long history of immigration[12]

The region of Nord-Pas-de-Calais,[13] to which Lille belongs, has had a number of waves of immigration over the last 150 years with people coming from different countries. The first wave was from its neighbours to the north, the Belgians, seeking industrial jobs. Before the Second World War it was the Polish who arrived to work in the coal mines. After the war the region welcomed the Italians, who helped rebuild a region that had been devastated by the fighting. And then, in the 1960s and 1970s, many Portuguese settled here, between the three cities of Lille, Roubaix and Tourcoing. These European immigrants were later joined by others from North Africa. First, the Algerians came in the middle of the 1960s, during the war in Algeria, followed by a second wave of Algerians in the first decade of the second millennium. The Moroccans started arriving in the region in the 1970s. In 2004, 74 per cent of the immigrants in the *département* of Nord-Pas-de-Calais came from one of these six countries.

Even though the region of Nord-Pas-de-Calais is a territory with a long history of immigration, the immigrants represent only a small part of the total regional population – 4.5 per cent in 2007 – which is a much lower percentage than the national average (8.3 per cent) and far behind the regions of Ile de France,[14] Alsace and the south-eastern part of France. But the immigrants of the region live mainly in the *départment* of Nord (81 per cent) and are essentially concentrated in the big cities and metropolitan areas. Thus Lille, Roubaix and Tourcoing[15] alone accommodate more than a quarter of the immigrants of the region, even though together they represent less than 10 per cent of the regional population. And it is here especially that the most recent waves of immigration (Algerians and Moroccans) are represented.

In proposing courses in French for foreigners LA CLE responded to a real need in the area, where it was the only association to offer free individual education courses. In addition to this, a thorough analysis of the group

12. The information that follows is derived from a study done for INSEE Nord-Pas-de-Calais (Institut National de la Statistique et des Etudes Economiques/National Institute of Statistics and Economic Studies) by Pierre Chaillot and Danièle Lavenseau, *Immigrés en Nord-Pas-de-Calais: une implantation liée à l'histoire économique en Nord-Pas-de-Calais* (*Immigrants in Nord-Pas-de-Calais: Settlements Linked to the Economic History of Nord-Pas-de-Calais*), Pages de Profils no. 89, February 2011. It is possible to download this document from INSEE: http://www.insee.fr/fr/themes/document.asp?ref_id=17070&reg_id=19.
13. France is divided into 22 administrative regions, each composed of a number of *départments* (counties). The region of Nord-Pas-de-Calais is made up of two *départments*: the Nord, which accounts for 64 per cent of the regional population, and Pas-de-Calais.
14. The region of Ile de France is made up of the capital, Paris, and surrounding *départements*.
15. The three cities form a conurbation.

welcomed by LA CLE during the school year 2009/2010[16] shows that the foreign population, or that of foreign origin, find here a genuine response to their needs, in three respects.

Out of 574 pupils,[17] 364 were foreigners from 70 different countries. Added to the French of foreign origin, this number jumps to 516, or almost 90 per cent. Obviously the majority of these people participate in programmes to learn French as a foreign language.[18] More than half had immigrated recently, and were referred to as *primo-arrivants* (newly arrived). But the foreigners and the French of foreign origin also represent three quarters of the group in the programme dedicated to those who already know how to speak French, but who have not mastered written French.[19] Finally, the majority (57 per cent) of the pupils who participated in LA CLE were young French with parents of foreign origin. Their parents often had difficulty helping them with their schoolwork, because they themselves had not mastered the language sufficiently or because they had little or no formal education.

Looking at the personal situation of the adult pupils, independently of which programme they had enrolled in, the importance of the support given to foreigners can be observed. Out of the 399 adults registered at LA CLE in 2009/2010, 81 had been granted political asylum or were waiting for their case to be processed. They came to LA CLE in order to integrate into society in the short term and perhaps to work towards professional advancement in the medium or long term. Among them were 66 housewives. They wanted to become more autonomous in their daily life, and some were considering taking up a professional activity in the medium to long term, while others were mothers who wanted to accompany their children in their schoolwork. The association did not inquire about the number of women who were foreign or of foreign origin, but the numbers previously cited allow us to conclude that this was also a high number.

Beginning in 2006, within the framework of the diversification of its activities, the association became part of the Équipes de Réussite Éducative[20] for children and adolescent *primo-arrivants* enrolled in nursery, primary or

16. These are the most recent data available at the time of writing.
17. LA CLE accompanied 607 pupils in all in that year. But 33 of them belonged to a special programme that requires confidentiality. Therefore they have been omitted from this analysis.
18. This means learning to speak, read and write French.
19. This programme enables the pupils to learn how to read, write and calculate.
20. Teams of Educational Success. These teams are multidisciplinary and aim to bring about an individualised solution to problems that the pupils may encounter in their daily life outside of the schools. The teams occupy themselves with children between two and 16 years of age, whose social and cultural environment does not always favour their well-being and who show signs of weakness and/or falling behind.

secondary schools who have not mastered the French language. It began offering workshops in French, in order to permit the pupils to be better integrated at school and to help them improve their schoolwork. This activity is still limited since there are only 25 young people involved in it so far, although this number is not negligible.

Sensitive to the Economic Realities in a Region in Transformation

As an area that has experienced immigration over many decades, this region has also known major economic upheaval. In the collective French imagination of the 1980s, the Nord was a stricken *département*, associated with unemployment. It was a time of crisis following the second oil crisis.

The region of Nord-Pas-de-Calais had been a powerful industrial region and an important demographic centre after the Second World War. But it was to be profoundly affected by the decline in its basic activities, something that had already started in the 1960s. The coal, textile and steel industries – all flagships of the local industry – were hit hard. The closure of factories multiplied to such an extent in the 1960s that the Nord-Pas-de-Calais was home to 50 per cent of France's abandoned industrial complexes. The engines that had made the local economy grow were no longer running.

The region of Nord-Pas-de-Calais addressed this crisis by undertaking a quite spectacular restructuring of its economy and expanding its service sector. Thus, in spite of its industrial decline, Nord-Pas-de-Calais never saw an employment slump greater than that of the national average between 1989 and 1994. The region began the second half of the 1990s by aiming even higher. Still, it was in the service sectors that the new jobs were created, while traditional industrial activities continued to disappear.[21] After 1998, the difference between the unemployment rate in Nord-Pas-de-Calais and the rest of France reduced,[22] but the region always maintained a lower level of unemployment than France as a whole. At the same time, there were many changes in the job market and these affected the types of skills demanded.

To go from an industrial workplace to a job in the service sector requires readjustment. This is true especially when it comes to mastering the spoken as well as the written language. The modernisation of industry with the

21. There was one exception to this, that is, the automotive industry, which managed to position itself in a fast-growing part of the market. See the results of a study done for the INSEE Nord-Pas-de-Calais by Pierre Maurin, *1989–1996: retrospective de l'emploi regional (1989–1996: A Retrospective on Regional Employment)*, Les Dossiers de Profils no. 45, 1997. It can be downloaded from: http://www.insee.fr/fr/themes/document.asp?ref_id=1857.

22. Results of a study done for the INSEE Nord-Pas-de-Calais by Raymond Bérard, *Douze ans de chômage (Twelve Years of Unemployment)*, Profils no. 1, March 2003. It can be downloaded from: http://insee.fr/fr/themes/document.asp?reg_id=19&ref_id=6066.

widespread use of new technologies is also moving in the same direction. Research carried out by the INSEE at the end of 2004 – Information et vie quotidienne (Information and Daily Life) – shows that there are greater problems with literacy (reading, comprehension and writing) in the region of Nord-Pas-de-Calais than in France as a whole.[23] The study measured above all the difficulties likely to hinder social relations or social integration. The results speak for themselves. While 80 per cent of the French population shows no difficulty in mastering the written French language in order to carry out their daily activities, that number falls to 75 per cent in this region. On the other hand, for those encountering partial difficulties (7 per cent) there was no difference between the region and that of France as a whole. The gap, however, widens as one compares the group of adults that experience significant problems (8 per cent in the region and 5 per cent for France as a whole), as well as the group made up of adults encountering serious difficulties (10 per cent in the region compared to 7 per cent across France). In case it might be thought that the number of foreigners born outside of France is the cause of this kind of problem in this region, it is worth noting that there is evidence that shows that those born in France to foreign parents also have a higher rate of difficulty (8 per cent) than the average of the equivalent group across France (4 per cent).

Furthermore, taking into account the fact that this region has greater barriers to entry to the job market than in France as a whole, problems with the written language translate into an even greater obstacle to finding a job. Thus, when the research was carried out, almost 20 per cent of the adults in this region who had serious problems were unemployed, compared to 10 per cent at national level.

This quick glance at regional characteristics when it comes to people's access to the written language shows how well the activity of LA CLE falls into the realm of the needs of the local community's social fabric. The analysis of the professional situation of the adults welcomed by LA CLE in 2009/2010 is also enlightening. Out of 399 adult pupils, 83 were employed and receiving a salary. They knocked on the door of the association in order to learn how to read and write or simply to improve their command of French. Many of them sought the assistance of LA CLE for professional reasons: to integrate better, to change job or to gain promotion. Another 112 people were

---

23. Study done for the INSEE Nord-Pas-de-Calais by Eric Vaillant, *Les difficultés face à l'écrit en Nord-Pas-de-Calais (Difficulties in Writing in Nord-Pas-de-Calais)*, Pages de Profils no. 12, October 2005. The document can be downloaded from: http://www.insee.fr/fr/themes/document. asp?reg_id=19&ref_id=9527.

unemployed. They came to LA CLE because they did not have access to the job market on account of their poor command of the French language. The situation certainly differs from one person to another, but many of the adults coming to LA CLE had professional objectives in mind.

A Recognised Local Partner

From the very beginning LA CLE was attentive to the needs of the people welcomed by the association. Aware of the fact that it could not grow indefinitely, the association developed its services in line with its initial intuition: helping women and men to get back on their feet, helping them to become autonomous and helping them to become responsible for their own lives in society. Beginning in 2007, the association began to employ a social mediator. The social mediator acts as a support while the person learns how to become autonomous. He helps people to understand government documents and to fill out different forms (for employment or housing, for example). Sometimes he acts as an interpreter in meetings with institutional representatives, facilitating the relationship of parents with the school, and similar events where such assistance might be very beneficial. Following this same logic, a psychologist was recently added to the team on a part-time basis. Social difficulties often accompany other difficulties.

The psychologist listens to the parents who encounter difficulties in the education of their children and offers workshops to help parents better assist their children in their schoolwork. Here again, it is not about becoming a crutch or substitute, but about guiding people in a specific situation. Because of these workshops, the value of the parents in the eyes of their children has increased and vice versa.

Since its inception LA CLE has been there for people who cannot find help anywhere else. The association thus has always welcomed people with learning difficulties. In 2009 14 such people visited the rue Jean Sans Peur premises. Four of them were in fact employees of an Établissement et service d'aide par le travail (ESAT).[24] The others had all taken courses of specialised education. But since no programme existed in the region for adults with these types of special needs, LA CLE offered them the opportunity to keep up and develop their skills. In a sense this was welcoming the poorest of the poor.

Over the past 30 years this work has gained the recognition and the support of local organisations, both public and private. The impressive list of

---

24. These establishments allow those with disabilities, who have not acquired sufficient autonomy to work in an ordinary context, to carry out an activity in a protected environment.

organisations that contribute financially to the functioning of the association is evidence of this. First, there are the local authorities that give subsidies to LA CLE, from the city of Lille to the regional council of Nord-Pas-de-Calais, including the General Council of the *département* Nord. They all contribute to the functioning of the association through different programmes and budget lines. A quick glance at the titles of these programmes shows the kind of activities for which LA CLE is recognised: social cohesion, integration and the fight against exclusion, the elderly and people with disabilities, families and parenthood, equal opportunities, territorial organisation, promotion of health etc. The French state, the European Social Fund and private donors also bring decisive support to the association.

Apart from the financial donors there is a whole group of partners who collaborate with LA CLE. The association and the activities it offers are better known today by the social stakeholders who work with people in difficult situations. This is notably the case with those in charge of the Revenu de Solidaritée Active (RSA),[25] the centre in Lille for asylum-seekers, and day care centres and sheltered accommodation, with whom collaboration is very active. LA CLE is also occasionally invited to meet people who do similar work in other structures and organisations. These contacts are useful in two ways. Firstly, they permit LA CLE to get to know other people who help those in the same type of situation, and, secondly, they permit LA CLE to understand their clients within a more global context and to be informed about the problems they may encounter. These contacts lead to a deeper knowledge of the different networks that contribute to the fight against exclusion. It also helps LA CLE to serve the people who come to the association for help more effectively, either by taking care of them on its premises or by referring them to the right person or organisation. Thus, since 2008, LA CLE has developed a partnership with an association offering classes in computer skills.

The long experience of LA CLE and its professionalism are bearing fruit beyond the traditional group it serves. During 2010, the public transport company of Lille contacted the director so that LA CLE could participate in a study to identify the current and future transportation needs of people living in precarious conditions. This is one way in which LA CLE contributes its expertise to the formation of certain public policies. The university in Lille also makes use of LA CLE's expertise. LA CLE has in fact become a

25. The RSA is a form of social assistance created in 2009, which replaces several earlier types of assistance.

recognised place of training for university students: 44 students approached the association in 2009/2010 with requests for internships. Thus the association also acts as a place of learning when it comes to social diversity.

CONCLUSION

Without losing any of the strength of the intuitions of its founders, LA CLE has known how to develop itself over the years 'in an attempt to grope for an answer to new needs', in the words of Sr Ancilla. In doing so it has become an important institution in the urban landscape of Lille. It is now recognised for its professionalism, and it has continued to increase the types of service that it offers, without reneging on the spirit of its foundation. On the contrary, it has preserved its identity, and above all it has allowed many people to regain their self-confidence, and to stride more confidently towards their future. In its own way LA CLE has thus contributed to the construction of the Kingdom of God.

BIBLIOGRAPHY

Berard, R., *Douze ans de chômage (Twelve Years of Unemployment)*, Profils no. 1, March 2003, INSEE Nord-Pas-de-Calais. http://insee.fr/fr/themes/document.asp?reg_id=19&ref_id=6066 (last accessed 28.04.12).

Chaillot, P. and Lavenseau, D., *Immigrés en Nord-Pas-de-Calais : une implantation liée à l'histoire économique en Nord-Pas-de-Calais (Immigrants in Nord-Pas-de-Calais: A Settlement Linked to the Economic History of Nord-Pas-de-Calais)*, Pages de Profils no. 89, February 2011, INSEE Nord-Pas-de-Calais. http://www.insee.fr/fr/themes/document.asp?ref_id=17070&reg_id=19 (last accessed 28.04.12).

Maurin, P., *1989–1996: rétrospective de l'emploi régional (1989–1996: A Retrospective on Regional Employment)*, Les Dossiers de Profils no. 45, 1997, INSEE Nord-Pas-de-Calais. http://www.insee.fr/fr/themes/document.asp?ref_id=1857 (last accessed 28.04.12).

Vaillant, E., *Les difficultés face à l'écrit en Nord-Pas-de-Calais (Difficulties in Writing in Nord-Pas-de-Calais)*, Pages de Profils no. 12, October 2005, INSEE Nord-Pas-de-Calais. http://www.insee.fr/fr/themes/document.asp?reg_id=19&ref_id=9527 (last accessed 28.04.12).

More information about La CLE : http://www.associationlacle.org/ (last accessed 28. 04. 12).

12

Dominican Sisters in Pakistan:
Upholding Women's Dignity
in a Muslim Environment

ANNA MORRONE.

Pakistan came into existence in 1947 after partition from India, with a constitution that upholds the principle of equality of all citizens before the law 'irrespective of sex, caste, creed or race' (art. 38). From 1980 onwards, however, under the dictator Zia-ul-Haq, Pakistani society was progressively islamised.[1] When the Shari'ah Act was passed in 1991, Pakistan became an Islamist state, leading to a deteriorating situation as regards the condition of minorities.[2] It is in the context of these developments that the Missionaries of the Schools, arriving shortly after the foundation of the new state in 1948, have been carrying out their mission.

THE BEGINNINGS OF A DOMINICAN PROJECT
OF JUSTICE AND PEACE IN PAKISTAN

In 1931, the Roman Province of the Order of Preachers agreed to take on what was then an Indian mission, sending a first group of friars with Fr Benedetto Cialeo as superior. Until that time, the Capuchins had jurisdiction over the diocese of Lahore, but after a brief period, Fr Cialeo was nominated apostolic administrator of that diocese. In 1939, the Diocese of Multan broke away from the Diocese of Lahore and set up independently, with Fr Cialeo as its first bishop. When the Second World War broke out, the Italian friars were interned in concentration camps for a good three years, but the Christian community, left without their spiritual guidance, remained united and faithful to the basic principles that the friars had taught them. The friars' joy was great when they were released and returned to find the community

1. On this point, see *Pakistan* in *The Oxford Encyclopedia of the Modern Islamic World*, ed. J. L. Esposito, New York-Oxford, Oxford University Press, 1995, vol. 3; 'Pakistan' in *Encyclopédie de l'Islam*, nouvelle édition, par C. E. Bosworth, E.van Donzel, W.P.Heinrichs et G. Lecomte, Leiden, E. J. Brill, 1995, vol. VIII.
2. Cf. the article of the FIDES news agency: *Breakdown of Christians in Pakistan.* http://www.fides.org/aree/news/newsdet.php?idnews=28452&lan=eng

not only still intact but larger than it had been. They asked for further help from their home province, and, in particular, that a congregation of sisters could come and work alongside them in their preaching, especially through education.

The provincial at that time, Fr Ludovico Fanfani, went to visit the mission personally, so as to understand what the real needs of the new missionary community really were. On his return to Rome, and as the co-founder of the Missionaries of the Schools, he could not help but think of these women. Having consulted with Mother Luigia Tincani, he asked them to go to Multan, still at that time a part of India. Ten sisters responded to the appeal; seven Indian sisters, who were in Italy completing their studies at the Catholic University in Milan and at the University of La Sapienza in Rome, along with three Italian sisters. Before they departed, however, they knew that the division between the two states had taken place, and that Multan would now be a part of Pakistan. This was very hard for the Indian sisters to accept, since they would no longer be returning to their home country and would have to opt for Pakistani nationality. This difficult choice, however, did not discourage them; they had already responded positively to God's call and would not turn back.

The first group, formed of three Indian and two Italian missionaries and accompanied by Fr Fanfani and Mother Tincani, set out from Venice for India on 10 January 1948, arriving in Bombay (Mumbai) after about a month.[3] In the meantime, on 30 January 1948, Mahatma Gandhi had been assassinated, one of the consequences of which was that it was no longer possible to travel by sea from Bombay to Karachi, but only to make the journey by land. After many days of tiring travel by train, they arrived at Multan, in the Punjab. They were warmly welcomed by Fr Agostino Pierini OP, who took them around the convent and school where they were to live and work, both of which had previously been occupied and run by the Belgian Sisters of Charity. They immediately saw the need for a school with teaching in Urdu for the children of the poor Christians and for the orphans. The school they set up, dedicated to the Sacred Heart, consisted of a few classrooms built from straw and mud. It was near the military zone, outside the city, and only a short distance from the cathedral, and they were lucky to have access to electricity and so to fans for cooling, which was a great help in temperatures that could rise to 45° or even 50°C. Two months later, a second group of

---

3. The issues of the missionary bulletin of the Missionaries of the Schools, *L'Arbore della carità*, for 1949 and 1950 were consulted for details on the origins of this mission, especially the articles by Fr Fanfani and A.M. Balducci.

Indian missionaries, with one Italian, arrived, and this allowed them to set up a second school, this time using English as the medium of instruction for the children of the military and for the Anglo-Pakistani families. This school was dedicated to the Virgin Mary, under the title St Mary's Convent School.

At the same time, the Dominican fathers would go out to the villages on a daily basis, often returning in the evening with orphaned children who had no one to look after them. They asked for help from the sisters and so two places were set up, one for boys and one for girls, so that they could be taken care of and supported at school. The sisters dedicated themselves to learning the Urdu language, the official tongue of Pakistan, which was hard for them but, they knew, essential to their mission. Through the school, they were immersed in the heart of the local culture and this offered them the chance to get close to the young people, both Catholic and Muslim.

Soon the two schools needed to be expanded to take the increasing numbers of orphaned children. One of the key issues was how to welcome the boys and girls that arrived at their door in a way that was acceptable to the local culture. This certainly meant that girls needed their own space so that, despite the discrimination against them, they could access the education that the sisters were offering. Pakistan is a country of the *pardha*, where a woman must not allow herself to be seen by a man, and must cover herself completely with a burqa. Thus it was clear that the girls and young women needed their own space. In the beginning the school had many boys and only a few girls; the only way to deal with this was to create different areas for them. As a result, the sisters allowed the boys to stay until the age of eight, after which they were required to find another school. It was not easy for them to make this choice, as they would have liked to keep the boys in the school, especially those who were making progress after a difficult start, but they had to keep in mind their overall aim of helping the girls and women to be better educated and, thereby, freer. With this decision, the number of girls in the orphanage and the school soon increased, so much so that they needed more space for them.

This presented the sisters with the problem of acquiring the funds needed and of gaining the necessary planning permission from the Muslim authorities. However, providence provided them with help: they did not need to get permission because there were already some structures on the site that could be modified, and the cost of the project was reduced as there was no need for a professional architect. The superior of the community, Carmelina Giambusso, though not a formally trained architect, was still able to carry out the tasks of one, as well as those of engineer and labourer, all at the same time, so that the building project was able to go forward little by little, tested by the monsoon rains, until the great day of its inauguration. In the first few years, the school had gone from about 60 pupils to 300, and it continued to increase in size. In 1953, a different but related project was achieved: the opening of a university residence dedicated to Our Lady under the title Regina Mundi.

There was also a need for a clinic. One of the sisters was a doctor and she dedicated herself to working with the women, who were in great need of her. At the beginning, they were unsure as to whether they should trust the sister-medic, but they soon realised that she was their great ally in dealing with family problems, especially with regard to violent and abusive husbands.

WOMEN AT THE HEART OF THE
CONCERNS OF THE MISSIONARIES

The educational work that the Missionaries of the Schools were doing was aimed at raising the cultural level of young men and women, since this was the only way open to them for improving the social position of Christians, and of women in particular. In doing so, they were following the ideas and practical approach of their foundress, Luigia Tincani,[4] aimed at forming young people, especially women, so that they could be capable of developing their freedom in a responsible and intelligent manner. In order to understand the peculiarity of the context in which they were operating, it is worth taking a historical excursus.

The Situation of Women in Pakistan

From the beginning of their mission in Multan, the sisters had realised that they needed to focus on women, often victims of the cultural situation, partly because of the practice of *pardha*, and partly due to tribal customs such as 'honour killing', where the guilty party – almost always a woman – is punished with death in order to re-establish the honour of the family. Another law, *samara*, allows for women to be used as scapegoats for faults committed, for the most part, by men; according to this law, even very small girls can be given in marriage to a man of the offended family to repair the damage done.[5]

4. See Chapter 20, 'Luigia Tincani: a Twentieth Century Foundress', pp. 394-413.
5. Istituto Sindacale per la Cooperazione allo Sviluppo (ISCOS), *speciale 8 marzo 2006*. http://www.iscos.cisl.it/

The situation of women in Pakistan, however, is varied. In the urban areas, especially in Islamabad, the capital of Pakistan, their situation is significantly better compared to that in the rural areas, and their rights are more protected. Their levels of instruction and employment give them the chance to have a career, and opportunities for participation in social life are more available. In the rural areas, however, women are seen as inferior beings who have to live in submission to men. They do tiring work that is poorly paid. Their role is largely in the home, taking care of the children and husband, while maintaining the house. If a woman has to leave the home, she must put on the *chador* or *burqa* to hide herself from the gaze of other men. At the same time, the poverty in which rural families live means that it is not uncommon for the woman to carry out remunerative work, in order to sustain the family budget. Often this work is of the type that can be done at home, such as weaving carpets and working with leather or embroidery, but which can often be bad for the health of the women themselves and, because they work alone, allows them to be exploited by unscrupulous middlemen.

Furthermore, in order to get their work done more quickly, they often get their children to help them, unwittingly contributing to their exploitation through child labour.

It is worth highlighting some particular groups of women:

* the **women labourers** have a hardworking life, but they are free of the law of *pardha* and can take control of their world, poor and limited as it is. They wear brightly coloured clothes with sparkling ornaments like bracelets, the tinkling of which accompanies their movements as they pick up or set down bricks or other materials needed for construction. These women are part of a tribe of nomads who are very numerous in Pakistan, and they dedicate themselves with much energy to the most diverse types of manual work, even those that we would associate more with men. Their work would be difficult to do alone; they are always together, with a rudimentary form of work organisation which is, nevertheless, effective. They can also be found working in the fields, harvesting corn or cotton. They accompany their work with songs that help them maintain the rhythm of their actions, whether it is cutting grass or corn, or transporting bricks or buckets of water. At sundown, they leave this work, taking their children who have been playing around them, going home to be with their husbands.

* the **women of the 'poor quarters'** (*basti*) are illiterate, and the most likely among those in Pakistan to be Christian. Their houses are made

of mud, without any sewerage system. The sisters have worked with these women to give them a basic education, including in the rudiments of hygiene, with the hope that they could arrive at the point of being able to set up little entrepreneurial activities that could benefit from microfinance and offer an alternative source of income to that of their previous activities.

* the **woman student and professional**, who can be either Muslim, with the *burqa*, or Christian. The sisters encourage both to debate problems and to participate actively in social life. Professional women are often teachers, lawyers and nurses, but they are to be found only in the urban areas, covering only 33 per cent of the territory of Pakistan.

The Saint Marth Centre for Domestic Science

At school, the sisters taught their pupils useful skills for keeping house, taking care of the sick and adding colour and life to the family home. Nevertheless, when the Saint Martha Centre for Domestic Science was set up between 1949 and 1950, it represented a little socio-cultural revolution. The first of its kind in Pakistan, and targeted primarily at women, it was a genuine justice project, giving dignity to women and raising their work in the family context to a level worthy of serious study. At the beginning, the centre opened its doors to Christian girls, but soon afterwards, at the insistence of Muslim political leaders, it started welcoming Muslim girls as well.

The students were given various tasks, such as furnishing various parts of the house: the kitchen with its various tools and appliances, the bedroom with space for a baby, a working room with sewing machine, embroidery frames or looms for weaving, as well as space for the children to play. All was done with simple instruments, helping these girls to prepare themselves to be good wives and mothers, able to manage their household budget effectively. The handiwork they produced was sold and the money given to the girls and women who produced it, thus setting up small commercial activities that they could later turn into their own businesses. The sisters gave them access to basic skills which, later, using their creativity and commitment, they could apply to developing little cottage industries as artisans.

In these ways, the sisters saw what they were doing as acts of justice and peace, promoting the freedom of religion and helping all to develop a culture of tolerance. They were much in agreement with the view of the universal Church that sees basic education as the first objective of a development plan, as put forward in *Populorum progressio*: 'Lack of education is as serious as lack of food; the illiterate person is a starved spirit. When someone learns how to read and write, he is equipped to do a job and to shoulder a profession, to develop self-confidence and realise that he can progress along with others' (n. 35). As such, the sisters wanted to be 'witnesses to love'[6] at the service of the Church, sent to all peoples as a 'universal sacrament of salvation'.[7]

Certainly, the opening of the School for Domestic Science was original and much appreciated and gave visible results as regards elevating the situation of women, but what was important was the overall educational plan, aimed at forming the intelligence and the will and educating consciences, in view of the global development of the whole person, along the lines of the Gospel. This was an arduous programme of justice and peace to put into action in a mission territory.

THE NEXT STEPS IN A COMPLEX MISSION:
CONCERN FOR THE POOR AND FOR EDUCATION

Openness to a mission beyond the walls of the classroom, remaining faithful to the charism of their foundation, was shown in the interest of the congregation in working directly with the poor. Mother Tincani wrote to one of the sisters: 'Hearing your description of the bastì, and of its poor people, I asked myself: what would be the true apostolic mission to them? To go and open a school there, among them; to stay there all day long and every day; a primary school; a school for the girls; clinics for all. To live there, if possible, in a house like theirs. This would be being missionaries and working to save the Christianity of these poor people!'[8] In another letter, she wrote: 'Cultural activities among the student body at university must have, in our hearts and in our work, one of the first places. With this I do not want to undervalue assistance to the poor, but we need both forms of work.'[9]

In the early 1970s, the American Dominican bishop of Multan, Mgr Boland, invited the sisters to open a centre in his diocese in the city of Khanewal. From there, they were able to visit the Christians spread across the city suburbs, the agricultural areas and in the desert nearby. A kind of avant-garde missionary community, they lived an itinerant life, moving from village to village, from *bastì* to *bastì* and from house to house. It was also around this time, however, that the congregation was forced to withdraw some Italian missionaries from the mission in Pakistan, in the

6. *Amata lex*, art.111 (Constitutions of the Missionaries of the School).
7. *Lumen Gentium*, n. 48.
8. Luigia Tincani, *Lettera*, 22 February 1955, ASMS 69 1.
9. Luigia Tincani *Lettera*, 27 September 1958, ASMS 48.

face of rising antipathy towards foreigners. In the General Chapter of 1975, Mother Tincani considered ways of being present in Pakistan, so as to continue to promote the liberation and the growth of women: 'As regards the past, the certainty that great good has been brought about through the school is a comfort. Looking to the future, as long as the government does not become openly hostile to missionaries, even if the possibility of keeping our schools were to be taken from us, we could dedicate ourselves to the wonderful apostolate among the poor in the villages and suburbs of the city, to teaching the catechism and to raising up women and families on human and Christian levels.'[10] We could say that those words, at that time, were truly prophetic. They came out of a close observation of developments in the ways of thinking and living in Pakistan, and the threat this posed to the future role of the sisters in the country, leading to the idea of preparing local people to become skilled in teaching and formation.[11] Although the role of the sisters was to become ever more difficult in this Muslim country, they could still dialogue on the practical level of faith, hope and love, and, by striving to live a coherent testimony to their faith, maintain the esteem of the people for the Christian religion.

With the arrival of General Zia Ul-Haq and the military regime in the 1980s, the 'madrassas', schools that promote conservative and sometimes extremist Koranic teaching, were established at many mosques in Pakistan. The Islamic identity of the country was reinforced to the maximum, with particular emphasis on the political, economic and educational spheres. The madrassas have played a central role in creating conflict in the country through their promotion of an intolerant and revolutionary Islam. The situation has continued to deteriorate to the present day.

In line with these developments, the general situation of women in Pakistan has not improved. They continue to suffer many injustices and to live in fear of violence. In such a context, the work of the sisters has continued in the area of education, which, according to the authorities, is the only justification for their presence in the country. General education for all, rather than religious formation, becomes the fundamentally important thing in such circumstances. Building relationships with girls and young women leads to long-term relationships. Many of the Muslim former students have invited the sisters to visit them in the institutions of tertiary education where they study after leaving school. In this way, the sisters have been to

10. Acts of the General Chapter 1975, pp. 67–69.
11. Cf. Luigia Tincani, *Lettera*, 13 July 1952, ASMS 64.3; *Lettera* 16 July 1959, ASMS 56.2.

visit the Nishtar Medical College in Multan, the prestigious universities of Lahore and Peshawar, and other centres of learning in Karachi, Dacca and Montgomery. The sisters also work hard for the possibility that Christian women too might study at university, thereby being able to contribute to the full in the Church and the wider society.

BELIEVING IN DIALOGUE

The small Christian community, 2 per cent of the population of Pakistan, faces intolerance, discrimination and acts of violence with alarming frequency. Nevertheless, it is not a hidden Church; it is well organised through its schools, whose pupils are almost entirely Muslim, its work in healthcare through hospitals, clinics and dispensaries, and its social activities, where it often collaborates with Islamic NGOs. During catastrophes, such as the devastating floods in 2010, Church organisations are in the front line in providing emergency assistance, thanks to the support of Caritas Internationalis.

There are also enlightened Islamic figures within the culture who make it possible for dialogue to take place, such as Asma Jehangir, the first woman president of the Supreme Court Bar Association of Pakistan. Overall, however, thanks to factors such as an illiteracy rate of 80 per cent across the country as a whole, and the effect of even more extreme forces in the neighbouring state of Afghanistan, genuine inter-religious dialogue is practically impossible in Pakistan. For dialogue to be able to take place, as the archbishop of Islambad, Anthony Rufin, points out, the equal value of the dialogue partners needs to be recognised, and they must be willing to understand and respect each other.

Unfortunately, much of the Islamic world in Pakistan is unable to do this. The blasphemy laws represent a serious obstacle to be overcome; so far, those who have tried to do so, such as the Muslim governor of Punjab, Salma Taseer, and the Christian minister for minorities, Shabaz Bhatti, have been brutally assassinated. However, there still remains the possibility of the 'dialogue of daily life', where we can find ways of agreeing and moving forward together.

CONCLUSION

Trying to carry forward action for justice and peace in the current Pakistani context is no easy task. The sisters aim to do so, especially for women, primarily through their schools, by doing all of the following: proclaiming

Christ openly to the Christians, through catechesis; helping Muslims to grow morally and spiritually through the teaching of morality and the example of a good life; liberating the poor, and Christians especially, from their misery, firstly through helping them to become literate and, secondly, through offering them good schools so that the Christian poor, in particular, can better understand the Word of God and the reality of the Church and society, and become active lay people, with proper professional training; liberating the rich from their prejudices, for example through bringing rich and poor, Muslim and Christian, to live together in the university residences and guiding them through a process of growing together; promoting the work and the freedom of women, with both prudence and audacity in the context of the surrounding culture, in a way that can be accepted by Muslims too, meaning in particular that work and freedom are compatible with the roles of wife and mother and so can be seen as true forms of development; helping the Muslim and Christian children in the schools to grow together day by day; proposing the Montessori method of education, which is suitable for very poor families but is also considered prestigious by many Muslims. In these, and other, simple and efficacious ways, the Missionaries of the Schools aim to carry out their daily mission and to promote greater justice and peace in Pakistani society.

13

Strengthening the Voice of Women in Iraq

MARIE THERESE HANNA, O.P.

Since their founding as a lay community in 1877 up until the present day, the Dominican Sisters of St Catherine of Siena of Mosul, Iraq, have served the people of Iraq, particularly women and girls, under the daunting challenges of war, poverty, violence and chaos. For the people of Iraq, the twentieth century both began and ended with the intense suffering of war and poverty.

At the start of the century, when the First World War broke out, genocidal massacres of Christians in the lands of the then Ottoman Empire made martyrs of untold thousands of Christians, including several of the early Dominican sisters. After the war, when the Allies partitioned the vanquished empire, establishing the modern state of Iraq under British rule, years of Arab revolt against the colonial power and Kurdish independence movements ensued. Eventually, Iraq won its independence, and successive governments, several overthrown by coups, assumed power. The politically turbulent century ended with an eight-year war against Iran, the Gulf War, and a severe decade-long economic embargo, which ended in 2003 with the US-led invasion and occupation of Iraq. The ongoing violence and chaos continues to take its toll on the Iraqi people, and the Christian minority again finds itself persecuted.

This brief overview of the last century to the present day hints at the highly complex geopolitical, religious and socio-cultural context in which the Dominican sisters have been labouring since their foundation in a predominantly Muslim region of the world. To appreciate the role of the sisters in strengthening the voice of women in Iraq during the twentieth century, it is important to understand this complex reality, as well as the long and rich history that is their legacy.

ROOTED IN ANTIQUITY

The St Catherine Dominican Sisters emerged out of a native community of Christians whose presence in Mesopotamia (the ancient name of Iraq) dates back to the early days of Christianity. Iraq's Christians are among the world's few remaining speakers of Aramaic, the language of Jesus. Similarly, the sisters' Dominican roots in the region stretch back to the beginnings of the Order of Preachers.

Dominic Guzman, the founder of the Order, had actually dreamed of opening a mission in Baghdad, then a brilliant centre of culture and study and the capital of the Islamic Empire. Five years after Dominic's death in 1221, a friend and contemporary of his set out with two other Arabic-speaking friars on a mission to the Holy Lands, travelling on to Baghdad in 1235. For the next 20 years, the Dominican friars served a small community of Christians. Eager to better understand the Muslim world, they engaged in studies at the newly established University of Baghdad, which is still operating today. The Dominicans remained until 1256 when they returned to Italy just two years before the city was ravaged by invading Mongols. Towards the end of that century, another Dominican missionary travelled to Mesopotamia, spending two years in Baghdad. In his chronicles, the friar records passing through Mosul on his way back to Italy in 1298.

It would be another 450 years before Dominicans returned to Mesopotamia, which by then was part of the Ottoman Empire. In 1750, Pope Benedict XIV sent a group of Italian Dominican friars to Mosul. Their papal mandate was to bring Catholicism to the Christian communities in the Ottoman lands and to strengthen the relationship between the Eastern churches and Rome. The Italian friars remained for a century and were replaced in 1853 by French Dominican friars who began to establish educational projects in Mesopotamia. Within 20 years, the friars decided to seek the help of their sisters in France, asking the Dominican Sisters of the Presentation of Tours to join them, so that girls might also be educated.

The sisters arrived in Mosul in 1873 and soon began to recruit local young Christian women of good character to help them as teaching assistants. The French sisters recognised the need to have native women who understood the language and culture to join them in the educational mission. It is from among these recruits that the indigenous lay Dominican community was born. Empowering women and girls with education was thus the foundational mission of the lay community that would become the Dominican Sisters of St Catherine of Siena of Mosul.

Among the earliest native women to serve as a teaching assistant was a young widow named Sausan (Susan) Semheiry. At the age of 30 she had lost her husband and all ten of her children to a ravaging infectious disease. In the wake of her great loss, Sausan asked the sisters if she might stay with them for several weeks to grieve and pray, seeking the consolation that only

God could provide. During her time in the convent, Sausan found comfort in the life with the sisters, and a desire to consecrate her life to God began to grow in her. As she spoke with other young women involved in the teaching mission of the sisters, she found that she was not alone in her yearning to live a religious life in community.

In 1877, in response to these expressed yearnings, the prior of the Dominican mission in Mesopotamia extended an invitation to these young women to join in creating a community of lay Dominicans in Mosul. Although no one had this in mind at the time, the establishment of this lay community was the first step leading to the foundation there of the Dominican Sisters of St Catherine of Siena and hence, 1877 has since been honoured as the founding year of the congregation. Formed under the guidance and administration of the Dominican friars in Mosul, the new community of young tertiaries pronounced private vows to their Dominican spiritual directors and engaged in ministry with the Presentation sisters as teaching assistants. Wearing the black clothing common to widows at the time, the lay Dominican women were known and referred to as 'Catherinettes', in honour of St Catherine of Siena, the most renowned tertiary in Dominican history.

Among those who joined the community of tertiaries were two other women named Susan – Sausan Kaka in 1890 and Sausan Jiji Mekhael in 1894. By 1900, each of the three Susans would be sent from Mosul to found a new convent and serve as teaching assistants in areas where the Dominican friars or Presentation sisters had missions. For this reason, the Susans, *Sausanat* in plural, are considered the founders of the Dominican Sisters of St Catherine of Siena. Only one of the Sausanat, Sausan Jiji Mekhael, would live to receive the white habit of the sisters of St Dominic in 1929, and then make profession as a member of the native Iraqi congregation.

The three founding Sausanat embodied qualities as women of faith that would become essential characteristics for the Dominican Sisters of St Catherine to witness to in their own lives, as they confronted the enormous challenges that lay ahead in the twentieth century. To help strengthen the voice of women in Iraq, the sisters first had to claim the power of their own voices.

IN SAUSAN KAKA, THE COMMUNITY GAVE WITNESS
TO THE POWER OF WOMEN'S COURAGEOUS LEADERSHIP
Sausan was serving as the prioress of the lay community's convent in Siirt, Turkey, where six Catherinettes taught more than 200 schoolgirls, when the First World War erupted. Almost immediately, the French Dominican friars

and Presentation sisters were sent to Syria to be deported back to France. The friars' house in Siirt was turned into a mosque and the sisters' house became an armoury. Left on their own, under Sausan Kaka's leadership, the Catherinettes began to endure the harassment of weekly police investigations. They had eight schoolgirls boarding with them. As the weekly interrogations continued into 1915, the Catherinettes began to grow more fearful; word of massacres in neighbouring Armenia was emerging.

The growing tensions exploded on the afternoon of 8 June 1915, when the Catherinettes heard sounds of gunshots, bombs and people screaming and crying in the streets. Running up to the convent roof to see what was going on, a chilling sight met their eyes. Right in front of their house, Christians fleeing for their lives were being gunned down and killed by angry soldiers, while others on horseback were galloping towards them. Running back downstairs, Sausan Kaka asked her sister Catherinettes to stay in the convent with the eight girls and not to leave. Sausan went out into the courtyard and bravely approached the gate, but before she got there, it was flung open and the guard was killed immediately. As soon as the soldiers saw the 60-year-old prioress, they grabbed her and began to beat her until she fell to the ground. Tearing off her rosary and ripping away her deep pocket, the soldiers took all the money she had and then stormed into the house. Sausan Kaka remained on the ground, lying still. Huddled inside, the Catherinettes and the schoolgirls watched the soldiers pillage the house, leaving neither furniture nor food behind. They even forced the girls to give up their shoes before they finally left.

As soon as the soldiers and horsemen galloped away, women and children from the town began to pour into the Catherinettes' courtyard, seeking protection and consolation from Sausan Kaka and the sisters. Chaldean, Orthodox and Armenian Christian women arrived, wailing over their lost husbands and sons. Earlier that day, the soldiers had murdered the town's bishops and priests and other Christians in high positions. Then they led away all the Christian men and boys over the age of 12, telling them they would return home. Instead, they slaughtered them outside the city.

The next morning, soldiers circled the Catherinettes' convent where, by now, several hundred Christian women and children had sought shelter under Sausan Kaka's leadership. The soldiers acted as if they were there to protect the townswomen and children; instead, they spent days humiliating, offending and mocking those inside. Some went even further in their savagery: many of the young women were raped. After 15 days of this siege, the

[233]

Turkish governor of the city ordered all the Armenian, Chaldean, Orthodox and other Christian women and children to Mosul.

On the morning of 29 June 1915, the governor's command was carried out with the shouted order: 'Move quickly! Take no possessions with you. Follow us!' By then, Sausan Kaka and the Catherinettes had more than 600 women and countless children under their wing. In the heat of the summer sun, with temperatures rising over 100°F/38°C, the women and children began the slow march to Mosul in a long human caravan. Trudging over rough roads through the mountains and valleys, the women endured extreme hardships during the day. At night, they were unable to sleep, on constant watch for soldiers who were looking for women to rape. To protect themselves, the Catherinettes agreed that each would walk with her own family so as not to appear to be religious. Sausan Kaka and another Catherinette from Mosul walked with the eight boarders, the youngest of whom was 14.

On the second day of the journey, emotionally and physically unable to continue, Sausan Kaka collapsed. The soldiers tore off her clothes until, naked, she fell on her knees praying. The soldiers shot the brave prioress dead, but her soul rose to eternal life that day.

IN SAUSAN JIJI MEKHAEL, THE COMMUNITY GAVE WITNESS
TO THE POWER OF WOMEN'S PERSEVERANCE AND FAITH

Sausan was 18 years old when she met the Dominican Presentation Sisters in 1879, during a visit to Mardin, some 80 miles south-west of her home town of Siirt, Turkey. It was then that she decided to become a sister. When she returned to Siirt, Sausan refused to marry, waiting patiently and confidently until the right time came for her to enter religious life. She waited almost 15 years! Some time in the early 1890s, realising there were Dominican Presentation Sisters in Mosul, Sausan asked to accompany her married sister to Mosul without revealing the real purpose for making the journey. After arriving in Mosul, Sausan met the Dominican friar who was then guiding the Catherinettes. With his assistance, she was accepted as a member in 1895. Years later, on 21 August 1929, after the lay community obtained canonical recognition as a religious institute, Sausan Jiji Mekhael – now Sr Diana – made her first profession of religious vows, publicly consecrating her life to God. She was 68 years old. Fifty years had elapsed since Sausan Jiji Mekhael, at the age of 18, had first met the Dominican Presentation Sisters and decided she wanted to make this consecration of her life.

IN SAUSAN SEMHEIRY, THE COMMUNITY GAVE WITNESS
TO THE POWER OF WOMEN'S CAPACITY TO BRING NEW LIFE
TO BIRTH OUT OF DEATH AND DESPAIR

The death of a child is so crushing a loss some mothers never recover. Sausan suffered the loss of not one but ten children, and then bore it alone when the ravaging disease that stole her children also robbed her of her husband. It is impossible to imagine the depths of Sausan's grief and despair. Yet, some-how, in the midst of that unutterable suffering, Sausan Semheiry found new life. Not only for herself but also for hundreds who would follow, consecrat-ing their lives to God and in service to all God's people in the lay community of Catherinettes that would become the Dominican Sisters of St Catherine of Siena of Mosul, Iraq.

The power of women witnessed to by the founding Sausanat became a legacy to which their successors have been called to witness in themselves over the past century – in courageous leadership, perseverance and faith, and in bringing new life to birth out of death and despair – as they served the people of Iraq in the midst of terror, poverty and war.

HONOUR AND RESPECT

The first ministerial work of the St Catherine Dominican sisters, as noted, involved empowering girls and young women through education. By 1913, within 36 years of their founding, the young community of Catherinettes had significantly expanded their mission and presence beyond Mosul. They had opened houses and schools for girls in a number of Christian villages in the Nineveh Plain surrounding Mosul, including Qaraqosh (1893), Telkeif (1900), Alqosh (1902), Tell Isqof (1907), Baqofa (1907) and Batnaya (1907). They also had missions in Jazeerat Ibn Omar (1891), Siirt (1895) and Ashita (1913) in modern-day Turkey, as well as in Faysh Khabur (1909), a town on Iraq's northern border with Syria and Turkey.

In addition to teaching schoolgirls in rural areas where there were few educational opportunities, the Catherinettes also reached out to the girls' mothers and other women. They met with women after Mass on Sundays when they had a few hours free from household chores and caring for the needs of their families. At these Sunday schools, the Catherinettes taught the women prayers, church music and how to sing the Psalms in Aramaic. They offered catechetical instruction and faith sharing, speaking of the Gospel, especially as it applied to daily life, and offering practical advice on how to raise their children. In addition, the Catherinettes opened their convents to women and girls, most of whom, but not all, were Christian. They gave lessons in sewing and needlepoint and how to manage a household responsibly, encouraging them also to learn more about their cultural heritage.

Fundamental to the approach the Catherinettes took in their work with women was that it was based on honour and respect. They always began by treating the women with honour and respect.

By the time the First World War was over, the lay Dominican community was reduced by nearly a half, from 59 to 34 Catherinettes. Five had been martyred during the death march out of Siirt that had claimed the life of Sausan Kaka; two others were martyred in genocidal attacks against Christians in Jazeerat. A number of others were killed or died during the war and some decided to remain with their devastated families.

In the midst of economic deprivation and the continuing political turmoil after the war, the Catherinettes persevered in their mission of teaching girls and in outreach to women. The blessings they received through the prayers and bloodshed of their seven martyred sisters helped them keep faith through the hardships of the war's aftermath. It also helped them to persevere in seeking canonical recognition as a native congregation of Dominican sisters.

When this cherished dream was finally realised in April 1928, more than 50 years after their establishment as a tertiary community, the Catherinettes achieved a significant breakthrough in strengthening the voice of Iraqi women in the Church, as well as in society as a whole. In the establishment of the Congregation of Dominican Sisters of St Catherine of Siena, not only were native Iraqi women able to take their rightful place among Catholic women religious worldwide, but the churches of the East and West were also brought together under one roof. Native Christian women, representing nearly half a dozen Eastern rites, joined to establish a Roman religious institute, within the global Order of Dominicans – a congregation that honours and celebrates the diverse rites, liturgical languages and traditions of its women.

In the years between the two world wars, the St Catherine sisters expanded their outreach to women in Kurdish areas, including the remote village of Mar Yaqob in the Kurdish region of Dohuk and the town of Qamishli in northeastern Syria, largely inhabited by Kurds and Syriac Catholics. They also reached out to women in Sinjar and Bashiqa, villages settled by Yazidis, members of an ethnic minority in northern Iraq who speak their own language and practise a unique religion, a people known for their kindness.

During these years, many of the girls attending the sisters' schools wished to consecrate their lives to God and become St Catherine Dominicans, but the congregation could not accept as many as wished to enter, for lack of financial resources. The sisters received no pay for their work in the schools or churches, or with the families they served, because most were in dire need themselves. The sisters got their food each day by begging for it from the people in the villages.

Nonetheless, the simplicity of life and the spirituality of poverty that the sisters lived had an impact on the people they worked with, helping to advance their mission, particularly in service to women and girls. Despite the economic hardships, the sisters continued to encourage young girls to come to their schools to learn and to educate themselves. Priests could not address the spiritual and intellectual needs of young girls, as was evident in villages where the sisters were not yet present. Once when a priest brought the daughter of a very good family to enter the community, they found that her religious education consisted of being able to recite the Our Father and half of the Hail Mary. Without faith formation and religious education in the villages, the women would never be able to assume leadership roles in the Church.

Increasingly, public schools were leaning towards secularisation, as was happening in neighbouring Turkey. This was a challenge to the Christian minority, especially in places beyond the Christian villages. Thus, in addition to feeling called to establish schools in villages where education was not available, the sisters also felt a need to increase the number of convents and faith activities in villages where there were schools, in order to help young girls and their families preserve and nourish their faith. But resources were thin, and soon another ravaging war would begin.

THE SECOND WORLD WAR

Although Iraq initially attempted to stay out of the Second World War, it was forced into the conflict by Britain, joining the Allies. During the war, the Iraqi people suffered many psychological and material hardships, including shortages of all the basic necessities of life. Because of malnutrition and bad living conditions during this time, many Dominican Sisters of St Catherine caught TB. Very few recovered and some died young, while still in their twenties.

Impoverished and lacking food, the community's leadership struggled to find ways to deal with the harsh material shortages and adversities faced by the congregation during the war years. Finally, as a way to address the enormous financial and emotional pressures bearing on the them, they made the painful and difficult decision to send all novices and temporarily professed sisters back home to their families. Some courageous sisters, however, opposed the leadership's decision. Determined at all costs to keep the congregation whole, they offered themselves in new ways of service. The sisters spoke of their readiness to work as housekeepers for wealthy families and to return to begging for food in order to make it possible for the women in formation to remain in the community. They also offered to find creative ways of putting their artistic talents to work for the good of the congregation. Gratified by this generous response, the leadership agreed to the ideas and the sisters began to implement them, working diligently on their sewing and embroidery, among other things. Through these efforts, the collective voice of the sisters within the community was strengthened and heard in a new way.

When the Second World War was over, the local churches in Iraq, as well as the Dominican Sisters of St Catherine and other religious, felt empowered by the spirit of the Gospel. Their apostolic activities began to flourish. With this fresh spirit and income from their new creative endeavours, the sisters were able to renew their efforts in Mosul and all the surrounding villages. Their numbers increased, nearing 70 members by 1952 when they outgrew their original home in Mosul and moved to a larger motherhouse in the Al-Jadida (New Mosul) neighbourhood.

It was at around this time that the congregation began to recognise the importance of obtaining higher education for its sisters, so that they would have the tools and training they needed to play stronger leadership roles in the country. Young sisters began to attend the newly founded Kuliat Al-Mosul (Mosul College), a high school established by the Dominican friars in 1944 to educate boys. The sisters were the only female students attending the Dominican high school. Sisters also began to be sent to public high schools for their secondary education. Prior to this, they studied in the convent, joining other students only when taking the state-sponsored final exams.

In 1957, for the first time, the Sisters of St Catherine sent some of their women to begin a mission in the nation's capital. Soon afterwards, in 1960, the congregation sent two young sisters to begin studies as secondary school teachers at the University of Baghdad, also a first.

In 1964, the congregation opened two schools of its own in Baghdad for children of all faith traditions. St Dominic was the name given to the co-ed elementary school. The other, St Thomas School for Girls, was a high school open to girls from all religious traditions and its first students included a number of Jewish girls. St Thomas School became known as one of the best schools in Baghdad, or even Iraq. The congregation also opened a boarding house in the Zaafaraniya neighbourhood of south Baghdad. The residence provided a home to female students of all faiths who attended the Jesuit Al-Hikma (Wisdom) University. The sisters' desire to serve the diverse peoples that comprise Baghdad's multicultural society found expression in a number of different foundations and ministries. The congregation borrowed money to build new schools and convents. Now compensated for their work in the schools, the sisters were able to pay back those loans as they generated income.

The congregation's new focus on obtaining higher education for their young sisters was complemented by a new spirit emerging in the Church in the 1960s. As Vatican II unfolded, the sisters engaged in rigorous study of the new Church documents as they were produced. The congregation began to develop a new vision of ongoing formation and openness to the world. The sisters looked to the signs of the times, the importance of study, and how to respond in new ways in mission to the needs of the world.

During this time, the congregation enjoyed an increase in the number of vocations. These young sisters were now being prepared not only to teach but also to work in the fields of health care and pastoral care and in a variety of administrative positions. Beginning in 1964, the congregation also took the initiative of sending several sisters to Europe to earn advanced degrees in theology, spirituality and other disciplines. The higher education they obtained in Europe, as well as in Iraq, would enable them to be present as women religious in a wider range of ministries.

The revolutionary fervour that gripped other parts of the world in the late 1960s, inciting in young people a desire for greater freedom, including liberation from religious traditions, also impacted Iraq. In the wake of the prolonged nationwide strike and student protests in France, 25 young sisters left the congregation between 1968 and 1970. The congregation's close ties to the French Dominicans made them acutely aware of this watershed event in promoting liberal secular social thought. The loss of so many young sisters created a large gap in the ages of the women in the community for a time.

Nonetheless, in the spirit and global vision of Vatican II, the congregation persevered and even began to look beyond Iraq's borders in its ministerial outreach. During this time, in response to mission requests, the congregation sent sisters to Bethlehem, Beirut, Cairo, Rome, Paris and Algiers to engage in ministry.

A NEW ROLE IN SECULAR IRAQ

In the 1970s, actions taken by the new government in Iraq had a significant impact on the mission of the sisters. In July 1974, the government nationalised all of the private schools. The action did not diminish the enthusiasm or the loyalty of the Dominican sisters. They remained as principals and teachers in the schools, working within the national framework, which focused on increasing literacy among Iraq's people. The sisters seized the opportunity presented by this literacy campaign to promote women's abilities and help women become more aware of their rights within the family as well as society. The change to nationalisation actually provided the sisters with new ways of being present to Iraq's secular society and, as women religious, to work in a more public way for the common good of the country. The sisters became more integrated with various sectors of society, gaining a greater awareness and understanding of the world in which they lived. Above all, they strengthened their presence in the professional fields of education and health care during this period.

In 1975, the congregation established a House of Prayer in Mosul in the sisters' original Al-Saah (The Clock) motherhouse, home of the Catherinettes dating back to 1913. For many, this location symbolised the sisters' return to their early roots in Mosul. At the House of Prayer, Mosul's Christians could join the sisters in their daily life of Dominican prayer and contemplation. It also offered opportunities for lay people, especially those working with the young, to experience day-long retreats. Those served were able to take these fresh, new experiences of prayer back to their parishes. Sisters in ministry at the House of Prayer also reached out directly to young people, especially young women, offering them a spiritual environment in which to pray and contemplate.

A house of prayer of a different kind was created in 1977, when the congregation rented a house in the Al-Jadida neighbourhood of Baghdad (New Baghdad), a highly populated Muslim area. Four sisters asked to be sent to Baghdad to live in a neighbourhood among the people with whom they were ministering. Although the Dominican Sisters of St Catherine had always invited non-Christians to attend their schools and participate in their outreach activities, this was the first time the congregation intentionally established a mission in a community that was not predominantly Christian. The sisters tried to make their house, St Catherine Convent, a peaceful, prayerful place for all who came to visit. For various reasons, including ones related to the Iran-Iraq war, the congregation had to close this convent in 1981. But the four sisters had a profound experience of witnessing to their faith and service in mission, while sharing in the simple daily life and difficulties of the people of Iraq, and most especially, of the women.

YEARS OF WAR

Whatever the political goals, the Iran-Iraq war had a devastating impact on ordinary people, especially the young and innocent. Although the war was fought on the borders of the country, many cities, residential areas and schools were destroyed. At the end of the war, the financial resources of both countries diminished significantly. The toll on human life was incalculable: no family in Iraq or Iran was spared the grief of losing a loved one, causing many tears and broken hearts. Even today, families and communities in Iraq that lost fathers, brothers and friends suffer the deep wounds this war created.

During the war, the Dominican sisters focused their mission on being a loving presence in solidarity with the Iraqi people, visiting and listening to them. The sisters opened the doors of their convents in Baghdad and Mosul to offer shelter to Christian and Muslim neighbours and anyone else who had no safe place to stay. They prayed and ate with the people, providing them with health care as needed. Treated with respect and care, the people grew closer to the sisters. The bonds between sisters and Iraqi families, as well as those between and among the multi-faith families themselves, became stronger. Iraq was like one family at this time.

Of course, the sisters also felt the cruel impact of the war in their personal lives and the lives of their families. The keen desire they felt to return to routine observances of their religious life after the war was thwarted, and has continued to be thwarted by years of subsequent war and strife. When the Iran-Iraq war ended, the Dominican sisters focused on healing and reconciliation, work that continues to this day.

In the mid to late 1980s, the congregation once again went to serve the people in the Kurdish regions. In 1986, the sisters opened a convent in Ankawa, just north of Erbil, teaching in the schools and providing pastoral services. Three years later, in 1989, the congregation opened the Mar Yaqob Convent in the city of Dohuk. Several sisters studied nursing in order to be able to offer health services to the Kurds and other people of Dohuk. The sisters also visited families and invited neighbours to join them in prayer. Today, the sisters in Dohuk teach in their own preschool and work in the public hospitals, serving primarily Muslim women, men and children.

Many reasons – historic, economic and hegemonic – are cited for Iraq's invasion of Kuwait on 2 August 1990. In the months leading up to the invasion, at an Arab nations' summit, President Saddam Hussein spoke against the increase in oil production that some Arab states had initiated, likening it to an economic war against Iraq. The production increase meant lower oil prices and, therefore, significant revenue losses for a nation massively in debt after eight years of war. In mid-July, Saddam publicly accused Kuwait of declaring economic warfare on Iraq and soon after began amassing troops at the border. On 2 August, Saddam invaded Kuwait, and four days later the UN, under US leadership, declared economic sanctions against Iraq.

The embargo immediately affected the country's economy, having a severe impact at all levels of society. Iraq became a recluse, shut off from the world. Ensuing UN negotiations with Iraq to withdraw its military forces from Kuwait were unsuccessful. In response, the US, along with 33 allies, launched a war against Iraq. On the night of 16 January 1991, US and allied military forces bombed Iraq's largest cities – Baghdad, Basra and Mosul.

Although what has come to be called the First Gulf War lasted only 42 days, it made the lives of ordinary Iraqis extremely difficult. The people, as well as the sisters, suffered immensely. Everyone lost electricity and water, as well as food. The sisters had to leave their convents in the large cities. Entire families were forced to evacuate their homes in Baghdad, Basra and Mosul and travel north to the safety of the Christian villages of Qaraqosh, Telkeif, Tell Isqof, Alqosh, Bartalah and Ankawa, among others. In each of these villages where the congregation had convents, the sisters, with the help of local priests and young people, played a major role in helping to provide many displaced families with daily necessities.

The war ended on 1 May 1991, but the embargo continued for another 12 years. Economic and social conditions worsened throughout Iraq, resulting in life-threatening shortages of medicine, food and other necessities.

SEVERE SANCTIONS

The Iraqi people endured tremendous hardships during the economic embargo, lacking basic necessities of life, such as food and medicine, as well as adequate means of communication. The sisters shared in all the difficulties. The congregation depended on two resources to meet their daily needs: the minimal salary the sisters received for their work and the food rations supplied by the Iraqi government. The rations, provided according to family size, were for flour, rice, oil, tea, sugar, green vegetables and dry milk. Sometimes the food was of poor quality but the people had no other choice. They had to have a ration card from the government to obtain even these items. Meat was very expensive and could be purchased only by families that had money. Many people, including the sisters, could not afford it. In addition, the value of Iraq's currency had plummeted. In 1980, one Iraqi dinar was equal to three US dollars; now 3,000 Iraqi dinar equalled one US dollar.

When the First Gulf War ended in May 1991, international relief organisations and religious congregations began coming to Iraq. Among them was Catholic Relief Services (CRS), which, in consultation with the Dominican sisters and others, determined where best to serve Iraqi families in need. The sisters volunteered to help CRS with the project, responding to the immediate needs of families in Baghdad, Mosul and the northern villages. Religious, priests and laity also helped, assisting and sharing resources with the very needy.

During those dire years, the congregation reached out, seeking help from many international non-profit organisations, churches and religious institutes, especially within the Dominican family. Thanks to the support that was provided, the sisters were able to enhance and expand their efforts significantly during these years of great suffering and isolation for Iraqis. They also were able to establish new relationships and forge deep friendships in mission with sisters from many other congregations around the world, helping to overcome their sense of isolation.

Striving to respond to the desperate, wide-ranging needs of the Iraqi people during the embargo, the Dominican sisters made strategic decisions about how to focus their efforts, centring their attention primarily on women and girls. The sisters decided to serve as witnesses of hope, to help young mothers and their babies, to offer women income-generating skills, to care for the most vulnerable young and to provide shelter for girls in need.

Witnessing to hope: At this time most workers in Iraq, especially women, were leaving their jobs because the government did not pay them a living wage. Their monthly salaries amounted to the equivalent of two or three dollars, which only covered a day's expenses. The sisters chose to remain in their ministries, working as teachers and state employees, in order to encourage their colleagues to do the same, witnessing to hope for a better future and motivating Iraq's young women and men to continue in their studies.

Offering maternity health care: The dangerous lack of health care and medicine caused by the sanctions prompted the sisters, in 1992, to convert one of their convents in Bagdad into a small maternity hospital. Sisters educated in nursing ministered in the hospital, alongside local doctors hired by the congregation, while other sisters helped run the hospital. Serving all women regardless of ethnicity or religious tradition, the small Al-Hayat (Life) Hospital opened with 12 bedrooms, later expanding to 22. By attending to the medical needs of mothers and babies, the congregation helped bring the joy of new life to the people during these harsh times. In 1995, the congregation opened the Al-Hayat Convent for sisters working in the hospital, making it easier for them to respond to emergencies. Since then, a new wing has been added to the hospital in response to growing needs. In the six years up to 2010, as many as 4,500 babies were delivered at Al-Hayat.

Creating small business centres for women: With the severe financial shortages, the sisters sought ways of helping families increase their incomes. Opening more than ten small business centres in their convents, the sisters offered free workshops to teach unemployed girls and women how to sew, do needlework and make flower arrangements. Some of the women sold their handmade articles at the sisters' centres, while others started their own small businesses or used their new skills to meet their own family needs. More than 3,000 women learned a craft at these centres.

Caring for small children: Since 1974, when the government nationalised all the Catholic schools, including those founded by the Dominicans, the sisters had stopped opening new schools, serving instead as teachers and principals in the nationalised institutions. In an effort to address the needs of very young, vulnerable children who were suffering from fear and terrible memories of war, the sisters opened pre-schools in the Christian villages and in Baghdad for children between the ages of three and six. The religious education focused on teaching the children Christian principles fostering peace. The kindergartens also provided the children with care equal to what other children in the world were receiving.

Housing girls in need: The congregation opened the doors of two of its convents, one in Baghdad and the other in Qaraqosh, to serve as orphanages. The sisters welcomed girls aged four to 18 who had lost parents or whose families were experiencing such hardship they could not care for them. Providing for their daily needs, the sisters ensured that the girls could remain in school, furthering their education through this difficult period, in the hope of a better future. These convents are still operating as orphanages today.

SOLIDARITY IN THE SISTERHOOD

Two days after the First Gulf War ended, leaving destruction at all levels of life in its wake, a mid-sized car stopped in front of one of the sisters' convents in Baghdad. It was full of food and other vital necessities, sent by the Franciscan Missionaries of the Divine Motherhood. The help that the Franciscan Missionaries offered immediately after the war continued during the next most difficult years of the embargo, given with love and respect, and deepening the friendship between the two communities.

During those early harsh years of the embargo, sisters from four congregations in Lebanon – Sisters of the Sacred Hearts of Jesus and Mary, the Antonine Sisters, Sisters of the Good Shepherd, and Sisters of St Thérèse the Little Flower – came to lend their support to the Iraqi Dominicans. Given the very difficult situations that these Lebanese sisters had faced during the previous 15 years of civil war in their country, their visits were a generous and vital witness to their sense of solidarity with the Iraqi sisters. The sisters from Lebanon spent time with the Iraqi Dominicans, exchanging spiritual, pastoral and apostolic experiences. Offering material as well as moral support, the Lebanese sisters gave talks to young women in formation, visited the congregation's ministries in the villages and supported the children in the sisters' kindergartens, as well as the students in elementary schools.

During this very difficult period, and despite all the expense involved, the congregation continued to send sisters out of the country to update their education and skills and to refresh their energy, relying on the generous help offered by other women religious in Europe, North Africa and the Middle East. Sisters also continued their higher education studies in Iraq, preparing themselves for teaching and other professional ministries. The congregation's continued focus on the sisters' education, a gift that would be put to the service of God's people, was a concrete sign during the difficult embargo years of their commitment to help build a better future in Iraq – and of the important role that women had to play in the country's recovery.

A key example of this was the congregation's opening of a house of studies for its student-sisters on the south side of Baghdad in 1999. It was located near Babel University, a school of theology and philosophy founded by the Chaldean Church and attended primarily by Chaldean seminarians, along with seminarians from other rites and a few lay people. It was a challenge for the young sisters to study in this nearly all-male environment, but they persevered, giving witness to their Dominican spirituality, love of seeking the truth through rigorous study, and intellectual equality as women. In fact, one among the several sisters who completed their degrees at Babel University graduated with the most outstanding academic record of the entire graduating class.

In the mid- to late 1990s, the oil-for-food programme was initiated, loosening the vice-like grip that the economic sanctions had had on the lives of the Iraqi people. With life slowly beginning to flow again, the congregation was able to seize further opportunities to serve the needs of the people and the Church in Iraq – and even begin to respond elsewhere.

At the end of the decade, in 1999, the Master of the Dominican Order, Timothy Radcliffe, arranged for the transfer of the San Domenico Convent in Pisa, Italy, to the Dominican Sisters of St Catherine. A year earlier, Friar Timothy had made a visitation of all the Dominicans in Iraq, gaining firsthand knowledge of their plight. The large convent in Pisa offered the Iraqi sisters the opportunity to establish an income-generating mission that could help them financially. The sisters began a mission of hospitality, hosting families whose loved ones were seeking medical treatment at the renowned University of Pisa Hospital. A separate wing would house female students enrolled in Pisa's universities. The convent also welcomed a number of Iraqi student-sisters, who helped in the mission while learning Italian prior to starting their formal studies elsewhere in Italy.

Committed to maintaining their global outlook and outreach to all people in need, the sisters responded to several new requests for missions abroad that came in the late 1990s. One of these involved joining Dominican friars in running a research library in Istanbul, Turkey, where they hoped to engage university students and scholars in interfaith dialogue aimed at building relationships across religions. For the friars, the three Iraqi Dominican sisters missioned there were a powerful presence, representing the seven Catherinettes who were martyred in Turkey during the First World War.

In 2001, the congregation was able to open a spiritual and cultural centre near Mosul University that it had tried to establish nearly a decade earlier. The Al-Kaleema (The Word) Centre was built on land owned by the Dominican friars. In addition to offering male and female students a place to gather for prayer and reflection, the Al-Kaleema Centre featured a library and a computer lab where students could work on their studies and do research.

GLOBAL DOMINICAN SISTERHOOD: 'I HAVE FAMILY IN IRAQ'
This period also marked the beginning of an important new relationship among Dominican sisters around the world; through it, many congregations

of Dominican women rose up to stand in solidarity with their Iraqi sisters.

In May 1995, a growing global solidarity among Dominican sisters quickened into an organisation. At a meeting in Rome, 80 Dominican prioresses general voted to establish the Dominican Sisters International (DSI). The aims of this blossoming new movement were to encourage Dominican sisters around the world to become more connected with one another, to help congregations that were isolated and in need, and to build common missions among two or more congregations.[1]

This international movement among apostolic Dominican sisters was a grace for the Sisters of St Catherine because it provided a key way for them to step out of the isolation caused by the embargo. Many Dominican congregations subsequently engaged with their Dominican sisters in Iraq in various ways, offering financial help, opening their doors to Iraqi sisters who were engaged in study and inviting them to participate in ministry. As noted, the leadership of the Dominican Sisters of St Catherine had been very aware for some time of the importance of having sisters earn higher academic degrees, enabling them to take leadership roles in the missions of the congregation and Church, as well as in public professional fields. Because of the support and new relationships being built among Dominican sisters through DSI, the congregation was better able to balance the reality of its challenging economic situation and isolation with what the leadership felt was essential preparation of its women for the future.

In the spirit of DSI's call to build common missions among congregations, in 2000, the Roman Congregation of St Dominic invited the St Catherine Dominicans to send sisters to live and work with them at their mission in Stockholm, Sweden. Iraqi sisters continue to serve there today, offering pastoral care in the parish and working with the community of Iraqi refugees in Sweden.

For the Iraqi sisters, another powerful witness to this new movement among Dominican women was a series of visits to Iraq made by delegations of (mostly) Dominican sisters from the US, the country bearing primary responsibility for the economic sanctions. In April 1999, the first of three 'Voices for Veritas' delegations of Dominicans, mostly from the US, went to Iraq to witness the pain and suffering caused by the US-led economic sanctions, to protest the embargo, and to show their solidarity with their Dominican sisters and brothers and the Iraqi people. The visit, in and of itself, was an

1. See Chapter 4, 'The Contribution of Dominican Sisters International to the Development of the Dominican Family', pp. 76-84.

act of civil disobedience with the possibility of serious legal consequences for the participants.

The relationships forged among the women through these visits helped open the hearts and minds of Dominicans around the world to the plight of their Dominican sisters and brothers in Iraq. In October 2002, at a meeting of the Dominican Leadership Conference, the leaders of US Dominican institutes agonised over how to respond to the Bush administration's threat of war against Iraq. Struggling over how best to express their relationship with their Iraqi Dominican sisters and brothers – and all the people of Iraq – the group came up with the phrase, 'I have family in Iraq'. Badges and banners bearing the slogan were created and distributed globally. Dominicans everywhere began to wear the badges as a sign of their concern for, and solidarity with, the people of Iraq.

Also through the Dominican solidarity movement, the St Catherine congregation was able to participate in DSI-sponsored programmess for Dominican formation directors from around the world, including one held in the Philippines in 2000. The Dominican family was holding its jubilee year celebration there at the same time, and one of the St Catherine sisters had an opportunity to speak about their mission in Iraq and the very harsh conditions suffered by the Iraqi people under the economic embargo.

Two years later, at the World Social Forum in Brazil, 45 Dominicans were among the more than 12,000 participants, mostly young people, who were present to hear the same Iraqi sister speak. Her words, giving participants firsthand news as an eyewitness to the pain and suffering that the Iraqi people were undergoing, moved many to tears. On the last day of the forum, when Mass was celebrated, two Dominican sisters – one Iraqi and the other American – offered the sign of peace. It was a powerful sign of friendship and reconciliation in the one human family and in St Dominic and St Catherine.

US INVASION

On 19 March 2003, the Iraqi people woke to the sounds of bombs exploding. US planes had started their bombing campaign against the nation's largest cities. The war did not come as a surprise because the US had been threatening Iraq since the US invasion of Afghanistan. But bombs that were meant to hit Iraq's army and infrastructure caused enormous damage to homes and neighbourhoods, and the deaths of a vast number of Iraqi citizens.

During the subsequent years of warfare and insurgency, the violence, terror, destruction, kidnappings, murder, rape and deteriorating security made life increasingly unbearable for the Iraqi people. Tens of thousands ended up fleeing the cities and the country. The violence also forced the closure of a number of the sisters' missions and convents.

By 2005, conditions in Baghdad were too dangerous to continue sending young sisters to study at Babel University.

On 19 October 2006, two car bombs exploded close to the congregation's Al-Kaleema Cultural and Spiritual Centre in Mosul, shattering glass, breaking computers and destroying several doors and an iron gate. In a neighbourhood nearby, increased violence and danger forced the sisters to vacate the Al-Hadba Convent in Mosul in 2007.

For the same reasons, the congregation had to close the Our Lady of Peace Convent in northern Baghdad that year, and in mid-September, the sisters were also forced to evacuate the children in their Baghdad orphanage. With the help of the late Chaldean archbishop of Mosul, Paulos Faraj Rahho, the congregation relocated the orphanage to the northern village of Telkeif, placing the children in two houses purchased and given to the congregation by the archbishop. Only five months after blessing these two houses as a new orphanage, Archbishop Rahho was tragically killed. On 29 February 2008, after celebrating the rite of the Via Crucis at the Church of the Holy Spirit in Mosul, Archbishop Rahho was kidnapped. Gunmen sprayed his car with bullets, killing his driver and bodyguards. The bishop was taken away in the trunk of a car. Two weeks later, on 13 March, his body was found in a shallow grave near Mosul. The beloved archbishop was 65 years old. Less than a year earlier, a priest, Fr Rageed Kenny, and three sub-deacons were killed leaving the same church after Sunday Mass; they had been told to convert to Islam or be killed. Grief and fear gripped everyone.

For the congregation's leadership, no decision was harder than the one to vacate the motherhouse in Mosul, especially because of its impact on the young women in formation. Like so many other Iraqis who received threats and were forced to leave their homes during this terrifying time, the Dominican sisters also were displaced and dispersed. No one has been exempt from the painful migrations except, perhaps, a few older sisters. Despite continued bombings and threats, four sisters remain at the motherhouse to this day, with three young men serving as guards. These Iraqi Dominican sisters remain as a presence of God's love in the midst of the violence, and a witness to their faith and vocation; they are ready to die in service of this mission. The congregation has long since stopped replacing the motherhouse windows; it is pointless. Most of the windows and all but one entrance have been cemented shut with concrete blocks.

Escaping Mosul, unfortunately, has not meant escaping violence. It has found its way to the towns and villages that many people, including the sisters, had considered safe. In Tell Isqof, the sisters who run a kindergarten in a building next to their convent fell victim to the violence. In early 2007, terrorists forced the sisters out of their car, stealing it and their belongings. Soon after, in April 2007, a bomb intended for the Kurdish party headquarters in Tell Isqof, near the kindergarten, exploded. It killed two adults and injured three sisters and 30 children. In November, early in the morning before school started, another bomb exploded nearby, blowing a massive hole in the kindergarten. This time the kindergarten was damaged beyond repair. The congregation rented a house in order to continue the children's schooling.

In the neighbouring village of Telkeif, several explosions occurred. The most severe was on 15 June 2008, when a car bomb exploded next to the convent, injuring three sisters and causing major damage to the building.

Throughout this difficult time, the Dominican sisters, like most Iraqis, have continued to live in fear and anxiety in a precarious environment where peace, security and basic modern necessities, such as running water and electricity, are absent. Because of the increased assaults on Christian communities, large numbers of Christians have been forced to leave their homes and country. Among them are family and friends of the sisters, especially among those who had been living in Mosul and Kirkuk and certain areas of Baghdad. An estimated 1.4 million Christians lived in Iraq before the US invasion; today, approximately 500,000 remain.

Recognising that the situation in Iraq over the past decade has worsened, the congregation created a new plan for mission aimed at helping to rebuild Iraq through efforts that honour the dignity and humanity of its diverse people. The congregation envisioned providing spiritual, intellectual and humanitarian support to the people of Iraq, through educational and health care services. One of the first steps taken to implement the new plan involved sending young sisters to Europe and the US to update their education and help them develop themselves intellectually, spiritually and personally for the great challenges that lie ahead.

Two Dominican congregations in the US – Springfield (Illinois) Dominicans and Adrian (Michigan) Dominicans – have taken in young St Catherine sisters as their own while they have pursued advanced degrees in education, theology, peace studies, medicine and psychology. Similarly, through the Union of Dominican Major Superiors of Italy and Malta, six congregations of Dominicans in Italy have offered hospitality to young sister-students. Other congregations, like the Bushey (England) Dominicans who have been supportive of the Iraqi St Catherine Dominicans for more than 40 years, have also continued to open their doors to the congregation's young sisters, offering hospitality and help in this critical educational mission.

In pursuing rigorous studies, in foreign languages in foreign lands around the world, the Iraqi student-sisters are continuing to equip themselves for ministry in disciplines that will help them respond to the spiritual, educational, psychological and medical needs of the Iraqi people. The young sisters have also come to know the larger Dominican family and its many gifts through their studies abroad. The Dominican Sisters of St Catherine are grateful to the many congregations of Dominicans and other women religious who have opened their hearts and homes to their Iraqi sisters – and to the entire Dominican family for the love and support they have shown them during this harrowing time. In the hospitality that has been offered, the young sisters have experienced a spirit of sisterhood and oneness, recognising the Dominican sisters with whom they live as their second communities and their homes on foreign lands as their second motherhouses.

While they have been studying and learning, the young sisters have also been serving as ambassadors for their country and as preachers of truth for their congregation, giving voice to the reality of the suffering of their people to audiences around the world. Through churches, social justice groups, conferences, the Internet, and a variety of other outlets, the young sisters have been speaking truth – letting the world know of the violence, instability and lack of security that continue to persecute the people of Iraq – and calling for justice.

Another key step has involved preparing the congregation's schools and health care facilities, where the returning student-sisters will minister, as places where the Iraqi people can experience healing and reconciliation.

In 2007, a key ministry to girls was revitalised when the Iraqi government returned the high school in Baghdad that the sisters had established in 1964 and the state had nationalised in 1974. The congregation repaired and renovated the building, changing the name of the school back to its original, St Thomas School for Girls. It reopened in September 2008. The sisters tried to keep a low profile for the safety of the students, accepting only two classes of eighth- and ninth-grade girls the first year it reopened. By the following academic year, the number of students, most of them Muslim, had increased to fill seven classrooms. Iraq's Ministry of Education has cited St Thomas as a model school. Demand for registration continues to increase through the witness of the girls and the words of their parents, whose relationship with the sisters is open and warm. One of the sister-students who completed her studies abroad recently returned to teach at St Thomas, where her training in peace studies is taking root.

In Baghdad, the congregation has added a new wing to its Al-Hayat Hospital, which, as noted earlier, is a maternity ward offering women a safe and joyful place in which to deliver their babies. The congregation sent a sister-student abroad to study medicine to provide another doctor for this hospital.

The sisters also obtained funding from an NGO that enabled them to offer courses in first aid and health care to women and young girls in rural villages of the north, empowering them to care better for themselves and their families. Also with the help of outside funding, the sisters were able to purchase computers for their convents in the northern villages. They then opened their doors, making the computers available to local women and offering training in basic computer skills and Internet use.

Other efforts focus on building hope. In 2010, for example, the congregation started a kindergarten in Batnaya, a village where services are few and the people have suffered greatly. A number of the village's young people have been killed or kidnapped; some are still missing. Most of the men in Batnaya, who had previously been self-employed in Mosul or Baghdad, have been unable to return to work because of the violence. The congregation is seeking to alleviate the many trials of the people of Batnaya so as to encourage them to remain in the country. By educating and caring for their children, the sisters are able to meet the children's parents, especially the mothers, offering them help and support as well. Young sisters, meanwhile, are educating themselves in Montessori methods, psychology/pastoral care and theology, gaining skills and expertise to serve Iraqis in dire need, like the people of Batnaya.

LIVING WITH FAITH INTO AN UNCERTAIN FUTURE
In July 2010, the congregation held its general chapter at the Al-Om Al-Tahrah (Immaculate Conception) Convent in Qaraqosh. It marked the second time in the history of the congregation that a general chapter was held outside the motherhouse in Mosul. The congregation's first general chapter, in 1933, was held in the village of Telkeif, where Marie Aimée Mousa Hindu

was elected as the congregation's first native prioress. The records do not reveal why the first general chapter was held there, away from the motherhouse, but the sisters know very clearly and painfully why this general chapter was held in Qaraqosh, a forced exile caused by violence. Still, the grace and blessings of a general chapter emerge, no matter where it is held.

Just prior to opening the chapter, sister-delegates and other members of the congregation gathered for a retreat. For the first time in the congregation's history, two Dominican sisters of St Catherine led the pre-chapter retreat – a role previously assumed by a priest or Dominican friar. Two student-sisters who were pursuing doctorates in biblical studies served as the retreat leaders. Focusing the retreat on the role of women in the Gospel of John, the young sisters raised self-reflective questions for the sister-delegates, including: Do you think the problems in our society are reflected in our lives in the convent? If so, how must we deal with them? The unsparing responses of the retreatants highlighted the deep dimensions of the trauma of war and the unrelenting violence impacting the lives of all Iraqis, including the Sisters of St Catherine.

At the beginning of the general chapter – which came after a year of study involving proposed changes to the constitution, a prayerful retreat and 12 days of further prayer, study and discussion – the sister-delegates re-elected Sr Maria Jebo Hanna to serve another six-year term as prioress. Although some of the most difficult decisions, including evacuating the motherhouse, have fallen during Sr Maria's term in office, she graciously acceded to the call of her sisters to continue shouldering responsibility for leading the congregation. By the end of the two-week session, the Dominican Sisters of St Catherine of Siena emerged from their general chapter steadfastly and resolutely committed to their mission of helping to shape a better future for Iraq and her people.

Despite the continuing danger, the persecution of Christians, and the great unknowns confronting Iraq today, the congregation's members – at the time of writing, including 128 solemnly vowed sisters and 13 sisters in temporary profession, with three novices in the wings – are committed to being a part of building a new future of peace and reconciliation in Iraq and around the world. Facing challenges as great as those of their martyred foremothers, without any idea as to when the daily bombings will cease and their country's streets and homes will be safe, the sisters continue the mission begun more than 130 years ago, with a central focus on empowering women and girls. In these most difficult and trying times, the Dominican Sisters of St Catherine draw deeply upon the legacy of their founding Sausanat, striving to give witness – in themselves and through other Iraqi women – to the power of women's courageous leadership, perseverance and faith, and capacity to bring new life to birth out of death and despair.

Editors' note: this contribution was one of the first to be completed for this project, in 2010. Obviously, there have been further developments in the Iraqi situation since then.

14

Sr Pétronille Kayiba Mukadi, O.P.
A Liberation Theologian
in the Democratic Republic of the Congo

ROGER GAISE, O.P.

BIOGRAPHICAL SUMMARY

Pétronille Kayiba was born in Kipushi in Katanga Province on 30 May 1954. When she finished her primary education at the age of 11 she wished to go to the convent to pursue her secondary education. She was then admitted to the novitiate of the Dominican Missionary Sisters of the Rosary and pronounced her first vows in Kinshasa on 1 August 1976. In the months that followed, she was sent to Cameroon, where she taught in Edea, Cameroon (1976–78). Then, she had to return to the Democratic Republic of the Congo (DRC) to work as a teacher at the Centre for the Disabled in Panda/Likasi (1978–83). During this period, she made her perpetual profession, also in Likasi, on the Solemnity of St Dominic, 8 August 1982. Two years later, in 1984, after the provincial chapter, she was appointed mistress of novices and postulants in DRC and Cameroon (1984–91) and, at the same time, pastoral animator of the parishes of Mater Dei and St Rita in Kinshasa (Diocese of Kisantu) (1984–90). These were probably the years in which she developed her inner strength and her commitment to struggle for justice and peace, especially through her relations with the basic ecclesial communities. Since then, having been won over by liberation theology, her commitment to justice and peace has grown continuously.

However, to gain a deeper theological understanding of this struggle for better social welfare for her compatriots, she was allowed to undertake theological studies. She did this with great success in the Catholic Faculties of Kinshasa from 1990 to 1995. Seeing the skills she acquired, her sisters did not hesitate to appoint her provincial secretary of the congregation in 1996. Three years later, she was elected provincial for a term of three years and, in 2002, was re-elected for another three years. During this time, her peers also elected her provincial superior of the DRC and president of the Union of Major Superiors of the DRC for two terms (1999–2005).

During her terms as provincial, she was noticed by members of the Dominican family, who unhesitatingly appointed her member of the International Commission Justice-Peace-Integrity of Creation (1998–2004) and co-promoter of Justice-Peace-Integrity of Creation for the Dominican family in Africa (1998–2004). When she finished her term as provincial, the Union of Major Superiors of the DRC called on her again in 2006 to lead its Commission for Justice and Peace.

During her ministry, Sr Pétronille Kayiba has launched all sorts of initiatives, not only in the struggle for a new socio-political order in the DRC but also for the advancement of African women. Among the initiatives undertaken, it is worth mentioning her active engagement in the Women's Movement for Justice and Peace (1997), the Institut de la Femme Kimpa Vita Béatrice (2000), the Centre for Women and Remedial Training, CE.FO. RAS (2007), and the Mgr Zubieta Development Project (2007). In addition, Pétronille Kayiba did everything in her power to speak effectively and efficiently in various intellectual circles in Kinshasa. Besides her work as a theologian, teaching at the Institut Saint Eugène de Mazenod in Kinshasa (since 1995) and at Kinshasa's Higher Institute of Religious Pedagogy (since 1996), she has also contributed significantly to the establishment of certain structures to promote women leaders in Kinshasa, co-founding and directing the Association of Women Theologians and Canonists of Kinshasa (ATHECAK). In the light of all these achievements, in 2006, she was named member of the Theological Advisory Committee of Women Theologians of the Dominican Family and, in 2007, member of the Dominican Family's International Commission for Preaching.

MAJOR APOSTOLIC DIRECTIONS

Taking into account the theories outlined by Clodovis Boff,[1] where the theologian can take a position either in the intellectual field, in the political field or in the pursuit of social inclusion, Pétronille Kayiba chose the last of these possibilities. In other words, she was convinced that a theologian in her position, who presents an understanding of the Christian faith in accordance with the mentality of African people, cannot remain silent in the face of injustices that affect the continent, on pain of failing in her mission to reach the concerns of the masses, to illuminate public opinion or to speak out.[2]

1. C. Boff, *Théorie et Pratique. La méthode des théologiens de libération*, Paris, Cerf, 1990, pp. 283–9.
2. Cf. R. Gaise, *L'Eglise Catholique et le processus de démocratisation au Zaïre. Essais et Témoignages* (24 April 1990–24 April 1995), Kinshasa, Facultés Catholiques de Kinshasa, 1996, pp. 245–9.

In the particular context of the deteriorating living conditions of the population in which she ministered, Pétronille Kayiba was engaged in the field of justice and peace as well as in working with women. She has always believed that in the DRC there is a link between the issues of justice, peace and development, on the one hand, and the issue of women, on the other.

COMMITMENT TO JUSTICE AND PEACE

Working in an Africa characterised by disturbances of all kinds (cultural, social, economic and political), Pétronille Kayiba, like other members of her congregation, made the border between life and death her central focus for preaching.[3] In this context, she endorsed the questions voiced by Cardinal Hyacinthe Thiandoum during the Special Synod of Bishops for Africa: 'In a continent full of bad news, how is the Christian message "good news" for our people? Amid pervading despair, where are the hope and optimism of the Gospel?' For Kayiba, the answer is quite clear: evangelisation must reach the African people in the midst of their anguish and torment. Consecrated among her own to the kingdom of heaven, she was convinced that the theologian must be of the people and for the people. That is why the theologian should constantly be aware of the aspirations of the masses. For, as the bishops of Africa and Madagascar have taught, 'the credibility and chances of evangelization will be the measure of solidarity with the legitimate aspiration of Africans to be responsible for their own destiny, the extent of its availability in the search for solutions to problems and the construction of the continent'.[4] Only to that extent can we avoid theology skilfully developed in libraries, with no impact on real everyday life.[5] In other words, someone who wants to do theology must work to raise awareness among pastoral workers in the DRC that the credibility of their message is conditioned by their involvement in concrete actions capable of transforming the socio-economic structures and policies of the country.

In such an environment, Pétronille Kayiba understands[6] Dominican preaching primarily as a requirement to promote justice and peace; the Dominicans, men and women, must see themselves as called to witness to

3. P. Kayiba, 'Pertinence de la prédication dominicaine en contexte africain', unpublished lecture given at the General Chapter of the Dominicans in Krakow, 2004.

4. Symposium of the Bishops' Conferences of Africa and Madagascar (SECAM), *Eglise et Promotion humaine en Afrique aujourd'hui, Exhortation Pastorale des évêques d'Afrique et de Madagascar*, Kinshasa, 15–22 July 1984, no. 77.

5. R. Gaise, *L'Eglise Catholique et le processus de démocratisation au Zaïre. Essais et Témoignages* (24 April 1990–24 April 1995), Kinshasa, Facultés Catholiques de Kinshasa, 1996, p. 246.

6. P. Kayiba, 'Pertinence de la prédication dominicaine en contexte africain', unpublished lecture given at the General Chapter of the Dominicans in Krakow, 2004.

their faith where people are still fighting for survival. Wanting to give an example of such a form of preaching, Pétronille Kayiba wrote:

> This option for Justice and Peace is so important that even our social, health, educational, pastoral and, in particular, catechetical service, bears this mark. This is why at the very heart of the Mobutu dictatorship, during the Second Republic in our country, one of our sisters characterized her vocation as preacher with the fact, both symbolic and physical, of 'making the chains fall' as a sign of fundamental human dignity and of our preaching. Here is one of her moving testimonies: 'I was allowed to visit the prisoners and bring them some medicine and food. I treated their wounds, cutting with simple scissors pieces of rotting flesh. I cleaned, disinfected, gave them antibiotics and vitamins. But I could not stand to see them with chains. I fought to have them removed … I took the saws, and in front of the guards and the prisoners, I started to saw the chains. Everyone looked at me, but nobody dared to stop me. After that, we buried the chains and objects of torture. We saw these brothers jump for joy at being freed from those chains. From that day on, we have never again seen in Makala [prison] instruments of torture or chains.'[7]

In other words, as she continues in the same text, 'the sisters' involvement in various movements for justice and peace has no other purpose than to give birth to life, and to protect, defend and offer it to God as a sign of His presence in Africa.'

A new phase opened up with the March of Christians on 16 February 1992. The active participation of Pétronille Kayiba in organising this march – with the Amos group, accompanied by Fr José Mpundu of the archdiocese of Kinshasa – contributed to its success and triggered the public manifestation of Pétronille's vocation as a courageous promoter of justice and peace.[8] Indeed, in the context of claims of a new socio-political order in the DRC, she became famous through her decisive involvement in Amos, which strongly contributed to the mobilisation of the masses in Kinshasa for the reopening of the Sovereign National Conference.[9] Here is what she said of

7. Ibid.

8. For more information about the Amos group, see http://fr.wiser.org/organization/view/eb7e3d39eb5a21ad2f2eb6921ff242f3 (last accessed 29.07.03)

9. Cf. R. Gaise, L'Église Catholique et le processus de démocratisation au Zaïre. Essais et Témoignages (24 April 1990–24 April 1995), Kinshasa, Facultés Catholiques de Kinshasa, 1996, pp. 88–100. See also 'Rethinking independence, the DR Congo 50 years on', Symposium on Fifty Years of Independence, Goma, June 2010, collection Cultures et Mémoires, Pole Institute. online: http://www.pole-institute.org/index.htm (last accessed 30.08.12), p. 49, and the article of Alexis Kabambi available at http://www.congonline.com/Forum1/Forum01/Kabambi01.htm (last accessed 29.07.13).

this experience:

> This period was a great moment for us, for our awareness individually and in community. We formed groups for animation in neighbourhoods. We participated, as communities in general and individuals in particular, in Church movements to fight for justice and peace. Our commitment to Justice and Peace became clear, at this time, as our distinctive characteristic. Our communities had influence, discreet, perhaps, but very real, in the circles of the diocesan church, in many religious communities and among the faithful of the Christian churches, especially in some neighbourhoods of Kinshasa where we are present.[10]

In the years that followed, Pétronille Kayiba engaged in unusual theological reflections in order to persuade various circles of the need to fight for a fairer and more equitable society, mentioning the places that are particularly important to access in order to liberate the people of Congo: family, hospitals, schools, churches, religious life, resistance groups and youth.[11]

With fellow members of the Amos group, Pétronille Kayiba was convinced that in order to introduce a new socio-political order in the DRC (at that time, still called Zaire,) several large-scale actions had to be undertaken:

1. Formation and conscientisation: Because the Church's primary mission in the promotion of justice is to raise the awareness of the population, it is evident that the faithful themselves must first be converted and formed before they can reach out to others.

2. Information: the members of groups should regularly inquire both about injustices committed and all actions carried out in favour of justice.

3. Action-transformation: this especially concerns actions promoting justice and peace, including concrete action in a liberation movement, official pronouncements on the major issues, reporting of social injustice, preparing the population for elections etc.

THE ADVANCEMENT OF WOMEN

For Sr Pétronille, it is not possible to talk about development without talking about women, who should be regarded as the pillar of all action to ensure the social well-being of humanity. That is why she is strongly committed

---

10. P. Kayiba, 'Pertinence de la prédication dominicaine en contexte africain', unpublished lecture given at the General Chapter of the Dominicans in Krakow, 2004.

11. P. Kayiba and F. Muzumanga, *Femme blessée, femme libératrice dans l'Église-Famille*, Ed. Baobab, Kinshasa 1995, pp. 26–9.

to everything that contributes to empowering women and making them really able to contribute to development. Indeed, she presents woman as the mother of life, understood in its dual dimension of individual and social; her mission is not only to bear life and give birth to it, but also to defend it against all threats.

Woman is made to receive, bear, protect and liberate life. This is her primary mission. The fact remains that she is then called to ward off everything that could lead to the destruction of life. Is this not the design and the conviction that gave rise to certain taboos imposed on women in particular cultures, such as the prohibition against breaking or eating an egg, or against cutting and burning trees? In other words, seen as a sign or sacrament of hope for life, a woman cannot kill, she cannot destroy life.

As a result of this, women should strive to defend life against anything that threatens it. So, in the midst of all the monstrosities that tend to destroy humanity and threaten life, women must truly step forward and offer themselves as a true sign of hope for life. This is a task that is obviously the opposite of violence. Pétronille Kayiba is adamant in her belief: 'In the feminine structure there is a predisposition to reject violence and to prefer non-violence. Although woman is the place where life and death come face-to-face, non-violence is inscribed in her being. In essence, woman is a living "contradiction-to-violence", and so to death, in favour of life. Consequently, any act of violence committed by a woman is inconsistent with her being.'[12]

This is why the promotion of a feminine spirituality, which draws its strength from femininity understood as a source of life, may bring hope to our society, in need, as it is, of life and peace for the third millennium.[13]

In any case, in order to accomplish her ministry for the promotion of the feminine genius and the role of women in society, Pétronille Kayiba has undertaken a number of activities: some are described in the sections that follow.

THE WOMEN'S MOVEMENT FOR JUSTICE AND PEACE (MFJP) (1995)

This movement, begun with the aim of giving women the opportunity to participate in the global movement working towards new, more humane social structures, strongly insisted on the importance of Dominican preaching

12. P. Kayiba, *La femme face à la violence*, on-line: http://www.afriquespoir.com/Ae09/index_fichiers/beijing.htm (last accessed 30.08.12).
13. Moreover, because of her commitment to the cause and advancement of women, she is sometimes asked to write prefaces for books. That was the case with Neno Gontran's book, *Ils vous ont guettées. 230 religieuses tuées en Afrique*, Ed. Afriquespoir-New People, Kinshasa-Nairobi, 2000, as well as Ofedico, *Chemin de croix de la femme congolaise*, Kinshasa, n.d.

on the value of life. In fact, the movement had national, continental and even international significance. For Pétronille and her congregation, the Dominican Missionary Sisters of the Rosary, in union with God's people, it was truly an apostolic *diakonia*.

This thirst to help women take charge of themselves and play their full role in the management of the city led Sr Pétronille to collaborate with several associations pursuing the same goal as the Women's Movement for Justice and Peace (MFJP), for example the RODHECIC (Network Organization of Human Rights and Civic Education of Christian Inspiration in the Democratic Republic of Congo[14]).

After a period of euphoria,[15] during which many women were involved, the MFJP group has decreased in size, although it remains very active. The movement aims at integrating the values of justice and peace, as well as freedom and fraternity, into society. Pétronille Kayiba sees this as another approach to the issue of the empowerment of women, because when there is talk about empowering women, many believe immediately that this means primarily formation in the field of development or economics.

THE INSTITUTE FOR WOMEN KIMPA VITA BEATRICE (2000)

Since the challenge to Dominican preaching in the current African context is in-depth evangelisation and explicit proclamation,[16] Pétronille Kayiba considered it appropriate to establish a research centre that was both an institute for women and a place where the service of the Dominican Missionary Sisters of the Rosary would be coordinated; this would give them a clearer identity as preachers, a prophetic identity. Situated in the suburbs of Kinshasa, the centre's main task is to programme the preaching of the congregation on the basis of the analysis of cultural, social and political

14. This association unites the following non-governmental associations and organisations: le Mouvement des femmes pour la justice et pour la paix (MFJP), led by Pétronille Kayiba; l'Organisation des femmes pour le développement intégral et communautaire (Ofedico), directed by Mrs. Marcelline Kisita; l'Association pour la promotion humaine (Aprohu), led by Bertin Kanyinda; la Fondation Bilenge ya Mwinda of Father Odon Miensea, Benedictine monk of Mambré.

15. Beginning in 1995: Message de la femme Zaïroise à la Nation (8 March 1995); 'Non aux billets de 1.000 NZ et de 5.000 NZ'; Message à toutes les femmes qui vivent au Zaïre (April 1995); Message à toutes les 'Mamans Religieuses' qui vivent au Zaïre (May 1995); Message à tous les habitants de Kikwit (22 May 1995); Message à toutes les 'mamans religieuses' de Kikwit (22 May 1995); '4ème Conférence mondiale de la femme de Beijing: pour quelle femme' (31 July 1995); 'Message aux femmes réunies à Beijing' (31 July 1995); 'Appel à toutes les femmes qui vivent au Zaïre' (16 February 1996); 'La force de la féminité: une espérance de vie'. Message à toutes les femmes qui sont au Zaïre (8 March 1996); 'Le cri des femmes du Zaïre: Nous voulons la paix' (7 November 1996); 'La voix des femmes du Congo-Zaïre' (23 May 1997); 'Le cri des femmes du Congo: Nous voulons la paix' (10 December 1998).

16. P. Kayiba, 'Pertinence de la prédication dominicaine en contexte africain', unpublished lecture given at the General Chapter of the Dominicans in Krakow, 2004.

ties. It also proposes collaboration with lay people and seeks to publicise its message. Finally, the *diakonia* projects should be composed of women formed in Dominican spirituality.

THE CENTRE DE FORMATION FEMININE ET DE RATTRAPAGE SCOLAIRE (CE.FO.RAS) (2007)

Called to challenge all forms of violence, because of its opposition to their own being, women must be seen as the motor of African development. Sr Pétronille is convinced that women are an opportunity and a hope for a future of peace; she sees African women as the midwives of society in all its components. To further this end, she designed a centre (CE.FO.RAS) intended to help women to take full responsibility for themselves and to help them advance in the area of education. Indeed, the Dominican sister notes that, since men have often wanted to dominate, and even take the place of women, relegating them to nothing more than an erotic function, these men have 'given birth' to a society that is a horribly violent monster. In the process, they forget that 'giving birth' is a singular privilege given to women by God. Therefore, combined efforts must be made to rehabilitate women so that they can regain their originality as intended by the Creator. Only under these conditions can African women be fully fertile and able to integrate fertility dynamically into the economic, political, cultural and religious dimensions.[17]

THE 'MONSIGNOR ZUBIETA' DEVELOPMENT PROJECT (2007)[18]

The project, named after Mgr Ramon Zubieta, is an agro-pastoral project, strengthening the capacity of the poor to provide for themselves through training in cultivation techniques, and promoting comprehensive and sustainable development that is not limited to the simple struggle for survival. To achieve this, several strategies are considered: coaching and training the beneficiaries in agricultural technology and farming; preparing

17. P. Kayiba, 'Essai d'approche féminine du problème africain', *Revue africaine des sciences de la mission* 7 (1997), pp. 55–72.

18. Mgr Zubieta y Les co-founded the Missionnaires Dominicaines du Très Saint Rosaire with Mother Nicole Goni in 1918. Soon after his appointment as apostolic vicar of Urubamba (Peru) in 1913, he had the merit of doing what no Dominican had dared to do: calling nuns of the second Order into the mission. After 28 years of contemplative life, Mother Goni became the first Dominican missionary to enter the Amazon forests previously explored by Bishop Zubieta, explorations for which he received the gold medal of the Geographical Society of Lima. Cf. Roger Etchegaray, 'L'effort missionnaire des Basques à travers les siècles', in VIIe Congrès d'Etudes Basques (2003), consulted on-line: http://www.euskomedia.org/PDFAnlt/congresos/07899912.pdf, (last accessed 31.01 11).

them to be in charge of the project through the creation of agricultural and livestock activities; generating revenue; mechanising agriculture for increased production; organising the beneficiaries into structured groups capable of defending their rights, and so on.

In other words, the Mgr Ramon Zubieta Project wants to develop a space for announcing the Good News and the Incarnation of the Good News in the concrete lives of the Congolese people today. It is to be a space for preaching that is both proclamation and *diakonia*, preaching that makes the human being stand tall, and permits him to be the subject of his own destiny.

CONCLUSION

Convinced that, in the specific context of Africa, Dominican apostolic preaching as *diakonia* focuses mostly on the struggle for life, Sr Pétronille Kayiba is currently developing what some have called a 'theology of life'. Here, women play a leading role: as the source of human life, they must also be its main liberating force. In other words, women have the responsibility to demonstrate that creation and salvation are part of the same fundamental mystery, in the self-communication of God through Jesus Christ and the Holy Spirit.

In this context, Dominican preaching must reach men and women of our times in the places where they are now fighting for life or even survival. Having found that the Dominican presence in theological education was largely unknown in the region, and especially in Kinshasa where decisions are made concerning the main directions of African inculturated theology, Sr Pétronille Kayiba met this challenge by organising conferences and sessions there. Theology, far from being confined to reflections on faith or culture, must now define a new kind of relationship between the Church and public social reality, between faith and the problems of our times. Behaving differently can only be detrimental to the Gospel of Christ and, of course, for the credibility of the Catholic Church. In this regard, two important poles of this struggle have attracted the attention of our sister: a commitment to justice and peace as well as to the empowerment of women in rural Africa in all its forms. These two challenges have occupied Sr Pétronille Kayiba's attention to such an extent that they appear in most of her writings or statements, making her a true African liberation theologian.

However, in the development of her theology, Sr Pétronille Kayiba has encountered resistance from some ecclesiastical circles, since, in their opinion, her focus was becoming unbalanced. In any event, Sr Pétronille

Kayiba remains unruffled when it comes to her initial intuitions: to continue fighting for the advent of a new socio-political order in the DRC. In this way alone can one claim to belong to a Church that is not only for the people, but is also with the people.

SELECTED BIBLIOGRAPHY

Boff, C., *Théorie et Pratique. La méthode des théologiens de libération*, Paris, Cerf, 1990.

Gaise, R., *L'Église Catholique et le processus de démocratisation au Zaïre. Essais et Témoignages* (24 April 1990–24 April 1995), Kinshasa, Facultés Catholiques de Kinshasa, 1996

—, 'Rethinking independence: the DR Congo 50 years on', *Symposium on Fifty Years of Independence*, Goma, June 2010, collection Cultures et Mémoires, Pole Institute. http://www.pole-institute.org/index.htm (last access 30.08.2012).

Gontran, N., *Ils vous ont guettées. 230 religieuses tuées en Afrique*, Ed. Afriquespoir-New People, Kinshasa-Nairobi, 2000 (Preface by P. Kayiba)

OFEDICO (Organisation des Femmes pour le développement intégral et communautaire), *Chemin de croix de la femme congolaise*, Kinshasa, n.d.

Symposium of the Bishops Conferences of Africa and Madagascar (SECAM), *Église et Promotion humaine en Afrique aujourd'hui, Exhortation Pastorale des évêques d'Afrique et de Madagascar*, Kinshasa, 15–22 July 1984.

P. KAYIBA'S WRITINGS

'Experiencia religiosa y mujer en África', in *Y Dios creo a la mujer*, Madrid, Evangelio y Liberación, 1992, pp. 107–24.

Kayiba P. and Muzumanga F., *Femme blessée, femmes libératrice dans l'Eglise-Famille*, Kinshasa, Baobab, 1995.

'Femmes africaines et combat non violent', in *Alternatives non violentes*, Ed. Odile Jacob, 105, 1997, pp. 46–8.

'Essai d'approche féminine du problème africain', in *Revue africaine des sciences de la mission*, 7, 1997, pp. 55–72.

'Catherine de Sienne: un défi pour le troisième millénaire', in *Perspectives*, Kinshasa, Ceril (Centre d'études et de recherches interdisciplinaires de Limete), 1, 1998, pp. 27–36.

'Nouvelles formes de pauvreté', in *Toujours en mission. Hommages posthumes aux pères Justin Alung Mpul et Giovanni Santolini*, Kinshasa, Baobab, 1998, pp. 151–63.

'Pour une inculturation de la ratio de formation à la vie consacrée', in *Inculturation de la vie consacrée en Afrique à l'aube du troisième millénaire*, Kinshasa, Carmel Afrique, 1998, pp. 299–310.

'La femme face à la violence', 2000, http://www.afriquespoir.com/Ae09/index _fichiers/beijing.htm (last accessed 30.08.2012).

'Pertinence de la prédication dominicaine en contexte africain', unpublished lecture given at the General Chapter of the Dominicans in Krakow, 2004.

'Le pardon ne signifie pas absence de justice', in Ngalula Josée (dir.), *Oser la défendre dans son inviolabilité*, Actes de l'Atelier 'Religion et violences faite aux femmes', Kinshasa, Editions Mont Sinaï, 2006, pp. 104–13.

'Nouvelles fondations', in *La vie consacrée dans l'Église du Congo. Bilan et perspectives*, Kinshasa, Médiaspaul, 2007, pp. 147–53.

'Rite de purification des veuves et le corps de la femme comme lieu de libération', in Ngalula Josée (dir.), *Le corps féminin lieu singulier de rencontre entre évangile et coutumes africaines*, Actes de l'Atelier théologique sur 'Rites de purification des veuves: des traditions africaines à la liturgie chrétienne', Vol. I, Kinshasa, Editions Mont Sinaï, 2008, pp. 23–7.

'Presencia liberadora del cristianismo en África', lecture given at the XXVIII Congreso de Teología: Laicidad y cristianismo, Madrid, 2008.

'Actualisation charismatique de la vie consacrée dans le contexte actuel', lecture given at the Colloque sur la formation dans la Vie consacrée: Quelle pédagogie pour la formation religieuse aujourd'hui?, Kinshasa, 2010.

15

The Story of the Dominican Sisters of Bethany

'Charity saves from death, and purges every kind of sin'[1]

HANNAH RITA LAUE, O.P., AND SVENJA BARBARA IBSCHER-HOLZ

The Dominican Sisters of Bethany, which is the focus of this contribution, were founded in 1866 in France from a women's prison. The historical circumstances were such that at the beginning of the twentieth century a second congregation with the same name came to exist. The French congregation, the Dominican Sisters of Bethany Montferrand, was contemplative, while the second congregation, which began in the Netherlands, the Dominican Sisters of Bethany Venlo, is apostolic in nature. Today, there is a good relationship between the two congregations and they are united in their original charism. Indeed, both congregations share the same historical beginnings.

In this article we will tell the story of the original beginnings as the story of both congregations before discussing them separately. We will deal with the apostolate of interior rehabilitation, which is lived by both communities, as well as the apostolate of the Children's Villages, which has been exclusive to the Bethany Sisters of Venlo.

The mission of Bethany is common to both congregations. The Bethany Dominicans were founded so that the mercy of God could be made visible to people who, because of their past lives, had been stigmatised or excluded from society. They were founded as a community for the 'incarnation of trust and hope.'[2]

THE 'REHABILITATED'

In 1864, a young Dominican priest, Fr Jean-Joseph Lataste, was asked by his superiors to give days of reflection at the Central Prison for Women in Cadillac.

Between 6.25 and 8.48 per cent of the women in this prison died every

---

1. Tobit 12: 9.
2. Jean-Marie Gueullette, *Jean-Joseph Lataste. Apostel der Gefängnisse*, Leipzig, Dominikanische Quellen und Zeugnisse 15, 2010, p. 109.

year, which was well above the average of 4.76 per cent for women's prisons at the time. The women were supervised during work, meals and rest periods by women from religious congregations. In the Cadillac prison the supervision was carried out by the Daughters of Wisdom.[3]

Before joining the Dominican Order, Lataste had worked within a conference of St Vincent de Paul. The members of the conference stressed the importance of engaging with people at a personal level and on an equal footing and within the conference there were no social barriers.[4] Even more important for Lataste's meeting with the imprisoned women, however, was his 'encounter' with Mary Magdalene while he was still a seminarian. He did not look on her, as was the custom of the time, as a penitent serving a lifelong sentence. For him it was her enormous love for Christ that counted, and that Jesus accepted this love. He was greatly impressed at how the mercy of God could be so great as to enable a former notorious sinner to become a witness to the resurrection.[5] His experience with this saint made him realise that 'the greatest sinners have the makings of the greatest saints'.[6] Gueullette, Lataste's biographer and vice-postulator in the process of his beatification, commented that the audacity of this saying is not in praising the capacity of God's grace to transform the sinner in some sort of external way,[7] but rather 'in believing that every person has this innate ability by virtue of creation itself. The flowering of holiness depends not exclusively on the good will of God but it also depends on how the person allows him or herself to be challenged in her or his environment by that grace.'[8]

In the prison at Cadillac Father Lataste was now confronted with the daily lives of these women, who were mostly convicted of child murder or theft.[9] They were roughly divided into three criminal categories: forced labour, temporary or lifelong, a prison sentence, or rehabilitation.[10]

During the two retreats that he held for the women in September 1864 and 1865, he surprised the women by speaking to them in a trusting way. He addressed them as his 'dear sisters'[11] and saw himself as their brother in Adam and in Christ Jesus.[12]

3. Ibid., pp. 128–131.
4. Ibid., pp. 33–46.
5. Ibid., pp. 112.
6. Ibid., pp. 108.
7. Ibid.
8. Ibid., p. 108f.
9. Ibid., p. 130f.
10. Ibid., p. 127.
11. Ibid., p. 134.
12. Ibid., p. 135.

A Decree of 10 March 1839 forbade prisoners to speak to Fr Lataste in the presence of others. The only opportunity for a conversation with him was thus limited to confession.[13] In these talks, he learned more about the backgrounds to the women's deeds, and that there were also other people who were responsible for the crimes committed who were never punished. These conversations brought him to the realisation that, '[I]n order to have the power to forgive one has to be innocent, or, if one is guilty, then one must have deep sorrow for his failing. Criminal hearts never forgive. But they [these women] forgive and that means in truth and in reality they are no longer criminals.'[14] Here he met women for whom what he had already found in his encounter with Mary Magdalene was true. At the same time, he saw very clearly how the miracle of this self-understanding of the religious sisters went against the world view of his contemporaries and French jurisprudence.

After this he was unable to rid himself of an idea, which he recognised as the will of God.[15] He wanted to overcome the barriers to changing society so as to take seriously the gift of rehabilitation that God had already given to these women. And so he said to the women in prison, 'Whatever your past might have been, please consider yourselves no longer prisoners, instead see yourselves as God's blessed souls in the same way as the souls in the convents.'[16] Such a remark, as Gueulette pointed out, was viewed as scandalous. It was unthinkable that these women could be given free access to life in a convent, especially when it meant joining a contemplative order.[17]

With the concept of 'rehabilitation', Fr Lataste developed an approach which still has a place in French criminal law today. In addition to a prison sentence, 'judicial social supervision' could and can be imposed. If a judge is dealing with a crime and not only a case of neglect, a form of 'judicial social supervision' for a period of up to 20 years can be imposed to begin *after* the custodial sentence has been served.[18] The additional penalties could and can relate to the 'deprivation of civic, civil and family rights'.[19] This means that one cannot vote, stand for election, get married or take any type of oath. The restoration of these rights is carried out through a public judicial act, the

13. Ibid., p. 129.
14. Jean-Marie Gueullette, op. cit., p. 138f., esp. p. 138.
15. Ibid.
16. Jean-Marie Gueullette, op. cit., p. 144.
17. Ibid., note XII.
18. Max-Planck-Institut (ed.): *Code Pénal. In Kraft seit 1992*, bilingual synoptic edition, 1999, Art. 131-36-1 and Art. 131-36 -5.
19. Ibid. Art. 131–26.

'rehabilitation'.

On 17 March 1865, the French interior minister issued an instruction emphasising to prison directors legislation enacted in 1852, which permitted inmates to avail themselves of rehabilitation after their period of incarceration, allowing them to regain their normal rights. During his second retreat day in Cadillac in September 1865 Fr Lataste spoke in his sermons about the idea of rehabilitation, which he had not mentioned in the previous year. But before he made this idea his central theme he changed it significantly. In his opinion, rehabilitation could not be reduced to a mere human act, but, instead, was helped by the grace of God. He saw rehabilitation as a *condition* of re-entry into society, while the judicial system saw the formal rehabilitation as a *confirmation* and sealing affirmation of the successful re-entry of offenders into society.

So as to show the mercy of God in the world, Fr Lataste wanted to create a community where former women prisoners and women who had never been in prison could live together, indistinguishable one from the other, in a religious community. He promoted this plan of God to the bishops and the public and spoke about the clear and ethical responsibility of society. The title of his booklet, *Les Réhabilitées*, seemed to play on the emotions and thoughts that were associated with *Les Misérables*,[20] and made clear the aspect of social criticism in the project. Fr Lataste knew that the work of God is always made manifest in society and is never independent of it. So, in his booklet, which was aimed at the wider public, he addressed his readers as 'My fellow citizens', and continued, 'I am aware of a terrible wound in society and no helping hand heals it, no heart cares for it with healing balm. Every year the big doors of prisons open and spew out poor creatures with pale and bowed heads. These women once did wrong; the justice system has punished them with the incarceration they deserved; but after they had been returned to duty through suffering and exhaustion, the justice system has not restored them to a position they deserved. They have suffered 10, maybe 20 years; they have paid a heavy price for their mistakes, and yet, when they return to society, all they bring with them is a tarnished name. Poor women ... A simple priest has thought ... it was time to redecorate their foreheads with the fallen crown. To unite them in a society of spotless souls, consecrated to God, who will take their hands like sisters and share with them their name, their religious habit, their vows, their entire lives, so that no one ever again can distinguish between those who have sinned and those

20. Victor Hugo, *Les Misérables*, Paris, 1862.

who have not sinned. So to rehabilitate them in the eyes of mankind as they already are in heaven's eyes.'[21]

Despite much opposition Fr Lataste, together with Mother Henri-Dominique, previously a member of the Soeurs de Charité Dominicaines de la Présentation de la Sainte Vierge, founded the Dominican Community of Bethany in 1866. In July 1868 the first two rehabilitated sisters were robed by Fr Lataste. Fr Lataste died on 10 March 1869, but Mother Henri-Dominique led the congregation with tenacity and far-sightedness until her death in 1907.

BETHANY AND ITS LINKS WITH THE PRISON

Conscious of the reasons for its founding, in their living together the sisters worked at building an 'interior rehabilitation', as well as their apostolate and the preaching of their community. As a result of this, their chief apostolate, prison work, was the main work of all the convents. Both areas – interior rehabilitation and prison work – developed along parallel lines, yet each of them had their own specific characteristics.

As a result of a decision of the leadership of the congregation, by 1877 permission was being sought from the French State Prosecution Office to visit women's prisons in France. The office was also informed that the Bethany-Montferrand sisters were 'prepared to take care of the young women prisoners under the supervision of the prison authorities'.[22] In the same month Mother Henri-Dominique received permission from the director of the Justice Department to visit all the prisons in France, accompanied by other sisters.[23]

During this work there was also close co-operation with the sisters who managed the prisons. In most cases, the supervision of the women's prisons came under the care of sisters, something that influenced the day-to-day running of the prison and not just its religious aspect. One example is the Filles de la Sagesse and the Soeurs de Maria Joseph working together in one prison.

Mother Henri-Dominique saw prison directors and chaplains as people who should be influenced by the ways and ideas of Fr Lataste. She did not see herself as the only person who could do this work. She saw to it that all Bethany-Montferrand convents adopted a prison and that the sisters living

21. 'Pater Lataste, Les Réhabilitées', in: Gueullette, *Jean-Joseph Lataste*, pp. 188–190.
22. Sr Pia-Elisabeth OP, *Entwicklung der Gefängnisbesuche in Bethanien Montferrand*, 2011, Archiv Bethanien Venlo, G 27 B, 1.
23. R.P. De Boissieu, *Béthanie. Les Madeleines réhabilitées*, Paris, Grasset, 1931, p. 193.

in that convent would care for the prisoners.[24]

Besides the development of a culture of visiting, at this time the French Justice Ministry decided in favour of internal rehabilitation. The sisters were allowed to take in women who had been released from prison on probation. According to documents from the general archives of the Bethany-Montferrand community, there were 38 such cases between 1874 and 1901. Boissieu writes in his book that, in the period from 1867 to 1908, 363 women entered Bethany-Montferrand, all of whom came directly from a prison.[25] However, 54 of these women did not come from French prisons but from similar institutions in Belgium and Germany. It can be seen from the Bethany-Montferrrand archives that 193 women stayed in Bethany and died as Dominican Sisters of Bethany. Between 1867 and 1908, 235 women with no prison history also entered Bethany. Of these, 201 remained, taking perpetual vows. The other 34 women left, either voluntarily or because they were asked to leave by the community.

Once they entered Bethany, those women who were under police supervision came under the care of the prioress.[26] Women who were in police custody were formally transferred to the legal custody of the prioress when they joined Bethany, both to clarify the legal situation and to make religious life possible for them. From the foundation of Bethany, the so-called 'little sisters' lived in the community until the period of their rehabilitation ended and it was possible for them to enter the novitiate. The 'little sisters' learned about the Order and received the religious habit. They were affiliated with the congregation with a promise and not by profession. This relationship with the congregation does not have the same legal meaning as profession, but in accordance with the constitution of the congregation they had a similar status in the everyday running of the congregation. This meant that from an outside perspective it was not possible to say who among those in the convent was on probation. The ideal situation was, and is, that discretion/confidentiality would be maintained in Bethany, so much so that sisters would not know about the past lives of other sisters. This means rehabilitation was, and is, anticipated by the convent.

24. Ibid.

25. R.P. De Boissieu, *Béthanie. Les Madeleines réhabilitées*, Paris, Grasset, 1931.

26. Both the fact that more women with a past in prison rather than without asked for entry in these years and that there was an almost balanced ratio among the sisters caused surprise in Bethany when it was discovered as part of Sr Hannah Rita Laue's research for her thesis on Church history, *Resozialisierung als geistliche Aufgabe. Die Geschichte der Dominikanerinnen von Bethnien in Stevensbeek/NL*, Bonn, 2012. It was not known before because the sisters' past lives had been treated discreetly for the purposes of internal rehabilitation.

The women who left Bethany had their probation conditions made easier, if not completely lifted. Indeed, they no longer needed to admit that they had been prisoners. Instead they could say that they came from a convent, which prevented any negative judgements being made about them. After 1908 women were still joining Bethany from prison. However, due to the discretion/confidentiality that was exercised, it is not possible to give any further information or details.[27]

At the beginning of the twentieth century, a Fr Williges Erren made contact, from Berlin, with Mother Henri-Dominique. He was inspired by the Bethany idea and asked if it would be possible to begin a community in Germany. Because of a personnel shortage and the difficult financial situation, his request was turned down. However, the community was open to the possibility of receiving German applicants and forming them in the spirit of Bethany.[28] The first German candidate went to France in 1903. Over the next ten years a further 16 women joined, of whom 12 stayed in Bethany.[29]

When the First World War started, these German women were considered citizens of an enemy state and had to leave France.[30] The refugees came to Venlo in the Netherlands in 1914 where they found accommodation with Fr Erren OP,[31] who was at the time prior of the Dominican Priory at Trans Cedron.[32] Because of the confusion of war, contact with the motherhouse was broken. It was important to create security for these women, all of whom, with the exception of the novice mistress, were still in the formation process. So a second Bethany congregation was founded in the Netherlands, the Dominican Sisters of Bethany in Venlo.

The mother congregation in France was, and is, mainly of a contemplative orientation, while the new community developed into an apostolic congregation. After the contact between both congregations was again established and trust in their relationship grew, they agreed on the verbal distinction between the Dominicans of Bethany Montferrand and the Dominicans of Bethany Venlo.

BETHANY MONTFERRAND

At the beginning of the twentieth century in France religious orders were

---

27. All information on this subject stems from the research of Sr Pia-Elisabeth, then prioress of the Dominicans of Bethany Montferrand. Her research is to be found in the archives there.

28. Alcide Postel, *Haus ohne Gitter*, Waldniel, Dominikanerinnen von Bethanien, 1954, p. 124.

29. Sr. Pia-Elisabeth, *Entwicklung der Gefängnisbesuche in Bethanien Montferrand*, op. cit., p. 4.

30. Alcide Postel, op. cit., pp. 125–136.

31. In the meantime, this secular priest had become a Dominican.

32. Chronik Bethanien Venlo, Buch I; Archiv Bethanien Venlo, p. 6.

forbidden to visit prisons. As a result of the separation of Chruch and state, many religious communities went into exile. Because of the vision of Mother Henri-Dominique, the Dominicans of Bethany were spared such a fate. In 1876 the founder had registered the Oeuvre de la Rehabilitation as a civil society, under which title it could continue in operation. The society was confirmed in 1891 and again in 1912.[33]

Between 1906 and 1932 Bethany Montferrand was affected by the ban on visiting prisons. In spite of this ban, many sisters managed to continue to write to the detainees and, indeed, some of them managed to continue visiting them in the centres of detention. While prison work in France experienced a setback, this provided the opportunity to expand it into Belgium. There, Dominicans who had fled France were able to preach the ideas that Fr Lataste had developed in Bethany, thereby inspiring tertiaries of St Dominic to visit Belgian prisons. As a result of this work two convents were founded in Belgium, Sart Risbart in 1898 (it closed in 1994) and Braschaet in 1905. Sixty-four women from the prisons visited by sisters from these convents joined the congregation.[34]

In 1932 the French Ministry of Justice again allowed the Dominicans from Bethany Montferrand to visit the prisons. But this time, each individual sister who wished to carry out this work was obliged to obtain permission to do so from the authorities and to renew the permit after a short period of time. In spite of this, visits to the prisons increased and all subsequent foundations were assigned a prison.

Even today, the Central Women's Prison in Rennes and the detention centre in Fleury Merogie, both in France, are visited by sisters of the Congregation of Bethany Montferrand. So, too, are the women's prisons in Hindelbank in Switzerland, in Gotteszell near Würzburg, Germany, and in Turin, Italy.

BETHANY VENLO

In this congregation the apostolate for inner rehabilitation and prison work was also developed, as fostered by the sisters from the French motherhouse. Former prisoners also joined the convent at Bethany Venlo, lived there in union with the sisters until their probation time had elapsed. Then they either took their vows or they left the community.

From the very beginning the prioress general of Bethany Venlo and later

33. Sr Pia-Elisabeth OP, *Entwicklung der Gefängnisbesuche in Bethanien Montferrand*, op. cit., p. 3.
34. Ibid., p. 3f.

other sisters visited the prisons in 's-Hertogenbosch/Den Bosch, Rotterdam, Amsterdam and The Hague.[35] Through magazine articles about the congregation written by others,[36] and the various books published by the sisters, they informed people about the ideas of rehabilitation as envisaged by Fr Lataste and as it is lived in Bethany Venlo.[37]

The foundation of the first filial house of Bethany Venlo in 1934, Maria Regina in Stevensbeek, was initially in the tradition of Bethany Montferrand, but it also developed an apostolic lifestyle because of its links with the foundation of a Catholic village[38] as well as its work in conjunction with the Dutch justice ministry. In 1933 Justice Minister Van Schaik offered the sisters the chance to take care of adult women and girls who had been prosecuted by the courts. Ten years earlier he had tried to link up with the sisters with respect to this issue, but at that time such a relationship was not possible.[39] At the beginning of the twentieth century, the Dutch state had taken up the issue of *reclassering* (reclassifying), which deals with the rehabilitation of convicts into society, and had tried to co-ordinate and control in a qualitative way the different private confessional organisations. More and more decisions were made as to how reintegration would be possible. The judges requested reports from the aforementioned organisations, which quickly led to the conclusion that people who worked in this area required a qualification. As a consequence, the task of rehabilitation became more and more the responsibility of trained social workers. For this, however, prison work and the possibility of reclassifying had to be part of their training. That naturally meant that they needed teachers who came from the former rehabilitation/resocialising organisations who could pass on the experience they had gained. In the debates in society about reclassifying, the effects of incarceration were discussed, leading to ideas for its reform, including measures to improve literacy and a reduction in the number of prisoners per cell. There was also a discussion about the introduction of what we today would call

---

35. See also: Sr Hannah Rita, *Rehabilitation; eine Lebensgeschichte. Oder der eine Cent von anderthalb.*, Archiv Bethanien Venlo, p. 4.

36. Sammlung: Bethanien in het wort. Archiv Bethanien Venlo, H 121.

37. For example: P. Willigis OP, *Unschuld und Busse als Schwestern*, Dülmen 1926;[3] Alcide Postel (ed.), *Verborgen Werelden*, Dominikanerinnen von Bethanien, 1939.

38. At that time there was a very strong confessional divide. The place where the village was to be founded was owned by Protestants and it was bought by the nearby village with the dream of a Catholic village being built there, with a church in the middle. For the emergence of the Stevensbeek village in connection with this foundation, cf. Sr Hannah Rita, Diplomarbeit: *Resozialisierung als geistliche Aufgabe. Die Geschichte der Dominikanerinnen von Bethnien in Stevensbeek/NL*, Bonn, 2012, Archiv Bethanien Venlo, Scr. 54.

39. Chronik Bethanien Venlo, Buch III, Oktober 1933, Archiv Bethanien Venlo, S. 660f.

probation officers.[40]

Bethany Venlo played an important role in the academic development and debate regarding reclassification and the reform of prisons, and also in the educational qualification of social workers. This led Dr N. Muller[41] to ask Sr Magdalena[42] to contribute to the book *Straffen en Helpen*.[43] In her contribution 'Vrouwen als Reclassenten' she made the observation that women, whether in prison or on their return to the community, should be treated differently from men because they have different needs.[44] Between 1955 and 1957 she taught Reclassifying at the R.K. School voor Maatschappelijkwerk. In her class notes she always referred to Maria Regina.[45]

The work at Maria Regina dealt more and more with under-age children. The sisters found themselves caring for young girls with behavioural difficulties who had been sent there by judges or their parents. These were not people who had been found guilty in courts. Maria Regina thus developed into a place of care and prevention. In 1946, of the 34 women who were there, 16 were minors, the youngest being 14.[46] Eventually, in 1972, Maria Regina officially changed from being an institution for reclassification to a place of care for children and young people.[47]

In order to allow the sisters to gain the necessary qualifications to work with children and young people, in 1948 the congregation began to run a course in different convents. The course was called Kinderbechmering A and B. This course was also open to women who were not members of the congregation. Course A included classes in 'pedagogy, psychology, children's rights, religious services, craft work, sport and games'.[48] To obtain the qualification, which was nationally recognised, candidates had to do a two-year practical course and pass an examination set by the State Examinations Board.[49] The sisters took this course when they opened their first Bethany Venlo community on German soil in 1952.

40. Sr Hannah Rita, *Diplomarbeit: Resozialisierung als geistliche Aufgabe*, pp. 42–54.

41. Nicolaas Muller was one of three men who worked out a concept for a reform of reclassification in the denominationally divided Dutch society through secret negotiations in 1940. This concept had a great influence on what happened after the Second World War. See Jean-Paul Heinrich, *Particuliere reclassering en overheid in Nederland sinds 1823*, Arnhem, Gouda Quint III., 1996, pp. 145–148.

42. Sr Magdalena was secretary to the General Prioress at that time.

43. Dr Nicolaas Muller (ed.), *Straffen en Helpen*, 1954.

44. Sr Magdalena, 'Vrouwen als Reclassenten', in : Nicolaas Muller (ed.), op. cit., 195 – 207.

45. Sr Magdalena, *Scripties van Lesen*, Archiv Bethanien Venlo, Scr. 53.

46. Sr Agnes, *Vijftig jaar hulpverlening: de stichting St. Joseph Patrocinium 1941–1991*, 1991, 12.

47. Brief, Ministerie van Justitie, Dir. Kinderbescherming, afd. Instellingen en Part. Inrichtingen, nr. KT 88-XII, 3. November 1972, Archiv Bethanien Venlo, Doc 1.

48. Sr Agnes, op. cit. p. 9.

49. Ibid.

In Germany, too, the prison apostolate had become a reality; in general, it was seen in a very positive light that sisters visited prisons near their convents. This was particularly so in the prisons at Willich-Anrath in Koblenz and Halle near Leipzig, where sisters worked as prison chaplains over a number of years. They also made it possible for prisoners to do craft work or sing in a choir. Many sisters were given full employment and others worked as volunteers in the prison service. The sisters who worked as prison chaplains were also involved in the different conferences of 'prison chaplaincies,'[50] where they were able to inform these groups of the work, ethos and spirituality of Bethany. Moreover, the convents in Germany were, and are, half-way houses for people who have just been released from prison. The Aldenhoven convent (1988–2002) is particularly noteworthy here because it was public knowledge that it was founded to admit people who had been released from prison for a specific period of time.

The internal rehabilitation offered in Bethany Venlo continues to be of great importance. In recent times Bethany has been the subject of much unexpected press attention, especially in France, but also in the Netherlands, Belgium and Germany. This was in the context of the case of Michelle Martin's early release from prison.[51] Even if Ms Martin did not come to Bethany, this is a clear example of how difficult it can be to live any kind of internal rehabilitation in our modern information age. It is not really possible to maintain discretion regarding the backgrounds of the sisters if information about individual cases is instantly spread worldwide.

DISCRETION

With reference to the apostolate of the interior rehabilitation and the fact that there is no distinction between the sisters regarding their backgrounds, discretion has an important role in Bethany. This discretion/confidentiality

50. Reference should also be made to the many years Sr Bonifatia worked as the diocesan delegate for prison chaplains in the diocese of Essen. See the Conference of the Catholic chaplaincy for Prisons in the Federal Republic of Germany, Published Notification, July 2011, p. 11.

51. Michelle Martin, the partner of Marc Dutroux, assisted him in his crimes against young women and children. Further information concerning this case can be found at Homepage der Dominikaner in den Niederlanden, 'Ex-vrouw Dutroux wil naar klooster Bethanie': http://www. dominicanen.nl/?p=47916 (last accessed 13.5.11); Michelle Martin niet naar Dominicanessen Bethanië: http://www.dominicanen.nl/?p=211378 (last accessed 31.7.12); Le Post, 'L'ex-épouse de Marc Dutroux aurait pu être accueillie dans un couvent près de Besançon': http://www. lepost.fr/article/2011/05/13/2493714_l-ex-epouse-de-marc-dutroux-bientot-dans-un-couvent-pres-de-besancon.html (last accessed 13.5.11); France soir, 'L'ex-femme de Dutroux aurait pu avoir sa place chez nous': http://www.francesoir.fr/actualite/societe/l-ex-femme-dutroux-aurait-pu-avoir-sa-place-chez-nous-101055.html (last accessed 13.5.2011); Domradio: 'Wie weit geht Gastfreundschaft'; http://www.domradio.de/aktuell/73533/wie-weit-geht-die-gastfreundschaft.html (last accessed 13.5.11).

is also in evidence in daily community life. Over the years, Bethany Venlo came to see this idea in different ways, just as there were changes in ordinary practical living.

First of all, discretion in Bethany meant complete secrecy about the former history of every woman from the moment she begins her life in Bethany. This would apply particularly in the public domain, so the general public are not informed about any details of the personal lives of people who live in Bethany.

Subsequently, internal discretion was given great emphasis. The sisters who entered in a particular year were of course aware of how other sisters came to Bethany, but there was no mention of any specific details about their past lives. Secrecy was so strict that it was even forbidden to mention anything to do with furnishings in family homes, as these could be a clue to the lifestyle of the person. For the sisters of subsequent generations the inner Bethany way of life was no longer visible because sisters who had a prison record and those who did not lived among both the choir sisters and the lay sisters, until these distinctions were abolished by Vatican II.

In a further development, discretion was seen as a means of protection from the outside, but the need for discretion within the convent lost its emphasis. The rule on keeping silent was seen as a negative experience as it created a distance between sisters which seemed incompatible with community living. The relaxation of this rule eventually led to people paying little or no attention to their own past lives and the histories of others.

Today it is impressive to see the understanding and experience displayed by the Bethany sisters with respect to the idea of discretion, navigating between the two extremes. A woman who comes to Bethany Venlo today may, of her own volition, explain as much as she wants to, but no one should ask her concrete questions. It is important to remember that vague answers are acceptable and that emphasis should not be placed on the responses to questions. This approach leads to a development in sensitivity towards internal discretion in the congregation and, furthermore, it means that sisters who have shared in this type of confidentiality with other sisters are well equipped to deal with broader aspects of confidentiality. In sharing information with one another it is important that no information about other people is released. This is especially important when new sisters or women interested in this life come to a convent. This confidentiality means that sisters may not expose the entire life stories of others, and when they are describing aspects of the lives of others, this must be done in such a way as not to identify the person. It is no secret that there are different ways within Bethany to serve God, either with the making of perpetual vows or by a temporary commitment. But it is important to note that this distinction does not allow us to know what had happened in the person's life before.[52]

The aim of internal rehabilitation was and is carefully mentioned in the self-portrayal that the Bethany sisters give of themselves, but the public has more widely perceived their apostolate in a different way, as described in the next section.

THE CHILDREN'S VILLAGES

The children's and youth villages are the best known apostolate of the Dominican Bethany Sisters of Venlo. But when Haus Klee in Waldniel was officially blessed on 11 February 1952[53] it was not a children's village but a home for girls. A long process preceded the opening of the girls' home and later the children's and youth villages.[54]

Bethany Venlo continued to develop between the two wars and even during the Second World War. As a result of the German occupation, the Dominican sisters were forced by the German army to leave their motherhouse in Venlo in 1940. They were evacuated to a convent in the village of Koningsbosch in the south of the country. In 1945, a small group went from there to Leyenbroek-Sittard.[55] Because women continued to join the congregation in the years immediately after the war, there was 'not enough work for them'.[56] This may well have played a role in their decision 'to become involved in social work in children's villages and, indeed, to develop this work'.[57] This meant it was possible for them to accept the invitation of the bishop of Roermond to care for children whose 'parents had been imprisoned for sympathising with the foreign rule/occupying force of the Nazis'.[58] There was some scepticism about taking on this work for fear that the com-

---

52. See in addition to this: Dominikanerinnen von Bethanien Venlo (eds.), Akten des Generalkapitels 1981, Empfehlung des Generalkapitels zur 'Diskretion',1981, Archiv Bethanien Venlo; Sr Laetitia OP, *Entwicklung der Handhabung von 'Diskretion' im Verlauf der Geschichte von Bethanien*, 2002, Archiv Bethanien Venlo, H 123a. Sr Hannah Rita OP, *Praktischer Leitfaden zur Diskretion*, 2005, Archiv Bethanien Venlo, H 123b.

53. Archiv Dominikanerinnen von Bethanien, Chronik, 31.13.1951.

54. As early as at the beginning of the twentieth century, German priest and chaplain Fr Erren had established contact with Mother Henri-Dominique; see the section of this article entitled 'Bethany and its Links with the Prison', p. 271.

55. Sr Agnes, op. cit., p. 24.

56. Dominikanerinnen von Bethanien, *Ursachen, Hintergründe und Umstände für die Séparation Bethanien-Montferrand und Bethanien-Venlo. Versuch einer Nacherzählung*, 2003, p. 24.

57. Ibid.

58. Dominikanerinnen von Bethanien (eds.), *25 Jahre Dominikanerinnen von Bethanien, Festschrift zum Jubiläum*, 1977, p. 18.

munity might not yet be ready for such an initiative. The sisters first cared for these children in Leyenbroek before moving to Baexem.[59] The convent in Baexem had formerly been owned by German Franciscans, but after the war it was confiscated by the Dutch government. The sisters moved to this building with the Catholic children, and children who were not Catholic lived in different establishments.

The Bethany Dominican Sisters in the Netherlands had developed a wide-ranging curative pedagogy that was tailor-made to support the individual needs of children in stress and difficulty. Hence, when setting up a home for girls in Germany, the sisters were able to draw on their experience of working in childcare.[60] To establish themselves in Germany it was important that a number of the sisters were in fact German citizens. After 1947 the general prioress and her assistant looked for a suitable house and grounds, finally finding it in Haus Klee in Waldniel, approximately 30 kilometres west of Düsseldorf.[61]

There were fundamental differences between the ethos of childcare in the early years of the Federal Republic of Germany and how the sisters approached this question. The leitmotif in Germany was 'the idea of the adaptability of the children to follow the norms, discipline and rules that were set down ...'.[62] Education in the homes was thus, above all, repressive. As had been the case before and during the war, children and adolescents were separated on the basis of gender, age and religion.[63] For the young people, this meant that they were not only separated from their family homes and familiar surroundings, but possibly also from their siblings. The daily routine in the homes was highly regimented. The needs of individuals were

---

59. Sr Agnes, op. cit., p. 24.

60. In his article Henkelmann emphasises that it was as early as 1951 that the first talks between the Landesjugendamt Rheinland and the Dominicans took place. See Andreas Henkelmann, 'Religiöse Erziehung in Anstalten der Kinder- und Jugendfürsorge in den 1950er und 1960er Jahren – Das Beispiel "Maria im Klee" in Waldniel', in: Wilhelm Damberg *et al.* (eds.), *Mutter Kirche – Vater Staat? Geschichte, Praxis und Debatten der konfessionellen Heimerziehung seit 1945*, Münster 2010, pp. 261–278, esp. pp. 263–264. According to the chronicle of the Dominicans of Bethany Venlo, the Zentrale des Kath. Fürsorgevereins für Mädchen, Frauen und Kinder in Dortmund, requested a sisters' house as early as in 1947. Cf. Archiv Dominikanerinnen von Bethanien Venlo, Chronik, 1947–52.

61. Ibid.

62. Markus Köster, 'Heimkampagnen – Die 68er und die Fürsorgeerziehung', in: Wilhelm Damberg *et al.* (eds.), *Mutter Kirche – Vater Staat? Geschichte, Praxis und Debatten der konfessionellen Heimerziehung seit 1945*, Münster 2010, pp. 62–77, esp. p. 66.

63. It was not until the 1970s that the denominational separation was gradually removed. See Andreas Henkelmann and Uwe Kaminsky, 'Die Geschichte der öffentlichen Heimerziehung im Rheinland (1945–1972)', in Andreas Henkelmann *et al.* (eds.), *Verspätete Modernisierung. Öffentliche Heimerziehung im Rheinland – Geschichte der Heimerziehung in Verantwortung des Landesjugendamtes (1945–1972)*, Essen 2011, pp. 43–150, esp. p. 82.

mostly not taken into consideration. The generally accepted educational phi-losophy, until the 1960s, was to see the individual in terms of what he could not do, rather than what he could.[64]

Wilfried Rudolf points out that the conditions in the homes were often similar to those evident in psychiatric institutions. For example, there were too few qualified personnel and the homes were run in an 'authoritarian fashion'.[65] The therapeutic approach was inadequate and the homes were constantly under-financed. The young people in the homes were cut off from the countryside and, finally, 'structures were anonymous, with large dormi-tories and without any room for any sort of individuality and intimacy'.[66]

According to Henkelmann and Kaminsky, it was in 1957 that the head of the Department for Youth Welfare, Jans, first spoke about transforming the homes, restructuring the existing mass accommodation into small units where children and young people lived with others of different ages and genders in so-called 'family groups'. This meant 'major reconstruction of buildings which were between 40 and 50 years old and an increase of finan-cial support to the private agency'.[67] This revealed that the relevant state authorities concerned with residential education (Landesjugendamt) had become aware of the shortcomings of the system. They sought to transform the homes in support of a person-oriented form of care, support and edu-cation, making use of new educational methods. In addition, the idea of a differentiation in residential care grew, in order to 'give adequate support to each young person'.[68] This finally led to the creation of homes or places that offered a therapeutic learning ethos.[69]

From the beginning, the Dominican Sisters of Venlo took a very different approach both in their homes for girls and in the children's villages. The founding mission of the congregation was central to the pedagogy of the Dominicans. 'Pater J.-J. Lataste is the founder of our congregation. For him the ideal was that women with fractured pasts would form a religious com-

64. Markus Köster, *Jugend, Wohlfahrtsstaat und Gesellschaft im Wandel. Westfalen zwischen Kai-serreich und Bundesrepublik*, Paderborn 1999, pp. 537–62.

65. Wilfried Rudloff, 'Sozialstaat, Randgruppen und bundesrepublikanische Gesellschaft. Umbrüche und Entwicklungen in den sechziger und siebziger Jahren', in Franz-Werner Kersting (ed.), *Psychiatriereform als Gesellschaftsreform. Die Hypothek des Nationalsozialismus und der Aufbruch der sechziger Jahre*, Paderborn, 2003, pp. 181–219, esp. p. 205.

66. Ibid.

67. Andreas Henkelmann and Uwe Kaminsky, 'Die Geschichte der öffentlichen Heimerzie-hung im Rheinland (1945–1972)', in Andreas Henkelmann *et al.* (eds.), *Verspätete Modernisierung. Öffentliche Heimerziehung im Rheinland - Geschichte der Heimerziehung in Verantwortung des Landes-jugendamtes (1945–1972)*, Essen 2011, p. 83.

68. Ibid., p. 84.

69. Ibid.

munity with women who came from ordinary or normal backgrounds. We believe his idea back then and even today is of great importance: every person has her or his unique value. We are all children of one father. It is not our status, the amount of money we have or our occupation that makes us good people, but what we are as human beings.'[70] As a consequence of this understanding of the person, it was possible to take an approach towards children and young people that was very different from that taken in other homes. Enriched also by the experience the sisters brought with them from their work in the Netherlands, the girls' home, and later the children's and youth villages, became the 'flagship project'[71] of the regional youth office. They differed greatly from other homes.[72]

The young women who moved into Waldniel at the beginning of February 1952 were between 15 and 25.[73] They were divided into groups, each group with a leader and an assistant. At the beginning four to five women shared a bedroom.[74] In time, with alterations to the building, every woman had her 'own small room with running water, a bed, table, chair and wardrobe'.[75] It can be assumed that children who grew up in their own families would not have known such luxury. The impact that this would have had on the young people in the homes can only be imagined. It certainly sent a message to the women that they and their privacy were being treated with respect.

The Dominican sisters aimed at empowering the girls and young women to lead independent lives.[76] According to an 'official rule',[77] every girl was re-

70. Anatol Feid and Florian Flohr, *Frohe Botschaft für die Gefangenen. Leben und Werk des Dominikaners Marie Jean-Joseph Lataste*, Mainz 1978, pp.178–179.

71. Andreas Henkelmann and Uwe Kaminsky, 'Die Geschichte der öffentlichen Heimerziehung im Rheinland (1945-1972)', in Andreas Henkelmann *et al.* (eds.), op. cit., p. 99.

72. In the following section(s), the intentions behind, and the concepts of, a children's village as developed by the Dominicans of Bethany will be presented. However, it is not possible to examine how they were realised, what could not be put into practice and what the children and adolescents themselves experienced in their time with the sisters.

73. There is contradictory information about the young women's ages. Alcide Postel assumes that the girls are 18–25, Heinz Theo Risse thinks that they are 15–25. *Haus ohne Gitter* was published in 1954, whereas Risse's article does not mention a publication date. However, Risse must have visited Haus Klee at the beginning of the 1960s because he produces very precise information about the girls' home and the children's village established in 1956. Furthermore, at the end of the leaflet *Sozialpädagogisches Werk Bethanien* there is a report on the college for home education, which was founded in 1963. Thus, Postel's book was published earlier than Risse's article. The discrepancy in the ages as between the two texts could thus be explained by the fact that the age of the young women admitted into the Dominican girls' home was lowered in the course of time. See Alcide Postel, *Haus ohne Gitter*, Waldniel, Dominikanerinnen von Bethanien, 1954, p. 157, and Heinz Theo Risse, 'Neue Wege der Resozialisierung', in: Dominikanerinnen von Bethanien (eds.), *Sozialpädagogische Werk Bethanien*, pp. 5–10, esp. p. 8.

74. See Alcide Postel, *Haus ohne Gitter*, op. cit., p. 157.

75. Heinz Theo Risse, 'Neue Wege der Resozialisierung', op. cit., p. 8.

76. Ibid.

77. Ibid.

quired to enter a profession between a year and 18 months after her arrival. Risse writes that 'alongside the preparation for a job or career, which more or less meets the personal aptitude – offers from the immediate surroundings of Waldniel are fortunately plenty – ... preparation for a good, settled married life with a family were of paramount importance'.[78] This idea has to be seen in the context of the time. For women and girls who had come from dysfunctional families the option to develop relationships and maybe to found a family themselves was a great opportunity.

At the opening of the girls' home in Waldniel, there was already talk of building an extension. The Dominicans took it to be the current house that should be extended. But the local youth office had focused its attention on the pedagogical approach adopted in the children's and youth villages. Eventually both concepts were realised. The girls' home was extended and, in 1956, the first German Bethany children's and youth village opened.[79]

The system used in the children's villages was based on how an ordinary family works.[80] The congregation had learned from experience that children from public residential homes became passive and dependent.[81] The sisters were convinced that the ideal pedagogical milieu for a child is the family, where she or he can develop in the best possible way.[82] They had learnt this from their observation centre in Nijmegen where 'child psychologists, teachers and experienced carers along with the Nuns had evaluated the "family system" ... .'[83]

But even when the children's villages created an atmosphere similar to family life, the Dominicans were very conscious that this was a mere substitute. The children and young people given into the care of the sisters were 'more or less emotionally disturbed; especially at the beginning, they had a lot to cope with: the separation from their families, settling into a new

78. Ibid.

79. Andreas Henkelmann, 'Religiöse Erziehung in Anstalten der Kinder- und Jugendfürsorge in den 1950er und 1960er Jahren – Das Beispiel "Maria im Klee" in Waldniel', in: Wilhelm Damberg et al. (eds.), *Mutter Kirche – Vater Staat? Geschichte, Praxis und Debatten der konfessionellen Heimerziehung seit 1945*, op. cit., p. 264.

80. The family system has remained the way of life in the children's villages of the Bethany Dominicans until today, see: http://www.bethanien-kinderdoerfer.de, last accessed 27.05.2013.

81. See: Heinz Theo Risse, 'Neue Wege der Resozialisierung", in: Dominikanerinnen von Bethanien (eds.), *Sozialpädagogische Werk Bethanien*, n.d., p. 7.

82. The concept of a family system was certainly not a solution for every child, but the Dominicans of Bethany did not claim that it was. Rather, they considered this type of educational care particularly adequate for groups of siblings. Cf. Heinz Theo Risse, 'Neue Wege der Resozialisierung', op. cit., p. 6.

83. Ibid., 7. However, it is unclear whether the family system was reflected on only after the foundation of the first children's village. The observation centres were established only after the first children had been accepted. Thus it can be assumed that the Dominicans first brought up the children intuitively in a family system and examined this in a more academic way at a later stage.

environment, the hesitant search for a personal relation with the new child care worker and for contacts with the other children'.[84] Unlike the situation in larger institutions, in these homes a carer or 'group-sister' would accompany up to 15 children from infancy to the age of 18.[85] She lived with the children in their own separate home and was therefore a constant person of reference. She filled the role of a mother.[86] The children and the sister in charge were to 'form a community and so create relationships which would last even after they left the structures of the children's and youth villages when they had reached adulthood ....'.[87]

Another difference from the institutions that were already in place was that siblings were not separated but, instead, lived together in a group. In the above-mentioned observation centre, they had found that it is 'dangerous to separate siblings'. By being kept together the siblings were spared yet further separation trauma. This meant there was no alternative but co-education.[88]

The education and general development of the children and young people were not just managed by the sister in charge. The Dominican sisters were conscious that the world outside the home had an important role to play. It meant that the children participated in church, cultural and public events. They attended a state school and were encouraged to have contact with people outside the home. So far as it was possible, the relatives of the children were involved in the lives of the children.[89]

The idea of the children's villages was very convincing. After the opening of the first children's village in Waldniel, Eltville-Erbach near Mainz opened in 1965 and Bergisch Gladbach-Refrath near Cologne three years later. All three homes, living their original ethos, are still up and running today.[90] In 1962 Bethany took over a children's home from the Caritas in Dalheim, a village near Aachen, which they transformed into a children's village. Ten

84. Mutter Magdalena OP, 'Möglichkeiten und Grenzen des familienhaft gestalteten Heimes', in: Dominikanerinnen von Bethanien (eds.), *Sozialpädagogisches Werk Bethanien*, p. 12.

85. Since the congregation is unable to provide a sufficient number of sisters today, lay persons adopt the role of 'group sisters'. However, their work as group leaders is identical to the task of the group sisters.

86. See Dominikanerinnen von Bethanien (eds.), *Die Kinderdorfarbeit der Dominikanerinnen von Bethanien. Auszug aus den Akten des Provinzkapitels 1975/76*, p. 9.

87. Ibid.

88. Mother Imelda also indicated that this was the main reason for introducing co-education. See Mutter Magdalena Nouwen OP, 'Möglichkeiten und Grenzen des familienhaft gestalteten Heimes', in: Dominikanerinnen von Bethanien (eds.), op. cit., p. 13.

89. Ibid., 18-19.

90. Bethanien Kinderdörfer gGmbH (eds.), *Leitbild der Bethanien Kinder- und Jugenddörfer*, 2006.

years later, however, this home had to be returned to the original patron.[91]

In 2001 the Dominicans founded Bethany Children Villages Ltd, which meant the finances of the limited company could be independent from the finances of the congregation. The children's villages remained under the patronage of the sisters. Today the children's villages can take up to 260 children and adolescents. They are cared for by roughly 230 staff members and 14 sisters.[92]

Qualified personnel were required to run the children's homes. For this purpose the Bethany Dominicans opened a state-recognised 'private college for the education of personnel'[93] in 1963. Again the Dominicans were in the vanguard. Up until then there had been no such schools in the diocese of Aachen or west of the Lower Rhine.[94] During their two-year course the trainees would 'learn about how to care for children in homes.'[95] In order to qualify for the course students had to have their secondary school certificate (Mittlere Reife) or the entrance qualification for a university of applied sciences (Fachschulreife), and have completed their eighteenth year.[96] Subjects included in the course were general ones such as German, youth literature and civic education. In addition, profession-related subjects, such as psychology, pedagogy, sociology, home and group dynamics, and some health-orientated subjects were taught. Also included were music and craft, gymnastics, event management and practical work in the day-to-day running of a home (housework, needlework, handicrafts, report writing, discussion work). A part of the course was work experience, which would last a number of weeks every year. A successful completion of the course entitled the qualified person to be a leader of a group of children and adolescents.[97]

Not only sisters of the congregation studied at the college – lay people were also accepted. As they came from all over the Federal Republic, it was possible for them to live at Haus Klee during their training. The first ten successful candidates, most of them young sisters,[98] qualified in 1965. The college was closed in 1971. According to the archives of the Dominicans, it

91. The home had to be returned due to a lack of sisters. In 1952 the Dominicans of Bethany founded another children's village in Aruba. In 1968, a children's village opened in Italy.

92. Bethanien Kinderdörfer gGmbH (eds.), *Leitbild der Bethanien Kinder- und Jugenddörfer*, op. cit.

93. The history of the private college has not been researched yet. Therefore it is possible to provide only a fragmentary overview here.

94. *Westdeutsche Zeitung – Mönchengladbacher Nachrichten*, 8 March 1965, Copy in the Chronicle of the Dominicans of Bethany, 1965.

95. Ibid.

96. Ibid.

97. Dominikanerinnen von Bethanien (eds.), *Sozialpädagogisches Werk Bethanien*, op. cit., p. 23.

98. *Westdeutsche Zeitung – Mönchengladbacher Nachrichten*, op. cit.

was closed because there were other places near Waldniel where one could study the same subjects.[99]

Both in their work as prison chaplains and in their care for young people in their homes and with the founding of their private college, the sisters showed they were pioneers in their work.

CALLED TO THE 'INCARNATION OF TRUST AND HOPE'[100]

As a result of his face-to-face contact with prisoners in the women's central prison in Cadillac and his readiness to meet them on an equal footing, Fr Lataste became a pioneer of practical charity. He founded a community that did not have a specific purpose in mind, for example the forming of young women or caring for the sick. The Bethany sisters rather had and have the purpose of creating a milieu where the mercy and love of God were and are made visible in places where people were made invisible and experienced social alienation.

Thanks to this, the sisters of Bethany Venlo were pioneers in their work. It was often uncomfortable for people to see how the sisters, instead of creating better living conditions for 'others' in some far-off remote place, were willing instead to share their lives with those 'others' and to become similar to them in such a way that it was no longer possible to make any distinctions between them. Meeting people such as prisoners in this way will lead to having to face frontiers and taboos set by society over and over again. And it also leads beyond them.

Through their practical living of the mercy of God in the here and now, the Dominican Sisters of Bethany show that there is a wound in the world that can be healed and overcome. The kingdom of God is among us where we are ready to believe that we can all do good and where we are ready to give witness with our lives to the hope for change and healing.

The preaching of Bethany is based on a belief in the future that comes from the death and resurrection of Jesus Christ, or, as Gueullette stressed, the 'Incarnation of trust and hope'.[101]

99. Archiv Dominikanerinnen von Bethanien Venlo, Chronik, 18 June 1971. It is impossible to determine here to what extent other factors contributed to the giving up of the technical college.
100. Jean-Marie Gueullette, *Jean-Joseph Lataste*, op. cit., p. 109.
101. Ibid.

BIBLIOGRAPHY

25 Jahre Dominikanerinnen von Bethanien, Festschrift zum Jubiläum, Dominikanerinnen von Bethanien, 1977.

Bethanien Kinderdörfer gGmbH (eds.), *Leitbild der Bethanien Kinder- und Jugenddörfer*, 2006.

De Boissieu, R.P., *Béthanie. Les Madeleines réhabilitées*, Paris, Grasset, 1931.

Feid, Anatol and Flohr, Florian, *Frohe Botschaft für die Gefangenen. Leben und Werk des Dominikaners Marie Jean-Joseph Lataste*, Mainz, 1978.

Gueullette, Jean-Marie, *Jean-Joseph Lataste. Apostel der Gefängnisse*, Dominikanische Quellen und Zeugnisse 15, Leipzig, 2010.

Heinrich, Jean-Paul, *Particuliere reclassering en overheid in Nederland sinds 1823*, Arnhem: Gouda Quint III, 1996.

Hugo, Victor, *Les Misérables*, Paris, 1862.

Köster, Markus, *Jugend, Wohlfahrtsstaat und Gesellschaft im Wandel. Westfalen zwischen Kaiserreich und Bundesrepublik*, Paderborn, 1999.

Max-Planck-Institut (ed.): *Code Pénal. In Kraft seit 1992*, bilingual synoptic edition, 1999.

Postel, Alcide, *Haus ohne Gitter*, Waldniel, Dominikanerinnen von Bethanien, 1954.

Postel, Alcide, *Verborgen Werelden*, (no place), Dominikanerinnen von Bethanien, 1939.

Willigis, P., OP, *Unschuld und Busse als Schwestern*, Dülmen, 1926.

ARTICLES

Henkelmann, Andreas, 'Religiöse Erziehung in Anstalten der Kinder- und Jugendfürsorge in den 1950er und 1960er Jahren – Das Beispiel "Maria im Klee" in Waldniel', in Wilhelm Damberg *et al.* (eds.), *Mutter Kirche – Vater Staat? Geschichte, Praxis und Debatten der konfessionellen Heimerziehung seit 1945*, Münster, 2010.

Henkelmann, Andreas and Kaminsky, Uwe, 'Die Geschichte der öffentlichen Heimerziehung im Rheinland (1945–1972)', in Andreas Henkelmann, Uwe Kaminsky, Judith Pierlings, Thomas Swiderek, Sarah Banach (eds.), *Verspätete Modernisierung. Öffentliche Heimerziehung im Rheinland – Geschichte der Heimerziehung in Verantwortung des Landesjugendamtes (1945–1972)*, Essen, 2011.

Heinz Theo Risse, 'Neue Wege der Resozialisierung', in Dominikanerinnen von Bethanien (eds.), *Sozialpädagogische Werk Bethanien*.

Köster, Markus, 'Heimkampagnen – Die 68er und die Fürsorgeerziehung', in Wilhelm Damberg *et al.* (eds.), *Mutter Kirche – Vater Staat? Geschichte, Praxis und Debatten der konfessionellen Heimerziehung seit 1945*, Münster, 2010.

Mutter Magdalena OP, 'Möglichkeiten und Grenzen des familienhaft gestalteten Heimes', in Dominikanerinnen von Bethanien (eds.), *Sozialpädagogisches Werk Bethanien.*

Rudloff, Wilfried, 'Sozialstaat, Randgruppen und bundesrepublikanische Gesellschaft. Umbrüche und Entwicklungen in den sechziger und siebziger Jahren', in Franz-Werner Kersting (eds.), *Psychiatriereform als Gesellschaftsreform. Die Hypothek des Nationalsozialismus und der Aufbruch der sechziger Jahre*, Paderborn, 2003.

Sr. Magdalena, "Vrouwen als Reclassenten", in Dr. Nicolaas Muller (ed.), *Straffen en Helpen*, 1954.

DOCUMENTS FROM THE BETHANY ARCHIVE IN VENLO

Brief, Ministerie van Justitie, Dir. Kinderbescherming, afd. Instellingen en Part. Inrichtingen, nr. KT 88-XII, 3 November 1972, Archiv Bethanien Venlo, Doc 1.

Chronik Bethanien Venlo, Archiv Bethanien Venlo.

Dominikanerinnen von Bethanien Venlo (eds.), Akten des Generalkapitels 1981, Empfehlung des Generalkapitels zur 'Diskretion', 1981, Archiv Bethanien Venlo.

Dominikanerinnen von Bethanien (eds.), Die Kinderdorfarbeit der Dominikanerinnen von Bethanien. Auszug aus den Akten des Provinzkapitels 1975/76.

Dominikanerinnen von Bethanien (eds.), Sozialpädagogisches Werk Bethanien.

Dominikanerinnen von Bethanien, Ursachen, Hintergründe und Umstände für die Séparation Bethanien-Montferrand und Bethanien-Venlo. Versuch einer Nacherzählung, 2003.

Sammlung: Bethanien in het wort. Archiv Bethanien Venlo, H 121.

Sr Hannah Rita OP, Diplomarbeit: Resozialisierung als geistliche Aufgabe. Die Geschichte der Dominikanerinnen von Bethnien in Stevensbeek/ NL, Bonn, 2012.

Sr Hannah Rita OP, Praktischer Leitfaden zur Diskretion, 2005, Archiv Bethanien Venlo, H 123b.

Sr Hannah Rita OP, Rehabilitation; eine Lebensgeschichte. Oder der eine

Cent von anderthalb, Archiv Bethanien Venlo.

Sr Laetitia OP, Entwicklung der Handhabung von 'Diskretion' im Verlauf der Geschichte von Bethanien, 2002, Archiv Bethanien Venlo, H 123a.

Sr Pia-Elisabeth OP, Entwicklung der Gefängnisbesuche in Bethanien Mont-ferrand, 2011.

Zr Agnes, Vijftig jaar hulpverlening: de stichting St. Joseph Patrocinium 1941–1991, 1991.

Zr Magdalena, Scripties van Lesen, Archiv Bethanien Venlo, Scr. 53.

Westdeutsche Zeitung – Mönchengladbacher Nachrichten, 8 March 1965, copy in the Chronicle of the Dominicans of Bethany, 1965.

WEBPAGES

Homepage der Dominikaner in den Niederlanden, Ex-vrouw Dutroux wil naar klooster Bethanie: http://www.dominicanen.nl/?p=47916 (13.5.2011); Michelle Martin niet naar Dominicanessen Bethanië: http://www.dominicanen.nl/?p=211378 (31.7.2012).

Le Post, L'ex-épouse de Marc Dutroux aurait pu être accueillie dans un couvent près de Besançon: http://www.lepost.fr/article/2011/05/13/2493714_1-ex-epouse-de-marc-dutroux-bientot-dans-un-couvent-pres-de-besancon.html. (13.5.2011).

France soir, 'L'ex-femme de Dutroux aurait pu avoir sa place chez nous': http://www.francesoir.fr/actualite/societe/l-ex-femme-dutroux-aurait-pu-avoir-sa-place-chez-nous-101055.html. (13.5.2011).

Domradio: Wie weit geht Gastfreundschaft; http://www.domradio.de/ak-tuell/73533/wie-weit-geht-die-gastfreundschaft.html. (13.5.2011).

http://www.bethanien-kinderdoerfer.de, (27.05.2013).

16

Portraits, Sketches and Snapshots:
Maryknoll Sisters around the World

BERNICE KITA, O.P., M.M.

In 1912 a small group of women, inspired by a strong desire to further the mission of the Church in foreign lands, came together in Hawthorne, New York, under the leadership of Fr James Anthony Walsh. Their immediate task was to help produce and distribute *The Field Afar*, a mission magazine intended to increase enthusiasm and generate support among American Catholics for foreign mission work. Their enthusiastic support enabled the Catholic Foreign Mission Society of America, later known as Maryknoll Fathers and Brothers, to ordain its first three foreign mission priests by 1917.

These pioneering women longed to serve in overseas mission themselves. In early 1921, 25 of them professed their first vows in the newly established Foreign Mission Sisters of St Dominic. Its founder, Mother Mary Joseph Rogers, became the first prioress. The sisters had deliberately chosen the Dominican family because contemplation in action would best suit their mission charism.

Four Maryknoll sisters travelled across the US to the cities of Los Angeles and Seattle to serve Japanese immigrants in Maryknoll parishes. Six others sailed to China where Maryknoll Fathers had recently established missions. Fr James Edward Walsh, ordained in 1915, wrote to Mother Mary Joseph from his mission in Kochow, China, of his hopes that 'the Sisters can begin to plan their work on the missions ... an orphanage, girls' schools, medical dispensaries and later hospital work'.

Mother Mary Joseph strongly believed that each Maryknoll sister is 'truly an apostle, commissioned by God in Christ, sent to the highways and byways of the world as a messenger of the Good News and a witness to God's Reign'. She believed that God's Reign begins right here on earth.

Then the king will say to those at his right hand, 'Come, you that are blessed by my Father, inherit the kingdom prepared for you from the foundation of the world; for I was hungry and you gave me food, I was thirsty and you gave me something to drink, I was a stranger and you welcomed me, I was naked and you gave me clothing, I was sick and you took care of me, I was in prison and you visited me.' ... 'Truly I tell you, just as you did it to one of the least of these who are members of my family, you did it to me.' (Mt 25: 34–36, 40)

The Maryknoll Sister pioneers in China carried the Good News to women and children, staying in villages for weeks at a time. They desired to save souls, yet saving lives soon became a large part of their work. From the beginning, spreading the Good News by word went hand in hand with spreading the Good News by deed.

For years after the fall of the Manchu Dynasty in 1912, warring factions and roving bandits disrupted the lives of thousands of Chinese villagers. Many families fled their homes and sought refuge in Maryknoll mission compounds. The sisters in Yeungkong were caring for babies, orphans, blind girls and old women. They also began a small school and initiated a catechumenate, producing their own catechetical material. Mother Mary Joseph visited the sisters in 1923 and recorded her experiences in her visitation diary: 'I spent the entire day watching and reporting movements while the Sisters made room in all our houses for the refugees who began to pour in ... These poor people with all their worldly treasures in a few baskets, abandoning their homes, seeking safety with strangers.'

Housing and feeding refugees, rescuing abandoned babies, aiding widows and orphans, caring for the suffering: these all became an integral part of the sisters' ministry. Although the term 'human rights' was not yet a watchword, the sisters' efforts to alleviate suffering truly were works for justice.

After Vatican II, followed by gatherings of bishops in countries around the world to implement its new vision of Church, Maryknoll sisters moved in new directions in mission based on 'the signs of the times'. Living in impoverished neighbourhoods and rural settings, sharing their neighbours' problems, many sisters realised a new vision of service. In the last quarter of the twentieth century, justice *per se* became a cornerstone of the Maryknoll sisters' ministries.

In 1978 their Eleventh General Assembly set equality for women in Church and society as a goal. In their Twelfth Assembly in 1984 they put forward eleven justice criteria for ministry. In 1990, in their Thirteenth Assembly, the delegates highlighted work for justice and peace, and an option for the poor, oppressed and alienated. 'We see the struggle for a just society with a new world order as integral to mission. Peace will come when hearts are transformed and when justice shines forth in social, economic, political, cultural and religious systems ... Our collective experience of physical and institutional violence has changed us irrevocably and strengthens our resolve to seek peace with justice'... We believe that true peace is based on justice and we choose to be doers of justice and peace ...'

The delegates to this assembly recommended that 'we continue to develop ministries of accompaniment which address the effects of domestic/political violence and militarization, e.g. with political, economic and environmental refugees/displaced persons'. They committed Maryknoll sisters to uphold the dignity of women and to work towards women's empowerment, to work for the elimination of the social sin of racism and to integrate ecology and environmental concerns into their ministries as justice issues.

Over the decades and across the globe, Maryknoll sisters have served victims of injustice and have laboured to bring the Reign of God on Earth by word and by deed.

PREACHING JUSTICE THROUGH HEALTH CARE
– KOREA, BOLIVIA, AND UNITED STATES, 1931–58:
SR MARY MERCY, M.M.

Within a few years of their foundation, Maryknoll sisters received requests for their missioners from several countries besides China. By 1930, they had missions in Korea, Manchuria, Hawaii, the Philippines and the US.

Many Maryknoll sisters went to learn basic health care techniques at the local hospital in Ossining, New York, before going to their missions. Some had come with backgrounds in the medical field, but none were medical doctors. In 1918 Sr Mary Joseph received a letter from Elizabeth Hirschboeck, a high school student with a strong desire to be a sister missioner. The women living at Mary's Knoll, however, were not yet recognised by the Vatican as a religious congregation. Elizabeth would have to wait a few years, Sr Mary Joseph replied. In the meantime, she suggested, why not study medicine? Sister-doctors were sorely needed on the missions.

Elizabeth accepted the suggestion as if it were her first assignment. Mother Mary Joseph sensed promise in Elizabeth and offered Maryknoll Sister support for her tuition at Marquette Medical School. Elizabeth fulfilled Mother Mary Joseph's and her own hopes. She graduated, completed her residency, and arrived at Maryknoll ten years later, medical degree in hand. She completed her novitiate training and professed her vows. Her new name, Sr Mary Mercy, prophetically summed up her life. Sr Mary Mercy became an iconic figure for Maryknoll sisters in the medical field.

Assigned to Korea in 1931, Sr Mercy joined other Maryknoll sisters in the northern town of Shingeishu. Korea had been a Japanese possession since 1910 and Japan treated Koreans and their ancient language and culture as inferior. Sr Mercy, on the other hand, saw the Koreans and the Japanese as beloved children of God. She studied the Korean language for five hours a day until she felt proficient enough to speak with her patients. She then opened a tiny dispensary under the church steps with only a table, a chair, some shelves, her doctor's bag and four types of medicine. Word quickly spread and soon 1,500 patients a month received her professional and compassionate care. When she closed the dispensary each day Sr Mercy made house calls all over town. Within two years of opening her makeshift dispensary, she had a brand new one built onto the convent. For nine years Sr Mercy lovingly dedicated herself to her Korean patients. Her love for God motivated all she did, and her personal relationship with Jesus shone through clearly. 'God has given us the privilege of caring for his poor,' Sr Mercy once wrote. 'It is nothing that we do for Him. It is, rather, another of His gifts to us.'

By 1940 Sr Mercy's health began to fail and asthma literally took her breath away. She left Korea on a steamer, intending to return after recuperating. However, the Japanese bombing of the US naval fleet at Pearl Harbour in Hawaii on 8 December 1941 plunged the US into war with Japan. Previously, Japan had tolerated Americans in Korea; now they were enemies. In a short time the Second World War had engulfed most of Asia and the Pacific islands, trapping many Maryknoll sisters in their mission countries and keeping Sr Mercy from returning to hers.

Doors soon began opening to Maryknoll sisters in Latin America and Africa. Sr Mercy's next assignment could not have contrasted more with Korea's temperate climate and ancient Asian culture. She would go to Bolivia, an extremely poor South American country, as head of a Maryknoll Sister medical team. Their task: to open a small hospital in the steamy tropical jungle town of Riberalta, on the Beni River. After studying tropical diseases in Panama for a few months, Sr Mercy and her team arrived in Riberalta at the end of 1943. They quickly set up a dispensary and learned some Spanish. Sr Mercy began visiting patients in their homes and planning for the new hospital.

The Maryknoll sisters provided the only medical care for hundreds of miles around. They served impoverished rubber and brazil nut gatherers who lived with their families in isolated villages strung out along the river. Undernourished and underpaid, with little schooling, the hard-working people lived in extreme poverty. Most patients had haemoglobin counts of 15 to 25 per cent, when a textbook case of 50 per cent was considered dangerously low. Malaria, hookworm, amoebas and intestinal worms were their constant companions.

The Maryknoll Hospital in Riberalta opened in January 1946, with Sr Mercy as administrator and physician. Maryknoll sister-nurses trained local staff and established the School of Practical Nursing. The sisters worked long hours in the hospital and travelled for days by horseback and river launch to hold clinics in isolated communities. With Sr Mercy setting the tone of Christ-like charity, Maryknoll and lay staff treated every patient with dignity and respect.

Sr Mercy loved these Bolivians, yet she longed to return to Korea. After seven years, she believed the Riberalta Hospital and the School of Practical Nursing could function quite well without her. A new Maryknoll sister-doctor, Maryknoll nurses and recently-graduated Bolivian practical nurses would take over. For Sr Mercy the parting was bittersweet. She was greatly loved and respected by the Sisters and the people of Riberalta, many of whom had signed a petition asking that she stay. She felt she had left a part of her heart in Bolivia, yet another part still remained in Korea.

But Korea had changed radically since she had left it in 1940. Japan had lost its colonies, including Korea, when it surrendered to the Allied Forces in 1945. The Allies divided Korea, with the north administered by the Soviet Union and the south by the US. In June 1950 the North Korean army, backed by China and the Soviet Union, invaded the south. US and Allied forces came to the defence of the South Korean army and evacuated all non-Korean civilians. As the war raged, refugees from the north fleeing Communism poured across the border. The nearest city, Pusan, with a pre-war population of 250,000, was being flooded with refugees who came with only what they could carry. Pusan's population in mid-1951 had already surpassed one million, and more kept coming.

Sr Mercy petitioned American General Douglas MacArthur, Supreme Commander of Allied Forces in Korea, for permission for a Maryknoll Sister medical team to return to Korea to serve the refugees. Amazingly, the general granted her request. In April 1951, these sisters became the first civilians to set foot in Korea since the war had started nine months earlier.

Maryknoll's two medical doctors, two nurses and one pharmacist had a lot of help in setting up their makeshift dispensary in Pusan. Twenty Korean Sisters of Perpetual Help, themselves refugees from the north, cleaned and scrubbed, made makeshift furniture and set up sterilisers. Military personnel volunteered as well. Medical donations arrived through Maryknoll and many charitable organisations.

The medical team began treating 500 patients a day. Smallpox, skin diseases, dysentery, worms, whooping cough, typhoid, pneumonia, tuberculosis and malnutrition were all seen in the course of a day's work. After the dispensary closed each day, the doctors would make house calls to the refugees' tiny hovels on the hillsides. At times, after taking off their shoes in respectful Korean fashion, they literally crawled into the shelters on their hands and knees. 'I had a call to the highest point on the highest mountain today,' Sr Mercy wrote to Mother Mary Joseph. 'The path is very narrow and overhangs a precipice. One of my companions would pull and the other push, both clutching my habit so that I would not fall. I have waddled through mud in my days in Bolivia, but Pusan's is tops. Soon I was coated with it but we kept going up and up ... The mother of the patient (a young man with TB) said she was sorry the sister-doctor who is so old (I like that – at 48!) was having such trouble puffing up the hill.'

Within a month the dispensary was treating a thousand patients a day. A year after the Maryknoll clinic opened Sr Mercy wrote, 'It is taking almost superhuman strength and energy to meet the crowds that come to us daily. The number at the clinic increase[s] every day. On busy days we have as many as 1,900, almost 1,950 one day this week. I don't know how the medicines last.' By October 1952, 35 medical personnel, including four Korean doctors, a Swedish doctor, and eight nurses worked in the clinic. Volunteer army and navy nurses came in their free time. The staff used whatever materials were at hand and provided food and clothing to the refugees.

Patients would begin lining up for a morning consultation the previous afternoon. A sister-nurse would go out after breakfast every morning to pluck the worst cases out of the line and put them first, lest they die while waiting. The line of destitute patients became famous as the longest charity line in the world. The highest number of patients treated in one day reached nearly 3,000. The dispensary grew to include an adult clinic and four paediatric clinics housed in prefabricated huts with packing boxes serving as examination tables. If a child was brought in suffering from smallpox, an immunisation team would soon be out in the neighbourhood vaccinating all comers. More than 50 per cent of the children had TB. By the end of 1952,

350 children with TB of the bone were in orthopaedic casts. In one year the children's clinics tended to over 95,000 children under the age of ten, more than any children's clinic in the US.

Sr Mercy took a break from her dispensary routine in June 1952. It was not a vacation. Rather, she went to receive the honorary degree of doctor of science, *honoris causa*, from her alma mater, Marquette University. She used the opportunity to speak to as many people, organisations and companies as she could, enlisting their support for the medical work in Korea. When she returned to Pusan, she brought with her donations and promises of help. In addition, six more Maryknoll sisters were assigned to the Pusan work.

The sisters kept dreaming up ways to help the refugees. Appeals went out to US citizens to 'Adopt a Korean family for $5 a week.' In September 1952, Sr Mercy wrote: 'Our latest project is a War Widows' Village … So many women with three or four children, destitute and starving, are living in the streets. We have already provided shelter for fifteen families and, with time, will provide room for forty-five. There will be a day nursery also where the children will be cared for so the mothers can work. At the present time we are supplying food for all.'

Three-and-a-half years after arriving in Pusan, Sr Mercy had the great satisfaction of attending the ground-breaking for the new Maryknoll Hospital. In all of Pusan there were many hospitals but only 40 hospital beds were available to the public. With land from the Korean government, materials contributed by the US Army and an enormous fund-raising campaign by seven volunteer agencies to pay for labour and equipment, the 160-bed Maryknoll Hospital would soon be a reality. But Sr Mercy would never attend patients at this long-dreamed-of hospital. Her health was breaking again. The day after the ground-breaking, carrying a letter of appreciation from South Korea's Ministry of Health, a citation from the governor of the province, a citation from the mayor of Pusan and the keys to the city of Seoul, South Korea's capital, Sr Mercy went home to Maryknoll to recuperate. She already knew her next job. A hospital in the middle of the US needed her healing skills, her love, her compassion and her example.

This time the healing would be not only physical but also societal. Sr Mercy and her newest Maryknoll Sister team would open the first racially-integrated hospital in Kansas City, Missouri, a part of the US where segregation of black people from white seemed a necessary part of life.

The invitation came from Edwin V. O'Hara, bishop of the Diocese of Kansas City. In 1951 he had been approached by leading white medical specialists who were completing training for several well-qualified black physicians. They were eager to practise according to the highest standards and work freely with their colleagues, but in Kansas City the only hospital that would admit black doctors and black patients did not have high standards. The physicians asked the bishop to open a hospital for blacks that would meet higher standards. However, Bishop O'Hara saw racial segregation as clearly unjust. He decided on a daring innovation: an integrated hospital, open to all. He invited the Maryknoll Sisters to accept the challenge of administering a racially colour-blind hospital in the segregated state of Missouri, and they did.

The 85-bed fully equipped general hospital, named Queen of the World, opened in 1954. A plaque on the wall just inside the door declared: 'These doors are ever open to all the afflicted regardless of race, creed or colour'. Maryknoll provided seven sisters, including a second doctor. Sr Mercy, who served as physician and administrator, set the tone. From the beginning, there were excellent relations between the sisters and the medical staff, who adhered to high standards. The hospital enjoyed the loyalty and the support of the staff. Sisters visited each patient every day, bringing comfort and encouragement, and quickly won their confidence.

'The Queen' began as the only interracial, non-sectarian hospital east of the Mississippi River in the state of Missouri. Within three years its professional reputation had been established. Its programme of complete integration of patients and staff proved that an integrated hospital was not only possible but also desirable. By mid-1956 the medical staff consisted of 183 white and 30 black physicians. The active staff, the backbone of the hospital, was 17 white and 17 black. As time passed, the Queen of the World's patient load started to drop, indicating that more hospitals were gradually opening their doors to all. After ten years, Maryknoll returned 'The Queen' to the diocese. The sisters had happily worked themselves out of a job.

Sr Mercy left 'The Queen' in 1958 when she was elected vicaress general of the Maryknoll Sisters. After serving two six-year terms, during which she strongly influenced the congregation's medical mission work and formation of its doctors, she retired. Leaving her life of intense activity, she joined two other sisters living in a small apartment in a poor neighbourhood of New York City to share their ministry of prayer. Sr Mercy once wrote, 'I consider my prayer presence the true fulfilment of my religious vocation.' She died 13 years later, fittingly on the Feast of the Korean Martyrs.

PREACHING JUSTICE THROUGH ACCOMPANIMENT
DURING WAR, US, 1942–45: SR MARY SUSANNA HAYASHI, M.M
AND SR BERNADETTE YOSHUMOCHI, M.M.

Japan's attack on Pearl Harbor in 1941 thrust the US into war. Maryknoll sisters who were US citizens and missioned in Korea, Manchuria, Japan and the Philippines suddenly found themselves in enemy territory. Japanese authorities searched their houses and placed many under house arrest. Several sisters were arrested, imprisoned and questioned for weeks in dank prisons. Forty-seven Maryknoll sisters in the Philippines were confined in Los Baños Prison Camp, where over 2,100 expatriate civilians suffered harsh treatment, hunger and deprivation until their liberation by US paratroopers and Filipino guerrillas on 23 February 1945.

The US also had its own shameful internment camps. Fearing that Japan would recruit spies from ethnic Japanese living near the Pacific coast, President Franklin D. Roosevelt issued Executive Order 9066 on 19 February 1942. It required all people of Japanese ancestry, US citizens as well as Japanese citizens, to be interned inland in camps or confined to select places. With little notice, innocent Japanese families had to sell all they had, pack just a few suitcases, and go to poorly prepared camps hundreds of miles from their homes. Approximately 120,000 people were forcibly relocated; two thirds were US citizens and half of them were children.

Maryknoll Sisters had been serving the Japanese communities in parishes in Los Angeles, California and Seattle, Washington since the missions opened. Twenty years later, their house diaries recorded the anxious days and weeks following Pearl Harbor and the subsequent uprooting of the parishioners. The Seattle diary kept a detailed account of their parishioners. The Maryknoll sisters, priests and brothers, all US citizens, longed to accompany their parishioners east to the camp in Idaho, but were forbidden.

The Los Angeles convent, however, was staffed by both US and Japanese sisters. The executive order permitted Japanese sisters Mary Susanna Hayashi and Bernadette Yoshumochi to be interned at the Maryknoll Motherhouse in Ossining, NY, but they chose to accompany their parishioners to the Manzanar Internment Camp in California. From 10 August 1942 to 28 October 1945, these Maryknoll sisters suffered the same hardships as the people they accompanied. Excerpts from the Maryknoll Sisters diaries and press releases follow.

Maryknoll Sisters Seattle Diary – 1941
    Dec. 7 – …we heard the radio broadcasts of the attack on Pearl Harbour.

Dec. 8 – …formal declaration of War between the U.S. and Japan.

Dec. 12 – Plans for organizing the second generation Japanese under the civil defense program were formulated by the Japanese American Citizens' League …

Dec. 16 - … representatives from all Japanese clubs and churches came to pledge their allegiance. … prominent American citizens … expressed their faith in the second generation Japanese.

Maryknoll Sisters Seattle Diary – 1942

Feb. 16 – We are troubled … papers talk of mass evacuation of aliens and citizens alike.

Feb. 21 – 101 more Japanese were interned today as FBI continues its search in the city.

Feb. 22 – We visited the Takisaki home … seven children. Mother died some time ago and the father has been interned … The two older girls carry the burden of the family … worried as to what to do with their home furnishing in the event of evacuation. They are Catholic and are not really alone as long as they have Maryknoll within call.

Feb. 28 – An important series of conferences opened today in Seattle regarding evacuation of the Japanese. Very little hope is held out for our people remaining here.

March 6 – Rumours of concentration camps for all causes much anxiety.

March 16 – The nursery babies were on the doorstep of the building where they were to be fingerprinted and tagged for identification this morning.

March 24 – Curfew for Japanese announced today …

March 26 – We took pictures of the different classes with their teachers to keep among our souvenirs … One curfew law is that no Japanese may move after Sunday night … people fearing concentration camp life are trying to get away before then.

March 29 – … our first farewells …

Apr. 18 – Father told us evacuation would begin next week.

Apr. 19 – … the ministers, preachers and heads of all the other Christian denominations are Japanese and so their work goes on in camp – which gives them an advantage over us.

Apr. 27 – A day long to be remembered. School closed at noon …

Apr. 28 – The first group for camp left in army trucks this morning …

May 19 – Word from the camp tells us of the deaths of two mothers and four new-born babies.

June 11 – Six of us, with Brother Adrian driving, visited our people for the first time ... we were greeted with the excited calls of the children lined up against the barbed wire fences ...

Nov. 15 – Our Japanese people in Idaho are beginning to feel the rigors of the climate. Last year the respective low and high in temperature were 25 degrees [Fahrenheit] below freezing for January and 105 degrees high for July.

Maryknoll Sisters Los Angeles Diary – 1942

Feb. 27 – A meeting was held at the Council of Social Agencies today to discuss plans for the evacuation of children living in Japanese homes.

Mar. 26 – Sr Susanna is busy packing. She expects to go to Owen Valley with Sr Bernadette.

Mar. 28 – Latest report: no Americans are allowed to go there and no resident priest.

May 16 – Long-awaited evacuation day – after wishing Sr Susanna and Bernadette Godspeed on their new adventure and trying to keep holy envy out of our voices and looks. It was long after 9 o'clock before the train pulled out for camp Manzanar. Truly an epoch-making day for Maryknoll history with two such ideal missioners voluntarily going forth to start a new kind of pioneer life with their own people. Though we are on this side of the Government Fence and can't get through to help them, our extra prayers and sacrifices can.

June – We frequently hear from the Sisters at Manzanar. Sr Susanna has been appointed Supervisor of the Summer School there ... Ninety-three pupils the first day marched into the barracks at the sound of the bell ... an empty tin can which, when struck with a stick, produces dead silence from the children. All of us are so happy.

Sept. 4, 1942 – Maryknoll Sisters press release, Maryknoll, New York

Given the choice of returning to the Maryknoll Sisters' Motherhouse near Ossining, New York, or being interned with their people at Camp Manzanar, California, two Japanese-born Maryknoll Sisters chose the latter as being more in keeping with their missionary vocation. Former teachers of Japanese children and adults in Los Angeles, Sr Susanna and Sr Mary Bernadette now find many opportunities to keep faith alive among their former pupils and parishioners interned with them in the camp. They have organized religious instruction classes for adults as well as children for each day of the week and were also instrumental in organizing a non-sectarian summer school for the internees. Assisting the Sisters in their catechetical work at Manzanar are several former pupils of the Maryknoll School in Los Angeles, who are zealous in interesting their relatives and friends in the faith ...

Aug. 11, 1944 – Maryknoll Sisters press release, Maryknoll, New York

Released for a fortnight from internment at Camp Manzanar where they are voluntarily interned for the duration, two Japanese-born Maryknoll Sisters were permitted recently to make a retreat at the Maryknoll convent here.

Under a convent roof for the first time in two years, the two internees gave an interesting account of camp conditions ... There, they live in barracks, divided into rooms, each family allotted one room.

'We have one of these rooms,' said the Sisters, 'where we sleep, have our recreation together and where we hold catechism classes for our Japanese pupils. There is no running water, and we walk the equivalent of a half block for hot water. The alternative is to go to the public showers. Meals are served in mess halls, each hall accommodating about two hundred people.'

It was further revealed that one of the Sisters' duties is to round up the people for meals, and thus they are always the last in line for their own portions of food. Each person is given one dish, and on it everything is served: rice and vegetables and dessert. Meat (never chops or steak) is served about three times a week. The Sisters have been given no special consideration or privileges, but they are respected by all in Camp, and they have made a great many converts. At the close of the retreat, the Sisters were returned to the Camp under official guard.

After the war, both sisters returned to Los Angeles and their parish work, welcoming many parishioners back from the camp. In 1950, Sr Susanna was assigned to Japan.

PREACHING JUSTICE BY TEACHING PEACE – OAHU, HAWAII, US, 1930–2000: SR ANNA McANANY, M.M.

'If you want peace, work for justice.' Pope Paul VI's famous formula, given on the Day of Peace, 1 January 1972, surely struck a chord in the heart of Maryknoll Sister Anna McAnany. She had been working for justice ever since she arrived on the island of Oahu, Hawaii in 1930 as a parish elementary school teacher. Yet she soon realised that, if you wanted justice, you had to work for peace, a task she took on early in her career. Whether breaking up fights in the schoolyard or visiting her pupils' families to talk over the children's progress, Anna came to see that violence frequently stemmed from injustices and discrimination. Domestic violence, she soon realised, frequently arose when a husband was treated badly by his employers. From her earliest years in Hawaii her heart so ached for the Filipino, Japanese and Portuguese sugar plantation workers that she became an advocate for them. She worked hard to place their children in secondary schools with high standards, and she found scholarships for many young students.

Soon after Vatican II, Anna took time off from teaching children in order to better educate herself. At St Mary's College, Notre Dame, she fed her great interest in religious studies. She delved deeply into Sacred Scripture with a focus on the prophets and her research greatly influenced her future endeavours. In 1966, at the age of 58, she earned a masters of arts degree in theology and catechetics. She carried with her the encouragement of a Scripture professor: 'When you go back to Hawaii, remember the prophets and speak out for truth and justice no matter how difficult it may be.'

Returning to Oahu, she moved to the Wai'anae coast, a neglected and impoverished area. She formed women's prayer groups, which gradually came to reflect on theology. At that time the Vietnam War was raging, as were anti-war sentiments. Anna, along with other religious leaders, began speaking out against the war. The desire to create peace united these leaders from many Christian faiths. They advocated non-violent protest against the war. Putting her body on the line, she took part in demonstrations outside military bases in Hawaii. She also demonstrated against the violence and injustice done to plantation workers.

While her reputation as a peace and justice educator spread beyond Hawaii, Anna continued to teach peace to children, devising a curriculum for middle school entitled 'Peace as a Way of Life'. She welcomed opportunities to speak on peace at schools and she fostered a peace farm, where classes of children from many public schools cultivated their own plots and cared for the soil. She was once invited to a conference in Yugoslavia to present a report on her peace work in the schools.

Anna was hitting her stride at an age when most others were enjoying a well-earned retirement. In 1984, when she was 76 years old, she underwent perhaps the most transformative experience of her life as a justice and peace educator. She was sent to Japan as a delegate to a nuclear freeze global conference. There she witnessed the devastation of Hiroshima and

Nagasaki and heard survivors speak of the horrors caused by the atomic bombs. Anna viewed the film *The Lost Generation*, made from footage taken by the US Strategic Bombing Survey Committee after the bombing of Nagasaki. Japanese citizens had organised to purchase the footage from the National Archives in Washington DC in order to make films based on it. That experience made eminently clear to her the nightmare of nuclear war that was threatening the community of nations. Anna purchased a copy of the film to use in her peace and justice work.

Because of her efforts to better the working conditions of Filipino farm labourers, Anna was selected as a member of a solidarity group sent to the Philippines to learn first-hand about the extreme poverty, the increasing malnutrition among children and the ravages caused by the government's takeover of the land. The delegation went in solidarity with the Filipino people who were working for the effective and peaceful reclaiming of their land and their future. When asked by some Filipinos if she would continue advocating for their cause, Anna promised she would, quoting the prophet Amos 9:15: 'I will plant them upon their land, and they shall never again be plucked up out of the land that I have given them, says the Lord your God.'

Anna was 88 years old when she received the *NETWORK* Women of Justice Award in 1996. *NETWORK* is the National Catholic Social Justice Lobby, sponsored by congregations of US women religious. The award recognised her long record of peace education and advocacy. That same year Anna, and the Peace Education Program of the Wai'anae Coast, published the fruit of her many decades of peace education, *Teaching Peace*, a teacher's manual with ten lesson plans for use in Hawaii's schools. In the preface, she wrote:

> After working for years in trying to resist violence, cruelty, hate, and torture, I decided to concentrate on peaceful, positive ways of trying to heal our confused and damaged world – nurture the children and challenge the teenagers, liberate the positive values hidden within them and inspire them to create a new world of peace, harmony, simplicity, and love. We need now a holistic type of education that embraces the wonder of the natural world, recognizes the importance of educating the heart to love and the mind to know, and strives to construct a new nation in which all the individual nations support each other, enrich each other and appreciate our differences.
>
> The root causes of war begin within ourselves. If we can overcome our selfishness and extend a helping hand, if we can appreciate the goodness

and talents of others, if we can acknowledge the value and dignity in each human person, and if we can realistically acknowledge and work for resolution of the conflicts that threaten to destroy us, then we can be assured we have done our part to bring about peace on earth.

When Anna McAnany finally retired to the Maryknoll Sisters' Centre she continued offering workshops on peace to interested groups and distributed her *Teaching Peace* manual. Until her death in 2000, she never wavered in her efforts to find non-violent means to resolve problems. The peace centre and farm she helped develop on Oahu continues to educate a new generation of peace activists and the manual *Teaching Peace* is still used in Hawaii's schools.

PREACHING JUSTICE FOR WOMEN IN PERU, 1954–2008:
SR ROSE TIMOTHY GALVIN, M.M., AND SR ROSE DOMINIC TRAPASSO, M.M.

Lima, Peru, boasts three canonised saints. The first, St Rose of Lima, was born in 1586. She chose a life of penance out of love for God. She refused marriage and at the age of 20 became a Dominican tertiary. Rose lived in a shack and ate meagrely. She made herself a bed that caused her pain and she dreaded to lie on it every night, yet she offered the pain to God. Her death at the age of 31 was doubtless caused in large part by the abuse she dealt her body. In the Spanish Catholic culture of her time, she was considered a holy woman. Her funeral was attended not only by family and friends but also by government and Church officials. Canonised in 1671, she is held up as a model to imitate.

In Lima, thousands of young women share some similarities with the famous saint. Their accommodations and their diet are poor. Doubtless, many dread their beds because they may suffer pain, abuse and even illness by lying on them. Theirs is not a penance offered to God but a service offered to men. Their paltry incomes barely support themselves and their children. When they die, few but family and friends may notice. They are definitely not held up as models to be imitated because these women, caught on the lowest rung of the social ladder, work in prostitution.

Two other 'Roses of Lima', Maryknoll sisters Rose Timothy Galvin and Rose Dominic Trapasso, provided an unintended link between the saint and the women in prostitution. They, like the saint, were Dominican women religious named Rose. They, like her, lived in a small house with few amenities. The Maryknoll Roses dedicated the greater part of their lives to serving the poor of Peru, especially Peruvian women. In the last decades of the twentieth century, these grandmotherly Roses befriended and aided hundreds of young women involved in prostitution. 'We have a sense that our presence among this particular group of women has made a difference in their lives,' said Rose Dominic, 'and it has made a difference in our lives.'

Lima continues to grow exponentially. Driven by economic necessity, indigenous people from the cold highlands of Peru's Andes Mountains continually migrate to the Peruvian capital hoping to find work and a better life. Unfortunately, thousands of unskilled and unlettered women can make a living only by selling themselves.

Prostitution has been legal in Peru since 1911, but the women the Roses served ply their trade illegally. Rather than working in licensed brothels they walk the streets in well-known red light areas of the city, selling their services to any man who will pay. As they are not registered and licensed by the government, they are subject to arrest, abuse, humiliation, imprisonment, disease and early death.

Through a programme called Creatividad y Cambio (Creativity and Change), which they began in 1973, and later, El Movimiento El Pozo (The Well Movement), founded in 1978 with three co-workers, the Maryknoll Roses spent the last quarter of a century promoting the cause of women's dignity and equality.

Rose Dominic and Rose Timothy were social workers with over 50 years of experience apiece. Their paths crossed and then joined in the 1960s and their deep concern for women was rooted in their experience. Rose Dominic spent three years in Honolulu's Catholic Social Services before her assignment to Lima in 1954. She initiated the social service centre in the parish of Santa Rosa de Lima and worked there until she began working in the archdiocesan Caritas de Lima in 1961. Rose Timothy had served migrant farm worker families in California and impoverished rural families in Bolivia before her assignment to Lima in 1961.

Rose Timothy joined Rose Dominic and three Peruvian social workers in initiating the Department of Social Promotion in Caritas of Lima. They worked in - with parish social workers, emphasising promoting volunteer services, workshops on social issues and other forms of community development. The successful programme reached many parishes that had no professional services and where trained volunteers were more essential.

In the 1960s and 1970s massive migrations of impoverished indigenous people from the Andean highlands began flooding the capital. Squatters raised huts of reed mats overnight on lands they invaded on the outskirts of Lima. The archdiocese of Lima responded to this new reality by creating

Misión de Lima, whose emphasis was primarily pastoral. The Roses visited new parishes and encouraged the pastors in setting up social services.

Rose Dominic taught in the School of Social Work that was affiliated with the Catholic University of Peru, instilling in her students the need for compassion and personal relationships with families as well as knowledge. She also supervised students from the National School of Social Service during the 1960s.

The Roses left their archdiocesan work in 1972. The following year they started Creatividad y Cambio, a small centre on a busy street in downtown Lima. Open to the general public, the centre offered a library and published pamphlets dealing with such themes as adolescence, ecology, population and human rights. The Roses participated actively in the feminist movement. They were interested in calling the attention of the general public to the sexism that was rife in society, as a means to creating changes in attitudes toward women. Much of their material focused on women and women's issues and was made available to many groupings of women.

The most important aim of Creatividad y Cambio, according to Rose Timothy, was to help the Peruvian woman become aware of herself as a person, of her value as a person and the contribution she can make to her family and society as a result of this awareness. Her early work with migrant farm families in California convinced her that it was unjust to expect women to do double work: all day in the fields, and then all the household duties at home. 'I am a feminist because I couldn't be anything else,' she said.

At the start of the UN Decade on Women in 1975 the Roses and like-minded companions wanted women in Peru to take specific action regarding the situation of women. They focused on women working in prostitution, calling attention to the large group in Peru who are exploited in this way. They gathered hundreds of signatures from women who saw the legalisation of prostitution as degrading and who demanded its reversal. After publishing the demands in several newspapers, the Roses and a few other women wanted to get in touch with some of these exploited women.

That led in 1978 to the birth of El Movimiento El Pozo, a centre promoting the human rights of women and a refuge for women who work in prostitution. At El Pozo they could meet with psychologists to talk about their problems, find solidarity with other women in their own position and search for alternative economic solutions. The centre offered opportunities for short-term study as well as part-time courses in crafts and income-generating occupations. The Roses and a staff of five Peruvian women offered counselling and courses in sex education, self-awareness and feminism.

A strong focus of the work of El Pozo was the promotion and liberation of women through an outreach programme. For several years Rose Dominic went weekly to sections of the city where women involved in prostitution 'worked out'. She and her co-workers showed interest in them as women, as mothers, as friends and not just as 'street walkers'. They offered information about different resources in the community to help them have more power over their lives and over what was happening to them. All this helped them integrate themselves into groupings of women and not to feel ostracised.

El Pozo is engaged in the ongoing struggle to eradicate sexist structures in society. 'We help the women to resolve problems they have with their children or with their legal situation,' said Rose Dominic. 'As a woman begins to have control over her life, she is able to make other kinds of choices and has a greater sense of her dignity. That, to me, is the first step to wanting to do something different.'

Because of the work done through El Pozo Rose Dominic accepted an invitation in 1983 to participate in a workshop to launch an international network against female sexual slavery and trafficking in women. Women from 18 countries gathered in Rotterdam to raise international awareness of the trafficking of women and girls.

For many years, the Roses wrote and spoke out against injustices done to women. In the journal *Christianity in Crisis*, Rose Dominic wrote: 'The women's movement in Peru – and the world – is part and parcel of the popular movement. Women's feminist agenda is a universal, global agenda because women's rights are human rights, requiring the total transformation of society' (6 February 1989).

In a 1990 interview for her golden jubilee, Rose Timothy reflected on her life as a Maryknoll sister. 'Perhaps the last years in Lima have been the most satisfying, as they led me to join in the women's struggles,' she said. 'Women had been denied their rights for centuries and need to become aware of this great injustice. Being able to be a part of this movement has given me the energy I need to grow myself and to participate in the growth of others.'

Sr Rose Timothy died in 2002, at the age of 88. Sr Rose Dominic retired from El Pozo in 2008.

PREACHING JUSTICE FOR THE OPPRESSED
– RHODESIA/ZIMBABWE, 1977–2008: JANICE McLAUGHLIN, M.M.
If ever a mentor could take pride in a protégé, Maryknoll sister Maria del

Rey could rightly do so in Sr Janice McLaughlin. Sr Maria del Rey had been a reporter for her hometown newspaper, *The Pittsburgh Press*, before becoming a Maryknoll sister. She wrote several books on the Maryknoll Sisters and opened the Maryknoll Sisters Publicity Office. In 1964 she took under her wing newly professed Sr Janice as her apprentice. Janice eagerly learned the journalist's trade on the job, interviewing, researching stories, writing press releases and delving into multimedia. She left the publicity office after three years to complete her studies at Marquette University, gaining a bachelor's degree in theology, anthropology and sociology.

Janice received her first overseas assignment to Kenya in 1969. She served the Kenya Catholic Secretariat as Director of Communications for the Catholic Church. For the next seven years she directed all radio, television, press, film and audio-visual productions for the Church. Following the example of her mentor, Janice found and trained her successors, all Kenyans, into these positions. Meanwhile, Janice kept herself informed on the political and social changes occurring on the African continent where African nationalism was growing by leaps and bounds. She followed the liberation movement in southern Africa with intense interest.

Southern Rhodesia's black population had its share of political and guerrilla activity for years, especially in the rural areas. That rogue colony of the United Kingdom refused to abide by the British policy prohibiting independence before the establishment of majority, meaning black, rule. In 1965 Southern Rhodesia's white minority government under Ian Smith unilaterally declared its independence from the United Kingdom. Although the declaration was condemned internationally and Britain never recognised its independence, the white minority instituted a policy of apartheid similar to that of South Africa, heaping restrictions and oppressive laws on the black majority. Finally, in 1970, Rhodesia declared itself a republic. Human and civil rights abuses by the minority white regime against the black majority escalated.

Rhodesia's five bishops, all of whom participated in Vatican II, had been strongly influenced by the views of other Church leaders from around the world. They realised that as leaders of the Catholic Church they had a great responsibility in the face of the continuing injustices perpetrated by the Rhodesian government. Under the leadership of Bishops Haene and Lamont, the Catholic Church of Rhodesia created the Justice and Peace Commission in November 1971. The Commission began by preparing sermons on the social teaching of the Catholic Church. In the highly polarised Rhodesian population, the sermons were largely rejected by whites as provocation and by blacks as weak. It was a beginning fraught with difficulty and danger as it investigated government injustices.

In 1977, at the height of Rhodesia's armed conflict, Janice received an invitation to serve as press secretary for the Catholic Commission for Justice and Peace, which was then documenting the atrocities of the Ian Smith government. Bishop Lamont, chairman of the commission, had been an outspoken critic of the government's oppression of the black population for years. Under house arrest when he interviewed Janice for the position, he told her never to fear telling the truth, no matter the consequences. Not long afterwards, Bishop Lamont was deported for speaking the truth. By then the Commission for Justice and Peace had become the government's strongest critic. Janice, with the permission of the Kenyan Episcopal Conference and the Maryknoll Sisters, accepted the position for a year.

As her first assignment, Janice helped investigate the murders of seven Catholic missionaries earlier that year. Indications were that the murders were the work of Rhodesian soldiers impersonating guerrilla fighters in an attempt to turn public opinion against the guerrillas. Shortly afterwards, Janice prepared a series of fact papers documenting the war crimes of the government forces against civilians. The documents were to be presented to a team of British and US diplomats hoping to negotiate a settlement to the armed struggle. The day before the diplomats were to arrive, Janice and several others of the staff were arrested by the Rhodesian secret service. She was charged with causing 'alarm and despondency', a crime under the regime of Ian Smith, and imprisoned in Chikurubi Prison for Women. In her recent book, *Ostriches, Dung Beetles and Other Spiritual Masters*, Janice speaks of her trial:

> As I was being taken to court, another prisoner bent over as if to tie her shoelaces and whispered to me, 'Not only the church supports you; the whole country supports you.' These words of encouragement enabled me to face the judge and speak the truth with confidence.
>
> As I stood in the packed courtroom, uncertain of what fate awaited me, the words of the gospel flashed before me: 'You will be dragged before governors and kings because of me, as a testimony to them and the Gentiles. When they hand you over, do not worry about how you are to speak or what you are to say; for what you are to say will be given to you at that time; for it is not you who speak, but the Spirit of your Father speaking through you.' (Matthew 10: 18–20)

Without fear I testified that I viewed the colonial system as unjust and that, indeed, I supported the cause of freedom. Accusing me of being a 'self-confessed supporter of communism and a terrorist,' the judge refused me bail and sent me back to prison. To my surprise the prison guards applauded me ... They told me that they only took this job because they had to feed their children but they also supported majority rule ...

The day that I was deported the other prisoners knew about it before I did. Mostly young women who were accused of feeding the 'terrorists' or trying to cross the border to join them, they smuggled letters to me to give to Amnesty International. Their letters told of the harsh conditions they were undergoing in prison and the beating and torture that they had suffered when they were captured. The Catholic Commission for Justice and Peace took these letters and made sure that they reached Amnesty and were widely publicized. (McLaughlin, pp. 90–91)

The government's attempt to suppress the truth that Janice and her co-workers had documented only served to spread it. Her arrest quickly became an international incident prompting her release. Upon her return to Maryknoll she was inundated with invitations to speak of her experience and the truth that had been documented. The crimes she investigated before her arrest were published in *Rhodesia, the Propaganda War*. For a year after returning to the US, Janice served in the Washington Office on Africa, a Church-based lobby group that helped to educate the US public and Congress about African affairs.

Janice returned to Africa in 1979. This time she went to Mozambique, Rhodesia's neighbour, where thousands of refugees had settled in camps. She spent two years as projects officer for the Zimbabwe Project, an initiative set up by a consortium of Catholic donor organisations to assist the refugees. She visited refugee camps, raised funds and purchased supplies, and came to be well known to the leaders of the Patriotic Front.

After Zimbabwe achieved independence in April 1980, the Patriotic Front leaders and many refugees and guerrillas recognised the Zimbabwe Project as an important contribution of the Church. Because of the good reputation the Zimbabwe Project had gained during the war, the government invited it to assist in the vital work of resettling ex-combatants. Janice also received an invitation to serve as educational consultant in the president's office. In that capacity she helped build nine schools for former refugees and war veterans. She also contributed significantly to the development of a new system of education linking academic subjects with technical training, a more realistic approach to education for the new Zimbabwe. In 1985 she helped establish the Mozambique-Zimbabwe Friendship Association to assist people displaced in Mozambique because of the war.

Janice took a break from her intense activity on the national level to educate herself further. Studying at the University of Zimbabwe from 1988 to 1991, she earned masters and Ph.D. degrees in religious studies. Her thesis was published as *On the Frontline: Catholic Missions in Zimbabwe's Liberation War*.

In 1992 Janice became communications director for the Maryknoll Sisters in New York and also wrote for *Maryknoll* magazine and other publications. After six years she returned to Zimbabwe to assume the role of training co-ordinator at Silveira House, a Jesuit leadership training and development educational centre for the economically poor and marginalised. She co-authored an advocacy training manual used throughout Zimbabwe to train local communities to lobby for changes in policies affecting their lives.

Janice has dedicated her life as a Church person in Africa to writing and speaking against colonialism and racism and in favour of independence and majority rule. *Marquette Magazine*, in its issue 'Women of the Times in Each Decade', said that Sister Janice '… was a child of the '60s and participated in the civil rights and anti-war movements on campus. She left Marquette convinced one person can make a difference and spent 30 years proving it.' While in Zimbabwe she encouraged young Zimbabweans to choose journalism as a career. 'It may be dangerous, but it's never dull,' she would tell them. 'And you just might be able to change the world!'

Although she loved her work at Silveira House and with various African groups working for justice and peace, Janice was pulled away in 2008 when she was elected president of the Maryknoll Sisters. In 2010 Marquette University, her alma mater, awarded her the honorary degree of doctor of religious studies.

PREACHING JUSTICE AS HUMAN RIGHTS – ECUADOR, 1974–2010:
SR ELSIE MONGE, M.M., AND SR LAURA GLYNN. M.M.

In the 1960s, winds of change were blowing in the western hemisphere as social activism reached new levels. Increasingly, groups were organising in demand of their rights. The changes brought about with Vatican II and the theology of liberation were also part of this context. Sr Laura Glynn and Sr Elsie Monge arrived in Santiago de Veraguas, Panama, in 1966, to teach in St Vincent High School after working with *campesinos* (poor farmers) in

Nicaragua and indigenous people in Guatemala. Within two years they had chosen a new educational tool for educating another group of people: radio.

The two sisters saw the creation of a radio school as a means of empowering campesinos to become subjects of their own destiny. In 1968 they integrated a team for the creation of Radio Veraguas under the auspices of the Diocesan Social Office and accepted the challenge of applying Paulo Freire's method of consciousness-raising through the radio school. Both sisters dedicated themselves to the education and organisation of the rural population of the province. They directed the educational team and, together with some local leaders, wrote radio programmes fostering consciousness-raising.

Fr Hector Gallegos, head of the evangelisation team, was a popular pastor of one of the extensive rural parishes. The young priest, a strong supporter of the rights of campesinos, was forcibly 'disappeared' in July 1971. His abduction profoundly affected Laura and Elsie as well as the rural communities. The sisters' investigation into Fr Gallegos' disappearance put them at odds with the new bishop, who told them to leave his diocese at the end of 1973.

Elsie, who was born in Ecuador, knew of the pastoral work of Bishop Leonidas Proaño among the rural poor of his diocese in Riobamba, Ecuador. In 1974 the two sisters accepted his invitation to get to know the Indian communities and his pastoral method of liberation theology. They accompanied Bishop Proaño in his rural visits and were inspired by his relationship with indigenous people who called him the Bishop of the Indians. The sisters found Bishop Proaño very open and understanding, and helpful in their discernment. They began working with the rural communities in Chimborazo but quickly realised that their inability to speak the Quichua language hindered them in providing popular education and strengthening the Indian organisations. Bishop Proaño advised the sisters to visit other pastoral areas in Ecuador.

On 1 May 1975, Elsie and Laura accepted an invitation to join INEFOS, a training centre for rural and urban leaders in Quito, where communication was in Spanish. The following year INEFOS formed two teams, one to work with labour unions and another with rural organisations. The sisters chose the latter, since they had broad experience with the campesino movement. They dedicated themselves to socio-organisational work with Afro-Ecuadoran communities in the Chota Valley where they helped form the Campesino Federation in Chota.

Five years later Elsie accepted an invitation to direct the newly formed

Ecumenical Commission for Human Rights (CEDHU). The commission was founded in 1978 during a harsh military dictatorship which committed many abuses against the poor, the most recent at that time being the murder of 100 sugar cane workers. In response, a Lutheran pastor in Quito urged other churches and popular organisations to join together in solidarity with the poor. They took a great risk to form CEDHU. Elsie and Laura threw themselves wholeheartedly into human rights education.

CEDHU's first priority was to promote the concept of human rights among social organisations as well as in society at large. The sisters started a bi-monthly publication, *Derechos del Pueblo* (Rights of the People), and travelled to various provinces to organise workshops with base groups, encouraging them to form their own human rights commissions. In 1982 four provincial human rights commissions met in Santa Cruz, Riobamba and established a network, Frente Ecuatoriano de Derechos Humanos (FEDHU), the Ecuadoran Human Rights Front. CEDHU itself was a founding member, and Elsie became its president in 1981. This human rights network became a strong support for all its members in the face of Ecuador's very repressive regime.

By 1986, the eight full-time staff members of CEDHU publicised human rights abuses in their bi-monthly publication, which had a circulation of 2,500. Besides producing radio programmes and audio-visual tools, CEDHU provided legal assistance and defence, investigation of abuses and a documentation service responding to needs or issues on the national scene. Every July CEDHU hosted a National Human Rights Forum and on 10 December, Human Rights Day, it organised a variety of human rights activities. Its biggest priority continued to be popular education and the promotion and defence of human rights.

Elsie, Laura and their co-workers denounced many cases of forced disappearances, extra-judicial killings, arbitrary detention, torture and other crimes against humanity. CEDHU gave its support to the formation of the Organization of the Families of Victims of Repression in Ecuador. Every Wednesday, members protested in the main plaza of Quito, the capital, seeking the truth about their disappeared loved ones and demanding that those responsible be brought to justice. From the early 1980s Laura and Elsie continued in solidarity with these families and every Wednesday one or both could be found linking arms with the families in the plaza.

The work done by Elsie and Laura during the last quarter of the twentieth century has broadened the understanding of human rights in Ecuador to include social, economic and cultural rights. It brought them threats as well as accolades. Elsie has twice been awarded the title Woman of the Year, once by a women's cultural club in Quito and later by a popular national magazine. In 1997 the Ecuadorean author Kintto Lucas included Elsie in his book of outstanding Ecuadorean women, *Mujeres del Siglo XX* (Women of the Twentieth Century). She was also one of the 1,000 Women for Peace nominated for the 2005 Nobel Peace Prize.

The Truth Commission of Ecuador was established in 2008 with Elsie as its elected president. Its investigations covered serious violations of the right to life and personal integrity committed during the period 1984–2008. In June 2010, the Truth Commission gave its Final Report to President Rafael Correa and the attorney general. Over 100 cases affecting 456 persons have been presented to the judicial system with the hope of banishing impunity and guaranteeing integral reparation for the victims.

Laura Glynn, Elsie's partner and support in the work for justice, would have rejoiced, but she died in 2004, while the Truth Commission's work was still in process.

PREACHING JUSTICE THROUGH HIGHER EDUCATION
– CAMBODIA, 1991–2010: SR LUISE AHRENS, M.M.

The concepts of social change and social ethics come into play both when society perceives a need for change and/or when the past social fabric has been destroyed. In Cambodia, after the murderous Khmer Rouge regime was ended by Vietnamese troops in 1979, at least two million Cambodians had died. Fewer than 15 per cent of Cambodians who had even high school education were still alive and present in the country. For the next ten years the US led an embargo against Cambodia, so the little aid that filtered through came only from the Eastern Bloc.

In 1991, Maryknoll Sisters began a new mission outreach to Cambodia. The choice was based on the strong impetus given in two previous general assemblies to continue to develop ministries of accompaniment that address the effects of domestic and political violence and militarisation. Luise Ahrens was one of four sisters assigned to collaborate with the Cambodian government's efforts to rebuild their ravaged country.

Luise specialised in higher education, having earned her PhD in English literature in 1973. Immediately after defending her thesis she left for a new Maryknoll mission in Indonesia where she played an important role in the Master of Arts Programme at the Provincial University of Java. She left that work 11 years later when the Maryknoll Sisters elected her their president.

Upon completing her term of office Luise and her Maryknoll Sister companions headed for Cambodia. While the other three served under the ministry of health in a community-based primary health care programme near Phnom Penh, Luise was assigned by the ministry of education to the Royal University of Phnom Penh. It was immediately clear to her that the all-pervasive educational devastation in the country was most deeply felt in higher education where academic levels were extremely low and modern management experience was totally lacking.

In the Khmer Rouge's effort to create a self-sufficient agricultural society, intellectuals and the educated populace had become the parasitic enemy. After just four years of their reign of terror only 36 students and two lecturers at the Royal University of Phnom Penh had survived the genocide. In 1991 when Luise arrived, about 800 students and many instructors were attempting to relaunch higher education at the university. Since 75 per cent of the students came from the provinces and many would become high school teachers, this was an ideal place to seed the social change of the future.

In hierarchical societies such as Cambodia's, social change generally comes from the top down, ideally meeting receptivity at lower levels. In other words, Cambodia had to have educated people open to creativity and ideas as well as a competent cohort of administrative and academic staff if the country were to have a future. Luise began slowly by re-training those studying to be Russian and Vietnamese language teachers, since those languages were no longer taught in the high schools. The English language opened the door to books in every discipline and, just a few years later, it opened the door to the Internet.

Luise trained the English teachers and supported the programme for many years with funds, staff development, management assistance and the provision of foreign language experts to interact with the young Cambodian staff. As student and faculty language improved, the university library, a deserted two-classroom storage area, also had to change. Luise worked with the university leadership, for whom libraries were as yet unknown riches, to lobby for a university library. In 1997 the first building was constructed. More than 800 students per day used the library, in a country of which many expatriates say: 'Cambodians don't read'. Cambodia's first master of library science is now working in the new library.

Change also comes through the exchange of ideas. Very early on, Luise recruited technical assistants in many academic disciplines. They worked with university staff to write textbooks in the Khmer language, train teachers in interactive pedagogy, design new laboratories and science curricula and help in departmental administration. In a place where children are taught not to ask questions in school in case the teacher does not know the answer and loses face, these were all social revolutions. She also sought and found graduate scholarships for promising young teachers.

From this platform, young Cambodian lecturers, many with advanced degrees facilitated by Luise, began organising conferences to discuss research and the creation of ideas; they were being sent both by Luise and by the university to participate in regional and international seminars; they were working with the Khmer Rouge Tribunal; they were also changing the ways in which courses were taught and quality assurance was achieved at the Royal University. The young graduates, many of them high school teachers, began changing both content and pedagogy in high schools across Cambodia. Questions were encouraged, discussion was valued and the classrooms were alive with 'what ifs'. Luise constantly travelled to see these young teachers. She worked with university lecturers and staff and also with the ministry of education in the area of higher education.

The university president, who was quite wary of the changes happening on the campus, visited the US for a month in 1995. On his return, he ran into Luise's office saying, 'Oh, Luise, I so amazing in US.' He was able to see and understand the changes that he and Luise had been working towards. Social change was a reality for him. Eyes alight, he brought his planning book to her saying, 'Let's begin'... and so they did.

In 1986, Manhattanville College, her alma mater, awarded Sr Luise the honorary degree of doctor of humane letters for 'the many bridges she has built between different cultures and peoples, for her unwavering commitment to the relief of poverty and suffering, for her love of learning and life of service'.

PREACHING JUSTICE FOR THE ELDERLY – PANAMA, 1990–2009:
SR GERALDINE BRAKE, M.M.
After living through a devastating earthquake and a civil war in Nicaragua, Sr Geraldine Brake thought life would be calmer when she moved to Balboa, Panama, in early 1989. She was wrong. She hadn't been in Balboa a year when the US invaded Panama on the night of 20 December 1989, to capture dictator Manuel Noriega on drug-related charges. A major target was Noriega's headquarters in the poor neighbourhood of Chorrillo, a

few blocks from the Maryknoll Sisters' home. Gerri recalled that night of bombing and terror as the longest night of her life. The terrible injustice done to innocent, defenceless and impoverished Panamanians during that attack fixed her direction in ministry for the conceivable future: to make the lives of elderly poor people safe and happy.

The people of Chorrillo lived in dilapidated barrack-like wooden structures built originally to house workers constructing the Panama Canal in the early 1900s. Many of the elderly residents living there in 1989 were sons and daughters of those workers. The US invasion left Chorrillo in smouldering ruins. Hundreds died and thousands became homeless. Six Maryknoll sisters who lived and served in the area joined hundreds of volunteers of various ethnicities, races and social backgrounds who helped in any way they could immediately after the invasion.

While Noriega found temporary refuge in the ample and luxurious residence of the papal nuncio, Chorrillo survivors lived in tents on the sports field of a neighbouring high school stadium. Volunteers supplied food, clothing and other necessities and provided friendship for 150 elderly men and women who had been rendered homeless overnight. A few weeks after the attack the refugees were relocated to a hangar at the nearby Albrook Air Force Station.

The role of Panama's air bases, built by the US decades earlier to protect the Panama Canal, changed dramatically after the invasion. Originally intended to launch fighter jets, some later served as housing for Panamanians. Albrook provided temporary shelter for thousands of the displaced. The Ministry of Health, with USAID, provided an indoor shelter there for sick and needy seniors. Howard Air Force Base would later become a permanent home for 80 elderly Panamanians. This ironic twist came about through the dreams, persistence and hard work of Sr Gerri Brake.

The metamorphosis took a decade. After the trauma of the invasion Gerri worked with many people of good will to respond to the desperate needs of the people of Chorrillo. They inspired one another to think of possibilities. Together they developed a dream whose realisation came gradually. During the year after the US attack on Chorrillo, some of the displaced people living at Albrook found homes with relatives. In 1991 the Panamanian government moved the remaining 50 elderly people to an old remodelled hospital near the Pacific coast. In 1992 Archbishop Marcos McGrath invited members of civic clubs, ecumenical groups and parishes to form a foundation to support the newly established residence for these Panamanian senior citizens. The foundation was named Fundación Nueva Vida (New Life Foundation).

Several years later the government decided to sell that site to a hotel chain. In exchange it offered four acres of Howard Air Force Base. What had been developed as housing on a temporary basis for an immediate situation gave way to the creation of permanent housing for the people of the 'third age', a place where dignity and peace could fill their lives.

With the amazing financial and moral support from ecumenical, civic and social groups, the new location at Howard Air Force Base, which had reverted to Panama on 31 December 1999, became a marvellous housing alternative for 55 people on 10 February 2000. On that special day a rainbow coloured the sky as the bus transported the group to their new home. It was also the birthday of Archbishop McGrath, who came to bless the new home. He died four months later, leaving his mark on all their lives.

The dream was kept alive and Gerri continued being a source of encouragement, inspiring others to work financially and actively to make the dream possible. The dedicated staff of 20 continued in the new location with Gerri as co-ordinator of the residence.

Fundación Nueva Vida completely renovated the buildings with the support of the ministry of public works, which provided all the labour. One structure has apartments for independent living; another has rooms for semi-independent residents, and a third, a former bunker, houses 28 people needing supervised care. Other buildings became the administration centre and a home for the Maryknoll Sisters. Gerri soon raised enough funds to construct an open-air chapel.

While none of the present residents date back to the original group, many of the 24 staffers do. They are united as a team in their efforts to provide compassionate care for the neediest. Besides the team, Nueva Vida counts on the services of physicians and therapists and on volunteers for such needs as hairdressing, entertainment and outings. Deep friendships have grown among staff and residents.

At the entrance to Nueva Vida stands a large sign with brightly painted butterflies. The sign reads: New Life Foundation – God is Love. 'That's really been our motivation and our hope,' says Gerri. 'The people here can feel the love and compassion of this God who is unconditional in caring for each one of us.' Gerri began planning a mausoleum on the property in 2008 and finished it in April 2009. Residents who die at Nueva Vida are never far from the friends who cared for them in life and pray for them after death. In May 2009 Gerri turned Nueva Vida over to a board of directors and the capable hands of the dedicated administrator and staff. Her next assignment: Administrator of the Maryknoll Sisters' Residential Care Centre at Maryknoll, New York.

In 2010 Sr Gerri Brake received the highest honour a civilian can receive in Panama: the Orden Vasco Nuñez de Balboa en el Grado de Caballero in recognition of her work with the elderly of Panama. It was signed by President Ricardo Martinelli, and presented to her in a ceremony at the Presidential Palace by Vice President and Minister of Exterior Relations Juan Carlos Varela on 2 June 2010.

PREACHING SOCIAL JUSTICE THROUGH BATTLING AIDS
– EL SALVADOR, 1994–2010: SR MARY ANNEL, M.M., SR LORRAINE
BEINKAFNER, M.M., SR BERNADETTE LYNCH, M.M.

In the early 1980s, Maryknoll sisters in the health professions in Africa began seeing people with 'slim disease', a new illness that looked like TB but which was universally fatal in young adults. Grandmothers bore the sad burden of caring for up to 20 grandchildren after the children's young parents had died. By 1984, when the disease was identified as AIDS, Maryknoll Sisters in Kenya, Tanzania, Zimbabwe and Namibia became involved in the care of terminally ill people and in responding to the educational, as well as health, needs of their orphaned children.

At the Maryknoll Sisters' General Assembly in 1990 every mission region around the world noted that the AIDS epidemic was demanding new responses in ministry. In the light of this crisis, the Sisters' Central Leadership Team commissioned a study of AIDS ministry. The recommendations produced by the study indicated placing multidisciplinary teams in countries near 'epicentres of AIDS', especially in Central America and Southeast Asia, where new epidemics were starting. In addition, a Maryknoll AIDS Task Force began sharing AIDS information and materials among missioners involved in this ministry and initiated advocacy work with the UN.

In El Salvador, Sr Mary Annel, a medical doctor specialising in public health, Sr Lorraine Beinkafner and Sr Bernadette Lynch, teachers with decades of experience in popular education, placed all their skills at the service of AIDS prevention. They began introducing AIDS prevention programmes in 1994 in the marginalised barrios on the outskirts of the capital, San Salvador. They offered innovative workshops to parish groups, schools and people in the prisons. AIDS theatre groups with pre-adolescents and teens performed for their peers and in street theatre. The sisters developed workshops for groups on masculinity and femininity which resulted in transforming unjust 'machismo' relations among women and men, boys and girls and, directly, in AIDS prevention. Soon a committed team of Salvadoran co-workers, many of whom were living with AIDS, dedicated themselves to preventing AIDS and to teaching about HIV / AIDS.

The same prevention activities, the AIDS clinic founded by Sr Mary Annel, and several of the projects on economic alternatives, were still going strong years later. Each of the 23 full-time employees and 250 volunteers has been a potent example of AIDS prevention and personal triumph. Not only do they transform their personal and ministerial lives, but they also become instant educators with others, as they travel on public transportation around the country. They are convinced that they can help other people transform their lives and prevent the spread of AIDS in El Salvador. In 1994, El Salvador was second highest in Central America regarding AIDS statistics, but since then it has been moving down the list. Much has been accomplished, and there is still much more work to be done.

In 1995, National Public Television producer Bill Mosher selected Sr Mary Annel and her team of HIV / AIDS prevention educators for a half-hour documentary titled *Yes to Life!* in his television series *Visionaries*.

PREACHING JUSTICE FOR EARTH – PHILIPPINES, 1990–2007:
SR ANN BRAUDIS, M.M.
In the latter part of the twentieth century Maryknoll sisters in many parts of the world engaged in ecological ministries. Many of them were aimed at protecting land and indigenous people's rights over their land and their culture in the face of government policies favouring resource extraction by powerful corporations. The devastation caused to the mountains by clear-cutting of forests and strip-mining became in itself a justice issue. Creation spirituality broadened the understanding of the role of human beings in protecting and reverencing Earth itself, and all of creation.

The latest and most multi-faceted ecological ministry is in the Philippines, in the mountain town of Baguio, north of Manila on the island of Luzon. This ministry ironically owes its existence to a devastation caused by the Earth itself in 1990: a killer earthquake. On 6 July 1990, in just 45 seconds, the rumbling Earth changed the Maryknoll Sisters' role in Baguio forever. The quake devastated the area, killing 800 people and destroying many buildings.

Maryknoll Sisters first went to the Philippines in 1925, in response to a request from the archbishop of Manila to open a teacher training institute. An elementary school and a high school soon followed. The sisters found that the hot, humid tropical climate took a toll on their health and their work. Doctors and friends advised them that the climate of Baguio, a town surrounded by a pine forest up in the mountains, was the perfect place to recuperate. In 1928 Maryknoll Sisters purchased land in Baguio and built a large convent on a hill overlooking Lingayen Gulf. For decades Baguio's cool pine-scented air and natural beauty proved restorative for the sisters' health and energy. The sisters who staffed the convent, as well as those recuperating, began visiting their Igorot and Ilocano indigenous neighbours, becoming fast friends. Five years after arriving in Baguio the sisters opened and staffed an elementary school.

Over the decades, nearly 300 Maryknoll sisters served in the Philippines, extending their ministries in education, health care, community development and various other works to other islands. Yet Baguio always felt like a home away from home – until the killer quake destroyed it.

Gathered in a regional meeting the year after the earthquake, the Maryknoll Sisters in the Philippines deliberated on their future in Baguio. The environmental degradation caused by human activity, the loss of forest cover due to logging and the disruption of the ecosystem in the area seemed to cry out for a response. A new ministry in favour of the Earth emerged from their discussions. At the meeting's end, the sisters voted to redirect their education energies. They would phase out the elementary school, since elementary education could be provided by others, and establish a centre for sacred ecology. It would provide environmental education at many levels, encouraging a change from destructive behaviours to those of reverence for all of creation. The idea was imaginative and daring.

To be prophetic, the new educational project would have to include the means for addressing specific issues and policies. It would have to be rooted in local geological and biological reality and contextualised by local culture. Carrying this project forward would require the right person, able and willing to dedicate several years to see it through to its completion. Providentially, that person, Sr Ann Braudis, had recently arrived in their midst.

Ann had requested assignment to the Philippines because she hoped to develop a ministry in ecology enlightened by the new cosmology. Suddenly the opportunity presented itself in its raw reality: could she envision a process to transform Maryknoll's Baguio property into a centre for the integrity of Creation?

After the earthquake, she quickly became aware of the potential the site offered for creating an outdoor exhibit of the evolutionary journey of the Earth. Her imagination recognised the place and knew its possibilities. She could almost hear the broken Earth lamenting its abuse, longing for the expression of its deepest identity in a form human beings could grasp, through the medium of art.

Ann accepted the challenge, with the full support of the Maryknoll Sisters. A task force was formed in 1991 to explore and critique ideas related to the project, search for funding and engage an architectural firm. Over the succeeding years, while the school was being phased out grade by grade, Ann researched, consulted, dreamed and planned. At a Maryknoll Sisters' regional meeting in 1994 the plan for environmental education to be offered by the new Centre for the Integrity of Creation (CIC) was approved.

In addition to theory, an ecological sanctuary would be developed on Maryknoll's 2.8 hectares, conserving the old growth pine trees and the native botanical species. An exposition area called the Cosmic Journey would invite visitors to ponder creation on a walk incorporating 14 stations reflecting significant stages in the evolution of the universe, the emergence of the Earth, its flora and fauna, and humankind. Near the end of the walk, environmentally friendly technologies would be presented which visitors could incorporate into their own daily lives. The culminating point of the Cosmic Journey would be the 'bio-shelter', the Maryknoll Sisters' home, which incorporates some features similar to those utilised by the indigenous peoples of the mountains. Solar panels harness the sun to heat water, while skylights provide abundant light, reducing the need for electricity.

It would take several years to phase out the school and build and equip the centre. In the meantime, Ann received many requests for lectures, seminars and workshops on ecology. In February 1999, the last graduating class of the elementary school formally transferred the school building to the Maryknoll Sisters' Centre for Justice, Peace and the Integrity of Creation. This act ended 66 years of Maryknoll formal education in Baguio, the longest-lasting Maryknoll Sisters ministry in the Philippines. However, this ending of one type of education gave birth to the beginning of Maryknoll's newest educational endeavour, a ministry to the Earth as well as to human beings. The school would be transformed into dormitories, seminar rooms, bathing facilities, a resource centre and a shop where visitors could purchase handicrafts such as pottery and handwoven cloth produced locally by the indigenous population.

Ann recalls her own learning experience while acting as guide for visitors to the Cosmic Journey:

> I was immensely challenged both to live the story and articulate the story ... in redirecting our endeavours away from formal schooling to a non-formal, alternative education, learning was intended to happen through experience, ritual and the senses. Little by little as I daily hiked the trail, the Earth's Journey invaded my conscious awareness, tickling my imagination and coaxing my capacity for ritual-making into action. To know myself as the Earth telling its story became my delight and my passion. I improved my skill at interpreting the meaning of the story, making connections with contemporary ecological issues. The response of the people was very affirming. Visitors began to return over and over, nourishing my hope that, eventually, knowing the story of the Earth's journey in an integral fashion would lead to aligning behaviour with what is experienced and understood.

The centre lent itself to the creative activities of dance, art, and music, as well as to classes and seminars. An art and photography gallery eventually developed. The centre aligned itself, and networked, with the Cordillera People's Alliance (CPA), an umbrella for several NGOs and people's organisations. CPA holds as basic tenets the indigenous people's rights to self-determination and defence of their land.

As Ann and the staff of the centre interacted and networked with the CPA's activities they learned, and were influenced by, CPA's philosophy. 'Some of our moments of most intense unity and joy happen as we network together in connection with events and demonstrations that draw attention to injustices and exploitation, whether caused essentially by the corporations or the government,' says Ann.

Planning into the future, Ann foresees the centre's staff plunging into university extension services, sacred ecology pilgrimages, justice and peace advocacy, alternative energy installation and staff forums. Two major developments she hopes for in the future are workshops to provide a more thorough exploration of the meaning of the Earth's journey and 'bioregion immersion', to help people reclaim a sense of affiliation with the Earth right where they live.

By 1999 the project was complete, and Ann looked to the new century with hope. Not the hope of holding on to this marvellous work of education, ecology and spirituality, but of turning it over to new leadership. She was convinced that new leadership was absolutely essential for the continued vitality and creativity of the project.

In 2007, Sr Ann Braudis joined the Maryknoll Global Concerns Office, and became the Maryknoll Sisters' NGO representative to the UN. She chairs the Committee on Sustainable Development.

BIBLIOGRAPHY

Braudis, Sr Ann Marie, M.M., 'Earthquake/Mindquake, Birthing the Maryknoll Ecological Sanctuary in Baguio, Philippines', unpublished thesis submitted in partial satisfaction of the requirements for the degree of Master of Liberal Arts in Creation Spirituality in the Graduate Division of Noropa University, California, May 2001.

Danforth, Sr Maria del Rey, M.M., *Her Name is Mercy*, New York, Charles Scribner's Sons, 1957.

McAnany, Sr Anna, M.M, *Teaching Peace*, Peace Education Program of the Wai'anae Coast, Wai'anae, Hawaii, 1996.

McLaughlin, Sr Janice, M.M., 'You'll be Back', in Geoffrey Bould (ed.), *Conscience be my Guide: an Anthology of Prison Writings*, London, Zed Books Ltd., 1991, pp.189–192.

McLaughlin, Sr Janice, M.M., *On the Frontline, Catholic Missions in Zimbabwe's Liberation War*, Harare, Baobab Books, 1996.

McLaughlin, Janice, M.M., *Ostriches, Dung Beetles, and other Spiritual Masters, a Book of Wisdom from the Wild*, Maryknoll, New York, Orbis Books, 2009.

DOCUMENTARY

Visionaries Series, show 111, *Yes to Life!*, 1995. Features Sr Mary Annel and her young AIDS prevention workers.

OTHER RESOURCES

Maryknoll Mission Archives, Maryknoll, New York, 10545.
Maryknoll Sisters Communications Office, Maryknoll, New York, 10545.

17

Dominican Sisters in Peru and the Truth and Reconciliation Commission

ELENA CORNEJO LUNA, O.P.

Peru is a country located in the western end of South America with a total population of 28.2 million. It has three natural regions: the mountain region, with a population of about nine million inhabitants; the jungle region, with around four million inhabitants; and the coastal region, with about 15 million inhabitants.[1]

1980 marked the beginning of Peru's internal armed conflict, which originated in the southern mountain region of the country, during the democratic government of Fernando Belaúnde Terry.

The southern mountain region shows the highest levels of poverty. Historically, this region has been the most abandoned and ignored by the state. The armed conflict had been in gestation for many years due to complex economic, educational and social conditions. These were aggravated by the state's lack of interest in this part of the country, mainly due to its being far away from the capital city, Lima.

It was in this context that a subversive and terrorist organisation called the Communist Party of Peru – the Sendero Luminoso – and a revolutionary movement, Túpac Amaru, initiated the armed conflict against the state and Peruvian society, and, in doing so, created a climate of urgency, uncertainty and terror.

This time of upheaval was characterised by constant terrorist incursions, using car bombs, murder of civil and police authorities, collective massacres and so on. These acts were all perpetrated in the rural region of the Andes.

Human rights violations committed by the armed forces were brought to light during the government of Alan García Pérez (1985–90). These violations were perpetrated while 'trying to eliminate terrorists', but in fact, they succeeded only in eliminating and massacring many communities of people from the Peruvian mountain range. Those killed were poor and illiterate,

---

1. Cf. National Directorate of Census and Surveys, *Final Results of the 2007 National Census*, Lima, Peru, 2008 http://censos.inei.gob.pe/censos2007 (Last accessed 14.04.12).

and could speak only their native tongue of Quechua.

The head of the Sendero Luminoso, Abimael Guzmán, was captured in 1992 under the government of Alberto Fujimori. This marked the beginning of the systematic dismantling of this subversive organisation.

Alberto Fujimori – then living in Japan – resigned as president of Peru at the end of the year 2000. After the fall of his authoritarian and corrupt regime, judicial investigations concerning the rampant corruption and human rights violations performed during his mandate began in earnest.

The Truth Commission was set up in 2001 during the transitional government of Valentín Paniagua, charged with investigating the facts and allocating responsibility for those human rights violations that could be attributed to either terrorist groups or the armed forces.

After democratic elections were successfully conducted, the Peruvian state – now under the government of Alexander Toledo – ratified and strengthened the original commission, changing its name to 'Truth and Reconciliation Commission' (CVR). Amongst its new responsibilities, the CVR was charged with determining the causes that gave rise to the violence and writing up viable proposals for possible reparations.

The CVR presented its final report to the government on 28 August 2003.[2] The report concluded that the insurgent violence and the tactics of counterinsurgency used by the government caused an estimated 69,000 deaths and disappearances, inflicted almost exclusively upon the indigenous communities. The commission recommended an exhaustive plan of reparation, criminal prosecution for those responsible, institutional reforms and a series of other related measures.

After the final report's presentation, numerous civil organisations came together to face the enormous challenges implied by the implementation of the plan. They made a further commitment to understanding the causes that gave rise to the lamentable and painful facts that destroyed many poor families in the country, as well as to preventing similar events ever happening again.

The genesis of the so-called Post-CVR in the affected zones was the result of assembling all civil society's networks with the Ombudsman (Defensoría del Pueblo) in the towns, in order to find the truth and promote reconciliation. This was done by following through the recommendations of the commission and by demanding their full implementation on the part of

2. Truth and Reconciliation Commission, *Final Report*, Lima, Peru, TRC, 2003, http://www.cverdad.org.pe (Last accessed 18.04.12).

the authorities.

In Cuzco, a region that had suffered terrorist incursions in many of its localities, the Post-CVR is still working on the elimination of discrimination, which leads to the most severe, lethal and frequent form of violence.

The Dominican Missionaries of the Rosary are part of this collective effort. They apply their charism through opting for the poor and through their constant work in the promotion of justice, peace and human rights. They challenge those authorities that forget their responsibilities before a God who, in the words of Bartolomé de las Casas, 'has an ever present memory of the smallest and the forgotten'.

Ever since this community of Dominican sisters discovered the work of the Post-CVR, it has been highly motivated to work together with other organisations – even with those not directly affiliated with the Church – whose contributions in the promotion of justice and peace are invaluable.

The presence of a prophetic and witnessing Church during the terrorist era was a great sign of encouragement in Peruvian society, and it helped the population at large to overcome those hard years. Today, this testimony inspires the Dominican sisters in Peru to follow in the footsteps of the many missionary brothers and sisters who, like Jesus, spoke of justice and peace. Those whose voices were extinguished in the process of doing so and whose memory and testimony remain with us until this day are especially inspiring.

As a religious community, the Dominican Missionaries of the Rosary have much to do and much to contribute, and they do it in various ways – from preparing the field to selecting the seeds to be planted. The sisters are convinced that an efficient way of continuing to animate this exhausting yet hope-filled work is by sharing *in it* and *sharing it* with others.

PAST HISTORY?

What do we want? ... We want that the truth be known about all these cases ... Truth, reconciliation and justice; we want that, yes! ... neither all the gold of the world, nor the silver, nor the diamonds, no! We are not after that, we want that the truth be known and, also, we want justice. As we have done during this time, we have always remembered everything that happened. We have remembered the solidarity of many people, as well as the indifference of those who did this. Truth and justice, ladies and gentlemen Commissioners ... .[3]

3. Truth and Reconciliation Commission, *Final Report*, p. 16.

When we utter the word 'violence' in Peru, it evokes a harsh reality for all of us: death and injustice. We thus arrive at the brutal realisation that a human being can stop being a human being and become the hunter of his brother or sister.

During the decades of the 1980s and 1990s, until 2000, the internal armed conflict in Peru had 69,280 victims – between those who were killed and those who vanished – and left profound psychological scars on those who survived.

According to recent investigations, the conflict sprang from the decision of Sendero Luminoso to initiate a popular revolt against the Peruvian state. This marked the beginning of an internal armed conflict that was the most intense and prolonged violent episode in the whole history of the Republic of Peru, and which had the greatest human and economic cost for the whole nation.

Throughout it all, it was somehow known that something was happening in Peru, but because news of terrorist attacks came from the poorest and most deprived regions (the majority of the victims were from the rural areas of the Andes, and from the jungle), they were largely ignored. These areas went unnoticed even among Peruvians themselves, those living in the north, in the coastal cities and in the capital.

Furthermore, the victims were essentially of indigenous origin (from the Andes, from the jungle, those called Quechua and Asháninka). Seventy-five per cent of all the victims spoke native languages and 79 per cent lived in the countryside.

According to the CVR, the terrorist group Sendero Luminoso was the main perpetrator of crimes and violations of human rights. The CVR used the known number of dead and disappeared as a way of bringing the group to justice. Sendero Luminoso was responsible for 54 per cent of all the fatalities. It used a systematic approach and methods of extreme violence and terror, without even the minimum respect or concern for either the basic rules of engagement during war or for human rights.[4]

The government did not have the capacity to halt the advance of the subversive army and, to aggravate matters, even the armed forces joined in the systematic violations of human rights, carrying out murders, disappearances, tortures and rapes.

There were many unfortunate consequences of the conflict, and even

4. Cf. Truth and Reconciliation Commission, 'Stages of Violence', chapter 1 in *Final Report*, vol. 1, Lima, Peru, TRC, 2003.

more questions ... driving us to an even greater commitment towards understanding what happened and to preventing it from ever happening again.

The CVR was created on 4 July 2001. Its mission was 'to contribute to the elucidation of the grievous violent incidents that occurred in Peru between the years 1980 and 2000; to establish responsibilities regarding the violations of human rights; and to propose initiatives that promote peace and national reconciliation, so that such a dramatic episode does not ever happen again in the history of Peru.'[5]

The CVR was created at a moment in which Peru needed to know what had happened – even though at the same time, deep down, the whole nation wanted only to forget. They wanted to forget the dark nights, the news of terrorist attacks, the deaths, and that the police and the military were both victims and perpetrators. But there were still many things for which there were no explanations, and explanations were necessary, since the only real means for achieving genuine peace and reconciliation was to build upon the explanations, that is, to build upon the truth.

Had death arrived as fast as the word arrives – lightly and shortly – it would have been a happy death. However, death arrived slowly, deliberately, making echoes, leaving marks ... and these marks last. Years have gone by since the submission of the CVR's final report and many more have passed since the beginning of the violence. Time has gone by, but in the memories of those affected the violence is still there because justice has not arrived, or is arriving only very slowly.

There are still mothers hoping to find out where the graves of their sons and daughters are so that they can bring flowers; there are still brothers and sisters looking for answers, who want to understand what happened; there are still eyes that become cloudy when they remember; there is still a society that is growing up without knowing (or wanting to know) what happened only recently, because this is, indeed, recent history.

THE SHADOW THAT SEPARATES: DISCRIMINATION

The State still continues discriminating, considering the Andean peoples not quite as citizens; when there are bomb explosions in Tarata and other places, society barely realizes that something is happening in the country; whatever was happening in the countryside, well, those were maybe

5. Centro Guaman Poma de Ayala, *Let us Break the Silence: Do not Discriminate and Do not Allow Yourself to be Discriminated Against. Methodology Guide*, Cuzco, Peru, CGPA, 2009.

'only Amerindian things ...'[6]

When the number of the dead or disappeared is reported, it is as if one is listening to a cold recounting. It is rather like hearing the results of a survey, or receiving the grade of a final exam. Numbers in themselves are 'cold'; after all, they are only numbers. However, when somebody mentions the more than 69,000 victims of this internal war, those numbers have faces, names, histories, dreams and hopes, all of which were cut off by their untimely and unannounced deaths.

From the beginning, this period of violence and destruction had a strong ethnic and racial component. This is nothing new for a country that, since the beginning of the Spanish colonisation, has known that it is different and distant. Our geography, however, causes distances to go beyond mere geography, and expand into racial and ethnic voids and chasms.

Since the beginning of the Spanish colonisation, the coast was favoured as the political and economic centre because of its connection with the sea and the potential for commercial exchange. The mountain range (at 2,500 to 6,700 metres above sea level) became Peru's most impoverished and marginalised zone because of its inaccessibility and harsh geography, and also because it had become the home of the largest indigenous population in the country – marginalised and exploited since the beginning – who had decided to settle there. The jungle was never a concern for the government – unless they wanted to exploit its mineral resources – because it was almost inaccessible due to its lack of transport infrastructure.

Currently, wealth – or lack of it – is what constitutes grounds for exclusion and marginalisation in Peru. 'Although there coexist more than 55 ethnic groups in the national territory and around a fifth of the population speaks an indigenous language, an explicit recognition of the original ethnic communities is still weak. Whoever speaks an indigenous language often prefers to hide his or her ethnic origins. This renders ethnic belonging invisible in the public arena.'[7] This has constituted, and still constitutes, a stumbling block to the enjoyment of social acceptance and the coexistence in equality of rights for these 55 ethnic groups, which should feel welcomed, accepted, and respected in their own country.

6. Edilberto Oré, 'Case 6: Testimony of Forced Displacement in Ayacuchana', in Truth and Reconciliation Commission, *Public Thematic Hearings. Political Violence and Displaced Communities,* Lima, Peru, Truth and Reconciliation Commission, 2002, http://www.cverdad.org.pe/ingles/apublicas/audiencias/atematicas/at05_sumillas.php. (Last accessed 25.04.12).

7. Truth and Reconciliation Commission, 'Violence and Racial and Ethnic Inequalities', chapter 2, section 2.2, in *Final Report,* vol. 8, p. 102.

In the past – and even now – the words *cholo* and *indio* were loaded with contemptuous and extremely humiliating connotations. They were, in fact, used to belittle others, justifying aggression and violence against them. Those called *cholos* and *indios* were rendered powerless and considered outsiders.

> This was a phenomenon that was present throughout the conflict, but in a covert way. Only at those moments in which physical violence was exerted did this type of discrimination become more evident, loading in that way the murders, tortures and violations with an explicit symbolic violence. Differences in power, wealth, status or geographic origin tended to be clustered and become – thanks to racism – categories of supposed inferiority or superiority.[8]

The belief that others (male or female) are inferior, can justify a plethora of discriminatory and violent actions against them, based solely on *who* they happen to be.

> … at night the torture began … with people belonging to the army, Alpha. A certain Juan Carlos even told me: 'you are brown and I belong to another race. I am "gringo". I have green eyes and now I am going to make you tell me all you know…' I remember the torture that they inflicted on me, the drowning, the *mace* and the red pepper; they threw all that together and warmed me up, then, they tied me and drowned me, securing me onto a table; then, they hanged me and applied electricity to my testicles … in *Los Laurels* all those things happened.[9]

We are bombarded with information that speaks of difference. Advertisements that promote Caucasian people have become one of the strongest mechanisms for maintaining stereotypes of beauty, success and happiness. Whatever looks *'mestizo'* or from *'los Andes'*, on the other hand, is associated with poverty and is frequently used only as 'exotic' propaganda.

> … ever since we arrived at our refugee camps, we suffered total marginalisation. It was as if we were worms; they saw us as if we were worms. We could not go into the city to look for something to eat or to look for a job. Since we did not have means to survive, we had to find little jobs in order to be self-sufficient … I would like to show you a newspaper from the year 1994. It says in here: 'the people from the highland towns invade Lima'. Do you see? They dealt with us in such a way: people from

8. Ibid.
9. Ibid., p. 122.

the highlands, *cholos* ... that's how we were treated in Lima.[10]

There are many testimonies to the presence of a racial and ethnic factor in the escalation of violence and in the procedures for selecting victims.

It is true that national reconciliation is necessary, but it will only be real when a collective identity is constructed. This collective identity must be based on the recognition of our cultural differences and in the discarding of everything that constitutes a danger for its construction, namely, ethnic and racial discrimination. This is, as CVR affirms, one of the biggest lessons we can learn from the perpetrated violence:

> The report that we present to you exposes, then, a double scandal: one of murder, disappearance and torture on a grand scale; and the one of the indolence, ineptitude and indifference of those who could have prevented this humanitarian catastrophe and did not do it ... The racial insult – the verbal offence against destitute people – resonates like an abominable refrain that precedes the beating, the kidnapping of the son, the firing at point-blank ... Much has been written on cultural, social and economic discrimination, which is prevalent in the Peruvian society. Little has been done by the authorities or the citizens to eradicate such a stigma from our community. This report shows to the country and to the world that it is impossible to coexist where there is scorn, because scorn is a disease that causes tangible and lasting damage. From now on, the names of thousands of people who are dead or who have disappeared will be here, in these pages, to remind all of us of this.[11]

After two years of gathering information, the CVR presented its analysis of the consequences of the armed conflict for Peruvian society. At the same time, it exhorted the authorities and civil society to work for the reconstruction of the social and political order, so as to look more realistically and seriously at this event, and provide solutions to the problems that had generated the internal conflict and the divisions in the country:

> This implies a deep institutional reform, the fulfilment of a plan of reparation in favour of the victims, and the application of penal sanctions against the people who committed crimes and human rights violations.[12]

10. Ibid., p. 110.

11. Salomón Lerner, 'Presentation of the Truth and Reconciliation Commission's Final Report', Lima, Peru, August 2003, www.cverdad.org.pe/ifinal/discurso01.php (Last accessed 14.04.12).

12. Delivery Commission of the Truth and Reconciliation Commission, *Hatun Willakuy. Abridged Final Report of the Commission of Truth and Reconciliation*, Lima, Peru, TRC, 2004.

The publication of the commission's final report marked the culmination of the process for many; for others, however, it was just the beginning of an even more arduous task: a long-lasting commitment to justice and peace.

The conclusions reached by the CVR[13] point to the great goal of national reconciliation, requiring personal and institutional commitment, as well as the political will to make it possible.

> The CVR understands that reconciliation must occur at a personal and family level; at the level of civil organizations, as well as in the reframing of the relations between the State and society as a whole. The three indicated plans must be adapted to a general goal, namely, the building up of a country that clearly and positively sees itself as multi-ethnic, multi-cultural and multilingual. Such recognition is the basis for overcoming those discriminatory practices that are the product of multiple discords throughout our republican history.[14]

Such an immense challenge points to the fact that it was, and still is, the state's obligation, as well as that of society and its various organisations and agents, to assume this task and to work towards the defence and promotion of human rights.

Answers to this challenge have been varied in the different regions of the country; however, as to the awareness raised about this terrible reality – which has been front and centre throughout this whole process – a clear certainty has been added: we must ensure that these crimes never happen again.

ENTHUSIASTIC RESPONSE TO A RECOMMENDATION

Cuzco is a state located in the south-eastern region of Peru. It encompasses several Andean zones and part of the high jungle. In times past, it was the state capital of the Inca Empire and during the time of the Spanish Colony it was one of its most important cities. It was precisely in this important region that the recommendations made by the CVR found an echo and, as a result, it was here that different initiatives were vigorously undertaken.

In 2004 – and at the initiative of the Defensoría del Pueblo in Cuzco – the CVR's recommendations made possible the creation of a forum where several civil institutions came together to elaborate a plan of action

13. The CVR presented 171 general conclusions in its *Final Report*, which correspond to each area of their investigation: www.cverdad.org.pe/ifinal/conclusiones.php (Last accessed 14.04.12).
14. Ibid., Conclusion no. 171.

that would ensure the implementation and promotion of the CVR's own recommendations.

Some of these institutions – the Defensoría del Pueblo, the Cuzco Regional Association of those Affected by Political Violence, the Bartolomé de las Casas Centre, *COINCIDE*, Vicariate for Solidarity, the Guaman Poma de Ayala Centre, the Association for the Defence of Human Life and Dignity, the Cuzco Civil Association 'Transparencia' among others – made a clear commitment to further the CVR's goals and mission.

This forum for reflection, which is called Cuzco's Post-CVR Inter Institutional Coordination, treated as a high priority task of analysing the structural causes that generated political violence in the country and their direct relation to the phenomena of marginalisation and social exclusion. This link became evident when considering the identity of the majority of victims: they were people who lived in the countryside, spoke native languages and were dedicated to farming activities.[15]

The community of La Pradera, located on the outskirts of Cuzco, was responsible for implementing the process, following the recommendations made in the CVR's final report. Their task was to co-ordinate efforts with other institutions working for the promotion of justice and the defence of human rights. For this reason, the community of La Pradera joined Cuzco's Post-CVR Inter Institutional Coordination in 2008.

Cuzco's Post-CVR Inter Institutional Coordination decided that it was necessary to face the problem of violence – translated into situations of extreme poverty, injustice, racism, discrimination and social exclusion – because it was still pervasive, or had worsened, in many regions of the country. This situation could generate new situations of direct violence. Thus, if we want to avoid going back to the grim reality of the terrorist years, we ought to work on raising awareness about human rights.

At the same time, it is of the utmost importance to identify and denounce signs of discrimination within our own families. These sow seeds of superiority and, at the end of the day, justify our indifference or, even worse, our forgetfulness. If they are not avoided, these realities will turn us into a society in which exclusion is the norm and where we become less and less human.

The pursuit of justice in this field has as its main goals the advancement of equality, the pursuit of truth, and the attainment of reconciliation. Among the main courses of action that the Coordination has proposed – and towards

15. Centro Guaman Poma de Ayala, 'Let us Break the Silence', unpublished document.

which it is still arduously working – we have the 'raising of awareness of the general population in order to create a historical memory of a traumatic period in the history of our country. This should be done through national, regional and local campaigns and training that looks to disseminate the truth and sensitize the population about it. Another way of achieving this is to appeal to the authorities – and in particular to government officials – to incorporate into their annual operating plans the recommendations made by the CVR.'[16]

Discrimination has always been present in our history and until we are fully aware that it is still a part of our milieu – in the most subtle and diverse forms – there will always be somebody who feels and believes that he or she is 'less than' someone else. At the same time, there will always be others who, taking advantage of the power of stereotypes, will marginalise and alienate those they consider inferior or different. This darkness – which breeds only inequality and poverty – will dissipate only when we become aware of how we marginalise others, or of how we are being marginalised in society.

A HURTFUL COMMITMENT

Brother, sister
of the downcast gaze, whose language often
I do not understand.
I want to understand your message
in real life,
learning to speak with you a same word,
a same feeling:
that of the proclamation of justice,
of dignity,
of memory.[17]

In 2008, Cuzco's Post-CVR Inter Institutional Coordination, with the support of the National Coordination for Human Rights, decided to address more directly the issue of inequality. They devised a regional campaign against discrimination: Let us Break the Silence: Do not Discriminate and Do not Allow Yourself to be Discriminated Against. The aim of the campaign was to bring to light something that is present in the darkest recesses of the human heart: our tendency to discriminate against others.

16. Centro Guaman Poma de Ayala, 'Let us Break the Silence', unpublished document.
17. Siembra, 'A Hurtful Commitment', in *Kjuyarikusun: Roads to Reconciliation*, Lima, Peru, Grupo Siembra, 2009, audio CD.

It is precisely when we believe we are so unique and important – even though that is part of what we are – that we lose sight of the fact that we are part of a community and that we need the other, the one who is different from us, to accomplish and build something in common.

The problem is not to acknowledge or recognise that we are different; the problem begins when we turn that difference into an excuse for excluding others and for feeling superior to them.

It is difficult to break this mindset because it is very much a part of our being. We can only break it when we are made aware of it, even by means of simple questions: How many times has a simple saying or proverb caught my attention and made me think about the fact that it excludes a whole sector of the population? How many people protest because in some form of advertising a group of people is turned into a mere object of pleasure or of ridicule? How many times has my academic background or my titles – or the lack of them – determined if I can sit in a 'special place' or not?

Reflecting on these 'small things' brings us the bigger picture. It is like the story of the mustard seed in the Gospel. Our present commitment is to make all these things evident, utilising the following very real facts: we all have been discriminated against, or have discriminated against somebody else, at some point in our lives; thus, we are aware of the fact that we live in a society that discriminates and that this is not the kind of society that we desire; finally, we must accept as indisputable that all sorts of discrimination separate and impoverish both the one who discriminates against another and the one who experiences the discrimination.

These facts served as inspiration for us, Dominicans, to begin working against discrimination.

An important group that was targeted by the campaign was young people. It is true that, generally speaking, young people are seen in our society as dangerous, different and unreliable. However, this view tends to ignore the fact that it is they who will carry our society forward. The campaign was essentially crafted around the formation of youth leaders with whom we conducted awareness sessions, targeting different sections of the population.

The young people who agreed to be part of the training process came from different social strata and various religious backgrounds. The environment was not really conducive to speaking about God, but we were already speaking about him from the moment we presented the goals to be achieved.

The greatest joy for us was to see in the faces of those young men and women the realisation that it was indeed possible to make a change because they themselves had been changed. How could one refuse to change after becoming acutely aware of what hurts and brings about discrimination? A young man said: 'We can be living our own internal war in such a silent way that we are never aware of all the deaths it can be causing.' This means that, in our unequal society, discrimination is evident only to those who endure it and to those who become aware of it.

Sometimes, it seems as if reality can no longer be changed because everything is based on indifference, competition and impunity. A single person will not be able to change anything and, apparently, society presents more problems than solutions. Thus, the rain of apathy and pessimism soaks us all and envelops us in what can truly become a dangerous mindset down the line: conformism. However, it is precisely when things seem most grim that hope appears on the face of a woman, a child, a young man or an elderly gentleman, compelling us to look at reality in a different way.

That is the kind of hope that moved – and still moves – this group to continue working in favour of justice and peace. Only with such will we be able to proclaim together 'that forgetfulness may not cover injustices, that exclusion may not move us away from our compatriots, that damage may be repaired, that life may continue to grow, that truth may always remain alight'.[18]

Painstakingly, and from the deepest recesses of the heart, the group elaborated a 'methodological guide' to move the campaign forward and to combine all the efforts, large and small, that were being made.

This campaign wanted to 'raise the awareness of those civil servants working in the public sector – mainly education, health and justice; all sectors in which the biggest number of complaints regarding discrimination are received – to adopt tactical measures in order to reduce discriminatory practices ... [and] to raise the awareness of the general population to face discrimination, not only when they are direct victims of it, but also when they witness, or are directly responsible for, acts of discrimination.'[19]

Several 'awareness fairs' were conducted in parks, on unmade roads and in places with the greatest pedestrian traffic. The young people utilised the arts – drawing, theatre, dance, group activities and puppets – to break the silence on this issue. This was far from easy because it required, first of all, drawing attention to something that is commonly lived but seldom perceived.

18. Siembra, 'Dreaming Utopias', in *Kjuyarikusun: Roads to Reconciliation*, Lima, Peru, Grupo Siembra, 2009, audio CD.
19. Centro Guaman Poma de Ayala, 'Let us Break the Silence', unpublished document.

Numerous groups of young people came together with this common goal in mind. Many ideas were shared for devising group activities and games that would encourage people's active participation, through which the spectators would realise how discrimination divides and damages. This means that the young had to abandon their 'anonymity' in order to turn their words into actions. It was a delight to see how much enthusiasm and dedication they put into their presentations.

The groups that took part in the training and in the fairs were looking for their own spaces of expression, which were naturally those closest to them. In this way, the group of university students organised their own fair in a more creative and 'spectacular' way, which suited the university milieu. Theirs was a real explosion of creativity! They started their fair with some trepidation on the university campus (having obtained the necessary permissions and authorisation) and, from there, they invited the whole student body, members of all the different faculties and from all social strata, to participate in different games and group activities aimed at raising awareness about this factor that divided and divides their country. The response they received was very positive.

Another group that participated was linked with education. These were mostly young people preparing to become teachers. However, they worked with people from other fields and decided to go to schools to do everything in their power to raise awareness. Theirs was an exhausting but very enriching experience. The co-ordinator for the use of materials collaborated in this project.

It was very good to see that some of the youth who participated in these fairs wanted to replicate them and share them with their school peers from lower grades. The end result was extremely creative and educational for all involved.

In fact, all suggestions were well received and, even though the young people had neither economic resources nor enough time – since most of them work or study – they made a real commitment, and made things happen. So, if it is true that youth is when people are intrepid, these young people manifested this by taking risks and by doing things boldly.

Our commitment 'hurts' – and will continue to hurt – as long as we remain conscious that there are discriminatory actions that hurt, divide and impoverish. It does, indeed, 'hurt', because to feel pain means doing something to stop it, and commitment springs from that. Peruvian young people have taught a lesson to the world: If you want to do something new

–even something that others thought impossible – it is indeed possible!

DREAMING UTOPIAS

> I love my land, my country
> that ties me and seduces me,
> that cheers me up and gives me peace
> because it contains in its bosom,
> dignity's dreams.[20]

Even if we are in the middle of nowhere and are surrounded by misery; even with dust on our hands and sweat running down our faces; even if the sores are still open, we can still dream, if only there is somebody else who dreams along with us.

Although discrimination is a problem that will not change overnight, and even if it fuels the pessimism of those who think that it will be the identifying mark of less developed societies, the facts show that it is possible to change when one begins with oneself, when one dreams of bringing about that change in the company of others who, even though they are different from us, also believe and trust that, in spite of all the differences, our blood is of the same colour.

The campaign and the work that is slowly being done give us the reassurance needed to keep believing.

CONCLUSION

The campaign gave us:
- Hope, which was experienced especially when we went into the streets without money – but with much creativity – and things happened and got done with everybody's enthusiastic contribution and collaboration.
- Commitment, realising that, more than in a political speech, it is our word, united with others, which brings about change. When we are aware of the bonds that unite us with others, we realise that those bonds are more fragile in times of upheaval, when everything changes, and it feels like 'every man is for himself'. Thanks to this campaign, however, the bonds went beyond last names, profession, age, political allegiance or even religion (in fact, many of the youth considered themselves to be agnostic!). The bonds were being built through our common efforts

---

20. Siembra, 'Dreaming Utopias', in *Kjuyarikusun: Roads to Reconciliation*, Lima, Peru, Grupo Siembra, 2009, audio CD.

and outlook on life. Out there on the streets we were one group with a common discourse and a shared vision. Our single commitment made us one!

- New paradigms that allow us to understand that 'the other', who 'has always been exploited, considered less, inferior', has a lot to say and to teach us. These are new times and 'the other' must be recognised and reinstated in his or her proper place in society.
- New awareness – we came out of this experience with 'new wounds' that became more acute as we confirmed their harsh correspondence with reality. Yes, we may have discriminated against somebody, but once we become aware of the damage inflicted by a discriminating word, we never utter that word again. In the words of songwriter and singer Mercedes Sosa, 'I only ask God that I may not be indifferent to discrimination ever again'.

In our present time, justice and peace are realities that some people believe unattainable or incredible. This may be because they are looking for grand results. It is possible to obtain them, however, through simple but incisive work. People are used to looking for bigger forums with more representation, and they tend to forget that the work done 'from below', among the little ones of the Gospel, produces better results.

The Dominican Missionaries of the Rosary in Peru, through the living out of their religious vocation, have made a total commitment to the promotion of justice, peace and reconciliation through dialogue.

BIBLIOGRAPHY

Centro Guaman Poma de Ayala, *Let us Break the Silence: Do not Discriminate and do not allow Yourself to be Discriminated, Methodology Guide*, Cuzco, Peru, CGPA, 2009.

Delivery Commission of the Truth and Reconciliation Commission, *Hatun Willakuy, Abridged Final Report of the Commission of Truth and Reconciliation*, Lima, Peru, TRC, 2004.

Peruvian National Directorate of Census and Surveys, *Final Results of the 2007 National Census*, Lima, Peru, 2008. http://censos.inei.gob.pe/censos2007 (Last accessed 14.04.12)

Siembra, *Kjuyarikusun: Roads to Reconciliation*, Lima, Peru, Grupo Siembra, 2009, audio CD.

Truth and Reconciliation Commission, *Final Report*, 9 vols., Lima, Peru, 2003. http://www.cverdad.org.pe . (Last accessed 18.04.12).

Truth and Reconciliation Commission, 'Political Violence and Displaced Communities', *Public Thematic Hearings*, Lima, Peru, TRC, 2002. http://www.cverdad.org.pe/ingles/apublicas/audiencias/atematicas/at05_sumillas.php. (Last accessed 29.04.12).

18

The Turning Tide:
Dominican Women and Reconciliation
in Northern Ireland

GERALDINE SMYTH, O.P.

UNDERSTANDING THE CONTEXT OF THE
CONFLICT IN NORTHERN IRELAND

Philosophers and historians debate the relative value of too much memory or too little.[1] Edna Longley, the Irish literary critic, reflecting on the tendency in Ireland to remember too much, once cryptically observed, 'We should erect a statue to amnesia and forget where we put it.' The stance in this essay is somewhere in between – one needs to remember ethically and self-critically, allowing oneself to be educated by the past in the service of a more inclusive narrative, one that values life even as it acknowledges the suffering and death of so many.[2] In particular, in exploring how Dominican sisters in a particular congregation tried to witness by their lives to Christ's reconciliation in a time of enmity and warfare, it may be helpful to look briefly at the context and historical development within which that witness found expression.

The roots of violent political conflict in Ireland reach back at least to the sixteenth and seventeenth centuries, with Ireland's colonial annexation and the planting of settlers from England and Scotland. Despite this long history, or perhaps partly because of it, at the time of the outbreak of this current period of the conflict 'in and about Northern Ireland',[3] beginning in the late 1960s, hopes were rising that a lasting peace might be secured. To gain some historical understanding of the past 30 to 40 years of violent conflict, one

1. See, for example, David Rieff, *Against Remembrance*, Melbourne, Melbourne University Publishing, 2011; Tzvetan Todorov, *Hope and Memory*, London, Atlantic Books, 2003, p. xv.
2. Cf. Geraldine Smyth, 'Telling a Different Story: Hope for Forgiveness and Reconciliation in Northern Ireland', in *Pathways to Reconciliation: Between Theory and Practice*, Philipa Rothfield, Cleo Fleming and Paul A. Komesaroff (eds.), Aldershot, Ashgate, 2008, pp. 67–78.
3. This designation of 'the conflict in and about Northern Ireland' has become an acceptable term in conflict resolution circles, by way of acknowledging that the trouble was not confined to the jurisdiction of Northern Ireland, together with the reality that even the name 'Northern Ireland' is not accepted by all – as it underwrites the creation of the jurisdiction in 1921 by an act of partition.

must at least look back to 1922, which witnessed Ireland's division into two parts: the six Northern counties became 'Northern Ireland', under British rule and with an assured Unionist majority, and the 26 Southern counties became the 'Irish Free State' (with dominion status, though later declaring itself the Republic of Ireland in 1949). This remained the constitutional situation until 1985 when the Anglo-Irish Agreement was signed by the prime ministers of Britain and Ireland, giving the Republic of Ireland a limited but real role in the government of Northern Ireland in recognition of the affinities of Northern Nationalists with the South.

In the six preceding decades, however, Anglo-Irish relationships had been deeply strained, while within Northern Ireland itself, life and politics were marked by Unionist ascendancy, sectarian division and recurring cycles of violence. The Nationalist population was denied civil rights and political equality, and there were extremist acts of violence on both sides. Peaceful civil rights protests in the 1960s were met with punitive suppression by local police and army reserves, and soon the dormant Irish Republican Army (IRA), no longer prepared to wait for civil rights by drip-feed, re-entered the stage with militant force. Unconvinced that an end to systemic discrimination would be delivered by constitutional means, they set themselves the task of ensuring that Nationalist districts would not be left defenceless against Loyalist pogroms. With the subsequent overrunning of Nationalist neighbourhoods by the British Army, internment without trial and the events of Bloody Sunday where the Parachute Regiment gunned down 13 innocent civilians at a civil rights protest, the IRA, which until then had had but a narrow base of support among the Nationalist population, began to gain ground among many. These people, until then law-abiding citizens, felt that the law and justice had deserted them.[4]

These years were marked by overt and covert sectarian events throughout Ireland, though more regularly in the North. It should be noted here that 'sectarian' and 'sectarianism' denote a volatile mix of 'politicised religion' and 'sacralised politics', interacting at personal, social and institutional lev-

4. Cf. Thomas Bartlett, *Ireland: a History*, Cambridge, Cambridge University Press, 2010, pp. 510–19, esp. p. 512; Paul Bew, *Ireland: The Politics of Enmity, 1789–2006*, Oxford, Oxford University Press, 2007, pp. 486–509, esp. p. 507. In 2010, the British Prime Minister, David Cameron, apologised for these deaths on behalf of the British government, saying that he was 'deeply sorry', and acknowledging that the killing of innocent civilians by the Parachute Regiment was 'unjustified and unjustifiable'. This unexpected, magnanimous public apology to the bereaved families was made in the Westminster Parliament, 15 June 2010, on the basis of the findings of the Saville Enquiry (1998–2010) which had recognised the innocence of the victims of Bloody Sunday, 1972. It represented a vindication of the victims and of their families' long struggle for justice and was an important milestone in the renewal of British-Irish relationships.

els in destructive, systemic ways. Cognisance must also be taken of post-colonial dynamics from the 1960s onwards, with reference to the long-post-poned recognition of human, democratic and civil rights for Nationalists/Catholics in Northern Ireland[5] (this was reinforced by resurgent nationalist movements elsewhere in Europe, reaching a new high in 1989, especially in South-Eastern Europe, with the break-up of the Soviet power bloc).

Coming back to the opening theme of memory, one must remember the long reach of history and historiography, shaping competing stories, myths and ideologies, which, in turn, influence the construction and reconstruction of history – and its distortions – primarily aimed at shoring up claims to legitimacy. Interpretations of past attack and counter-attack, defeat and victory are often magnified through the lens of exclusivist narratives, symbols, legends and norms. Furthermore, these historical narratives are further entrenched in the present by geographical and social segregation, as well as religious sectarianism. Still, such an outcome was not inevitable. In the South of Ireland, for instance, Protestants, though a small minority, are fully integrated into social and political life, despite the fact that sectarianism can still manifest itself on occasion.

Between the 1960s and the 1990s, Northern Ireland suffered waves of atrocious violence at the hands of feuding paramilitaries. Though by far the greatest number of deaths was inflicted by the IRA – condemned by Irish and British governments alike – many were also brutalised or killed by the British Army and the Royal Ulster Constabulary, generally now accepted to have been a partisan police force (until the implementation of the findings of the Patton Report, 1999, and the subsequent Bill on Police Reform, 2000). The accumulated human cost has been incalculable – close to 4,000 lives were lost, leaving behind scores of thousands of bereaved family members. More than 40,000 people were severely injured, and countless others, less visibly affected, still carry the painful scars and hidden wounds.[6]

A breakthrough occurred in 1994 with a ceasefire that was declared by the Provisional IRA on 1 September, with Loyalist paramilitaries following suit a month later.[7] In April 1998, after four years of 'off again-on again'

5. Cf. Frank Wright, *Northern Ireland: a Comparative Analysis*, Dublin, Gill and Macmillan, 1992. The alignment of 'Nationalist' with 'Catholic' is an approximation, as is the equivalent linking of 'Unionist' with 'Protestant', the other power bloc in Northern Ireland.
6. Verifiable figures can be found in the monumental and definitive documentary study, David McKittrick, Seamus Kelters, Brian Feeney, Chris Thornton and David McVea (eds.), *Lost Lives*, Edinburgh and London, Mainstream Publications, 1999, with an updated edition in 2006 that takes account of those who were killed subsequently – after the ceasefires.
7. The way had been paved by the ground-breaking *Joint Declaration on Peace: The Downing Street Declaration, Wednesday 15th December 1993*, signed by the British and Irish prime ministers

ceasefires, the Good Friday Agreement (or Belfast Agreement), sponsored by the Irish and British governments, was signed and overwhelmingly endorsed in referendums held in the Republic of Ireland and, the following month, in Northern Ireland. This peace agreement definitively changed and expanded the political relationships on three levels – between the Irish and British governments, between Northern Ireland and the Republic of Ireland (which dropped its constitutional claim on the North), and structurally, within Northern Ireland, through a power-sharing government executive. The latter, after several collapses and negotiated compromises, has settled into a form of normal politics that includes former paramilitaries in government, together with massive reforms: these were provided for by legislation towards a more balanced police service, respect for human rights, equal opportunities and parity of esteem. Although dissident rump elements of the IRA even today mount lethal attacks by bomb and bullet, and cycles of feuding violence rear up within the ranks of Loyalist Unionism, the perpetrators are relatively few in number and narrow in range of influence. The political framework for peace is now established.

The period since 1998 has been characterised by phenomenal, if precarious, progress in transitional justice and post-conflict peacebuilding.[8] As in all conflicts, when the fighting stops, the legacy of the past must be faced. Attempts need to be made to acknowledge the residual trauma and loss, and to redress grievance and injustice. After the political peace, the building of community peace remains an immense challenge. The discipline of peace studies makes clear that the larger challenge of building trust and relationships at civic and inter-community levels is a slow and halting process. Peacebuilding needs to be envisaged as inter-generational work, requiring multi-level, multi-agency and time-phased processes embracing society as a whole – including the Churches and faith communities.[9] It must take ac-

at that time – John Major and Albert Reynolds. Paragraph 4 states: 'The Prime Minister … reiterates, on behalf of the British Government, that they have no selfish strategic or economic interest in Northern Ireland.'

8. 'Transitional justice' is the term now assigned to the interdisciplinary field that engages the dilemmas of the past in post-conflict societies. Here, contested and complex issues come to the fore, such as truth recovery processes (the relative merits of truth, or truth and reconciliation, commissions, trials, tribunals or restorative justice processes, for example); the role of commemoration and story-telling initiatives; state accountability for human rights abuses; the role of apology and the possibility of forgiveness, the role of commemoration, apology and forgiveness; sanctions, convictions and rehabilitation of former combatants; justice and redress for victims and survivors. Cf. Nir Eisikovits, 'Transitional Justice', in *Stanford Encyclopedia of Philosophy*, Stanford, USA, 2009, http://plato.stanford.edu/entries/justice-transitional/ (last accessed 04.05.12); also, Daniel Philpott (ed.), *The Politics of Past Evil: Religion, Reconciliation and the Dilemmas of Transitional Justice*, Notre Dame, Indiana, University of Notre Dame Press, 2006.

9. See, for example, John D. Brewer, *Peace Processes: A Sociological Approach*, Cambridge, Polity

count of the cognitive, affective, ethical, social, political and spiritual aspects of social life, and of the local and wider contexts and their history. At the same time, such mediating networks and leadership are not new; they have long been at work, even in the midst of the worst times of violence, encouraging risk-taking, creating neutral spaces for clarifying non-negotiable positions, facilitating 'back channels' and 'talks about talks' and paving the way to ceasefires and ultimate negotiations.

DOMINICAN LIFE IN THE CHURCH IN NORTHERN IRELAND

It is the purpose of this piece to explore the contribution of Dominican women, living and working in the North of Ireland, to ecumenism, peace and reconciliation. Aware of their call to be preachers of truth, they can recount experiences of grace and blessing, even in periods of abysmal suffering, as they seek to understand the past and read the signs of the times today, in what remains, perhaps inevitably, an ambiguous, even murky, moral landscape. Northern Ireland finds itself in an uneasy position between war and peace, or between endemic violence and the last-ditch stands of 'No Surrender'. In this time of transition, many are torn between remembering and forgetting. Symptoms of trauma are still widespread and the pain of many victim-survivors remains to be acknowledged. Ireland – and the focus here will be mainly Northern Ireland – will have to cope with the legacy of bitter violence and tragic loss for a long time yet.

Dealing with the past, overcoming sectarian hostility, and engaging the multifarious challenges of transitional justice and reconciliation are a social challenge that should be a primary concern of the Churches – theologically, ethically, ecclesiologically and pastorally. Young people are largely educated in segregated settings, at least until university. Although there has been progress in ecumenical encounter, it has been painfully slow. Perhaps we can give it two cheers, for although some have persevered, including some deemed noteworthy here, there is still a widespread lack of understanding, enthusiasm and comprehensive commitment. Churches remain to be fully reconciled and ecumenical relations are not consistently encouraged by word or example. In Ireland, one cannot overstate the urgency of the witness to ecumenical reconciliation, both in terms of the *esse* and the *bene esse* of the Church itself, and also for the sake of social reconciliation and peace. In Ireland, divided Churches have cost lives, and continue to share responsibility

---

Press, 2010; also John Paul Lederach, *Building Peace: Sustainable Reconciliation in Divided Societies*, Washington, United States Institute of Peace, 1997.

for estranged communities and sectarian division. Dominican sisters working in Northern Ireland since 1870 find themselves alongside many others at the heart of this story of estrangement and brokenness.

This contribution is drawn from the work of a small steering group that met over a period of several months.[10] All had lived in several Dominican communities in the North of Ireland for at least part of this period and been involved there in educational and ecumenical ministry. It was agreed that it would be important to canvass wider experiences of Dominican involvement beyond our own perspectives. A questionnaire was devised, which duly elicited fruitful responses from sisters who had lived and worked in the North of Ireland during these decades. Certain theological motifs will be visible in the paper – such as the Church viewed through the lens of the Pilgrim People of God, or ecumenism construed as a call to unity in difference. The essential spirit of the Dominican congregation in Cabra is a dynamic and shared mission reality – when one acts, it is on behalf of all, since all are one in Christ Jesus, and all variously express and rejoice in the same charism.

The aforementioned questionnaire elicited thoughtful memories from more than a dozen sisters who had lived in one or other of our three larger foundations in Belfast: St Mary's Dominican Convent, Falls Road, was founded in 1870 in the predominantly Catholic West of the city, from Cabra in Dublin; Dominican Convent Portstewart on the North Antrim coast was founded in 1917; and Dominican Convent, Fortwilliam Park, in the socioreligiously mixed North Belfast, was founded in 1930. In the Falls Road, the central focus of ministry was educational, with sisters involved in first- and second-level schools and a third-level college of education. Some sisters later ran a small school for hearing-impaired children. Pastoral care of hearing-impaired adults represents another ministry outreach over many years. Fortwilliam Park was located near the infamous 'murder triangle', scene of some of the most appalling events of the entire 'Troubles'. Through various periods, this community had in its care a first-level school, two second-level schools and a commercial college. Of all the sisters' schools, Dominican College Portstewart was the only one with a sizeable proportion of Protestant and other religious traditions (now 40 per cent of students). Staff, too, have been denominationally mixed, and recent principals have included a Presbyterian elder who had had a long prior association with the school as a teacher.[11] The college has earned accolades as a beacon to the actual possibil-

---

10. The steering group included Sr Maeve McMahon, Sr Maris Stella McKeown and myself.
11. The sisters departed Portstewart in 1999. These Dominican schools are served now by other principals, although the sisters maintain connections variously – as trustees, management

ity of Catholic, Protestant and Dissenter being educated together, yet in a Catholic ethos. Staff and students who do not belong to the Roman Catholic tradition treasure and engage in the Dominican vision – to praise, to bless, to preach – and its educational philosophy focused on the value of the human person, the search for truth and justice and the affirmation of all God's creation.

Also represented in the responses are contributions of sisters whose ministry was associated with one of several small communities since the 1970s. These largely sprang out of the existing larger communities. Sisters who moved to these were involved variously in parish pastoral work, social outreach and faith formation. Cavendish Square (1987–2001), and the Lanthorn Community was especially dedicated to sustaining a parish-based programme of faith formation and friendship across several dioceses according to the method known as SPRED (Special Religious Education).[12] In itself, the Lanthorn Community consisted of Sr Criona Considine, who had pioneered it, and Sr Margaret Purcell, with up to four other adults in a L'Arche-type community that was always a tonic to visit. The Currach Community was a bold initiative founded by Sr Noreen Christian in 1992. Something of its ecumenical peace witness and of her outstanding contribution to cross-community and interchurch reconciliation will be explored below. Later still, Lecceto was founded, a community of two sisters who believed in the value of being a Dominican presence in the predominantly Protestant-Unionist East Belfast, while engaging in broader areas of ministry – educational, cross-community and ecumenical.

Many seeds, scattered and nurtured, have taken root and borne fruit, seen

board members, in chaplaincy, retreat work and various kinds of staff and student support. The longest serving principal was Sr M. Lucina Montague, who served as principal for 12 years in Dominican College Portstewart from 1974, and with the whole staff ensured an ethos and embodiment of interchurch respect and understanding. Later, she worked ecumenically in the pastoral context of Queen's University Chaplaincy in periods that were both politically turbulent and a constant challenge to the Churches to make unity visible. Sr Margaret Purcell carried on the Dominican torch there as a chaplain in the mid-1990s.

12. While they may not seem to be directly focused on peace and reconciliation, these broke new ground educationally and modelled collaboration and ecumenical hospitality, ensuring opportunities of inclusion and reciprocity among children and adults whose disability has often caused them to be overlooked in Church and society. It is in part thanks to the exemplary role of such initiatives that the crafters of the Good Friday Agreement (section 75) provided within the *peace agreement* for protective and inclusive legislation for people with disability. This demonstrates the integral connection between human rights, equality, justice and peace. Acknowledgement is due to Sr Sadoc Lynch (d. 1983), Sr Maolíosa Byrne and Sr Lorna Ridley for their work in deaf education and in pastoral and liturgical ministry with adult deaf people. The impact of the work of SPRED was true to its name through the pioneering work of Sr Bernadette O'Sullivan (d. 1993) and Sr Criona Considine, Sr Kate McGlynn, Sr Lorna Ridley, Sr Lambert Gahan and Sr Margaret Purcell, among others.

or unseen, throughout the decades of violence and into now more than a decade of peacebuilding. Whatever their different points of entry, Dominican women have found that within their context in the North of Ireland, ecumenical reconciliation and social justice are two sides of one coin. Ecclesial unity and social reconciliation imply each other and are at once mutually sustaining and mutually challenging. Such reflection also yields the realisation that in the diverse range of contributions to reconciliation and justice over these years, both the inner meaning and outward focus have been at one with the witness of the whole Dominican Order to the reconciling heart of Christ's mission – in whose mission we are all called to participate.

MISSION AND MOBILITY FOR MISSION

Mobility for mission represented one of the concrete expressions of the renewal of mission and ministry in the Church and in the Order following Vatican II. One outstanding prioress general of the Cabra congregation from 1974–86 – Sr Jordana Roche – led the way in encouraging or 'volunteering' sisters to greater mobility in mission. Often this involved smaller groups living in the middle of housing estates in new areas, or, somehow, on the margins – St Martin's in the troubled Turf Lodge area of Belfast comes to mind. Some who made the move continued to teach in local schools and colleges – not necessarily those under the congregation's jurisdiction, but sometimes in new community school or co-educational ventures, including collaboration with the friars – reflecting a more pluralist Ireland and an ever greater demand for education. Some sisters, after undertaking higher studies and specialist courses in pastoral ministry, biblical studies or catechetics, moved into parish-based pastoral roles or into educational chaplaincy. Sr Jordana Roche is remembered for her claim that every sister should have experienced at least two cultures before she was 40. During her double six-year term of office scores of sisters were sent out to South Africa, to new mission ventures in Argentina, Louisiana, Brazil and Lisbon, or to involvement in contextually inserted evangelisation at home. Sent in the name of the congregation, the mission of one was the mission of all. In these years, where responsibility for schools and colleges was increasingly ceded to lay principals, many undertook a more visible witness to social justice and the option for the poor, both before and after formal retirement age, whether by direct evangelisation, human rights action or simple accompaniment of the people in their search for education, for racial justice, for equality and liberation. Some who were moved from the Republic of Ireland to the different jurisdiction of Northern Ireland, were not slow with the riposte, 'Never mind Latin America; aren't we already involved in our second culture?' Irony aside, this was not without truth because, at least until the war in Bosnia and Herzegovina, these decades were witness to the worst violence in Europe since the Second World War.

The 1980s saw the increased interest in devising and adopting mission statements. The one developed at the 1986 General Chapter stands the congregation in good stead to the present day:

> Our mission as Dominican Women is to study, share, proclaim and witness to the liberating Word of God, in order that right relationships be restored between God, people and the earth, where these are broken due to lack of knowledge and distortion of the truth.

The ongoing affirmation of the reality of the Order of Preachers as the 'Dominican family' (General Chapters of Friars, Tallaght, 1971, and Naples, 1974), and, later, the new language of 'Frontiers for Mission' (Avila General Chapter of Friars, 1986) was embraced and lent fresh impetus to mission. These emphases were underscored in letters and visits of successive Masters of the Order, particularly Fr Damian Byrne, and through collaborative projects grounded in the charism of preaching (as advocated by the General Chapter of the Friars, Rome, 1983). In these closing decades of the century, some sisters who had been part of the new wave of mission abroad, and others who had gone out soon after profession, found an Ireland socially changed, almost beyond recognition, on their return. Ecclesially, their transition back to Ireland was sometimes difficult, since change within the Church had been slower on many levels in Ireland, not least in the scope for women in leadership, in contrast to their previous mission contexts.

In apartheid-riven South Africa, for example, ecumenical co-operation and action for social justice had been commonplace; in Argentina, following the episcopal conferences at Puebla and Medellin and during successive military dictatorships, commitment to structural justice and solidarity with the poor were viewed as constitutive of the Gospel in the context of solidarity with marginalised people and the potential of basic Christian communities. Action for human rights and the search for a transformed ecclesial reality as the Church of and for the poor were seen by them as normative. Sisters also continued moving in both directions to and from communities in Lisbon and in New Orleans, both of which continued a dual track commitment to formal education and to initiatives of social justice and the dismantling of attitudes and structures of racism, whether against African-Americans, Native Americans or other minority communities.

The 'encounter of cultures' could be more daunting in reverse – when sisters who returned to Ireland voiced comments or critical questions arising from their experience of such intercultural encounter, or, in certain contexts, counter-cultural witness to the transcending values of the Kingdom of God, at the other side of the world and on the underside of history. There were many discussions at chapters and community meetings about the relative priorities of community and mission, and about what has since been appositely termed 'constants in context'.[13] Mission was the guiding constant.

COMMON DOMINICAN MISSION:
UNIQUE CALLS AND DIVERSE FORMS OF MINISTRY

A Paradigm of Diversity in Unity: Prophet, Priest and King

The theological vision of faith, hope and love gives an underlying orientation to Dominican mission. More widely, in these years many tensions arose regarding diverging attitudes to increasing pluralism, and there were debates about contested priorities and preferential options.[14] Old arguments were rehearsed around the apparent polarities of charism versus institution, liberal and traditional views of religious life, and clashing tastes for the prophetic, the pastoral and the institutional, whether in community life-style, in educational forms or liturgical practice. Reading back from a twenty-first century vantage point, one seeks for some integrative paradigm for construing the contribution of Cabra Dominicans to social ethics within Northern Ireland, yet resisting the impulse to smooth away the conflict of interpretations and the tensions arising from this. Clearly one needs a framework that can accommodate the divergent and even the contentious, that can shed light on the complexity of social and ecclesiological context and the diversity of views and expressions; a framework that holds together the vital potential of diversity in the kind of unity that does not totalise any one model of faith and ethics, any one way of living a religious ministerial life-form and witnessing to Christ's creating, saving and sanctifying mission.

The threefold symbol structure of Prophet, Priest and King (the latter con-

13. Stephen B. Bevans and Roger P. Schroeder, *Constants in Context: A Theology of Mission for Today*, Maryknoll, NY, Orbis Publications, fifth printing 2009 (2004).

14. One of the finest studies on the theology of ministry, grounded in a Thomistic theology of grace and sensitive to changing understandings in history and culture, is that of Thomas O'Meara, *Theology of Ministry: Completely Revised Edition*, NY, Paulist Press, 1999. The original volume of the same name, published in 1983, was also at the time a most significant resource.

strued variously as King/Shepherd/Sage) has been used by Christian think-ers reflecting on Jesus and his way of communicating the manifold love of God for the world.[15] In one place, he stands in the paradigm of Good Shep-herd; in another his actions are those of the perfect High Priest; in another he is portrayed through his words and action as the Prophet. The Pauline writ-ings are shot through with allusions to this typology. As a methodological device, it may help to do justice to the diversity of ministries within a com-mon mission. To this end, in the three following sections the contributions of different congregational initiatives and the profiling of some particular sisters will be explored, under this threefold symbolic expression – Prophet, Priest, Shepherd-King – as a way of presenting the variety of work for recon-ciliation in a time of shared trouble and search for peace. Such times required each kind of witness, both variously and in interrelationship. Firstly, under the image of Shepherd-King, the way the sisters worked through education-al structures to promote peace and reconciliation will be presented, since this involves shepherding the young through to maturity.

Shepherd-King: Dominicans in Education and Pastoral Ministry

Education was the matrix of mission within the congregation. It was ex-pressed mainly through teaching – as a service of truth enabling young people to succeed and equipping them as citizens and leaders in various fields in the secular world and in the Church. Teaching also took the form of pastoral care, and extended to many extra-curricular activities oriented to social justice, spiritual maturity and engagement in the public sphere. Some sisters took prophetic steps in opening minds to think and act counter to the conventional grain and by promoting opportunities for inter-communi-ty engagement and mutual understanding. So, too, Dominican education is deeply oriented to the sacred, the sacramental and the spiritual (emblematic of the priestly). But within the schema employed here, it most aptly reflects what has been associated here with the role of shepherd-king – guiding, teaching, leading and nurturing others in the ways of wisdom, but with a mind also to reciprocal relationships and mutual care. Dominican schools sought to provide for this, alongside aiming for the academic excellence and sound knowledge that is assumed in most Dominican centres of learning.

In times of violence and conflict, and with the competing ideologies of

15. See, for example, Yves Congar, *Lay People in the Church: a Study for a Theology of the Laity*, where the author relies on this *tripos* for the deep structure of his theologising of the role of the People of God. From a Jewish perspective, the work of Jacob Neusner may also be mentioned.

justice and peace that characterised Northern Ireland, this was more than ordinarily demanding in scope. In these years Dominican schools, like many others, were not only centres of learning and of the search for truth, but also communities of pastoral care and community outreach. So often in Belfast, when buses were burning, or local shops and pubs were bombed, or when students' own homes were seized by paramilitary gunmen or kept under military curfew, the school was the only safe space, a haven from the terror of violence and political contention. Communities and the staff in the schools became a kind of collective 'Good Shepherd', providing a secure ethos and steadying hand, keeping young people safe from harm, seeing them home. During prolonged bomb scares or violent attack, school halls were transformed into overnight shelters for families. In the particularly appalling summer of 1969, when Catholic homes in West Belfast came under arson attack, hundreds of families fled, terrified, making their way across the border to the South. Through Dominican networks, many found their way to refuge in Dominican and other religious communities, in convents and school halls, until temporary housing could be found for them by the state authorities.

Protection of, and provision for, families were all part of the educational pastoral ministry in those days. And in the daily routine of school life, promotion of peace and reconciliation was a constant, through '[i]nvolvement of the whole staff in promoting a spirit of understanding and openness as part of the ethos of the school', as well as through embracing the challenges of tolerance and peace, through curricular and extra-curricular programmes for mutual understanding.[16] Curriculum options for A level (matriculation equivalent) included a specialist focus on the Celtic Church or on Scripture, with a view to revealing deep shared foundations and a common heritage. So, too, 'cross community contacts were very important and actively promoted', including shared projects with several schools of different traditions, as were ecumenical services to which 'Ministers of Religion were invited to address assemblies and other gatherings'.

One might also make reference to the influential role played by the teaching of history in the contexts of state-building, in post-conflict societies, or in situations where there is little awareness and practice of gender equality and the values supported by healthy pluralism. Nowadays there is fairly widespread acknowledgement of more balanced approaches to history writ-

16. Reported by Sr Jacqueline O'Reilly, long time principal at intervals in Fortwilliam Park and St Dominic's Belfast, and now chairperson of the governing body of the strongly inter-denominational Dominican College Portstewart.

ing and teaching and to the disciplines of historiography and hermeneutics. Dr Margaret (formerly Benvenuta) MacCurtain, a well-known historian and lecturer in University College Dublin, must be particularly mentioned for her leadership in this field, developing and teaching the history curriculum in second-level schools in the 1970s in a more inclusive and nuanced direction. Still recalled affectionately by thousands of her university students over these decades as 'Sr Ben', in her near and post-retirement years she was crucially involved in the setting up of a Centre for Women's Studies in the university. She led the way, seeing to it that women's voices, so often written out of history, were brought into the domain of higher education and research, through her own publications, international women's history conferences and in her mentoring of young academics in their scholarship and publishing endeavours (including publications on the historical contribution of women religious in Ireland and Irish missionary movements). She is still much sought after by the media for interview, or as a panelist at key turning points in Irish life and society, on the importance of inclusive reconciliation. She is a recognised 'wisdom figure' in the true sense of the term.

In these years of turmoil many Cabra Dominicans, South and North, involved themselves in structured attempts – often in partnership with others – to show solidarity in practical ways. Sr Margaret MacCurtain, writing about the introduction of internment without trial by a Special Powers Act in August 1971, tells of her involvement with such intellectual and civic leaders as Liam De Paor, Austin Flannery and Seán Mac Réamoinn from the South, who, together with a Northern Nationalist MP, Paddy Devlin, set up a small North-South benevolent association – Association of Committees for Aiding Internees' Dependents (ACAID). She became its treasurer and border-crossing ambassador, travelling the hundred miles north from Dublin to Belfast each month to hand over a cheque to provide these distressed families with £20.[17] Sr Cornelia Dooley (d. 2010) and Sr Simeon Tarpey (d. 1997) – both of whom had been principals of St Mary's College of Education in Belfast in these decades – ensured that financial and other support was made available unobtrusively to families under duress, as did other principals and teachers, through their own pastoral attention and networks. Sr Simeon maintained contact through visits and letters to former students who were serving long

---

17. Dr Margaret MacCurtain, in her questionnaire response, notes that Paddy Devlin's daughter, Anne Devlin (herself a Dominican former student and now a well-known playwright and screenplay writer), found material about this work of ACAI, 1971–73, when the first constitutional power-sharing executive in NI was brought down by Unionist determination. ACAID formally closed the following spring.

sentences for involvement in acts of terror. She did not agree with their political stance nor with the hunger strike they embarked upon, but she never
turned away from them in their own times of desperation: 'I was in prison
and you visited me' (Mt 24: 34–36).

So too, the pastoral, sapiential responsibilities led on into the sacramental
and priestly, in the daily spiritual formation through the surrounding ethos
or in such ordinary events as weekly or seasonal liturgies, school retreats,
and class Masses. In times of deep sorrow, as when students were injured
or killed or lost relatives, the convent chapel or a local church became sites
of lamenting, grief and prayer for peace, where stories of loss and anguish
were gathered into the paschal mystery of Christ's death and resurrection.

So, too, the prophetic dimension was in evidence, as sisters sought educational opportunities to overcome the inevitable estrangement arising from
segregated neighbourhoods and schools. Dominican schools led or joined
in initiatives providing different kinds of inter-cultural contact, friendship
and learning through the school year. Often this was publicly acclaimed. Sr
Helen O'Dwyer (d. 2009) as principal of St Rose's High School, Belfast, was
named in the Queen's Honours List and awarded the OBE for her outstanding service to young people and leadership in the field of education.

Sr Maris Stella McKeown describes how, as a young Dominican teacher
back in 1974, she, along with other sisters, promoted whatever passing possibilities were at hand – through sports or debating societies, for example. At
the same time, she and Sr Marie Therese Martin sought for something more
wide-ranging and sustained. Writing in the *Dominican Newsheet* in 1974,
Maris Stella spoke of the huge obstacles, making it all the more important
to 'mak[e] a beginning no matter how small'. They organised a week's holiday for students from St Dominic's and St Rose's Dominican Schools, and
Methodist College, catering for second-level students in Belfast who had few
other opportunities for meeting each other. With their teachers and the Corrymeela Centre staff, all 44 teenagers worked together, enjoying themselves
in the ethos of trust for which Corrymeela is now internationally renowned.
They prepared services of worship together and enjoyed barbecues and discussions alongside international visitors. The date of departure, she wrote,
brought tears and clasped hands, but also the realisation that 'Corrymeela
begins when you leave'.

Social psychologists writing about segregation in Northern Ireland have
suggested that the kind of 'contact' that such holiday adventures allow
has minimal value. They have claimed that afterwards – pleasant holiday

memories aside – people revert to their segregated ways. But that has not proved to be the case where there is purposeful and participative preparation and sustained reflective follow-up and support. In the long, tense summer months students were helped to avail of summer holiday adventures in Belgium or the US, for example, giving them undreamed-of opportunities for gaining the kind of culturally diverse experience impossible at home. Such adventures, being somewhat removed from the prevailing dangers, gave them deeper resources to help them in facing the hard underlying dynamics of institutionalised sectarianism.

There are further examples of initiatives that, far from withering on the stem, grew apace and scattered seeds towards more far-flung development. Sr Patricia O'Reilly's account for a congregational newsletter in the 1980s tells of an interchange between 38 Belfast schoolchildren and their teachers from St Catherine's Primary School, Falls Road, and Fane Street Primary School (a state school in a totally Protestant enclave a few miles south). Following a series of tentative inter-class gatherings and projects such as tree planting in a large suburban park, trips to the city-centre YMCA and a shopping trip, the staffs of the schools, now bolder in vision, organised a trip to the Corrymeela Community of Reconciliation, 60 miles away on the North Atlantic coast. Sr Patricia describes how, at the end of the year, the fruits of the initiative were brought into the wider civic sphere. The teachers – Sr Patricia, Louise, Hugh and Bertha – mounted a display of the student's joint work at Queen's University, where parents were invited to come and see what happens when the impossible is imagined in the search for the greater good. Sr Patricia claims that even if it 'melted the tip of the iceberg' it embodied in a few hundred children and their teachers and parents, 'hope for the future'.[18]

This is typical of initiatives in other Dominican schools, North and South, which have grown apace from the seeds sown by Dominican teachers in the 1980s. Sr Elizabeth Smyth, who, as a student in St Rose's High School, Belfast, participated in some of these 1980s initiatives, has expanded this model

18. A brief addendum might be added here: 25 years later, the Fane Street teacher Bertha McDougall went on to become a victims' commissioner for Northern Ireland, giving leadership in addressing the needs of victim survivors from all sides of the community. At the time of writing, I found myself in Fane Street School to meet several principals and representatives of the Irish School of Ecumenics (ISE). (ISE is a graduate institute, now part of Trinity College Dublin, in which Irish Dominicans have been focally involved, and, for this reason, it will be featured later in more detail.) The meeting was convened to plan a boundary-crossing educational initiative through art, aiming to involve and integrate disadvantaged local and 'newcomer' children from diverse ethnic backgrounds. It can be seen from this that the seeds of the 1980s initiative are flourishing still.

to create opportunities for Dominican students in Ballyfermot, Dublin, Belfast and in Iguape, Brazil, where she spent six years. The aim is to allow students to experience and learn about one another's contexts, share experiences, build educational links of solidarity and foster community leadership capacities for a global world and a new millennium.[19]

Sr Margaret Hegarty speaks of her time working in pastoral ministry in St Martin's community, beside Holy Trinity Parish Church (1972–79 and 2005–08). The community of three to four other sisters was involved educationally and pastorally there. She describes living in a neighbourhood with huge social problems – mass unemployment, addiction, marriage breakdown and inability to cope with the violence and the permanently tense situation: 'There was palpable tension at all times ... aggravated by the constant twenty-four hour presence of the army on the streets. Many parishioners were murdered ... Many were totally innocent ... others unfortunately were involved in paramilitary activity.' Here the main apostolate of the sisters was 'to minister to the bereaved families and to many families without fathers, as many were interned without trial. Support was also given to mothers concerned about the activities of their teenage sons.'

The sisters there were new to this kind of pastoral setting, but they stayed close to the people and their educational expertise was quickly called upon when they were asked to open a crèche for families, 'as mothers were now the chief breadwinners'.[20] The needs of women were given close attention, and Sr Margaret drew in the help of others in setting up courses in personal development and relationship skills, practical skills, cookery and budgeting. These courses enabled women to raise their own educational expectations, leading to further educational and job opportunities and empowering them to cross boundaries into intercommunity ventures, participating with Protestant and other Catholic women in community development programmes in the Corrymeela Centre for Reconciliation.

19. Among the peace and reconciliation programmes in which Sr Elizabeth has become involved and opened up to Dominican youth, we may note: 'Our town, your town' (St Dominic's Ballyfermot and North West Educational Board, Northern Ireland); NICH – Cross-border Leadership Programme; Civic Link Cooperation Ireland; and International Exchange (involving Irish, Brazilian and Argentinian young people from Dominican schools and parishes).

20. Sr Ultan Smyth, Sr Nuala McKinstry and Sr Noeleen Fitzpatrick were all active in nursery education in these years, both in St Martin's and St Agnes's Parish, Andersonstown, and in Sr Nuala's case, as lecturer in the Education Department of St Mary's University College. Sr Brighde O'Kane, a few miles away on the Falls Road campus, ran Bible study and faith formation programmes for staff and parents of children in St Catherine's Primary School, though this was also a point of entry for sustained pastoral support for these (mainly) women who lived locally under heavily militarised and disadvantaged conditions.

PRIESTLY PEOPLE

Again, it should be stressed that there is no partition between the pastoral, priestly and prophetic call and mission. They can be imagined perhaps as tributaries of one stream, now intersecting and forming a confluence, now breaking off in a different direction – attending to the sacred and reconciling bonds between earth and heaven and within the whole community. It should again be underlined that, for this purpose and context, the priestly appeals in broad terms to a sense of the sacred, openness to the transcendent and to making visible the divine *communio* in our human and ecclesial relationships. It is used here as emblematic of the sharing by all the baptised in Christ's unique priesthood, bringing forth Christ's healing love to people who are bereaved and broken, raising hands in prayer with them, repenting, interceding, thanking and glorifying God, in times of shame, pain, joy and longing. So-called 'ordinary Christians' across Northern Ireland have risen to this priestly call to bear witness to Christ's desire for the oneness of his Church and its embodiment in Christ's reconciling mission for the whole world. It has been heartening to see many Dominicans among them.

HOSPITALITY, HOLINESS AND HEALING:
BREAKING OPEN THE DIVIDING WALL

It was such motivation that led Sr Maris Stella McKeown to take pen in hand and write to the letters page of *The Belfast Telegraph* in January 1976. She wrote of the approaching Week of Prayer for Christian Unity, and the need for prayer *and* work together for more tolerance and understanding: 'I would like to make a practical gesture of reconciliation towards neighbours who are not members of the same Church as I, by inviting anyone ... to reply to the address below,' if only in 'simple acknowledgement, accepting this gesture from one Christian to another', though going on to invite readers who wished to come and meet together in dialogue as a way of dispelling misunderstandings and stereotypes about one another, and in preparedness to both pray for reconciliation and to work for it. 'This is one way,' she continued, 'that the silent, nameless majority can become vocal and reveal themselves to one another', and concluded with a quotation from 1 Jn 4: 20: '... those who do not love a brother or sister whom they have seen, cannot love God whom they have not see.' More than 50 people replied, and about 25 gathered with Sr Maris Stella and Sr Maeve McMahon at Corrymeela's Belfast centre. For some, there followed their first visit ever to a convent, giving shared witness to the Johannine text. The summer of 1976 saw an appalling series of sectarian murders and bloodletting on an unprecedented scale.[21] But following the escalation of violence on the part of antagonistic paramilitary groups, people came onto the streets in peace rallies, marches and prayer vigils in which large numbers of Dominican sisters participated.

In September, Sr Maeve McMahon introduced peace and reconciliation into her curriculum in the adjacent St Catherine's Primary School, and not long after was invited by the Irish Commission for Justice and Peace (a commission of the Roman Catholic Bishops' Conference) to work ecumenically alongside representatives of the Irish Council of Churches (Protestant) to write a peace and justice education programme for primary schools in Ireland. Out of that emerged a permanent desk at the Irish Council of Churches (ICC) building in Belfast, where joint efforts in developing resources, further projects and training continued under joint ICC-RC Episcopal Conference auspices right into the new millennium.

It was impossible for Dominicans in Northern Ireland not to have been close to the unspeakable suffering and trauma on the long journey to peace. They took part in the seemingly endless funeral rituals associated with colleagues, students and their families, neighbours, and, indeed, their own relations. They also followed mourners not personally known to them, as a result of atrocities that tore apart other ordinary families, other cultural communities and other confessional traditions. Sr Noreen Christian was active in the Falls-Shankill Fellowship at the time, some of whose members (Protestant and Catholic ministers) had committed to visit together every bereaved family on either side of the divide, to offer condolence and – if acceptable – to pray with them.

A few personal memories come to mind: on the morning after the bombing of a fish shop on the Unionist Shankill Road, Belfast, in October 1993 (a bomb planted by an IRA volunteer, which killed nine Saturday shoppers, as well as himself), I was worshipping at the Sunday service in Fitzroy Presbyterian Church a few miles away.[22] Towards the end of the service, Reverend

21. On St Dominic's Day, 1976, buses and cars were ablaze outside the Falls Road convent gate, as Dominican and family visitors, as well as friends, took hurried leave after the author's final profession ceremony.

22. As a student at the Irish School of Ecumenics some years earlier, I had engaged in ecumenical fieldwork in Fitzroy Presbyterian Church, which at the time was in an 'interchurch fellowship' with Clonard Monastery close to the Shankill 'Peaceline' wall, dividing it from with greater Falls Road (Nationalist area). Sr Noreen Christian was a member. Clonard was the home of a Redemptorist community, which ministered to a local congregation. Their crypt sheltered local Protestants and Catholics alike during the Second World War Belfast blitz, as it gave refuge in 1969 to Catholics from neighbouring Bombay Street whose homes were set ablaze by a Loyalist mob on rampage. Clonard was also the site of early meetings between Protestant and Catholic Church people with members of Sinn Féin – the political wing of the IRA.

Ken Newell asked the congregation to come forward with ideas – 'As well as sending flowers and praying, how can we show them that we care, that we are mourning with them?' Out of this appeal, it seemed to me that it was necessary to go to the Shankill Road that night, to one of the evening services, to pray alongside a grief-stricken people there, to express repentance for what some members of my community had done, and simply to say, in the timeworn Irish way, 'I am sorry for your trouble'. Other Dominicans did the same, whether personally, or as members of Religious for Justice, or of the Dominican Justice and Ecumenism Group (an initiative of about ten sisters founded as a result of the encouragement of Fr Albert Nolan during a Dominican assembly at Tallaght in the late 1980s).[23]

Lethal retaliation was swift, both in Belfast and in a rural area in Co. Down. In the wake of this tit-for-tat cycle of violence, members of religious orders and other church groups met with trades union leaders and middle-ground political leaders to plan a consensual protest. On the decided day and hour, tens of thousands gathered at city halls and town squares, to listen to calls for sober reflection and fresh deliberation, embodied symbolically by a time of shared silence and ecumenical prayer. Noreen Christian and I, representing Religious for Justice, were members of the planning meetings, and many sisters either participated at the lunchtime gatherings or organised parallel services of quiet reflection in college chapels or assembly halls. Similar public events occurred following the Omagh bomb in August 1998. This bomb, planted by dissident Republicans determined to wreck the precarious peace process, killed 29 people, including a mother carrying unborn twins. Just as an indiscriminate bomb made no exceptions in snatching lives, conversely, the power of a collective prayerful act of worship that transcended the old religious divisions brought some consolation to the traumatised communities and bereaved families from Ireland, North and South, and from Britain and Spain. Attending one of the many funerals a few days later, I learned again that there was no difference between Protestant and Catholic tears and such experiences of communion in suffering reminded us that we were all finding comfort and communion of heart in the same Christ, knowing the

---

23. The core members included Sr Aine Killen, Majella Fitzpatrick, Lelia Newman, Noreen Christian, Miriam Weir, Elizabeth Smyth, Geraldine Marie Smyth, Fiona McSorley (d. 2008). Some friars joined – Fr Redmond Fitzmaurice and, later, Fr Donal Roche. Among other things, the group engaged in ecumenical justice actions, including against the use of lethal plastic bullets, and for prison reform; campaigning on a civil liberties platform for the release of a number of unjustly imprisoned young people from both sides of the community; study and seminars on topics such as the relevance of South Africa's *Kairos Document* for Northern Ireland, and support of ecumenical activities, such as a local Presbyterian church flower festival.

need of a consoling, empowering Spirit, lifting our hearts to the same God.

PREACHING RECONCILIATION

Some sisters were particularly involved in the mission of ecumenical reconciliation based in interchurch prayer, charismatic renewal or interchurch retreats and study groups. All the communities were houses of hospitality for ecumenical prayer or Bible study groups. Sr Teresa Morgan (d. 2007), with her natural sister, Sr Ann Patricia Morgan (d. 2005), and Sr Marie Therese Carvill (d. 2010) were keenly involved and, each month, during the mid-1980s, hosted the charismatic and ecumenical Community of the King in the Dominican Convent, Falls Road. A number of sisters have been faithful participants in the weekly ecumenical service of healing in the Anglican city centre cathedral since the 1970s, worshipping alongside Christian sisters and brothers and building reconciliation in prayer, friendship and conferences that interconnect faith and healing.

In 1996, I contributed a lecture in a Lenten series sponsored by the Anglican St Anne's Cathedral, Belfast. An initiative of the cathedral's Catalyst group, which was committed to the cathedral's ministry of reconciling study and cross-community outreach, its theme was: 'Brokenness, Forgiveness, Healing and Peace in Ireland'.[24] I also spoke in those years at similar conferences, hosted variously by Corrymeela, Protestant and Catholic Evangelical Encounter, the Presbyterian Church at Fortwilliam Park, and, further afield, in the Irish School of Ecumenics and in Irish, British and US universities on topics such as 'Reconciling Memories', 'Moving Beyond Sectarianism' and 'Religion and Civil Society'. Sr Brighde Vallely, Sr Noreen Christian and I responded often to invitations to speak, or to preach at denominational or ecumenical services.

Brighde, as Head of the RE department at Dominican College Portstewart and, later, as lecturer in the Religious Education Department and dean of student services at St Mary's College of Education, devised inter-college events promoting 'Education for Mutual Understanding', including retreats and pilgrimages to ancient Celtic or Roman sites. There, in such liminal and

---

24. In this series, a theologian delivered a paper each week on the given theme, with responses from politicians or members of political parties. A publication resulted, under the title *Brokenness, Forgiveness, Healing and Peace in Ireland: What Can the Churches Do?* The contributors were Victor Griffin, Enda McDonagh, John Dunlop, Johnston McMaster and Geraldine Smyth, and the collection was published by the Community Relations Council, Belfast, in 1996. The respondent to my paper was Mitchell McLaughlin, a former Maze-Long Kesh political prisoner. Today, 15 years later, he is a Member of the Legislative Assembly for Northern Ireland, and National Chairperson of the Sinn Féin Party.

hallowed spaces, the participants discovered untapped sources of alternative thinking, friendship and communion that encouraged them to keep seeking a different way that was rooted in a broader and deeper tradition. The same resourcefulness was evident when she later assumed the role of directing the Conference of Religious of Ireland (CORI) Northern Ireland desk, convening sisters and brothers of different religious congregations with Christians of all confessions to find ways of engaging more effectively together in the search for the peace and unity that Christ intended.

As Director of the Irish School of Ecumenics, invitations came to me to preach in various Anglican and Reformed churches, including St Patrick's Cathedral Dublin, Canterbury Cathedral, Coventry Cathedral and St Giles Cathedral Church, Edinburgh, which I welcomed all the more as a way of following Dominic's way of reconciling through the preaching of the word. I also worked with Reverend Doug Baker, a Presbyterian minister, on a peace-building project entitled Partners in Transformation, helping clergy of different denominations to meet on a regular basis and to find nourishment in one another's company by bringing their own desire to be reconcilers into dialogue with the Word of God, broken and shared together. Another dimension of this project was to bring senior Church leaders together with leaders of Church-connected organisations for peace and reconciliation, with the purpose of creating space, and process, for building mutual understanding over a few days. Because of the political pressures at home, such meetings of necessity took place in a sequestered place in Scotland. But the participants testified that the time spent together in informal conversation, reflection and prayer provided a human basis of mutual concern and solidarity that they carried home, in the confidence that they could build upon it.

In witnessing to the peace of Christ that makes all one, a meditative being present to the inner prompting of the Holy Spirit, and to the presence of Christ at work within us and around us, is a *sine qua non*. Sr Noreen Christian was highly sensitive to the untold stresses on families in troubled interface areas, and particularly to the needs of women. So often the ones who hold the fabric of family and community together, these women needed a space for peace and quiet, for trusted ways of meditation and healing in times of nerve-racking pressure. She helped them to shape or find a sustaining form of symbolic retreat away from the endless drone of overhead helicopters, nightlong gunfire, petrol-bombing and army raids, and some temporary respite from the anxieties about the safety of their children and menfolk. She enabled them to create oasis resources for themselves, and introduced them to old and new ways of spiritual renewal for the body and the soul that were at once refreshing and empowering.

In so doing, she was testifying to the fact that, for peace to bear fruit, the inner life must be nurtured, and that one needs to create space for the Spirit of peace to heal and guide. One memorable example of this was in 1987, when, with some others, Noreen organised an open-air Good Friday Stations of the Cross for Reconciliation around the streets, going from Clonard monastery to a park in the Shankill area. It was a risky act, and not all the stares of passersby were friendly. But it gave testimony to faith in the suffering Christ as the peace between us, breaking down the dividing walls and making, out of the two, one people (Ep 2: 14).

Over several years in the 1980s, as a member of the Eckhart House Community founded by Miceál O'Regan in 1980, I co-ordinated guided meditation weekends with other Eckhart House associates in a rural Passionist Monastery in Crossgar, Co. Down. I also engaged in a ministry of psychotherapy for individual persons, and group facilitation of religious communities living in troubled situations, such as North Belfast or Portadown, who were dealing, day by day, with violence, harassment and trauma. This work started from the theory and practice of meditative self-presence, bringing together the wisdom of spiritual traditions and the insights of modern psychology, and developed with those seeking in their own inner depths some middle ground between the institutionalised aspects of religion and a personal experience of a lived and living tradition in openness to the divine and to the other. More recently I have been involved in other initiatives that bring together professional psychologists with therapeutic backgrounds and those working in spiritual ministries of healing within Church contexts, with a view to sharing and learning from their respective approaches and recognising the significance of the spiritual in the path to healing for many. Another personal involvement is with the organisation Healing Through Remembering which aims to raise awareness and to facilitate healing by encouraging open but sensitive public activity in dealing with the past, leading to the construction together of a more integrated and open society in which all can share and belong.[25]

So too, Sr Brighde Vallely, working through CORI as a committee member of an initiative called Journey Towards Healing, has brought this work

25. Cf. www.healingthroughremembering.org (last accessed 04.05.12) for the range of Healing through Remembering published and web-based research, practical guidelines and other resources for approaching contested issues and processes of commemoration, story-telling, truth recovery, annual days of reflection and living memorial museums.

further through sustained structured events. In 2005, assisted by government funding, a publication – *Journey Towards Healing: A Faith-based Resource on Trauma* – was launched, and this was succeeded by a series of training days in which religious, clergy and other practitioners further explored the significance and impact of trauma on a person's faith. In her response to the questionnaire about her own experience, Brighde, who, like Noreen, had also been in leadership in CORI, Northern Ireland, speaks of using this role intentionally to open up ways 'to support victims of the Troubles on their journey towards healing', as well as ways for religious life itself to witness through 'a hospitality that welcomes both "the other" and the newcomer to Northern Ireland'.

Although there were many and various ways in which Dominicans have lived their priestly calling, and sought to bear witness to their baptismal faith in 'one Lord, one faith, one Baptism', and to Christ's desire that the whole world be reconciled, the portrayal in the above section has centred on a few people whose work thrust them more into the public domain. So also in the final section focusing on the prophetic sphere, the work of these three will again come to the fore: Sr Noreen Christian's work as founder and leader of the Currach Community in the shadow of a 40-foot 'Peaceline' Wall and redoubtable gates of steel; Sr Brighde Vallely's mediating initiatives while leader of CORI NI; and my own contribution to ecumenical and educational reconciliation through the structure and activity of the ISE.

PROPHETIC IMAGINATION

The term 'prophetic' is here used cautiously, because it has sometimes been too glibly used, indicating rather an individualised path, or a *modus operandi* separate from the Church – a term thereby reduced to meaning 'institution' – implying a generalised declaration against the status quo, without qualification. The idea of 'prophetic' resistance or protest needs to be kept in interdependent relationship with the community and its needs, in openness to the fullness of God's purposes. Such historically complex symbol structures as Covenant or Reign of God are meaningless outside God's relationship with the community, and require a proper understanding of the often ambivalent biblical prophets (such as Ezekiel or Jeremiah), in their histories and traditions. In Ireland we have learned that the prophetic challenge is not immune from grey moral edges, and the prophetic call involves a return to spiritual and moral renewal of the whole community.

Northern Ireland was in a situation that called for prophetic resistance, through faith, to the unquestioned certainties of a dominant ideology and the intellectual search for truth. This involved entering into collective expressions of suffering in cries of anger and lament that gave birth to hope when all seemed beyond hope, and taking the risk to open up and reach across boundaries of enmity, believing that love could be real, across the grain of tribal convention. Furthermore, in Northern Ireland, such prophetic gestures and processes could be transformed by being grounded in the person, teaching and actions of Jesus Christ, the Way, the Truth and the Life.[26]

The Currach Community has already been mentioned. Situated on the Springfield Road-Workman Avenue 'Peaceline' in Belfast, its founding by Sr Noreen Christian was an act of prophetic imagination.[27] On her return to ministry in Northern Ireland, after 25 years' teaching in South Africa, Noreen worked with other Christians in the mainly non-resident ecumenical Cornerstone Community, which had grown out of an interchurch prayer group in Clonard Monastery close to a Unionist/Nationalist interface. On completing a term as prioress of the Falls Road community (1987–91), Noreen continued discerning with other colleagues. Thus, with an underlying vision of being an ecumenical residential community on the 'Peaceline', Currach Community was opened in 1992. The name Currach (the Irish word for a small boat or coracle) evokes images of the created seas, the Celtic past, and of the boat symbolising the ecumenical movement. It was mixed as to gender, ethnic background and confessional belonging, with both religious and lay members.

With reconciliation a key directive from successive regional and congregational chapters, Noreen's vision and the ongoing mission of Currach had the support of regional and congregational leadership. Appropriate premises had, providentially, been purchased and refurbished by the Methodist Church (its Belfast Central Mission). The property was adjacent to Springfield Road Methodist Church, which, owing to the accidents of history, now lay inconveniently for its parishioners on the Catholic/Nationalist side of the wall and gates. Currach thus provided a garden path throughway to the side door of the Methodist church, with Noreen symbolically as the gatekeeper![28]

Another founding member was Fr Redmond Fitzmaurice. Until his death

26. See, for example, Walter Brueggemann, *Hope within History*, Atlanta, John Knox Press, 1987.

27. See Walter Brueggemann, *The Prophetic Imagination*, Philadelphia, Fortress Press, 1978; *Hopeful Imagination: Prophetic Voices in Exile*, Philadelphia, Fortress Press, and London, SCM Press, 1986.

28. Funding was provided by the Dominican congregation, Cabra, the Irish Dominican province of the friars, and the nearby sister-community, Cornerstone.

in 1999 Redmond also lectured in the postgraduate ISE, as a specialist in Islam and Interreligious Dialogue. Redmond lived at Currach during his sabbatical year, and the two Dominicans were joined by another male colleague and by a married couple just returned from working overseas to take up positions as doctors in the nearby Royal Victoria Hospital. The fledgeling group committed to living there as an ecumenical community for one year and to contributing in some way towards the ministry of healing and reconciliation in the local area. Noreen relates that they also 'sought to build healthy relationships with each other and with the surrounding community, on both sides of the divide, whilst also searching for an appropriate way of praying together.' Over time, the community became the gathering place for children's homework and reading clubs, art groups and women's groups. The house also aroused suspicion and even hostility, and was frequently the butt of stoning, paint-bombing and, indeed, a rocket attack, as at certain times of the year tensions in the neighbourhood ran perilously high. Some people simply had no way of imagining how such a community group – mixed confessionally and culturally – could actually coexist, and doubted that they could be trusted. But that changed gradually as new projects with local people took shape. The main one was the Forthspring initiative, in which Currach, Cornerstone, the Methodist Church and the Mid-Springfield Community Association joined forces, with the aims of community development, peace and reconciliation foremost, soon employing youth and community workers, cafeteria workers and volunteers to coordinate a range of local projects.

Soon, Sr Noreen, with Fr Brian Lennon SJ, set up and co-directed an office on behalf of CORI in Belfast – next door to the nearby Methodist church on the Nationalist side of the wall. Other plans grew apace, including the development of Religious for Justice and Peace, and much later, of Embrace Northern Ireland, to provide structured practical and personal support to migrants and asylum seekers in Northern Ireland.[29] Later, in the period following the Good Friday Agreement, when the peace process was to know a decade of constant instability, Sr Noreen and Fr Brian joined energies again,

---

29. Sr Catherine Campbell, one of the founders, who had recently returned from many years in South Africa where she had been active in the anti-apartheid movement, was well poised to give leadership. A number of Dominicans were the driving force and providers of woman-power in the early days of EMBRACE (www.embraceni.org, last accessed 04.05.12). Other Dominicans too have been active in an island-wide ecumenical initiative, which began as the Churches Commission on Racial Justice, and now operates as the All Island Churches Consultative Meeting on Racism, focusing on research, conferences, collaborative action and publications on intercultural relations.

setting up Community Dialogue – a civic movement aimed at assisting people to analyse, dialogue and make responses to the fast-moving political shifts and social changes that the community was experiencing, through structured and safe opportunities for dialogue. Training and direct work on behalf of the NGO Mediation Northern Ireland was another fruitful and challenging activity, and Noreen in due course served as a board member.[30]

All these processes and encounters enriched and expanded the life of the Currach Community and of the Dominican family, with whom connections were sustained through visits and the hosting of meetings of common interest, including, for example, the Dominican Ecumenism and Justice group, and Religious for Justice. Noreen describes a high point in her Currach years as the day in 1991 when the Dalai Lama visited Forthspring, and the iron gates were flung open to welcome this ambassador of peace. He had come to speak at an international conference at Belfast's Waterfront Hall (I was privileged to share the platform with him in a panel conversation on 'The Things that Make for Peace'). Noreen's leadership was indeed prophetic, not least in her capacity to draw others together in the hopeful search for a new, shared vision. That leadership received public, and indeed royal, recognition, for she was cited in Queen Elizabeth's Honours List and received an OBE at Buckingham Palace in 1998; the following year, she also received the US President's Prize Award at the White House. The Currach Community continues today, now under the care of Marist sisters, but Noreen Christian stands out as a counter-cultural Dominican who has left behind her a legacy of the spiritual and social fruits of reconciliation, when all the historic odds seemed stacked in favour of violent division.

When responsibility for CORI's Northern Ireland work fell to Sr Brighde Valleley in the post-conflict period following the Good Friday Agreement in 1998, she met the new historic challenges with insight and vigour, creating openings for bold politically-informed initiatives that were both ecumenically and community-based. A few examples among many can be noted for their prophetic significance. Sr Brighde knew that sectarian fears and ani-

---

30. Mediation Northern Ireland (MNI) is a mediation organisation that played a pivotal role in resolving conflicts and mediating acceptable solutions in major stalemate situations, such as those associated with annual Orange parades at Drumcree, south-west of Belfast, with accompanying violence, siege and arson. Sr Brighde Vallely later became a board member of MNI, and Sr Geraldine Smyth collaborated with this organisation on Partners in Transformation, 2002–05, sponsored jointly by Mediation Northern Ireland and the ISE. Noreen's mediation training and skills were called into play in 1994 when she was invited by an interchurch group to return to South Africa to work as a peace monitor in the six weeks leading up to the first inclusive free elections there, which saw in the presidency of Nelson Mandela and generated hope in the heart of every peacemaker.

mosities were deeply embedded, making it essential to work with statutory bodies such as the Good Relations Council and the Office of the Police Ombudsman, to ensure structural change. But she was also alive to the transforming power of symbolic imagination for moving towards a shared future. A small digression may illustrate, but it provides an apposite analogy.

Former Irish President Mary McAleese and Queen Elizabeth II were hailed for their prophetic gesture in coming together at Messines in Belgium in 2006 to dedicate a peace park jointly, in honour of the Irish and British soldiers who had fallen together in the Second World War.[31] Their gesture bridged a centuries-old chasm in British-Irish relationships, and in Dublin in May 2011, president and queen repeated the gesture of joining together in shared remembrance of those Irish volunteers who died fighting to overthrow the British yoke in 1916, and later of those who had died fighting in the British Army during two world wars. Their symbolic gesture was justifiably hailed by the media and by people of every political stripe as historically momentous.

Sr Brighde Vallely was possessed of a similar sense of the transformative power of symbol in the work of assuaging fears and reconciling those at enmity. This was evident when she and a senior official in the Police Ombudsman's office prepared a group of young Loyalists and accompanied them on a field trip to Belgium. She explained that relationships were not yet sufficiently formed to embark on a purposeful venture with their opposite numbers from a Republican background. Peace comes dropping slowly. But this was a stage in a journey that crossed deep-dividing boundaries, inspired by a prophetic vision that guided that intensive week-long visit, 'to a country', as Brighde described it, 'with three official languages and three identities, yet little conflict and with the reality of peaceful co-existence, safety and tolerance'. Equally important, on their return home, Brighde continues, 'we were able to focus on helping the members of the community to which the group belongs to move beyond their fears and prejudices and begin the process of creating a new future'.

Another, and more highly contentious, example can be given, though the project was to take five years to come to fruition. In 2001, global media beamed pictures of terrified youngsters being prevented from going to

31. Professor Mary McAleese, long before becoming president, had been committed to ecumenical reconciliation. *Inter alia*, she had been a member of the Working Party on Sectarianism of the Department of Social Issues of the Irish Inter-Church Meeting (IICM). This is a national ecumenical body in Ireland. The publication that emanated from the IICM Working Party has been published as *Sectarianism: A Discussion Document*, Irish Inter-Church Meeting, 1993.

their local primary school though a Loyalist street by local Loyalist protesters, who were using this as a platform for many genuine grievances of a small beleaguered Protestant community who were at the time hostage to a nightly barrage of bottles and other projectiles from the Republican side of the 'Peaceline'. They had had enough, and determined on blockading the throughway to the Catholic Holy Cross Primary School along their street.

Some of the children's parents forced the issue, flanking or carrying their children to school through a military-shielded corridor of steel. It was an appalling sight – terrorised children caught as pawns betwixt clashing ideologies and competing rights – on the children's part, the right to education, and on the part of the protesters, the right to live in safety from nightly attacks in their own homes. The 'two Churches', despite their best efforts to build bridges, found themselves mired in a morass of misunderstanding, trauma and recrimination. So Brighde and her Protestant colleague worked for a year in a facilitating role with a small group of people from the Catholic Holy Cross Church and Immanuel Anglican Church. Slowly, fears were overcome, hurts acknowledged and, through table fellowship and shared worship, relationships were formed which would carry through into the Immanuel-Holy Cross Initiative in succeeding years.

Its culmination was a St Patrick's Day Celebration Breakfast in 2006, in a hotel on the other side of the city. Children from the two local schools travelled there together and entertained 200 guests, where hearts were warmed to see the happy commingling of the yellow and red uniforms. Brighde shared the address that day with Reverend Dr Ian Paisley. Her inclusive and prophetic words elicited a poem written on the spot by the representative of the Irish foreign minister, praising Brighde for her seeing further than others could see:

> But you brought us on your magical mind journey …
> From India to your final destination.

Tellingly, however, Sr Brighde reserves her praise for the many who participated in the five years' painstaking and risky work, and particularly, the two school principals, 'for their courage and determination to bring healing to the Ardoyne area of North Belfast'.

To conclude this section I add some comment about my own, and Dominican involvement generally, in the ISE, a cross-border institute of Trinity College Dublin, with a small campus also in Belfast. In point of fact, many other Dominicans have been part of the life and work of ISE. Among its earliest supporters were several Dominicans, of whom Austin Flannery deserves particular acknowledgement. When I became Director of ISE for the first time (1994–99),[32] Fr Austin Flannery was the longest serving person on ISE's steering committee and also a member of its academic council. Sr Margaret MacCurtain was also a council member and had contributed to ISE's research project, *Reconciling Memories*.[33]

For almost a quarter of a century, I have found many openings for formal and informal collaboration between Dominicans and the ISE, especially in Northern Ireland but also in broader ecumenical initiatives – as, for example, with the World Council of Churches and the Pontifical Council for Christian Unity. The Irish Region Council, the Congregation Council of the Cabra Congregation, and the Irish Province of the Friars, have, at different times, contributed generously to educational and research initiatives, including jointly creating and funding, with ISE, an adult theology lectureship in 'Education for Reconciliation'. Local Dominican communities have also been generous, and made of their communities or halls hospitable meeting places for Protestants and Catholics to come together for courses in peacebuilding from the perspective of ecumenics and social ethics in a divided society. The sisters' community in Aquinas House, Belfast, was one such as this, where Sr Olive Cooney, Sr Antoinette Doherty, Sr Teresa Pender, and Sr Rosaire Boden sustained the ethos of an ecumenics programme led by Dr Cathy Higgins – a young teacher with lifelong associations with all the Dominican educational institutions in Northern Ireland, and also a graduate of ISE. Through the creative ecumenical vision of Fr Ben Hegarty (another ISE graduate) and Fr Redmond Fitzmaurice, St Catherine's Friary in Newry, on the border with the Republic of Ireland, worked with ISE staff over several years, joining hands across the border with the priory in Dundalk. To this day, one encounters in significant interchurch and intercommunity leadership roles folk who began their ecumenical journey in programmes such as these, some of whom proceeded to take higher degrees in ecumenics or reconciliation studies at ISE, or who undertook community-based restorative justice projects or conflict resolution work on sectarian interfaces in crisis events to come.

The support of the wider congregation was always significant, but part-

32. Cf. Geraldine Smyth, 'Challenge and Change: 1994–1999, in Michael Hurley SJ (ed.), *The Irish School of Ecumenics: May it Flourish in Order to Perish*, Dublin, Columba Press, pp. 159–92. My chapter in the founder's edited collection is one among successive directors of ISE, giving an overview analysis of our respective periods in office.

33. See Alan Falconer (ed.), *Reconciling Memories*, Dublin, Columba Press, 1988; an updated and fuller edition was published a decade later under the same tile, edited by Alan Falconer and Joseph Liechty. Margaret MacCurtain's chapter is entitled 'Reconciling Histories'.

nership with others in both civic-based and Church-related endeavours has also been crucial for Dominican sisters in setting free prophetic vision and the courage to take risks. Dominicans working in the North of Ireland have faced many challenges in bearing witness to the Spirit blowing in unfamiliar and unlikely quarters. In retrospect, prophetic witness to the signs of the times and to God's saving grace, unsurprisingly, has involved welcoming the light from any quarter. The leadership of the Cabra congregation has been magnanimous in freeing some sisters for mission beyond the normal institutional contexts to work in co-operation with others in the secular sphere, from other Churches or in ecumenical settings. It is not surprising, on reflection, to find that prophetic imagination called us not only to challenge denominational and sectarian divisions, but also led us to creative initiatives that actually embodied ecumenical relationships and partnership with the 'un-churched'. The prophetic vocation, whatever the times of loneliness, actually implies that we do not go it alone, and that the future is not determined by the prevailing or dominant expectations: Sr Noreen Christian leading the Currach Community or working with the Methodist Church or with Jesuit colleagues; Sr Brighde Vallely and her colleagues working their way indefatigably through a community impasse; Dominican leadership in joint commitments with the ISE towards reconciling truth and memory, faith and politics, justice and peace – these have witnessed to the deep power of prophetic collaboration.[34]

The prophetic call opens us up to the possibility of new creation and of journeying forward in faith. It is worth recalling here what was said earlier about the catalysing influence towards peace and justice of those sisters who returned from mission abroad and who had themselves been changed by the wider encounter of cultures and religious visions in dialogue and struggle together. These have brought to Dominican mission in Ireland an enlivening vitality, a breadth of perspective and a readiness to take risks for peace because it is the Gospel way. Although their questions may not always have been immediately appreciated, the dynamic conversations that the questions provoked between themselves and the many sisters who had wrestled

34. Another collaborative venture of note is the Interchurch Group on Faith and Politics closely associated with the ISE and the Corrymeela Community (I have been a member since 1993). This group grapples with specific cultural and theological aspects of Church and society through debate, structured meetings with political and Church leaders, and publications. See for example, *Doing unto Others: Parity of Esteem in a Contested Space*, Faith and Politics Group, Belfast, 1997; *Boasting: Self-righteous Collective Superiority as a Cause of Conflict* (1999); *Doing unto Others: Parity of Esteem in a Transition*, Faith and Politics Group, Belfast (2001); *A Time to Heal: Perspectives on Reconciliation* (2002). After several years in abeyance the group re-formed in 2010. All its publications are available on www.irishchurches.org/resources (last accessed 30.07.12).

continuously with contemporary challenges or made innovative moves to engage frontier issues of peace and reconciliation closer to home, opened up a broader sense of the Catholic Church and of alternative ways of being a more participative church, of the potential for leadership-in-solidarity and of the urgency of working for unity and peace in an ever more plural yet also globally interconnected world.

CONCLUSION

In these decades under review, Dominican sisters of the Cabra congregation participated in many 'small circles and quiet processes' (an apt Quaker term) in classrooms and churches, on the street and behind closed doors. They saw themselves as part of the long journey into reconciliation, seeking to be part of a social ethic that engaged inherited alienation and enmity, refusing to be captive to them. Their outreach was made possible by the faith conviction that 'in Christ, God was reconciling the world to himself, not counting their trespasses against them, and entrusting the message of reconciliation to us' (2 Cor 5: 19). Whatever the failures along the way, and the unknown journey ahead, we have learned that compassion towards others' suffering opens up hope, and have known God's love through partaking of ecumenical hospitality.

Such circles and processes have evolved in symbolic public initiatives of protest against atrocious scenes of murder and mayhem, and in witness for peace, offering simple but necessary counter-signs of cross-community interdependence and avowal of the sacredness of all life. In this *Kairos* moment on the journey into peace, when New Creation once more seems possible, Dominicans know the need for continued truth-filled reflection – the work of faith, of compassionate involvement in the pain of the other – for the hope that makes forgiveness possible, and for the moral engagement and embodiment of inclusive risk-taking for reconciliation in Church and society – for the transcending power of love.

Irish Nobel Laureate Seamus Heaney, in a number of poems penned during times of terror and bloodshed, explores the deep kinship between old histories of invasion and resistance, and the multifarious wealth of language that has issued forth from the clash of tongue and clash of sword[35] – at once a legacy and an 'imaginary'. Whatever history's apparent hopelessness, the hope endures, he claims

---

35. Among the best known is 'North' – the title poem in the collection (Seamus Heaney, *North*, London, Faber & Faber, 1975, pp.19–20).

> ... once in a lifetime,
> That justice can rise up,
> And hope and history rhyme. [36]

Such intimations may suffice in place of any attempt to sum up the voices and words that have flowed into this analysis. In drawing the essay together, and hinting once more at the many unnamed, unspoken voices that have inhabited the story of these years, strangely apt is the insight of another poetic voice from Ulster – Moya Cannon.[37] Her vision transcends the rote-learned, worn-out grammars of violence, victory and defeat and shapes a different, creative world. In her curiously titled poem 'Murdering the Language', with ingenious word play, Cannon brings into dialogue her schooldays love of language-learning and the unfolding recitations of Ireland's bloody history with its syntax of invasion, defeat and rebellion:

> Mood, tense, gender,
> What performs the action, what suffers the action?
> What governs what?
> What qualifies, modifies?

The taut diction betokens the tense, tidal yearnings for freedom and order:

> ... why victories won in blood are fastened in grammar
> And in grammar's dream of order ...

Her imagining of the 'long and tedious campaign' of language in its ebb and flow around the Irish coastland, becomes an articulation against the tide of the still surging violence, and a way of speaking up for a new learning of a grammar of compassion:

> Laws learned by heart in school are the hardest to unlearn,
> But too much has been suffered since
> In the name of who governs whom.
> It is time to step outside the cold schools,
> To find a new, less brutal grammar
> Which can allow what we know:
> That this northern shore was wrought

---

36. Seamus Heaney, *The Cure at Troy: a Version of Sophocles' Philoctetes*, London, Faber & Faber, 1990, p. 77.
37. Moya Cannon taught adolescent travellers in St Bridget's School, Galway – incidentally, alongside sisters from the congregation, including Sr Bridget O'Driscoll and Sr Aideen McMahon, who were successive principals there in the 1980s and early 1990s.

> Not in one day, by one bright wave,
> But by tholing the rush and tug of many tides.[38]

Such poetry intimates God's grace flowing ever ancient, ever new, and making out of many one. In the ebb and surge of new tides, in the drama of many voices, gestures and protagonists, the divine imagination will continue to summon forth wisdom for a new day of peace. In that wisdom, may there be found many Dominicans 'stepping outside the cold schools' of divided memory, seeking and shaping together with others a fresh language of reconciliation through the pastoral, priestly and prophetic ministries which the Spirit has prepared for them.

BIBLIOGRAPHY

Bevans, S. B. and Schroeder, R. P., *Constants in Context: A Theology of Mission for Today*, Maryknoll, N.Y., Orbis Publications, fifth printing 2009 (2004).

Brewer, J. D., *Peace Processes: A Sociological Approach*, Cambridge, Polity Press, 2010.

Brueggemann, W., http://books.google.it/books?id=x7wlSBj0XwsC&hl=it &sitesec=reviews*Hope within History*, Atlanta, John Knox Press, 1987.

Brueggemann, W., *The Prophetic Imagination*, Philadelphia, Fortress Press, 1978.

Brueggemann, W., *Hopeful Imagination: Prophetic Voices in Exile*, Philadelphia, Fortress Press, and London, SCM Press, 1986.

Eisikovits, N., 'Transitional Justice', in *Stanford Encyclopedia of Philosophy*, Stanford, US, 2009. http://plato.stanford.edu/entries/justice-transitional/ (last accessed 04.05.12).

Lederach, J. P., *Building Peace: Sustainable Reconciliation in Divided Societies*, Washington, United States Institute of Peace, 1997.

MacCurtain, M., 'Reconciling Histories', in Alan Falconer (ed.), *Reconciling Memories*, Dublin, Columba Press, 1988.

McKittrick, D., Seamus Kelters, Brian Feeney, Chris Thornton and David McVea, *Lost Lives*, Edinburgh and London, Mainstream Publications, 1999, updated edition, 2006.

O'Meara, T., *Theology of Ministry*, Completely Revised Edition, NY, Paulist Press, 1999.

38. Moya Cannon, 'Murdering the Language' in *The Parchment Boat*, Oldcastle, County Meath, Ireland, The Gallery Press, 1997, pp. 14–15. The word 'tholing' – a linguistic residue of ancient Viking invasions – is still current in Ulster common speech, apt for expressing a rude capacity for holding out and enduring with resignation.

Philpott, D. (ed.), *The Politics of Past Evil: Religion, Reconciliation and the Dilemmas of Transitional Justice,* Notre Dame, Indiana, Univ. of Notre Dame Press, 2006.

Smyth, G., 'Telling a Different Story: Hope for Forgiveness and Reconciliation in Northern Ireland', in Philipa Rothfield, Cleo Fleming and Paul A. Komesaroff (eds.), *Pathways to Reconciliation: Between Theory and Practice,* Aldershot, Ashgate, 2008.

Smyth, G., 'Challenge and Change: 1994–1999', in Michael Hurley SJ (ed.), *The Irish School of Ecumenics: May it Flourish in Order to Perish,* Dublin, Columba Press, 2008, pp. 159–92.

ONLINE RESOURCES

www.embraceni.org (last accessed 04.05.12) *Embrace Northern Ireland,* to provide structured practical and personal support to migrants and asylum seekers in Northern Ireland.

www.healingthroughremembering.org (last accessed 04.05.12) for the range of Healing through Remembering published and web-based research, practical guidelines and other resources for approaching contested issues and processes of commemoration, story-telling, truth recovery, annual day of reflection and living memorial museum.

www.irishchurches.org/resources (last accessed 30.07.12), Faith and Politics Group, Belfast, documents available online: *Doing unto Others: Parity of Esteem in a Contested Space* (1997); *Boasting: Self-righteous Collective Superiority as a Cause of Conflict* (1999); *Transitions,* Faith and Politics Group, Belfast (2001); *A Time to Heal: Perspectives on Reconciliation* (2002).

19

Active Resistance against Nuclear Weapons in the United States

MARY PATRICIA BEATTY, O.P.

The ministry of active resistance to nuclear weapons and war of Dominicans sisters Ardeth Platte, Carol Gilbert and Jacqueline (Jackie) Hudson (1934–2011) is summed up in their statement: 'As Dominicans we hope to learn truth, preach truth and live truth in these present times.'[1]

The early years of their ministries, as members of the Dominican Sisters in Grand Rapids (Michigan) congregation, were in the field of education. Ardeth Platte, who entered in 1954, taught junior and senior high school, served as a principal and created an alternative school. Carol Gilbert, who entered in 1965, taught junior high school. Jackie Hudson, who entered in 1952, taught piano, vocal and instrumental music. Education was the setting for their mission to 'praise, bless and preach'.

After Vatican II, many congregations of Dominican sisters in the US shifted their ministries from work focused primarily on education and healthcare, expanding into fields such as parish ministry, social work and social justice advocacy. Dominican women were responding to 'the signs of the times', as called for by the Council documents. The US role in the Vietnam War, the Cold War and the build-up of nuclear weapons, which increased the threat of nuclear war, were all 'signs of the times' that called forth a response by Dominican women's congregations in the US.

SIGNS OF THE TIMES AFTER VATICAN II

The 'signs of the times' in Saginaw, Michigan, motivated Sr Ardeth and Sr Carol to expand their ministry beyond the classroom. From 1966–71, Sr Ardeth was the principal at St Joseph High School in Saginaw. St Joseph Parish, which had originally been a parish of Irish ethnicity, was changing into a parish with a mix of Euro-Americans, Hispanic and African-American

---

1. Hudson, Jackie, Gilbert, Carol and Platte, Ardeth. *Praising, Blessing, Preaching on the Way to Jerusalem*, from the *DSI Newsletter*, May 2010, http://www.dsiop.org/web/index. php?option=com_content&view =article&id=881:praising-blessing-reaching-on-the-way-to-jerusalem&catid=18&Itemid=42. (Last accessed 10.04.12).

Catholics. The high school was transformed from a traditional high school for grades 9–12 to one that had an adult education night school, a school for drop-outs and a retrieval programme and family education. Sr Carol taught at the Alternative Learning Centre at Sacred Heart Parish from 1977–79.

Sr Ardeth took another step beyond the traditional role of women religious when she was elected to the Saginaw City Council in 1973. She served on the council for 12 years. In 1983, she served as mayor pro-tem for Saginaw, Michigan.

Sr Ardeth and Sr Carol established the Home for Peace and Justice in Saginaw's inner city. The centre was a place for analysing the 'signs of the times', reflecting on them and then planning a course of action to transform society into one that was more just and peaceful. The home became a gathering place for peacemakers from around the state of Michigan. Nonviolent resistance communities were formed to protest the manufacture and deployment of nuclear cruise missiles.[2]

MINISTRY OF ACTIVE RESISTANCE IN OPPOSITION
TO NUCLEAR WEAPONS AND WAR

In the early 1980s, nuclear Cruise missiles were deployed on B-52 bombers at the two Strategic Air Command bases in Michigan (Wurtsmith Air Force Base in Oscoda and K.I. Sawyer Air Force Base near Gwinn), defying an initiative passed in Michigan by 56 per cent of the voters. Sr Ardeth, Sr Carol and Sr Jackie, with other peacemakers, organised Faith and Resistance retreats and held protest vigils at the two air force bases in Michigan.

They formed a coalition of Michigan peacemakers, held vigils, displayed banners and carried out non-direct action. Because of these actions, they were arrested, presented court testimony and served jail terms. Their full-time commitment to active resistance in opposition to nuclear weapons and war had begun.

The nonviolent civil disobedience actions of the three sisters prompted the leadership of the Dominican Sisters in Grand Rapids to write guidelines that recognised the following: that civil disobedience, in a democratic society, is an inherent right of citizens; that an act of civil disobedience is a matter of individual conscience; that the decision to commit an act of civil disobedience must be weighed carefully; and that such an act is not done in the name of the congregation.[3] Thus, those sisters who engage in civil disobedience are

2. Carol Gilbert, O.P. and Ardeth Platte, O.P, *Risking Time in Jail to Build a Nonviolent World.* http://hillconnections.org/ri/gilbertplatte9ap.htm (last accessed 12.04.12).
3. Dominican Sisters in Grand Rapids Archives, *Policies and Procedures,* Chapter I, Part B:

bona fide members of the congregation. While living in various resistance communities over the years, Sr Carol, Sr Ardeth and Sr Jackie have been faithful members of the Dominican Sisters in Grand Rapids, participating in the life and ministry of the congregation.

After seven years, Sr Carol and Sr Ardeth moved from Saginaw to Oscoda, Michigan, continuing prayers and actions at the base. The Faith and Resistance movement continued until all nuclear cruise missiles were removed from the State of Michigan. Wurtsmith Air Force Base closed in June 1993 and K.I. Sawyer Air Force Base closed in 1995.

Nuclear weapons were removed from one state but still existed in other parts of the US. The sisters' full-time commitment to active nuclear resistance had just begun. Sr Ardeth and Sr Carol continued their commitment by moving to Jonah House in Baltimore, Maryland, in March 1995. Sr Jackie moved to Poulsbo, Washington, in October 1993, to join Ground Zero for Nonviolent Action, founded in 1977. Ground Zero's property adjoins the US Naval Base Kitsap-Bangor, the home port for eight US Trident nuclear submarines and site of the largest nuclear weapons storage facility in the world.

The three sisters joined with resistance communities that live a lifestyle similar to the Dominican way of life; a life of prayer, study, community and ministry. The Jonah House community and the Ground Zero community imitate our founder, Dominic Guzman, who studied and prayed Sacred Scripture, thus gaining the courage to live the values of the Gospel. He 'shared the fruits of his contemplation' with his companions and with all to whom he preached.

The pillars of Jonah House are: community as vital to nonviolence and resistance; nonviolence as a way of life; resistance as a practice of opposition to nuclear weapons and war. The house was set up in 1973, during the Vietnam War, by Philip Berrigan, Elizabeth McAlister and other peacemakers. It is a faith-based community, primarily Catholic, but people of all faiths are welcome. The community prays together and studies Scripture. 'We delve into the Scriptures wholeheartedly and make the necessary changes in our own lives according to the way of the nonviolent Jesus and prophets of the past and prophets in these times. Besides studying the Scriptures and writings of Scripture scholars, we study the signs of the times, read and listen

---

'Policy on Balancing Protection of Expression of Individual Conscience and the Common Life', pp. 13–18. Quoting from the policy: 'This policy is meant to help a sister in any situation where she believes she must act out of a conviction of conscience ... acts of civil disobedience, addressed specifically in this statement, are one type of such actions ... the primary purpose of this statement is to assist a sister in discernment through a demand of conscience ... each of us must respect the sister's decision resulting from such prayerful consideration.'

to the news from all sides and perspectives.' The house welcomes people for retreats, as well as college students who come for a week to experience a nonviolent lifestyle.

The members live a simple life. They cultivate a large community garden of vegetables and fruit. They preserve food for themselves and for the hundreds who visit them each year. They also sponsor the Jonah House Food Pantry, serving more than a hundred homeless and needy persons each week.

The Jonah House community preaches God's Word through faith and resistance retreats and other nonviolent actions. Their yearly calendar consists of actions during Holy Week, the anniversary dates of the atomic bombs dropped on Hiroshima and Nagasaki during the first week of August and the Feast of Holy Innocents in December. Regular actions take place at the Pentagon, the White House, the National Security Agency, the Department of Energy and other places where military decisions are made. Their civil resistance actions often result in arrests, imprisonment or community service in lieu of a custodial sentence.[4]

Sr Jackie lives at the Ground Zero Center. As stated on their website, the centre offers 'the opportunity to explore the meaning and practice of nonviolence from a perspective of deep spiritual reflection, providing a means for witnessing to and resisting all nuclear weapons, especially Trident. We seek to go to the root of violence and injustice in our world and experience the transforming power of love through nonviolent direct action.'[5] The focus of the community's resistance has been the Trident submarine and the Trident D-5 Missile System. Trident nuclear submarines form the sea-leg of the US triad of land, air and sea. Sr Jackie continues preaching the Gospel through speaking engagements, television and radio interviews, keeping vigil at the gates to the base and in the local communities, displaying banners, participating in the nonviolent direct actions scheduled three times a year at the entrance to the base, and providing support during the court proceedings that result from these actions.

SACRED EARTH AND SPACE PLOWSHARES II ACTION

Ardeth Platte, Carol Gilbert and Jackie Hudson are known for the Sacred Earth and Space Plowshares II action, which took place on 6 October 2002.

---

4. The information on Jonah House in Baltimore, Maryland, can be found at www.jonah-house.org (last accessed 07.04.12).

5. *About Ground Zero. Ground Zero Center for Nonviolent Action.* http://www.gzcenter.org/ (last accessed 22.05.12)

This action led to their long-term imprisonment in the US federal prison system. The news of their trial and sentencing spread throughout the world. Individuals and groups from around the globe sent words of encouragement and support for their opposition to weapons of mass destruction and the threat to use them. They were especially grateful to the worldwide Dominican family for their encouragement, prayers and presence.

The Sacred Earth and Space Plowshares II action of 2002 was inspired by the first Plowshares action in September 1980 at the General Electric Plant in King of Prussia, Pennsylvania. Philip Berrigan and seven other persons hammered and poured their blood on the Mark 12A nuclear missile components.

The sisters chose 6 October 2002 for the action in remembrance of the anniversary of the US bombing of Afghanistan and to protest the US threat to invade Iraq. They cut through a chainlink fence and entered the Minuteman III missile silo N-8 in Weld County, Colorado. They wore mop-up suits like those used by toxic clean-up crews, with 'Disarmament Specialists' written on the front and 'CWIT' (Citizen Weapons Inspection Team) across the back. The suits mimicked those of the UN teams who had scoured Iraq for weapons of mass destruction but found none. The sisters inspected, exposed and symbolically disarmed the weapons of mass destruction that exist on US soil.

Resistance actions require prayer and study before an action and are always carried out in a prayerful manner. The sisters hammered the top of the silo and the tracks that carry the lid to its firing position with household hammers, symbolic of Isaiah's prophesy that 'they shall beat their swords into ploughshares' (Is 2: 4). They had drawn their own blood before the action and they poured this on the silo's lid and tracks in the shape of a cross. The blood represented the violence towards and the deaths of those who would be killed in Iraq. They left a rosary and legal documents on the silo lid.

After 45 minutes, the military entered the area in force. They immediately detained and arrested the sisters and delivered them to the Weld County Jail.

After ten days, the US Government charged the sisters with two felonies: destruction of government property essential to national security and obstructing national security; both counts are to be found under the same US code that covers sabotage. This charge has a sentence of up to 20 years in prison. The sisters pleaded 'not guilty', citing international law and Article 6 of the US Constitution.

The jury trial took place in March and April 2003 in Denver, Colorado. Defence attorneys argued that the sisters were not a threat to national security. The military officers testified that the sisters had done nothing that would have interfered with the use of the silo even if the weapons had needed to be launched.

The defence lawyers had two professors of international law testify that the action was legal under US and international law. International treaties declare that the threat to use, or the use of, nuclear weapons is illegal. The US Constitution, in Article 6, Section 2, declares all laws and treaties made under the authority of the state to be the supreme law of the land. The Plowshare sisters and the defence lawyers contended that the US violates the law because it possesses illegal nuclear weapons and has threatened the use of these weapons. The judge did not allow this defence to be heard by the jury.[6]

The US District Attorney prevailed with his national security obstruction charge. The government wished to punish the action of the three sisters severely, as a deterrent to them and to other protestors. The jury brought in a verdict of 'guilty as charged'.

On 25 July 2003, the judge sentenced Sr Jackie Hudson to 30 months, Sr Carol Gilbert to 33 months and Sr Ardeth Platte to 41 months in federal prison. The difference in the individual sentences was due to prior convictions.

By sentencing them to long prison terms, the government hoped to deter them and others from protesting against weapons of mass destruction. Their hope was not realised. Many 'plowshares' actions have taken place in the US and in other countries since the Dominican sisters' plowshares action. In her statement in front of the Federal District Court House in Denver, Colorado, on 25 July 2003, Sr Carol Gilbert noted: 'We have read in the press and in our pre-sentencing report that the lengthy sentence is for deterrence—both for ourselves and others. But, what the government fails to recognize is that long prison sentences will only energize the movement.'[7]

Sr Jackie Hudson was released from federal prison on 4 March 2005, while Carol Gilbert's release was on 23 May 2005 and Ardeth Platte's on 21 December 2005. Even after their release from prison, the sisters were not free of the criminal justice system. They had to serve three years on probation, restricting their freedom of movement. They owed $3,082 dollars in restitution to the US Air Force for damaging government property. The sisters refused to pay restitution in the form of money, but were willing to pay 'restitution' in a

---

6. Strabala, W., *WMD, Nukes & Nuns*, New York, Algora Publishing, 2006, pp. 71–72.

7. Palecek, M. and Trettien, W., *Cost of Freedom: the Anthology of Peace & Activism*, Berthoud, Colorado, Howling Dog Press, 2007, pp. 104–5.

creative manner. Canned goods for the children of military families on food stamps were presented to the US Attorney in November 2006. Diane Carman, writing for *The Denver Post*, commented that the occasion brought out humour as well as protest. The judge and the US Attorney would not accept the canned goods in lieu of money. 'This is a grace-filled holy action,' said Gilbert. 'Our conscience does not allow us to participate in war by providing any money for bombs or violence.'[8]

SUPPORT FROM THE DOMINICAN ORDER

The sisters received thousands of letters of support and encouragement from around the world. The worldwide Dominican family was very supportive. The Master of the Order, Carlos Azpiroz Costa, sent a letter from Rome on 19 April 2003. He wrote:

I want you to know that your symbolic stand for a world without war has been for me a wonderful Christian message of action. And, like Jesus, you have shown a willingness to suffer because of that prophetic action so that a new kind of world might be born ... In the name of the Order, I thank you for your powerful preaching![9]

The Dominican Promoters of Justice, Peace and the Integrity of Creation, who were at a planning meeting in Elkins Park, Pennsylvania, published an affirmation atatement in support of the three sisters. The North American Co-promoter, Judith Hilbing OP, attended their sentencing in Denver, Colorado, at the request of the International Commission and the US Justice Promoters.[10]

Their non-violent resistance actions were recognised by the International Physicians for the Prevention of Nuclear War and by the Seventh Generation Fund of California. The Nuclear-Free Future Award honours individuals, groups and communities who have worked with tireless commitment to create a world free of nuclear weapons. On 12 October 2003, in Munich, Germany, Sr Diane Zerfas, the Vicaress of the Dominican Sisters in Grand Rapids, accepted the award in the name of the three Plowshare Sisters. The award was given to 'Carol Gilbert, Jackie Hudson, Ardeth Platte – USA, for

8. Carman, D., 'Nuns' Canned-food Offer Isn't Up to Prosecutor's Palate', *The Denver Post*, 16 November, 2006, http://www.denverpost.com/ci_4668314 (last accessed 10.04.12).

9. Azpiroz Costa, C., *Letter to Sisters Ardeth Platte, Jackie Hudson, Carol Gilbert*, Rome, Convento Santa Sabina, 19 April 2003, Dominican Sisters in Grand Rapids Archives.

10. Hibing, J., *Letter; Reports on the Sentencing of the Three Sisters*, 27 July 2003, North American Co-Promoter of Justice, Peace, and the Integrity of Creation, email, Dominican Sisters in Grand Rapids Archives.

working to transform swords into plowshares as an act of conscience out of love for humanity'.[11]

After their release from prison in 2005, the International Commission for Justice, Peace and the Integrity of Creation of the Order of Preachers sent a letter of support from Santa Sabina in Rome on 13 January 2006. 'As members of your Dominican family, we want to tell you how grateful we are to you for your witness to truth and how indebted we are to you also for your suffering and imprisonment. We praise and honour you for your heroic stand against the development and use of weapons of mass destruction, which by their existence alone threaten weaker nations and impose unjust controls ... Your convictions witness to the belief that the only ways to promote and achieve peace are not through violence, bloodshed, destruction of economic structures, and personal property but through dialogue, international consensus and compliance with the decisions of the International Court of Law.'[12]

On 30 January 2007, Dominicans gathered at the Assembly of CODALC (Confederation of Dominican Sisters of Latin America and the Caribbean) in Lima, Peru, wrote a letter of support to the Plowshare sisters: 'Your witness helps us to be aware of our responsibility to speak with conviction against the militarisation of our world ... We support and affirm your belief that militarisation is not the answer to frayed relationships between peoples, the earth and space. Our faith recognises that another world is possible. "Otro mundo es possible."'[13]

AFTER RELEASE FROM PRISON

The commitment of these three women to 'active resistance in opposition to nuclear weapons and war' inspired the Dominican women in the US to make a greater commitment to work for nuclear disarmament. Their ministry was formally recognised by the US Federation of Dominican Sisters at the Third Convocation of Dominican Sisters USA on 28 April 2008. Ardeth Platte told the group: 'We are excited that so many Dominican women in the Federation join this public commitment. We feel our work empowers

11. Zerfas, D., 'Nuclear-Free Future Award Given to Three Imprisoned Dominicans', Munich, Germany, *Nuclear-Free Future Award*, October 2003, http://www.nuclear-free.com/eng/zerfas.htm#lark (last accessed 10.04.12).

12. International Commission for Justice, Peace and Care of Creation of the Order of Preachers, *Letter to Srs Ardeth Platte, Jackie Hudson, Carol Gilbert*, 13 January 2006, found on: http://www.domlife.org/Justice/Disarmament/Disarmament.html (last accessed 10.04.12).

13. *Letter to Grand Rapids Dominicans Carol Gilbert,OP, Ardeth Platte, OP and Jackie Hudson, OP from Dominicans in Latin America and the Caribbean*. Lima, Peru January 30, 2007. http://www.domlife.org/LatinAmerica/2007CODALC/Letter_CODALC_toCarol_Ardeth_Jackie_ENG.html (last accessed 10.04.12).

everyone to act together in whatever way possible to speak the truth about nuclear arms. The nuclear arms industry is a devastation of our economy, our planet and our people.'[14]

CORPORATE STANCE FOR THE ABOLITION OF NUCLEAR ARMS

Inspired by the actions of these three sisters, the US Federation of Dominican Sisters wrote and endorsed a public corporate stance calling for the abolition of nuclear arms and encouraged their member congregations to do the same. Two thirds of the member congregations of the federation have passed resolutions.

The Dominican Sisters in Grand Rapids took a public stance on 15 November 2007, the feast of St Albert the Great.

> The Dominican Sisters in Grand Rapids call upon the United States government to lead the way for the global abolition of nuclear and all weapons of mass destruction by adopting a plan to lock down, dismantle, reduce, and eliminate nuclear and all weapons of mass destruction.
>
> We call for immediate development, adoption and implementation of a plan that will ensure that there will be no new nuclear weapons, no new materials for nuclear weapons, and no testing of nuclear weapons.
>
> We will work with all people of goodwill until there is no chance that a nuclear weapon or other weapon of mass destruction can come into the hands of anyone wishing to do harm.[15]

Specific Actions: Sisters who participate agree to take one or more actions from a list that includes prayer, study, action and advocacy on behalf of the issue.

CATHOLIC CHURCH'S STANCE ON NUCLEAR
DETERRENCE AND NUCLEAR ARMS

Theological considerations play an important role in the Dominican Sisters' motivation to work toward the elimination of all weapons of mass destruction. Statements from Vatican II documents, papal encyclicals and other Catholic Church teachings guide and encourage us in our work for justice and peace.

---

14. *Grand Rapids Dominicans Recognized for Work on Nuclear Disarmament. Dominican Life USA.* http://www.domlife.org/2008Stories/GrandRapids_Award_Federation.html (last accessed 10.04.12).

15. Corporate Stance on Nuclear Disarmament. Dominican Sisters in Grand Rapids: http://www.grdominicans.org/index.php/who-we-are/call-to-justice/corporate-stances/stance-on-nuclear-disarmament/ (last accessed 10 April 2012).

The US Bishop's pastoral letter *The Challenge of Peace* encouraged us. Many US Catholic peace groups, including members of the Dominican Sisters of Grand Rapids, assisted the bishops in the writing of this document. The peace groups and other persons made critiques of several drafts of the document before the final version was published in 1983.[16]

The Pastoral Constitution *On the Church in the Modern World* (Vatican II, 1965) links the preparation for war with the problems of development: 'The arms race is an utterly treacherous trap for humanity, and one which ensnares the poor to an intolerable degree.'[17]

The *Compendium of the Social Doctrine of the Church* (Vatican City, 2004) states:

> The Church's social teaching proposes the goal of general, balanced and controlled disarmament. The enormous increase in arms represents a grave threat to stability and peace. ... Policies of nuclear deterrence ... must be replaced with concrete measures of disarmament based on dialogue and multi-lateral negotiations.[18]

The Catholic Church took an even stronger stand against the policy of nuclear deterrence at the United Nations Seventh Review Conference of the Non-Proliferation Treaty. On 4 May 2005, Archbishop Celestino Migliore, Vatican representative to the UN, made an impassioned plea for nuclear disarmament.

> The Holy See emphasises that the peace we seek in the 21st century cannot be attained by relying on nuclear weapons [19] ... When the Holy See expressed its limited acceptance of nuclear deterrence during the Cold War, it was with the clearly stated condition that deterrence was only a step on the way towards progressive nuclear disarmament. The Holy See has never countenanced nuclear deterrence as a permanent measure, nor does it today when it is evident that nuclear deterrence drives the development of ever newer nuclear arms, thus preventing genuine nuclear

---

16. US Conference of Catholic Bishops, *The Challenge of Peace: God's Promise and Our Response*, Washington, DC, US Catholic Conference, 1983.

17. Vatican II, *Gaudium et Spes*, n. 81.

18. Pontifical Council for Justice and Peace, *Compendium of the Social Doctrine of the Church*, n. 508. *http://www.vatican.va/roman_curia/pontifical_councils/justpeace/documents/rc_pc_justpeace_doc_20060526_compendio-dott-soc_en.html* (last accessed 10.04.12).

19. Statement by H.E. Archbishop Celestino Migliore, Apostolic Nuncio, Permanent Observer of the Holy See to the UN. The Seventh Review Conference of the States Parties to the Treaty on the Non-Proliferation of Nuclear Weapons (NPT). May 4, 2005. http://www.holyseemission.org/statements/ statement.aspx?id=195 (last accessed 12.04.12).

disarmament.[20]

A statement made by Bishop Gabino Zavala, the Pax Christi USA president, in an address given at the University of Great Falls, Montana, has further motivated the Catholic peace movement in the US. In his address on 11 March 2009, Bishop Zavala called for the elimination of all nuclear weapons.

Last December [2008] in Paris, one hundred international, political, military, business and civil leaders came together to launch a new initiative called GLOBAL ZERO, which includes a new high-level policy work and public outreach to achieve a binding agreement to eliminate all nuclear weapons through phased and verified reduction ... It is my deepest hope that the Catholic Church in the United States will embrace this new moment and play an important role in education on these critical issues.[21]

NUCLEAR WEAPONS IN THE TWENTY-FIRST CENTURY
From the beginning of the 'nuclear age', citizen groups have pressured the US government to curb the threat of nuclear weapons. The mobilisation of public action helps reduce the threat of nuclear war. In the late 1950s and early 1960s, peace activists worked to 'ban the bomb'. Many peace organisations mobilised in the 1980s to support the 'nuclear freeze campaign', prompted by factors such as the US Senate's failure to ratify the SALT II arms control agreement and President Carter's directive that allowed for a 'first strike' nuclear war. By the 1990s, thanks to citizen pressure and the ending of the Cold War, a nuclear weapons freeze was achieved: no nuclear production, no testing and no new deployments.

The destruction of the World Trade Center in New York City on 11 September 2001 returned the nuclear weapons question to the forefront of US foreign policy. The government put more pressure on non-nuclear nations to stop building facilities that could produce nuclear weapons, searched out weapons of mass destruction in countries such as Iraq and sought to tighten control over nuclear material to prevent terrorist groups securing it to make small portable nuclear devices. The policy of former administrations that tried to stop the spread of nuclear weapons through diplomacy and treaties was changed to a policy of using military means to overthrow offending governments. The Bush administration declared a permanent 'War on

20. Ibid.
21. Zavala, G., *Living With Faith and Hope: Reflections on the U.S. Bishop's Peace Pastoral*, 11 March 2009, http://ncronline.org/news/peace/full-text-speech-bishop-gabino-zavala (last accessed 10.04.12).

Terror' against Afghanistan and other countries that harboured terrorists. Nuclear non-proliferation activities were placed as a sub-department of the 'War on Terror'.

SHIFTS IN DOMESTIC POLICY REGARDING
THE NUCLEAR ARSENAL OF THE US

Complex 2030, later renamed Complex Transformation, was the plan of the administration of George W. Bush to rebuild and reorganise the Nuclear Weapons Complex by 2030. The complex, administered by the National Nuclear Security Administration within the Department of Energy, is a network of facilities that develop and maintain the US nuclear weapons system. The new plan would consolidate weapons-grade nuclear material into fewer locations. It also called for a new nuclear weapons production facility to be built. The new facility would increase the weapon production capacity of the US. The goal was to have a level of capability comparable to what the US had during the Cold War. The Complex 2030 plans were defeated in Congress.[22]

The Bush administration also formulated a 'Vision for 2020' that would facilitate US control of space for military operations and determine which nations would or would not have access to space.[23]

At first, the new administration of President Obama brought a sense of euphoria. Peacemakers had hoped that the new administration would curb runaway military spending, design nuclear policies that were more reasonable and stop the Complex Transformation projects and the US domination of space.

In the early days of President Obama's administration, it pledged to:
- Secure loose nuclear materials from terrorists
- Strengthen the Nuclear Non-Proliferation Treaty
- Move towards a Nuclear-Free World by: stopping the development of new nuclear weapons; working with Russia to take US and Russian ballistic missiles off hair-trigger alert; seeking dramatic reductions in US and Russian stockpiles of nuclear weapons and material; and setting a goal to expand the US-Russian ban on intermediate-range missiles so that the agreement could become global.[24]

22. 'Complex Transformation', Friends Committee on National Legislation, http://fcnl. org/issues/nuclear/action_guide__complex_transformation_q__a/index.html (last accessed 22.05.12).

23. Gagnon, B. K., *Space Domination: Pyramids to the Heavens*, 1999, Global Network Against Weapons and Nuclear Power in Space, http://www.space4peace.org/articles/domination.html (last accessed 10.04.12).

24. Barack, O., and Biden, J., *Obama-Biden Foreign Policy Agenda, January 2009- Nuclear Weap-*

There was one sign of hope when President Obama and the Russian President signed the START Treaty (Strategic Arms Reduction Treaty) on 8 April 2010 in Prague. The treaty limits the number of deployed strategic nuclear warheads to 1,550. This is almost a two-thirds reduction in the number that was part of the 1991 START Treaty. The START Treaty was ratified by the US Senate on 22 December 2010.

Other pledges made by the Obama administration have not been fulfilled. For example, President Obama pledged to take ballistic missiles off hair-trigger alert. However, in a vote held on 27 October 2010 in the United Nations General Assembly First Committee on Disarmament, the US voted 'no' to a resolution that called for nuclear weapons to be taken off high-alert status.[25]

The Obama administration is implementing the Complex Tranformation plan, constructing three complexes at Los Alamos, New Mexico, Kansas City, Missouri and Y12 in Oak Ridge, Tennessee.[26]

Peace groups will continue to pressure the present and future US government administrations to: further reduce the US arsenal of nuclear weapons; pledge never to use nuclear weapons against any nation; reduce the amount of money spent on nuclear weapons and nuclear facilities; take ballistic missiles off high alert; and not use space for military operations.

The Global Zero initiative is the newest movement used by peace activists to pressure governments to curb the threat of nuclear weapons. The International Global Zero movement, launched in December 2008, includes more than 300 political, military, business, faith and civic leaders, and hundreds of thousands of citizens working for the phased, verified elimination of all nuclear weapons worldwide. Global Zero members believe that the only way to eliminate the nuclear threat, including proliferation and nuclear terrorism, is to stop the spread of nuclear weapons, secure all nuclear materials and eliminate all nuclear weapons. The international Global Zero Commission of 23 political and military leaders has developed a practical step-by-step plan backed by hundreds of former heads of state, foreign ministers, national security advisers and military commanders to achieve this goal over

---

ons, 21 January 2009. http://www.cfr.org/us-strategy-and-politics/obama-biden-foreign-policy-agenda-january-2009/p18307 (last accessed 10.04.12).

25. *US Votes Again to Keep Nuclear Weapons on High-Alert*. Sunflower Newsletter Issue #160 November 2010. Nuclear Age Peace Foundation. Found on: http://www.wagingpeace.org/menu/resources/sunflower/ (last accessed 10.04.12).

26. Information on Nuclear Weapons Modernization Complex found on various websites: NTI Global Securities Newswire at http://www.nti.org/gsn/ ; Y12 National Security Complex, U.S. Department of Energy http://www.y12.doe.gov/ Nuclear Watch New Mexico at: http://www.nukewatch.org/; TriValley Cares at: http://www.trivalleycares.org/ (Last accessed 01.07.15).

the next two decades.[27]

CONCLUSION:

DOMINICAN PREACHERS CREATING A CULTURE OF PEACE

Ardeth, Carol and Jackie continued to preach the way of nonviolent living, by their words and actions, as the US Government continues spending trillions of dollars updating the US nuclear arsenal. In 2010, Sr Ardeth and Sr Carol faced trial hearings for their witness to stopping an enriched uranium processing complex at Y12 in Oak Ridge, Tennessee. The refurbishing of nuclear arms and nuclear facilities in the US motivates Dominicans to continue to advocate and pray for the complete abolition of all weapons of mass destruction.

Carol's Poem

Order of Preachers
Dominicans
Dominican Preachers—
Itinerants, Mendicants, Beggars

Dominican Preachers
We preach where we stand—
War zones, inner cities, countries made poor,
refugee centers, gun shows, air shows
stockholder meetings, military bases,
nuclear-weapons sites, executions,
courts, jails, prisons,
places of power.

Dominican preachers
Speaking truth
Not with words but with actions—
Vigils, demonstrations, boycotts,
nonviolent civil resistance,
recycle, live simply,
plant gardens,
live in community, beat swords into plowshares.

---

27. Global Zero website: http://www.globalzero.org/ (last accessed 01.07.15).

Preachers
Dominican Preachers
We contemplate. We remember.
We preach with our lives.
We create a culture of peace.
We risk all in faith.

Carol Gilbert, Lent 1999
Kent County Detention Center, Chesterton, Maryland[28]

Sr Carol speaks eloquently in her poem. Dominican preachers 'create a culture of peace'. We seek to live a nonviolent life; a life that preaches and lives God's way of peace. Even if the earth were free of nuclear weapons, our world would not be peaceful. We will live in peace only when we respect all of God's people and all God's creation.

The Sacred Earth and Space Plowshares Sisters placed that vision before all Dominicans and the world in their statements published in *Dominican Life USA*:

How fitting it is for Dominicans to unite in this kairos time to nourish our love-force taught by Jesus, our truth-force taught so eloquently by Dominic and Gandhi, and our soul-force practiced by Martin Luther King Jr. and a large cloud of witnesses. In every ministry, we have opportunities to plant the seeds for life, the concepts that bring about collegiality, mutuality, and self-worth. With all our courage and strength we say "no" to death-dealing weeds that have grown up to strangle any nation's resources or people. We are living on one planet—Earth. We are one family, each member is our brother, sister, mother, father and child … Communities of sisters are affirming corporate stances against nuclear weapons which are the taproot of so much violence. This proclaims a loud and clear message that our security is in God, not in weapons of mass destruction. The closer we draw to Earth and each other, the more furiously we will work to leave a gentler footprint.[29]

Peacemakers leave 'a gentler footprint' on the earth. Warmakers leave a 'heavy, destructive footprint'. The footprints of warmakers destroy people,

---

28. Carol Gilbert, OP and Ardeth Platte, OP *Risking Time in Jail to Build a Nonviolent World*. Hill Connections. http://hillconnections.org/ri/gilbertplatte9ap.html (last accessed 12.04.12).

29. Hudson, J., Gilbert, C., and Platte, A., *Disarmament and the New Creation*. http://www.domlife.org/2007Stories/Essay_Disarmament.html (last accessed 01.07.15).

our planet and all of God's creation.

'Peacemaking with justice is not an easy road to travel. It is a slow lifelong journey to Jerusalem and the most blessed way to give our lives. Thanks be to God.'[30]

Our founder Dominic would encourage all Dominican men and women to learn truth, preach truth and live truth in these present times. He prays that we leave a 'gentler footprint' on creation as we travel together on our 'journey to Jerusalem'.

RESOURCES

BOOKS

Palecek, M. and Trettien, W., *Cost of Freedom: the Anthology of Peace & Activism*, Berthoud, Colorado, Howling Dog Press, 2007.

Strabala, W., *WMD, Nukes & Nuns*, New York, Algora Publishing, 2006.

Schell, J., *The Seventh Decade: the New Shape of Nuclear Danger*, New York, Metropolitan Books, 2007.

US Conference of Catholic Bishops, *The Challenge of Peace: God's Promise and Our Response*, Washington, DC, US Catholic Conference, 1983.

FILMS

Fox, Brenda Truelson, *Conviction: a Documentary Film*, Boulder, Colorado, Zero to Sixty Productions, 2006.

Hansen, Barbara, *Earth and Space Plowshares II*, Grand Rapids, Michigan, Grand Rapids Television, 2003.

WEB ARTICLES

About Ground Zero. Ground Zero Center for Nonviolent Action, http://www.gzcenter.org/ (last accessed 22.05.12).

Barack, O., and Biden, J., *Obama-Biden Foreign Policy Agenda, January 2009- Nuclear Weapons*, 21 January 2009. http://www.cfr.org/us-strategy-and-politics/obama-biden-foreign-policy-agenda-january-2009/p18307 (last accessed 10.04.12).

Carman, D., 'Nuns' Canned-food Offer Isn't Up to Prosecutor's Palate',

---

30. Hudson, Jackie, Carol Gilbert, and Ardeth Platte. *Praising, Blessing, Preaching On the Way to Jerusalem*, from the *DSI Newsletter* May 2010. http://www.dsiop.org/web/index.php?option=com_content&view%20=article&id=881:praising-blessing-preaching-on-the-way-to-jerusalem&catid=18&Itemid=42 (last accessed 12.04.12).

16 November 2006, *The Denver Post,* http://www.denverpost.com/ci_4668314 (last accessed 12.04.12).

Carol Gilbert, OP and Ardeth Platte, OP, *Risking Time in Jail to Build a Nonviolent World.* Hill Connections. http://hillconnections.org/ri/gilbertplatte9ap.htm (last accessed 12.04.12).

'Complex Transformation', Friends Committee on National Legislation, http://fcnl.org/issues/nuclear/action_guide__complex_transformation_q__a/index.html. (last accessed 22.05.12).

Dominican Sisters of Grand Rapids, *Corporate Stance on Nuclear Disarmament.* http://www.grdominicans.org/index.php/who-we-are/call-to-justice/corporate-stances/stance-on-nuclear-disarmament/ (last accessed 10.04.12).

Gagnon, B. K., *Space Domination: Pyramids to the Heavens,* 1999, Global Network Against Weapons and Nuclear Power in Space, http://www.space-4peace.org/articles/domination.htm (last accessed 10.04.12).

Grand Rapids Dominicans Recognized for Work on Nuclear Disarmament, http://www.domlife.org/2008Stories/GrandRapids_Award_Federation.html (last accessed 10.04.12).

Hudson, J., Gilbert, C., and Platte, A., *Disarmament and the New Creation.* http://www.domlife.org/2007Stories/Essay_Disarmament.html (last accessed 10.04.12).

Hudson, J., Gilbert, C., and Platte, A., *Sacred Earth & Space Plowshares III. Citizen Weapons Inspection Team Disarms Weapons Of Mass Destruction,* 5 November 2002. Global Network Against Weapons and Nuclear Power in Space. http://www.space4peace.org/reports/3sistersplowsharesb.htm (last accessed 10.04.12).

Hudson, Jackie, Carol Gilbert, and Ardeth Platte. *Praising, Blessing, Preaching On the Way to Jerusalem,* from the DSI Newsletter May 2010. http://www.dsiop.org/web/index.php?option =com_content&view=article&id=881:praising-blessing-preaching-on-the-way-to-jerusalem&catid=18&Itemid=42 (last accessed 12.04.12).

International Commission for Justice, Peace and the Integrity of Creation of the Order of Preachers, *Letter to Sr Ardeth Platte, Jackie Hudson, Carol Gilbert,* 13 January 2006, found on : http://www.domlife.org/Justice/Disarmament/Disarmament.htm (last accessed 10.04.12).

Letter to Grand Rapids Dominicans Carol Gilbert, OP, Ardeth Platte, OP and Jackie Hudson, OP, from Dominicans in Latin America and the Caribbean, Lima, 30 January, 2007, http://www.domlife.org/LatinAmerica/2007CODALC/

Letter_CODALC_toCarol_Ardeth_Jackie_ENG.html (last accessed 10.04.12).

Migliore, C., *Statement by H.E. Archbishop Celestino Migliore, Apostolic Nuncio, Permanent Observer of the Holy See to the United Nations The Seventh Review Conference of the States Parties to the Treaty on the Non-Proliferation of Nuclear Weapons (NPT)*, 4 May 2005, http://www.holyseemission.org/statements/statement.aspx?id=195 (last accessed 12.04.12).

McElwee, J., 'U.S. Nuclear Weapons Policies Headed in Opposite Directions', *National Catholic Reporter*, 22 January 2010. http://ncronline.org/news/peace/contrary-directions-nukes (last accessed 10.04.12).

Pontifical Council for Justice and Peace, *Compendium of the Social Doctrine of the Church*, *http://www.vatican.va/roman_curia/pontifical_councils/justpeace/documents/rc_pc_justpeace_doc_20060526_compendio-dott-soc_en.html* (last accessed 10.04.12).

Roberts, T., '"Terrorist" Nuns Put Spotlight on Homeland Security', *National Catholic Reporter*, 26 December, 2008. http://ncronline.org/node/2866 (last accessed 10.04.12).

Roberts, T., 'Thirty years of Speaking Peace to Power', *National Catholic Reporter*, 26 December, 2008. http://ncronline.org/node/2868 (last accessed 10.04.12).

The 2010 Nuclear Posture Review. United States Department of Defense. http://www.defense.gov/npr/ (last accessed 10.04.12).

US Votes Again to Keep Nuclear Weapons on High-Alert. Sunflower Newsletter Issue #160 November 2010. Nuclear Age Peace Foundation. Found on: http://www.wagingpeace.org/menu/resources/sunflower/ (last accessed 10.04.12).

Zavala, G., *Living With Faith and Hope: Reflections on the U.S. Bishop's Peace Pastoral*, March 11, 2009, http://ncronline.org/news/peace/full-text-speech-bishop-gabino-zavala (last accessed 10.04.12).

Zerfas, Diane. *Nuclear-Free Future Award Given to Three Imprisoned Dominicans*, Munich, Germany. Nuclear-Free Future Award. October 2003. http://www.nuclear-free.com/eng/zerfas.htm#lark (last accessed 10.04.12).

DOMINICAN SISTERS IN GRAND RAPIDS ARCHIVES:

Azpiroz Costa, C., *Letter to Sr Ardeth Platte, Jackie Hudson, Carol Gilbert*, 19 April 2003, Roma, Convento Santa Sabina, Print.

Geary, Maureen R. Message to Mary Brigid Clingman, O.P., Councillor for Mission and Advocacy, Grand Rapids Dominicans. 8 July 2003. Email.

Geary, Maureen R. Affirmation statement of Dominican Promoters of Justice, Peace And Care of Creation. 8 July 2003. Email.

Grand Rapids Dominicans. Dominican Sisters Face Sentencing July 25, 2003. Grand Rapids, Grand Rapids Dominicans, 14 July 2003. Print.

Grand Rapids Dominicans. Policies and Procedures. November 1990.

Hibing, J., *Letter; Reports on the Sentencing of the Three Sisters*, 27 July 2003, North American Co-Promoter of Justice, Peace, and Care of Creation. Email.

20

Luigia Tincani: Worker for Justice and Peace

'Justice is the queen of virtues, and the majesty of the good.'[1]

CESARINA BROGGI

The Servant of God, Luigia (Gina) Tincani (1889–1976), foundress of the Dominican congregation known as the Union of Missionaries of the School of St Catherine of Siena, lived as a child in Bologna, Cuneo, Messina and Rome, the cities to which her father, a professor, was transferred periodically. In Rome, she obtained a master's degree in education in 1916 and a licence in literature in 1917. After that, she studied philosophy at La Sapienza University and, in 1925, graduated in philosophy at the Catholic University of Milan. She taught philosophy and pedagogy in institutes of higher learning.

In 1908 she became a Dominican tertiary. In 1924 she made her religious profession to Fr Lodovico Fanfani OP, her spiritual director and co-founder of the Union of Missionaries of the School of St Catherine of Siena. She adopted the motto of Fr Hyacinth M. Cormier OP: *caritas veritatis*.[2]

HISTORICAL CONTEXT

The story of Luigia Tincani is intertwined with the wider histories of the Church, of Italy and the world, and of spirituality and education at that time. She lived through the years of the unification of Italy, under the monarchy, followed by the First World War, Fascism, the Second World War and, finally, the establishment of a democratic and republican government.

The first years of the twentieth century were marked in Italy by strong anti-clericalism and a prohibition on Catholic participation in political elections, in protest against the liberal state.

At the same time, in the period following Vatican I, there was growing

---

1. L. Tincani, *La giustizia*, 1 August 1954, Archivio Storico Missionarie della Scuola (ASMS), p. 200.

2. Fr Cormier encouraged the foundation of the Union. Cf. P. Fanfani, testimony in the Roman Process of Beatification of Bl. Cormier, p. 78; testimony of L. Tincani, *Positio* (1972), pp. 202–03.

awareness of the identity of Christians in the world; people were beginning to speak about the laity in the Church and to value their active presence.

Those years saw the emergence of the most important issues facing feminism: the public presence of women in society was developing, with the consequent need for centres of formation and places for women to work for justice in the secular sphere and in the Church. Tincani took this seriously and launched a serious effort for the secular and religious advancement of women.

The state school system had been deeply affected by the anti-clerical political climate of the time. During those years, the teaching of religion in state schools was hotly debated; the state schools themselves were being used to draw people away from the Church.[3] In order to help young people encounter God, Tincani modified the structure of her new religious congregation. She entered the state school system with companions who shared her ideals, and fully consecrated religious sisters thus entered into the heart of secular culture, but without any distinguishing signs such as a religious habit.

The school was, as always, the instrument of those in power, firstly of the anti-clerical monarchy and then of Fascism. In a spirit of freedom, Tincani transformed teaching into an instrument in the service of apostolic zeal, moving in two directions simultaneously: widespread penetration of the structures of society, and the organisation of initiatives for promoting human development.

The position that Tincani took up with regard to the problems posed by Fascism for school education was complex, prudent and intelligent. She collaborated actively with Catholic Action, and through her membership of the Executive Committee of the Diocese of Rome, the Pro-Schola Secretariat, the Council of the National Association of Private Educational Institutions (ANISP) and the Central Office for Italian Educational Institutes at the Congregation for Seminaries.[4] During these years the Catholic school system began to develop, slowly and painfully, and was eventually recognised by the National Education Ministry after a legal victory. Afterwards, it had to defend itself and its rightful autonomy continually, in the face of pressure

---

3. L. Tincani spoke out on the issue of teaching religion in *Fondazione di Scuole catechistiche e di religione*, Bologna, 1913, p. 60 (manuscript and printed proofs), ASMS 5, 2.

4. Cf. Letter of Appointment: Commission Pro Schola e cultura, 11 April 1923, ASMS 22.1.1; Segretariato Centrale di Azione Cattolica per la scuola, 27 June 1930, ASMS 22.1.2; Member of the Commissione competente di problemi scolastici presso l'Ufficio centrale per le Scuole e gli Istituti Cattolici d'Italia, within the Congregation for Seminaries, 26 September 1932. ASMS 24.1.1, 4.

from the Fascist state.[5]

Tincani was always cautious and prudent as regards the schools. She knew the idealist philosopher Giovanni Gentile, a theorist of Fascism in the field of education and her former professor at the University of Rome. Realistic in assessing and accommodating the improvements offered by the regime to the school system in general, Luigia Tincani always showed respect for law and authority, but she did not give up her freedom to judge to what extent the claims of the totalitarian state should be accepted or rejected when they interfered with choices in the private Catholic schools. In this sense, she guided the sisters in charge of Catholic schools. She distinguished herself particularly by her sense of justice and prudence when, in 1938, the Ministry of National Education established ENIM (Ente Nazionale Insegnamento Medio; National Association for Middle School Teaching) as a new means of centralisation, and Catholic schools found themselves at a crossroads: either stand apart and isolate themselves or join the new body with the risk of losing their autonomy.[6] Tincani helped religious sisters at that crucial time to study the government regulations and to accept what was necessary so as to avoid cutting their schools off from the rest of the school system, while vigorously resisting the more or less overt attempts at ideological interference. The University College for High School Teaching of Maria Santissima Assunta, now the LUMSA, played an interesting role in this socio-political context, which will be discussed later.

Throughout both world wars, Tincani engaged in works of service, and with her sisters she offered her prayers and suffering to implore God for peace. She participated actively in post-war reconstruction efforts. Instead of engaging in politics directly, she helped to prepare and form her students to take an interest in the common good and the need to pursue just policies in the new republic that was being formed. With Mgr Montini (later to become Pope Paul VI), she started training women who were Christian intellectuals for positions in the parliament and in the professions, where they could make a new contribution to the life of the nation.

After the Second World War, in the face of the shifting balance of international power, Tincani's apostolic vision expanded to include other places around the globe with a cosmopolitan and missionary spirit. Her earlier work in Italy prepared her to launch similar efforts of evangelisation in other European countries, and in Africa and America, where the sisters

---

5. Cf. B. Papasogli, *Luigia Tincani, l'oggi di Dio sulle strade dell'uomo*, Rome, Città Nuova Editrice, 1985, pp. 305–06.

6. Ibid., p. 309.

were sent for individual apostolates and temporary positions. In Asia, she opened missions in India and Pakistan.

When the student protests struck around the world in 1968, Tincani was very attentive to the new leaven of autonomy and freedom that animated young people in those years, and she saw in these upheavals an invitation to accomplish the work of justice, through formation, in new ways.

EDUCATION FOR PEACE AND JUSTICE: *CARITAS VERITATIS*

Luigia Tincani defined her evangelical and Dominican vocation by truth. Her originality consisted in bringing the Dominican ideal – the love of truth – into the state schools. Tincani's name is not tied to any grand gestures for justice and peace, but her deep hunger and thirst for righteousness, lived with sacrifice and under the weight of responsibility, are expressed in the silent work of the daily discipline of study and teaching. The scope of Luigia Tincani's work of justice and peace is best represented by her efforts towards full and integral human formation: physical, spiritual, social and cultural, earthly and supernatural. This is how her programme presented itself:

> Apostolic truth and true contemplation pours the truth known and loved on the poor, especially those who are poor in spirit, whom the Father has given us to feed. Listen to Jesus in order to understand the seriousness of the poverty of those who do not have the truth. How does Jesus respond to the disciples of John the Baptist? *Go and tell John what you see and hear: the blind see, the deaf hear, the dead are raised, the lame walk, lepers are cleansed and the good news is announced to the needy* (Mt 11: 5; Lk 7: 22).[7] The Union has been developed to evangelize the poorest of the poor, who are poor in soul, poor in truth.[8]

Where should this training in righteousness and peace be done? In school, the 'gathering place for all young people, who precisely there are bound by social laws to receive their principal and almost only food.[9] She felt the urgency to 'penetrate into this vast universal emporium of the intelligence and the spirit to bring to it the work of the Christian apostolate, not only by teaching but also with all those forms of assistance that the circumstances may make necessary and possible.'[10]

---

7. L. Tincani, *Contemplazione, amore, apostolato*, 8 May 1934, ASMS 200.
8. L. Tincani, *Condivisione con le Novizie*, Gubbio, 19 July 1942, ASMS 200.
9. L. Tincani, *Lettera circolare*, 7 December 1941, ASMS 200.
10. Ibid.

LUIGIA TINCANI'S CONCEPT OF JUSTICE

Tincani's thought has a solid foundation in philosophy and theology, developed along Thomistic lines and with careful consideration to what would later be called 'the signs of the times'.[11] With Thomas, Tincani states that, above all, if the act of justice consists in giving to each his own, the object of justice is obviously the right.[12]

Living the charism of a founder

Inspired by the Dominican motto 'Contemplate and hand on to others that which has been contemplated', Tincani felt that her first duty was to nourish those in need of the Word of God, giving to them freely, in participation with the Church's work of justice. She approached law and justice from a theological rather than a philosophical perspective.[13] One particular statement clearly expresses her ideas on the subject:

> In order to be, justice requires the existence of something absolute that it can lean on and from which beings may draw their dignity and rights. The concept of justice vanishes when the concept of God disappears. If there is no notion of an Absolute, independent of everything else, all is relative; for example, in its interests the state can do whatever it wants with the citizens, killing or condemning them to hard labour, for the simple fact that it finds its interest in doing so. When there is a concept of God's existence and of human beings as children of God, and of everything being conformed to God's will, then there is respect for the rights of others, there is justice.[14]

Justice towards God

In Tincani's spiritual experience, the first demand of justice was in regard to what she herself owed to God. From her youth, Tincani had shared St Catherine of Siena's insight concerning the position of the creature before God. The creature recognises that God is the author and source of all there is, and that she owes everything, including her own existence, to God. This leads to a spirit of adoration that submits everything to God.[15] Tincani

---

11. Cf. G. Dalla Torre, 'Tincani: in cattedra per i poveri', *Avvenire*, 6 July 2000.

12. Cf. *S.Th.*, II–II, 57, 1, available at: http://www.newadvent.org/summa/3057.htm (last accessed 27.01.16).

13. Cf. G. Dalla Torre, *Commemorazione di L. Tincani*, Roma, 16 June 2007, *Pro manuscripto*.

14. L. Tincani, *La giustizia*, op. cit.

15. Cf. *S. Th.* II–II, 81–85, available at: http://www.newadvent.org/summa/3081.htm (question 81); http://www.newadvent.org/summa/3082.htm (question 82); http://www.newadvent.org/summa/3083.htm (question 83); http://www.newadvent.org/summa/3084.htm (question 84); http://www.newadvent.org/summa/3085.htm (question 85). All of these pages were last accessed 27.01.16.

wanted to make a religious consecration, to consume that holocaust of love that 'is the religious act *par excellence*'.[16] She lived her consecration through 'progressive detachment that leads step by step to intimate annihilation, so that the soul comes to feel, to think, and actually to say with all its soul the word that St Catherine never tires of repeating, because it sums up correctly all perfection: "I am nothing, God is everything".'[17]

In a growing acceptance of the mystery, Tincani discovered that 'in the soul of Jesus resides the answer to this full duty of the creature to give glory to God. Jesus's soul is the Temple of the glory of God.'[18] 'In Christ's soul, personally assumed by the Word, all justice is accomplished.'[19] 'We take our place before God; we really place ourselves in justice if we succeed in living no longer for self but simply for Christ.'[20]

Tincani believed that, through Jesus, souls in adoration fulfilled the noblest act of justice. She extended this insight to her entire family's spirituality: 'It would be a very good thing if we could all give our spiritual life this form ... [that of being] worshipping souls! I think that our whole life would take on a character of order and justice, a luminous order full of love.'[21]

Justice towards Others

The relationship with others is a hallmark of justice, which always has a social note because it requires respect for the rights of others. Since justice is a function of respect for, and guarantees rights, rights precede and specify justice.[22] Attention to the individual and his rights, Tincani's first and foremost interest, prevented her from committing any abuse.

All human beings are placed in that immense temple of God that is created to fulfil a law of love: they have rights that are also duties. We too have no right which is not also a duty. Let us examine our way of being and acting with others. If God gives us the task of guiding other souls, heaven help us, let us do this task; woe to us if we attract these people to us for our personal satisfaction, for our benefit or interest.[23]

Tincani was convinced that helping someone to grow as a person meant

---

16. L. Tincani, *Vita religiosa, olocausto a Dio*, December 1919, ASMS 200.
17. Ibid.
18. L. Tincani, *Consumate a gloria di Dio*, 27 March 1934, ASMS 200.
19. L. Tincani, *Psallite sapienter*, 7 October 1945, ASMS 199.4.
20. L. Tincani, *Nell'Anima di Gesù*, 28 August 1961, ASMS 201.2.
21. L. Tincani, *Lettera*, 1 June 1929, ASMS 70.
22. Cf. *Contra Gentiles*, 2, 28, available at http://dhspriory.org/thomas/ContraGentiles2.htm#28 (last accessed 27.01.16).
23. L. Tincani, *Umiltà e carità*, 6 May 1934, ASMS 200.

freeing him or her, making them able to develop a personal identity, to know themselves in truth: only the person who knows the truth about him or herself is free and becomes capable of justice and of acting accordingly. She considered the teaching of personal responsibility and the formation of consciences as the sure way to building strong personalities and, thus, to renewing society.

Mother Tincani had various ways of working for justice, including evangelising and humanising through the school and culture.

Evangelising First, for Tincani the teacher was the proclamation of the Gospel, 'that Vatican II stressed as the divine mission of the entire Church,[24] as the testimony of the religious,[25] and as the responsibility of the lay faithful, who are often the only ones able to act in some environments.[26] It is in fact a clear and firm idea, in Luigia Tincani's thought and action, that announcing the Gospel is the work of justice.'[27] We read in Pope Benedict XVI's Apostolic Exhortation *Verbum Domini* that evangelisation is a commitment to justice and to the transformation of the world.[28]

For Tincani the strongest right of others, even if they are unaware of the fact, is to know God and his love, to know the truth about life, and the beauty and grandeur of its being in time and eternity. Therefore, the first duty with respect to others is to respond to their deepest need, expressed or implicit, to find God, the truth.[29] In an integrated spiritual approach, she presents the apostolate as an act of justice that takes into account the rights of God over the soul.[30] She writes:

> The call to the apostolate is, after the Redemption, the greatest sign of love that the Creator can give to his poor little creature. With this He raises him to the highest dignity, asking in some way for help, allowing him somehow to share in his divine work! … The apostolate requires a purity

---

24. Pastoral Constitution *Gaudium et spes*, n. 89, available at http://www.vatican.va/archive/hist_councils/ii_vatican_council/documents/vat-ii_const_19651207_gaudium-et-spes_en.html (last accessed 27.01.16).

25. Decree *Ad gentes*, n. 40, available at http://www.vatican.va/archive/hist_councils/ii_vatican_council/documents/vat-ii_decree_19651207_ad-gentes_en.html (last accessed 27.01.16).

26. Decree *Apostolicam actuositatem*, passim, available at http://www.vatican.va/archive/hist_councils/ii_vatican_council/documents/vat-ii_decree_19651118_apostolicam-actuosi-tatem_en.html (last accessed 27.01.16).

27. G. Dalla Torre, *Commemorazione*, op.cit.

28. Benedict XVI, *Verbum Domini*, 100, available at http://w2.vatican.va/content/benedict-xvi/en/apost_exhortations/documents/hf_ben-xvi_exh_20100930_verbum-domini.html (last accessed 27.01.16).

29. Cf. L. Tincani, *Contemplazione*, op. cit.

30. G. Mazzotta, *La giustizia nel pensiero e nella vita di L. Tincani, fondatrice della LUMSA*, Palermo, 5 April 2003.

of intention, with a complete detachment from any taste or interest, with a sacred respect for God's rights over the soul.[31]

Proclaiming the Word in the state schools began as early as 1917, when she denounced the situation in the schools and proposed to the lay Dominicans who were with her, young educated women like herself, a silent revolution in the education offered in state schools.[32]

Humanising The second aspect of Tincani's work for justice concerns humanisation, a kind of pre-evangelisation in the ambit of the school and of culture. Professor Dalla Torre, speaking of Tincani's accomplishments, notes:

If the commitment to the school and to culture was a dominant and characteristic feature in Tincani's life, we must recognize that it was nothing more than the obvious and necessary consequence of a strong conviction: that the lack of education and ignorance were the most severe forms of poverty and that, in a reflexive way, education and training were – on the natural level – the highest forms of charity. For education and training accomplish the process of the individual's humanization and of its revelation, firstly to his or her own consciousness, of the superior dignity of the human person. That dignity, which is proper to man as created in the image and likeness of God and perfected fully only in Christ as God incarnate, can only assume human nature in its perfection, revealed to humanity. But in her view, charity is justice. As we have noted, her reasoning is theological. Yet a closer look reveals that this way of thinking about education and training responds precisely, on a juridical level, to the values that have now become part of the heritage of modern democracies and constitute the pillars of our constitutional order: the right to education and instruction,[33] as well as to the removal of barriers that prevent the exercise of this right[34] as manifested in positive law. The binding obligations of economic, political and social solidarity[35] are precisely the secular expression of charity.[36]

Teaching, a duty of justice As a teacher of teachers, Tincani felt a responsibility to highlight the serious duty of teachers as a duty of justice. She proposed

31. L. Tincani, *La chiamata all'apostolato, dono di Dio*, 30 January 1927, ASMS 200.
32. L. Tincani, 'Conferenza alle Terziarie domenicane nel VII Centenario dell'Ordine', Florence, 29–31 December 1916; published in *Bollettino del Terziario Domenicano*, 5, 1917, pp. 29, 34, 49, 60, 66.
33. Cf. Italian Constitution, arts. 30 and 33.
34. Cf. Italian Constitution, art. 3, par. 2.
35. Cf. Italian Constitution, art. 2.
36. G. Dalla Torre, *Commemorazione*, op. cit.

anew 'the metaphysical and logical necessity of the concept of education' and faced the 'problem on the basis of Thomistic philosophy, with insistence on the duty, the right, the need and the possibility to educate'.[37]

Education is an act of justice towards those who have a right to be educated. The basis of that justice is the universal law of life that is

> ... [a] law *of cooperation and mutual aid*; each person, being limited, can and must be thought of as a reality that *tends to self-perfection* and in order to improve needs outside help, because he cannot find in himself what is necessary for his growth. ... . The fundamental law of being is not only *in receiving* but also *in giving*; not only to receive, i.e. to educate one's self, but to give, that is, to educate. We remain always as learners and always as teachers.[38]

Tincani proposes a form of teaching that will help the young to grow only if the teacher tries honestly to be the living model that they have the right to see in him or her.

> The truth is this: we never do any good around us, we are never educators, if not through the substance of our moral value, the strength of our convictions, and the reality of our actions that our moral ideal has achieved in us. So if we want to be educators, we need to take care of our lifestyle, rather than trying to make others live according to our ideals.[39]

The main responsibility of the teacher is a competence full of passion and faith. Tincani read in St Jerome that 'learned justice teaches righteousness to man'.[40]

The best means of communication and the different media to use, in accordance with times and places as well as situations – for example the classroom, the pulpit or a conversation– are then taken into consideration:

> The lesson should be the bright centre of your teaching. During class, you have the grace of state. You can speak as if invested with a kind of priesthood, and are sent in the name of the Lord. Full application, all desire and love, must be assembled in the lesson, so that it may be beautiful, well made, without neglect of any kind. The lesson must be surrounded

---

37. Cf. L. Tincani, *Note di pedagogia generale*, Milan, Università Cattolica del S. Cuore di Milano, 1925, p. 12.

38. Ibid., pp. 10–11.

39. Ibid., pp. 95–98.

40. Jerome, *Letter* 53, 3, available at: http://www.newadvent.org/fathers/3001053.htm (last accessed 28.01.16).

– before, during and after – with sacred care, because this is really the performance of one of the highest duties that can be accomplished on earth.[41]

The pulpit is a great means of apostolate; this is why it was given the primary place ... But the primary place is not the only one.[42]

In the years of the student revolution in the late 1960s, Tincani perceived the existence of new needs on the part of the students that could not be met by the classical type of lesson alone: they wanted the teacher to be close to them, as a witness to a different kind of life.

There is a need for something new: the need for us to work among the masses, not with our teaching authority, not from on high, but rather with an authority that can only rely on the personality we have formed in ourselves. There is an obligation for today's Missionaries to be what they are – to be wholly, to be totally – the representation of a complete Christianity, to be faithful, evangelical; only this permits us to penetrate into the soul of young people who approach us. In the midst of the masses, we must try to be 'living grounds of credibility' and the 'aroma of Christ' ... Young people like courage, loyalty and the manifestation of open-mindedness![43]

Political and social justice For Tincani, the above-mentioned criteria of justice were those of every job and profession. Her days, and those of the missionaries, were lived in the light of justice.

I would like you to develop the habit of asking yourself, before taking the decision to say and do anything: Is it right or not? We are in the service of justice, at the service of God.[44]

Too often we forget to exercise the true Christian virtues in our profession or social relations. Yet it is precisely in the exercise of these social relations that Jesus wants to recognise us as His; and He wants us to let others recognise us as His.[45]

She lived out her responsibility for educational work, exercising authority as a service to justice and charity. She asked those who manage labour to

41. L. Tincani, *L'apostolato dell'insegnamento*, 5 September 1936, ASMS 200.
42. L. Tincani, in *Atti del Capitolo Generale* del 1955, 16 August 1955, p. 41.
43. L. Tincani, *Conversazione*, August 1968, ASMS 148.
44. L. Tincani, *Condivisione con le Novizie*, 21 August 1933, ASMS 200.
45. L. Tincani, *Lettera*, 13 October 1954, ASMS 49.1.

respect the rights of the individual employee, organising work on a human scale[46] and honouring the rightful autonomy of each person.[47]

In 1969, with realism and balance, she faced the problem of the teachers' strike. A letter to her sisters on the right to strike, dated 5 June 1969, can be considered a fundamental document for deciphering Tincani's thought on social rights and the position of the missionaries in relation to their duties as teachers and the needs of the school. Such thinking is a prelude to concepts applied today, such as self-regulation of the right to strike and the possibility of conscription in the case of essential public services; but in the 1950s and 1960s this thinking clearly went against the mainstream. Her reflection on this matter seems significant and prophetic.

> The right to strike is now proclaimed and fully accepted, regardless of whether the benefits of a particular group of people may bring harmful effects on our society and on those in other groups. ... But in a well-ordered society, it would be fair for this right to be limited by the rights of others, namely the good of all, as in any other social legislation. ... We, in our case – as teachers and educators – weigh up, on the one side, the financial and practical good of our group and, on the other, the moral good that we should instil in the young, the good moral and financial support of families, especially the poor, and also our own moral good, our dignity as educators.[48]

Justice and charity Those who knew Tincani appreciated her ability to balance charity and justice by harmonising the two virtues. Professor Luigi Gedda, who saw her working towards the Maria Santissima Assunta University College for High School Teaching, wrote that:

> When an apostolic work is institutionalised, the dangers of bureaucracy begin, and so the problems of justice emerge everywhere and often take precedence over charity. In the difficult relationship between these two virtues, Mother Tincani was a master.[49]

Justice in Relation to Nature
With respect to justice in the thought of Luigia Tincani, there remains one final point concerning the relationship with nature, a subject of great

46. Cf. L. Tincani, *Lettera*, 31 July 1957, ASMS 57.1
47. L. Tincani, *Lettera*, 20 April 1952, ASMS 51. 1.
48. L. Tincani, *Lettera circolare*, 5 June 1969, ASMS 201.
49. L. Gedda, 'La Madre Tincani', in *Traspontina*, Magistero Maria ss. Assunta, n. 21, Rome, 1976, pp. 24–25.

relevance today.

> Strictly speaking, there is no question of justice, if not with regard to rational beings, because only these are capable of having rights. However, in a larger sense we can say that all created beings are entitled to reach that goal for which they were created and that is their nature. So one could say that a plant has the right to be watered in order to flourish; a dog has a right to be cherished. Treating animals or plants poorly is an offence against divine art. Animals and plants must be treated in accordance with the requirements of their nature.[50]

Here we see a striking anticipation of today's environmental sensitivity, in which

> a right is understood in a non-positivistic sense, not as the mere will of the human legislator, nor the external form of the will of those who are stronger (right is right because commanded *jus quia iussum*), but rather as designated from the perspective of natural law, i.e. the law as such which pursues justice (*jus quia iustum*). Hence a certain justice, that '*omnium est domina et regina virtutum*',[51] which is the will to give to each what is his. Tincani, a woman of culture, was certainly well aware of this distilled wisdom of the Roman law ... In the passage Tincani shows how natural law is understood with respect to living in accordance with the personal dignity of each individual, in a hierarchy of dignity where mankind is at the top because created in the image and likeness of God; a theory of natural law which posits that every living being must be treated in accordance with the requirements of its nature. Here the student of legal science grasps, with a few surprises, the singular similarity of Tincani's thought with the most modern and bold expressions of the philosophical and legal doctrine that look to the natural law in an ontological and relational perspective.[52]

LUIGIA TINCANI'S CONCRETE ACHIEVEMENTS

Let us now follow the path of Tincani the worker of justice and peace. In fact, her thought 'is strongly oriented to action and practice by its solid doctrinal foundation'.[53]

---

50. L. Tincani, *La giustizia*, op. cit.
51. Cicero, *De off*. 3,6,28, available at: http://www.constitution.org/rom/de_officiis. htm#book3 (last accessed 28.01.16).
52. G. Dalla Torre, *Commemorazione*, op. cit.
53. Ibid.

The academic world: Beware the woman who studies

In 1912, Luigia Tincani found her first field for promoting justice in the Istituto di Magistero (Institute of Education) and at Sapienza University.

In 1913–14, she established the first of many institutions, the Catholic University Women's Club in Rome,[54] and then an Institute of Religion for Women University Students, something unthinkable at that time.[55] Backed by Giustiniani Bandini, Tincani organised the Catholic women university students, opening a new way forward for the promotion of women and the achievement of their dignity and rights in the Church and in society. The students she supported in turn went on to become the founders of university clubs in their home towns. In a lecture she delivered in 1916–17, on learning to study, she exhorted them to form themselves in a culture based on truth, and to assume personally the individual and social responsibility of those who choose a life of study. She invited them to live their femininity and to be fulfilled as women, with the mission of maternity, in a broad sense, entrusted to them by God. She called on them to live their faith in an enlightened, conscious and firm way.[56]

We should remember that Tincani was evangelising these young people, with freedom and fresh courage, at a time and in an environment where the very name of God was banned. One of her companions wrote about her in these terms:

> In her heart and in her eyes there was something deep and a light that we didn't have! There was a true, living and working faith ... a serene joy, almost luminous, that distinguished her from others. We felt that she was superior to us, and not only because of her intelligence, but for something that we perhaps did not know how to define; but this made us feel her elevation, in a sphere where she – quite obviously – wanted us to join her![57]

Promoting women spiritually and culturally was a duty for Tincani, an act of social justice. In the aforementioned meeting in Florence, in 1917, with

54. Cf. *Annuario* of the Federazione Universitaria Cattolica Italiana (FUCI) 1927, where mention is made of Fr L. Fanfani OP, Assistant, and of Gina Tincani, first President. *Ricordi di vita*, 25th Anniversary of the 'Unione Donne Cattoliche', 1934, pp. 27–29. *Statutes* of *the Circoli*, 1918. Copies of the membership cards of the Circolo signed by Tincani, ASMS 42.

55. The teachers were significant personalities: Mgr P. Paschini, Fr G. Mattiussi SJ and Fr L. G. Fanfani OP.

56. Cf. L. Tincani, *Discorso alle universitarie*, 1916–17, autograph on pages used for school notes, ASMS 12.2.

57. B. Stagno, *Ricordi*, ASMS 116.

the Dominican students and professors, she spoke of the 'new duties' of women, taking a firm stand against anarchist feminism, but inviting them at the same time not to ignore that

New customs impose new duties on Christian women ... pretending not to see the changed conditions of things, not to see the new duties they would impose, would be a lazy and slothful attitude, contrary to charity; it would be blameworthy. This exalted and much feared feminism has perhaps brought a little good and much evil. So let us, Christian women, make ours the bit of good and right that is in it; as to the evil, we should study it, get to know it and try to repair it. We cannot oppose it totally; nor would it be right to do so. Some irresistible currents are not overcome by fighting against them directly, but by guiding them into a solid and secure direction. Therefore, if we wish to fulfil our duty as Dominicans, we must necessarily consider and understand this.[58]

In 1924, she offered very effective collaboration in the foundation of the Association of Catholic Women Graduates, of which she was a councillor. She commented that the 'movement, small and humble but vital, [was] the expression of an intrinsic, long felt need ... We need to enlighten minds and spread among collaborators the wisdom drawn patiently and courageously from austere studies. This is the task of Catholic graduates.'[59] Thus, Tincani opened the way for the promotion of women's rights to study and do academic research. This was a typical expression of her work for justice. She wrote:

There is a special vocation, which women – with few exceptions – have believed, up to today, to be foreign to them: I am speaking of the intellectual vocation. I use the word *vocation*, because I intend to talk about study understood as the fundamental work of their lives and practised as a liturgical *cult* and an *apostolate*. To engage in study with humility and fervour, sensing that every little truth conquered is a step toward the ultimate truth. To feel that knowledge is like a path that lies hidden in God: every natural being bears the mark of the vestiges, every facet of human history conceals the secret, every property of beings reflects the eternal light, and every gift of the soul reveals its infinite greatness. Studying, therefore, – for the love of God – in search of the life divine

58. L. Tincani, *Alle Terziarie domenicane di Firenze*, op. cit.
59. L. Tincani, 'La pagina delle laureate. Il nostro compito', in *L'Azione Muliebre*, January 1925, pp. 50, 53.

hidden in what we know, worshipping this kind of incarnation of God's power, wisdom and love in every creature; seeking the truth, with purity of heart and humanity, in nature; hearing the universal presence of God, transforms scientific and academic study into a continuous act of worship and love. And then one humbly takes one's place, with the arms that the Lord has given, to serve Him in our brothers and sisters.[60]

She took part in the debate that the journal *Studium* introduced on the issue of professional women, and promoted women's access to the professions, without neglecting the duties of a wife and mother.

Wherever women have been placed, they have generally proven their value. Female intelligence has shown itself capable of that force, of that order, of that constant enlightenment that, even prior to studying, the high professions require. ... Women have always been able to demonstrate their capacity for heavy responsibility; we can say that what harms them is precisely not having it. ... But certain professions or offices, as well as trades or businesses, remove women completely and systematically from the family, preventing the fulfilment of a fundamental task in social life; that is not good, and it is contrary to the providential order of human society.[61]

From 1925 on, in accordance with her specific vocation and in full harmony with the wishes of Pope Pius XI, she turned her attention to the opening of university residences.[62] She opened residences for women students in Italy, Pakistan and India. The following were opened by Tincani in Italy: Maria Clotilde (Milan 1925–30), Santa Francesca Romana (Rome, 1926–37); Casa Bianca (Palermo, 1920–28), St Catherine of Siena (Bologna, 1930–57); Casa Regina del SS.mo Rosario (Parma, 1947–52); Regina Mundi (Rome, 1938–). In addition to the house for university students, a teachers' residence, St Catherine of Siena, was opened in Rome (1930–42, 1948–74).

In Pakistan, she opened a house for Christian and Muslim high-school students in Multan, Sahiwal, Karachi, beginning in 1950.[63]

Teaching

From 1916 to 1929, Tincani taught philosophy and pedagogy in several schools of higher learning. Her colleagues saw her as a professional

---

60. L. Tincani, 'Vocazione intellettuale', *L'Azione Muliebre*, January 1925, p. 50ff.
61. L. Tincani, 'La donna e le professioni liberali', *Studium*, XXX, no. 2, 1934, pp. 87–98.
62. Cf. L. Tincani, *Lettera circolare*, 7 December 1941, ASMS 200.
63. See Chapter 12, 'Dominican Sisters in Pakistan', pp. 220–229.

Christian committed to proclaiming justice in schools: the right to education, the competence of teachers, the necessary cooperation of parents, and the participation of students in certain decisions concerning them.[64] With the opening of the Armanni Classical High School in Gubbio in 1923, 'the foundations of a radical social, cultural and moral change in the population were laid. This was a true revolution.'[65]

In 1924, she founded the Union of Missionaries of the School of St Catherine of Siena to work for the promotion of justice for the young in the state school system and for human and Christian growth.[66]

CATHOLIC SCHOOLS

In the context of the Catholic school system, Tincani had a special role in the advancement of women religious. Thanks to her legal training and knowledge, regarding both state legislation and the canon law of religious life, responsibilities in this area were entrusted to her, as we have already seen, and she performed a valuable work of justice for women within the Catholic school.

The work that more than any other expresses Mother Tincani's love for justice is the Maria Santissima Assunta University College for High School Teaching. It was founded with the intention of raising the cultural level of the sisters decisively, so as to have a profound impact on the quality of the Catholic school.

As a member of the commission responsible for problems in the schools, the Central Office for Schools and Institutes of Catholic Italy, instituted at the request of the Holy Father within the Sacred Congregation for Seminaries, Tincani was appointed in 1932 to carry out an inspection of schools run by religious institutions. She was to verify the level of education imparted, the quality of the formation offered, the adequacy of school facilities and the professional preparation of teachers. She noted the advantages and limits of the private Catholic schools run by sisters and, in order to bridge the gap she saw between the professional training of religious and the levels required by the Italian school system, she had the idea of founding in Rome, together with Cardinal Pizzardo, the University College of Maria Santissima Assunta,[67] where the young religious – intelligent, motivated and spiritually

---

64. Cf. *Testimonianze del Liceo Armanni di Gubbio*, ASMS 275.

65. V. Baldelli, Dean of Armanni High School, Gubbio, 'Luigia Tincani, La scuola come vocazione', *Studium*, 1998, p. 286.

66. Cf. documents of the foundation in ASMS 144.

67. Paul VI highlighted Tincani's role as foundress of Maria Santissima Assunta: 'To you, Mother Luigia Tincani, goes the incomparable merit not only to have been the foundress of the

prepared women – were able to receive a serious university education, on both cultural and professional levels, and also earn degrees with 'legal value', in relation to the provisions of the Concordat.[68]

Tincani's actions grew out of her concern for justice and in response to the ecclesial and political context of the time. 'The "Maria Santissima Assunta" University College for High School Teaching represented, historically, a very important step forward in the cultural and professional training of women, and in the more general process of women's empowerment.'[69] Tincani's plan was in harmony with that of the restoration of Catholic education as foreseen by Pope Pius XI in his *Divini illius Magistri* (1929). Different types of Catholic organisation were developing in the field of education and instruction, for different reasons and with different commitments, and Tincani was a part of this. At that time, the dictatorships that would characterise the twentieth century and make uncompromising demands in the educational field were growing strong.[70] In 1939, not long after Tincani had founded Maria Santissima, the Fascist state, in the person of Giuseppe Bottai, promulgated the *Carta della Scuola* (Schools Charter),[71] and Tincani, with the whole Catholic world, was warned of the imminent danger that the state could gradually close down the Catholic schools. Concretely, as mentioned above, Tincani helped the Catholic schools to keep aloof from the harmful influences of the Fascist regime by preparing the sisters to be responsible for the direction of the schools through the study of the laws concerning them. Opening professional schools for women in Bergamo, Gubbio and Palermo, she went beyond the desire to prepare the students to be domestic workers and good mothers, according to the wishes of Fascism; she worked, rather, to make them capable of dealing with the 'hard problems of the life of the Nation', valuing 'women's minds, opening them wide to the specific problems of

Institute, but also to have been until now its intelligent and untiring animator' ('Audience with the Academic Body', 15 May 1971, in *Insegnamenti di Paolo VI*, vol. IX, p. 424). Mgr G. B. Montini participated closely in the establishment of the LUMSA (Cf. G. Dalla Torre, 'Le origini e lo sviluppo del Magistero "Maria Ss. Assunta"', in L. Tincani, *La scuola come vocazione*, op. cit., p. 109ff.).

68. Cf. A. Talamanca, *Libertà della scuola e libertà nella scuola*, Cedam, Padova, 1975, p. 265ff. The idea of the 'legal value' of a degree has no counterpart in the English-speaking world. In Italy, and in many other countries, one must have a legally valid degree in order to be able to take up employment in the public sector, including a teaching post in a state school. It is still possible to obtain employment in the private or civil sectors with a degree without legal validity, such as those offered by 'foreign universities' on Italian soil (in this sense, the Pontifical Universities in Rome are considered 'foreign universities' by the Italian State).

69. Cf. G. Dalla Torre, 'Le origini', op. cit.

70. Cf. G. Dalla Torre, loc. cit.

71. Cf. F. De Vivo, *Linee di storia della scuola italiana*, Brescia, Editrice La Scuola, 1983, p. 99ff. and bibliography.

women.'[72]

In order to give sisters access to university level formation in the Maria Santissima Assunta University College of High School Teaching, she also opened the institute Sedes Sapientiae, where they could acquire high school diplomas; some 8,000 sisters passed through these institutions, and all of them were able to grow culturally, deepen their spiritual commitment and gain new responsibility and dignity. In these projects, Tincani was supported by Popes Pius XI, Pius XII, John XXIII and Paul VI.[73]

A very important gesture towards the promotion of justice in religious life, closely linked to the establishment of educational institutions for the sisters, was Tincani's commitment to support the establishment of the juniorate in women's congregations, i.e. to reserve, as in the religious life of men, the first years after profession for sacred and profane studies, to help young women grow fully and to train them for the apostolate.[74]

THE CENTRE FOR CATHERINIAN STUDIES

In 1963, Tincani decided to take the direction and management of the National Centre – now International – of Catherinian Studies, offered to her by two renowned scholars of St Catherine, Senator Carrara and Commander John Smith, the founder. With this gesture, Tincani, pursuing her interest in the growth of women, devoted herself to disseminating that model represented by Catherine of Siena, the ingenious saint and socially active woman. With the collaboration of the Catherinian scholar Giuliana Cavallini, she organised a library, now among the most famous in the world in this field, as well as meetings for disseminating knowledge of the saint's life, and for publishing the thought of St Catherine.

LUIGIA TINCANI'S CHARITABLE WORKS

In 1911–12, Luigia Tincani had encountered the suffering of the many orphans of Messina, where her father had been transferred to reorganise the schools after the historic earthquake of 1908; there, amid the rubble of this city, engaged alongside Don Orione in an intense work of assistance, she decided to devote herself to the 'poor of truth'.

From 1931 to 1946, she took on the responsibility of caring for the

---

72. Cf. *Relazioni sulla scuola professionale di Palermo* ASMS 311–312; L. Tincani, *Commento alla 'Carta della Scuola'*, ASMS 25.1. 'Dissertazione su "La Carta della Scuola"', *L'ORA – Il giornale del Mediterraneo*, PA 1, 2 June 1939.

73. Cf. *Corrispondenza di Luigia Tincani con i Pontefici*, ASMS 74.

74. Cf. *Atti del Capitolo Generale del 1967–68*, p. 105.

orphaned children of aviators at the Istituto Baracca in Loreto, an institute that depended on the Air Force for funding. Tincani and her missionaries worked hard to develop in those children, tried by family tragedy, an integral education on all levels.[75]

TRAINING FOR CIVIL AND POLITICAL JUSTICE

During the First World War, along with other university students, Tincani worked as a volunteer nurse with the Red Cross to alleviate the sufferings of the soldiers.[76]

During the Second World War, with the greatest discretion and secrecy, commissioned to do so by Pius XII, she worked with Cardinal Pizzardo to give aid and shelter in her houses to victims of political persecution, without distinction, and to Jews, disaster victims or whomever was oppressed by hunger or the Nazi occupation of Italy.

In the post-war years, Tincani expressed her genuine interest in peace, as she considered the problem of the moral and material reconstruction of the Italian nation, in the name of the 'principle of mutual solidarity among all people, also in the moral life and in the practice of social life'.[77] She collaborated with the Ministry of Education and the Regional Education Office of the American Allies to rebuild the state school system in Italy, as well as devoting herself to updating the cultural dimension of the Catholic school and the related bureaucratic aspects of this issue.[78] She supported the return of the Italian Guides Association to Italy and, with the help of the Honorable M. Unterrichter Jervolino and the Honourable G. Gonella, the return of the educator Maria Montessori to Italy. In Baden Powell's formation to responsible freedom and the Montessori method, which considers the child as a source of renewal for society as a whole, she saw great help for the reconstruction of Italy through the formation of young people.

She was in close contact, particularly in the years of the Constituent Assembly that drafted the post-war Italian constitution, with Maria Jervolino Unterrichter and Maria Badaloni, as well as with other women who had prepared themselves for political life, sustained by the force of their faith.

She worked hard to teach women the importance of being able to exercise, for the first time in the history of Italy, the right to vote. To reach as

---

75. Cf. *Relazioni dell'Istituto Baracca*, 1935–42, ASMS 350.1.

76. Cf. Service rendered by L. Tincani in the Leoniano military hospital, Rome, August and September 1915, ASMS AA1, VII.2.1.

77. L. Tincani, *Solidarietà sociale*, 1960, ASMS 201.

78. See the *Acts* of the meetings in ASMS 23.2; Agenda of L. Tincani, ASMS 31.

many women as possible, she organised meetings in various cities of Italy to form the superiors of religious congregations who could, in their turn, give formation to others.

Her compassion for those who were marginalised and weak led Tincani to raise awareness among her friends in power so that they might assist the poor who were asking for help and seeking employment.[79]

She grasped the chance to be present in schools in the poorest countries: in 1948, she accepted the invitation of the co-founder of the Union of Missionaries, Fr Fanfani, and the Dominican Bishop of Multan (Pakistan), Mgr Cialeo, to open schools in this mission land.[80]

From 1950 onwards, along with many others in the Church, she sensed a new urgency to be present to the masses, to know them and to contribute to their advancement with the power of grace and culture. She found herself, with the originality of her Dominican and ecclesial charisma, in tune with a new, pre-conciliar Church, closer to the people and more integrated into everyday life. With great courage and determination, she continued to accomplish her mission and, like St Dominic, sent out her missionaries in small groups, into the hearts of the cities – as teachers in the state schools – to be the yeast in the dough, *living reasons of credibility* among the people in the world. The sisters formed small communities, serving the suburbs of large cities such as Rome and Palermo, and in Bologna the younger missionaries collaborated with Cardinal Lercaro in the apostolate in the suburbs.

In conclusion, Tincani's work consisted in the vigorous and concrete promotion of justice through the formation of teachers and youth. Quiet and respectful of the other persons,

[S]he chose to enter into the world of culture discreetly, not with the idea of converting but rather to understand, to know this world and herself. She realized that, in modernity, the value of the person, of the 'I,' the subject, was essential, and that in teaching one was required to put aside any idea of uniformity, of homogenization of culture: teaching would now be precisely through interpersonal relationships, through the discovery of the individual, as an expression of the spirit, but above all, as an exchange; formation would take place in a reciprocity of interests, proposals, and availability.[81]

---

79. Cf. *Testimonianze sulla carità di Madre Tincani*, ASMS 82.
80. For more on this, see Chapter 12, pp. 220-229.
81. G. De Rosa, *L. Tincani, La scuola come vocazione*, pp. 309ff.

21

A Century of Dominican Sisters
Promoting Justice in the United States

KAYE ASHE, O.P. (1930–2014)

'Those who are wise shall shine like the brightness of the sky.' This verse from the Book of Daniel (12: 3) appears on the base of a sculpture of the founder of the Sinsinawa Dominicans, the Venerable Samuel Charles Mazzuchelli (1807–1864). He is seated in front of a telescope and is pointing to the stars as he instructs one of his sisters and a young student of St Clara Academy. The group is placed in front of the academic building on the campus of Dominican University in River Forest, Illinois. It reminds all who pass it of the long history of Sinsinawa Dominicans who, inspired by their founder, have instructed others unto justice at every level of education and in a variety of other ministries. The six members of the congregation who are profiled here represent the more than 3,000 daughters of Fr Mazzuchelli who have preached, taught and worked for justice for more than 150 years.

PREACHING JUSTICE THROUGH EDUCATION:
SR JOAN SMITH (1890–1976) AND SR MARY NONA McGREAL (1914–2013)

Sr Joan Smith
Ann Smith, the third of five daughters of John and Elizabeth Smith, was born and grew up in Kilkenny, Minnesota. After graduating from Mankato State College in 1914, and teaching in the Le Suer public school, she entered the Sinsinawa Dominican Congregation of the Most Holy Rosary. She knew the congregation by reputation only, having never met a Sinsinawa Dominican. As a postulant, Ann was sent to teach at the Sacred Heart Academy in Washington, DC, and took to heart the advice of Mother Samuel to further her education by seeing everything the capital city had to offer. Returning to the novitiate, she received the name Mary Joan. After profession in 1916, she was sent to teach first grade at St Thomas Apostle Parish in Chicago. While maintaining her teaching position, she earned a BA in philosophy from the University of Chicago in 1927. That same year, she became supervisor of the elementary schools of the Archdiocese of Chicago, a post she held until 1940.

In 1934 she earned an MA at the Teacher's College of Columbia University.

In 1936, the Chicago archdiocese agreed to release Sr Joan for a year to co-found a model of progressive education at Corpus Christi Grade School in New York City. In 1937, she initiated a similar programme for Mgr T. V. Shannon at St Thomas Apostle Parish.

Her work in Chicago and New York attracted the attention of Mgr George Johnson, PhD of Catholic University, who, in 1939 invited her to become part of the Commission on American Citizenship, which was in the process of being formed. Her task was to build a curriculum for Catholic schools that would centre all of the child's learning experiences on basic human relationships, emphasising moral education for social justice. She would soon be joined by Sr Mary Nona McGreal, her colleague at St Thomas Apostle School from 1937 until 1941.

After completing her work on the curriculum, Sr Joan was assigned to Edgewood College in Madison, Wisconsin. From 1946 to 1969, she taught curriculum, served as registrar, and was deeply involved in the academic and physical growth of the college. Wholly engaged in the ministry of higher education, she nevertheless continued to serve the Commission on American Citizenship in various ways. In 1969, she retired to the motherhouse where she served as director of studies for the northwest province and the assistant director of studies for the congregation.

Sr Joan died of pneumonia at St Dominic's Villa in 1976, at the age of 86.

Sr Nona McGreal
Mary McGreal was born in Chicago, Illinois, the eldest of six children of Thomas and Margaret (Kehoe) McGreal. After attending Immaculate Conception Elementary School and Holy Child High School in Waukegan, IL, she was received into the Sinsinawa Dominican Congregation of the Most Holy Rosary in 1932 as Sr Mary Nona, and made her final profession in 1936. She received a BA in English from Rosary College (Dominican University) in 1942; an MA in Education in 1946 from Catholic University of America; and a PhD in the same field and from the same institution in 1951.

After teaching in two Catholic elementary schools in Chicago, Sr Nona joined Sr Joan at St Thomas Apostle School in 1937 as a first grade teacher. She entered with enthusiasm into the progressive curriculum introduced by Sr Joan. It was designed to nurture in every pupil his or her highest level of intellectual, moral and spiritual potential. Soon it attracted educators from all over the city. They came to observe and to take notes on a programme that emphasised children's active role in the process of education and introduced grade school children to Christian social principles. From 1941 to 1949, Sr Nona joined Sr Joan at the Catholic University of America in Washington, DC, serving with her on the Commission on American Citizenship. Together they wrote the three volumes of *Guiding Growth in Christian Social Living,* destined to have a profound impact on elementary Catholic education in the US.

In 1950, Sr Nona joined Sr Joan at Edgewood College. She served in this capacity until 1967, when she was called to be Vicaress General of the Congregation, a post she held until 1977. Subsequently, she researched and wrote extensively about the life of Fr Samuel Mazzuchelli OP, the founder of the congregation, and in 1989 presented to the congregation for the Cause of Saints the *Positio Super Vita et Fama Sanctitatis Caroli Samuelis Mazzuchelli, O.P.* While continuing to work on the cause of Fr Mazzuchelli, in 1984 Sr Nona launched the ambitious Project OPUS, a collaborative effort to trace the history of the Dominican Order in the US. In 2007, she went to St Dominic's Villa in Sinsinawa, and died in March 2013, just a month before her ninety-ninth birthday.

GUIDING GROWTH IN CHRISTIAN SOCIAL PRINCIPLES

The genesis of this work, a curriculum for Catholic elementary schools, lies in a letter of Pope Pius XI written to the bishops of America on the occasion of the fiftieth anniversary of the Catholic University of America. In it he included a request 'to evolve a constructive program of social action ... which will command the admiration and acceptance of all right-thinking men'. The bishops set about at once to fulfill this request. They wrote to the Catholic University, directing the administration to design a programme that would emphasise the social teachings of the Church at all levels of education. The administration formed the Commission on American Citizenship to oversee this task.

The Right Reverend George Johnson PhD set the stage with his book *Better Men for Better Times,* in which he outlined the basic principles of a curriculum focused on social principles and action for justice. These included the familiar ones of the dignity of every human person; the sacredness of the family; the dignity of work and the worker; the importance of using the earth's resources according to God's plan; the obligation of peoples and nations to relate in justice and charity; and the unity that binds the human race together. He entrusted to Sr Joan and Sr Nona the task of applying his visionary philosophy to a curriculum for elementary schools.

There was no model, no established guide, for carrying out this challenging assignment. Fortunately, Sr Joan and Sr Nona were already practised in nurturing in children the understanding, desire and habits that would enable them to live as true Christians. They brought to their work a profound reverence for the child, a solid grounding in pedagogical principles, and the conviction that creative self-activity was the key to learning. Rote learning found no place in their classroom. Children would master the truth by doing the truth.

All of this, and more, is reflected clearly in the original editions of the three volumes of *Guiding Growth in Christian Social Living*, published by the Catholic University of America Press between 1943 and 1946. Reprints and numerous new editions, with additions and revisions, appeared throughout the 1950s. In 1960, complete revisions and reprints of the curriculum were issued. By this time appreciative teachers in Catholic schools throughout the country had been referring to the work for a long time as 'The Green Bible' – an allusion to the colour of the binding.

One is struck at once by the scope and the philosophical and theological depth of the three volumes. The authors adapt to elementary education the tradition of Christian ethics and social thought from Aquinas through the encyclicals, dealing with the topic through the nineteenth and twentieth centuries. It is striking how thoroughly the principles permeate the entire curriculum. They were not simply to be 'covered' and memorised in religion lessons; they were to be incorporated throughout the curriculum from first grade religion to fifth grade science and eighth grade physical education. Furthermore, through various learning activities, the child was meant to encounter the vitality and universality of the tradition again and again.

Volume 1 deals with grades 1–3; Volume 2, grades 4–6; and Volume 3, grades 7 and 8. Each volume begins with a preface by Sr Joan and Sr Nona, and a commentary on 'Education for Life' by Mgr Johnson. In the preface, the authors define the curriculum as 'all the guided experiences of the child under the direction of the school'. They explain that the curriculum is broader than a course of studies: 'It is a guide for directing the child's living in the light of Christian principles, with a detailed plan of the learning activities that are basic to that living.'

Each volume of the work is organised under three headings:

Part I is the same in each volume and covers the Child in Relation to God and the Church, to Fellow Men, to Nature, and to Self; the Principles of Christian Social Living; a Summary of Habits to be Developed; and The

Evaluation of Child Growth. It is in the sections on the Principles and Habits of Christian Social Living that the Thomistic influence is most clearly felt.

Part II deals with the Objectives and Organization of the School Program (the same in each volume) and then covers each discipline, including Health and Physical Fitness, according to the grades featured in the volume. It is obvious in this part that each subject is considered in the light of the child's fundamental relationships. The heaviest emphasis is on religion, social studies and science, precisely because of their direct relationship to God, others and nature.

Part III offers Supplementary Materials and Procedures, tailored to the various grades, under the titles Study Tours, School Assemblies, School Enterprises, Parent-Teacher Conferences, and a Bibliography for Teachers. This section is extensive and extremely practical. It profits from the fact that the authors draw on materials that had been used effectively in numerous parochial schools.

There are reminders throughout the curriculum that we are called to develop right relationships with all because of our common humanity, without reference to colour or nationality. The charming full-page photographs of children engaged in many activities include children of minority groups. There is an emphasis on our right to the truth and our right to justice; the right of workers to a just wage; our obligation to share our goods with those less fortunate; and the evils caused by greed, the uneven distribution of wealth and unjust wars among the nations of the world. These concepts would come alive through the lessons, stories and activities adapted to each grade level.

Throughout the curriculum there are repeated references to joy, delight and beauty. The classroom was to be a happy place that the children looked forward to coming to every day. They were to avoid rivalry and help one another in learning; 'competition with self; cooperation with others' was the order of the day. Reading was to be experienced as a pleasurable skill, with younger children taking delight in recognising familiar words and learning new ones, and older ones relishing the vicarious experiences offered by many kinds of literature. Painting, etching and music, too, were to be sources of pleasure, and in studies of the wonders of nature, children were encouraged to rejoice in the stars, seeing in them a manifestation of God's beauty and wisdom. Clearly, learning was meant to be enjoyable and living happily was not to be reserved to the 'ever after'.

The value and popularity of *Guiding Growth* can be judged by the fact that

Sr Joan and Sr Nona were called upon for years to give courses at universities and to plan and direct institutes, seminars and courses in archdioceses and dioceses throughout the country to help teachers incorporate the curriculum materials of *Guiding Growth* into existing curricula. They were assisted in this effort by several other Sinsinawa Dominicans and by sisters of other congregations as well. The effort was, in fact, a broad collaborative one at a time in which this was not commonplace. The work, furthermore, was translated for use in Germany, the Netherlands, Burma and various countries in South America. Although the commission also published an experimental high-school curriculum for use in four dioceses, ultimately the elementary level materials were the most widely used and the most highly regarded.

THE FAITH AND FREEDOM READERS
Closely related to the three volumes of the curriculum were the *Faith and Freedom Readers,* designed to bring Christian social principles alive through stories, articles and poems. These were written, or chosen, both to develop reading skills and to implant Christian relationships and principles in the minds of Catholic children. The writers of the series, Dr Mary Synon, Sr Mary Marguerite SND, Sr Mary Thomas Aquinas OP of the Newburgh Dominicans, and Sr Mary Charlotte RSM, worked closely with Sr Joan and Sr Nona. This ensured that the readers would effectively reinforce the purpose of the entire curriculum, namely, to help children see how intimately related are the love of God and love of neighbour, and to inspire them to translate into their young lives the truth of the Gospel and of the social teachings of the Church.

The series is designed to follow the development of the child's consciousness as it broadens out from home and family, classroom and playground, friends and neighbours, to town, city and nation, and, finally, to the wider world of international relations. Sr Joan in her analysis of the series writes in a presentation designed to introduce teachers to the series: 'They definitely are *not* public school readers sprinkled with a little Catholicity of content, usually of verse alone. They are *not* assemblages of words chosen only for the development of reading skills. They are one of the great pillars in the structure of Christian social living which the Catholic Church is building for the betterment of American citizenship.'

The officers of the Commission on American Citizenship point out in their description of the commission's work that the trivial and the mediocre were winnowed from the series, 'leaving stories, poems, and articles of high dramatic interest and of literary quality rarely found in school readers'. Teachers' *Manuals* suggested ways to approach each selection and specified each one of its Christian social living objectives, thereby assuring the conscious application of the philosophy laid out in the curriculum guide.

Like *Guiding Growth*, the *Faith and Freedom Readers* caught on quickly in Catholic schools throughout the US. The 1947 report on the commission notes that within a year of the appearance of the first edition, the series had been adopted by more than 6,000 of the 8,000 Catholic schools in the country. The readers became popular further afield as well. They were widely used in the Philippines and in Hawaii and soon enquiries came from educators in schools that were not Catholic, who wanted to examine the series as possible models for their own school systems. The commission also received enquiries from military authorities involved in revising systems of education in the occupied countries of Japan and Germany, and Catholic educators in Belgium, France and the Netherlands made use of the series in their plans for revising their curricula.

It is interesting to note that the Seton Press printed new editions of the *Faith and Freedom Readers* between 2000 and 2009. These apparently are being used primarily by children who are being home-schooled. The effort begun in the last century, therefore, extends into the new millennium, another tribute to the tireless and fruitful effort of Sr Joan and Sr Nona, in collaboration with many others, to infuse elementary Catholic education with the love, truth, and pursuit of justice that distinguishes the true Christian.

SEEKING JUSTICE FOR WOMEN IN THE CHURCH:
SISTER ALBERTUS MAGNUS MCGRATH OP (1911–1978)

Marion Cecily McGrath was born in Chicago, the last of seven children of Michael and Nora (Keane) McGrath. Through grade school, high school and college she was educated by Sinsinawa Dominicans. She admired the joyful, well-educated women who were her teachers; they exerted a powerful influence upon her. It came as no surprise, therefore, that upon graduation from Rosary College (later Dominican University), she entered the Congregation of the Most Holy Rosary at Sinsinawa, Wisconsin. Her novice mistress suggested the name Albertus Magnus, recognising in her, no doubt, a lively intelligence and an independent spirit of enquiry.

Sr Albertus Magnus was assigned to teach at Edgewood High School and Edgewood College in Madison, Wisconsin. In 1937, while continuing to teach in both schools, she was asked by her superiors to enrol in the history department of the University of Wisconsin. She welcomed the opportunity to devote herself to study in a milieu of progressive and reformist thinking, an atmosphere she relished. She earned an MA in history in 1942 and a PhD in history and English in 1947, having written her thesis on the nineteenth-century Anglo-Catholic movement.

She joined the history department at Rosary College in River Forest, Illinois, in 1946, and would teach there until 1976. While she taught with enthusiasm, her appetite for learning continued unabated. During summer sessions she studied at the University of Fribourg in Switzerland, and at Columbia and Harvard Universities. In 1965/66, she was granted a research fellowship at Yale Divinity School, where she studied the apostolate of women after the Industrial Revolution. Her interest in the history of women in the Church and in society at large predated the second wave of feminism, but the new research in women's history sparked by that movement deepened and widened her interest and strengthened her determination to speak out for justice for women.

Invited in 1967 to give the keynote address at the national convention of Kappa Gamma Pi (the Catholic women's graduate honour society), she introduced for the first time themes she would develop fully in her book *What a Modern Catholic Believes about Women*, published by Thomas More Press in 1972, and reprinted by a division of Doubleday in 1976 as *Women and the Church*.

In a 1974 interview in *St Anthony's Messenger*, 'Are Women Oppressed in the Church?', Sr Albertus Magnus, who seldom minced words, answered with a resounding 'Yes!' and did not hesitate to say that her energy was often directed to challenging oppressive structures in the Church which deprived women of full equality and the full exercise of their gifts. Her book is an engaging study in which she documents the legal, economic and social subordination of women and reveals the depth of the misogyny that has permeated philosophical, scriptural, theological and historical texts through almost all of historical time.

In the very first chapter she traces 'the Eve syndrome' in the earliest agricultural societies and the earliest religious traditions, whether Buddhist, Shinto, Islamic or Jewish. In all of them, she notes, women are seen as unclean and dangerous and are held in contempt. In the Hebrew scriptures she lingers over the ugly story of the Levite in Judges 19 who hands over his young wife to sodomites who abuse her all through the night. The husband finds her dead on the threshold the next morning. 'The Levite's reaction? He takes the poor, violated body and cuts it into twelve pieces for distribution among the tribes of Israel. His property has been destroyed, his honor must be avenged' (p. 19). Woman, then, is seen as property; she can be divorced for little cause or no cause at all; if she commits adultery, she can be beaten or stoned to death; if accused, she cannot give evidence in court; a widow could not inherit and could well become destitute unless she had borne a son.

Conscious of the social, legal and economic disadvantages of women in ancient Israel, Sr Albertus Magnus points out the ambiguities of their religious position. She quotes scholars who insist that women had no part in the cultic and ritual life of the community, and were considered unclean and dangerous. Since they were not circumcised they were not part of the covenant, not included among the 'people of God'. In the pre-exilic history of Israel, though, she finds and lists various texts in which we find women prophets, women participating in various rites and pilgrimages, attending weddings and entering the sanctuary on festival days. She notes that women could be present at the reading of the law on the Feast of Tabernacles, a concession that came around only once in seven years, however, serving 'to emphasize the exclusion of women from the ordinary worship service and from the knowledge of the Torah' (p. 22).

Turning to the post-exilic books, Sr Albertus Magnus finds a virulent strain of misogyny. A case in point is Ecclesiastes 7: 26–29:

> I found more bitter than death the woman who is a trap, whose heart is snares and nets, whose hands are fetters; one who pleases God escapes her, but the sinner is taken by her. (...) One man among a thousand I found, but a woman among all these I have not found.

Worse still is Ecclesiasticus 25: 19 and 24:

> Any iniquity is small compared to a woman's iniquity; may a sinner's lot befall her!
> From a woman sin had its beginning, and because of her we all die.

This, precisely, is what the author means by the Eve syndrome: 'the projection on to women of cosmic guilt' (p. 23), a burden lifted by Jesus, but one which, nevertheless, persisted, and through the writings of the Church Fathers and of the scholastics, heavily influenced Church tradition.

In subsequent chapters, Sr Albertus Magnus details the revolutionary change in attitudes towards women so apparent in the ministry of Jesus and in the early Christian communities. It takes the mind and eye of a feminist to highlight the exquisite gender balance struck by Jesus both in his teaching through parables and in his actions. In the parables, if Jesus speaks of a man losing one sheep of a hundred, he will also speak of a woman losing one of ten drachmas. If he breaks the Sabbath to feed his disciples, he will also break it to cure the woman bent double, rebuking the rulers of the synagogue 'for valuing the letter of the Law above the needs of "a daughter of Abraham"' (p. 27). It is characteristic of Sr Albertus Magnus to suggest that in his gentle rebuke to Martha for being worried about many things, Jesus was actually encouraging her to 'seize the freedom to cultivate her gifts of mind and spirit' (p. 29). And she highlights the fact that it was to Martha that he disclosed the mystery of his resurrection, winning from her the same kind of fervent confession of faith that Peter made when Jesus asked his disciples, 'Who do you say that I am?' (Mt 16: 15).

In recalling story after story of Jesus' interaction with women, Sr Albertus Magnus marvels at the warmth, strength and beauty of the relationships he forges, beginning with that with his mother. He would insist, she points out, that his mother's true worth lay not in the fact that she bore and suckled him, but in the fact that she heard the word of God and kept it. In this retort Sr Albertus Magnus finds 'the doctrine of woman's true liberation' (p. 36). While we value and revere woman as bearer and nurturer of life, a woman 'is more than a womb. She is a fully human person with intelligence to understand and strength to fulfil the word of God' (p. 37).

Sr Albertus Magnus takes evident pleasure in outlining the role of women in the early Church, a role that included their active participation in teaching, prophesying, spreading the good news of the Gospel and participating equally with men in prayer and the breaking of bread. She also recognises and analyses at length some of the ambiguities in St Paul's teaching about women and the debate in the teaching of theologians and Fathers of the Church about whether woman is made in God's image. Jesus claimed women as friends and called them to be disciples, but the hierarchy gradually eliminated women from official service as the organisation and structure of the Church came to resemble that of the Roman Empire. She refers to an entry in the 1960 edition of *The Catholic Dictionary* which demonstrates how stubborn in the Catholic tradition is the idea that while women and men are equally endowed in terms of intellectual virtues, women are inferior to men in the cardinal virtues (prudence, justice, fortitude and temperance) as well as in the theological virtues of faith, hope and love, all of which are found to a higher degree in men because St Paul had said that '[M]an is head of the woman' (p. 57).

As Sr Albertus Magnus continues her narrative we learn a great deal about the role of deaconesses in the early Church, nuns, women mystics, Dominican and Franciscan tertiaries and the Beguines. We also learn of the persistent, morbidly negative view of sex, strangely viewed down the ages as a monopoly of women, and the identification of women with evil and lust of the flesh. Particularly distressing is her account of the witch hunts related to such views, which resulted in the burning, beheading and hanging of thousands of women over three centuries. While the craze had been fed by the book *Malleus Maleficarum* written by two Dominican inquisitors, the Church would be the first to condemn the vicious trials and punishment that the Reformation failed to address. In regard to women, claims Sr Albertus Magnus, the Reformation was, in fact, a step backwards, relegating them to silence, the home and the rearing of children. At the same time, she credits sects like the Brownites and the Quakers with recognising women as men's equals and entrusting them with the work of preaching and evangelisation.

Throughout her account of the long struggle that accompanied the effort to gain ecclesiastical approval of apostolic congregations of women, we sense both the admiration of the author for the men and women who persevered in the effort and her dismay with the obstacles put in their path. It took three centuries for the Church to finally recognise active congregations of women religious and to grant them a certain amount of autonomy. Bishops would maintain full control, however, of cloistered communities.

Tracing rapidly the movements of the eighteenth, nineteenth and twentieth centuries, Sr Albertus Magnus places the feminist movement in the larger context of the Enlightenment, the Industrial Revolution, the nineteenth-century missionary movement, the Suffragette movement, and the two world wars of the twentieth century. She notes the vigorous opposition of the Church to most of these movements, which benefited women in numerous ways. Churchmen lamented the emancipation of women. An article on 'Women' in the original *Catholic Encyclopedia* stated that women's demands were 'not compatible with the standard of the Gospel' and claimed that women should not challenge men, but be subject to them (p. 107).

Welcoming the unambiguous recognition in the documents of Vatican II of the absolute equality of man and woman as made in God's image, Sr Albertus Magnus called, nevertheless, for more than lip service to this conviction. In her introduction she reminds us that at the council itself women were at first totally excluded; a handful were later admitted as silent observers. The brilliant economist Barbara Ward was not allowed to read her own paper; it was delivered by a man. Physical force was used to prevent Catholic women journalists receiving communion; they would, presumably, 'contaminate the male participants who were also receiving the Eucharist' (p. 7). She points to stubborn inequities in the employment of women in the Church, a tokenism in the appointment of women to decision-making positions in parishes and dioceses, and she traces the arguments against women's ordination and finds them wanting.

In support of women's ordination, Sr Albertus Magnus attended the Women's Ordination Conference in 1976 and by this date was seen as a leading voice for Catholic women. Chicago Catholic Women, a feminist organisation, chose her to chair a meeting of women in Chicago for the purpose of gathering testimony to be transmitted to the National Call to Action. This position placed her in the centre of a supercharged, emotional debate within the Church, since the Call to Action was a nationwide assembly of Catholics called by the bishops of the US, with the responsibility of hearing from all sectors of American Catholicism.

Women and the Church concludes with the words, 'the Church has righted wrongs, has evolved in new directions many times in the past under the guidance of the Spirit. Women of prayer and of purpose can be fit instruments of the Spirit to hasten this development in the direction of justice and love' (p. 143).

Already a popular speaker, after the publication of her book Sr Albertus Magnus was invited to present at numerous sisters' councils and councils of laywomen throughout the US. The mood at these settings was one of excitement, discovery and growth, as women began to see through and to reject damaging stereotypes that deprived them of full and free personhood.

Sr Albertus Magnus hunger for justice extended beyond the cause of women in the Church. She was an ardent proponent of the Equal Rights Amendment (ERA). She strongly supported Susan Catania, a Catholic laywoman, mother of seven daughters, lawyer and a member of the Illinois General Assembly from 1973 to 1982, who was the principal sponsor of the ERA. After Sr Albertus Magnus death, Ms Catania wrote to Sr Candida Lund, president of Rosary College, that 'the best way for us to honour her [Sr Albertus Magnus] is to carry on her crusade for equal rights for women in the Church and for the women's movement in general' (Catania to Lund, October 23, 1978, Rosary College Archives). Consistent with her belief that higher education was one of the most effective tools for attaining equal rights for women, Sr Albertus Magnus participated in 1971 in an institute sponsored by the US Office of Education where she advocated for stronger federal support for higher education and for equal opportunity for women. Yet another avenue for 'preaching justice' was offered to her by the Archdiocese of Chicago. Recognising her experience, her scholarship, her probity and objectivity, the Archdiocesan Board of Conciliation and Arbitration invited her to join the board. There she played a leading role in resolving disputes ranging from financial and personnel issues to theological and liturgical ones.

World peace was another social and political issue that engaged Sr Albertus Magnus dedicated attention. In 1958, she was invited to participate in a symposium sponsored by the ecumenical Church Peace Union, entering with her accustomed vigour and wit into a wide-ranging discussion of foreign policy and world affairs.

In the last two years of her life, Sr Albertus Magnus was diagnosed with chronic hydrocephalus. She died at the Mercy Health Centre in Dubuque, Iowa, and is buried in the cemetery at Sinsinawa, Wisconsin.

It was during her long tenure at Rosary College that she exercised her most profound influence. It was here that she challenged successive generations to use their intelligence to its fullest capacity and to use their hearts, daring and instinct to transform unjust ecclesial and social structures. Her students, their daughters and their granddaughters, while recognising that progress has been made, realise that much remains to be done. They honour her memory now by carrying on the work she did for so long and with such eloquence, persistence and devotion.

SEEKING JUSTICE BY ADDRESSING PREJUDICE AND RACIAL MYTHS:
SR MARY ELLEN O'HANLON (1882–1961)
Catherine O'Hanlon, one of seven children of Joseph and Ellen Frances (Sullivan) O'Hanlon, was born on a farm in Johnson County, Iowa. She attended a public one-room country school and upon graduation from eighth grade, entered St Agatha Seminary, a Catholic girls' private school sponsored by the Sisters of Charity of the Blessed Virgin Mary (BVMs). There she was taught by Sr Mary Hortense, who had earned a degree from the University of Iowa. Impressed by this liberally educated woman who taught nearly all of the subjects, Catherine would herself become a teacher. She taught first at St Agnes Seminary in Iowa City. After summer study at the University of Iowa and having passed the state examination, she began teaching eighth grade in Coon Rapids, Iowa. She returned to the University of Iowa for fur-

ther study in the summer of 1908, and the following April left Coon Rapids to take a position in the Des Moines public school system.

While in Coon Rapids, Catherine had begun to ponder a call to religious life. Now, in a larger city with greater opportunities to participate in parish life and Catholic-sponsored activities, Catherine gave it more serious thought. The question soon became not whether she should become a religious, but to decide which congregation to join. She admired the BVMs who had educated her, but, after a visit to St Clara Academy at Sinsinawa, Wisconsin, where her sister Genevieve was a student, she knew that it would be with the Sinsinawa Dominicans that she would cast her lot. She entered the congregation in August 1912, and received the religious name of Mary Ellen. After teaching briefly as a postulant at a Catholic girls' academy in Bloomington, Illinois, Sr Mary Ellen returned to St Clara College (on the same site as the Academy) where she received a bachelor's degree in home economics in 1917. It became clear that she had neither appetite nor aptitude for that field, however, whereas she had a natural talent for science. She received a master's degree in botany from the University of Madison in 1919.

In September 1922, St Clara College moved to River Forest, Illinois, and was renamed Rosary College. Sr Mary Ellen was assigned there as chair of the new department of botany. Even as she accepted this appointment, she continued her education as a doctoral candidate at the University of Chicago, receiving her PhD, *magna cum laude*, in 1925. By this time, she had become interested in orthogenesis (organic evolution), finding in it a way to reconcile scientific discoveries with her religious convictions.

In 1934/35, Sr Mary Ellen was granted sabbatical leave, which she spent in Europe. She lived with her Dominican sisters at the Institut des Hautes Etudes (Villa des Fougères), a junior year abroad sponsored by Rosary College (now Dominican University) in Fribourg, Switzerland. She was befriended by Professor Uhrsprung of the botany department at the University of Fribourg and was granted the privileges of a visiting professor at the same university. She enjoyed similar privileges at the Universities of Bern and Zurich. During the year, she took full advantage of these privileges, especially in Fribourg where she attended classes. She also took advantage of the opportunity to travel to various European cities. It was while attending an International Congress of Botanists in Amsterdam that Sr Mary Ellen was jolted into an awareness of the realities of racism in America. In a casual conversation during which she was asked about her impressions of life in Europe she said she was struck by what she termed 'the caste system' and the sharp distinctions between classes that persisted there. She was asked in return, 'What of the Negro in America?' (*Three Careers*, p. 204). This question startled her into what she termed an 'awakening'. She began to realise that her experience had shielded her from examining the gross injustices faced by blacks in her own country.

Soon after Sr Mary Ellen's return to the US, Rosary College enrolled its first African-American women. They were religious of the Oblate Sisters of Providence, one of three congregations of African-American women religious. Sr Mary Ellen became friends with one of them and this friendship, no doubt, deepened her insight into racism in America. She began to turn her attention to the intersection between science and social realities, and became more and more determined to combat prejudice through a scientific and ethical approach to race.

This change in direction is what Sr Mary Ellen termed her 'third career', the first one being her call to religious life and the second her professional work as a biologist. While some might think her career as biologist was the 'glamorous' one, she insists in an unpublished autobiography that for her it was subordinate to her call to serve God in a special way as a Third Order Dominican sister, 'a most precious gift from God' (*Three Careers*, p. 2). She would study both God and the works of God's creation through the eyes of faith. 'Without a doubt,' she writes, 'there is much matter for serious and reverent thought for the student of nature who knows and loves God first of all and, consequently, all His creatures and the many wonderful manifestations of His creation, each in its proper order' (p. 4). It was her third career as a humanitarian, though, that she finds the most prominent, the most interesting, and the most soul-satisfying. 'It has provided for a fuller life—a life in which the love of neighbor, in the love of God, are fast-knit both in truth and in deed' (p. 4).

The first article of her new career, 'Genesis and Human Traits', appeared in the December 1943 issue of the magazine *Thought*. This led to speaking engagements on the topic to graduate students at De Paul University in February 1945. She would expand ideas developed at De Paul in her booklet, *Racial Myths*. It enjoyed a wide circulation and led to invitations to speak throughout the Chicago area, at Loyola University, Friendship House, the Catholic Interracial Council of Chicago and the Shiel School of Social Studies. It took some courage in the mid-1940s for a white woman to speak of white privilege and of racism in America. Segregation in both public and white schools was still common and separate was definitely not equal. Jim

Crow laws, of course, were still firmly in place in the South.

In the booklet, Sr Mary Ellen covers a lot of territory. She dismisses the term 'race' itself as having no reliable source or accurate meaning. She then enters into a discussion of the myths of racial blood, human surface characteristics, skin colour, skin odours and the notion of inequality among the so-called races, noting that 'Some of the absurdities which are rife even among influential and otherwise enlightened people would at times be downright humorous were they not at the same time so tragic in their import' (*Racial Myths*, p. 9). Her conclusion is that the superficial traits and characteristics of the so-called 'races' have little significance scientifically; that we are all descendants of a common ancestry; and that we all belong to a common species, namely, *Homo sapiens*.

In her next booklet, entitled *The Heresy of Race*, Sr Mary Ellen retraces some of the same ground covered in *Racial Myths*, but here the emphasis is on the place of religion in identifying and uprooting the 'contagious pestilence' of racism to which 'most of its victims have succumbed before they were conscious of what was happening to them' (p. vii). She concedes that the word 'heresy' is a strong one, but explains that she uses it not to identify a doctrine condemned by the Church, but to errors in the physical sciences, social sciences, in civil law and in education 'which impinge upon the Faith or affect adversely the practice of virtues which should mark a Christian' (p. 6). She includes an extensive bibliography and in her introduction recommends particularly books by black American scientists, poets, novelists, statesmen, and historians. Her own experience had taught her that there was no substitute for firsthand accounts if one wished to gain insight into the 'frustration, the strivings, the courage, the fortitude, and finally, some of the triumphs of the Negro American' (p. viii).

In both of these booklets and in her many speeches and presentations it was evident that Sr Mary Ellen brought to her observations a strong background in science, and a sharp eye not just for discriminatory laws and policies, but also for social behaviour and casual conversations that were cruel and betrayed a wilful ignorance of the realities of racism.

Sr Mary Ellen's work for justice for African-Americans extended, naturally, to the question of prejudice against Jews. Through her friend, Sr Mary Henry Gibbs, a professor of sociology at Rosary College, she made the acquaintance of Stella Counselbaum, and they became staunch friends. Mrs Counselbaum was active in numerous organisations working for the rights of all, irrespective of religion, national origin or race. These organisations included the Anti-Defamation League of B'nai B'rith, the Commission on Human Relations of the city of Chicago, the National Conference of Christians and Jews, and the National Conference of Negro Women. Mrs Counselbaum invited Sr Mary Ellen to address the Midwest Educators' Committee on Discrimination in Higher Education, a two-day conference held at the University of Illinois; a group of Jewish women, members of the KAM Temple of Sisterhood of Chicago; and an event at the International House of the University of Chicago sponsored by the Chicago B'Nai B'rith's Council and focused on 'International Relations on Your Own Street'. Sr Mary Ellen accepted these invitations with pleasure. Always strong in her convictions, in her talk on discrimination in higher education she told her audience:

> We must strive to eradicate all of the noxious weeds of injustice which are strangling the very essence of human brotherhood. This is a big order and, if higher education is to function fully in meeting it, all subject matter which is presented and discussed in our classrooms must be purged of all bias, bigotry, and belligerence. In all fields we must deal openly with the truth, in justice, sincerity, and with human understanding. For too long our textbooks have reeked with half-truths, distorted views and, most of all, conspicuous lacunae, all of which contribute to, and confirm, the ignorance about facts which every student should know. (*Three Careers*, p. 237)

Another friendship was influential in drawing Sr Mary Ellen further into the burgeoning civil rights movement. As the recently named president of the Cowles Botanical Society of Chicago in 1944, she was responsible for finding good speakers to address the society. She turned to her friend, Sr Mary Henry, for suggestions. The latter suggested Dr Percy Julian. Sr Mary Ellen had met Dr Anna Julian, a sociologist, at human rights meetings at Rosary College, and been impressed with her, but was unaware that she was married to Dr Percy Julian. She was unaware as well of the stature of Dr Percy in the field of chemistry, where his work on steroid hormone-based drugs was widely recognised and appreciated. Sr Mary Ellen acted at once on Sr Mary Henry's suggestion, convinced that Dr Percy, as a graduate of Harvard University (an MS degree) and the University of Vienna (a PhD degree in chemistry), would attract not only botanists but chemists and intellectuals generally. She received a prompt and courteous reply in which Dr Percy accepted the invitation. 'I was most happy,' writes Sr Mary Ellen, 'because I knew that here was someone who would bring a fuller house than we had yet enjoyed and send his audience away with more to think about than the ordinarily good speaker could do. My assumption came true one hundred percent in every respect' (*Three Careers*, p. 213). From this first meeting, a close friendship developed between Dr Julian and Sr Mary Ellen. She was eager to introduce him to the faculty and students of Rosary College and did so in the course of the year. His first talk there was devoted to 'Negro Inferiority in American Thought'. In her appraisal of the presentation, Sr Julie, an English professor on campus, wrote:

> With a consummate mastery of language and perfect ease in the communication of thought and experience, Dr. Julian, capable of both laughter and compassion, presented, with a strong appeal to the emotions, a perfectly logical argument ... Dr. Julian described the paradox which has manifested to the whole world the monstrosity of a democracy whose black armies represent and reflect the discrimination and segregation policies which have grown out of the concept of Negro inferiority and which have led us into an injustice that will destroy us, physically and spiritually, unless our Christianity is strong enough to save us ... Dr. Julian recounted the story of his slave grandfather who had mastered the art of writing and was prevented by his white master, in the most merciless and irrevocable way, from exercising it ... The audience who listened to Dr. Julian might well question whether any one of these defamers who sowed the bitter seed which has swollen into injustice, could match the fine power, and the beautiful Christianity, of this Negro scientist. (*Three Careers*, p. 215)

The Julians themselves would face violent resistance to their purchase of property in 1950 in the all-white suburb of Oak Park, adjacent to the suburb of River Forest. Before they moved in, a fire-bomb had been thrown at the house, and after they moved in, the house was dynamited. Through all of this, the Julians and their children stood firm, and community members, scandalised at the violence, came to their support. Sr Mary Ellen was, of course, among them.

It was Dr Julian who opened Sr Mary Ellen's eyes to pockets of bias that she might otherwise not have noticed in herself. She recognised the validity of an observation of Dr Julian's concerning her views on interracial marriage. In regard to her remarks on this topic in *Racial Myths*, he wrote to her, 'It is hardly enough for one of the Catholic faith to leave this question resting largely upon the statement that "negroes do not wish it any more than white". That is an emphasis upon the schism between the races rather than upon the fundamental principle of mutual respect ... If two people of like tastes, similar ideals, mutual respect and love wish to marry, it is time that the Catholic Church should say "God bless them"' (*Three Careers*, p. 219). Dr Julian acknowledged that she had inferred this principle, but felt that she could have been more blunt. Rather than resenting this insight, Sr Mary Ellen welcomed it as part of her journey to become fully and truly Catholic. In her article 'Color, Caprice, and Circumstance' (*Today*, 1 December 1947) she took a much firmer stance with regard to interracial marriage. Once again she was far ahead of the general public in a country where interracial marriage was still against the law in 29 states.

A trip in 1947 to the Deep South with her friend, Sr Mary Henry, deepened Sr Mary Ellen's understanding of race relations. Both of them had a sharp eye and exchanged insights along the way. 'What one of us did not observe, the other one did,' she wrote (*Three Careers*, p. 228). They were impressed by the dedicated work of their Sinsinawa Dominican Sisters in Mobile, Alabama, where African-American students received an excellent education in the grade school of Pure Heart of Mary parish. They met students at the St Joseph High School in Tuskegee, as well as the diocesan high school for African-American students in Tuskegee, another school where their sisters taught. In the 1950s and 1960s, these sisters (and their successors) would play a significant role in the Civil Rights Movement. In Tuskegee, Sr Mary Ellen and Sr Mary Henry were welcomed by the faculty of the renowned Tuskegee Institute and visited the graves of Booker T. Washington and George Washington Carver. In New Orleans, they visited the Sisters of the Holy Family, one of the three congregations of sisters of African-American ancestry. Two of them had been students at the Graduate School of Library Science of Rosary College.

In 1949, Sr Mary Ellen welcomed the opportunity to address a large audience through a radio interview conducted by Mgr Arthur F. Bukowski, President of Aquinas College in Grand Rapids, Michigan. Asked to account for the existence of racial prejudice, Sr Mary Ellen responded with her accustomed clarity and verve, that it was the progeny of pride, greed and selfishness. The white American, she said, 'has exploited the Negro, first, as his slave, and since, as cheap labour, and has employed various intrigues to maintain this despicable practice of injustice. One of his methods ... has been his desperate efforts to keep the Negro in ignorance, in subordination and oppression' (radio interview, 1 December 1949, WLAV, Grand Rapids,

Michigan). She urged her radio listeners to combat this deep-seated vice so offensive to both justice and charity.

Sr Mary Ellen continued to teach at Rosary College and to promote interracial justice and harmony through numerous speaking engagements until 1954 when, because of a fractured hip, she went to the congregation's infirmary, St Dominic's Villa in Dubuque, Iowa. She was released in April and spent the next four years at the motherhouse at Sinsinawa, serving the community there until ill health obliged her to return to the infirmary in 1958. In 1961, complications due to anaemia and arthritis confined her to bed. She died on 25 August 1961, at the age of 78.

A woman of great intellect and warm heart, Sr Mary Ellen O'Hanlon entered into each of her careers with dedication and devotion. In her third career as a recognised leader in Catholic social action for interracial justice, she influenced students, educators and social activists who would help move forward the civil rights agenda of the 1960s. If she were alive today, she would be the first to recognise that the work of 'justice for all' is far from finished.

SEEKING ECONOMIC JUSTICE AND PEACE:
MARY ELLEN BUTCHER OP (1936–1992)

Mary Ellen Butcher was born in Ottumwa, Iowa, the only child of Harold and Bernice (O'Brien) Butcher. Before she reached school age the family moved to Omaha, Nebraska, where her father managed the Regis Hotel. Living in the hotel and taking meals in the hotel dining room, Mary Ellen early on became accustomed to adult company and to participating in adult conversations. She proved a precocious pupil at the local Catholic elementary school and at Duchesne Academy. After her graduation at the age of 16, she enrolled at Rosary College (now Dominican University) in River Forest, Illinois.

The Sinsinawa Dominicans who taught there, she said, gave her three invaluable gifts: 'a love of the intellectual life, a realization of the possible freedom of the spiritual life, and a passion for social justice' (profile in *Edgewood College Today*, fall 1982.) She entered the Congregation of the Most Holy Rosary at Sinsinawa in 1955, before completing her BA degree. She finished her degree after her first profession in 1957 with a major in history and minors in English, French and philosophy. From 1957 until 1974, Sr Mary Ellen served as teacher or administrator in a number of secondary schools. At Sacred Heart in Washington, DC, she combined teaching with study at the Catholic

University of America, where she earned a PhD in Economics in 1969. From 1974 until 1984, she served either as assistant or as the general finance officer of the congregation, and from 1985 to 1988, was assistant professor in the area of finance at Providence College, in Providence, Rhode Island. Recognising her passion for both peace and justice, Timothy Radcliffe, Master General of the Order, asked her to serve in 1985/86 on an eight-person committee on peace. She was the only woman on the committee. From 1988 until her death she served as the Executive Director of the National Association of Treasurers of Religious Institutes, based in Silver Spring, Maryland.

In all of these ministries, Sr Mary Ellen was a witness to the truth and an advocate for the underprivileged and for peace; in all of them, as one admirer said, she 'strengthened the weak and challenged the strong'. She was steeped both in Thomistic theology and in the encyclicals and other documents devoted to modern Catholic social teaching. The latter are sometimes referred to as the Church's best kept secret; Sr Mary Ellen would do her best to bring them into the public domain. She shared her research in classes for Sinsinawa Dominican novices; for the Internovitiate Program in the Dubuque area; for the Continuing Education Program at Clarke College in Dubuque; and for deacons in the Diocese of Tulsa. She lectured on the topic of the Church's social teaching to various audiences, including the Parable Conference on 'Doing Justice', which, in 1988, brought Dominicans from around the country to the Rosary College campus. There her topic was 'Integrating Principles for Action'. Finally, in a series of 11 videotapes she traces, succinctly and beautifully, the themes that have dominated the tradition of social teaching from Aquinas to Vatican II, noting how the themes have changed over time. She includes in that series the social teaching of the Church in Latin America, the US and Canada.

Sr Mary Ellen's paper/lecture on the 'Influence of Thomas Aquinas on Modern Catholic Social Teaching' summarises some of the materials she treated at length in the series of videotapes. The paper is an elegant demonstration of the influence of the Summa Theologiae on the entire body of Catholic social teaching. The Summa, she was fond of pointing out, furnished the structure and the basic themes of these documents, beginning with Leo XIII's *Rerum Novarum*.

Sr Mary Ellen outlines how, in that encyclical, Leo XIII departed from the practice of his predecessors who condemned the exaggerated rationalism of the eighteenth and nineteenth centuries and what they saw as the dangers of modern thought. Rather than condemning the errors of his time,

Leo XIII would offer an alternative to them by applying and adapting Thomistic principles to the realities of the modern world. The first and most basic of these principles is the dignity of the human person who is unique but bound irreversibly to all beings 'coming from and destined for God' (p. 3). Sr Mary Ellen finds this principle to be the distinguishing mark of the Church's social teaching through the centuries. In the first videotape of the series on the Church's social teaching, she offers some touching medieval expressions of the dignity bestowed by God on the universe and all of its creatures by the simple fact of creation. She describes the North door of the Cathedral of Chartres depicting the Creation. God smiles, she says, thinking of the human person, the crowning glory of creation, and 'It is in that smile of God for each person that we find the key to Christian social teaching.' She refers as well to Thomas Aquinas' reference to the Seventh Day of Creation as 'God's day of joy'.

A second principle is that of the common good, the need to balance individual rights with the welfare of society as a whole. In 'The Influence of Thomas Aquinas', Sr Mary Ellen emphasises that, while Aquinas recognised the individual's right to private property, he saw it as a relative right rather than an absolute or primary one. It is to be exercised in relation to the welfare of society as a whole, and so is limited in the light of society's needs, rights and responsibilities. This principle, rooted in Aquinas' teaching on justice, had particular appeal for Sr Mary Ellen, who mourned the growing economic disparity among people around the globe. She notes that while *Rerum Novarum* and *Quadragesimo Anno* seemed to affirm the right to private property more strongly than Aquinas, John XXIII's *Mater et Magistra* and *Pacem in Terris* returned to 'a more relativized notion of private property ... more closely related to the teachings of Aquinas' (p. 6). One senses in Sr Mary Ellen's tracing of the influence of Aquinas on the modern social teaching found in papal and other documents a regret that some of his concepts have been rather watered down. She notes that in *Rerum Novarum* and *Quadragesimo Anno*, the exhortation to governments to remember their responsibilities to workers are 'somewhat mild', and their hope that Christians would work to form neo-medieval organisations resembling guilds 'somewhat unrealistic' (p. 7). And while Aquinas' 'just war' theory clearly influenced John XXIII's *Pacem in Terris* and the US bishops' *The Challenge of Peace*, she finds it lacks some of the clarity and force of Aquinas' expression. Even less visible is Aquinas' principle that people, acting with due prudence, have the right to overthrow a tyrant who fails to govern in the interest of the common good (p. 8).

It is the Thomistic assertion that justice is the essential element in social relationships that Sr Mary Ellen finds to be most clearly and consistently echoed in modern Catholic social teaching. It is this concept that 'determines the content and even the existence of the documents which form this contemporary body of teaching' (p.9). The reminder that justice is the fundamental and essential virtue, the basis of law and the guarantor of the common good, is one that is relevant in every nation and in every age. Sr Mary Ellen was acutely aware of its relevance in her own country, where in 1980 corporate executives earned 42 times as much as the average worker. What would she think had she lived to see the day when they would make over 500 times as much, or the day when more than four fifths of the total increase in American incomes goes to the richest 1 per cent?

Although Sr Mary Ellen's emphasis in regard to the social teaching of the Church was on its historical development and its economic aspects, she also presented and published papers on its relationship to racism, sexism and classism in contemporary society.

Sr Mary Ellen's grasp of the central place of justice in the moral and spiritual life was not simply intellectual. She hungered for it, she preached it, she lived it out in her own life, in the classrooms where she taught, on the boards on which she served, and in the offices she directed. John E. Corrigan, who served with her on the Finance Committee of the Board of Trustees of Rosary College (Dominican University), wrote of their work on that committee:

> We battled frequently. Her views were constant and vigorous. The company [in which they were considering an investment] had to meet high standards of social justice, or we would have nothing to do with it. After several years of working together we became steadfast friends, and I held her in highest respect. Social justice transcended profit, whether profit for the company or profit for us as a potential owner. (Quoted in *Enriching Many*, p. 8)

When, in 1988, the National Association of Treasurers of Religious Institutes (NATRI) invited her to accept the position of director, Sr Mary Ellen was obliged to weigh that invitation against her desire to continue teaching both graduate and undergraduate students at Providence College. In the classroom she delighted in the opportunity to open her students' eyes to the ethical and social justice dimensions of financial management and investment. On the other hand, she had been instrumental in the formation of NATRI and had served for two terms on its board. She knew the kind of service it offered to the finance officers of religious congregations, and knew how badly such service was needed. She was aware, as well, that her schedule as Director of NATRI would be more flexible than her teaching schedule and easier to coordinate with the many invitations she received to lecture, participate in workshops, and serve on numerous boards and committees.

Her position as Director of NATRI brought Sr Mary Ellen back to Washington, DC. She had loved the city since her days of teaching at Sacred Heart Academy, when she had lived in an old convent in a multicultural neighbourhood, protesting the injustices she perceived there, marching in peace demonstrations and taking full advantage of the cultural advantages. Now, from 1988 until her death in 1992, she would focus her attention, energy and considerable gifts of mind and heart on serving the treasurers of more than 550 institutes of religious women and men. She had already served as one of the ten original members of a task force established in 1983 by the National Conference of Catholic Bishops, the Leadership Conference of Women Religious and the Conference of Major Superiors of Men to act as consultants to religious institutes experiencing financial concerns. She brought to NATRI the experience gained in assisting these institutes in financial planning and management, and in designing educational programmes for their leadership and membership. Her leadership, her clarity and her vision were greatly appreciated at a time when religious congregations were facing an ageing and diminishing membership, with difficult negotiations involved in the sharing of facilities and in mergers of provinces and of entire congregations. Mary Swain SL, a member of the NATRI Board, wrote of her work as director:

> I always think of Mary Ellen as the one who began finding the smaller, poorer communities, particularly contemplatives, and getting them into the consultation process and the supplemental grant process.
>
> What I really appreciated about Mary Ellen was what she brought to the position of executive director of NATRI. She brought intelligence, experience, vision, imagination, courage, a strong sense of justice and of concern for those with less monetarily than many of us. (Quoted in *Enriching Many*, p. 11)

It's clear that Sr Mary Ellen's profound understanding of the close relationship joining justice, peace, love and compassion affected every aspect of her life. It coloured her ministries: her teaching, her research, her position as General Finance Officer of her congregation, her work on boards, her position as Director of NATRI. It also imbued the way she understood and lived out her religious vows. Her article 'Dominican Poverty: A Somewhat Radical Reflection', prepared for the Leadership Conference of Women Religious and the Dominican Leadership Conference of 1990, places the vow in the context of Gospel values, the Dominican tradition and the effort of women religious after Vatican II to refound, re-imagine and renew their congregations and way of life.

She emphasises the fact that the refounding for Dominicans takes place in the context of their history as a mendicant order whose founder understood voluntary poverty as essential to the preaching. Dominic and his followers understood that those on fire to preach the Word could not be burdened with excessive baggage; they knew that voluntary poverty would add credence to their message. It is up to us to reflect on how it is to be lived in the context of our own time, as members of a society marked by extremes of wealth and deprivation and as members of a Church that 'has proclaimed its preferential option for the poor, a Church that struggles with its own landed wealth, with its own dependence on the generosity of the rich and powerful, with the dilemma of how and where to allocate its resources' (p.15), and as congregations of ageing members and diminishing membership, with the challenge of providing for the future of our life and mission from a fundamentally inadequate earning base.

In an inspiring reflection on the vow within these contexts, Sr Mary Ellen sketches the fundamental meaning of the common life. It is a life free of clutter, a life in which all we have or earn or receive belongs to all and is available to each according to individual need; it is a countercultural life in a society in which the accumulation of wealth and power are primary goals. She calls us today to the asceticism of 'responsible, participative and collaborative planning for the use of our resources' (p. 18). She foresaw as part of collaborative planning the pooling of resources among Dominican congregations and the mergers of provinces and of entire congregations, all in the context of the shared charism of preaching, teaching and sharing the fruits of our contemplation.

Through all of this runs the thread of compassion, compassion for ourselves, for one another and for our world. 'Living the common life opens us to a new compassion for our world. When we allow ourselves to have nothing, to be dependent and give over control of material resources to others, our hearts are opened in new ways to those for whom this is a way of life by necessity' (p. 21).

In his book, *Sing a New Song*, Timothy Radcliffe OP emphasises the need for sisters and brothers of the Order to be trained in serious economic and political analysis of the causes of injustice. Throughout her adult life, Sr Mary Ellen answered that need, and she did it, persistently and brilliantly, through the prisms of scripture, Thomistic theology, papal encyclicals and bishops' pastoral letters on justice and peace. She read these documents with the eyes of a scholar and researcher and the heart of someone who was touched both by the beauty and the suffering of all of God's creation.

In 1986, Sr Mary Ellen underwent surgery for breast cancer. She recovered quickly and returned to teaching at Providence College until her appointment as Director of NATRI. In September of 1992, the cancer returned. She was hospitalised in Louisville, Kentucky, and died there on 6 November 1992. There, as Sr Electa Armstong noted in her homily at the wake service at Sinsinawa, Sr Mary Ellen and the Sinsinawa Dominicans attendant on her, were ministered to by the sisters of Loreto, the Ursuline sisters, the Kentucky Dominicans, Baptist friends, and her long-time Dominican friend and brother, Archbishop Thomas Kelly. The latter wrote of the accumulated grace and wisdom that was so evident in her living and in her dying, and concluded: 'She was, in life and in death, a bright shining star' (quoted in *Enriching Many*, p. 15).

SEEKING JUSTICE FOR ALL:
SR DOLORES BROOKS (1928–2002)
Sr Dolores Brooks (Laurus) was born in Chicago, Illinois, the third of four children born to Robert Patrick and Della (Storin) Brooks. She attended grade school and high school at the Academy of Our Lady, sponsored by the School Sisters of Notre Dame. After her third year at St Mary's of Notre Dame in Notre Dame, Indiana, she entered the Congregation of the Most Holy Rosary at Sinsinawa, Wisconsin, making her final profession in 1953. She completed her undergraduate study at Rosary College, River Forest, Illinois, with an emphasis on history, sociology and political science, while carrying on her ministry of teaching. In 1957, she was granted a BA degree from Rosary College (now Dominican University), and later received MAs in history (University of Notre Dame) and divinity/theology (Weston School of Theology).

Sr Dolores brought to her study and to her various ministries acute intelligence, warm compassion, boundless energy and a longing for, and strong commitment to, justice. She inherited her hunger for justice, she often said, from her father. Robert Brooks was avidly interested in world affairs and read them through the lens of justice. It was he who put into her hands a book on the Holocaust. She was 12 years old at the time, and would never forget the book whose images remained forever engraved on her mind and heart. Her father would acquaint her with injustices closer to home as well. As a union leader on Chicago's south side in the 1930s and 1940s, he was well versed in the long hours, low pay and dangerous working conditions experienced by the working class.

For 23 years (1950–73), Sr Dolores brought to classrooms across the US her compassion for the exploited and disenfranchised and her commitment to peace and justice. Whether she was teaching fifth graders at Our Lady of Refuge in New York, or high school students in Cheyenne, Wyoming, Whitefish Bay, Wisconsin, River Forest, Illinois, or Minneapolis, Minnesota, Sr Dolores introduced her students to the social issues of the times and the Christian principles that addressed them. She awakened them not just to the social and political realities of the US, but to the cries of the poor all over the world. Former colleagues and students attest to the fact that she made history come alive and engaged students in proactive learning. They speak of her as a remarkably gifted teacher who engendered in her students a joy and enthusiasm and a positive sense of self that made them eager to come to class.

From 1973 to 1976, Sr Dolores was engaged in graduate study, after which she joined the pastoral team at St Clement's Parish in Chicago as an associate pastor. She was the only woman, serving with Fr John F. Fahey, pastor, and with several other associate pastors. It took some effort, both on the part of Dolores and of the priests, to adapt to a shared ministry, as Fr Fahey recalled in a testimony to Sr Dolores included in the booklet *Loving Life, Doing Justice, Dedicated to Dolores Brooks, O.P.* 'Dolores learned quickly, with surprise and frustration, that we did not measure up to the standards of her Dominican Sisters or of her Jesuit mentors in Cambridge' (p. 30). Fr Fahey described the priests as 'entrenched' and Sr Dolores as 'determined'. After some dialogue, which we may imagine was spirited, they came to agree that she would join them for three meals a day in the rectory, if she chose to do so. They would all decide how, given their interests and gifts, they might best serve the parish, whose needs were many and diverse. St Clement's, an urban parish with a population of 40,000, included three hospitals, several nursing homes, many young singles, conventional and unconventional families, well-educated professionals and homeless indigents. In their desire to serve a variety of needs, the team gained mutual trust and began to work in harmony. This was not lost on the parishioners, who volunteered even more generously and enthusiastically.

During her ten years at St Clement's, Sr Dolores served as leader of the Confraternity of Christian Doctrine, director of the Rite of Christian Initiation for Adults, and active participant on the Peace and Justice Committee. With her usual penchant for collaboration, she became involved with interfaith programs including the Lincoln Park Shelter and the Lincoln Park Food Bank. Fr Fahey notes, 'Almost every one of these programs struggled into existence, meeting obvious needs that had been long recognized but just as long ignored. With the care Dolores gave to these programs they grew year by year; instead of growing tired of them, she grew with them' (*Loving Life, Doing Justice*, p. 30). She visited the nursing homes weekly, took an active part in the weekly meeting of the liturgy committee and met with parishioners for counselling and spiritual direction.

Sr Dolores, a qualified, effective and much-appreciated preacher, wanted not only to work for justice but also to preach justice. She asked to preach on one Sunday a month and was scheduled to do so. When the archdiocese objected to this arrangement, she preached on weekdays and special occasions. She would advocate, not only for women's right to preach, but also for the right to have their call to priesthood tested. She served on the task force that planned and organised the Women's Ordination Conference held in Detroit, Michigan, 28–30 November 1975. It called for 'Women in Future Priesthood Now: A Call to Action'. She saw the movement as central to the renewal of Church structures, comparing it to the effect of Paul's mission to the Gentiles, another cultural question dealing with full membership in the Christian community. Sr Dolores was a member of the core commission which would make of the Women's Ordination Conference a national organisation and served on the task force that organised the second Women's Ordination Conference, entitled 'New Women, New Church, New Priestly Ministry'. It was held in Baltimore, Maryland, 10–12 November 1978. Her deep commitment to justice for women in the Church led her to play a central role in establishing the Women of the Church Coalition in 1977, a group that sponsored the first Women Church Conference in 1983. Sr Dolores' ardour for real equality for women everywhere was unfailing. Fr Fahey, in an article published in the *St Clement's Journal*, winter 1986, noted that: 'Dolores particularly feels for women in the church. She weeps and fights for her sisters and, in so doing, strikes a deep resonance with other women – young, old, religious and lay.'

Sr Dolores left her ministry at St Clement's in 1986, much appreciated and loved by the people she had served so faithfully and compassionately for ten years. In 1987 she joined the staff at the Chicago headquarters of the 8th Day Centre for Justice, an organisation founded by six Catholic religious communities in 1974. Today there are nine congregations listed as sponsoring members, 14 as member friends and 28 as contributing members. The centre has constituents in every state and in more than 36 countries.

The vision and goals of the organisation matched Sr Dolores' own desire to promote peace and justice, equality and human dignity, in a world free from oppression. As co-coordinator of the centre, she would bring her penchant for collaboration to a centre committed to coalition building and networking, and her experience as a teacher to its educational outreach. Her gifts of critical social analysis and of theological reflection would enhance the centre's goal of fostering 'critical analysis and awareness out of a spirituality of nonviolence and to model this in our work and in society'. Sr Dolores threw herself wholeheartedly into the work of the centre, helping to organise, and participating in, peace protests, calling in the media to draw public attention to oppressive systems, pushing for social and economic reform through legislative action, challenging corporations who exploited labourers in Central and South America, standing with the people of El Salvador, Haiti and Iraq against oppressive regimes and supporting and publicising the School of the Americas (SOA) Watch.

The SOA Watch is an advocacy organisation founded to protest the training of mainly Latin American military officers by the US Department of Defense at Fort Benning in Georgia. Some of the graduates of this centre, originally called the School of the Americas, are guilty of human rights abuses, including rape, torture and contraventions of the Geneva Accord. SOA Watch lobbies Congress to close the school and has won support from many members of Congress, but never enough to bring about the closure of the school. The name of the school, however, has been changed and it is now known as the Western Hemisphere Institute for Security Cooperation. 'Different name, same shame', was the reaction of members of SOA Watch. Another concession to the protestors was the addition of an obligatory class on human rights and the principle of civilian control of the military. Sr Dolores participated year after year in the marches and protests organised by SOA Watch and encouraged others to join in the effort. When she could no longer march because of a recurrence of cancer, she showed up at the annual November vigil in a wheelchair, as feisty and committed as ever.

Another organisation in which Sr Dolores played an active leadership role is the Interfaith Centre on Corporate Responsibility. Members of this religious coalition buy shares in certain companies in order to introduce shareholder resolutions designed to address the abusive and exploitative practices of these companies whether in the US or abroad (see the contribution on socially responsible investing in this volume). She regularly attended meetings of ICCR and collaborated in the writing of the booklet *Principles of Global Corporate Responsibility*. Timothy Smith of Walden Asset Management, in a letter to Sr Toni Harris, then prioress of the congregation, wrote that Dolores 'pressed for creative and aggressive strategies', and 'gave generously of her time and wisdom in the governance of ICCR' (24 January 2002). The Executive Director of ICCR, in another letter to Sr Toni Harris, dated 25 January 2002, spoke of Sr Dolores as a visionary who, 'In the true Dominican fashion ... was known to speak truth.' Efforts by ICCR and others have resulted in moves by several international companies to new levels of social responsibility, if not out of conviction then as a defence against bad press. Sr Dolores also served for many years as the co-chair of the Illinois Committee on Responsible Investment, where she helped develop global principles for workers' rights and investments.

Sr Dolores' commitment to the pursuit of justice brought her to various parts of the world. She visited El Salvador on several occasions, while associate pastor at St Clement's, she accompanied parishioners on trips to acquaint them with both the beauty of the people and their suffering at the hands of a brutal regime, supported in part by the US government. In November 1989, the staff of the 8th Day Centre held a rally in Chicago outside the El Salvador consulate to commemorate the death of the Jesuits, their cook and her daughter, who had been murdered by right-wing death squads. Sr Dolores spoke of the occasion as a 'chance for grace in which God calls us to take up the cause of right ... an opportunity to amend the sins of history ... to honour the blood of so many heroes and martyrs in Central America' (*The New World*, 24 October 1989). In 1991 she travelled to Iraq with Sr Kathleen Desautels, a staff member of the 8th Day Centre. They joined others on a tour of Iraq and the West Bank organised by the National Assembly of Religious Women, distributing $22,000 in medical supplies purchased with donations collected by the Assembly and other religious organisations. In 1995 Sr Dolores joined with women from around the world at the NGO Forum and the Fourth UN Conference on Women held in Huairou and Beijing. She, together with 150 women religious representing 69 congregations from around the world, issued a statement to the delegates of the UN Conference declaring solidarity with the women participating in the NGO Forum. It reads, in part: 'Our commitment to live out the Gospel impels us to raise our voices with theirs and to insist that the delegates to this U.N. Conference ratify and implement a platform of action which effectively addresses the militarization, racism, structural adjustment programs, narrow fundamentalist interpretations and patriarchal structures which contribute to the feminization of poverty and do violence to women and girl children everywhere.'

In 1999, at its January commencement exercises, Dominican University in River Forest, Illinois, bestowed an honorary degree on Sr Dolores, in recognition of her dedication and commitment to justice issues. The university lauded her work 'for systemic change at the local, national and international levels on a variety of issues including economic justice and poverty, peace and human rights, and women's issues'.

Sr Dolores' unflagging commitment to peace and justice is all the more inspiring when one considers that she lived with the effects of cancer which recurred in different parts of her body over a period of 18 years. Neither this illness, nor the ills of the world she worked so hard to address and alleviate, deprived her of a sense of humour and a spirit of fun. These, her friends and God's grace sustained her to the end.

22

A Pioneer of Inter-religious Dialogue:

Rose Thering

MICHELLE OLLEY, O.P.

CHOICE FOR A LIFETIME

When Dr Rose Thering addressed the graduating class of 2000 of the State University of New York, she quoted her friend, Elie Wiesel, who in his writings and lectures emphasised the importance of questioning. In her own words, Rose underscored Wiesel's advice when she passionately declared to the graduates: 'You have completed one milestone today, but you have many more goals to attain. As you do this, you must question, everything and always. When you and I stop questioning, you and I stop learning. It is that simple!'[1]

'Question everything and always' was a steady theme throughout the lifetime of Rose Elizabeth Thering. As a small child she questioned her parents, teachers and pastors regarding the Benziger Brothers *Bible History for Children*, which portrayed the Jews as the killers of Christ and, therefore, eternally doomed. Why did the Jews commit the great sin of putting God himself to death? Why did the Jews murder the Messiah? Often her questions went unanswered or she was told to be quiet. She was puzzled by these questions because she had been taught that everyone was created by God and that God loved his creation. Rose was disturbed by the negative teachings about the Jews and other faith traditions in her religion books throughout her Catholic grade and high school years.

Albert and Elizabeth Thering, second-generation German Catholics, raised their 11 children in Plain, Wisconsin, where Rose was born on August 9, 1920. With the exception of one Protestant family, the entire farming community was Catholic. All of the Thering children attended St Luke's School where the Racine Dominicans taught. The whole family loved the sisters and often took the fruits of the fields to them to show their appreciation. Even as

---

1. This and other quotations in this contribution are taken from various documents at the Siena Center, which is the motherhouse of the Racine Dominicans, and can be found by contacting the archivist. One source that is particularly important, and which is used with permission, is an interview of Sr Rose Thering by Sr Immaculata Schmidt OP; it can be found in the same archives.

a young child, Rose knew that she wanted to become a sister in a teaching community, and her parents knew that this was her desire. After ninth grade she began preparations to enter the Racine Dominican community.

However, her mother had three sisters who were Franciscans in Milwaukee and they came to visit the Thering family that summer. Rose's three aunts invited her to visit their convent. Rose told them that she was all packed and ready to go to the Racine community. They said that she could use all the things she had packed for their community in Milwaukee as well, so Rose accepted their invitation, to please them, and accompanied them back to Milwaukee. After her Milwaukee visit, Rose was still determined to enter the Racine Dominican community, even though she had never even visited the convent in Racine.

It was in August 1936 that the family gathered together for their traditional morning prayer. It was a rather sad scene because everyone was crying through their prayers. Her father finally stopped the crying when he said, 'I am ready to leave for Racine. Who is going with me?' Rose and her mother followed him out the door and joined him for Rose's first trip to Racine. Some members of her family didn't think she should become a nun. One of her sisters and her husband showed up at the convent within a week after her arrival in Racine and offered to take her home. Rose told them she was staying.

Rose spent her first two years as a postulant attending St Catherine's High School, sponsored by the Racine Dominicans. She graduated in June 1938. In August, she became a novice and received the name Rose Albert. In 1940, she made her first profession of her vows. From 1940 to 1957, Sr Rose was a teacher at two Catholic grade schools and at St Catherine's High School. She also served as a principal in a Catholic grade school. During this period of time she earned her bachelor's degree from Dominican College and her master's degree in education from the College of St Thomas in Minnesota.

A PROPHET SEARCHING FOR TRUTH

In 1957, Sr Rose Albert went to St Louis University to continue her education and to pursue a doctorate. At that time, St Louis University was engaged in a study of the textbooks and materials used in Catholic schools and how they viewed religious, racial and ethnic groups. However, in the beginning, the research was limited only to materials used in the areas of English and social studies.

Rose told her mentor, Mgr Maher, that the real problem existed in the books used for teaching religion. The study would not be complete unless an examination of religious teaching materials was included. However, this would be a major decision, since religion books had already received a *nihil obstat* and an *imprimatur*. After much discussion the decision was made to do a complete study by including the religion department, and the research moved forward. At the same time, similar studies were undertaken for Protestants, by Dr Bernard Olson at Yale University, and for Jews, by Dr Bernard Wineryb at Dropsie College.

Sr Rose Albert was given an office at St Louis to work on her research on high school textbooks, manuals and related materials, covering those that were the most widely used in Catholic high schools. When the dissertation was finished, she had to code all the materials that she had studied so that only she and the respective publisher would know the results of the study of its particular books, manuals and materials. Each company received a copy of the study of its publications.

Rose concluded that the Jews were the most visible group in this study who were presented in a negative light. The Catholic teaching materials portrayed the Jewish people as unfaithful, hypocritical and as God-killers, reducing the human dignity of the Jews and creating attitudes among children that would make reprisals against them seem like doing God's will. In the Good Friday liturgy the Church prayed for the 'perfidious' Jews. Some Christian groups were also treated with disrespect. Two examples of such texts are: 'The Catholics are the only truly Christian group. Other Christian groups are not really Christian because they do not truly follow Jesus'; and: 'The Protestant groups are working havoc in Latin America by taking the people away from the Catholic Church.'

When the university studies of the departments of English, social studies and religion were completed, St Louis convened a special conference on education and invited all the superintendents of Catholic schools in the US and a few interreligious leaders. This conference included presentations on the results of the studies, with opportunities for discussion.

The day before the conference, Sr Rose Albert warned Mgr Maher that she expected that her presentation would be the only controversial one, and that there would probably be some trouble after it. He replied that he saw no problem coming up.

Both the English and social studies presentations were well received. However, after Rose gave her report on the textbooks used for the teaching of religion, the reaction was so strong that she felt that she was on trial, and being tarred and feathered. One priest commented on her arrogance in criticising books that had the imprimatur of the Church. Another asked for the criteria used in her study, but was not satisfied with the answers he was given. In general, there was a lot of mumbling and grumbling throughout the audience. Finally, one of the bishops stood up and said that if the books used for teaching religion contained such negative teachings about the Jews and other faith traditions, as the analysis presented by Sr Rose Albert indicated, it was not possible to continue using such materials. Following this, a bishop from Kansas City got up and remarked that he had been hearing a lot of prejudice expressed in the room and he challenged the priests there to examine their consciences. After the conference, a bishop from Milwaukee asked her not to publish her work, saying that she should not 'hang out our dirty laundry'. Sr Rose Albert reported later, 'I listened to what he had to say, and then I hung it out.'

After such a gruelling session, Rose concluded that, with only two positive responses, she ought to suspend her research. She was very discouraged, and she did not return to her office for several days.

A week later Mgr Maher told Rose that he had missed her because he had been waiting to tell her some good news. Two magazines wanted to publish the talk that she had given to the superintendents. Rose said that she could not allow that. She believed that it would not be accepted with her name as the author. Maher asked Rose if she would be willing to let him put his name on the article. Rose agreed with Maher's suggestion, since it was important to get the information out to the public. So the article was sent to religious education magazines. The response to the publication of her article was positive, Rose rediscovered her courage and was able to finish her research in 1961.

This research on the most widely used religion teaching materials demonstrated that, prior to Vatican II, the Catholic Church did have 'contempt teachings' between the covers of some of its religion textbooks. Vatican II made a major breakthrough, however, with its promulgation in 1965 of the Declaration of the Relation of the Church to Non-Christian Religions, known as *Nostra Aetate*.

John XXIII had been pope for only 90 days when, on 25 January 1959, he made the unexpected announcement of his plan to convoke an ecumenical council. After nearly four years of exhaustive preparation, Vatican II finally opened on 11 October 1962.

When the council was working on the document on 'The Relationship of the Church to Non-Christian Religions', Cardinal Augustin Bea of Germany requested a copy of Rose's dissertation, which was taken to Rome by Rose's friend, Rabbi Mark Tenenbaum. It was also read by Mgr John H. Oesterreicher, one of the main figures behind the drafting of the document.

Rose's dissertation was needed at the council for the cardinals to see the proof that there were 'contempt teachings' in our Catholic textbooks that needed changing. With the promulgation of *Nostra Aetate* during the final session of Vatican II in 1965, the Church unequivocally condemned anti-Semitism in every shape and form and forever laid to rest the 'deicide' charge. Never again could the Church blame the Jews for the death of Jesus. The document also recognised God's enduring love and covenant with the Jewish people.

After the council had approved *Nostra Aetate*, Cardinal Bea said, 'Through our negative teachings we have promulgated hatred against the Jews culminating in the Holocaust.' It was only after *Nostra Aetate* had been issued that publishers, editors and authors of textbooks for religious education began to revamp their previous negative treatment of Jews and Judaism and to publish new materials.

Mgr Oesterreicher was the same John Oesterreicher who was hunted all over Germany by Hitler during the Second World War, but who had been able to escape to the US. Later he became a Catholic and a priest. Sometimes he is compared to St Paul, who brought Christians to a better understanding of the Jews. Mgr Oesterreicher's mission was to have Christians understand the Jews as the Jews understood themselves. Later on, in 1968, he would hire Rose to work with him in Seton Hall University at the Institute of Christian-Jewish Studies.

DOMINICAN COLLEGE AND CHICAGO ARCHDIOCESE

Whether her role was teacher, researcher, social justice advocate, student and/or preacher, Dr Rose Thering was most diligent and meticulous in her pursuit of education, research and accompanying preparation, as well as extensive foreign travel. After she received her doctorate at St Louis University, her next two assignments (1961–68) were somewhat related to the focus of her dissertation regarding racial and religious discrimination and poverty.

Rose was appointed to Dominican College in Racine, Wisconsin, to serve as the Chairperson of the Department of Education from 1961 to 1965. Among her activities, Rose developed a programme of special summer school classes for disadvantaged children, in collaboration with Catholic schools in Racine. The programme would enrol 150 disadvantaged children in grades 1 through 6. Rose also developed and administered a nine-week programme for teachers and teacher-supervisors of disadvantaged youth, in collaboration with the Racine Unified Public School District, funded by the National Defense Education Act (NDEA). During the final year of her tenure, she also served as co-ordinator of Racine's Catholic elementary schools.

From 1965 to 1968 Sr Rose Albert served as Director of Special Programs in the Catholic Adult Education Centre of the Archdiocese of Chicago. Rose developed programmes and sponsored conferences in special areas, including Catholic-Jewish relations, summer biblical institutes, ecumenical relations and black studies.

With the encouragement and financial help of Reverend Louis Luzbetak, Director of the Centre for Applied Research in the Apostolate (CARA), Sr Rose Albert submitted a proposal for a research survey of the inner city activities of religious communities of women, which was accepted. On 1 August 1966, Rose completed the project and presented the results of the research survey in an impressive 85-page publication entitled *The CARA Survey of Inner City Activities of Religious Communities of Sisters: A Preliminary Study*. The principles of renewal suggested by Vatican II in *Perfectae caritatis*, or the Decree on the Appropriate Renewal of the Religious Life, were directly related to this survey research.

Beginning in 1968, each Racine Dominican had the opportunity and responsibility to search out her own individual ministry, one which reflected and promoted the community focus and mission, in dialogue with the community's leadership. While Rose was working in the Chicago archdiocese, she heard about a new position available at Seton Hall University in the Institute of Jewish-Christian Studies. She felt that her background and experience fitted the position, and she was more than ready to focus on this area. The Racine Dominican leadership encouraged Rose to apply to Seton Hall. That was the same year she reassumed her baptismal name, Rose.

AN ENDURING LEGACY

In 1953 Mgr John Oesterreicher founded Seton Hall University's Institute of Judeo-Christian Studies and became its first director.[2] In 1968 he wanted to expand the work of the institute by developing a summer programme for teachers to learn about the history of anti-Semitism, the Holocaust, Israel,

2. For the story of Seton Hall University's Institute of Judeo-Christian Studies and the Sister Rose Thering Fund, see: http://www.shu.edu/academics/artsci/sister-rose-thering/history.cfm (last accessed 12.09.12).

Jews and Judaism. He chose Sr Rose Thering to be the programme co-ordinator for that new position. Given her educational background in Jewish-Christian studies and her keen interest in the Jewish roots of Christianity and the state of Israel, she seemed to be the ideal fit.

Shortly after Sr Rose came to Seton Hall University, she began teaching in the School of Education and worked on developing the programme, which was to be run jointly by the institute and the Anti-Defamation League. Sr Rose believed in the power of teachers, and she was confident that teachers in public, private and parochial schools, with scholarship assistance, would be able to enrol in the Jewish-Christian studies at Seton Hall University and stem the tide of ignorance in schools and in society. In 1970, Sr Rose went on the first of her 54 study trips to Jerusalem, and eventually she studied at Yad Vashem, the Holocaust Memorial Museum there.

In 1975 a masters programme in Judeo-Christian studies was designed and Mgr Oesterreicher became the first chair of the programme. Eventually the institute became the Department of Jewish-Christian Studies. Sr Rose served as professor of secondary education and was also instrumental in establishing the university's department of Jewish–Christian studies. At this time she earned a master's degree in Jewish-Christian studies from Seton Hall University. In 1988 David Bossman PhD, a scholar in Jewish-Christian studies, became the department chair.

Rose continued teaching until 1989 when she retired to become executive director of the National Christian Leadership Conference for Israel (NCLCI).

In the NCLCI position, Sr Rose conducted strategy sessions and conferences to enable Christian leaders from many denominations to become better acquainted with one another and to strengthen each other's efforts. She arranged briefings both in the US and in Israel with government officials and experts on Middle East issues and advocated for US policies that would promote peace, justice and security in that region. She also worked with the major newspapers to publish the statements produced and signed by interfaith leaders and scholars. Letter-writing, emails and phone campaigns to Congress and other political leaders were organised during crises through her New York and Seton Hall offices.

In the 1990s, Sr Rose, Professor David Bossman and a group of friends began discussing the need for teachers to take more courses in Jewish-Christian studies and to work towards a graduate degree so that they could take the significant history and/or interreligious insights they would learn back to their many students. Since tuition costs had always been, and continue today to be, problematic for teachers, the concept of a fund to defray these costs was born. The 'founders' wanted to name it after Sr Rose. She did not agree with such a suggestion, urging other names instead. She was overruled and gave in only because she felt so strongly that a fund should be created to help teachers.

The Sister Rose Thering Endowment (SRTE) was established in 1993 to honour Sr Rose by providing scholarships for teachers of pre-school and primary school children in public, private and parochial schools in New Jersey, so that they could gain graduate education credits in the department of Jewish-Christian studies at Seton Hall University. Later, the SRTE Board officially changed the name to the Sister Rose Thering Fund (SRTF) to reflect its purpose and activity more precisely. The board of the fund has 70 members, reflecting the community at large, as well as an honorary board of present and past elected officials and leaders of both Jewish and Christian communities. The SRTF Board carries out the mandate of the State of New Jersey to teach about the Holocaust in all schools,[3] as well following Pope John Paul II's call to 'teach about the Shoah', so that it may never be forgotten.

The SRTF Board continues to work closely with the Department of Jewish-Christian Studies to assure the continuity of the programme. In its first 17 years (to 2010) nearly 400 teachers had been enrolled in its programmes. The teachers, in turn, have had a significant impact on more than 150,000 students. Each semester the SRTF publishes a course brochure and distributes it through all the New Jersey diocesan school districts, through public and private schools via their superintendents and principals, as well as to several New Jersey education and teacher associations and the New Jersey Commission for Holocaust Studies.

Awards for promoting Jewish-Christian relations, the honorary degree of doctor of humane letters, as well as the 'Humanitarian of the Year Award' are conferred upon individuals who have demonstrated outstanding passion, altruism and courage in various endeavours. Sr Rose Thering is one of those who received an honorary degree of doctor of humane letters in 2000.

Other examples of those honoured at the Evening of Roses[4] include:

---

3. See: http://www.state.nj.us/education/holocaust/about_us/mandate.html (last accessed 12.09.12).

4. 'The Evening of Roses is the major fund raising vehicle for the Sister Rose Thering Fund for Jewish-Christian Studies. Its aim is to promote the Fund's work by honoring outstanding scholars in the field of Jewish-Christian relations and conferring honorary Doctor of Humane Letters as well as Humanitarian of the Year awards upon individuals who have demonstrated outstanding compassion, altruism, and courage in various endeavors.'; see: http://www.shu.edu/academics/artsci/sister-rose-thering/evening-of-roses.cfm (last accessed 12.09.12).

- In 2005, Sylvia and David Steiner for their significant role in helping produce the award-winning short documentary film, *Sr Rose's Passion*, which was shown to a large, receptive audience honouring Sr Rose for her lifetime achievements.
- In 2006, Lee and Toby Cooper, for their generous donation of $1,750,000 towards the establishment of an endowed professorial chair in honour of Sr Rose, who had passed away earlier that year.
- In 2007 Mgr Robert Sheeran, President of Seton Hall University, with the Sister Rose Thering Award for Exemplary Leadership, the highest award available, for his untiring support of the fund and Sr Rose's work.

In 2007 Eric and Lori Ross added their own gift of $1,250,000 to the endowed chair, making it now fully funded at $3 million. The first professor to hold the title of the Cooperman/Ross professorship in Jewish-Christians Studies in memory of Sr Rose was Dr Alan Brill, who began to teach in the first semester of 2007/8.

The Sister Rose Thering Fund and the undergraduate programme in Jewish Christian studies (now part of the Department of Religions) have been called the 'hidden jewels' of Seton Hall University, since this is the only university in the US that offers a master's degree in Jewish-Christian studies. However, they are no longer 'hidden jewels', but rather 'treasures found', since the fund contributes more than $60,000 annually in scholarship funding to the university, and the programme continues to educate teachers and scholars to promote understanding between Christians and Jews.

IN HER OWN WORDS

Even though Sr Rose spent 37 years in New Jersey, she kept in close contact with the members of her Racine Dominican community and her family by phone, letters, emails and regular visits. She kept them up-to-date on her busy life and was always interested in their lives as well. She was an active participant in annual meetings of her community. Several family members, including her mother, and Racine Dominicans were able to travel with her on the Seton Hall study tours to Israel.

Each year, every Racine Dominican sister is expected to write an annual report of her ministry for the past year as well as her plans for the future and to send it to the leadership team. In Rose's 2003 annual report to the Racine Dominican leadership, she expanded on her involvement in interreligious dialogue and also revealed her initial involvement in what would become the film, *Sister Rose's Passion*:

I am responding to the letter that you received from the Dominican Priests in Rome regarding the possibility of creating a permanent committee composed of the brothers and sisters involved in Islamic-Christian ministry in order to promote and sustain the involvement of the order in Islamic-Christian dialogue. I have served on the Archdiocesan Committee for Interreligious Dialogue for 24 years. We are commissioned to have dialogue with the Muslim communities and we do. I served as Consultant and Advisor to the U.S. Bishops' Secretariat for Catholic-Jewish Relations for 20 years. The Leadership Conference of Women Religious invited me to serve on its Committee on Ecumenism and Catholic-Jewish Concerns for 8 years.

At Seton Hall University we have had programs of discussion with representative Imams of the Arab communities. At Drew University we had an entire day devoted to Christian-Islam dialogue. This is of great concern to us.

Just two Sundays ago we had a discussion in New York City with presentations on Judaism, Orthodox and Conservative, Islam, Hindu, Christianity, etc. I gave the introduction and invocation. So you can report to the Dominican fathers that one of the Racine Dominicans is involved in this area in a very special way, serving the Newark Archdiocese. The task is urgent but is not one of conversion of the Muslims but in helping them to be aware of the "love" readings in the Koran. The Arab religion texts also need to be examined as we did ours.

You can see that I am involved with many groups that show my interest in how healthy are our relations with all the world religions.

Last, but not least, I have been asked to have a video done of my commitment to Jewish-Christian studies. A team of professionals have done about six hours of interviewing in New York and at Seton Hall University ... The video will be used in our New Jersey schools, teaching teachers and students about the Holocaust and Jewish–Christian relations. One of the team members will need to raise $400,000 to make this video. All profits from the finished video should be going to Sister Rose Thering Endowment to give tuition assistance to teachers who take courses at Seton Hall in the Department of Jewish–Christian studies. Hence, from this you can see that my mission will continue here at Seton Hall University after I am gone.

The 2003 filming mentioned above resulted in a remarkable award-winning 39-minute film, *Sister Rose's Passion*. This film won the best Documentary Short Film prize at the 2004 Tribeca Film Festival in New York. It was also nominated in 2005 for an Academy Award in the short documentary category. *Sister Rose's Passion* was a production of the New Jersey Studios and Storyville Firms, produced and directed by Oren Jacoby, who is highly respected in the film world. The film-makers returned with Sr Rose to visit the current Racine Dominican motherhouse convent and contrasted it with archival film footage showing the old convent scenes where Rose took her first vows in the 1940s. It traces Rose's courageous lifetime mission to reform Church doctrine and improve Jewish-Christian relations.

Oren Jacoby said, 'At a time when people are willing to use religion for their own calculated political reasons, it's an honour to tell the story of Sr Rose Thering, a true woman of conscience.' This film and an accompanying study guide have been distributed to all middle and high schools in New Jersey. It is also widely distributed in the US by the Anti-Defamation League.

GOING HOME

In November 2005, with her health declining, Rose moved back home to Siena Center in Racine. Even there, her passion and her work continued. She travelled to Hales Corner and gave the last lecture of her life in April 2006, at Sacred Heart School of Theology, less than a month before her death.

Rose's final days were spent at All Saints Medical Center. Even there, the day before she died, Rose rang her bell for the aide. When the aide arrived, Rose invited her to sit down so they could talk a bit and told her she really didn't need anything. When a visitor stepped in, she discovered Rose conversing with the aide about Seton Hall and her mission. Rose did her last preaching at the pulpit of her bed.

Sr Rose Thering, 85, died peacefully in the early morning hours of 6 May 2006, with her friend, Sr Michelle Olley, at her bedside. On the evening of 9 May her funeral celebration was honoured by the presence not only of her family and her Racine Dominican community, but also by her friends and colleagues from New Jersey and New York. Those attending noticed that Rose was wearing her familiar jewellery, a cross fused with the Star of David, a symbol of her life's mission.

Her friend and colleague, Reverend David Bossman of the Graduate Department of Jewish-Christian Studies at Seton Hall, presided and preached at her funeral Mass. The next day Rose was laid to rest at Holy Cross Cemetery. At the graveside, her Jewish friends carried out Rose's wishes to pray Kaddish over her body just before the burial.

REMEMBERING SISTER ROSE

In Seton Hall Archives there is a collection of the media coverage of the life of Sr Rose. A few statements that were published in the New Jersey *Jewish News* on 11 May 2006 follow. She was an amazing woman who received 80 awards during her life.

Mgr Robert Sheeran, President of Seton Hall University, labelled her death 'an immense loss for the entire Seton Hall family, indeed, for all men and women who seek to forge a world of greater understanding. For a half century Rose was an inspired voice of reconciliation and dialogue among Christians and Jews. Her support for the nation of Israel, her determination to root out anti-Semitism wherever it exists and her commitment to educating new generations about the evils of the Holocaust forms her lasting legacy.'

Paul Winkler, Executive Director of the New Jersey Commission on Holocaust Education, remembered Rose as a mentor and a leader, someone who pushed not only for Holocaust education but also for education to make all humanity better.

Luna Kaufman, Chair of the Sister Rose Thering Fund, remarked: 'At first when I met her, I couldn't believe that a Christian would be that passionate about fighting anti-Semitism. Even the Jewish community at first was a little mistrustful about what she was doing, but that mistrust turned into great admiration over the years and the Jewish community feels a tremendous loss. Her leadership is absolutely irreplaceable.'

To be a persevering, passionate person in pursuing a lifelong mission takes a very strong character with unwavering commitment. That was Sr Rose Thering. Her friends in New Jersey experienced Rose as such a woman during her 38 years in that community. Her family knew her as one who was always present or in touch by phone or email when she was needed. Both groups knew her inside out, through and through, and loved her unconditionally. Their presence and testimony at her funeral was a priceless tribute to her.

23

Witnessing in a Multicultural Society: Dominican Sisters in Sweden

MADELEINE FREDELL, O.P.

INTRODUCTION

During an extended general council meeting in 1995, I was dumbfounded when our prioress general addressed me with these challenging words: 'But you are not integrated into Sweden!' For I was Swedish, and, at the time, the majority of the sisters were also of Swedish origin! Just a couple of years later I was prepared to give credence to her surprising statement. We did not mirror the actual situation in the country, and even less did we mirror that of the Catholic Church! In understanding what a process of integration really means, the Dominican sisters in Sweden slowly moved from living *in* a multicultural context to an intercultural life as such *within* their community. At the same time, they revisited their history in the country to better understand their main task as Dominicans today. They realised that their history had prepared them for this kind of intercultural living within a local community.[1]

This essay is an overview of the history of a group of Dominican sisters in Sweden from two particular perspectives. In the first, the way the sisters have handled intercultural encounters in a broad sense, including ecumenical, interfaith and socio-political dialogues, since they were established in Stockholm in 1931, is addressed. The purpose here is to study how the sisters integrated into a new country and how this process developed once the first sisters of Swedish origin had made their final profession. In the second perspective, we look at how the sisters have succeeded or not in being a mirror of the growing Catholic Church since the end of the Second World War. How did the sisters interact with a society that went through both a cultural and social transformation, from a homogeneous religious and ethnic reality to a multicultural and multifaith country in a very short space of time? Some tentative conclusions will be outlined concerning the challenges of an inter-

---

1. As a writer as well as a member of this group of Dominican sisters I am aware that I am interpreting this revisited history from 'inside' and that I cannot possibly be fully objective. Reports, chapter minutes and chronicles have been used as background material.

cultural lifestyle within a religious community today and what might be the way forward for Dominican religious life in this respect.

It is evident that 'intercultural' is a recent concept. It describes how different cultures interact in a particular setting. For a long time we have used 'multicultural' to describe how different cultures co-exist in a specific context. 'Multicultural' did not necessarily mean that interactions took place between the cultures, therefore those who used that term tended not to notice the formation of a 'new' culture as a result of these encounters or lack of them. This essay will outline the interactions that the sisters have had with different cultural phenomena, through ecumenical dialogue, interfaith encounters and action in the political sphere, and how these interactions have modified their own Dominican religious lifestyle.

The essay will only cover the Dominican sisters belonging to St Dominic's Roman Congregation (CRSD),[2] who have been, or are still, living in Sweden. It does not say anything about the other Dominican congregation, present in the south of the country, nor about the Dominican friars.[3]

The very first group of French Dominican sisters who came to Sweden in 1931 had to adapt not only to a new country, culture and language, but also, first and foremost, to a population that was close to 100 per cent Lutheran. This invited them, although it was rather unusual at the time, to an ecumenical outlook from the start, which grew and was broadened, eventually to include all Christian denominations. These first ecumenical contacts were in fact also intercultural and slowly changed the way the sisters were living their Catholic faith and Dominican life.

Since the Second World War, the Catholic Church in Sweden has been steadily growing, with members coming from almost all corners of the planet. Each and every parish is a laboratory of intercultural encounters, with the Swedish language, apart from our shared faith, the only common denominator. Since the year 2000, Dominican sisters in Sweden have tried to live interculturally within their own community, so as to be an integrated part of the Catholic Church in Sweden.

Some of the experiences of the specific community lifestyle that developed from intercultural encounters, and from intercultural living as such, will also be described. Along the way, the sisters have gone through several integration processes, trying to be a mirror of the Catholic Church, while building bridges to Swedish society. The sisters have continually been

2. The official name of the congregation in French is Congrégation Romaine de Saint Dominique and it will be referred to as CRSD.
3. Dominicaines de Sainte-Marie des Tourelles.

searching for ways to respond to the cultural challenges in their surroundings, and not least to the growing secularisation Sweden is experiencing.
Today, these challenges are quite different from those of only 20 years ago.

This essay will try to show both how the sisters have concretised the
motto of Truth and Mercy in their mission in a multicultural context, and
how they have tried to live it in an intercultural way as a community. This
has also been done in relation to the congregation as a whole, which clearly
defined itself as international, as one of its basic characteristics, at its general
chapter in 1987. This had become a fact in the life of the congregation since
the creation of autonomous provinces and vice-provinces in 1966 and 1969.
The sisters living in the different entities of the congregation are Japanese,
Brazilian, Canadian and so on, and they have been relatively free to develop
their own specific lifestyles and missions in order to be faithful to their own
contexts. From 1995 onwards, the impact of the formation and growth of the
network of Dominican Sisters International (DSI), and its regional and local
organisations, has also played an important role in the life of the Swedish
Dominican sisters.

AN INTERTWINED HISTORY OF THE DOMINICAN SISTERS,
THE CATHOLIC CHURCH AND SWEDISH SOCIETY SINCE 1931

The Dominican Sisters of St Dominic's Roman Congregation established a
community in Stockholm in October 1931. There were five sisters who were
the founders: three French, one Swiss and one Belgian,[4] from the Dominican
Congregation of Notre-Dame of the Holy Rosary and of St Thomas Aquinas.[5]
They had been invited to start a community by the apostolic vicar, Bishop
Johannes Erik Müller, and were closely connected to the French Dominican
friars who also established a community in Stockholm in the same year. The
sisters' congregation amalgamated in 1956–57 with four others to form the
current CRSD. These congregations were all of French origin but had mis-
sions in different parts of the world and a large number of local vocations.
This led to the formation of autonomous provinces and vice-provinces after
Vatican II. The sisters in Sweden became a vice-province in 1969.

The sisters had come to a country where there was no religious freedom
and which had only about 5,000 Catholics at that time. There were quite

4. The sisters who have lived and worked in Sweden will not be mentioned by name in this
essay. On the other hand, other persons will usually be identified.
5. The official name in French was the Congrégation Dominicaine de Notre Dame du Saint
Rosaire et de Saint Thomas d'Aquin. This congregation later merged with others to form the
CRSD.

heavy restrictions for non-Lutherans and it was not until 1952 that the law of full religious freedom came into effect. Even if, in their hearts, the sisters, and especially their superiors in France, as well as the Catholic bishop in Stockholm, were focused on proclaiming the Catholic faith, everything they did in their apostolate was also influenced by the idea of spreading French culture. It is worth noting that Sweden had been a country of emigration, not immigration, until the 1930s, and only a very small minority had sufficient language skills to communicate with people from other countries.

The sisters recruited Swedish members almost from the start. Quite a number of well-educated women combined their spiritual search with an interest in French culture, and they were also drawn to the new theological strands emerging in France in the 1940s. However, even with Swedish members in their midst, the Dominican sisters in Stockholm were seen as French for a long period, and the common language in the community was French. According to the testimony of a French sister who died in 2006, French was spoken on a daily basis in the community until 1966! Not without reason, therefore, both religious convents and parishes were seen to be foreign in the eyes of the Swedish population, although most of them were German.

During and after the Second World War the demographic situation changed drastically in Sweden, with a great impact on its Catholic minority. A few Catholic immigrants, mainly from Italy, had come at the beginning of the century, but they did not play an important role, either in society or in the Catholic Church. During and immediately after the war, Sweden received many refugees, a large number of whom were Catholic. Most of them came from European countries and they integrated quickly into Swedish society.

To begin with, the refugees and labour migrants, the latter of whom arrived until 1965, thanks to a government policy encouraging them to do so, did not have any direct influence on the life of the Dominican sisters. The sisters were mainly focused on recruiting young Swedish women and on carrying out a mission to the Catholic minority scattered all over the country. It was only occasionally that the effects of the war years had a direct impact on the lives of the sisters. However, things would take a decisive turn with the revolution in Hungary in 1956 and the subsequent arrival of about 13,000 Hungarian refugees. Quite a few of them settled in the western part of the country, in and around the city of Karlstad. This led to the foundation of a second community of Dominican sisters, and a very conscious mission among newly arrived Catholics in the country. This move coincided with the fact that the number of sisters of Swedish origin had grown considerably.

In the 1950s and 1960s a large number of Swedish intellectuals entered the Catholic Church. There was an interesting osmosis going on during these two decades. It was as if, all of a sudden, the Catholic Church had become a force to be reckoned with from a Swedish perspective. It was no longer a small and totally foreign minority. The immigrants arriving to answer the needs of the labour market were claiming their rights, and some of the Swedish Catholics were already well known through the mass media. The impact of Vatican II, not only as it concerned ecumenical and interfaith theology, but also in its more general theological achievements, not least in ecclesiology and the dialogue with the world in a broad sense, also had a strong influence on the Swedish Lutheran Church. This gave way to new ecumenical projects in which the Dominican sisters were involved from early on.

Sweden was not marked by the political events of 1968–69 to the same extent as other countries in Europe. Even if both the outcome of Vatican II and the 1968 revolution had considerable implications for the lives of the Dominican sisters in France, it would take another five to ten years before any deep consequences were felt in the lives of the sisters in Sweden.

On the other hand, the impact of the Fourth General Assembly of the World Council of Churches in Uppsala in 1968 was groundbreaking for ecumenical life in Sweden and consequently changed the lifestyle of the sisters in many ways. The Dominican sisters took an active part in a number of events in Uppsala, and it quite clearly changed their mission as a community.

From the 1970s onwards, waves of political refugees have obtained asylum in Sweden and transformed the religious map of the country in a radical way. After the military coup in Chile in 1973, around 14,000 Chileans arrived, followed by other Latin Americans fleeing political turmoil and persecution on their continent. In the middle of the 1970s about 16,000 Christians of different denominations came from Turkey and the Middle East. Roughly 5,000 Vietnamese obtained political asylum at the beginning of the 1980s. To this we should add thousands of Eritreans, Iraqis and Iranians. During the war in the former Yugoslavia, close to 85,000 refugees came to Sweden, although a large number of them eventually returned to their former countries. Since the 1990s, refugees mainly from Iraq, Iran and Somalia have arrived, and continue to do so.

Taking a look at different studies on future trends done by the Dominican sisters in Sweden or evaluating the restructuring of their entity since the 1970s, we find that they have always tried to interact with the changes in the surrounding society. However, this interaction did not always have an immediate or direct influence on the sisters' own lifestyle. Most interactions in the late 1970s and the 1980s were either in relation to people affected by a secularised society and an uprooted personal or family history, or in relation to a 'Swedish' ecumenism, or in supporting new organisations within the Catholic diocese.

Studying the Catholic Diocese of Stockholm, which covers the whole country, it is only during recent years that its leadership has, in any deep sense, reflected on, and taken action in regard to, the urgent and new inter-cultural situation. Today, the Catholic Church in Sweden comprises 12 linguistic missions of the Latin Rite, a vicariate of Oriental Catholic Churches with five different rites, and, in addition to this, there is the Gheez Rite with, of course, the Latin Rite in Swedish. The bridge-building between all these groups, including the Swedish one, is still rather weak but is well on its way.

The leadership of the Catholic Diocese of Stockholm approached the vice-province of Dominican sisters in 1997, encouraging them to found a new community in an area of significant immigration in the west or south of the country. They also offered help in inviting sisters from other Dominican congregations, from countries represented among the refugees, as partners in collaboration. This led to visits to Iraq in 1999 and Vietnam in early 2000. As a result of these visits, contracts of collaboration were drawn up between the Dominican congregations in these countries, the Swedish vice-province and the Catholic Diocese of Stockholm.

Today, there are two main groups within the Catholic Diocese of Stockholm, one from the Middle East, mostly from Iraq, using a non-Latin Rite liturgy, and another belonging to the Latin Rite. There are up to one hundred different languages spoken within the whole Catholic Church in Sweden. At this point, the Swedish Catholic Youth Movement is the only Catholic organisation where interaction takes place between these groups on a daily basis. All of the three Iraqi Dominican sisters who live and work with the Swedish Dominican sisters are engaged in this intercultural work, with a wide diversity of activities all over the country.

FIRST INTEGRATION PROCESS:
BUILDING BRIDGES THE FRENCH WAY
To make their living, the Dominican sisters opened a hostel for students and young professional women in central Stockholm in 1939, soon after they arrived. They also started two groups where young girls and women, both

Protestant and Catholic, would meet to discuss French poetry and art, as well as social, youth and women's issues. Despite the fact that everything took place in French, it was a unique endeavour from an ecumenical perspective, as there were no other meeting-places between the two denominations at that time. Over the years, the composition of these groups changed and developed into several others, including more specialised ones.

As can be expected, the sisters were not working for ecumenism in a conscious way in the early 1930s. Nevertheless, they certainly laid the groundwork on which the Swedish sisters could continue to do so later on. The French-speaking sisters were remarkably open to learning about their new country and the Swedish Lutheran Church. The young Protestant women, who wanted to practise their French and know more about French culture and spirituality, became, in their turn, doors into the Lutheran culture. In the sisters' archives we also find notices of meetings between the Dominican sisters and the Lutheran deaconesses in Stockholm and with officers in the Salvation Army. Still, we must admit that the chronicles also show a kind of self-sufficient attitude among the sisters, echoing the official tone of the Catholic Church at that time.

The sisters also offered courses in liturgical Latin, Thomistic philosophy and, above all, in the French language. With the return of the two first Swedish-born sisters in 1940, after their formation in France and Switzerland, Swedish literature and culture in a broader sense were introduced, and a real integration process started. In the same year, the community was established as a regular convent, giving the sisters larger autonomy. By 1949, one of the Swedish sisters had been elected prioress, reinforcing the processes of inculturation that were already in action.

It is clear that the sisters dealt with an elite in Swedish society, never doing any direct social work among the poor in Stockholm. At the same time, the ecumenical and intercultural value of their work should not be underestimated. During the 1950s, the sisters prepared young adults to present stage plays in French, such as *Dialogues des Carmélites*, with complete scenery and costumes. On one occasion, a comedy was reviewed, in a very positive way, in one of the biggest daily newspapers. It was certainly a surprise to the wider Swedish public that religious sisters would train young people in this way, and organise this kind of entertainment.

It was the Second World War and the arrival of refugees in Sweden that started to change the focus of the sisters. During the war they received some refugees from Poland and Finland in their student hostel. There is a special notice in the chronicles of a Mass in the sisters' chapel for the Polish refugees, just at the time of the outbreak of war. At the end of the war, the prioress went to the south of the country to meet French women who had been rescued from concentration camps by the Swedish Red Cross. This was the closest they had come so far to a new reality slowly installing itself in Sweden in 1945, but it would quickly grow and influence the Catholic Church in the country.

During the 1950s, the work and life of the Dominicans was flourishing. The hostel was well known, and was also used as a guesthouse when the young women were on holidays with their families. The convent was not only a French cultural centre; it had quickly become a study centre as well, where famous international theologians, historians and social workers stayed during congresses in Stockholm. The sisters used these occasions both for their own ongoing formation and for public lectures and debate. This contributed to a change in the outlook of the Catholic Church in Sweden and led to new ecumenical encounters. For a culturally homogeneous country like Sweden this meant that the convent of the sisters had become an international meeting place, even if the sisters themselves would not have defined it as such at the time.

In 1956, the sisters and the whole Dominican family celebrated 25 years of presence in the country. A quick look at the programme of the jubilee, which took place over four days, points clearly to the achievements of the sisters thus far. The keynote speech was given by one of the Swedish sisters on the theme of *Veritas*. This was unique from many points of view. Firstly, one of the Dominican friars could easily have been appointed to do this, as they were celebrating the jubilee together with the sisters. Secondly, even in Sweden at that time, there would have been few women theologians available to give public lectures at all. It was not until 1958 that the first women were ordained priests in the Lutheran Church. The sister who delivered the speech had completed a theological degree at the University of Uppsala. Thirdly, the whole Dominican family, around 60 persons in total, obtained the permission of the Lutheran parish priest in Sigtuna to celebrate Mass in the Lutheran parish church, the Maria Church, on the last day of the jubilee. The church had been built by the Dominicans in 1247, together with the adjacent medieval convent. This was a groundbreaking ecumenical achievement at the time, and the Mass itself had to be celebrated behind locked doors. After this, they all went to a big restaurant and continued the celebrations in a more public way. Since then, several Dominican events have taken place in this church in Sigtuna but now they are always together with the Lutheran parish!

The internal lifestyle of the sisters did not differ in any important way from the one that was common in the rest of the congregation. However, even early on, they benefited from some dispensations. They were allowed to leave the convent for their apostolate to a much greater extent than was usual in any other community in the congregation. The Swedish-born sisters had also obtained permission to visit their families, which was not common at that time. This was a very conscious decision, in order to build confidence between Catholics and Lutherans, especially as almost all Swedish-born sisters came from Lutheran families. As a community, they would also take time to walk in the public parks and gardens, and even in the forests, in and around Stockholm. They also spent a week of holidays together in a summer cottage, something quite unique for religious sisters in those days. In addition to this, the Swedish sisters were allowed to take a swim in the summer.

These details might sound rather unimportant, but they highlight two important differences between the situation of the sisters in Sweden and the rest of the congregation that would develop into an updated form of religious life long before the effects of Vatican II. Firstly, the work with the student hostel within the premises of the convent never took on such dimensions as to prevent the sisters from responding to appeals from the Catholic parishes, as well as from society as a whole. This was something new for a congregation that had a rather strong monastic tradition, and opened up new areas of the apostolate. It also required an open spirit on the part of the sisters, and a willingness to learn about new and different ways of understanding faith and culture. Secondly, the dispensations also supported the sisters in their personal development and work. The demands from the surrounding society were such that they could never rely on one another to help in the execution of different apostolic assignments. They simply had to work on an individual basis. This was an early, pre-Vatican II 'emancipation'.

SECOND INTEGRATION PROCESS:
BUILDING BRIDGES THE SWEDISH WAY

Even if the Swedish language was not regularly spoken in the community of the sisters until 1966, we can already sense a certain alteration in their approach to the surrounding culture by the late 1950s. They were invited to participate in several ecumenical contexts. They conducted morning prayers in state schools, or gave lectures on the Catholic faith in the context of religious education. The French Dominican theologians Yves Congar and Marie-Dominique Chenu were invited to the community, where they introduced the sisters to a new ecumenical theology that would eventually be taken up in the official teaching of the Catholic Church at Vatican II. Three sisters also took part in a specialist course on Luther in 1958–59.

With the second community in Karlstad, founded in 1956, and the combined effects of Vatican II, the Fourth General Assembly of the World Council of Churches in Uppsala in 1968, and the student upheavals of the same year, French hegemony in the community was definitively broken down. The complete consequences of this would not become fully apparent until the second half of the 1970s, but fundamental changes were already taking place during the late 1950s and the 1960s.

The foundation of the community in Karlstad had given the sisters the opportunity to engage in a new kind of pastoral work among immigrants in Sweden. In 1956, the Catholic parish in Karlstad had around one thousand members, of whom 950 had arrived from 14 different countries. They were mostly refugees and had arrived since the end of the war or because of the political consequences of the division of Europe into East and West. The sisters did social, as well as catechetical, work among Hungarians, Poles, Germans, Czechs, Dutch, Austrians and Lithuanians. This apostolate most definitely changed the lifestyle of the sisters, although they were not aware of this until many years later. Some of them had to take driving lessons, since they had to buy a car to be able to reach the various parts of a parish that was bigger than Belgium. The readiness to travel that one sees among the sisters in Sweden has its origin here.

The sisters also continued some of the more intellectual activities that characterised the convent in Stockholm. They held language courses, but now they were teaching English, Italian and German, as well as French. This had become possible with the arrival of one sister from Italy and another one from a German-speaking part of Switzerland. One of the Swedish sisters was also employed in a state high school to teach Latin and French. This was a consequence of the new law on religious freedom coming into effect. It was also in this region that the sisters became involved in ecumenical encounters on the local level between the Catholic and the Lutheran Churches and also with one of the free churches of the reformed tradition. And this was all before Vatican II!

In Karlstad it was natural for the sisters to speak Swedish in daily life. The new convent was still an international meeting place but of a totally different kind from the one in Stockholm. Here they had to meet with refugees and socially marginalised people, as well as with a working-class Swedish population. From 1962 to 1974, an English Benedictine served as parish priest, introducing the sisters to the Catholic Church in England. From this time onwards, one of the Swedish sisters regularly went to a Dominican convent in London to practise her English.

It was at this point that the sisters came into closer contact with the Dominican friars, nuns and sisters in Oslo,[6] as the distance from Karlstad to Oslo was shorter than the distance to Stockholm. This led to inter-Nordic collaboration between the different Dominican branches. There were regular meetings until the beginning of the 1980s, and an attempt to restart them was made in the early 1990s, mainly among the sisters. The whole Dominican family has only come together on a few occasions since the 1980s.

In the early 1970s we read the following from a community project in Karlstad: 'In our community life we want to take advantage of the richness of our different national origins.' At that point, the community comprised eight sisters from five different countries. This is the first time that we see the sisters becoming aware of being an intercultural reality within the community, and that living this reality is a mission in itself. Despite this, as time goes by and the implications of Vatican II influence the life of the community, there are also growing tensions among the sisters. Experiences of an intercultural lifestyle in a multicultural context were not common at this time, and there was not much support or understanding from superiors in these matters.

The community in Stockholm continued a more traditional way of living the Dominican mission. With more young Swedish sisters returning after their formation in France, Italy and Belgium, apostolic activities were broadening in the second half of the 1960s and the beginning of the 1970s. The Catholic publishing sector was growing, as was the catechetical area, and ecumenical work took on a more formal structure. The sisters were actively promoting all these sectors and were highly appreciated by the Swedish public.

Without making too much of this, we can see more of a tendency at this time in the Stockholm community to focus on Swedish Catholics, and on a general Swedish Christian public in Stockholm, than was present in the community in Karlstad. The latter had become a mirror of the surround-

---

6. The sisters in Oslo belong to the congregation of the Dominicaines de Notre-Dame de Grâce.

ing society, characterised by immigration. The community in Stockholm was still marked by a French culture, while the sisters in Karlstad, in some way, used their different national origins to become more Swedish, even if they also engaged more directly with the newcomers in the country.

A crucial step in the integration process was taken in 1967 when the sisters in both communities changed from Latin to Swedish when praying the daily office. This was easily effected, as the Swedish Lutheran Church could already offer the necessary translation with music. Praying Lauds, Vespers and Compline has a long tradition in the Lutheran Church in Sweden.

During the second half of the 1960s, the sisters also tried to respond to the call of Vatican II. They regularly participated in official ecumenical celebrations from 1966 onwards, as in the Week of Prayer for Christian Unity and the International Women's Day of Prayer. Justice and Peace issues are also mentioned regularly in the chronicles from 1966 onwards, although this subject was not treated by the congregation as a whole until the 1987 General Chapter. One of the sisters was also preaching a retreat as early as 1966.

During the 1974 canonical visitation of the community in Stockholm by the prioress general of the congregation, a Spanish sister, it seems to have been regarded as normal that she should spend almost a whole day with the Lutheran parish priest, Reverend Margit Sahlin, who was the first woman to be ordained a priest in 1958. In her visitation report, the prioress general wrote half a page on this experience and expressed her joy and gratitude in knowing more about the parish in which the sisters were living. She was greatly impressed by the collaboration that had been established between the sisters and the Lutheran parish, and wanted the rest of the congregation to know about it.

A new project was undertaken in 1969 at the initiative of the Catholic Diocese of Stockholm. The sisters were asked to run the diocesan centre, Marielund, situated 30 kilometres to the west of Stockholm, on one of the islands in Lake Mälaren. Three or four sisters from the community in Stockholm would spend an extended weekend at Marielund caring for, and sometimes also moderating, groups. The project continued in this form for ten years and, in 1979, it was time to open a third community at Marielund.

From the beginning of the 1970s the sisters engaged in all kinds of preaching activities. They gave public lectures in churches of all Christian denominations, participated in debates, gave interviews, preached on television and radio, and published books and articles in both ecclesial and secular contexts. In the project of the vice-province from 1975, the sisters stated that their intra-ecclesial mission sometimes needed to take second place, with priority given to providing trustworthy witness to Christian faith and life to non-believers and the religiously indifferent.

Marielund became a more-or-less totally Swedish project, especially during the 1980s. It was also established as a novitiate for the Swedish sisters. The sisters did everything from cooking, gardening and moderating groups. Roughly a thousand people would visit the house each year, for one reason or another. The community offered courses in Zen-inspired meditation, study weekends in theology, not least in feminist theology, as well as discussion weekends on justice and peace issues. The participants were almost exclusively Swedish, and the majority belonged to Protestant denominations or did not have any religious affiliation at all. Groups who came with their own leaders were also Swedish. The sisters assigned to the community from 1979 onwards were Swedish, with one or two exceptions.

On the one hand, Marielund became a kind of showcase for the Catholic Church in Sweden. This was the *Swedish* Catholic Church! On the other hand, over a period of more than 20 years, Marielund attracted neither the older immigrants nor the newer ones. It was certainly an important place for people with existential questions but it never functioned as an intercultural meeting place.

Looking back on that period, it can be seen that at the beginning of the 1980s the sisters had arrived at a stage in their Dominican history in Sweden where the three communities mirrored the surrounding society in three different ways. Stockholm was still a cultural centre, with a strong French touch to it; Karlstad was living and working interculturally, with a burgeoning awareness of this, while Marielund was consciously Swedish.

A SWEDISH CATHOLIC CHURCH OR A CATHOLIC CHURCH IN SWEDEN?
During the 1980s the Dominican sisters in Sweden were consciously striving to become Swedish, and also emphasising the development of a *Swedish* Catholic Church. Marielund benefited from strong support from the vice-province. The community in Karlstad had to close in 1983. The vice-province had not foreseen this, and did not look for it, but a conflict with a new parish priest had taken on a character such that the best solution seemed to be that of moving the sisters to a new project.

The next step was to reinforce their ecumenical work, so the sisters in Karlstad were invited to found a community in Rättvik, at a Lutheran retreat and meditation centre. While this meant a close ecumenical collaboration, it also cut off the intercultural contact with which the sisters had earlier been engaged in Karlstad. At the time, this was never expressed as a problem in any formal document, but sisters sometimes complained that they were missing this specific pastoral work.

To a certain degree, the Catholic Church became Swedish in the 1980s, at least in a limited geographical area, mainly in the three largest cities and in the university cities of Uppsala and Lund. Many Swedes were introduced to a Catholic spirituality translated into Swedish, not least through the publishing activities of some of the religious communities. Both at Marielund and in Rättvik, many people would take part in the daily prayer life of the sisters, and this was also the case in several other places where religious communities were present. The Dominican sisters also continued to present new international theological literature to the Swedish public, not least within the area of feminist theology. In 1984, the community at Marielund started a series of booklets called *Women in the Church: Contributions to a Catholic View*, and the weekends on feminist theology attracted both Catholics and Protestants, including a number of Lutheran women preparing for the priesthood. One Dominican sister represented the Catholic diocese in a commission that was working on a common hymn-book for several Christian denominations. In 1987, it was approved and published and is still in use in the Catholic Church at the time of writing. A number of new organisations were established by the Catholic diocese in the 1980s, among them the Swedish Justice and Peace Commission, which was headed by a Dominican sister from the start.

It would be too early to draw the conclusion that the Catholic Church had finally become rooted in Sweden during this decade. Maybe it could be said that it had become a little less exotic and a little less foreign. The Catholic diocese was represented by a number of Swedish-born persons, not least in the ecumenical area. Some small groups, like the Dominican sisters, had become inculturated, in the sense that they were really rooted in the country. Nevertheless, the number of Catholics from other national origins still constituted a large majority. Many new nationalities were also arriving in the country, not only Catholics but also Orthodox and Oriental Christians, as well as Muslims. Swedish society had drastically changed between the beginning of the 1970s and the 1990s, while the Catholic Diocese of Stockholm and the Dominican sisters had become, somewhat ironically, more and more Swedish.

The official recognition of the work of the Dominican sisters in Sweden was the doctorate in theology that was awarded *honoris causa* to one of the

Swedish sisters by the University of Uppsala in 1989. The reason was that she had 'actively worked to introduce a Dominican perspective into Swedish cultural life', and she responded with a lecture on the usefulness of a practical and living theology in contemporary society. We can view this event as the culmination of the interaction between secular society, recognising the richness of a Catholic, and in this case Dominican, cultural contribution, and the Catholic community, which had become open to dialogue with Swedish society in a comprehensible way.

It was also in 1989 that Pope John Paul II made a pastoral visit to the Nordic countries. This was exceptional from both religious and political points of view. All these countries had strong socialist groupings, a widespread secular culture, and an established Lutheran Church. Nevertheless, the pope was highly acclaimed by the population, Christian as well as secular, in all five countries during his visit. In the eyes of the population in general, the Catholic Church in Sweden reached its apogee around the end of the 1980s and the beginning of the 1990s. Since then its popularity has declined considerably.

The main challenge for the vice-province at the end of the 1980s and the beginning of the 1990s was to respond faithfully to a new face of the Catholic Church in the country, and to a society in stark transformation. The fall of the Berlin Wall in 1989 led to new contacts between Sweden and its close neighbours, not least the Baltic States. This was also the beginning of the end of Sweden as a neutral state and of the more than 40-year political hegemony of the Social Democrats. Joining the European Union in 1995 was a cultural break for Sweden, almost like the falling of a cultural iron curtain that so far had protected a homogeneous Lutheran population and a Swedish welfare model. European integration, globalisation and capitalism were rapidly transforming Swedish society.

The Catholic diocese in Sweden took a very active part in the First European Ecumenical Assembly in Basel in 1989, on the theme Peace with Justice. It had its clear focus on the divide between East and West in Europe. A Swedish Dominican sister was part of the delegation of the Catholic Diocese of Stockholm, and Dominicans from all over Europe also participated in the meeting. Dominican sisters from Sweden were also part of the official delegations at the Second Assembly in Graz in 1997 and at the Third Assembly in Sibiu in 2009. 1989 signified a new and wider European outlook for the Swedish Dominican sisters, both from a religious point of view and from a political perspective. Everything that happened in 1989 was a good preparation for what would take place during the first half of the 1990s.

The arrival of immigrants and refugees from the 1970s onwards had radically changed the religious map of Sweden. It also transformed the face of the Catholic Church, albeit at a slower pace. It was a surprise to many Catholics that all of a sudden the face of the Catholic Church in Sweden was not only 'Latin', but also 'Oriental', with a considerable number of Chaldeans, Syrian Catholics, Maronites and Melchites. A legitimate question was how far the Catholic Church should become *Swedish* in this new situation. Would it not be more justifiable to develop a *Catholic* Church in Sweden, underlining its catholicity from both theological and cultural aspects? And how should the vice-province of Dominican sisters respond to this period of transformation? At that time they were probably one of the most deeply rooted Swedish Catholic groups in the country.

SWEDISH DOMINICAN SISTERS OR DOMINICAN SISTERS IN SWEDEN?
The three-year mandate between 1988 and 1991 was a crucial turning point in the history of the vice-province. The most thoroughgoing decision was to sell the house in Stockholm with its student hostel and cultural centre and close its community. The building was in great need of renovation and did not fulfil the regulations for a hostel anymore. As the sisters were growing older, they considered it was no longer possible to continue working there, even under modernised conditions. In 1988, the community in Rättvik was also closed, mostly due to the fact that the sisters wanted to do other things, and because they felt too isolated in the countryside.

In 1990, a complete restructuring took place, with two new communities besides Marielund, one in the central part of Stockholm, in the form of a number of apartments in one and the same building at Västmannagatan, and the other in a developing suburb, Märsta, close to the international airport of Stockholm. The community at Västmannagatan would continue some of the activities that had been carried out before in Stockholm, like the courses in the French language and culture, as they had also acquired a meeting hall in the same building.

The project that had been elaborated for Märsta changed drastically during its first year of existence because of the bankruptcy of a new technological centre planned to occupy the space between the airport and the residential area of Märsta. The dream had been to offer 'a soul' to this new technological area and also to help with the chaplaincy at the airport. Instead, the mission-challenge would be a small group of Catholics from all over the world that did not have a space of their own to celebrate Mass, or any other sort of meeting place in Märsta.

The Catholics in Märsta formed a microcosm of the Catholic Church in Sweden at the beginning of the 1990s. The sisters organised regular Sunday Masses, catechesis for the preparation of first communicants, and social events. After some time, they became annexed to one of the parishes in the city centre of Stockholm. The experiences from the work in Karlstad of building up a parish of geographically and culturally scattered Catholics was invaluable, as were their ecumenical contacts when it came to gaining access to a Lutheran church for Masses and social events. However, the Catholics did not come from Europe this time, but from Latin America, Africa and the Middle East. And there were new ecumenical contacts to make with the Syrian Orthodox, who also made up a considerable part of the local population.

To start with, the sisters in the community of Märsta were of Swedish origin. They considered themselves to be bridge-builders in a multicultural context. There were very few Swedish Catholics in Märsta and the sisters had to handle a number of non-European cultures with their own liturgical customs and create a unity from this surprising diversity.

Another restructuring of the vice-province took place in 1994, four years after the previous one. During the intervening years, it had become evident that the vice-province could no longer maintain three communities. The decision was taken to continue with Västmannagatan and Märsta and return to the way Marielund was run from 1969 to 1979, as a weekend project, but with the addition of some help from several employees.

An interest in interreligious dialogue had started with the Zen-inspired meditation learned and taught by some of the sisters. Contact had been made with Buddhism already in the early 1970s, at least on an intellectual level. This was then deepened during the 1980s and 1990s, including visits and longer stays in Japan, especially by one of the sisters. She also wrote her doctoral dissertation on the spiritual dialogue with Zen Buddhism in 1998. In addition to this, some sisters have been active in the Swedish Jewish-Christian Council. As a follow-up to the interfaith meeting in Assisi in 1986, the community at Marielund organised an interreligious weekend with participants from the Jewish, Muslim, Buddhist and Hindu communities in 1989. This was something quite new in a Swedish religious context at that time. One sister also took the initiative to establish a Commission for Interreligious Dialogue in the Catholic Diocese in 1998.

But it was in Märsta that the more social aspects of interfaith dialogue with Islam were developed on the local level. To start with, this was a collaborative effort between the immigration office of the municipality, the Syrian Orthodox community, the Muslims living in Märsta and the Dominican sisters. The initiative came from the municipal authorities when they turned to the Dominican community in Brussels to invite a Dominican friar and sister to help with building dialogue and understanding between the different religious communities in Märsta. The friar, Br Khalil Kochassarly, was of Iraqi origin, and the sister, Marianne Goffoël, was from the congregation of Missionnaires de Notre-Dame de Fichermont, and had lived in Iraq with the Iraqi Dominican sisters for several years. This became the starting point of a deep relationship with the Iraqi Dominican sisters that is still ongoing.

From an academic point of view, one sister submitted a dissertation for a PhD in 1990, comparing the religious identity over two generations of two sampled groups, Croats and Swedish converts, within the Catholic Church in Sweden. In 1993, the same sister published her research on religion, ethnicity and European integration, having visited a number of European institutes and organisations related to one or other Christian denomination and engaged in various interactions on a political, ecumenical and interfaith level. Both these studies are typical of Swedish interests at that time, when Swedish society was looking towards its membership in the European Union.

In many ways, it was in the 1990s that the vice-province of Dominican sisters began to wake up to the transformation that had taken place in the society around them. Interactions with other faiths and with political groups, with different immigrant groups, and a wider ecumenism, grew and intensified every year. Here we may mention only very few of their wide range of interactions with others in the 1990s, interactions that had a direct impact on their life.

Two Justice and Peace projects engaged the vice-province directly. The first one was small and local, and concerned mostly the sisters at Marielund. It had already started during the second half of the 1980s. The sisters were connected to an ecumenical movement that both imported and sold craft products from co-operatives in developing countries, and the sisters put up a small shop in collaboration with this movement. At the same time they organised sessions aimed at raising awareness of the structural injustices within the system of international trade.

In the second project, the vice-province committed itself to supporting local development projects financially, in collaboration with Dominican sisters' provinces in Brazil and Benin, through Caritas Sweden. This not only led to new contacts within the CRSD, but it also meant that some sisters travelled to these places to see and appreciate the work that was taking place in the field. These projects continued for almost a decade.

A wider international, and a more specifically European, awareness among the sisters in the vice-province, and the recruitment of sisters with other cultural backgrounds into their midst, now led to new collaborations and interactions with other Dominican sisters. Since the sisters had left Karlstad in 1983 there had been only a few contacts with the Catholic Church in England, and even less with the English Dominican sisters. This changed from 1994 when the contacts were renewed, first with the English Dominican Congregation of St Catherine of Siena, with its generalate in Stone, Staffordshire, and, a bit later, with the congregation of St Catherine of Siena of Newcastle, Natal, South Africa, with its generalate in Bushey, Hertfordshire.[7] In fact, the Stone Dominicans had a community in Bodö in northern Norway, but as there had only been a few occasions for the whole Dominican family in the Nordic countries to come together, relations with this group of sisters were almost non-existent at the beginning of the 1990s.

There were two more or less immediate issues that pushed the sisters of the vice-province to contact the Stone congregation. First, the sisters were looking for English-speaking possibilities for their ongoing formation, as it became more and more difficult to do this in the French context of the congregation. Secondly, new members needed relations with other young Dominican sisters with whom they could share in a language other than French. The vice-province became a member of the Dominican Association of the British Isles and Ireland, which offered regular sessions on theological and Dominican topics. In 1995–96 the vice-province was also part of the joint-novitiate of Stone and Bushey, and sent one novice to do her novitiate with sisters from these two congregations in England.

A number of other collaborative efforts at this time enlarged the international outlook of the sisters in Sweden. One sister was a member of the International Justice and Peace Commission of the Dominican Order between 1993 and 1999, with the special task to promote Justice and Peace issues in the Dominican family in Northern Europe. This led to a European Dominican session on labour market issues in Ireland in 1996, organised together with ESPACES, the Dominican organisation that tries to respond to the challenges of European integration.

7. The two congregations will be referred to as 'Stone' and 'Bushey'.

The Maria Church in Sigtuna celebrated its 750th jubilee in 1997, and the Dominican sisters were invited to share in the festivities with the Lutheran parish. As this was a unique ecumenical event, the vice-province invited members of the Dominican family from northern Europe to take part in a session on Dominican spirituality in Sigtuna, with Fr Tom Jordan and Sr Marian O'Sullivan, both from Ireland, as keynote speakers. About 60 Dominicans participated in the four-day seminar.

During the 1990s, Sweden became part of the European Union. This was a period of learning on the international level for the Dominican sisters in Sweden. Even if the majority of the sisters were of Swedish origin, they realised that they could no longer act in a monocultural way if they were to be credible from a Catholic point of view, let alone from the perspective of the Gospel. These insights were not voiced at the time, but circumstances emanating from this reality would soon have decisive consequences in the life of the vice-province. The former tendency to emphasise the *Swedish* character of the life and work of the sisters was definitely over. The sisters had become Dominican sisters in Sweden.

TOWARDS A NEW FACE OF THE CATHOLIC CHURCH
AND OF THE DOMINICAN SISTERS, IN SWEDEN
The need for structural change was quickly realised at the end of the 1990s. On the one hand, there were some new vocations, not only of Swedish origin. Over a couple of years, one young woman came from South Korea, after having completed some years of university studies in Sweden; another had an English background, while a third had grown up in Syria, although she was of Armenian origin; a fourth was Swedish. The arrival of these women led to the decision to establish a house of formation at Västmannagatan in Stockholm, and to appoint a mistress of novices.

Even if the numbers of younger sisters seemed to be increasing, there were also sisters growing older, and some were suffering from serious illnesses. There was a large generation gap, as well as new intercultural challenges within the group of sisters. In 1999, the decision was taken to leave the diocesan centre at Marielund and to put new energy into an 'open house' project at Västmannagatan.

In the same year, the previous recent contacts with the Dominican sisters from different congregations in England and Ireland resulted in a regional collaboration within the structure of Dominican Sisters International (DSI). DSI had its first constitutional meeting in 1995 and its second general assembly in 1998, when over 80 Dominican congregations took part. In many parts of the world, there already existed organisations of collaboration between Dominican sisters, such as in Latin and North America, or within linguistic zones like Italy, France, Spain and German-speaking Europe. But many Dominican sisters were not affiliated to any regional or linguistic grouping and needed to build up some sort of structure. This was true for many countries in Northern Europe and also for Europe as a continent. The Stone Dominican sisters and the Swedish vice-province of CRSD took the initiative to invite all those regional Dominican groups in Europe that could communicate in English to a founding meeting of the English Speaking Zone (ESPZ) of Dominican sisters in Europe in 1999. This was one of the last events that the sisters facilitated at Marielund. The ESPZ includes Dominican congregations in Ireland, England, the Netherlands, Norway and Sweden.

As mentioned earlier, the Catholic Diocese of Stockholm and the Dominican sisters of the Swedish vice-province were now making contact with Dominican sisters in Iraq and Vietnam to see if they latter could send some sisters to Sweden to work with Catholic refugees and immigrants. During the general assembly of DSI in 1998, one of the sisters of the vice-province had the opportunity to meet one of the Dominican prioresses general from Vietnam, as well as with the prioress general of the Dominican sisters in Iraq. It was with great enthusiasm that the Catholic Diocese of Stockholm, the sisters in Iraq and Vietnam and the Swedish vice-province drew up the main lines for this new project.

The first three sisters arrived during the second half of the year 2000, two from Iraq and one from Vietnam, and, together with the young sisters in formation, there were two quite lively communities in Stockholm and Märsta that started a new journey in the history of the vice-province. The report to the vice-provincial chapter in June 2001 speaks of a fresh start and a deep hope of becoming a better mirror of the Catholic Church in Sweden and of reaching out to people from many different cultures. The goal was expressed of promoting a new culture in Sweden. But behind the enthusiasm there was also a shadow: the health problems and the advanced age of some of the sisters.

Obviously, the Dominican sisters and the Catholic Church in Sweden are two very different kinds of entity, but it is not totally wrong to compare them from a cultural perspective. The famous Swedish converts from the 1940s to 1960s were growing old and did not play the same role any longer. The leading sisters of the 1950s to 1970s were also ageing and, even if they still enjoyed great influence in the community, they would no longer take the initiative in any new projects. In the Church, new people had arrived from all over the world and the receiving partner was now too small and weak to offer a stable community in which to settle. The generation that had taken over in the vice-province during the 1990s and the first years of the new millennium was also very small in number and had to fulfil many different roles at the same time: caring for the older generation, forming the younger ones, continuing their own theological formation, working professionally and taking on leadership. It was no longer a very stable community into which the younger ones or the sisters from Iraq and Vietnam could settle. Enthusiasm and hope were strong, both in the Church and in the religious community, but there was a tendency not to take the deeper cultural differences sufficiently seriously, and some problems and tensions were not attended to in time.

HOW TO MIRROR A NEW CULTURE IN SOCIETY AND CHURCH:
EXPERIENCES OF INTERCULTURAL COMMUNITY LIFE

In 2003, it was time for another restructuring of the Swedish vice-province. A second sister from Vietnam was about to arrive and a third sister from Iraq. The Catholic Diocese of Stockholm had renewed its request that the vice-province found a new community in some area with significant immigration. There were different opinions regarding whether it was opportune to respond to such a request. Overarching questions among the sisters were: How to live a visible and attractive Dominican life? In which setting could this be best done? There was still a dream of a life like the one at Marielund that had been more conducive to the contemplative side of the Dominican life. It was difficult to realise this in central Stockholm or in Märsta, where the sisters were engaged in work and activities in all kinds of sectors and all over the country, sometimes even over the whole of Europe. Travelling and absences added neither to the visibility nor to the attractiveness of Dominican community life! But this was obviously part of postmodern society, even if it was not easy to handle.

In 2002 the Catholic Diocese of Stockholm made a formal request to the vice-province to move to the diocesan centre at Johannesgården in a suburb of Gothenburg, the second largest city in the western part of Sweden. This corresponded with some of the aspirations among the sisters. It would be a setting similar to Marielund, although not in the countryside but in a suburb with quite a few Christians from the Middle East and Vietnam. It would offer the possibility to develop an apostolate in which the whole community could take part, and could be a good way of integrating the sisters from Iraq and Vietnam, and also the sisters in formation, into the country. The place would be conducive to an intercultural community life in many ways, and it would also introduce the Dominican sisters to a new part of the country.

After many deliberations, and not without some fear, the vice-province decided to take on the leadership of Johannesgården in the autumn of 2003. In order to constitute two communities of roughly the same size, Märsta was closed and the community in Stockholm refounded at the same time as the opening of the new community at Johannesgården. Both communities were intercultural in their composition, although Johannesgården also offered an intercultural annex parish. The running of the diocesan centre demanded more administrative skills than Marielund had required, but the cooking and cleaning were handled entirely by employees.

The sisters were relatively free to organise weekends on topics of their own choice and visiting groups often took an active part in the prayer life of the community. The annex parish that gathered at Johannesgården for Sunday Mass was a lively group of mostly young families from all over the world, with the majority from Vietnam, Germany and the Middle East. This was the focal point of the community, while the opportunity to gather groups for retreats, meditation and theological or cultural subjects interested only the Swedish sisters. Over time, this gave rise to some tensions within the group.

The Iraqi and Vietnamese sisters worked quite a lot among their own cultural groups, both at Johannesgården and in the wider area of Gothenburg. The novitiate of the vice-province was transferred to Johannesgården, since this kind of community offered a better setting for a novitiate than a community in apartments in central Stockholm. However, it was not easy to motivate the younger members of the community to share all the manual chores that a house like Johannesgården naturally demands of its inhabitants.

It was during this period at Johannesgården, between 2003 and 2008, that the sisters finally became aware of living interculturally as a community. Once the external and more exotic aspects of cultural difference have been brought to the fore, enjoyed by all, and given their rightful space and time in daily community living, deeper and more serious differences emerge. Sometimes we allow these to surface and are able to talk about them, but at other times they are kept behind thick walls so that we do not have to confront our own weaknesses, or those of our sisters.

As some of the sisters in formation chose to leave religious life for various reasons, and some of the older sisters became frailer, and with the ecclesial situation changing drastically in the Catholic Diocese of Stockholm with some thoroughgoing changes in the Gothenburg area, the vice-province once again had to restructure its life. The two Vietnamese sisters returned to their congregations in Vietnam. One of them had obtained a masters' degree in social work at the University of Gothenburg and was eager to try using her skills in her own country. The other sister was needed to found a new community and to take care of aspirants. The decision was made to move all the sisters back to Stockholm, and to found a new and small community close to the one at Västmannagatan.

After 2008, the number of different nationalities declined in the vice-province. Three Iraqi sisters continued living and working together with the Dominican sisters in Sweden. The Iraqi sisters began experiencing an intercultural mission as such, not only as a result of interactions with Swedish Catholics but also with Catholics coming from a large variety of cultures. One of the Iraqi sisters became chaplain for the Catholic Youth Movement and worked with young people from all cultures, and has helped with bridge-building inside the Church as well as between the youngsters and the wider society. Another Iraqi sister prepared young people, most of them born in Sweden but of parents who come from different countries, for the sacrament of confirmation in the Latin Rite. She worked in a parish in one of the poorest suburbs of Stockholm. In that parish, the Catholic priest from Poland, the Swedish Lutheran priest and the Muslim imam tried to create an understanding for, and dialogue with, the youngsters from these three religious families. The third Iraqi sister began moderating a number of groups of Iraqi people, dealing with catechesis, youth and women, and was also helping families with conflicts, mediating between spouses and between parents and children.

Intercultural living among the sisters has become something normal, even if we are still discovering misunderstandings and difficulties. At the same time, we have learned to live with certain tensions. Above all, we have accepted that we are not equal and that we can never pretend to live like equals either. This may sound shocking, but if an intercultural relationship should ever be fruitful and create something new, we have to be humble enough to accept some fundamental facts of a specific situation. Living fraternal justice then, with generosity and love in the biblical sense of these words, is to realise the Dominican motto of Truth and Mercy.

TRUTH AND MERCY – SOME CONCLUSIONS

During this period of more than 12 years, we have learned the hard way how difficult it is to integrate into a given context. It is obvious that the sisters coming from different cultures have had to integrate into a new country when settling into Sweden. But the Swedish-born sisters have also had to do this, and it took some time to admit that this was so! There would simply be no cultural interactions, or personal interactions for that matter, if actors on both sides are not actively trying to integrate into a new context. The context becomes new simply by the fact that there is a new person entering into it.

But we are not equals in this new contextual setting. The sisters belonging to the Swedish vice-province will always be laying the groundwork for the agenda of the community. They have the financial responsibility for the common project. They are also its juridical owners, and rightly so, because they are the only ones who cannot leave it. They also have the linguistic prerogative and, at least in the beginning, they will set the limits of the newcomer's room for manoeuvre. If we are not humble enough to recognise this superiority or power, we will most certainly commit serious injustices.

However, the sisters coming from other cultures also have to admit this, otherwise it will be tempting to use this unavoidable inequality as an inverted power, making oneself a victim of the situation. If this happens, and it is easily done, the newcomer is opting out of the necessary integration process and will never engage in an intercultural action. This will lead to a self-imposed segregation, harming any religious community life.

To live truthfully is to recognise this inequality between the members of a community. To live mercifully is to try to find ways to compensate handicaps where possible, and not to do so where it is useless to try. Firstly, the receiving community must give time and economic resources to the sister from another culture, so that she can learn the language and be professionally introduced into the culture of the new country. Secondly, the purpose of the mission of the sister must be crystal clear even if the concrete activities she carries out may vary a lot. It is important that the sister personally applies for a job within the parish or diocese, as this will strengthen her independence. Thirdly, the sister must be granted dispensations from regular community life more often than the others in order to relate to her friends and colleagues within her own cultural group. Fourthly, the sister has to enjoy the same economic rights and duties as the other members of the community.

Then there are various cultural 'traps' to avoid in daily life. For some people, an honest Swedish 'no' may be understood as a personal insult. Others will say 'no', expecting you to coax them into finally accepting, say, another cup of coffee. It becomes more delicate when the community has to make a decision on a common venture of some importance. Our decision-making processes may look alike in the Dominican family but they can be experienced differently all the same. We are all proud of our Dominican democracy, but there are several different ways of realising it!

There is an integration process to be made by all actors in every new community setting. However, integration does not mean arriving at the same perceptions of things. The more we can openly admit that we have different perceptions of events within the Church, as well as within society, the more truthfully and mercifully we will live in a community. This is especially important when it comes to the history of the receiving community. The only truthful and merciful way to find out what the differences are between us is to talk about them. This intercultural action is about good conversation, and good conversation will always lead to good conversion.

The Dominican sisters in Sweden have been living a continuous integration process since the first sisters arrived in Stockholm in 1931. They have always been engaged in dialogue with the surrounding society, whether this was related to ecumenism, interfaith contexts, religiously indifferent people or social policy. Their faith, as well as their theological and ecclesiological perceptions, has always been in a process of change and renewal. This is their fundamental characteristic and this always has to be revisited and renewed in each new integration process, if they are to be truthful and merciful to themselves.

24

The Dominican Charism Lived with and from the Perspective of the Poor

BEATRIZ ALICIA AND MARIA LEONOR CHARRIA ANGULO, O.P.

WHERE THERE IS LIFE, THERE IS STILL HOPE!

The first community of Dominican Sisters of Apostolic Life arrived in Colombia in 1873 (the Dominican Sisters of Charity of the Presentation[1] originally from France). This community has been a steady evangelising presence in Colombia since then. The sisters have tried to remain faithful to their original charism (as outlined by Marie Poussepin) throughout all the historical changes and adaptations that have happened in the country. However, faithfulness to the ideals of their foundress has not prevented them living in the present and attentively scrutinising the signs of the times.

This essay looks at the concrete reality of Latin America – and specifically that of Colombia – paying special attention to the lived reality of the most vulnerable groups, namely, the excluded. Among those, we will describe the concrete circumstances of a group of women who live in a destitute part of the city, Altos de Cazuca, which is located a few kilometres outside Bogotá, the capital city of Colombia.

The experience of being and working with these groups is shared, relived and reinterpreted through the eyes of two Dominican sisters – who happen also to be twins. These sisters have worked in this destitute area for more than ten years. The situation of extreme poverty and exclusion – affecting women in particular – has transformed the way these two sisters conceive their own vocation as Dominicans. It has also forced them to read, assume, feel about and experience this reality in a different way.

A GLANCE AT THE LATIN AMERICAN (COLOMBIAN) REALITY

A close look at the Latin American (Colombian) reality must be hope-filled. There is a need to rekindle the fire that sparks back to life from the ashes of poverty, death and exclusion in the lives of the poor, yet entrepreneurial,

---

1. In 1696 Blessed Marie Poussepin founded the Congregation of the Dominican Sisters of Charity of the Presentation in France.

joyful and caring, people. A desire to find solutions and alternatives, and to create something new, can still be found in the hearts of many of these people. They still believe that it is possible to create a different reality – especially for Colombia – where justice and solidarity can reign supreme. After all, it will only be with this mindset that we will be able to find new ways to reconstruct the social fabric of our country. At the same time, we may also ask ourselves: is it really possible to look at this reality with hope-filled eyes?

It is only possible to hope when we are directly immersed in the concrete reality we hope to change. In other words, in order to be truly hope-full, one has to experience at first hand the reality of the unjust and premature threat of death that hangs over the heads of the poor of this continent; one must know the continent's increasing inequalities.

It is necessary, then, to read and to interpret this reality in a horizon of hope and through the wisdom that comes from faith. The constant challenge that we sisters face is to be messengers of hope, as well as joyful followers of Jesus Christ, and to preach and work towards the Kingdom in the midst of this reality. Our present challenge is to respond to God's call faithfully and to help further the quest for the construction of a better future.

From a biblical perspective, to hope means to be attentive to what is happening, to be able to see beyond immediate experience, and to believe in things not yet seen (Cf. Heb 11: 1). This is the attitude that is requested of us – what the Liturgy of the Hours calls Vigil: to be alert because the Kingdom of God comes. Thus, hope implies vigilance. We must be vigilant about repeatedly analysing current events in a reflective and critical way, in order to bring about viable change.

A hope-full glance that springs from the concrete, lived reality is neither the promotion of an illusion, nor a Utopian ideal that distorts or diverts our desire to improve our country, nor is it the resigned passivity of those who accept whatever happens as 'the will of God' or a preordained destiny. A hope-full glance is the effective, affective and laborious work that aims to transform injustice into justice, misery into dignity, war into peace. It is, in sum, a call to give up one's life for the promotion of those values that, through solidarity, bring about a truly humane reality.

This is not an easy task, especially when the social fabric is wounded, fractured and fragmented. It is not a facile endeavour when unity is broken and the resulting divisions are used to further the individual interest of small and select groups that take advantage of the situation to increase their wealth. But it is precisely because of this reality that we must redouble our efforts to cure wounds, build bridges and promote bonds that facilitate encounter, convergence and dialogue. The carrying forward of these tasks presupposes a process of personal conversion, structural change and commitment on the part of all of us.

At the Medellin Conference (1968),[2] the Church in Latin America and the Caribbean chose a particular method to analyse the reality in the continent and to identify key pastoral needs and ways to meet them. This method is called: 'see – judge – act'. It will constitute the substratum of this essay.

LATIN AMERICA (COLOMBIA): BETWEEN HOPE AND OBLIVION
Latin America has had a long history of dependent relations with international markets. From the very beginning – and for more than 300 years of colonisation – Latin American economies have been based on the export income from primary goods, rendering them vulnerable to the capricious will of external economic powers. Internally, Latin American societies – even after almost 200 years of independence – have been characterised by a rigid system of social stratification, which begets inequalities, power struggles and fragile democratic systems.

Although most Latin American nations have economies that are currently integrated into the global market, their internal socio-economic conditions are still seriously marred by high rates of poverty and social exclusion. These conditions are nothing new in most Latin American countries. However, it is necessary to ask ourselves if globalisation is accelerating positive change regarding these conditions or if, on the contrary, it is negatively contributing to the stagnation of the socio-economic situations across the continent.

The impoverishment of the population has accelerated in recent years, due to the increasing concentration of wealth in fewer hands. As a matter of fact, 10 per cent of the population (the wealthy) holds 48 per cent of the nations' wealth, while another 10 per cent of the population (the poorest) must survive with only 1.6 per cent of that wealth.

The GINI coefficient, a measure of inequality between the richest and the poorest in a particular country (higher GINI coefficients indicate more unequal distribution), indicates that countries like Brazil, Paraguay, Chile, Guatemala and Colombia are amongst the nations of the world with the greatest levels of inequality.[3]

In the context of our present economic crisis, it seems obvious that if we want to live in a developed and equitable society, we must look at the roots

2. CELAM, *Medellín*, Medellin, CELAM, 1969.

of the present system and implement some structural changes. Unfortunately, that does not seem to be happening. How does this continental reality – inequality – manifest itself in Colombia?

A COUNTRY THAT OSCILLATES BETWEEN SHADOWS AND LIGHT
A cursory glance at the Colombian reality in the early part of the twenty-first century shows an acute situation of impoverishment, generalised violence[3] and a general deterioration of basic standards of living.

The most serious analyses of the causes of our present crisis show that such a disastrous reality is the result of the implementation of wrong approaches to promoting development and of wrong mechanisms that were implemented long ago and have stayed ingrained in our society throughout our history. The following is a case in point.

The Spanish Conquest, through the greedy and brutal behaviour of the *conquistadores*, showed that profit was their primary value, over and above the life of the natives. Later on, during the time of the Spanish Colony, a good deal of exploitation and misappropriation went on. It was also during this period of our history that the thirst for wealth gave rise to diverse forms of slavery. From the period of independence until the Republic (1819–86), an inadequate transference of political and executive power caused an abysmal and chaotic jump from a pre-Columbian model of societal organisation to a complex and chaotic model of 'modern' society that survives until this day.

As a result, Colombia is a country of many contrasts. One of them is the fact that while the economy grows, generally speaking, it benefits only a few, while the immense majority lives in extreme poverty. For this majority, poverty takes the concrete form of undernourishment, lack of housing and unemployment. Monopolised wealth – kept in the hands of a very few – has turned Colombia into a country filled with injustices and inequalities. Recent years have seen growth in the economy and a reduction in poverty levels in general, but a concurrent increase in extreme poverty. The ruptures and the ever-growing divisions in the social fabric have turned our country into a divided and broken nation, marked by seemingly hopeless and bleak

3. See the World Bank data at http://data.worldbank.org/indicator/SI.POV.GINI (last accessed 03.09.12). Colombia still faces a dire situation of armed conflict and violence. Ours is the oldest internal conflict in America, perhaps in the world. Nevertheless, it was only between the years 1985 and 2000 that the internal war became more visible, because it was circumscribed in a clearly delimited territory. The Colombian government has crafted various peace proposals during the past 30 years, trying to find some concrete answers. Unfortunately, all have failed. At the same time, peace proposals – and the demands for peace – have multiplied, mainly coming from civil organisations 'from below'. But again, very little has been achieved. Nevertheless, in recent years the number of armed groups in the country has decreased.

situations. However, we must still find reasons to keep hoping.

Some hard data[4] shed further light on the real magnitude of the problem: Many Colombians still live in poverty today. For those who live in the countryside, the situation is still more alarming: 65 out of 100 Colombians who live in the countryside live below poverty levels – compared to 39 out of 100 for those who live in the cities.

According to the data regarding poverty and inequality in Colombia (from the *Misión para el Empalme de las Series de Empleo, Pobreza y Desigualdad, Nacional*), more than 46 per cent of the population live in poverty and 17 per cent have to beg on the streets in order to survive.[5] In other words, 20.5 million Colombians are poor and 7.9 million live in destitution.

At the time of writing, a home would be deemed poor in Colombia when, if it includes four people, its members receive a combined income that is below 1 million Colombian pesos per month (the equivalent of 500 US dollars). As far as destitution – extreme poverty – goes, we would be talking about a home with four members in which there is not enough income to buy basic products, especially food. In Colombia, at the time of writing, this would be a monthly income below 450,000 Colombian pesos (approximately 225 US dollars).

POVERTY AND EXCLUSION:
A HURTING REALITY THAT DEMANDS COMMITMENT
There is nothing new to be said about issues relating to poverty and the poor; after all, they have been among us throughout the whole of human history! History, in fact, shows a marked dialectic reaction regarding inequality, injustice and oppression. At times, for instance, there has been a radical denunciation of the trampling upon human dignity; at other times, however, these same realities have been justified and people have even learned how to coexist with them, as if they were just part of the norm.[6]

For many years now, it has been clear that poverty is a multidimensional phenomenon, closely related to the so-called process of exclusion. Thus, a multidimensional approach that focuses on the dynamics that prevent hu-

4. University of the Andes, 'La Pobreza en Colombia no Cede', *Redacción Bogotá/Vanguardia Liberal,* 14 February 2010, http://www.vanguardia.com/historico/53402-la-pobreza-en-colombia-no-cede (last accessed 30.08.2012).

5. DANE y DNP, *MESEP/Misión para el Empalme de las Series de Empleo, Pobreza y Desigualdad. Resultados cifras de pobreza, indigencia y desigualad 2009,* Bogotá, DANE y DNP, April 2010.

6. Ana María Leonor Charria, 'Haciendo visibles a los invisibles. Una mirada a Medellín y Aparecida desde la perspectiva de los pobres y excluidos', in Amerindia, *Esperanza en Contraviento. Medellín 40 años,* Bogotá, Indo-American Press, 2008.

man development and directly challenges the marginalisation and exclusion that prevents people participating at all in socio-economic, political, cultural and religious levels is needed to address the situation.

It is important to state that drastic neoliberal socio-economic and political measures during recent decades have aggravated the structures of injustice, inequality and exclusion. Furthermore, it would be hard to argue that they have not contributed to the reinforcement of an environment of misery, hunger, impatience and delinquency in our country.

The number of people excluded from participation in the economy – and in social affairs – is growing exponentially. Many people have been excluded from having a stable job, land, a house, sound credit, proper education, adequate health services and a healthy environment. Their committed participation in the decision-making process regarding the construction of a healthy society has been jeopardised.

Social exclusion has caused serious damage to our social cohesion: it has raised the levels of insecurity, marginalisation, environmental degradation and criminality. At the same time, many Colombian citizens find it impossible to exercise their democratic rights in order to protect the environment, to receive adequate health care, to contribute to the local economy and to obtain good employment and dignified social services.

Social exclusion is the result of the increasing concentration of wealth in the hands of very few. These few refuse to make a conscious effort to allow all sectors of society to benefit from economic growth and to help increase our capital and our social cohesion. They refuse to ensure the protection of human rights and of the environment. It is worth remembering that the more close-knit the government's economic and political measures have been, the more fragmented and disintegrated our society has become.

In this country, poverty often has the face of a child, of a teenager, of a woman, of people of colour. In a world in which all nations have made a commitment to respect gender equality, to end racial discrimination and to defend the rights of children, the fact that living conditions are worse for these groups than for others is plainly intolerable.

Exclusion, as a reality, is the result of various factors that converge and are parts of a whole. On the one hand, there are structural elements, namely, the way in which societies organise their relations and social, political and economic agreements, as well as the way in which they distribute income, develop public policies, establish relations with other countries, reinforce values and adopt relationship models and cultural ideas. On the other hand, there are personal factors and individual characteristics that influence how an individual resists or adapts to change.

Based on all of the above, it is possible to affirm – without fear of being mistaken – that current Colombian structures and policies tend to be more exclusive than inclusive. In this context of poverty and exclusion, what alternative roads can we find for our daily-lived reality in the life and actions of Jesus?

CHRISTOLOGY AND ECCLESIOLOGY AS A POINT OF REFERENCE:
JESUS' ACTIONS INTERPRETED FROM A LATIN AMERICAN PERSPECTIVE

Latin American theology has repeatedly affirmed that Christians must follow a liberating Jesus, a living God who, in the words of Jon Sobrino,[7] gives life. Jesus teaches us to live a simple and dignified life, a meaning-full and hope-full life.

At the same time, it is not until we approach the person of Jesus to discover how he was able to live a life of poverty and how he situated himself in relation to this option[8] that we are able to understand the real meaning of his choice.

'Jesus Christ ... though he was rich, yet for your sakes he became poor.' (2 Cor 8: 9) It is necessary to highlight the fact that Jesus lived a poor existence and lived among the poor. This fact is impossible to hide and has, first of all, an anthropological meaning: poverty was Jesus' chosen way to live his human existence, his way to express a way of being and doing. In other words, Jesus chose to live as a poor man.

In this sense, Fr Federico Carrasquilla indicates that, at an *anthropological* level, being poor was Jesus' way of being a man; at a *spiritual* level this fact expresses his humility; and at a *sociological* level, being poor meant living like the poor live.[9]

These three dimensions appear in the letter to the Philippians: 'Let the same mind be in you that was in Christ Jesus, who, though he was in the form of God, did not regard equality with God as a thing to be grasped, but emptied himself, taking the form of a servant, being born in the likeness of

---

7. Jon Sobrino, *Jesús en América Latina: su significado para la fe y la Cristología*, Santander, Sal Terrae, 1985, p. 158.

8. The contributions and reflections shared at different times with the Colombian priest Federico Carrasquilla were a powerful point of reference for the writing of this chapter. Fr Carrasquilla is deeply committed to working amongst the Church's poor in a suburb of Medellin, Colombia.

9. Transcript, Federico Carrasquilla, *Antropología del Pobre*, 1996, by Luz Stella Múnera, available at: http://caritasmardelplata.org.ar/?page_id=638 (last accessed 25.10.10).

men. And being found in human form, he humbled himself and became obedient unto death, even death on a cross' (2: 5ff).

The *spiritual* dimension is shown in the fact that 'he emptied himself'. The *anthropological* dimension is shown in the fact of his 'taking the form of a servant, being born in the likeness of men' and 'becoming obedient unto death [he chose death], even death on a cross'. The *sociological* dimension is shown in his decision to live as a poor man amongst the poor. If we want to understand the full meaning of Jesus' existence, we ought to take these three dimensions into consideration.

Jesus decided to live a life of poverty

The life of poverty that Jesus lived was the result of a personal choice and, thus, it was pure gratuity. That is what we read in 2 Corinthians: 'For you know the generous act of our Lord Jesus Christ, that though he was rich, yet for your sakes he became poor, so that by his poverty you might become rich' (8: 9). Jesus remained steadfast in his decision to live a poor life throughout his earthly existence; it was a lifestyle that he chose to assume.

Jesus chose to live a life of poverty in the way the poor experience it

Jesus lived a life of poverty in the way the poor do. This insight is the greatest Latin American contribution to theological reflection, the so-called *irruption of the poor into the Church*.[10] The fact that Jesus lived a poor life out of humility had always been remarked upon; however, the fact that he did so in a sociological sense (he was a poor man living amongst the poor) was something new. This realisation was novel because it moved poverty out of the spiritual realm and into the concrete lived-reality of many poor people.

Jesus decides to live a life of poverty because he gives poverty a new sense and meaning. In other words, he presents poverty as an ideal way of living. This is new, especially since poverty was considered to be an evil in the Old Testament (Deut 28: 48; Pr 10: 4, 15) and thus was never proposed as an ideal way of living. This new paradigm is proper to Jesus' lifestyle. He directly and repeatedly presents poverty as an ideal way of living (Mt 5: 3; 18: 3; 19: 16 etc.), especially during the Sermon on the Mount: Blessed are the poor in spirit, for they make the Kingdom come about. He does not say, 'blessed are the poor because they are going to stop being poor!' Thus, if Jesus proposes poverty as an ideal way of living, it is because he sees a value

10. Numerous Latin American theologians have pondered this expression for a long time. Some of these theologians include Gustavo Gutiérrez, who made this expression famous in his book *Teología de la Liberación*, Salamanca: Sígueme, 1972. In the same vein, see P. Casaldalica and J.M. Vigil, *Espiritualidad de la Liberación*, Santander, Sal Terrae, 1992.

in being poor.

Jesus, not only chooses to live a life of poverty, but he also goes on spending his life fighting in favour of the poor and against marginality, hunger and disease.

We can see two fundamental characteristics in the way Jesus acts: firstly, everything he did in favour of the poor, He did as a sign. For this reason, for instance, after the multiplication of the loaves of bread, when people were looking for him, he clearly told them the meaning of his sign: 'Very truly, I tell you, you are looking for me, not because you saw *signs*, but because you ate your fill of the loaves.' (Jn 6: 26; Mt 11: 2; Lk 4: 16). Secondly, Jesus' main goal was to help people assume their own destiny and to recover their dignity, more than to offer immediate solutions to their needs – although he also did that from time to time.

Jesus' option in favour of the poor: a sign of the Kingdom

Jesus came to propose a new way of life, a new society; he brought us a community project that is called the Kingdom. It is because of this that his main goal is not simply to free the poor, but to create a new society (Cf. Rv 21: 1–8; Is 11: 1–9; 65: 17–25).

Jesus did not look directly to changing structures, although this does not mean that he was not interested in the transformation of the reality of his time. He came to create a new society, not simply to change individuals. His proposal is clear: the Kingdom. The preference for the poor is the option for a new society, built upon the basis of equality, justice and love.

This reflection regarding Jesus and his option for the poor frequently questions our way of being and acting in a world marked by poverty. Where to begin? How can we do it? What does it mean to help the poor live a dignified life? Does our commitment demand our direct participation in order to change unjust structures?

Little by little one realises that the ideal response is to take a two-sided (inseparable and non-contradictory but clearly differentiated) perspective. That is to say, we need to employ a different perspective in which it is possible to work in favour of the poor from the point of view of the person and from the point of view of the structures. From the point of view of the person, we have to focus on personal change and, from there, we have to bring about structural change. What is most important in this approach is personal accompaniment, 'one-on-one presence', the furthering of individual education, and the raising of awareness about the importance of participation in social organisations. From the point of view of structures, it is necessary to orient our action towards the struggle against the structures that oppress the poor. Political struggle reigns supreme on this level, thanks to its ability to denounce oppressive and unjust structures and situations.

These two approaches (beginning with the person or with the structures) are equally valid and complementary. When working in favour of the poor from the point of view of the person, it is necessary to consider the structures, and when working in favour of the poor from the point of view of the structures, it is necessary to consider the person.

In this way, it becomes clear that our commitment to further the cause of the poor must be oriented to the recovery of their identity and dignity, both as human beings and as sons and daughters of God. Our commitment should promote their personal values, which, in turn, will allow them to fight and to defend their rights. It should help them realise that poverty is something to fight against and not an ethical category that deems them 'evil'. Our commitment, in sum, should teach them to take responsibility for their ethical task: to thrive and to work in order to be fully recognised as persons in society.

THE LATIN AMERICAN CHURCH IN THE MIDST OF THIS REALITY

The Church in Latin American and the Caribbean, through its various conferences, has clearly analysed and denounced the increasing inequality. Aparecida's final document[11] (beginning at n. 62) indicates that globalisation is driven by a tendency to privilege profit and that this causes a dynamic of the concentration of power and wealth into the hands of a few – not only of natural resources and money, but also of information. This in turn causes the exclusion of those who are not sufficiently trained or informed, increasing inequalities and the conditions that prevent a multitude of people getting out of poverty.

Immediately afterwards, the document invites us to look at the faces of those who experience material or moral poverty and are excluded from society. It also speaks of new types of poverty and shows that they are mainly the fruits of globalisation without solidarity. The excluded are not only 'the exploited'; they also become 'the left-overs', the 'disposable ones'.

After clearly establishing these facts, the bishops have indicated the urgency of a preferential option for the poor in the final documents of their previous conferences. This preferential option goes beyond mere rhetoric and becomes a demand for commitment on the part of those who want to

11. CELAM, *Aparecida*, Bogotá, CELAM, 2007.

remain faithful to the Gospel of Jesus and to respond to the urgent cries of our present historical moment.

In this regard, Puebla's final document, echoing the call issued in the Last Judgment passage from the Gospel of Matthew, invites us to recognise in the faces of the poor 'the suffering face of Christ, the Lord, who questions and challenges us' (n. 31). Further, Santo Domingo's final document affirms that, 'to discover in the suffering faces of the poor the face of the Lord (cf. Mt 25:31–46) is something that challenges Christians to a deep personal and ecclesial conversion' (n. 178). Aparecida's final document indicates: 'Today, we want to ratify and to harness the option of the preferential love for the poor, which was adopted in previous conferences' (n. 396). This 'is a characteristic aspect of the face of the Church in Latin America and the Caribbean' (n. 391).

It is worth remembering how Pope Benedict XVI, in the inaugural speech of Aparecida, wanted to support and promote this option for the poor, based in our faith. He clearly showed how this option is not something marginal but something that 'is implicit in our Christological faith, in our faith in a God who has become poor for us, to enrich us with His poverty' (n. 392). The option for the poor, then, is neither 'the result of an ideology' nor of a certain philosophy or a socio-political optimism; 'it is born from our faith in Jesus Christ, the God made man, who has become our brother' (n. 392).

The face of Jesus Christ and the faces of the poor are inseparable, because one is reflected in the other. We contemplate 'in the suffering faces of our brothers, the face of Christ, who calls us to serve Him in the poor' (n. 393). Furthermore, 'in the face of Jesus Christ, in that suffering and glorious face, we can see, with the eyes of faith, the humiliated faces of so many men and women of our lands' (n. 32). 'Everything that has to do with Christ has to do with the poor and all that has to do with the poor relates to Jesus Christ' (n. 393).

Along these same lines, religious men and women living a consecrated life in this continent have been trying to determine how to emphasise the way in which they 'live and proclaim' Jesus' Kingdom in Latin America.

RELIGIOUS LIFE IN LATIN AMERICA:
ITS PROPHETIC AND MYSTIC DIMENSIONS

In recent years, the Latin American Conference of Religious (CLAR) has been reflecting on the need for a mystical and prophetic religious life.[12] How has this impacted our journey? From our point of view as Dominican sisters, it

12. M. *Víctor Martinez, Mística y profecía en la vida religiosa*, Bogotá, Paulinas, 2005.

seems that to be a mystic and a prophet in the midst of this reality demands that we possess an open and merciful glance. It is all about being able to see and to listen to the pain of our brothers and sisters, just as Jesus did. Being a mystic demands being a prophet and vice versa. From this springs the need to attain wholeness in one's own life through a deep experience of the Lord and through the proclamation of the Gospel, which denounces everything that goes against the Kingdom.

An 'open-eyed' mystic attitude that leads towards God – as it has been called in Latin America – has a point of departure in so-called 'stillness', but promotes a critical attitude and the boldness of allowing the Spirit to lead one's own life.

A hope-full prophetic attitude chooses the essential in life and looks at reality with a new glance, the glance of change and commitment. This attitude helps create new realities and turns those who allow themselves to be seduced by God into people who are more human, just and caring. At the same time, a mystical and prophetic attitude demands that we be welcoming and that we work in favour of the values of the Kingdom. It demands that we read the signs of the times in a concrete place and constantly recommit ourselves to the promotion of a kind of peace that springs from justice and charity.

Charity is, in fact, that kind of shared love that becomes real brother/sisterhood in favour of life, equality, freedom and unity. At the end of the day, it is all about creating, with the help of our brothers and sisters, another reality, a reality that is closer to the one portrayed in the Gospel of Jesus. Living our lives based on a mystical and prophetic perspective, in a coherent way, is a constant challenge for us. But it is this 'Utopia' that animates every day of our lives and for which we work with optimism and faith. This way to understand and to live Jesus' project among the poor has become – and it is still – a call, an imperative for us, Colombian Dominican Sisters of the Presentation.

We have taken a cursory look at the Latin American (Colombian) reality. We have reviewed the main premises of the Church and of those living religious life in Latin America and the Caribbean. Keeping all that in mind, it is now time to look at other realities that impact and confront our lives as Dominican Sisters of the Presentation here in Colombia.

A BELT OF EXCLUSION AND MISERY:
ALTOS DE CAZUCA, COMUNA 4 DE SOACHA

Altos de Cazuca, in Comuna 4, is one of the poorest places in Soacha. One of the biggest belts of poverty in the city and in the country is found in this municipality, which is adjacent to Bogotá (Cundinamarca State).[13] It is located on the edge of the hills of this municipality. People began arriving in this area from around 1975, and they have not stopped coming ever since.

There are approximately 45 *barrios* (districts) subject to constant migration, thanks ultimately to violence or neglect on the part of the state. The 'houses' are illegal establishments with meagre infrastructure, mostly uninhabitable. The inhabitants of these slums have very limited or no access to the general system of social security. They come from many different places; thus, there is a huge diversity of habits and cultures, which renders the processes of integration and community organisation almost impossible. This area receives a high percentage of displaced people from different areas of the country. Here, the newcomer gets quickly lost in a vast sea of misery and marginality.

It is not easy to live in this place for those who are displaced from the various regions of the country because, as a displaced woman from Tolima says, 'in the countryside one does not suffer this much ... one has simple clothing but does not need much anyway, except for one set of nice clothes to go to Sunday Mass ... we never lack for food; neighbours are good and we help one another ... in contrast, here in the city, from time to time, there is nothing to eat ... we are six or seven people living together ... the only food we can get here are potatoes and rice ... there is no meat or eggs – which we used to eat in the countryside ... in addition, to find a job here one needs to wear decent clothing; otherwise, if one is poorly dressed, they do not give you a job ... leaving one's own small piece of land is very hard.' Besides poverty, these families have to endure the loneliness and anonymity that come from living in big cities.

According to the experimental census carried out in May 2003,[14] the Comuna 4 (which includes los Altos de Cazuca) had 63,308 inhabitants – making it already the second most populated area in this municipality, with a population that continues to grow at a considerable rate.

---

13. Although Soacha and Bogotá are independent cities from an administrative point of view, geographically, Soacha is a continuation of the capital city, Bogotà.
14. Carried out experimentally in preparation for the 2005 National Census.

A DOMINICAN PRESENCE AMONGST THE POOREST

The Dominicans of the Presentation arrived in San Mateo, Soacha in 1997. They came to respond to the Archdiocese of Bogotá's call for help[15] and as a result of their own province's search for a place to do mission work in Bogotá. They arrived in Altos de Cazuca two years later. Since the foundation of the community, Sr Beatriz Charria and three of her community sisters have been present here and have offered permanent support to the people in this area. They have been accompanied in this endeavour by Sr María Leonor and a big group of sisters, and by the Dominican friars, young women in formation, the Dominican family, and various volunteers who spend time with them, especially during the most important liturgical moments of the year – Holy Week and Christmas.

El Arroyo – Altos de Cazuca

A discernment process began from the moment the sisters arrived in Soacha. They began to identify which sectors of the population were more depressed and in dire need of attention. The reality of all these settlements – rapidly and exponentially growing – was a constant call to respond but ... to respond to what? Where? To which pressing need first? Helped by whom? Choosing what to respond to was not an easy task, especially since poverty is ubiquitous here.

The Lord who accompanies these discernment processes, however, showed us the way. A community sitting at the top of the hill was singled out. They had literally nothing: no school and no running water; their houses were built of cardboard or plastic ... However, in the midst of such misery, the sisters found joyful people, open and eager to work and to improve their living conditions; these were sharing and caring people who believed in the God of life who accompanies them and helps them, but who also asks them to do their part. This barrio is called El Arroyo. Here the sisters have done more than ten years of joint work, of promotion and integral evangelisation.

A Dominican community that wants to live up to its own identity

The small community, formed by four sisters, live in the El Arroyo, meaning 'The Stream'. The irony of this name is heavy, since the only access the inhabitants of El Arroyo have to drinking water is for two hours per *week*. What they found here cannot be called poverty; it is downright misery! Basic services are very deficient. Unemployment rates are very high. The majority

---

15. In those years, Soacha belonged to the Archdiocese of Bogotá. Today, the municipalities of Soacha and Bosa form a diocese in their own right.

of the people work in recycling, construction, domestic service or informal commerce.

A firsthand encounter with this reality becomes a challenge for any Dominican sister who, on the one hand, must show the same predilection that Jesus showed for the poor, and, on the other, has to walk with these families, helping them recognise their dignity, potentialities and values. The experience is challenging because it entails proximity to a marginal reality, to a place where the excluded, the poor, have names and faces. It is challenging because we are talking about families with many children – most of them very young – who live in crowded houses in a marginal zone of the city. It is challenging because we are talking about houses generally made of mud or zinc, where there are not even basic services.

Speaking to the International Congress of Historians of the Order of Preachers in Santo Domingo about the need to experience this reality directly in order to be able to evangelise it, Fr Gustavo Gutiérrez OP said:

> The proclamation of the Gospel cannot be done without direct contact with the reality of the people to whom we are sent to preach. We preach to real human beings, to their daily-lived reality, to real people who are full of joy and hope, who suffer. The proclamation of the Gospel must consider these situations. It seems obvious, naturally, but sometimes we proclaim the Gospel as if reality did not have any major incidence in the daily life of people. I remember what a friend used to say: 'we would be so good but for reality!' And this is, of course, true ... we would be very good, but as soon as reality shows up, along come the questions.[16]

El Arroyo: a community that is being built one day at a time

The El Arroyo barrio was born approximately 20 years ago, when a group of people from the M19[17] was reintegrated into society. Their leader, Álvaro Arroyo, named the barrio after himself. He and his bodyguards took over these lands and started building small houses made of tin cans, wood, plastic and other very low quality building materials. When other families starting arriving in the area, Mr. Arroyo sold them small land parcels at relatively cheap prices – or just gave them the land outright, depending on the case. There is no one left here of that first group of settlers.

16. Gustavo Gutiérrez, '500 Años de lucha pro la justicia. Los Dominicos y la UASD' (inaugural speech at the International Congress of Dominican Historians, Santo Domingo, Dominican Republic, 14 October 2010), Charria's personal notes.

17. The M19 was a leftist political movement that was disbanded and reintegrated into civil society during the 1990s.

The second group of inhabitants was made up of families that had some savings and were able to buy a piece of land and build a house. (Since the land is not legally owned, the document the 'owner' receives is only a piece of paper with little or non-existent legal weight. However, this 'title of property' is considered valid by all the inhabitants of the area.) A few of this second group of inhabitants remain here, but they have since improved their living conditions.

A significant number of families have settled here more recently. They have been displaced because of the violence that ruins this country.[18] Generally speaking, these families have relatives already living here. Thus, they move in and slowly start building small houses. The community is always open to welcome these families. They are all united by the same situations of poverty and displacement and that gives them a sense of solidarity with one another.

The inhabitants of this area are open, welcoming people who value the aid they receive from inside or outside their community. However, they do not accept dishonest manipulation or mishandling (the kind that 'politicians' sometimes try to offer to them).

A few families are formed by young couples with four or five small children, but there is a growing number of women who have become the heads of their households[19] because of the death – generally violent – of their partner or because their partner has left them. These women work as housemaids or in the so-called *rebusque*.[20] Very few have a decent job. Martha[21] is one of them.

Martha, her husband and her four children fled from Tolima state – where they were farmers – over 15 years ago. While sitting in her house in Altos de Cazuca, sector el Arroyo, she shared her history with us, a story that will allow us to get a glimpse into her reality:

> When we lived in Tolima, we cultivated our own food, so we never had to buy anything. We lived peacefully. We had what we needed. Both the paramilitaries and the guerrillas were present in the area. One day, a group

18. Cf. note 5, *supra*

19. According to researcher Martha Bello, women are the sole heads of three out of ten homes that have been victims of forced displacement in Colombia. Six out of ten people who have been displaced are women. Cf. Martha Nubia Bello (ed.), *Desplazamiento forzado. Dinámicas de guerra, exclusión y desarraigo en Colombia*, Bogotá, UNHCR, ACNUR, Universidad Nacional de Colombia, 2004.

20. A term used in Colombia to identify a variety of informal economic activities that help people earn some income in order to subsist. It would be possible to say that the term refers to all kinds of activities that are not considered a formal job.

21. A fictitious name is used to protect the person's identity.

of guerrilla fighters showed up and demanded my husband pay a kind of 'tax'.[22] My husband did not want to pay but they threatened him and beat him up. After that, we were forced to pay a higher amount than the one originally requested, even though it was impossible for us to pay it. Soon after, we received a warning: 'either leave your property in the next 12 hours or be killed, you and your family.' We fled that same day and arrived in the middle of the night at a bus station in Bogotá. We did not know a single soul here. All we managed to bring with us was some little money, two mattresses, some clothes, and nothing else.

Martha's situation is symptomatic of the reality faced by hundreds of thousands of people who are forced every year to leave their homeland in Colombia because of the violence that still prevails, even if now on a smaller scale, in this country. Martha and her husband, however, were among the few lucky ones from among the thousands of displaced people in Colombia. They befriended a man who helped them find jobs and thus, soon they were able to find decent lodgings for themselves and their children. Martha found a job working as a housemaid for a rich family in the north of Bogotá and things began to improve for them. However, Martha continues:

One day, my husband returned to Tolima to find out what had happened to the belongings we left behind ... somebody let the Paras[23] know that he was around and, that same night, they came and killed him ... when I told my employers what had happened, they told me that I was a supporter of the guerrillas, and threw me out on the street. Later on, my friends asked me why I had been such an idiot as to openly speak about what had happened to me. But I do not have anything to hide or anything to be ashamed of! I am not a member of the guerrillas! It was the guerrillas that forced me to move here. I am innocent! I am a victim! Today, I feel an inner force that compels me to continue fighting, to continue supporting my children.

With these words Martha ends her story.

The experience of accompanying this people over many years allows us to point out that women living in these barrios are victims of intra-familiar

22. A sum of money to be given to an armed group, in order to be allowed to remain in one's house.

23. This is a common expression used to designate members of a paramilitary group, which are armed civil organisations, frequently allied with the army. These groups were created to repress subversion because of the state's inability to do so. The groups frequently exert extreme violence against the civil population, which has nothing to do with the armed conflict.

violence and abuse; however, they are the ones who – paradoxically – are in charge of all community processes. In other words, women are the ones in charge of starting projects from below; they are the ones working to further the recognition and respect of their rights; they are the ones who are fully committed to seeing through their productive initiatives; they are the ones who are getting qualified and who are acquiring basic formation, in order to be able to find better jobs, jobs other than domestic work.

It is important to emphasise that, generally speaking, women are the leaders of all community projects in El Arroyo. They are the ones who have been able, progressively, to acknowledge their potentialities and their limitations. They are assertive and are able to set challenging, clear and attainable goals for themselves. They have skills to face life's challenges and are willing to share their talents with others. This way of being and acting is what has been called *resilience*.[24] During the past years, we have undertaken a process of accompaniment and formation with them. It has been with them and from their daily-lived experience that, somehow, we have seen some positive results. Nevertheless, we are still very far from having a big number of women who have managed fully to develop their potential or to explore further the whole array of possibilities available to them.

There is a question that people who work on the frontiers or among the marginalised – especially people belonging to religious communities – frequently ask: Is living among the poor – accompanying them – a sociological/political option? Is it a sort of protest against the injustice, poverty and structural violence in which many people live in the world? Or is there something else, which moves and supports this type of commitment?

How has our journey been during these past years? First of all, we have listened to the people; we have shared their pains and needs; we have helped them look for ways out of their situation of marginality and exclusion. At the same time, we have formed a small faith- and hope-full community with them, centred on the Lord Jesus. We have learned to read the Word with them, and from their perspective, and to use it as a point of reference for our daily living. This 'being with the poor' has helped those of us who share in this experience to undertake a new spiritual journey. It has helped us learn with and from them and to experience a kind of God who is always on the side of the poor and who speaks from their point of view.

---

24. This is a term used for the first time during the 1940s by American psychologists, and later in France at the beginning of the 1980s, to designate women who, in the midst of struggles and difficulties, have learned how to survive and even how to thrive after the crisis is over.

WALKING THE WALK: 2000–2010

When the sisters first arrived in El Arroyo, their recurrent question was: where do we begin, especially when there are so many pressing needs at all possible levels? After a series of town hall meetings with the inhabitants of the community, we decided to help them build a school, in order to give an education to the many school-aged children in the area. Up to that moment, the only thing they had was a two-wall classroom and a water tank, donated by Doctors without Borders. The commitment was mutual: we, the sisters, would get the money for purchasing construction materials; they, the community, would provide the labour needed to build the school. Since then, and over recent years, our presence in, and commitment to, the area has taken the form of three clearly articulated goals.

Our first goal has been to help the people who live in this marginal and deprived area to find answers to their real and heartfelt needs. Sr Beatriz and Sr Margot (a young professed sister) are primarily in charge of this task. They are supported in their efforts by several organisations, volunteer groups, university students and people from the barrio.

The increase in the demand for, and requirements of, our work led us to create a small legal entity to give stronger support to our projects. Thus, an NGO was created, under the acronym FUNDEHI (Corporation for Integral Human Development). This was done in collaboration with a group of committed lay people who, without being part of this district, feel identified with it, and called to collaborate with our evangelising presence. They have supported, undertaken and created new projects, in co-ordination with members of this community. They are clearly aware of the nature of their commitment and the perspective from which we are all working.

Over recent years, some fruitful projects have been developed thanks to the support of FUNDEHI and of its president, Sr Beatriz. These projects employ a group of mothers who are the heads of their families. One such project is a cookie factory called Corazones de Cazuca. The name 'corazones' was chosen because both the cookies and their wrappings are made in the shape of a heart. Cazuca is the name of the area to which El Arroyo belongs. As mentioned before, the authorities stigmatised this area as being very violent, with high rates of poverty, marginality and destitution. The cookie factory provides jobs for ten mothers; however, as the demand for cookies rises, new opportunities are created for more mothers to support their households. Distribution is the most difficult part of this process, even though we have already secured the required permits to do so. A percentage of the proceedings is earmarked for building safe and sturdy houses in the barrio, which at present are very much needed because more than a hundred families have lost their humble abodes due to the harsh weather conditions.

Another project that offers jobs to mothers who are the heads of their households is the so-called Tampografía (screen printing). A printing machine was donated to the foundation and the women use it to print designs on pens, T-shirts, key chains etc. The market is very competitive – especially because Chinese-made products are ubiquitous and much cheaper. However, we have personally spoken with many business owners, explaining to them the goal of our project and, little by little, we have been able to secure their support.

The 'opportunities bank' is another of our projects. It offers loans to families, especially for those times of crisis (sudden illness, calamity) in which they would have no other means to survive. This project includes a savings programme, which is administered by the community itself and grows thanks to their bi-weekly contributions, which they fondly call 'investments'. This project has been very well received, especially since it allows members of the 'bank' to secure small loans. The sisters monitor this project closely.

There are other projects that are more tailor made. One such is a small school that serves 250 children. They receive not only academic formation at the school, but also breakfast and lunch. The total cost of this project is only $5,000 per month. We are able to offer this help to the children thanks to the support of a large number of 'godfathers' and 'godmothers who have each adopted a specific child as godchild.

Our kindergarten hosts 85 children under the age of five. This centre also serves as a nursery and the children are well fed and taken care of, thanks, again, to the help of more of our 'godfathers' and 'godmothers'.

We also have a dining hall called El remanso de los abuelos [the grandparents' oasis], which serves elderly people – one of the most vulnerable sections of our population, because of poverty and because they are neglected by their own children. Thirty-five senior citizens are fed there on a daily basis. They also receive psychosocial help and the opportunity to participate in handcraft activities and workshops.

Our second goal aims to form a critical awareness among these people of their individual dignity and of their rights, along with welcoming the participation of all the members of the barrio in the community organisations. Sr María Leonor was in charge of this work up until the time in which she was asked to serve in the general government of our congregation, due to her expertise on socio-political and human rights issues.

This work is at present animated by some sisters from our congregation and by university students from the areas of sociology, communications and social work. Inroads have been made progressively through the creation of spaces in which members of the barrio can participate, become more aware and be better prepared for the defence of the rights of their community. Now, whenever the members of the community feel that their rights are not being respected, they get together and organise a protest march against the decisions made by the state. This is not an easy task, especially since most members of the barrio were raised and formed in a culture of submission.

Our third and last goal – as important as the two previous ones – is to build faith communities around the Word, communities where service, solidarity and pardon can somehow express a different way of being and living in this place.

The three goals are equally important and mutually dependent on each other. At times – and depending on diverse circumstances – one has to take precedence over the others; however, the three together are the point of reference that guides our daily actions.

It is obvious that our commitment to evangelise and liberate, as well as to make present the Kingdom amongst the poorest, is of the utmost importance to us. The presence of a community of Dominican sisters here is, in and of itself, a testimony to, and a way of announcing, the Kingdom. However, we also engage in concrete work and action that is worth our while, and worth sharing.

An example of one concrete effort is the Bible study group that was formed five years ago with the intention of looking at the Sunday readings and linking them with the daily lived reality of the people of this place. Some time later, some members of this group, composed of about 40 members, asked us if they could have more time to receive more in-depth Christian formation and to deepen their knowledge of the Holy Scriptures.

Another example comes from the fact that priests can come only twice a week to celebrate the Eucharist. For that reason, our sisters are in charge of sacramental preparation, which they do in tandem with a catechist from the barrio and in close collaboration with the parents of the children.

A final example comes from the work done during the high points of the liturgical year (Lent/Holy Week and Christmas). At these times, Dominican sisters and friars come to help us, especially because there is a lot of work to be done in the other eight surrounding barrios that have nobody to offer them spiritual care.

Formative and organisational processes have been lived with the people of this area – especially with women – in our search for answers and solutions to their concrete needs. We have motivated them to be aware of the situation of marginality and exclusion in which they live, as well as of its causes. We have encouraged them to work for the construction of a more just and caring environment.

From its very beginning, our community, which is known as 'House of Preaching', has tried to be an evangelising and prophetic presence. It has achieved this through our testimony of life, a simple, austere and welcoming life; through the proclamation of the Word; and through the integral promotion of the human person. In this way, we have been able to respond to the new challenges that arise from the situation of vulnerability lived by the majority of the inhabitants of this area.

CONCLUSION

The lived experience of these past years has given us a wealth of learning that we consider worth sharing. Our presence among the poor has worked as the leaven hidden in the dough. We are called to render Gospel values ever more visible through our commitment to the poor, through our work in favour of justice, through our participation in initiatives in favour of the promotion of peace and of the defence of human rights. The Word of God, read, shared, prayed and celebrated, in and from this reality, maintains and animates our journey.

There is a need for a contemplative glance that neither errs on the side of fatalism nor strays on the side of idealism. This glance helps us to see beyond mere appearances to discover what lies underneath each attitude, each word, each gesture and each situation experienced by the inhabitants of these marginalised places. This profoundly contemplative attitude will allow us to discover, from the point of view of God, the true meaning of even the smallest things, of each fact, of each event, of history. It is necessary to enter into dialogue with reality, to pay attention to the 'signs of the times' in order to perceive what is urgent. Our operative words must be insertion, inculturation and ecclesial harmony

The Word and the concrete reality of the people invite us to become witnesses to a God who becomes flesh, who becomes one of us. This invitation demands that we denounce everything that goes against the salvific plan of God. In order to do that, it is essential that we do not conform to the world, or to the ways of the world, as St Paul has said (Rm 12: 2).

Our evangelising processes have to be integral. They must help members of the barrio/community to grow, to mature and to take charge of their own development. The commitment and experience gained while working amongst the poor demands that we not only become the voice of the voiceless, but also that we help them recover their own voice so that they can speak up for themselves and demand respect for their own rights.

It is imperative that we learn, progressively, how to let go of our need to be protagonists, of our need to be the centre and axis of the work being done. The members of these communities are the ones who must be the protagonists, the ones to bring about all the necessary changes to their environment and to their life. It is therefore necessary that they grow, that they become empowered and ready to be in charge of all these processes. At the end of the day, we ought not to forget that those of us who come from outside are only accompanying them for a limited period of time. And, as somebody said a long time ago, we must learn how to live simply, 'so that others can simply live'.

The mission has to be lived and undertaken in community. In our case, our community of Dominican sisters has tried to improve the life of our brothers and sisters who are victims of poverty, injustice and exclusion. Networking with other organisations in the Church, the Order, other religious congregations, and the civil society, is also very important because only in this way will we be able to address all the different realities of this place. The values of gratuity, justice, service and solidarity must be a fundamental part of our daily actions.

Contemplating this reality, one feels called once again to be a witness and a messenger of our God of life. One also feels called to be a witness in each and every moment and place in which the mission is lived and implemented. Nonetheless, we frequently experience our own smallness and our own weaknesses, especially while confronted with the huge challenges that call into question our ability to respond adequately to the mission that has been entrusted to us. It is then that we discover with greater force the need for a deep spiritual life and for the support of our religious community. It is only with the support of these two key elements of our religious life that we will be able to carry on faithfully Jesus' project: the coming of the Kingdom amongst us.

BIBLIOGRAPHY

Amerindia, ¿Es posible 'Otro mundo'? Reflexiones desde la fe cristiana, Bogotá, Indo-American Press Limitada, 2004.

Bello, Martha Nubia (ed.), Desplazamiento forzado. Dinámicas de guerra, exclusión y desarraigo en Colombia, Bogotá, UNHCR, ACNUR, Universidad Nacional de Colombia, 2004.

Carrasquilla, Federico, Antropología del Pobre, transcript by Luz Stella Múnera, 1996, available at: http://caritasmardelplata.org.ar/?page_id=638 (last accessed: 25.10.10).

Casaldaliga, P. and Vigil, J.M., Espiritualidad de la liberación, Santander, Sal Terrae, 1992.

CELAM, Aparecida, Bogotá, CELAM, 2007.

CELAM, Medellín, Bogotá, CELAM, 1969.

Charria, Beatriz, La primera comunidad dominica. Defensora del indígena, Bogotá, CELAM, 1987, (Colección V Centenario).

Charria, Beatriz, Jesucristo ungido y liberador. Una reflexión cristológica desde América Latina, 3rd ed., Bogotá, Indo-American Press, 1992.

Charria, Ana María Leonor, 'Haciendo visibles a los invisibles. Una mirada a Medellín y Aparecida desde la perspectiva de los pobres y excluidos', in Amerindia, Esperanza en Contraviento. Medellín 40 años, Bogotá, Indo-American Press, 2008.

DANE y DNP, MESEP/Misión para el Empalme de las Series de Empleo, Pobreza y Desigualdad. Resultados cifras de pobreza, indigencia y desigualad 2009, Bogotá, DANE y DNP, April 2010.

Gutiérrez, Gustavo, '500 años de lucha por la justicia. Los Dominicos y la UASD', Inaugural speech at the International Congress of Dominican Historians, Santo Domingo, Dominican Republic, 14 October 2010.

– Densidad del presente, Lima, Cep, 1996.

– En busca de los pobres de Cristo, Lima, Cep, 1992.

– Beber en su propio pozo, Lima, Lima, Cep, 1985.

– Teología de la Liberación, Salamanca, Sígueme, 1972.

Madera, Ignacio V., 'Luces y sombras de la vida religiosa en América Latina en los últimos 200 años', Revista Testimonio, Santiago de Chile, Julio-Agosto 2010, núm. 240.

Martinez, Víctor M., Misión continental y vida consagrada, Bogotá, Paulinas, 2009.

– Mística y profecía en la vida religiosa, Bogotá, Paulinas, 2005.

Müller, Gerhard L. and Gustavo Gutiérrez, Del lado de los pobres, Lima, Instituto Bartolomé de las Casas, 2005.

Posada, Félix, Conferencia inédita, Amerindia, Bogotá, July 2008.

Prebisch, Raúl, *Capitalismo periférico. Crisis y transformación*, México, D. F., Fondo de Cultura Económica, 1981.

Sobrino, Jon, *Fuera de los pobres no hay salvación*, Madrid, Ed. Trotta, 2007.

Sobrino, Jon, *Jesús en América Latina. Su significado para la fe y la cristología*, Santander, Sal Terrae, 1985.

Universidad de los Andes, 'La pobreza en Colombia no cede', *Redacción Bogotá / Vanguardia Liberal*, 14 February 2010, available at: http://www.vanguardia.com/historico/53402-la-pobreza-en-colombia-no-cede (last accessed: 30.08.12).

25

Promoting an Ecological
Spirituality and Lifestyle

HONORA WERNER, O.P.

The ecological crisis facing the human community threatens most of life on Earth as we know it. The devastation attributable to human activity violates our call to be good stewards of creation and the responsibility we have towards future generations for the goods that we hold in common, such as the Earth. Responses to this crisis, therefore, can be understood as exercises in the virtue of justice. The Catechism of the Catholic Church defines justice in this way:

> Justice is the moral virtue that consists in the constant and firm will to give their due to God and neighbor. Justice toward God is called the "virtue of religion." Justice toward men disposes one to respect the rights of each and to establish in human relationships the harmony that promotes equity with regard to persons and to the common good.[1]

This concern for the common good must of necessity include concern for the good of the Earth, the source of all the material goods needed by earthly creatures, including human beings. It follows that to act justly includes establishing right relationships with all creatures for the sake of the common good.

In December 1989, Pope John Paul II noted that a new ecological awareness was beginning to emerge as a moral issue.

> In our day, there is a growing awareness that world peace is threatened not only by the arms race, regional conflicts and continued injustices among peoples and nations, but also by a lack of due respect for nature, by the plundering of natural resources and by a progressive decline in the quality of life. The sense of precariousness and insecurity that such a situation engenders is a seedbed for collective selfishness, disregard for others and dishonesty.

1. *The Catechism of the Catholic Church*, English trans. United States Catholic Conference, Inc., New York, Doubleday, 1994, Part 3, Section 1, Chapter 1, Paragraph 1807.

Faced with the widespread destruction of the environment, people everywhere are coming to understand that we cannot continue to use the goods of the earth as we have in the past. The public in general as well as political leaders are concerned about this problem, and experts from a wide range of disciplines are studying its causes. Moreover, a new ecological awareness is beginning to emerge which, rather than being downplayed, ought to be encouraged to develop into concrete programs and initiatives.

Many ethical values, fundamental to the development of a peaceful society, are particularly relevant to the ecological question. The fact that many challenges facing the world today are interdependent confirms the need for carefully coordinated solutions based on a morally coherent worldview.

For Christians, such a worldview is grounded in religious convictions drawn from Revelation.[2]

Then, in November 1991, the United States Bishops Conference issued a pastoral letter, *Renewing the Earth,* calling for reflection and action based on Catholic social teaching to reverse the terrible devastation of the earth by human action. They cited six goals for this letter:

1. To highlight the ethical dimensions of the environmental crisis.
2. To link questions of ecology and poverty, environment and development.
3. To stand with working men and women and poor and disadvantaged persons, whose lives are often impacted by ecological abuse and trade-offs between environment and development.
4. To promote a vision of a just and sustainable world community.
5. To invite the Catholic community and men and women of good will to reflect more deeply on the religious dimensions of this topic.
6. To begin a broader conversation on the potential contribution of the Church to environmental questions.

'Above all, we seek to explore the links between concern for the person and for the earth, between natural ecology and social ecology. The web of life is one.'[3]

However, the issues at the root of this crisis are not new, nor are they un-

---

2. John Paul II, *The Ecological Crisis: A Common Responsibility,* nn. 1–2, 8 December 1989.
3. USCCB, *Renewing the Earth: An Invitation to Reflection and Action on Environment in Light of Catholic Social Teaching,* Washington, DC, US Bishops' Statement, 14 November 1991, available at http://www.usccb.org/issues-and-action/human-life-and-dignity/environment/renewing-the-earth.cfm (last accessed 28.01.16).

familiar to members of the Order of Preachers. It will come as no surprise, then, that before the leaders of the Church spoke out, members of the Order were active in the study and preaching needed to call people to the Truth.

DOMINICAN TRADITION AND RESPONSE

The Albigensian heresy that ravaged southern Europe in the late twelfth and early thirteenth centuries challenged the traditional Jewish and Christian belief that all creation as it comes from the Divine Hand is good, or, as the first chapter of Genesis puts it, 'very good'. The Albigensian dualistic world view saw all material as evil and only the spiritual as good. Preachers supporting this errant belief appeared credible; they dressed simply, eating and drinking little and travelling on foot. They offered stark contrast to the official preachers of the Church, bishops and abbots, who arrived in towns on horseback, attended by an impressive retinue, dressed in fine garments and obviously well fed. As they travelled through southern France, Bishop Diego of Osma, Spain, and his companion, Dominic Guzman, a canon of the cathedral at Osma, became convinced that credible preachers of the orthodox tradition could help repair the damage done to the faith of the people by the heresy. Thus the Order of Preachers began, not only with the men who walked the roads of Europe in pairs, preaching the Gospel and challenging the heretics in public disputations, but also with the women of Prouilhe, forming what became known as The Holy Preaching, communities of people living the Gospel message and preaching or supporting the preachers by prayer and hospitality. The writings and teachings of Albertus Magnus, Thomas Aquinas and Meister Eckhart offer early testimony to the truth of the goodness of creation and expose the errors of dualistic thought that would deny this. Clearly, a correct understanding of creation forms an important part of the Dominican tradition right from its beginning, although attention to this dimension of the tradition has waxed and waned across the centuries.

The latter third of the twentieth century saw intense activity, especially among the women of the Order, regarding the Earth, our place in the community of creatures, and a cosmology arising from the new scientific knowledge available to the human community. War, industrialisation, consumerism, greed, wanton use of resources, ignorance and apathy have all contributed to the degradation of the environment. Dominican women have studied, prayed and worked against this evil and the threat it represents to the health of the planet's ecosystems and the very survival of the many species, including human beings, who inhabit it. Passing on a compromised

environment to subsequent generations is an injustice that we cannot ignore. In response to these signs of the times, the women of the Order have:
- founded Earth literacy centres
- established farms using sustainable methods of agriculture
- published works in theological and biblical studies
- offered retreats and spirituality programmes
- designed curricula used at every level of education
- begun a centre promoting and advocating environmental legislation
- preached the Gospel and taught in a variety of venues calling people to ever greater communion with, reverence towards and respect for all creation as a revelation of the Divine.

GENESIS FARM AND MIRIAM MacGILLIS OP:
SEEDBED AND SOWER OF GOOD NEWS FOR THE EARTH

Miriam MacGillis is a member of the Dominican Sisters of Caldwell, New Jersey. She lives and works at Genesis Farm, which she co-founded in 1980 with the sponsorship of her Dominican congregation. In 2005 she received the Thomas Berry Award, and in 2007 was named among the top 15 green religious leaders by *Grist* magazine. She lectures extensively and has conducted workshops in the US, Canada, Europe, Asia and the Pacific.

Sr Miriam Therese MacGillis (Caldwell), was educated as a teacher and a fine artist, with degrees from Caldwell College and the University of Notre Dame. She taught young children, high school girls and college students for a number of years. Her passion for justice was fired through her work with an organisation called Global Education Associates and, as a result of this, she became the Director of the Archdiocese of Newark's Office of Peace and Justice. In 1977 Global Education Associates convened a conference at Maryknoll, Ossining, NY. They invited Thomas Berry CP to address the gathering. Fr Berry began by identifying himself as a 'geologian', as he explored, through study, the revelation being discovered by the current study of the universe and the Earth in particular. At Maryknoll he presented a paper, 'Contemplation and World Order', in which he asked: 'What world order are we contemplating?' He referred to the two great works of revelation: Scripture and the natural world. This insight is clearly present in the writings of Thomas Aquinas:

For [God] brought all things into being in order that [divine] goodness might be communicated to all creatures, and be represented by them; because [God's] goodness could not be adequately represented by one creature alone, [God] produced many and diverse creatures, that what was wanting to one in the representation of the divine goodness might be supplied by another. For goodness, which in God is simple and uniform, in creatures is manifold and divided, and hence the whole universe together participates in the divine goodness more perfectly and represents it better than any single creature whatever.[4]

Berry noted that our knowledge and understanding of the natural world had changed dramatically in recent decades, but he wondered whether these new understandings had affected our contemplation.

MacGilllis had been reading the work of Teilhard de Chardin and Berry's words deeply challenged her. Under Berry's tutelage, she began studying his writings, which took the work of Teilhard de Chardin and the insights of modern science to a new level of understanding of cosmology and its implications for human life, including religious life. For example, MacGillis notes, modern telescopes have taken the human eye further than ever before possible. People can see light that left its origin billions of years ago. This ability to see includes a sacred call to one who believes in a Creator God. Contemplating the universe like this enables human beings to create new meaning for themselves.[5] Far from perpetuating the dualistic thinking resulting from the days of the Black Death in Europe, through the Industrial Revolution of the eighteenth century and beyond, in which faith and science became antagonists for many people, this new avenue of contemplation can bring faith and empirical knowledge together as partners in receiving the revelation coming from God as reflected in the universe.

When her congregation invited proposals for the use of a newly inherited property in rural New Jersey, MacGillis described a vision of a centre where Berry's insights might be lived out and taught. This idea was endorsed by the congregation and thus, in 1980, Genesis Farm, an Earth literacy centre, began.

At Genesis Farm people raise serious questions about the global crises and evoke the rich spiritual insights that are within the hearts of all people. Focusing on connections between improving the state of the environment and the health of human communities within particular bioregions, they address the basic issues of our time in concert with all people of good will,

---

4. Thomas Aquinas, *Summa Theologiae*, I, 47, a 1, tr. Fathers of the English Dominican Province. New York: Benziger Brothers, 1947, available at: http://www.newadvent.org/summa/1047.htm (last accessed: 28.01.16).

5. Miriam MacGillis OP, 'Contemplating Universe and Earth: Charism, Call and Commitment', talk given at Mt. St Dominic Motherhouse, Caldwell, NJ, 13 November 2010.

learning together how to become part of creating that health, both inwardly and outwardly. The writings of biologists, physicists and other scientists make it ever clearer that human society must alter its perceptions about how their actions and choices affect the earth. The survival of the human species must be seen as depending upon the quality of air and water. Echoing Berry's thinking, MacGillis calls on all human institutions – religious, governmental, economic and educational – to reform their thinking and actions so as to express these new understandings adequately, and reverse the rush towards destruction currently caused by ignorance and inaction.

There are no easy or quick answers. At Genesis Farm, people try to learn more, and to experiment with changing themselves and their own behaviour. This is difficult, and demands that people encourage each other to be creative and hopeful rather than discouraged or paralysed into non-action.

Genesis Farm is rooted in a belief that the universe, the Earth, and all reality are various reflections of God's infinite goodness and beauty. All the ecological and agricultural work done there is rooted in this deep belief. This sacred mystery, known by so many religious names, is the common thread in all their efforts.

The approach to learning at the farm is holistic – a way of seeing all people and human cultures, in addition to the lands, waters and creatures of the planet, as an evolving, interconnected web of life. We are more than the sum of our parts. Each of us, in our unique body, mind, and spirit, is connected to, and responsible for, the larger community and the goods we hold in common, including the Earth. The programmes of Genesis Farm encourage the integration of body, mind and spirit within this unity.

Genesis Farm is located on 231 acres of preserved farmland and open space in the beautiful ridge and valley region of northwest New Jersey. While trying to become more Earth-enhancing in patterns of living, it offers hospitality and shared learning experiences through a variety of residential and non-residential programmes, courses, hands-on workshops, and film and lecture series.

Curricula at Genesis Farm are based on the insights and work of hosts of thinkers, scientists, artists, ecologists, activists and religious pioneers, and most especially on the work of Thomas Berry and Brian Swimme. Gardening there involves working with the soil and with the energies of the land and the universe itself. This biodynamic approach finds its roots in the work of Austrian metaphysician Rudolph Steiner. It is not a simple method and requires specialised training to implement well. Swiss master gardener, Heinz

Thomet, introduced this method in the early days of Genesis Farm.

MacGillis lectures and offers workshops in many countries, and her recorded presentations are widely distributed as well. In addition, people have come from Europe, Australia, Southeast Asia and all over North America to study, live and work at Genesis Farm. Many have returned to their homelands to begin Earth literacy centres or work in such centres based on their experience and study at Genesis Farm.

Buildings in the grounds express in wood and stone the principles being taught and lived there.[6] A farmhouse built in the 1830s with a kitchen added more than 150 years later offers the warmth of age along with plenty of space for meal preparation and cooking classes. There are five guest rooms with three bathrooms, and a composting toilet was installed in 1987. A guest house, Bread and Roses, has welcomed programme participants since 1990 and can accommodate 12 guests. Wildwood Hermitage, a cosy, simple structure, offers hospitality to those seeking silence and solitude. The library is home to over 2,800 books, journals, and other resources pertaining to Earth literacy. This former tractor shed was renovated in 1991 to provide classroom and library space for Earth literacy students and, in 2009, additional space and technology upgrades for teaching were added. A former farm building renovated in 1998 provides staff working spaces and a small conference room. A small greenhouse serves as a space for sprouting seeds and storing garden tools. The Strawbale Hermitage, built in 1992, is a simple, peaceful sanctuary at the edge of the forest. The house, built of straw bales, demonstrates beautiful, yet energy-efficient, sustainable building. Construction was started in 1993 by teams of international volunteers, also providing an opportunity for local community members and builders to work and learn together. The house has a composting toilet and grey water waste system. A solar space-heating panel was added to the roof in 2007. The barn's lower level, which once housed dairy cows and stored milk, now offers space for workshops and storage. The upper level is an open space for programme activities. Its post and beam construction, with the date 1836 carved into one of the major beams, offers another reminder of the history of this place. The Garden House, the heart of the community supported garden, contains a root cellar and a distribution centre, where garden members pick up their weekly produce. The second level houses an office, a kitchen and a workspace where seeds are saved. Attached is a greenhouse used to start seeds in

6. The information about the buildings and grounds of Genesis Farm is taken from its website: www.genesisfarm.org (last accessed 27.06.12).

the spring and grow summer vegetables and herbs and winter salad greens.

The beauty of the farmland and the creativity of its friends continue to be cultivated, and they reveal the influence of MacGillis' artistic eye and skill. An art studio offers people a work space in which to express their visions. *Lychtos*, a sculpture by Frederick Franck, is the centrepiece of the flower and herb garden. The Memorial Garden, designed as a 'river of life', is planted with wild flowers whose seeds are sown during the growing season in memory of those who have died. An underground spring feeds a pond and then winds through the woods into the meadow and wetlands. The water flow varies with the seasons and weather, but the stream bed is always visible. Frogs, turtles, fish, herons and the occasional swimming bear inhabit or visit the pond. With a dock and boathouse, this is a favourite place for summer swims and restful canoeing. The acres of wetlands, a rich ecosystem, offer young summer campers close-up encounters with the web of life – turtles, frogs, birds, cattails and more.

New life and insights from modern science enhance the farm. A kiwi orchard, planted in 1986, provides grape-sized kiwis after the first ripening frost of autumn. The Tea Garden, made with wood milled on the farm, features raised beds containing a variety of herbs that are used in the farm's kitchen. The Seed-Saving Sanctuary Garden was created in 2001 for cultivating, saving and distributing 15 varieties of heritage tomato seeds. The solar panels, installed in 2005, provide electricity for the farmhouse, library, office and the Strawbale Hermitage.

Even mealtime finds people living the principles being taught: vegetarian meals, served buffet style at the farmhouse, consist of fresh, organic (whenever possible) fruit and vegetables with a variety of grains, beans, seeds and nuts. Eggs and small amounts of dairy foods, including cheese and yogurt, are used occasionally. Every effort is made to use seasonal and locally grown foods.

The Dominican Sisters of Caldwell have placed all but five of these 226 acres into farmland and woodland preservation, with the hope that the community of all life will be nourished by this place long into the future. Many congregations of religious in the US have found themselves holding title to rich farmlands and other valuable properties as part of their stable patrimony. A number of them have decided to take legal steps to preserve the land for healthy use and prevent wanton development.

The community-supported garden at Genesis Farm came into being more than 25 years ago and feeds about 300 families annually. Members buy 'shares' and pick up their vegetables at the distribution building weekly or bi-weekly, depending on the size of their share. Cultivating approximately 35 acres, three gardeners and their apprentices grow vegetables, beans, grains, herbs, fruit and flowers, using biodynamic methods. Members and other volunteers often help with weeding and harvesting. The gardens and fields of Genesis Farm also serve as an outdoor classroom for the local charter school

GENESIS FARM LEARNING CENTRE PROGRAMMES

Transformation of a culture's awareness, beliefs and stories about the universe, and the place and purpose of human beings within it, is the foundation for any deep change in the world. This understanding is core to the farm's mission as staff work with others to transform the ecological devastation being caused by the western industrial economy. Through its educational programmes and its commitment to action, Genesis Farm offers diverse and innovative educational experiences that inspire a comprehensive approach to change, both personal and social.

Earth literacy is the primary focus of the programmes offered at the farm. Students explore the mysterious unity and relationships binding the Earth and the totality of life under conditions out of which the Earth has emerged within a single unfolding universe. Simultaneously, Earth literacy is a movement of people who understand that any viable future for the human species depends completely upon the viability of the planet. This movement arises from a desire to work not just for the Earth's survival, but for the transformation of all the limited beliefs, values, institutions and structures that promote domination, violence, destitution and powerlessness among people, and between people and the natural world.

Now celebrating its thirtieth anniversary, Genesis Farm works with people in other movements towards a sustainable future for the Earth and all its inhabitants. Transition Towns, responding to the reality that the Earth's oil supply has already peaked, climate unpredictability and both ecological and economic instability, engages people in responding to questions like: How are we to live into such a moment with intention and hope? How can we act on our commitment to life and the common good? A network of imaginative and locally focused initiatives, Transition Towns supports local leadership efforts to engage people to take the far-reaching actions that are required to mitigate the effects of these crises and build community resilience. These efforts are designed to result in a life with greater social connection, vibrancy, equity and fulfilment. This community-wide process for creating 'energy descent pathways' has spread around the world.[7] Genesis Farm is a natural partner in such a movement.

Permaculture methods taught through programmes at the farm show participants how to grow plants native to their bioregions that can supply food for their families and beautify their environment while respecting the natural properties of the soil. Programmes teaching more careful use of water and even construction and use of rain barrels are on the calendar of events.

MacGillis still directs the farm, but with the support of a maturing board of trustees looks to a succession plan that ensures the vitality of Genesis Farm into the future.

BRANCHES, FRUIT AND NEW PLANTINGS
A number of other congregations of Dominican sisters, many as a result of MacGillis' influence, have established farms and Earth literacy centres of various types in various parts of the world. Some of these include:
- An Tairseach (Wicklow, Ireland) – farm, centre and land for learning
- Catherine's Well (Trinidad-Tobago), focused on the theology of creation, with emphasis on ecology
- Churches' Center for Land and People (Sinsinawa), supporting rural life and farming;
- Crown Point Ecology Center (Akron – now Peace)
- Dominican Community Garden (Houston) – food for those in need
- Eckhart Community (East London, South Africa)
- Eco-Justice Center (Racine) – Education and care of the Earth
- Heartland Farm and Spirituality Center (Great Bend, now Peace) – organic agriculture and holistic health
- Homecoming: Sophia Garden and Learning Center (Amityville) – unity of human life and all of creation
- Ilanz (Switzerland) Motherhouse of the Dominican Sisters of St Joseph
- Jubilee Farm (Springfield) – ecology and spirituality
- Kormiko Centre (New Zealand) – preaching, teaching, reflecting and political action on behalf of the Earth
- Maryknoll Ecological Center (Baguio City, Philippines) – A 'secret garden' taking visitors on the cosmic evolutionary journey, with 14 'stations' along the way.[8]

7. www.genesisfarm.org (last accessed: 27.06.12).
8. See Chapter 16, 'Portraits, Sketches and Snapshots: Maryknoll Sisters around the World', pp. 289-323.

- Masiphuhlisane Catholic Project (East London, South Africa)
- ROAR: Religious Organizations Along the River – network of religious (including the Dominicans of Hope) and organisations along the Hudson River Valley of NY State – protecting the ecosystem in this bioregion
- Schlehdorf (Germany) – interfaith 'Sustainable Churches'
- Shepherd's Corner (Peace) – harmony between human beings and all creation
- St Catharine Farm (Kentucky, now Peace) – Collaborating with the University of Kentucky to demonstrate 170 acres of sustainable cattle-grazing techniques.

As members of the Order grew in consciousness and knowledge of the realities of the revelation available through the universe and the human activity threatening life on Earth, other Dominican responses have been characteristically diverse and creative. In this variety of responses Dominicans address the four groups of human institutions that Berry and MacGillis have identified as needing reform. The following sections sample their efforts.

WRITERS

Theologians and writers have used the power of the pen to preach Truth regarding issues of all sorts, and in this the issue of ecology is no different.

Sharon Therese Zayac, a Dominican sister of Springfield, Illinois, is the author of *Earth Spirituality: In the Catholic and Dominican Traditions.*[9] As the title implies, Zayac succinctly traces the spiritual traditions both of ecology and of the Dominican and the wider Christian traditions. After study, including time at Genesis Farm with Miriam MacGillis and a master's degree in Earth literacy from Saint Mary-of-the-Woods College in Indiana, she became the director of Jubilee Farm, her congregation's centre for ecology and spirituality. She skilfully weaves together papal and episcopal statements, reaching back to *Rerum Novarum* in 1891 and including writings of John Paul II and contemporary bishops from several countries. She cites the wisdom of the Catholic tradition as well as the fallacies that have enabled our destructive behaviour. She then shows how the work of early Dominicans, especially Albert, Thomas and Eckhart, offer foundational support for contemporary scholars and preachers. She devotes particular attention to the work of reading the Scriptures in the light of the ecological crisis. She notes six principles

9. Sharon Therese Zayac, OP, *Earth Spirituality: In the Catholic and Dominican Traditions,* Boerne, Texas, Sor Juana Press, 2001.

used by contemporary scholars in reading biblical texts:

- The principle of intrinsic worth. The universe, the Earth, and all of its components have intrinsic worth and value.
- The principle of interconnectedness. The Earth is a community of interconnected living things that are mutually dependent on each other for life and survival.
- The principle of voice. The Earth is a subject capable of raising its voice in celebration and against injustice.
- The principle of purpose. The universe, the Earth, and all its components, are part of a dynamic, cosmic design within which each piece has a place in the overall goal of that design.
- The principle of mutual custodianship. The Earth is a balanced and diverse domain where responsible custodians can function as partners, rather than rulers, to sustain a balanced and diverse Earth community.
- The principle of resistance. The Earth and its components not only suffer from injustices at the hands of human beings, but also actively resist them.[10]

This book makes the case for Dominicans, indeed all Catholics, to take seriously the traditions of our faith in facing the ecological crisis of today.

Besides presenting hundreds of programmes, days of reflection, retreats, workshops and study sessions on topics related to Earth literacy, spirituality, religious life and ecological issues, Zayac has also participated in training sessions presented by Al Gore in preparing to present his award-winning film, *An Inconvenient Truth.*

Theologian Mary Catherine Hilkert (Dominican Sisters of Peace) writes and speaks extensively of the challenges the universe offers theologians. In her writing, although the focus is not specifically the crisis of the Earth, she voices the laments of the powerless and thus offers a template for doing theology that attends to the ecological crisis. Rooted in the tradition of the Order, she integrates respect for creation into her work.[11]

Biblical scholar Carol Dempsey OP (Caldwell) has written extensively on these issues. After inviting her university colleagues to reflect on ecology from the vantage point of their disciplines, she has edited and published their contributions.[12]

10. Norman Habel (ed.), *Readings from the Perspective of Earth*, Sheffield, Sheffield Academic Press, 2000, 24, quoted in Zayac, op. cit., pp. 64–65.

11. For example, Mary Catherine Hilkert, 'Bearing Wisdom – the Vocation of the Preacher', *Spirituality Today*, vol. 44, no. 2, pp. 143–60.

12. Carol Dempsey OP and Mary Margaret Pazdan OP (eds.), *Earth, Wind, and Fire: Biblical and Theological Perspectives on Creation*, Collegeville, MN, The Liturgical Press, 2004; Carol J. Dempsey

Linda Gibler OP (Houston, Texas), formerly a student and intern at Genesis Farm, and then a graduate of the California Institute of Integral Studies, addresses sacramental theology in her book *From the Beginning to Baptism: Scientific and Sacred Stories of Water, Oil, and Fire.*[13] She explores the elements of the sacrament of Baptism in light of the evolving story of the universe. She traces those elements from their earliest appearance in the universe to their use in contemporary sacramental celebrations. She includes their functions in the community of creatures, their use by human beings from the earliest times, biblical and patristic reference to them and the understandings of them in the prayers of the liturgy of the Church. Gibler also includes comments on insightful and outdated references in liturgical texts.

Combining the roles of theologian, writer, preacher and justice promoter, Margaret Galiardi OP (Amityville, NY), invites readers and hearers to 'ponder the question of just what it is that constitutes the way of living and acting that typifies true discipleship, not in abstract historical time, but rather at *this* moment.'[14] She echoes the understanding of many theologians when she remarks that the cosmological story emanating from the universe today confirms her suspicion that the God often preached is 'much too small!'[15] The wonder and awe of the story invites us deeper into the depths of the Mystery of God.

Poet-professor Elizabeth Michael Boyle OP (Caldwell), in *Science as Sacred Metaphor: An Evolving Revelation,*[16] offers an invitation to begin with the science unfolding before us and follow its lead to a stance of contemplative wonder. Structuring her reflections on the liturgical year, she reflects with poetry on the theological mysteries she encounters through her wrestling with the truths taught by science.

An even greater commitment to preaching the Word regarding ecology was made by Carol Coston OP (Adrian) and Elise Garcia OP (Adrian) in founding the Sor Juana Press. Both women had begun as advocates for jus-

---

and Russell A. Butkus (eds.), *All Creation Is Groaning: An Interdisciplinary Vision for Life in a Sacred Universe*, Collegeville, Liturgical Press, 1999; Carol Dempsey, 'Creation, Revelation, and Redemption: Recovering the Biblical Tradition for Ecology', in Edward Foley and Robert Schreiter, *The Wisdom of Creation*, Collegeville, MN, The Liturgical Press, 2004, pp. 53–64; Carol Dempsey, 'Ask the Animals, and They Will Teach You: The Gift of Wisdom and the Natural World', *The Bible Today*, vol. 35/3 (May/June, 1997), pp. 147–51.

13. Linda Gibler OP, Collegeville, MN, The Liturgical Press, 2010.

14. Margaret Galiardi, OP, *Where the Pure Water Flows: The New Story of the Universe and Christian Faith*. San Antonio, TX, Sor Juana Press, 2008.

15. Galiardi, written response to a questionnaire circulated in 2010 by Honora Werner OP. Her response was written in November 2010.

16. Elizabeth Michael Boyle OP, *Science as Metaphor: An Evolving Revelation*, Collegeville, MN, The Liturgical Press, 2006.

tice at the national level (NETWORK, Partners for the Common Good, and Common Cause). In addition to publishing those writing on theological aspects of ecology, Sor Juana Press dedicates its energies to publishing the work of women of colour and women religious on topics arising from women's spirituality and the relationship with the Earth. The press was named in honour of Sor Juana Ines de la Cruz (1648–1695), a Mexican nun, scholar, poet and playwright, musician and scientist, who, although silenced for advocating for women's rights to education, continued to voice concern for their right to learn. The press as a pulpit allows women's preaching voices to be heard in defence of the ecological movement and in leading others to reflect upon our evolving common origin story. For a number of years these sisters also directed Sanctuario Sisterfarm, celebrating the rich diversity of life on Earth. They collaborated with the Latinas of the Texas-Mexico border to demonstrate living lightly on the land while honouring the wisdom of the Latina women of the area.

A LEGAL INITIATIVE

Patricia Siemen OP (Adrian) entered the arena of ecology from her training as an attorney. Her work with Latino and African-American communities struggling for dignity, racial respect, equality, empowerment and economic justice led her to law school in order 'to better represent "the voiceless" – those who had no access to the legal system or remedies.'[17] Subsequently she worked with the US Department of Justice, the Civil Rights Division and the Voting Rights Division, and then moved on to represent farm workers in Immokalee, Florida. She served a few years in congregational leadership and became more aware of environmental degradation. She studied Berry's work, becoming aware of the sacred dimension of the earth. After a year of study at Sophia Center, Holy Names College, Oakland, she went to Genesis Farm, New Jersey. There she became aware of MacGillis' work with the Earth Ethics Institute at Miami Dade College in Miami, Florida. She became its director, working to infuse Earth literacy and ethics into the curriculum.

In 2005 her congregation received a bequest to advance Catholic education in Florida. She wrote a proposal that they start a centre for Earth jurisprudence at the two Catholic law schools in Florida: Barry University and St Thomas University. Inspired by Berry's thinking, she explained that the legal system sustains and legitimates the processes of ecological destruction,

---

17. Patricia Siemen OP, written response to a questionnaire circulated in 2010 by Honora Werner OP. Her response was written on 13 March 2011.

is not equipped to address issues of climate change, ecological refugees, the end of peak oil, increased accumulative poisons, soil erosion and desertification and massive loss of species. She proposed that the centre prepare lawyers to address these critical issues from a sensitive and skilled position, regardless of the type of law they might practise. As graduates of a Catholic law school, she maintained that the students needed to be aware of the moral, ethical and legal implications of ecologically overstressed systems.

Upon receiving a grant for five years, Siemen began the Center for Earth Jurisprudence in August 2006. A curriculum of courses and seminars, annual colloquia and conferences and a quarterly newsletter form parts of the programme. Both law schools have received recognition from the profession and academic bodies for their work on Earth jurisprudence. Although other law schools offer environmental certificate programmes, this centre is the only one of its kind in the US offering degrees in Earth jurisprudence.

Siemen collaborates with centres, institutes and movements to advance legal protection of nature in Australia, Bolivia, Ecuador, Ethiopia, India, Kenya, the Philippines, South Africa and the UK. Most of the efforts towards providing legal representation of ecosystems, forests and marine mammals are led by indigenous people.

When reflecting on her work in the light of her Dominican vocation, Siemen notes that, 'either we Dominicans understand the massive ethical, moral and legal challenges facing our ecological demise or we abandon our moral standing as having anything to say to the greatest threat to the survival of Earth.'[18] She goes on to reflect that seeking and preaching truth would be meaningless if the home in which we celebrate God's goodness and beauty is destroyed. She wonders if we will be the ones to allow the face of God known only through the revelation through creation to be marred beyond recognition. She summons us to be hospice workers and midwives, accompanying the death and dying while bringing forth new life and alternatives for life on Earth.

EDUCATION FOR THE GOOD OF EARTH AND EARTHLINGS

Gervaise Valpey OP (San Rafael, California), reflecting upon her work as a Dominican woman in education, refers to the first intentionally sustainable communities of the Order: the medieval monasteries and convents. She notes that Dominican women, recognising our interconnectedness with all of creation and our corresponding responsibility for its future well-being, have

18. Ibid.

studied and called one another to focus on this issue as congregations and in our schools.[19] Study at Genesis Farm with Miriam MacGillis added impetus to the motivation she had from her childhood in an agricultural community. Sharon Zayac and Carol Coston also provided her with inspiration and example. Valpey developed a programme for a school incorporating many facets of social ethics into its spirituality, its curriculum and its practices. With a grant from her congregation and the help of green architect Sim van der Ryn, she and her colleagues launched Sustainable San Domenico in San Anselmo, California, in September 1994. The school educates children from pre-kindergarten through grade 12, with boarding (high school only) and commuting students. On 512 acres of land San Domenico boasts a Garden of Hope featuring organically grown fruit trees, vegetables and flowers, irrigated using a drip system. Buildings include:

- a tool shed made with cob and recycled wood (teaching students how people around the globe build)
- covered outdoor classrooms, kitchen and compost bins
- a secure chicken house built by faculty and students
- a cob oven and benches for baking foods for the school community.

In addition, straw bale and tree stump circles were created for use in poetry, reading, writing and religion classes. Students' artwork is displayed throughout the garden. Summer programmes, after-school classes, gatherings of parents and the larger community, and festivals take place there. Produce from the garden that is not used at San Domenico and bread baked by the students is shared with local facilities that offer food to people in need, where students also help to serve.

The school's food service buys from local farmers' markets and prepares healthy meals for the entire school community. Cleaning and supplies used for maintenance comply with ecological best practices. To reduce the number of vehicles used to transport students, a programme with an independent bus company provides transport for all students. This very expensive service is included in tuition. The school is working to extend the use of the water from their artesian well to water the playing fields and plantings around the buildings. In partnership with a solar energy company, the school has installed solar panels that provide about 85 per cent of their energy. This project was also a part of the school's curriculum.

All of this work has been done while providing in-service and faculty de-

19. Gervaise Valpey OP, written response to a questionnaire circulated in 2010 by Honora Werner OP. Her response was written in November 2010.

velopment opportunities through the Center for Ecoliteracy in Oakland and the Sophia Center at Holy Names University, with guest speakers Thomas Berry, Miriam MacGillis, David Orr, Mary Evelyn Tucker and Brian Swimme. The Dominican Sisters of San Rafael have adopted the Earth Charter so that incorporating this wisdom into the students' studies is organic too.

Sustainable San Domenico is but one example of Dominican women developing curricula for all levels of education that incorporate ethical principles addressing the ecological crises of these times.

Some sisters work in programmes that are not academic in nature, but serve to educate people about sustainable living appropriate to their situations. One such is EarthLinks in the city of Denver, Colorado. Here women from the Hope and Sinsinawa congregations work with people who are homeless, helping them connect with the natural world. The project involves teaching people skills for beekeeping, worm farming and marketing, vermin-culture and organic gardening. Prior to working in Denver Julie Schwab (Sinsinawa) had ministered in Guatemala, teaching women there to raise and plant trees in an effort towards reforestation. The women's co-operatives there also became successful micro-economic projects. Subsequently, Schwab has worked with her congregation to transition their farmland to organic farming.

DOMINICANS IN HEALTH CARE AND THE HEALTH OF EARTH

In comparing contemporary times with the thirteenth century Mary Ellen Leciejewski OP (Adrian) notes many similarities:

- illiteracy – today, this is less verbal and more ecological
- hunger for truth – although flooded with data today, it is often difficult to find truth (e.g. food labelling is often insufficient)
- helplessness in the face of people with power – then feudal lords, now multinational corporations
- dualistic thinking – then Albigensian heresy, now belief that the earth is to be exploited without limits, for and by human beings.

She sees in all this an opportunity for the power of Dominican preaching to bring good news.[20]

Leciejewski began to be drawn into working for the Earth's health when she encountered Miriam MacGillis at a conference on the fate of the Earth in 1982. She continued her study at several ecology centres, including Genesis

---

20. Mary Ellen Leciejewski,OP, written response to a questionnaire circulated in 2010 by Honora Werner OP. Her response was written in November 2010.

Farm, and finally earned a master's degree in ecology from the University of Illinois. The following year she began serving as the Ecology Program Coordinator at Catholic Healthcare West (CHW), working out of San Francisco, California. CHW is the fourth largest not-for-profit health care system in the US, and includes 41 hospitals in California, Nevada and Arizona. Theirs was one of the first hospital systems to employ ecology and sustainability administrators. As healing occurs in the hospitals' surgical suites and patient rooms, they make the connection with the healing needed in local communities and on the planet.

Employees are trained to reduce, reuse, recycle, reprocess, redesign and restore. Leciejewski coordinates this education and other activities, promoting good planet health. She ensures the use of environmentally safe products and processes, and educates vendors and suppliers about these sustainability policies while enlisting their support and co-operation. These policies result in such practical applications as food waste reduction, reduction or elimination of chemicals, green building, data collection and education. Leciejewski incorporates the spirituality of oneness with all creation into discussions and presentations at the hospitals. She receives reports from the green teams in each hospital detailing their goals and progress and she posts them on the CHW website. She has organised a CHW Sustainability Team at the administrative level to ensure that CHW's vision for the future continues to be implemented and integrated into the culture of the organisation. She has assisted the Food and Nutrition Council at CHW in developing a vision statement that helps CHW support food and agricultural systems that are healthy for human beings, animals and the land. CHW hospitals use locally produced foods – organically grown, fish and meat from animals free from unnecessary hormones, pesticides and antibiotics, Fair Trade coffee – do composting, support on-campus farmers' markets, create hospital gardens and use the produce grown there. Minimising the use of disposables and bottled water, and taking public stands against genetically modified sugar beets and animal cloning are all part of the efforts she has led in hospital communities. Efforts to reduce the waste of materials generated in the hospitals during a variety of activities have proved successful: using reusable sharps containers, participating in needle take-back programs, switching to DEHP/PVC-free intravenous bags (thus reducing the carcinogens released when they are manufactured or incinerated), and encouraging manufacturers to develop computers using less toxic chemicals. She notes that they work both 'upstream and downstream', that is, in receiving goods made in unhealthy ways and in disposing of materials to ease abuse of the earth.

Despite all this work done in a short time span, Leciejewski sees that there is yet much to be done. For example, in 2010, 80,000 chemicals were manufactured and used in the US, but the Environmental Protection Agency of the federal government required comprehensive testing of only 200. In collaboration with other hospital systems and national organisations, she and other Dominican women, including Roselli Tria (San Rafael), continue to educate and advocate for ecological concerns.

PRAYING AND PREACHING WITH NEW AWARENESS OF THE UNIVERSE
Dominican women administer and programme many retreat centres where people come to be refreshed, to reflect and often find new ways of viewing their world. These centres have become places where retreatants hear the invitation to come home to Earth and realise their rightful place in creation. In centres like Mariandale, Ossining, NY (Hope), Springbank and Spirit Mountain (both Adrian), Heartland Center (Great Bend, now Peace), Siena Center (Racine) and Santa Sabina (San Rafael), programmes are run to help people connect their spirituality with the spirituality that reveres the revelation that comes through all creation and draws people more deeply into the Divine Mystery. Many Dominican sisters, like Nancy Erts (Hope), Margaret Galiardi (Amityville), Honora Werner (Caldwell), and their lay associates, having studied at centres like Genesis Farm, now preach and lead these retreats and invite other people who are similarly prepared to present programmes also. Some Dominican women, like Werner, engage in teaching preachers to use the cosmic lens for reading Scripture and for interpreting the lives of their hearers. These Dominicans are part of a groundswell of awareness that captures imaginations and feeds the hungers of people of diverse faith traditions. Celebrating the liturgical year and its festivals, the sacraments in their fullness and tapping into the Dominican tradition of incarnational spirituality, these programmes and this preaching also continue the ancient and ever new approaches of the Catholic tradition. When people encounter the Universe Story and ponder its implications for their own lives, the moral imperatives emanating from it challenge them and often channel a divine invitation to conversion.

CONCLUSION
Any attempt to overview the work of Dominican women addressing the moral and ethical issues arising from the study of ecology will be a faint re-

flection of the reality. As can be seen from the foregoing, the women tend towards itinerancy, moving from one area of endeavour to another in response to the needs of the time and the situations in which they find themselves. New projects arise continually and are given over into the hands of others, not Dominicans, so the work continues. Collaboration with people who are not members of the Order sometimes causes the identity of the Dominican women to be hidden from public view. Work in some areas of the globe precludes use of the Internet, thus depriving researchers of information about activities that are under way. Therefore it is difficult accurately to report the work being done by Dominican women in ecology. That being said, it is clear that the women of the Order have responded, and continue to respond, creatively and effectively to what many consider the most serious threat to life on Earth, the destruction of the planet by human actions and neglect. These women study assiduously the Book of Nature, the works of scientists, cosmologists, theologians, ethicists and others, contemplate deeply the data from their study, and preach the Good News to all of creation by their stamina, creativity and zeal, and through projects as diverse as the Order itself.

BIBLIOGRAPHY

Aquinas, Thomas, *Summa Theologiae,* Tr. Fathers of the English Dominican Province. New York: Benziger Brothers, 1947, available at http://www.newadvent.org/summa/1047.htm (last accessed 28.01.16).

Boyle, Elizabeth Michael, OP, *Science as Metaphor: An Evolving Revelation,* Collegeville, MN, The Liturgical Press, 2006.

The Catechism of the Catholic Church, English trans. United States Catholic Conference Inc., New York, Doubleday, 1994.

Dempsey, Carol, OP, and Pazden, Mary Margaret, OP (eds.) *Earth, Wind, and Fire: Biblical and Theological Perspectives on Creation,* Collegeville, MN, The Liturgical Press, 2004.

Dempsey, Carol, OP, and Butkus, Russell A. (eds.), *All Creation Is Groaning: An Interdisciplinary Vision for Life in a Sacred Universe,* Collegeville, The Liturgical Press, 1999.

Dempsey, Carol, OP, 'Creation, Revelation, and Redemption: Recovering the Biblical Tradition for Ecology,' in Edward Foley and Robert Schreiter (eds.), *The Wisdom of Creation,* Collegeville, MN, The Liturgical Press, 2004, pp. 53–64.

Dempsey, Carol, OP, 'Ask the Animals, and They Will Teach You: The Gift of Wisdom and the Natural World', *The Bible Today,* vol. 35/3 (May/June,

1997), pp. 147–51.

Galiardi, Margaret, OP, *Where the Pure Water Flows: The New Story of the Universe and Christian Faith*, San Antonio, TX, Sor Juana Press, 2008.

Gibler, Linda, OP, *From the Beginning to Baptism: Scientific and Sacred Stories of Water, Oil, and Fire*, Collegeville, MN, The Liturgical Press, 2010.

Habel, Norman (ed.), *Readings from the Perspective of Earth*, Sheffield, Sheffield Academic Press, 2000.

Hilkert, Mary Catherine, OP, 'Bearing Wisdom – the Vocation of the Preacher', *Spirituality Today*, vol. 44, no. 2, pp. 143–60.

John Paul II, *The Ecological Crisis: A Common Responsibility*, nos. 1–2, 8 December 1989.

MacGillis, Miriam, OP, 'Contemplating Universe and Earth: Charism, Call and Commitment', talk given at Mt St Dominic Motherhouse, Caldwell, NJ, 13 November 2010.

United States Conference of Catholic Bishops, *Renewing the Earth: An Invitation to Reflection and Action on Environment in Light of Catholic Social Teaching*, Washington, DC, US Bishops' Statement, 14 November 1991, available at http://www.usccb.org/issues-and-action/human-life-and-dignity/environment/renewing-the-earth.cfm (last accessed 28.01.16).

www.genesisfarm.org (last accessed: 27.06.2012).

http://storygroups.org/html/CosmicWalk.htm (last accessed 03.09.12).

Welcome to the Community Supported Garden at Genesis Farm!, CSG Handbook, Genesis Farm, Blairstown, NJ.

Werner, Honora, OP, unpublished survey of Dominican women in ecology done by circulating a questionnaire, November 2010.

Zayac, Sharon Therese, OP, *Earth Spirituality: In the Catholic and Dominican Traditions*, Boerne, TX, Sor Juana Press, 2001.

26

Preaching Justice through Socially Responsible Investing

PATRICIA DALY, O.P.

EMERGENCE OF CORPORATE RESPONSIBILITY

Dominican women were not the first to translate the axiom 'money talks' into 'money preaches'. In the US, as early as the seventeenth century, Quaker and Methodist congregations preached justice to those companies that employed slave labour by withholding investments from them. At other times throughout early modern history, religious groups have used the power of the boycott in an effort to exert control over entities that they considered socially dangerous, like gambling and alcohol. Fortunately, modern promoters of social justice have expanded the concept of moral responsibility considerably beyond narrow areas of personal sin to include collective crimes like war, economic exploitation and ecological degradation. Dominican women of the twentieth and twenty-first centuries entered socially responsible investing in the early 1970s as a preaching ministry by honestly acknowledging that the first audience for authentic preaching is always the preacher. Hence, Dominican finance officers introduced the concept by first educating the consciences of their members and all those within their spheres of influence to accept the Gospel dimensions of economic justice. By engaging with each other in a process that demanded candid self-evaluation, Dominican women became leaders in the movement known as Socially Responsible Investing (SRI).

Using graphs like those with which analysts critique federal budgets, Dominican treasurers and investment managers challenged the corporate consciences of their communities by showing how budgets are eloquent numerical statements that prove whether or not a community has translated purported values into action. After such enlightening demonstrations, most members eagerly embraced the concept of transforming the congregational portfolio into a tool for preaching justice.

Soon, by uniting in the joint strength of coalitions of investment power, religious investors were able to command attention in the financial community and to preach directly to those in powerful positions with the greatest potential to change corporate behaviour.

Founded on the premise that economic justice requires the ethical transformation of the corporate forces which control the world's resources, SRI
can be defined as *the use of investment power to promote the values of peace,
justice and integrity of creation by speaking the language that corporate economic
forces understand.* SRI advocates also recognise the need to use language that
members of religious congregations understand even better. When speaking or writing for a religious audience, Corinne Florek OP further nuances
general definitions of the term with words that boldly underscore SRI's demand on investors who profess a vow of poverty: '[SRI is] an economy of
solidarity that is critical of the present economic system … and that calls us
to put our resources … at the service of the most vulnerable' ('Investing in
Justice: Using Our Common Monies to Promote Our Critical Concerns'[1]). To
this end, Dominican women of the twentieth and twenty-first centuries have
strengthened their traditional and expanding apostolic roles with a new
model of preaching that directly addresses audiences, not in churches and
classrooms, but in corporate boardrooms.

In 1971, the World Synod of Bishops endorsed this form of preaching in
its historic document *Justice in the World*:

> Action on behalf of justice and participation in the transformation of the
> world appears to us as a constitutive dimension of the preaching of the
> gospel or, in other words, of the Church's mission for the redemption of
> the human race and its liberation from every oppressive situation. (n. 6)

By 2012, Dominican congregations of women involved in the SRI ministry can point to four decades of studying the most urgent economic and
environmental issues of our time through the lens of Gospel values and of
using their collective investment power to draw attention to the ethical consequences of many corporate business practices. In collaboration with social justice activists of other faiths, Dominican women have not limited their
preaching to 'consciousness-raising' through public protests and demonstrations. Following the Gospel injunction to learn from 'the children of this
world', they have become adept in various strategies for bringing financial
pressure to bear on business executives and their governing boards. At this
time, their principal methods of communicating this pressure are:

Screening. Religious investors draw up a policy specifying products and

---

1. http://www.mercyinvestmentservices.org/storage/documents/Investing_in_Justice.pdf
(last accessed 01.07.15).

business practices that they will not support and instruct their portfolio managers to use the policy to 'screen out' companies from current and/or future investment. Such screens may also be used to identify corporations that actively support the investor institution's values, for example progressive labour practices, independence from the military industry and sustainable environmental policies.

Shareholder resolutions. These offer the socially responsible investor the greatest opportunity to compel concern for consequences of a product or service beyond the 'bottom line'. Resolutions appear in the annual proxy, for vote by all the shareholders, thus educating investors and requesting the board of directors to act on various concerns. Investors present resolutions at annual stockholder meetings in language designed to win shareholder approval by linking moral issues with sound economic policy. Even 3 per cent of the vote would be a tremendous success and would enable the resolution to return to the proxy the next year (gaining perhaps 6 per cent and then 10 per cent in the second and third years). For the first 15 to 20 years of the movement, faith-based initiatives were not joined by serious investment power. The support of public pension funds and other large funds was not consistently forthcoming until well into the global warming strategy. Even the South Africa campaign did not garner great support until later. While many of our resolutions now receive 30–50 per cent of the votes, we are happy even today with a 3 per cent vote regarding a new, little-known concern.

Corporate dialogue. Over the years, SRI practitioners gradually replaced methods like boycotts with more sophisticated 'insider' strategies. Today, most of the work of corporate responsibility takes place in regular corporate dialogues with management teams that most often address a range of sustainability concerns with complex metrics to determine a company's progress.

Proxy voting. Religious investors are diligent in their voting on annual proxies, addressing not only social and environmental concerns, but also weighing in on important corporate governance issues.

Community investments. As sisters began to specialise in the SRI ministry, some congregations chose to invest not only in corporations but also in community-development projects, low-interest loans, co-operatives and partnerships.

DOMINICAN WOMEN ACTIVE IN SRI

This contribution will trace how Dominican women, individually and/or collectively, developed the concept of SRI from a short set of portfolio guidelines for congregational finance officers into full-time ministries for one or more members. Many Dominican women's congregations achieved a presence in spheres of influence far beyond the traditional parochial and campus territories familiar to teaching sisters, nurses and pastoral associates. This account of the scope, diversity and intensity of SRI activities by individuals and congregations is intended to be suggestive rather than exhaustive.

In general, it can be said that each congregation began by formulating a screening policy and then proceeded gradually to invest funds and/or personnel in the SRI ministry. Such investment first required the education of each congregation's membership through the assignment of individual members to study the moral implications of economic issues and then to educate their communities, trustees and colleagues regarding the relevance of these issues for the preaching of the Gospel.

In 1971 the Episcopal Church became the first religious institution to present a shareholder resolution asking General Motors to leave South Africa. Thus SRI became a tool widely used for social justice advocacy.

Additionally it was in 1971 that the Corporate Information Center (CIS) provided the first database for religious groups to begin implementing SRI policies for educating and influencing government and business executives to accept responsibility for policies whose consequences extended beyond corporate profits. Two years later, in 1973, CIS expanded into The Interfaith Center on Corporate Responsibility (ICCR). Organised Catholic involvement in this movement became apparent in 1973 with the formation of its Catholic arm, the National Catholic Coalition for Responsible Investment (NCCRI).

Also in 1971, the Adrian Dominican administration assigned Louise Borgacz OP to 'investigate the role that the Church, as investor, has in proclaiming the gospel'. Her 1972 study, 'Report on the Moral Responsibility of Corporate Investors', launched the Adrian Dominicans' deep and continuing commitment to SRI as a way of involving the whole congregation in 'preaching justice' by establishing 'consistency between its stated values and its financial resources'. Unsurprisingly, as soon as Louise Borgacz completed her report, the Adrian congregation promptly recognised its call to educate others in the concept of using investment-power to preach social justice. In the autumn of 1973, Louise Borgacz and Kathleen Noonan held a symposium on SRI at Adrian. As first steps toward enlisting a congregation's investment power for the preaching ministry, they advised finance administrators to:

- develop social-justice criteria for a congregational investment policy
- include fair employment practices; sensitivity to racism, sexism and ecological impact; economic opportunity for deprived populations; and a focus on businesses that support peace rather than war
- review portfolios regularly to determine that investments support these criteria
- initiate and/or co-operate with both positive and negative actions taken regarding corporations in relation to these criteria
- appoint a representative to the NCCRI.

Congregations who had attended the 1973 Adrian symposium left with such concrete guidelines for integrating policy and practice that the widespread adoption of action plans was virtually assured. Less than a year later in Sinsinawa, Mary Ellen Butcher OP and Mary Paynter OP implemented their action plan as they prepared the congregation's first shareholder action. At Gulf Oil's next annual meeting, Mary Paynter presented a shareholder resolution on labour concerns.

There are many ... questions, but ultimately, one must ask – and ask in a way that searches for truth without a preconceived answer – is the large corporation capable of responding to moral pressure? This is a frightening question not only because it admits no simple answer, but even more because to have asked it carries with it the responsibility of seeking an answer and then of acting on it.[2]

From 1974 onwards, the history of Dominican women's involvement in SRI paralleled and derived significant impact from its affiliation with the ICCR. This interfaith umbrella organisation represents the significant investment power of nearly 300 religious groups of many faiths who share its motto: 'Inspired by Faith, Committed to Action'. The following Dominican sisters congregations are listed as ICCR members either directly or through Catholic regional Coalitions for Responsible Investment: Dominican Sisters of Hope (originally Dominican Sisters of the Sick Poor and Newburgh), Dominican Sisters of Peace (most of the seven founding communities), Adrian Dominicans, Amityville, Blauvelt, Caldwell, Edmonds (now Adrian), Grand Rapids, Houston, Maryknoll, San Rafael, Sinsinawa, Sparkill, Springfield, Houston and Takoma, all sharing ICCR's declared mission: 'Through the lens of faith, ICCR builds a more just and sustainable world by integrating

---

2. Mary Ellen Butcher OP, Sinsinawa Dominican *exChange Magazine*, Dec. 19, 1974. See more about Mary Ellen Butcher in this volume, pp. 433-439.

social values into corporate and investor actions.'

DOMINICANS AND ANTI-APARTHEID

For many religious groups, the anti-apartheid movement was the first experience of using investment power to influence social policy. In solidarity with our Dominican sisters in South Africa taking the first steps to desegregate schools,[3] Dominicans in the US became active in filing shareholder resolutions and attending annual meetings of stockholders asking corporations to leave South Africa. It was during this period, and in conjunction with the apartheid protest also, that Dominican women at the Adrian motherhouse in Michigan first demonstrated the power of creative ritual to advertise a moral stance. In a unique ceremony with the artistic flair characteristic of women religious, the sisters symbolically destroyed hundreds of Shell Oil cards. Their well-publicised performance drew secular attention to a public denunciation of a company with ties to the South African police and military. Similar demonstrations created heightened awareness on numerous university campuses. Slowly but surely, disinvestment across the globe proved effective. International news media noted that for the first time in financial history, stock market prices declined for companies doing business in South Africa.

But even with international participation in the movement, it took decades to force the South African government to abandon its system of racial apartheid. In 1993, when Nelson Mandela stood before the UN to request the lifting of economic sanctions in view of the upcoming first democratic elections at that time, Dominican women could share in the triumph of social activists all over the world. No one can deny that moral pressure on multinational corporations brought that nation to a new place. Since then, the influence of religious investors in other social justice issues has been frequently acknowledged by major American and international news media. *Time, Forbes, Business Week, New York Times, Wall Street Journal* – all have publicised the influence of interfaith investors with headlines like 'Nuns vs. Bankers: The Shareholder Proxy Wars'.

Although, at the time of writing, the desired transformation of corporate values has not yet been achieved, over the past 40 years solid evidence has accrued attesting to the investment power of religious congregations and their associates and its significant impact. For example, pressure from reli-

3. See Chapter 6, 'The Story of the Cabra Dominican Sisters in the Struggle against Apartheid in South Africa', pp. 108-137.

gious investors has placed environment, social and governance (ESG) analysts in many major investment firms, and actions by SRI groups often make headlines in major national and international news media. Most notably, by the dawn of the twenty-first century, an estimated one in every eight dollars under professional management in the US is involved in socially responsible investing. ('2001 Report on Socially Responsible Investing Trends in the United States', Social Investment Forum, 2001).[4]

ADRIAN: EARLY AND SIGNIFICANT LEADERS

Among the numerous religious entities – Protestant denominations, congregations of women and men and organisations which spearheaded the SRI movement in the US – several congregations of Dominican women offer outstanding examples of initiative, dedication and effectiveness. Of these, the Adrian Dominican Sisters of Michigan deserve special mention for their organisational leadership and consistent commitment of personnel and resources. Adrian's history in the SRI endeavour parallels that of the organisations to which its sisters gave early leadership. Between 1975 and 1976, the Adrian Dominican pioneers, through their affiliation with the leadership of other congregations, moved swiftly from formulating criteria for monitoring investments to setting goals in new areas: investigating banks, evaluating alternative investments and identifying strategies for using investment power to address evolving and newly urgent issues of social concern.

DOZENS OF CONCERNS BECOME ISSUES OF SUSTAINABILITY

In the midst of the work on South Africa, Dominican women, together with their ICCR colleagues, expanded the work of corporate responsibility into a remarkable array of concrete activities: dialogue with banks on an array of concerns involving access to capital; work with agribusiness companies on labour, safe foods and water contamination; low-cost housing and minority-owned banks; shareholder initiatives with multinational corporations like IBM, General Electric and 3M; attendance at stockholder meetings.

Dominican women communicated the following priorities, among others, to those businesses in which they invested:

- human rights
- labour rights and justice in the supply chain
- board representation from a broad social spectrum
- affirmation of human dignity in advertising

4. http://www.ussif.org/files/Publications/01_Trends_Report.pdf

- just and equitable distribution of corporate profits
- direction of products and services toward consumer health and welfare
- conversion of major operations from military to peaceful purposes
- cessation of exploitation in developing economies
- ecological sustainability in lending practices, energy, operations and consumer products.

In solidarity with others at ICCR, Dominican women confronted corporations on issues where corporate profits conflicted with human health and the health of the planet. Although it is common practice today for corporations to weigh issues like climate risk and human health in conjunction with their fiscal plans, this was not always so. These considerations became normal practice after a series of socially responsible shareholder pressures. For example, shareholder resolutions with Abbott Labs, American Home Products and Bristol Myers called on these corporations to cease using marketing techniques in Developing World countries that encouraged mothers to move away from breastfeeding and to embrace Developed World infant formula that was often detrimental to newborns. As a result of persistent SRI activities, there are now international codes that control the marketing of breast milk substitutes. Health issues have included marketing of tobacco products, access to HIV/AIDS medications in developing countries, affordable access to pharmaceuticals in the US and the health impacts of toxins in products.

For six frustrating years, from 1976 to 1982, Meg Andrezick OP, Margarita Ruiz OP and Annette Sinagra OP exposed Gulf & Western's mistreatment of cane workers in the Dominican Republic. Through a series of meetings, they brought together government officials, community activists, cane workers, union leaders, Adrian sisters and the local bishop. Together they prodded human resource managers to adopt policies that would replace insanitary hovels and cruel employment practices with housing, health care and compensation commensurate with human dignity. As a result of this collaboration, for the first time the powerless workers had a voice representing their plight at a Gulf & Western shareholders' meeting. This historic confrontation regarding conditions in the Dominican Republic echoed the first social protest in the western hemisphere when sixteenth-century Dominican missionaries interceded with the Spanish *conquistadores* for the rights of indigenous slaves in 1511.

In anticipation of the Jubilee Year of 2000, SRI representatives worked with banks and multilateral entities to forgive inappropriate debt that continued to strangle developing economies. A proposal emanating from a PREACHING JUSTICE THROUGH SOCIALLY RESPONSIBLE INVESTING conference on globalisation sponsored by the North American Dominican Promoters of Justice and Peace was later passed by the members of the Dominican Leadership Conference, calling on congregations to commit 5 per cent of their investment portfolios to community investment in the Developing World.

REGIONAL INITIATIVES

As the SRI ministry expanded, individual sisters and groups became compelled to focus on a few issues from a list of needs too numerous to address effectively. Hence, social justice promoters in each congregation found themselves attracted to, or uniquely positioned to represent some specific issues more than others. The geographic location of a congregation often influenced these priorities. For example, the Sinsinawa Dominicans, active members of ICCR since 1975, felt a special responsibility to represent the rights, resources and priorities of their Native American neighbours. Toni Harris OP remembers the first shareholder meeting she attended in 1980, after Mary Ellen Butcher OP asked her to work on shareholder actions for the Sinsinawa community. Toni presented her congregation's shareholder resolution concerning predatory mining on Native American lands. For several years, Sinsinawa Dominicans became the voice of the indigenous tribes of Wisconsin on this issue. Respect and appreciation for Native American spirituality made the Sinsinawa Dominicans especially sensitive to the impact of corporate practices on environmental integrity. Through active membership in ICCR, Sinsinawa Dominicans contributed greatly to the development of an international eco-justice agenda.

The Dominican congregations in the New York area, together with other Tri-State CRI members and led by the Caldwell Dominicans, began to address the polychlorinated biphenyl (PCB) contamination in the Hudson River by General Electric (see below).

PRIORITIES OF THE EARTH EMERGE

Beginning early in the 1980s, Dominican women throughout the US also began to use SRI to persuade specific corporations to address environmental concerns. While energy around these concerns merged with earlier concerns about pollution and toxic contamination, this focus also paralleled the study of the new cosmology and the deeper understanding of our connection to the planet. A few examples will serve to highlight the scope of SRI preaching for eco-justice. These examples also demonstrate the kind of study, patience and perseverance that this ministry demands of the preacher.

- Largely because of the influence of religious investment power, Dow Chemical ended US sales of certain herbicides similar to Agent Orange.

- Later in the 1980s, shareholder resolutions with food companies prevented irradiation of foods and food ingredients and the serving of irradiated products in restaurants.

- ICCR and its affiliates began dialogue with DuPont and Monsanto, who were investing heavily in genetically modified organisms with a view to transforming themselves into life-science companies. Begun in the 1980s, that debate has not yet been satisfactorily resolved. The Adrian and Caldwell Dominicans stand out in this initiative, mirrored by corporate stances in their congregations and their commitment to community-supported gardens and organic gardening.

- In 1990, the Caldwell Dominicans were among the first to file resolutions with utility companies concerned with global warming. These first resolutions focused on the demand side of management programmes, energy efficiencies and investment in renewable energies. By the mid-1990s, with many Dominican congregations active on this issue, resolutions extended to oil and gas and motor companies. Today, thousands of companies now understand climate risk, report their greenhouse gas (GHG) emissions and publish goals to reduce emissions. Shareholder resolutions continue to ask companies to set reduction goals for GHG emissions, in both operations and products. While national and international policy addressing global warming has often stagnated in the past, corporations have learned that reducing GHG emissions, together with investments in new energy-efficient technologies, makes good business sense in energy savings and reduced potential risks.

- Under the leadership of Caldwell Dominican Patricia Daly, members of the Tri-State Coalition for Responsible Investment led a national campaign to exert public pressure on General Electric to remove poisonous PCBs from the Hudson River. Decades after PCBs were outlawed by the Environmental Protection Agency (EPA) and, despite a mandate from the same agency in 2000, that clean-up had scarcely begun by 2010. Shareholders worked to invite the company to warn area residents of dangers, while demanding transparency in the monies spent in advertising, misinformation and delaying tactics. While Caldwell Dominicans were united with Dominican congregations and ICCR members and associates across the nation in these two efforts, they are credited with a leadership role in the Hudson River and global warming issues.

- In California, Dominican women found a way to combine ecological concerns with attention to vulnerable populations through WAGES, a non-profit organisation that develops eco-friendly house-cleaning co-operatives for low-income Latinas. Corinne Florek (Adrian) served as WAGES board treasurer.
- In 2007, Toni Harris (Sinsinawa) extended her ministry beyond the Americas as she became International Dominican Promoter for Justice and Peace. In this position she continued to preach to multinational corporations on morally sensitive issues like extraction of resources (mining) and use of hydroelectric power in Latin America.

Under the SRI umbrella, a remarkable combination of criticism, confrontation and collaboration has taken Dominican women into preaching opportunities unheard of before the late 1960s: from street demonstrations, to the marketplace, to board rooms, to union halls, to the legislative chambers of local, state and national governments. It is not surprising that corporate executives did not always welcome the challenging presence of religious stockholders at shareholders' meetings. All of a sudden, exploited workers, undervalued female executives, underserved populations and devastated landscapes spoke up in the voices of women with advanced degrees in economics, law, history, ethics, theology and political science. As more and more sisters attended shareholders' meetings, they began to put a human face on the victims of corporate policies that were heretofore indifferent to 'unintended consequences'. Nevertheless, the most effective influence of this preaching continued to reside in the collective investment power of ICCR's 300 members.

INVESTING IN COMMUNITY ECONOMIC DEVELOPMENT:
A PROACTIVE APPROACH

Exerting moral pressure on multinational corporations often proved to be somewhat frustrating, however. SRI advocates gradually began to make more pro-active contributions to social and economic change by investing directly in small businesses and by a variety of actions for reinvigorating distressed communities. Community-development lending puts money directly back into poor communities in a way that calls the recipient to fiscal responsibility. Since these are loans, not give-aways or grants, recipients are obliged to pay interest until the money is repaid. Moreover, the investor is committed to ongoing communication with the recipient. This establishes a reciprocal relationship. By securing accountability for what happens as a result of the loan, the religious community shares in the struggles and accomplishments of the group they are assisting. What happens as a result of the loan often extends the investor's outreach beyond the traditional roles of Dominican women by creating jobs, building affordable housing, providing job training and day care, and by extending credit.

Making loans through community-development banks, aligning themselves with worker-owned corporations and ecumenically supported housing projects, and working with people who would usually have been excluded by traditional lending institutions, the sisters were not surprised to find links between racial justice and economic opportunity. Maureen Fenlon OP and Carol Coston OP visited an African-American credit union in Mississippi that had been discriminated against by the white business and banking communities, employing segregationist tactics against their economic progress. A deposit of $50,000 into its lending capital made the Adrian Dominican sisters partners in the empowerment of this minority community.

Dominican congregations have also been long-time investors in community development in regional initiatives such as the Leviticus Fund, founded by the members of the Tri-State CRI. Since 1984 $36.7 million has been invested in various initiatives in New York, New Jersey and Connecticut, creating businesses, housing, childcare and social service centres, new jobs and new businesses.

LARGER CONGREGATIONS TAKE A LEAD:
THE CASE OF THE ADRIAN DOMINICANS

Larger congregations with more substantial resources gradually expanded their support by financing their own SRI ministry. The history of SRI in the Adrian Dominican congregation offers an outstanding example.

In 1975, Adrian created its Portfolio Advisory Board (PAB) whose task was to direct the congregation's investment power as a concrete expression of the its Gospel values. The group began with an annual budget of $4,550 to cover board activities. Within 25 years, those activities gradually persuaded the congregation to increase the annual budget to $77,000. In 1978, the PAB made its first alternative investments in widely separated locations: Chicago's South Shore Bank, a credit union in Texas, an ecumenical coalition in Ohio, and St Mary's Development Center in South Carolina, directed by Ellen Robertson OP. The PAB became an eminently successful leadership training school for Dominican women, who soon began reaping dividends for the SRI ministry, far beyond their congregation and far beyond Michigan.

Adrian's commitment of personnel extended its preaching power, as members of the PAB went on to be of service to religious and civic communities throughout the US. This outstanding performance of Adrian Dominicans in the SRI ministry is perhaps best illustrated in the careers of Carol Coston OP and Corinne Florek OP. Each of these sisters deserves special mention for exemplifying the remarkable scope of SRI activities as well as the most effective policies and practices of this unique ministry. One of the founding members of the Adrian Portfolio Advisory Board in 1975, Carol served subsequently as chair, director and board member until 1991. In 1988, after two decades in social justice ministries including NETWORK and Adrian's Portfolio Advisory Board, Carol brought her financial experiences to Christian Brothers Investment Services (CBIS), a for-profit business founded to help other religious congregations manage their investment portfolios. Carol suggested to CBIS a design for community development lending similar to the one created during her PAB service. Carol then directed the Partners for the Common Good Loan Funds until 2001, investing over $11 million in loans to low-income businesses and housing, minority banks and credit unions, and micro enterprises.

In 2001, Partners for the Common Good received the Presidential Award for Excellence in Microenterprise Development. That same year Carol received the Presidential Citizens Medal from President Bill Clinton for her leadership in social justice and economic development.

By 1980, when Corinne Florek finished her MBA from Notre Dame, Carol Coston and her colleagues had inspired Adrian sisters with fiscal talents to explore many possibilities in an SRI ministry. Corinne chose to put her financial education to work by creating economic opportunities for the poor in the hills of Appalachia. Eventually, as a member of Adrian's Portfolio Advisory Board for 15 years, her perspectives broadened. She subsequently brought her Michigan experiences to Kentucky, California and beyond, by bringing her indefatigable energies to a series of administrative positions: director of Economic Development Programs for the Campaign for Human Development; manager of a micro-enterprise loan fund for Women's Initiative for

Self-Improvement; executive director of JOLT (Justice Organizers Leadership Treasurers), treasurer of WAGES (a non-profit organisation supporting the labour of Latina women mentioned above) and monitor of the $6 million Mercy Partnership Fund. In one of her reports to the Sisters of Mercy, Corinne described how their investment fund gave them a geographic outreach that empowered even their retired sisters to minister to people from New Orleans to Haiti to Thailand to Ghana. In San Francisco in 2000, when Corinne received the Ned Gramlich Lifetime Achievement Award in recognition of her long-time dedication to community investment, she accepted the award in the name of US Catholic women religious who were among the first to invest in non-profit community organisations.

Among other Adrian Dominicans who began on the PAB and then conferred the benefits of their service there on people and organisations far from Michigan, were Maureen Fenlon, who began by educating other congregations in SRI strategies and then went on to work for the Ecumenical Development Cooperative Society (now Oikocredit), a $100,000,000 international lending fund. Judy Rimbey's experience on Adrian's Portfolio Advisory Board prepared her to direct a multi-million dollar alternative investment fund for Catholic Healthcare West, co-sponsored by eight religious congregations.

DOMINICAN CONGREGATIONS IN REGIONAL COALITIONS

As the ICCR began to form from the leadership of the Protestant denominational members of the National Council of Churches in the US, it was difficult not to have Catholics overrun the organisation with hundreds of autonomous institutional investors (most Protestant denominations have national pension funds). Most of the Catholic institutions formed regional coalitions; the largest of these regional affiliates is the Tri-State Coalition for Responsible Investment located in the New York metropolitan area. Founded in 1975, Tri-State CRI is an alliance of Roman Catholic investors in the tri-state area of New York, New Jersey and Connecticut. All of the Dominican women's congregations in the tri-state region are members of Tri-State CRI: Amityville, Blauvelt, Caldwell, Hope (formerly Newburgh and Dominican Sisters of the Sick Poor), Maryknoll and Sparkill. Tri-State CRI's actions have attracted national media attention, and CEOs of major corporations, like Ford and General Electric, have acknowledged its influence. In fact, when *The New York Times Magazine* ran a feature article on investors' growing concerns with Exxon Mobil, the article soon evolved into an admiring profile of Patricia Daly, a Dominican of Caldwell, New Jersey, and Executive Director of Tri-State CRI since 1994.

Tri-State CRI was only two years old and Patricia Daly was a mere novice when she represented the Caldwell congregation at a shareholders' meeting at J.P. Stevens Company. In 1977, J.P. Stevens was engaged in anti-union activities in the South to such an extent that people had actually been killed. This dramatic workers' struggle was immortalised in the film *Norma Rae*. At the meeting Patricia attended, the ICCR shareholders joined the unions in filing a resolution in support of workers' rights. Together they were finally successful when ICCR convinced banks to refuse additional loans to the company. The J.P. Stevens episode is a good example of how the SRI process works to bring moral pressure to bear on big business. The idealism and enthusiasm of ICCR members opened up for Patricia Daly the possibility of fulfilling her vocation to preach justice through the medium of SRI. While active since her novitiate, corporate responsibility has been her full-time ministry for almost 20 years.

In a recent interview, Patricia explained how socially responsible investing connects with her vocation to preach the gospel:

> I understand Jesus to be a prophet in his day – and a reformer who addressed corruption in the religious and political systems of his society. One could also argue that Jesus also took on economic concerns. "The worker is worthy of his hire," ... In 2011, we continue to watch and understand new dimensions of the 13.7 billion year history of the universe – what we can now understand as the primary expression of our Creator. Socially responsible investing, and especially the work of engaging with the companies, is one way of preaching in the market place, addressing the economic and political powers which control the riches of creation. Our preaching is a struggle to be faithful to the primary revelation of God: food, water, the livelihood and survival of various species, and especially the basic rights of humans.

On the Pacific Coast, the outstanding regional coalition which merits special mention is JOLT, for which Corinne Florek of Adrian served as executive director. JOLT solidifies the SRI activities of all the West Coast congregations of Dominican women with other faith-based organisations in the region. In her interaction with the business communities there, Corinne recognised how a pat on the back can prove not only more pleasant but also more persuasive than a twist of the arm. Hence, policies of affirmation became the hallmark of her leadership style. Publicity surrounding JOLT's influence on two national corporations drew attention to the impact of its methods. After a successful campaign that exposed Nike's violation of fair employment standards at 700 factories, JOLT coalition members wrote letters of appreciation to Nike executives for revising their policies to recognise workers' dignity. Further co-operation with national corporations was assured in 2005 after JOLT constituents, by working with farm workers' organisations to address issues of wages and working conditions in the tomato industry, publicly cited Taco Bell for 'setting a new standard of social responsibility for the fast food industry'. The voices of socially responsible Dominicans and their collaborators could be clearly heard in a resolution that applauded the fast-food giant for working conditions that represented 'human dignity, democratic participation, solidarity with the poor, and the elimination of slavery and trafficking of human persons'.

In addition to educating corporate consciences, JOLT members support non-profit organisations like Rubicon Programs, Inc. This organisation assists over three thousand poor and homeless people in the Bay Area by creating affordable housing and providing job training, legal counselling and mental health services.

CHALLENGES OF THE NEW MILLENNIUM
Dominican congregations and all ICCR members continue to take public positions and rally moral pressure from investors, supported by investment strategies whenever corporate policies and behaviours have social implications. Among the issues that have dominated the news media recently have been healthcare reform, ecological sustainability, predatory credit card practices, full disclosure of pay disparity excesses and taxpayer bail-out of failed banks and corporations. Almost every issue that dominates the political news cycle is promptly analysed for its social impact. In 2010–11, US health care reform was such an issue. After years of working with corporations within many industries to prepare for health care reform in the US, health insurance companies prominently opposed the passage of what became known as 'Obamacare', and congressional opponents posited its prohibitive cost to taxpayers. In its analysis of this cost, ICCR targeted sky-rocketing compensation packages for health insurance executives and, by contrast, for their clients and employees, a shift of burden from insurer to the insured. SRI investors were soon joined in their demand that insurance companies publish compensation data.

In 2009, ICCR launched a year-long series of podcasts chronicling its history of shareholder activism by religious congregations and organisations. These podcasts clearly demonstrated the practical consequences of SRI insights in resolutions on corporate practices related to economic and environmental sustainability. In that year, Dominican congregations who participated in ICCR shareholder resolutions could point to their prophetic early warnings on the global economic catastrophe of the 2008 sub-prime lending meltdown and the environmental disaster in the Gulf of Mexico. The following year, ICCR filed 283 shareholder resolutions with 188 companies throughout the US and Canada.

To date, most SRI preaching has been addressed to executives, shareholders and governing boards of large companies based in the US. In the future, Patricia Daly, for one, would like to see Dominicans who lead faith-based communities in developing countries mentor people in ways to engage with their local economies and the government entities that oversee them. Thanks to new technologies, religious on the ground in developing countries are at meetings with company executives speaking firsthand to conditions and the concerns they face due to corporate practices. The communications technology industry has been swift to seize upon the opportunities for profit in developing nations. Patricia points out that the same technology can also be a tool for exposing policies that have abused workers and a resource for liberating populations who have been entrapped by multinational predators. There is reason to hope that the same technology will become an instrument for preaching socially responsible economics and for publicising the positive activities of its Dominican preachers.

PROMOTERS OF A GLOBAL ECONOMY THAT
SUPPORTS THE EARTH AND HER PEOPLE

It is safe to say that no individual Dominican or her congregation, acting alone, could have exercised sufficient influence on any company to modify its policies or practices to accommodate ethical values. Hence, it is also safe to say that almost all Dominican SRI initiatives were implemented with ICCR members. Having collective assets of $110 billion, ICCR speaks very fluently the language that multinational corporations understand. At the turn of the century the mission of corporate responsibility and SRI had securely emerged into an industry beyond the members of the faith community. As investment analysts have become fluent in the integration of social and ecological risks and investment managers comfortable in managing portfolios with social screens, even corporations are now skilled in reporting on their environmental, social and governance commitments. Sustainability managers within corporations now push management within companies to attend to social and environmental concerns clearly connected to the reputation and financial risk of the company. As the United Nations Framework on Business and Human Rights implements its guidelines for corporations, investors continue to push for compliance from smaller corporations throughout the world.

In the end, Dominicans and other faith communities have played a profound prophetic role in recreating business practices on this planet. It is obvious to all that our preaching must continue.

Index

Aachen (Germany), 283, 284
Abbott Labs, 536
Abizeramariya (Rwandan congregation), 153
Abraham, 423
active religious life ('third state'), 48–51, 56–57
Adoula, Cyrille, 140, 141
Adrian, Br, 299
Adrian (Michigan) Dominicans, 39, 65, 250–251, 520–522, 524, 526
  Portfolio Advisory Board, 540–541, 542
  socially responsible investing (SRI), 532–533, 534, 535, 536, 539, 540–542
Afghanistan, 228, 248, 379, 386
Africa, 30–31, 68, 69, 70, 71, 73, 74, 75, 79, 80, 112, 146, 257, 258, 292, 307, 309, 310, 396. *see also individual countries*
African Bishops' Conferences, 132
African Catechetical Institute (Rwanda), 141, 150
African National Congress. *see* ANC
African nationalism, 112
African-Americans, 428–429, 432, 521, 540
Afro-Ecuadoran communities (Chota Valley), 311
Agent Orange, 538
aggiornamento, 177, 182, 205
agriculture, 262–263
Ahrens, Sr Luise, 313–315
AIDS. *see* HIV/AIDS
Albert the Great, St, 383, 510, 518
Albertus Magnus, Sr. *see* McGrath, Sr Albertus Magnus
Albigensian heresy, 510, 524
Albizzi family (Florence), 46
Albrook Air Force Station (Panama), 316
Aldenhoven convent (Germany), 276
Alexandra, Sr, 98
Alford, Helen, OP, 13
Algerian migrants (France), 213
Algiers, 240
Al-Hadba Convent (Mosul), 249
Al-Hayat Convent (Baghdad), 244
Al-Hayat Hospital (Baghdad), 244, 252
Al-Hikma University (Baghdad), 239
Al-Kaleema Centre (Mosul), 246, 249
All Island Churches Consultative Meeting on Racism (Ireland), 365n
Allied Forces, 293
Al-Om Al-Tahrah Convent (Qaraqosh), 252
Alqosh (Iraq), 235, 242
Al-Saah (Mosul), 240
Altos de Cazuca (Colombia), 483, 495
  Dominican sisters, 496–505
Amapá (Brazil), 200

Amazon (Brazil), 196
American Home Products, 536
Amityville (New York), 517, 520, 533, 542
Amnesty International, 309
Amorim, Jeronimo Alves, 202
Amos group, 258, 259
AMREF Health Africa, 150
Amsterdam (Netherlands), 274
An Tairseach (Wicklow, Ireland), 517
Anastasie, Mother, 203
ANC (African National Congress), 113, 114, 115, 126, 129, 130, 131, 132, 133, 135
ANC Youth League, 112
Ancilla, Sr (LA CLE), 205–206, 207, 208, 219
Andean peoples (Peru), 304–305, 327, 328–331, 332
Andrezick, Sr Meg, 536
Angers (France), 50
Anglo-Irish Agreement (1985), 342
Angola, 129
Ankawa (Iraq), 241, 242
Annel, Sr Mary, 318–319
anthropology, 55, 58–60, 489, 490
anti-apartheid movement. *see* apartheid struggle
Anti-Defamation League (USA), 430, 451, 455
anti-Semitism, 37, 429–430, 445, 447, 449, 450–451, 456. *see also* Holocaust
Antoinette, Sr (Rwanda), 150
Antonine Sisters (Lebanon), 245
Anunciata congregation, 65
apartheid struggle (South Africa), 24, 25–26, 109–137, 151, 349, 534–535
apostolate of women, 48–51, 56–58
Apostole del Sacro Cuore, 56
apostolic congregations, 21, 24, 78, 80, 83, 266, 424. *see also* Dominican Sisters International (DSI)
Aquinas, Thomas. *see* Thomas Aquinas, St
Aquinas College (Grand Rapids), 432
Aquinas House (Belfast), 369
Araguaia guerrilla movement (Brazil), 197
Ardoyne (Belfast), 368
Argentina, 79, 348, 349
Arizona (USA), 525
Armanni Classical High School (Gubbio), 409
Armenian Christians, 233, 234
Armenian massacres, 233
Arminjon, Blaise, 154
Armstong, Sr Electa, 439
Arnauld, Angelica, 45
Arusha (Rwanda), 146
Asháninka, 327
Ashe, Kaye, OP, 13, 35–36

Table of Biblical References